Make the Most of Your Windows PC

Sherry Kinkoph, et al.

201 W. 103rd Street
Indianapolis, Indiana 46290

Make the Most of Your Windows PC

Copyright © 2003 by Que Publishing

International Standard Book Number: 0789-72944-X

Library of Congress Catalog Card Number: 2003101770

Printed in the United States of America

First Printing: May 2003

06   05   04   03   4   3   2   1

Que Publishing offers excellent discounts on this book when ordered in quantity for bulk purchases or special sales. For more information, please contact

U.S. Corporate and Government Sales

1-800-382-3419

corpsales@pearsontechgroup.com

For sales outside of the U.S., please contact

International Sales

1-317-581-3793

international@pearsontechgroup.com

Trademarks

Warning and Disclaimer

Associate Publisher
Greg Wiegand

Acquisitions Editor
Stephanie J. McComb

Development Editor
Kevin Howard

Managing Editor
Charlotte Clapp

Project Editor
Elizabeth Finney

Copy Editor
Seth Kerney

Indexer
Erika Millen

Technical Editors
Galen Grimes, et al.

Team Coordinator
Sharry Lee Gregory

Interior Designer
Anne Jones

Cover Designer
Anne Jones

Contents at a Glance

Introduction 1

Part I Windows Basics

1 The Basics 5

2 Up and Running 25

3 Using the Windows XP Desktop 49

4 Working with Files and Folders 75

5 Printing 105

6 Working on a Network 123

7 Working Away From the Network 145

8 Having Fun with Windows XP 161

9 Changing Windows XP Settings 177

10 Optimizing Your Computer 211

11 Installing New Software and Hardware 227

12 Troubleshooting Your Computer 245

13 Back Up and Restore Your Computer 257

Part II Using the Internet

14 Connecting to the Internet 277

15 Browsing and Searching the World Wide Web 293

16 Protecting Yourself on the Web 329

17 Communicating with Electronic Mail 349

18 Sending and Receiving Instant Messages 377

19 Participating in Chat and Online Communities 387

20 Participating in Usenet Discussion Groups 399

Part III Being Productive with Microsoft Office XP

21 Using Common Office Features 417

22 Using Word to Create and Edit Documents 447

23 Using Outlook for Email, Contacts, and Scheduling 507

24 Using Excel Spreadsheets 539

25 Creating Presentations with PowerPoint 601

26 Making Databases with Access 643

27 Working with Office's Graphics Tools 669

Glossary 689

Index 707

Contents

Introduction   1

Part I: Windows Basics

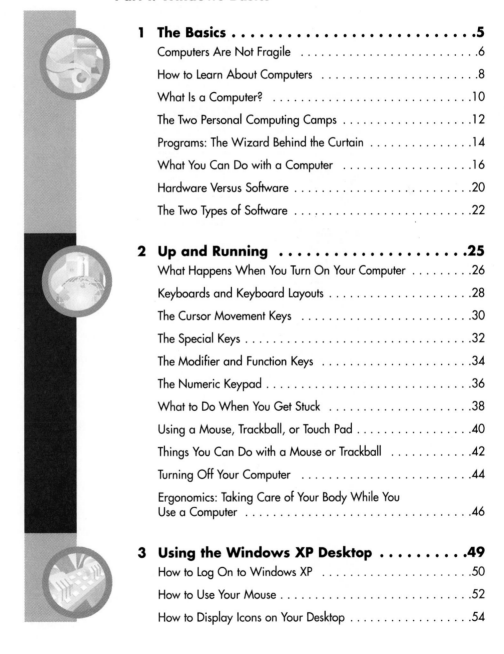

1 The Basics 5
Computers Are Not Fragile 6
How to Learn About Computers .8
What Is a Computer? 10
The Two Personal Computing Camps 12
Programs: The Wizard Behind the Curtain 14
What You Can Do with a Computer 16
Hardware Versus Software 20
The Two Types of Software 22

2 Up and Running .25
What Happens When You Turn On Your Computer 26
Keyboards and Keyboard Layouts 28
The Cursor Movement Keys 30
The Special Keys 32
The Modifier and Function Keys .34
The Numeric Keypad 36
What to Do When You Get Stuck 38
Using a Mouse, Trackball, or Touch Pad 40
Things You Can Do with a Mouse or Trackball 42
Turning Off Your Computer 44
Ergonomics: Taking Care of Your Body While You
Use a Computer 46

3 Using the Windows XP Desktop 49
How to Log On to Windows XP .50
How to Use Your Mouse 52
How to Display Icons on Your Desktop 54

How to Start a Program 56

How to Arrange Windows on the Desktop 58

How to Switch Between Programs 60

How to Use the Notification Area 62

How to Browse Your Disk Drives 64

How to Get Help 66

How to Use the Recycle Bin 68

How to Log Off Windows XP 70

How to Turn Off Your Computer 72

4 Working with Files and Folders 75

How to Use Windows Explorer .76

How to Search for a File or Folder 78

How to Create a Folder 80

How to View Items in a Folder .82

How to Create a File 84

How to Open a File 86

How to Save a File 88

How to Create a Shortcut to a File or Folder 90

How to Rename a File or Folder .92

How to Delete a File or Folder 94

How to Move or Copy a File or Folder 96

How to Format a Floppy Disk 98

How to Send a File to the Floppy Drive 100

How to Open a File with a Different Program 102

5 Printing 105

How to Print a Document from a Program 106

How to Print a Document from Windows 108

How to Manage Documents Waiting to Print 110

How to Change Printer Settings 112

How to Share a Printer with Others 114

How to Install a Local Printer 116

How to Set Up Your Computer to Use a Network Printer 120

6 Working on a Network **123**

How to Set Up a Small Network 124

How to Set Up Additional User Accounts 128

How to Share an Internet Connection 130

How to Use My Network Places 132

How to Add a Network Place 134

How to Find a Computer on the Network 136

How to Find a File on the Network 138

How to Share a File or Folder with Others 140

How to Map a Network Drive 142

7 Working Away from the Network **145**

How to Create and Fill a Briefcase 146

How to Take a Briefcase with You 148

How to Update Files in a Briefcase 150

How to Make Items Available Offline 152

How to Use Offline Items 154

How to Synchronize Offline Items 156

How to Change Offline Settings 158

8 Having Fun with Windows XP **161**

How to Play Music and Movies 162

How to Record Music 164

How to Find Music Online 166

How to Make Movies 168

How to Work with Pictures 172

How to Play Games 174

9 Changing Windows XP Settings **177**

How to Change the Volume 178

How to Set Up a Screen Saver 180

How to Change Your Desktop Theme 182

How to Change Your Wallpaper 184

How to Change Desktop Appearance 186

How to Change Display Settings 188

How to Change Mouse Settings 190

How to Change Keyboard Settings 192

How to Customize the Taskbar 194

How to Change Folder Options 196

How to Change Power Options 198

How to Change System Sounds 200

How to Add an Item to the Start Menu 202

How to Add an Item to the Quick Launch Bar 204

How to Start a Program When Windows Starts 206

How to Set Accessibility Options 208

10 Using the System Tools 211

How to Free Up Space on Your Hard Disk 212

How to Defragment Your Hard Disk 214

How to Schedule a Task to Occur Automatically 216

How to Use the Windows Troubleshooters 218

How to Get System Information 220

How to Use System Restore 222

How to Compress Files and Folders 224

11 Installing New Software and Hardware . . .227

How to Add a Program to Your Computer 228

How to Change or Remove a Program 230

How to Add Windows Components from the CD 232

How to Add Windows Components from the Internet 234

How to Find Out About Your Installed Hardware 236

How to Tell Whether a Windows Service Pack is Installed 238

How to Install Windows XP Service Pack 1 240

How to Set Program Access and Defaults 242

12 Troubleshooting Your Computer 245

How to Clean Up the System Tray 246

How to Boot Selectively 248

How to Stop a Service 250

How to Uninstall a Program 252

How to Use the Event Viewer .254

13 Back Up and Restore Your System **257**

How to Back Up Your Files 258

How to Restore Files from a Backup 260

How to Use Automated System Recovery 262

How to Upgrade to Windows XP .264

How to Install Windows XP on a Blank Hard Drive 266

How to Activate Windows XP 270

How to Create Setup Floppy Disks 272

Part II: Using the Internet

14 Connecting to the Internet **277**

How to Set Up an Internet Connection 278

How to Choose an Internet Service Provider 282

How to Connect to the Internet 286

How to Connect to the Internet Through a Proxy Server 288

How to Load a Web Page 290

15 Browsing the World Wide Web **293**

How to Use a Web Site 294

How to Visit a Web Site When You Know Its Address 296

How to Revisit Your Favorite Web Pages 298

How to Load a Web Page for Faster Viewing 300

How to Pick a New Home Page for Your Browser 302

How to Change Internet Explorer's Settings 304

How to Print a Web Page 306

How to Save a Web Page to Your Computer 308

How to Find a Site When You Don't Know Its Address 310

How to See Pages You Have Recently Visited 312

How to Search for a Specific Topic on the Web 314

How to Search Through Millions of Web Pages 316

How to Find Software on the Web 318

How to Find a Company on the Web 320

How to Find a Person on the Web 322

How to Find a Job on the Web 324

How to Find Your Ancestors on the Web 326

16 Protecting Yourself on the Web 329

How to Choose a Security Setting 330

How to Customize Your Security Setting 332

How to Block Objectionable Content from Being Viewed 334

How to Use Security Certificates .336

How to Disable Cookies in a Web Browser 338

How to Make Your Internet Connection More Secure 340

How to Install Antivirus Software 342

How to Check Your Computer for Viruses 346

17 Communicating with Electronic Mail 349

How to Set Up Outlook Express for Email 350

How to Send Email 352

How to Receive Email 354

How to Send a Web Page Using Email 356

How to Send an Attached File 358

How to Receive an Attached File 360

How to Find Someone's Email Address 362

How to Subscribe to a Mailing List 364

How to Set Up a Free Web-Based Email Account 366

How to Set Up Hotmail in Outlook Express 370

How to Use Your Free Web-Based Email Account 372

How to Print an Email Message .374

**18 Sending and Receiving Instant
Messages 377**

How to Add Someone to Your Contact List 378

How to Invite Someone to Use Messenger 380

How to Send Someone an Instant Message 382

How to Prevent Someone from Sending You Messages 384

**19 Participating in Chat and Online
Communities 387**

How to Create an Account to Chat on MSN 388

How to Chat for the First Time on MSN 390

How to Participate in a Chat on MSN 392

How to Join a Community on MSN 394

How to Read and Send Messages in an MSN Community . . .396

20 Participating in Usenet Discussion Groups ....**.399**

How to Set Up Outlook Express for Usenet Newsgroups 400

How to Read a Newsgroup 402

How to Read Newsgroups You Have Subscribed To 404

How to Post a Message to a Newsgroup 406

How to Find a Newsgroup 408

How to Search an Archive of Past Newsgroup Discussions 410

How to Decrease the Junk Email You Receive 412

Part III: Being Productive with Microsoft Office XP

21 Using Common Office Features 417

How to Start and Exit Office Applications 418

How to Navigate Office Applications 420

How to Work with the Task Pane 422

How to Work with Menus and Toolbars 424

How to Customize Toolbars 426

How to Start a New File 428

How to Save Your Work 430

How to Open and Close Files 432

How to Print a File 434

How to Find Files 436

How to Use the Office Help Tools 438

How to Cut, Copy, and Paste Data 440

How to Link and Embed Data 442

How to Add and Remove Office Components 444

22 Using Word to Create and Edit Documents .447

How to Use Word's Views 448

How to Enter and Edit Text 450

How to Select Text 452

How to Move and Copy Text 454

How to Use Templates 456

How to Work with AutoText 458

How to Format Text 460

How to Copy Text Formatting 462

How to Insert Symbols 464

How to Set Margins 466

How to Set the Line Spacing 468

How to Align and Indent Text 470

How to Work with Bulleted and Numbered Lists 472

How to Set Tabs 474

How to Create Columns 476

How to Insert a Table 478

How to Add Borders and Shading to Text 480

How to Use Headers and Footers 482

How to Insert Comments, Footnotes, and Endnotes 484

How to Insert Page Numbers and Page Breaks 486

How to Use Styles 488

How to Work with Drop Caps and Text Case 490

How to Add a Watermark 492

How to Find and Replace Text 494

How to Check Your Spelling and Grammar 496

How to Work with AutoCorrect 498

How to Track and Review Document Changes 500

How to Change Paper Size 502

How to Print an Envelope 504

23 **Using Outlook for Email, Contacts, and Scheduling** 507

How to Get Around the Outlook Window 508

How to Schedule an Appointment 510

How to Set a Recurring Appointment 512

How to Schedule an Event 514

How to Plan a Meeting 516

How to Create a New Task 518

How to Create a New Contact 520

How to Import Contact Data 522

How to Organize Items 524

How to Compose and Send a Message 526

How to Read an Incoming Message 528

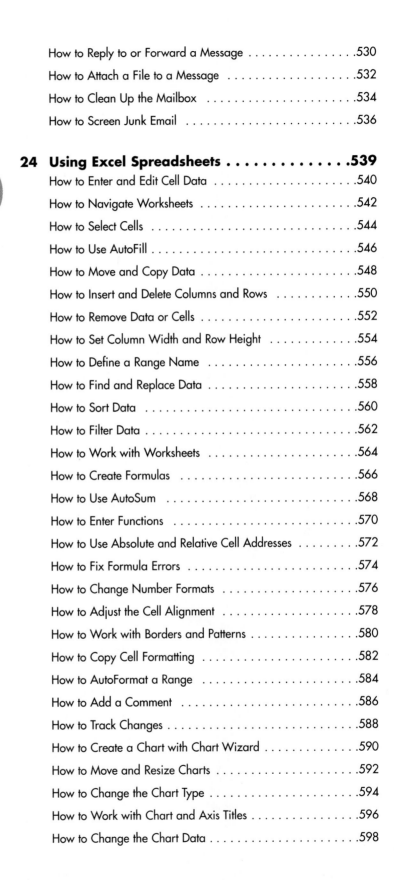

How to Reply to or Forward a Message 530

How to Attach a File to a Message 532

How to Clean Up the Mailbox .534

How to Screen Junk Email 536

24 Using Excel Spreadsheets 539

How to Enter and Edit Cell Data 540

How to Navigate Worksheets .542

How to Select Cells 544

How to Use AutoFill 546

How to Move and Copy Data .548

How to Insert and Delete Columns and Rows 550

How to Remove Data or Cells .552

How to Set Column Width and Row Height 554

How to Define a Range Name .556

How to Find and Replace Data 558

How to Sort Data 560

How to Filter Data 562

How to Work with Worksheets .564

How to Create Formulas 566

How to Use AutoSum 568

How to Enter Functions 570

How to Use Absolute and Relative Cell Addresses 572

How to Fix Formula Errors 574

How to Change Number Formats 576

How to Adjust the Cell Alignment 578

How to Work with Borders and Patterns 580

How to Copy Cell Formatting .582

How to AutoFormat a Range .584

How to Add a Comment 586

How to Track Changes 588

How to Create a Chart with Chart Wizard 590

How to Move and Resize Charts 592

How to Change the Chart Type 594

How to Work with Chart and Axis Titles 596

How to Change the Chart Data 598

25 Creating Presentations with PowerPoint . . .601

How to Use the AutoContent Wizard 602

How to Start a New Presentation Based on a Design
Template 604

How to Build a Presentation from Scratch 606

How to Use PowerPoint's View Modes 608

How to Understand Slide Elements 610

How to Add and Edit Slide Text .612

How to Format and Align Slide Text 614

How to Add New Text Boxes 616

How to Add an Illustration to a Slide 618

How to Add a Chart to a Slide 620

How to Insert a Table in a Slide .622

How to Change the Slide Layout 624

How to Change the Slide Background 626

How to Insert and Delete Slides .628

How to Reorganize Slides 630

How to Define the Slide Transition 632

How to Add Animation Effects 634

How to Run the Slide Show 636

How to Create Speaker Notes and Handouts 638

How to Use Pack and Go 640

26 Making Databases with Access 643

How to Understand Database Basics 644

How to Use the Database Wizard 646

How to Enter Data in the Database 648

How to Add New Tables 650

How to Modify a Table in Design View 652

How to Create a New Form with the Form Wizard 654

How to Make Changes to a Form in Design View 656

How to Sort Records 658

How to Filter Records 660

How to Perform a Simple Query .662

How to Create a Report 664

How to Modify a Report in Design View 666

27 Working with Office's Graphics Tools **669**

How to Draw Basic Shapes 670

How to Insert Clip Art 672

How to Insert an Object 674

How to Insert a WordArt Image 676

How to Move, Size, and Rotate an Object 678

How to Change Image Formatting 680

How to Add Shadow Effects .682

How to Group and Ungroup Objects 684

How to Insert a Diagram 686

Glossary   689

Index   707

About the Authors

Sherry Kinkoph has written more than 30 computer books and has taught thousands of new computer users how to make the most of their computers.

Walter Glenn is an independent writer, editor, and networking consultant who has helped thousands of people learn more about using Windows. He is a Microsoft Certified Systems Engineer, Internet Specialist, and Certified Trainer.

Rogers Cadenhead is the author of 12 books on the Internet, Java, and Web design and is a Web publisher whose site receives 7.3 million visits each year. Other books by this author include *Sams Teach Yourself Java 2 in 21 Days* and *Sams Teach Yourself FrontPage 2002 in 24 Hours*.

Lisa Biow is a computer trainer and consultant to small and medium-sized businesses in Oakland, California. She has taught everything from introductory computer classes to advanced database management courses at the college level.

We Want to Hear from You!

As the reader of this book, *you* are our most important critic and commentator. We value your opinion and want to know what we're doing right, what we could do better, what areas you'd like to see us publish in, and any other words of wisdom you're willing to pass our way.

As an associate publisher for Que Publishing, I welcome your comments. You can email or write me directly to let me know what you did or didn't like about this book—as well as what we can do to make our books better.

Please note that I cannot help you with technical problems related to the *topic* of this book. We do have a User Services group, however, where I will forward specific technical questions related to the book.

When you write, please be sure to include this book's title and author as well as your name, email address, and phone number. I will carefully review your comments and share them with the author and editors who worked on the book.

Email: feedback@quepublishing.com

Mail: Greg Wiegand
           Associate Publisher
           Que Publishing
           201 West 103rd Street
           Indianapolis, IN 46290 USA

For more information about this book or another Que title, visit our Web site at www.quepublishing.com. Type the ISBN (excluding hyphens) or the title of a book in the Search field to find the page you're looking for.

The Complete Visual Reference

Each chapter of this book is made up of a series of short, instructional tasks, designed to help you understand all the information that you need to get the most out of your computer hardware and software.

 Click: Click the left mouse button once.

 Double-click: Click the left mouse button twice in rapid succession.

 Right-click: Click the right mouse button once.

 Drag: Click and hold the left mouse button, position the mouse pointer, and release.

Each task includes a series of easy-to-understand steps designed to guide you through the procedure.

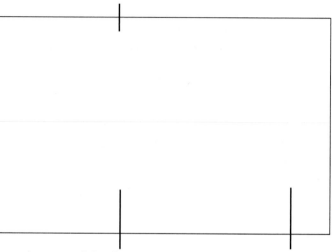

Each step is fully illustrated to show you how it looks onscreen.

Extra hints that tell you how to accomplish a goal are provided in most tasks.

 **Pointer Arrow:** Highlights an item on the screen you need to point to or focus on in the step or task.

 **Selection:** Highlights the area onscreen discussed in the step or task.

 Key icons: Clearly indicate which key combinations to use.

 Type: Click once where indicated and begin typing to enter your text or data.

Menus and items you click are shown in **bold**. Words in *italic* are defined in more detail in the glossary. Information you type is in a `special font`.

 **Drag and Drop:** Point to the starting place or object. Hold down the mouse button (right or left per instructions), move the mouse to the new location, and then release the button.

Introduction

You're new to computers and you want to get started fast. You don't want to spend a lot of time buying books on different topics, studying them for weeks before you can get something accomplished. This book will guide you through the basics and the critical tasks that you'll need to accomplish what you want to do. We'll cover Microsoft Windows, the Internet, and Microsoft Office, the major topics any computer user needs to know.

Fortunately, Windows XP is designed to be easy to use, and this book is designed to make it even easier. Whether you are completely new to Windows, or feel at home clicking your way through all those dialog boxes, you are likely to have questions, all of which you will have answered here:

- How do you search for a file when you don't know its name?
- How do you install a network printer?
- How do you manage documents that are waiting to print?
- How do you work with files on the network?
- How do you make a movie?
- How do you set permissions on a file?
- How do you change the way your mouse works?

You've heard a lot about the Internet, and this book will make it easy to put it to work for you. Here you will learn the following:

- How to choose an Internet provider
- How to connect to the Internet
- How to revisit your favorite Web pages
- How to find a company on the Web
- How to send an email message
- How to send an attached file
- How to chat online in real time

You have a computer that can handle each of these things, and a thousand other useful and fun features of the Internet. Now you will have the knowledge to benefit from it!

When you are ready to get productive, you can move on to the Microsoft Office XP section. Here, you'll learn how to use Microsoft Word, Excel, PowerPoint, Access, and Outlook. In no time you will be a confident, efficient computer user. Some of the tasks you'll learn include the following:

- How to create and format Word documents
- How to work with Excel formulas and functions
- How to create slideshow presentations with PowerPoint
- How to use Access to organize your data
- How to send and receive email with Outlook
- How to use the Office graphics tools to add pictures and shapes to your files

Each topic is presented visually, step by step, so you can clearly see how to apply each feature to your own tasks. The illustrations show exactly what you'll see on your own computer screen, making it easy to follow along.

You can use the book as a tutorial, working through each section one task at a time, or as a reference, looking up specific features you want to learn about. There's no right or wrong way—use the method that best suits your own learning style.

Whatever your level of expertise and for whatever reason you use your computer, you will find this book a useful tool. Whether you read it cover to cover, or set it aside for reference when you come across a specific task with which you need help, this book provides you with the information you need to complete the task and get on with your work. Enjoy!

Windows Basics

1 The Basics **5**

2 Up and Running **25**

3 Using the Windows XP Desktop **49**

4 Working with Files and Folders **75**

5 Printing **105**

6 Working on a Network **123**

7 Working Away from the Network **145**

8 Having Fun with Windows XP **161**

9 Changing Windows XP Settings **177**

10 Optimizing Your Computer **211**

11 Installing New Software and Hardware **227**

12 Troubleshooting Your Computer **245**

13 Back Up and Restore Your Computer **257**

1 Computers Are Not Fragile 6

2 How to Learn About Computers 8

3 What Is a Computer? 10

4 The Two Personal Computing Camps 12

5 Programs: The Wizard Behind the Curtain 14

6 What You Can Do with a Computer 16

7 Hardware Versus Software 20

8 The Two Types of Software 22

1

The Basics

Learning to use computers is like learning a new language. Along with the new vocabulary and skills, you will inevitably acquire some new ways of thinking about and interacting with the world. Even if all you learn to do is plug in the computer and compose letters, the computer might change your writing process by making it much easier to revise what you've written.

Learning about computers will also give you access to new ways of obtaining and working with information. After you know how to operate a computer, you can easily use it to chat with people across the country or the globe, about everything from international politics to recipes for bouillabaisse to Chinese word processing programs. If you have an office job, computer literacy might enable you to carry out some or all of your work from home—letting you communicate with the office computer using your own computer and a telephone. Finally, you might gain glimpses of what the future will be like, when computers are sure to be even more ubiquitous and more capable than they are today.

In short, learning about computers will probably change your life, at least a little. Consider it an adventure.

Computers Are Not Fragile

Before you start using your computer, you should know one critical thing. Contrary to popular opinion, computers are hard to break. There is no key or combination of keys that you can press that will damage the machine. Shy of dropping the computer on the ground or spilling soft drinks on it, there is little havoc you can wreak that is irreversible or even more than annoying.

① **Protect Your Disks**

The one fragile part of the whole setup is your computer's disks, which do not take kindly to vibration, dust, smoke, magnets, extreme heat, or spilled coffee. But for the most part, your computer is a sturdy object, without any auto-destruct sequence or ejector seat.

② Most Mistakes Aren't Fatal

If you issue an instruction to your computer that doesn't make sense, it will usually let you know by displaying a message on the screen. As soon as you acknowledge the message (often by pressing another key), it disappears and the computer discards all knowledge of the misdeed.

③ Fixing Mistakes

Computers are also very forgiving. Even if you blindly press every key in sight, the most likely result is that you will just delete some of the information you just entered. (Even this will take a little effort, and if you notice the mistake right away, it can often be corrected with a single command.)

If you see a button like this, you can click it to undo what you just did.

④ Try Again

You might inadvertently tell the computer to do something other than what you intended. After you notice the problem, you can almost always find a way to undo what you just did and then try again.

How-to Hint

Why Computers Break Down

I don't mean to imply that computers never break down. They do. But they break because of electronic or mechanical failure, rather than because you pressed the wrong key at the wrong time.

How to Learn About Computers

The prospect of learning about computers can be intimidating for these reasons:

- People who already know about computers speak a dialect guaranteed to frighten off newcomers.

- It seems that everyone else, including every five-year-old on the block, already knows how to use computers.

- Maybe it's been awhile since you've explored such thoroughly new terrain.

For those of you who feel a little anxious or inadequate at the thought of "learning computers," here are some suggestions for approaching the learning process itself:

① Assume That You Have the Capacity to Do This

Just about anyone can learn to use a computer. You don't need to be good at math or have mechanical aptitude. You don't need to be geared toward logical or linear thinking. You do, however, need some patience, self-confidence, and determination not to give up when something doesn't work the first (or even the second or third) time you try it.

② Acquire New Knowledge in Bite-sized Pieces

Don't try to absorb everything at once. Learn only as much as you can comfortably assimilate in a single session, and then review and practice until you have mastered the material. Then go back and learn some more.

③ Make It Concrete

Whenever possible, put at least some of the information or skills you acquire to immediate use. Your new knowledge is much more likely to "stick" if you find some way to put it to work. When you read about computer equipment, see whether you can locate the various components in your own computer system. When you read about a particular type of computer program, imagine how you (or other people or businesses) might use such a program (or whether you'd have any use for it at all).

4 Cultivate Curiosity

The best way to get good at computers is to experiment, to question, to wonder if you can do *x* or what would happen if you did *y*. Don't just passively accept what you read here or in computer manuals. Try to figure out some things on your own.

5 Don't Try to Be Productive Immediately

If possible, keep the learning process free of deadline pressure. (Don't decide to learn how to produce a newsletter the day before the newsletter needs to be finished.) Try to make learning about computers a task in itself, not a means to an immediate end. Schedule plenty of time for the process and, if possible, work on something that interests or amuses you.

6 When in Doubt, Don't Panic

Your aim in learning about computers should be not to avoid mistakes, but to discover what to do when they happen. I'll give you lots of hints for what to consider when things go wrong, and suggestions about where to go for more help.

Thousands of people have learned to hate computers at the hands of well-meaning friends, relatives, and co-workers—someone who tries to tell them everything they need to know about computers in 15 minutes, or who forgets there was ever a time when they didn't know what a CD-ROM drive was. If you feel stupid every time a certain someone tries to teach you about your computer, the problem probably lies in the teaching, not in you or the subject matter. If you want someone to hold your hand while you learn computers, choose someone you can ask "stupid questions," someone you don't need to impress—for most of us, this means avoiding a teacher who's either a boss or an employee, and quite possibly a spouse or child as well.

7 You Don't Need to Be a Computer Expert to Use a Computer

The purpose of the computer is to help you do something. You don't need a Ph.D. in electrical engineering to get some work done. Although you can make a career or a hobby out of learning about computers, it's fairly easy to do the basic things. If you just want to use your computer to compose and print simple letters, you can probably learn everything you need to know in an hour or two. To learn to produce a professional-looking newsletter, expect to spend weeks. (To learn to converse with computer salespeople, you may need months.) In any case, learning everything you want to know about computers might take awhile, but you can fairly quickly learn enough to get some work done.

8 Have Fun Whenever Possible!

If you merely relax and learn, you'll come to enjoy the many things your computer can do. Try not to stress about little problems or things you don't yet understand. Have fun!

How-to Hint

Computers Are Literal

As you may have already heard or experienced, computers are completely and often maddeningly literal. There's an old phrase in computer lingo called GIGO: garbage in, garbage out. In some cases, if you spell something wrong or accidentally press the wrong key, the computer won't even *try* to guess what you mean. However, when you do everything correctly, computers provide immediate and decisive feedback. When you press the right keys, you get the right results; when you don't, you don't.

What Is a Computer?

A computer is a general-purpose machine for storing and manipulating information. Beyond this, there are two very different schools of thought: 1) Computers are dumb but very fast machines equivalent to extremely powerful calculators. 2) Computers are thinking machines capable of awe-inspiring, almost limitless feats of intelligence. Actually, both statements are true.

**You see text and images and hear sound.
Inside, all information is handled as numbers.**

1 How Computers Work

By themselves, computers have a very limited set of skills. They can add, compare, and store numbers. This probably seems very strange because the computers we see each day seem to do far more than this. They manipulate text, display graphical images, generate sounds, and do lots of other things that seem nonmathematical.

2 Information Is Numbers

Internally, the computer handles all information as numbers, and everything it does involves storing and manipulating those numbers. In this sense, computers are like fancy adding machines. But if you know how to "talk" to a computer in the language of numbers, as programmers do, you can get it to do some amazing things. Any kind of information that can be represented numerically—from music to photographs to motion picture videos—can be manipulated via a computer, assuming someone knows how to provide the computer with the proper instructions.

3 Don't Need to Learn Programming

This does not mean that you need to know how to program computers (write your own instructions) to use them. You will buy and use programs that other people have created. You need to learn how to use those programs—a task that is far easier and less demanding than learning to write programs of your own.

4 Computers Are Everywhere

You probably deal with computers on a daily basis, whether you want to or not. Every time you use an ATM, watch the checker scan the bar code on your milk carton into an electronic cash register, or use a hand-held calculator, you are using a computer. Some of those computers—such as the calculator—are designed to do a specific task, and the instructions for performing that task are built into the equipment itself. The type of computer you will be using at your home or office is probably more general purpose. It can do just about anything, provided it is given appropriate instructions.

5 Shapes and Sizes of Computers

Computers come in a multitude of shapes, sizes, and types, ranging from those that fit in the palm of your hand or hide in the corner of your microwave or VCR to those that occupy entire rooms; from ones generally used by one person at a time to those simultaneously used by dozens or even hundreds of people. This book is about personal computers—computers primarily designed for use by one person at a time.

6 Personal Computers

Personal computers are relative newcomers to the computer scene. Although the first computers were built in the 1940s, the first personal computers were only introduced in the 1970s and didn't come into widespread use until the 1980s. The speed and capacity of the machines has continued to increase almost as fast as their size and price shrinks, making them all the more practical and popular. Today's personal computers are hundreds of times more powerful than those sold 10 or 15 years ago, cost less, and can fit in packages the size of a notebook.

The First Friendly Computer

In 1984, Apple introduced the original Macintosh computer, specifically designed to be easy to learn, fun to use, and non-intimidating for the nontechnical user. Although not all this technology was original with Apple, this "user friendly" computer design has come to be the standard for most personal computers.

Computer Networks

Just because personal computers are "personal" doesn't mean they can't talk to each other. Computer networks are groups of computers that are linked together so they can share information, programs, and/or equipment. You'll learn more about networks in Chapter 6, "Working on a Network." Today, a PC can talk to millions of other computers over the Internet as well. You'll learn more about the Internet in Chapter 14, "Connecting to the Internet."

The Two Personal Computing Camps

The majority of personal computers currently fall into two camps: IBM PCs/compatibles and Apple Macintosh computers (often referred to as "Macs"). Although at one time these types of computers were at opposite poles, in many ways they're growing more and more similar.

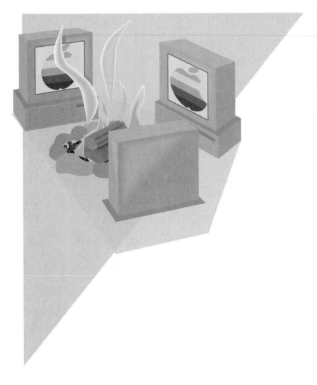

1 IBM Clones

The terms IBM clone and IBM compatible mean a computer that uses similar components and a similar design to IBM-manufactured PCs, and therefore can use the same type of programs as IBM computers. When it first created the PC, IBM decided to allow others to imitate its machines. The theory was that the more IBM imitations there were, the more likely it was that IBM-type systems and the software that runs on them would become the business standard. This strategy spurred the development of literally thousands of brands of IBM "workalikes" (also known as clones).

2 User Interfaces

For a while, the main difference between PCs and Macs involved the user interface—the way they presented information on the screen and solicited and responded to your input. In general, Macs had a more playful, less intimidating interface, centered around pictures and menus (lists of options) on the screen. The PC interface tended to be starker and more text-oriented. Today PCs employ a graphical user interface much like the Macs. (You'll learn all about this interface, called Windows, in Chapter 3, "Using the Windows XP Desktop.")

③ How to Choose a Computer

If you are planning to buy a computer, one of your big decisions will be whether to get a Mac or a PC. If possible, try playing with both types of computers and see whether you prefer one of the two. See whether you can get a special deal on one type of computer through your school or job. Don't forget to consider whether all the applications you want are available for the platform you select.

④ Computers for Work and Home

If you use a computer at work and have any plans to bring work home, you might want to get the same type of computer you use at your job. If your friends are willing to help you learn about computers and ride to the rescue when something doesn't work, you might want to get the type of computer they use.

⑤ How Will You Use Your Computer?

If you plan to use your computer for a fairly specialized task—like editing video or managing an auto repair shop—start by selecting the program you want to use, and then choose the computer the program will run on. These days, many programs have both Mac and PC versions, but some will only work on one type of computer.

⑥ What Computers Are Used in Your Field?

Even if what you're doing is not all that specialized, you might want to find out what type of computer most people in your field are using. Most graphic designers use Macs; most tax and financial consultants use PCs. If you stick with the computer most of your colleagues are using, you're more likely to find a wide range of applicable programs, and people who know both your business and your computer, in case you need help.

How-to Hint

What PC Means

Although the term *PC* (short for Personal Computer) was coined by IBM as the name for its first personal computer, its meaning has expanded over the years. Some people use PC to mean any personal computer. Others, including myself, use it to mean IBM-type computers, including IBM compatibles. In this book, PC means any computer designed to work like an IBM personal computer and able to run programs designed for such a computer.

What This Book Covers

When it comes to specific details about how computers work, this book covers PCs only. However, much of the general information applies to Macs and other personal computers as well.

⑤ # Programs: The Wizard Behind the Curtain

People new to computers sometimes think that computers come ready and willing to do anything they want them to do, like electronic Wizards of Oz. Although computers can theoretically do just about anything, by themselves they do nothing at all. They are like VCRs without tapes. What allows your computer to actually do something is a program—that is, a set of instructions that tell the computer what to do and how to do it. A program is like the man behind the curtain, turning the knobs and pulling the levers, making your computer perform or seem to perform magic.

Now I'm a word-processing machine

❶ How Programs Work

For example, to use your computer to compose and print documents, you use a word processing program. The word processing program contains instructions that tell the computer what colors, characters, and images to display on your screen and how to respond to your actions (such as pressing various keys). When you run this program, your computer is temporarily transformed into an electronic typing and word processing machine. Your screen appears largely blank, the electronic equivalent of a blank sheet of typing paper. You will see a list of options at the top of the screen that enable you to perform word processing tasks, like setting margins, underlining, or adding footnotes.

❷ "Playing" Programs

If you want to do something else with your computer— keep track of customers, for example, or play a game of solitaire—you need to find a program designed for that purpose. The computer is not "set up" to do that task, or any other task, on its own. In a sense, you could say that the basic function of a personal computer is to "play" different programs—just as VCRs are designed to play VCR tapes.

③ Using Multiple Programs

A single computer can, and usually does, hold several programs at once. In fact, these days you can run two, three, or more programs at once on your computer, and switch between them just by clicking with your mouse.

④ How Many Programs Can You Run?

The number of programs that you can run at once is limited only by the amount of "memory" your computer has. You'll learn the ins and outs of computer memory in Chapter 4, "Working with Files and Folders." (In computer lingo, memory is often called RAM, for "random access memory.")

⑤ Installed Programs

When you buy a computer, it commonly comes with many programs already installed—that is, already on your computer and set up to work with your equipment. You can install new programs whenever you like, and after they are installed, they remain stored inside the computer, ready for you to use.

⑥ How Many Programs Can Your Computer Store?

The number of programs that you can store in a single computer is limited only by the amount of disk space you have. You will learn about disks and disk space in the next chapter.

How-to Hint

Don't Open Too Many Programs at Once

Although most computers can now run several programs at the same time, it's better to run just the programs you are actually working with. Running lots of programs can make your computer run slowly.

6 What You Can Do with a Computer

You can run dozens of types of programs on a personal computer, from ones that teach typing to ones that prepare your tax returns to ones that let you play video games. For now, we'll just outline some of the major categories.

PRINTER

Hello Jane,
Just got your memo about the upgrade program. It sounds interesting. I will run the idea by the managers at the monthly sales meeting. Please keep me posted of any other programs that are likely to be helpful in the future. Thank-you.

Sincerely,

Jack McGrive

Hello Paul,
Just got a memo about an upgrade program. It sounds interesting. I will run the idea by the managers at the [...]

1 Word Processing Programs

Word processing programs such as Microsoft Word let you use your computer to compose and print letters, papers, reports, and other types of documents. They offer much more extensive editing capabilities than typewriters—such as allowing you to insert new characters, delete existing ones, and move blocks of text from one part of the document to another without retyping. Most word processing programs have features for handling page numbers and footnotes. They also generally include a mail merge feature that enables you to generate personalized form letters by "merging" a letter with a set of names and addresses.

2 Desktop Publishing Programs

Desktop publishing (DTP) programs such as Quark enable you to combine text, pictures, graphics, tables, lines, boxes, and other design elements in a single document. They let you perform the type of page layout operations required to produce documents such as newsletters, books, and flyers—operations otherwise performed in a typesetting shop. These days, the most popular word processing programs include extensive desktop publishing capabilities.

HOW TO...

③ Spreadsheet Programs

Spreadsheet programs such as Microsoft Excel are number crunchers. They let you perform almost any kind of mathematical calculation. Although they are most often used for financial calculations (budgeting, financial analysis, and forecasting), they can be used for scientific or engineering calculations and sorting other types of data as well. Besides the familiar ledger format, most have built-in graphics capabilities, permitting you to transform a set of numbers into a bar graph or pie chart, for example.

④ Accounting Programs

Accounting programs such as Quicken help you manage your money. They let you track and categorize income and expenses, reconcile your bank statements, and produce standard financial reports such as income statements and balance sheets. At one end of the spectrum are simple personal money management programs that let you balance your checkbook and track personal expenses. At the other end are sophisticated business accounting programs that generate extensive financial reports, produce invoices and statements to customers, handle accounts payable and receivable, print payroll checks and payroll reports, and track inventory.

5 Database Management Programs

Database management programs such as Microsoft Access let you store, retrieve, and manipulate large collections of information, such as mailing lists, inventories, student rosters, and library card catalogs. They enable you to keep your data up-to-date, sort it, generate statistics, print reports, and produce mailing labels. Database programs also let you extract portions of your data based on certain selection criteria—all your customers in Oregon with a credit limit over $100, for example, or all the inventory items of which there are fewer than three in stock.

6 Graphics Programs

Graphics programs such as Adobe Photoshop let you create pictures, slides, or designs to display onscreen or to print. This category includes painting and drawing programs that let you combine and modify existing pictures or construct your own. This category also includes programs that let you edit and enhance photographic images.

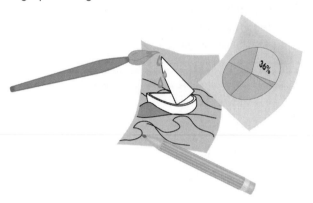

7 Browsers

Browsers such as Internet Explorer are programs that let you access and use the Internet. Most let you send and receive messages via electronic mail, as well as surf the World Wide Web for information on everything from politics to yoga, stock prices to recycling. (You can also use online services such as CompuServe and America Online to send and receive electronic mail.) You can access library card catalogs, locate airline schedules, and order products from the millions of companies that now sell their products online.

8 Presentation Programs

Presentation graphics programs such as PowerPoint create line graphs, pie graphs, organizational charts, and other types of diagrams, and, in many cases, combine these images into slideshows for use in business presentations.

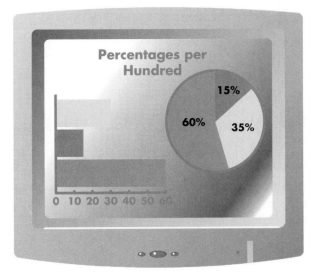

9 Game Programs

Game, entertainment, and educational programs (sometimes called *edutainment programs*) let you do everything from playing backgammon to doing battle with computer-generated dragons. There are programs that let you step inside detective and science fiction novels, work on your golf swing, and attempt to save the world from ecological disasters. There are also dozens of games for children, many of them educational, such as programs that "read" children's stories, highlighting each word on the screen while pronouncing it through the computer's speakers.

Hardware Versus Software

Now that you know what a program is (a set of instructions), you are ready for your first two pieces of computer jargon. In computer terminology, all computer equipment is referred to as *hardware* and all computer programs are known as *software*. These two terms emphasize the fact that the equipment and program are two essential parts of a working computer system. Hardware is the machinery and its physical accoutrements, including the keyboard (the part that looks like a typewriter), the screen, and the printer. Software is the set of coded instructions that brings the machinery to life.

1 **Hardware Versus Software**

Some people get a little confused about the difference between hardware and software. Part of this confusion has to do with the way software is packaged and sold.

2 **What You Get When You Buy a Program**

If you buy a new program, you get a box with one or more manuals explaining how the program works, plus either a CD-ROM or one or more floppy disks on which the program is stored.

Software is more elusive. It is like the music recorded on a CD rather than the CD itself. You can't touch it, you can only see or hear its results.

Hardware is the machinery and its physical accoutrements. It includes all parts of the computer system that you can touch.

③ Disks and CD-ROMs Are Hardware

When you get back to your home or office, you install the program by copying its instructions from the CD-ROM or floppy disks to your computer. As a result, many people think of disks as software. If you've never encountered floppy disks, they are round, flat wafers—kind of like small and flimsy records—that are encased in square plastic wrappers. They are used to store both programs and data.

④ Software on CD-ROMs

Most programs are now available on CD-ROMs—special types of compact discs that are meant to be "played" on a computer. You'll learn all about floppy disks and CD-ROMs in Chapters 2 and 3.

⑤ Hardware Rules

In fact, disks and CD-ROMs are hardware. The basic rule of thumb for determining whether something is hardware or software is whether you can touch it; and because disks and CD-ROMs can be touched, they're in the hardware camp. Software, on the other hand, is much more elusive. You can't touch, see, or taste it; you can only witness its results.

Programs Are Software

From here on, I will be using the words *program* and *software* virtually interchangeably.

Hardware and Software Work Together

The terms *hardware* and *software* emphasize the fact that the equipment and program are two essential parts of a working computer system.

The Two Types of Software

As mentioned, the native language of computers consists solely of numbers. Because few of us are able (or patient enough) to speak to a computer in this language, we almost never interact with the computer directly. We always "speak" to the computer through an intermediary, namely, a program whose function (among other things) is to translate our requests to the computer. Programs enable the computer, by telling it how to display text or pictures on the screen, produce sounds, or print characters on paper, to "speak" back to us.

① Applications Software

There are actually two different types of software: applications software and operating systems. Applications software is the software that you use to actually perform your work. This includes the types of programs previously described under "What You Can Do with a Computer," such as word processing or spreadsheet programs.

② Operating Systems

Operating systems are programs that act as the intermediary between you and the hardware and, to some extent, between the hardware and the applications software. You'll learn a great deal about how to use one particular operating system, Windows, in Chapter 3. This book doesn't go into detail about DOS, or the Macintosh operating system.

③ Operating Systems Run Your Hardware

As you will learn in Chapter 3, operating systems serve several functions. For starters, the operating system controls various parts of the machine and allows them to talk to one another; in effect, it operates the hardware. Your operating system is the essential program that makes your computer "go."

4 What You Can Do with Your Operating System

Operating systems include various "housekeeping utilities" that allow you to find out what programs and data are stored on a disk, to copy programs and data to and from your computer, and to delete programs and data.

5 Starting Applications

The operating system allows you to start up application programs. If you want to play chess on your computer, for example, you issue a command that tells the operating system, "Go find the chess program and fire it up." Then the operating system acts as an intermediary between the applications and the hardware, by making sure they understand the requests they make of each other.

6 Different Operating Systems

Different operating systems are designed for different types of computers. If you are running a PC, you will probably use an operating system named Windows. The latest version of Windows is Windows XP. Depending on the age of your computer, you might be using Windows Me, Windows 2000, Windows NT, Windows 98, or Windows 95.

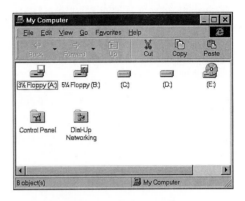

7 How DOS Worked

The Windows operating system employs pictures and menus to help you manage your application's programs and data. In contrast, DOS, which before the advent of Windows was the most common operating system on PCs, used a command-driven interface—whenever you wanted the computer to do something, you needed to type in a command. Because there were no visual cues on the screen, you needed to either memorize all the commands or look them up in a book as needed.

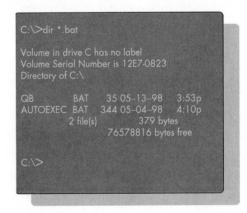

1. What Happens When You Turn On Your Computer 26

2. Keyboards and Keyboard Layouts 28

3. The Cursor Movement Keys 30

4. The Special Keys 32

5. The Modifier and Function Keys 34

6. The Numeric Keypad .36

7. What to Do When You Get Stuck 38

8. Using a Mouse, Trackball, or Touch Pad 40

9. Things You Can Do with a Mouse or Trackball 42

10. Turning Off Your Computer 44

11. Ergonomics: Taking Care of Your Body While
You Use a Computer .46

Task

Up and Running

This chapter discusses several things that are essential to know before you can operate your computer. Much of the information you'll learn here—such as how to turn the machine on and off and how to find your way around the keyboard—might seem obvious to those of you with even a small amount of computer experience. At the same time, these pages might reveal some new twist that you didn't know about, such as a new keyboard strategy for getting yourself out of trouble.

First, you'll learn what exactly happens when you turn on your computer—how to decode some of the sounds you'll hear and messages you'll see. Then you'll get some in-depth information about keyboards and keyboard layouts. You'll find out how to make your way around with the cursor movement keys. You'll also learn the ins and outs of some special keys, particularly the **Delete** and **Backspace** keys. In addition, you'll discover how and when to use the function keys, either by themselves or in combination with modifier keys such as **Ctrl** and **Shift**. As you'll see, you can enter numbers speedily with the numeric keypad, which can typically double as a set of extra cursor movement keys as well. Some of the most valuable keys and key combinations you'll discover are those that help you get unstuck.

You can also communicate with and control your computer via the mouse or its stand-ins: the trackball or touch pad. In this chapter, you'll learn the full variety of mousing techniques. After that, you will find out the proper way to turn off your computer. Finally, you'll learn some tips for arranging the different parts of your computer system for maximum comfort and minimum back, wrist, and eye strain.

What Happens When You Turn On Your Computer

Many personal computer systems are set up so that all the components, including the system unit and the monitor, are plugged into a single power strip. In this case, you turn on your computer (and everything else in sight) by throwing the switch on the power strip itself. If you don't have a power strip, you'll have to turn on the components one at a time. As you'll learn here, a whole sequence of events happens next.

❶ What Happens First

Your computer hardware can't do much of anything without instructions. When you turn on a computer, the first thing it does is go searching for a program that can tell it what to do next.

❷ The Boot Program

The program the CPU is looking for is a very small part of the operating system known as the boot program. This program is stored in ROM and is known as the boot program because it essentially helps the computer "pull itself up by its own bootstraps," by loading (booting) the rest of the operating system into memory. The basic input/output system (BIOS) is part of the operating system that is stored in ROM. It runs the basic startup tests for your computer.

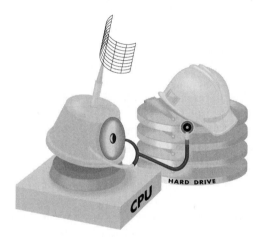

The CPU makes sure the disk drives and other components are working. The CPU takes an inventory of memory.

3 The Power On Self Test

Under the direction of this boot program, the CPU performs what is known as a *power on self test (POST)*. During this stage, the CPU tests to see whether the various parts of the system are still alive and well. You will see a progress report during this phase. At a minimum, you will probably notice the computer counting up its memory. You might also see messages as the CPU checks out various peripherals, and little lights on your keyboard and printer might turn on and off. Finally, a beep will indicate that everything seems to be okay.

4 Searching for the Operating System

After the CPU has finished its internal inventory, it goes hunting for the rest of the operating system: the part that is stored on disk. The first place it looks is in the floppy disk drive. (If you have a PC with two floppy disk drives, it looks to the one named drive A—which is usually the leftmost or uppermost drive.) If the floppy disk drive is empty, the CPU continues its search on the hard drive.

The read/write head, under instructions from the CPU, locates the operating system on the hard disk.

5 If You Have a Disk in the Floppy Disk Drive

If there is a disk in the floppy disk drive, your computer checks whether it contains the operating system. If it doesn't, the computer informs you that you have an invalid system disk or a non-system disk or disk error. Just open the floppy disk-drive door or eject the disk and then press any key on your keyboard to have the CPU resume hunting for the operating system on your hard drive. (The moral of this story is that if you plan to work with a floppy disk, postpone inserting it until your system is done booting.)

6 When Windows Starts

As soon as the CPU locates the operating system, it loads it into memory. If you are running Windows XP, you'll see the message `Starting Windows XP` and then the Microsoft Windows XP logo. (If you are running another version of Windows, you will see that version's logo and name at this point.) If you are not part of a network, you'll probably go immediately to a screen known as the *Windows desktop*. (You learn all about the desktop in Chapter 3, "Using the Windows XP Desktop.")

7 Logging In to a Network

If you are on a network you'll need to enter your name and password before you arrive at the desktop. This process is known as *logging in*.

Keyboards and Keyboard Layouts

Before you can use your computer effectively, you need to know your way around the keyboard. Your computer keyboard is very sensitive; you don't need to bang or lean on the keys, placing unnecessary stress on both your own wrists and the keyboard's innards; your computer recognizes and responds to the lightest key press. If you hold down a key for more than a second, your computer will respond as though you had pressed it several times in rapid succession. The effect will depend on what that key actually does in the program you are using, but it's unlikely to be the intended result. If you're not accustomed to typing at all, experiment to find the lightest touch that will work on your machine.

① The Standard Keyboard

Close to a dozen different styles of computer keyboards are available. One of the most common keyboards is shown in the figure below. Although almost all keyboards have the letter and number keys in the same places, the location of other keys can vary.

② The Feel of a Keyboard

Different brands of keyboards can also have a very different feel. On some, the keys click when you press them and on some they don't; the keys feel stiffer on some keyboards and looser on others. The nice part about this variety is that you can choose the feel and the layout you like. The unfortunate part is that if you switch computers at some point, you might need to spend some time getting used to the feel of the keyboard and searching for keys.

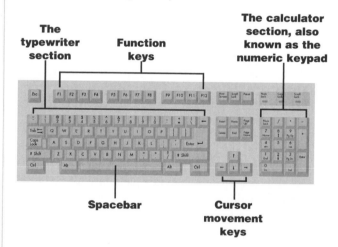

The typewriter section   Function keys   The calculator section, also known as the numeric keypad

Spacebar   Cursor movement keys

Your keyboard might have a different arrangement of keys. If you are using an older computer, or a laptop or notebook computer, you might have fewer keys altogether.

❸ The Caps Lock Key

Caps Lock is what is known as a toggle key—a key you use to alternately enable and disable a particular feature. You press it once to turn the feature on and again to turn it off. Unlike the **Shift Lock** key on a typewriter, **Caps Lock** on a computer keyboard affects letters only. This means that typing a dollar sign requires holding down the **Shift** key while you press the 4 at the top of your keyboard, even if **Caps Lock** is on.

❹ The Enter Key

If you first learned to type on a typewriter, you'll find that the **Enter** key works something like a carriage return: You press it to move to the next line when you get to the end of a paragraph. However, you don't need to press **Enter** at the end of each line in word processing programs; the program automatically "word wraps" text to the next line when you reach the right margin. You still need to press **Enter** to force the cursor to a new line before you reach the right margin, however. You also sometimes use **Enter** to select options from a menu (onscreen list of options) or to indicate that you are done entering instructions or data and want the program to respond. (Not sure just what the cursor is? You'll learn in a moment.)

❺ The Tab Key

On some older PC keyboards and many laptops, the **Tab** key doesn't actually say Tab. It just has two arrows pointing in opposite directions, such as → ←. In some cases you get both the text and the arrows.

How-to Hint

Different Names for the Enter Key

The **Enter** key is labeled Return on certain older PC keyboards. In addition, some keyboards label the **Enter** key with the ↵ symbol. This symbol is used to indicate "Press the Enter key now" in many software manuals. Your keyboard also might have an additional **Enter** key, at the right of the numeric keypad, for entering numbers.

The Cursor Movement Keys

In most programs, a symbol indicates where you are on the screen at the moment—like a "you are here" indicator on a map for a park or shopping mall. When you are entering text in Windows, the "you are here" symbol is a blinking vertical line known as the *insertion point*. (Its DOS equivalent was the cursor.) On most keyboards, there are two groups of keys designed to move the cursor or insertion point around the screen: the **arrow keys** and another set of keys called **Home**, **End**, **Page Up**, and **Page Down**. You might also have a duplicate set of cursor movement keys on the numeric keypad. You can move the cursor or insertion point by using either the cursor movement keys or your mouse.

The insertion point or cursor indicates your current position on the screen.

① The Arrow Keys

The **arrow keys** move the cursor/insertion point one character or one unit at a time in the direction of the arrow. To move one character to the left when you are entering text in a word processing program, for example, you press the left **arrow key**. On most keyboards, the arrows occupy keys by themselves.

② Additional Navigation Keys

The other cursor movement keys (**Home**, **End**, **Page Up**, and **Page Down**) let you make larger jumps across the screen. On some laptop keyboards, there are no separate cursor movement keys; they are always part of the numeric keypad (the calculator section). You'll discover how to use these dual-purpose keys when you learn about the numeric keypad.

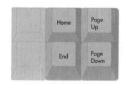

③ The Home Key

The **Home** key is often used to move to the beginning of some set of data—such as the top of a document, the beginning of a line, or the upper-left corner of a spreadsheet.

④ The End Key

The **End** key is often used to move to the end of some set of data—such as the bottom of a document, the end of a line, or the last number or character in a particular block of data in a spreadsheet.

⑤ The Page Up Key

The **Page Up** key is usually used to move up one page or one screenful of data. (This key is often labeled **PgUp**.)

⑥ The Page Down Key

The **Page Down** key is usually used to move down one page or one screenful of data. (This key is often labeled **PgDn**.)

⑦ Moving the Insertion Point with the Mouse

You can also move the cursor or insertion point by using a mouse. Typically, you do this by clicking where you want the insertion point to go.

The Cursor

If you're still using DOS, the "you are here" symbol is a little blinking line or rectangle, known as a cursor. Keys for navigating in Windows programs are still called "cursor movement keys," even though they're actually moving the insertion point. You might occasionally see the insertion point referred to as the cursor.

The Cursor Versus the Insertion Point

You'll never have both a cursor and an insertion point. You always have one or the other, depending on the type of computer and the program you are using.

The Special Keys

The special keys include all the keys other than normal typewriter keys, cursor movement keys, the numeric keypad (the set of keys resembling a calculator), and function keys. These keys are scattered around the keyboard, and they generally perform some operation other than displaying a particular character on the screen.

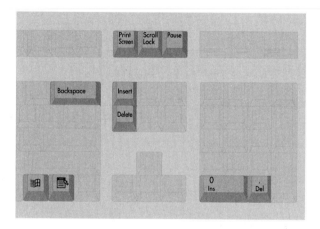

The Backspace key gobbles characters to the left of the cursor or insertion point.

The Delete key (sometimes abbreviated Del) gobbles characters to the right of the cursor or insertion point.

1 The Backspace and Delete Keys

Most PC keyboards include two keys for erasing. The key labeled either **Delete** or **Del** generally deletes the character immediately to the right of the insertion point. The **Backspace** key deletes the character to the left of the insertion point. (On some keyboards, the key doesn't say "Backspace"; it shows a left-pointing arrow.)

2 Deleting Selected Text

In most programs, you can also select a group of characters to erase using either your keyboard or the mouse. Pressing either the **Backspace** or the **Delete** key will delete any currently selected characters. (In case you don't already know, you'll learn how to select shortly, in the task "Things You Can Do with a Mouse or Trackball.")

3 The Insert Key

The **Insert** (or **Ins**) key is a toggle that determines what happens when you type new characters within existing text or numbers. If the Insert feature is on and you type new characters in the middle of a paragraph, for example, the old characters are pushed to the right to make room for the new ones. With Insert off, the new characters replace the old ones. In most programs, Insert might be set on by default, so you don't accidentally overtype what you've already entered. On some keyboards, Insert shares a key with the number 0 on the numeric keypad.

4 The Windows Logo Key

Some keyboards designed specifically to work with Windows contain two extra types of keys— **Application** keys and **Windows Logo** keys—that provide fast keyboard alternatives to many operations you'd usually perform with a mouse. For example, you can use the **Windows Logo** keys to open the **Start** menu, instead of clicking the **Start** button at the lower-left corner of the desktop.

5 The Application Key

You can use the **Application** key to bring up a shortcut menu relevant to what you're doing at the moment (it's the equivalent of right-clicking). If you're not sure whether your keyboard contains these keys, look a bit to the left and right of the spacebar. The **Windows Logo** keys contain the Windows logo (surprise). The **Application** key looks like a menu with an arrow pointing to it.

How-to Hint

Backspace Versus Left Arrow

Don't confuse the **Backspace** key and the **Left Arrow** key. Both of these keys contain left-pointing arrows. Although both of these keys move the insertion point to the left, the **Left Arrow** (like all arrow keys) doesn't change anything. In contrast, the **Backspace** key moves and erases at the same time. Every time you press the key, the character to the left of the insertion point is deleted and the insertion point moves left one space to take up the slack.

The Modifier and Function Keys

All PC keyboards contain three types of special keys that you use almost exclusively in combination with other keys. They don't do anything by themselves. (Many keyboards contain two keys of each type—two **Shift** keys, two **Control** keys, and so on.) This book will refer to these special keys as *modifier* keys. Occasionally, the modifier keys are used with a row of keys called *function* keys—labeled **F1**, **F2**, and so on—that you'll probably find across the top of your keyboard.

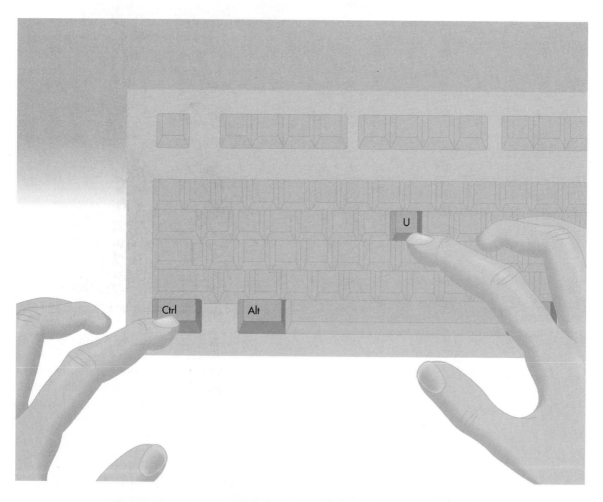

When you use key combinations, you always press the modifier key (in this case Ctrl) first and hold it down while you press the other key.

① Modifier Keys

For those of you who've used typewriters, the **Shift** key on a typewriter is an example of a modifier key. Pressing the **Shift** key by itself does nothing. But if you hold down **Shift** while pressing the letter **A**, you get an uppercase A instead of the lowercase a you get by pressing the **A** key by itself.

② The Shift, Control, and Alt Modifier Keys

Similarly, on a PC keyboard, nothing happens when you press **Shift**, **Control** (**Ctrl**), or **Alternate** (**Alt**). But in many application programs, holding down a modifier key while pressing another key is a way of issuing a command. In some word processing programs, for example, holding down the **Ctrl** key while pressing **U** issues the command to underline any currently selected text (while pressing **U** by itself would generate a letter U, and pressing **Ctrl** by itself would do nothing). These key combinations are often called *hot keys* or *keyboard shortcuts*.

③ Using Modifier Keys with Cursor Movement Keys

Often you can also modify the way the cursor movement keys work by using them in combination with one of the modifier keys. For example, in Microsoft Word, pressing **Home** moves the insertion point to the beginning of the current line, whereas pressing **Ctrl+Home** moves the insertion point to the beginning of the document. **Shift+Home** selects a block of text from the beginning of the paragraph to the insertion point.

④ What Is a Key Combination?

A *key combination* is a combination of two or more keys (at least one of which is a modifier key) to perform an operation. To use a key combination, you press the modifier key first and hold it down while you press the other key. Don't try to press both keys at once; you might press the second key slightly before you press the modifier key, which has the effect of pressing that second key by itself.

⑤ How Key Combinations Are Notated

When computer books or manuals refer to key combinations, they sometimes combine the names of the keys with commas, hyphens, or plus signs. In other words, if you're supposed to hold down **Alt** while you press the **Backspace** key, you might see **Alt,Backspace**, **Alt-Backspace**, or **Alt+Backspace**.

⑥ Function Keys

The function keys are the keys labeled **F1** through either **F10** or **F12** and are usually located at the top of the keyboard. In many application programs, function keys are used to issue commands. For example, **F1** frequently invokes an application's Help system, which provides you with information on how to use the program. **F10** sometimes activates the program's menu system. Surprisingly, in many programs many of the function keys have no function at all.

How-to Hint

Function and Modifier Keys Together

The function keys are sometimes used in combination with the modifier keys. For example, in a number of word processing programs, pressing **Shift+F7** invokes the thesaurus.

The Numeric Keypad

Currently, two basic layouts exist for PC keyboards: one, often called the *extended keyboard*, for desktop PCs, and another for laptops. The main difference is that most desktop keyboards have both a numeric keypad and separate groups of cursor movement keys, while most laptops have a numeric keypad that doubles as a set of cursor movement keys.

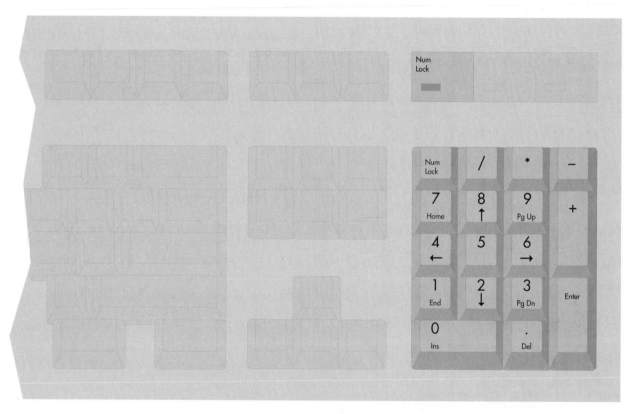

You can use the numeric keypad either for typing numbers or moving around the screen, depending on the current status of the Num Lock setting.

① The Two Ways to Use the Numeric Keypad

On all keyboards, you can use the numeric keypad for either of two functions: typing numbers or moving around on the screen. The status of the Num Lock (number lock) setting—which you control by pressing the **Num Lock** key—determines the function.

② The Num Lock Key

Num Lock is a toggle key: Each time you press it, the status of the Num Lock feature changes, from off to on or on to off. When Num Lock is on, the keys on the numeric keypad generate numbers. When Num Lock is off, they change to cursor movement keys. The **7** key acts like a **Home** key, for example, and the **8** key serves as an **Up Arrow** key. The function of each key is spelled out on the key itself. (The effect of the cursor movement keys was covered earlier in this chapter.)

③ Other Keys on the Numeric Keypad

The keys other than the **Num Lock** key around the outside of the numeric keypad work the same regardless of the Num Lock setting. You can use them to enter mathematical symbols such as + and -. (In a number of applications, the / symbolizes division and the * symbolizes multiplication.)

④ The Enter, Insert, and Delete Keys on the Numeric Keypad

The **Enter** key on the numeric keypad works just like the **Enter** key in the main section of the keyboard. (If you're typing lots of numbers, you might want to use this **Enter** key rather than the one that's in with the typewriter keys.) The **Ins** and **Del** keys work just like the **Insert** and **Delete** keys typically found to the left of the **Home** and **End** keys.

⑤ How to Tell Whether Num Lock Is On

You can usually determine whether Num Lock is on in several ways. On most keyboards, there is a little light on the key itself or a light labeled Num Lock above the key. If the light is on, the feature is on. Many application programs also display the words Num Lock or Num on the screen when Num Lock is on. If needed, you can check by pressing one of the arrow keys and see whether the cursor moves or a number is generated.

⑥ Turning Off Num Lock

Why would you want to turn off Num Lock? On many laptops, there is no separate set of arrow keys; you have to choose between using the cursor movement keys and using the numeric keypad to type numbers. If you don't need to do a lot of moving around at the moment, you might turn Num Lock on temporarily to enter a set of numbers, particularly if you're a touch-typing wiz on calculators. Otherwise, leave Num Lock off and use the number keys at the top of the keyboard to enter numbers.

How-to Hint

Entering Arithmetic Operators from the Numeric Keypad

It's often easier to type arithmetic operators (such as + and *) using keys at the side of the numeric keypad rather than keys at the top of the keyboard. If you use the keys at the top, you need to remember to hold down the **Shift** key; otherwise, you'll get = when you mean +, or 8 when you mean *.

Options for Navigating

The **Num Lock** key was carried over to the newer keyboards primarily to accommodate people who were already used to navigating with keys on the numeric keypad. Some people also prefer the layout of arrow keys on the numeric keypad (with the **Up Arrow** key above the **Left Arrow** and **Right Arrow** keys).

What to Do When You Get Stuck

Never turn off your computer in the middle of an application if you can avoid it. (Turning off your computer is covered later in this chapter.) It can damage data and, at the least, cause you to lose any unsaved data in memory. Occasionally, however, you might just get stuck. There might be a "bug" (glitch) in the program you are using, causing an error message that won't go away; or the program might stop responding to your commands. Here are some techniques to try if you do get stuck, listed from the least drastic to the most.

❶ The Escape Key

In many application programs, the **Escape** (or **Esc**) key is a general-purpose "get me out of here" key—used to cancel or back up a step in the current operation.

❷ The Break Key

If the **Escape** key doesn't solve your problem, you can try the **Break** key. On most keyboards, either the **Scroll Lock** or **Pause** key doubles as a **Break** key. (You should see the word Break either on top of the key or on its front edge. If you don't find Break on either key, you can use **Scroll Lock** for this purpose.) By itself, **Break** does nothing, but holding down a **Ctrl** key and pressing this key will interrupt some programs or commands. This key combination is referred to as **Ctrl+Break** (pronounced "Control Break").

③ Rebooting Your Machine

If neither of the preceding techniques works, you can reboot your computer by holding down the **Ctrl** and **Alt** keys and then tapping the **Del** key. This opens a window that allows you to close specific programs or to reboot the machine by pressing **Ctrl+Alt+Del** a second time. Rebooting erases memory and reloads the operating system; you lose any data currently in memory. In some programs, you can damage data as well, so only use this key combination when you can't think of any other solution. Although fairly drastic, rebooting is still a bit safer than the next two options.

④ The Reset Button

Many PCs have a **Reset** button that lets you restart your computer without actually flicking the power switch. The main power to the computer's components is not interrupted. This saves wear and tear. (Some, but not all, **Reset** buttons are actually labeled Reset. If you can't find yours, check in the documentation for your computer.)

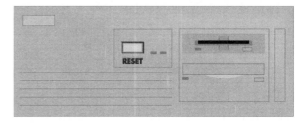

⑤ If All Else Fails

If all else fails and your computer does not have a **Reset** button, turn off the computer by switching off the power supply switch, wait at least 30 seconds, and then turn it on again.

How-to Hint Closing Programs and Rebooting in Windows

If you are using Windows, pressing **Ctrl+Alt+Del** invokes a **Close Program** dialog box. From there, you can select the program you suspect is causing the problem and click the **End Task** button. If that doesn't work, click the **Shut Down** button. If you still have no luck, press **Ctrl+Alt+Del** again.

Using a Mouse, Trackball, or Touch Pad

Keyboards are only one of the tools available for talking to your computer. The other main tool is a mouse or trackball. A *mouse* is a hand-held pointing device that lets you point to, select, and manipulate objects on the screen. As you move the mouse around on your desk, a special symbol, known as the *mouse pointer*, moves in an analogous direction on the screen. If you move the mouse forward and backward, the mouse pointer moves up and down on the screen; if you move the mouse left and right, the mouse pointer moves left and right. Although the mouse pointer most often looks like an arrow, it can assume many other shapes, depending on which program you are running and what operation you are performing.

❶ Using the Mouse

You can hold the mouse in either hand. Most people prefer to use their dominant hand—the right if right-handed or left if left-handed. (Most computer stores offer left-handed mice.) Make sure the mouse cord is pointing away from you. Then just glide the mouse lightly over the surface of your desk or mouse pad.

❷ Moving the Mouse

If you reach the edge of your desk or mouse pad before you reach the desired point on the screen, just lift your mouse up and move it. The mouse pointer only moves when the mouse is flat against a hard surface; the ball underneath rolls as you move the device. If you want to move the mouse pointer to the bottom of your screen, for example, and you reach the front edge of your desk when the mouse pointer is still an inch above the desired spot, just lift the mouse, move it up a few inches, put it back down again, and continue moving it down.

❸ Using a Mouse Pad

If your computer didn't come with one, you will want to purchase a *mouse pad*, a rectangular piece of nylon-covered rubber that you place on your desk as a platform for your mouse. A mouse often gets better traction and therefore moves more smoothly on a pad than directly on a desk, particularly one with an uneven surface.

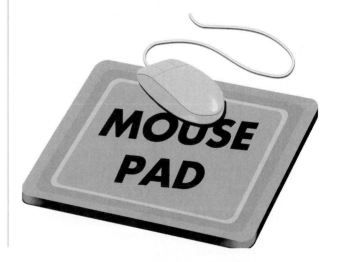

④ Trackballs

A *trackball* is essentially an upside-down mouse. Instead of having a ball on the bottom, it has a ball on the top, set inside a square cradle. Rolling this ball has the same effect as moving a mouse.

⑤ Pointing Sticks

Laptop computers sometimes sport yet another type of pointing device, known as a *pointing stick*. This is a small cylindrical piece of plastic that looks like the eraser on the end of a pencil. It is usually positioned in the center of the keyboard. By pushing the stick in various directions, you can control the movement of the mouse pointer on your screen. (The stick itself does not actually move when pushed, but it does respond to the pressure of your finger.) Computers with pointing sticks generally have two buttons near the bottom of the keyboard that you can press to simulate left and right mouse clicks.

⑥ Touch Pads

A touch pad is a small rectangular area on some keyboards. Moving your finger across the touch pad causes the pointer to move across the screen.

⑦ The Two Mouse Buttons

Many of the operations that you perform using a mouse, trackball, or touch pad involve pushing buttons. Mice designed for PCs typically have two buttons: a left button and a right button. The buttons on a trackball are usually positioned at the far end of the device. You can press them using either your thumb or forefinger. On a touch pad, you can click by either tapping the pad with your finger or pressing the left button.

⑧ Cleaning Your Mouse

If your mouse pointer starts moving in fits and starts or moves in one direction but not another, it's probably time for a mouse cleaning. Turn the mouse upside down. Next, either slide the round lid down until it pops open or turn it counterclockwise until it reaches the open position. Drop the ball out into your palm. Clean the rollers inside the mouse using a cotton swab dipped in alcohol. Clean the ball using a soft, dry cloth. Replace the ball and the lid and you're ready to go. To reassemble a trackball after cleaning, place the ball in one hand, with your other hand, place the mouse part on top of it, and flip your hands over.

Things You Can Do with a Mouse or Trackball

Moving the mouse pointer where you want it is just the first step. After you've done so, you need to use one of the available buttons, depending on which type of action you want to carry out. When you read software manuals, you are likely to encounter the following terms for the various things you can do with a mouse or trackball.

1 Pointing

Point means position the mouse pointer over a particular word or object on the screen. If the mouse pointer looks like an arrow, you need to position the tip of the arrow over the desired object. Pointing is usually the precursor to actually doing anything by using one of the mouse buttons.

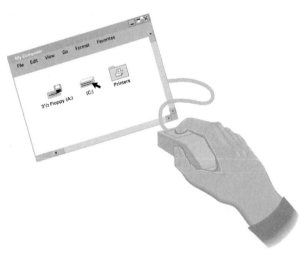

2 Pressing the Mouse Button

Press means press and hold down the mouse (or trackball) button. You need to press the mouse button in preparation for dragging, which is described in a moment.

3 Clicking

Click means tap the button—pressing it in and then releasing it quickly. The term *click* generally means click the left mouse button. *Right-click* means tap the right mouse button. Often you click to initiate some action, such as pulling down a menu of choices. In Windows, right-clicking typically displays a shortcut menu of choices relevant to the object you clicked.

④ Double-Clicking

Double-click means click the button twice in rapid succession. Double-clicking often initiates some action right away; for example, if you have a program icon on your desktop, double-clicking that icon will launch the program.

⑤ Dragging

Drag means move the mouse or trackball while holding down the button. (*Right-drag* means move the mouse or trackball while holding down the right button.) Dragging is frequently used to move or resize items on the screen, as well as to select text or other items. When you've dragged the item to its new location, you drop it by releasing the mouse button. This procedure is called *drag-and-drop*.

Click Means the Left Mouse Button

When you see instructions to press or click the mouse button, assume that you should use the left mouse button unless explicitly told otherwise. If you are supposed to click the right mouse button, for example, the instructions will say "right-click" or "click the right mouse button" rather than just "click."

How to Click the Mouse

To click the mouse in a particular spot, move the pointer to that spot and then, without moving the mouse, just use your index finger to press the mouse button. (Some beginners try to jab the mouse key from on high, which usually jettisons the mouse pointer away from its target.) If you're double-clicking, be sure to keep the mouse in the same spot between the first and second click.

Adjusting the Double-Click Speed

If every time you try to double-click, the computer responds as if you'd only clicked once, chances are you're waiting too long between the first and second click. If you're using Windows, you can adjust the double-click speed—that is, the amount of time you're allowed to leave between clicks. To do this, open the **Start** menu and select **Control Panel**. Then double-click the mouse icon, and you'll be there.

⑩ Turning Off Your Computer

The first thing to know about turning off your computer is not to do it too often. In general, you should turn it off only when you don't plan on using it again for several hours. If you're going to lunch, leaving the computer on causes less wear and tear than turning it off and then on again. (Some people even leave their computers on night and day, presumably with the thought that this is easier on the machine in the long run, even though it might not be easier on their electricity.) However, you might want to turn off your monitor temporarily, to protect the screen and to turn off the electromagnetic radiation. The monitor also consumes the most energy.

① Saving Your Work

When you are done using your computer for the day, save any unsaved data that you want to be able to use in future work sessions.

② If You Close Before You Save

If you are using Windows and forget to save something, the program double-checks with you before discarding your changes.

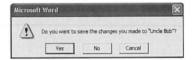

③ Shutting Down

After confirming your choices, click the **Start** button in the lower-left corner of the screen to display a **Start** menu. Click the **Turn off Computer** option.

Turning Off Your System

When Windows displays a box with the title Turn Off Computer, click the button labeled **Turn Off**. In a moment, you'll see the message `It's now safe to turn off your computer` and you can flip the on/off switch or press the power button.

5 **Automatic Shut Down**

Some laptops and desktops are smart enough to turn themselves off automatically. All you do is choose the Turn Off Computer option; you don't need to flip an on/off switch or press a power button.

6 **When You Can Turn Your Computer Back On**

If you turn your computer off and then decide to turn it on again, wait for 30 seconds first to let all the electrical charges dissipate from the machine.

How-to Hint

Shutting Down

In versions of Windows before XP, the Turn Off Computer sequence was known as Shut Down. If you are using Windows 98, for example, you will see Shut Down instead of Turn Off Computer. The end result is the same either way.

Safe Mode

If you turn off your computer without shutting down properly in Windows, when you turn your computer on again, you might see a message indicating that the computer is starting in "safe mode." If so, let the computer finish booting, and then shut it down properly. When you see the **Turn Off Computer** dialog box, choose **Restart** and then click **OK**. When your computer restarts, it should be in regular (rather than safe) mode.

Ergonomics: Taking Care of Your Body While You Use a Computer

You'll never learn to love (or even tolerate) a computer if it causes you discomfort or pain. If you plan to spend hours at the keyboard, it's worth taking time to make the experience as comfortable as possible. Setting up your workstation properly isn't just about feeling good (although that's a worthy goal). It's also a way of preventing painful and potentially debilitating conditions like carpal tunnel syndrome, tendonitis, repetitive motion disorder, and chronic back pain. The figure shows how to arrange your computer to cause minimum wear and tear on your body. The basic rules of thumb are as given in the following paragraphs.

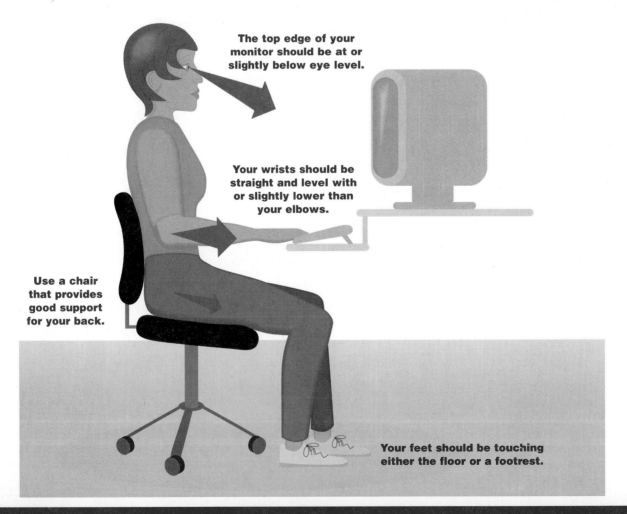

The top edge of your monitor should be at or slightly below eye level.

Your wrists should be straight and level with or slightly lower than your elbows.

Use a chair that provides good support for your back.

Your feet should be touching either the floor or a footrest.

1 Your Monitor

The top edge of your monitor should be at eye level or a little below, so you're looking down just slightly. (You might need to prop up the monitor with a large book or a monitor stand.) The front edge should be 20–30 inches from your eyes.

2 Desk Height and Posture

Your wrists should never be higher than your elbows. Ideally, your elbows should be bent at a 90° angle and your wrists should be straight, not flexed upward or bent downward. If you can't achieve this position using your desk, your desk is too high (or your chair seat too low). Try a typing desk or a keyboard drawer that allows the keyboard to sit lower than the desktop. Your feet should touch the floor or a footrest and the angle between your thighs and spine should be 90° or a bit more.

3 Proper Mousing

Keep your mouse close to the keyboard so you don't have to reach far to use it. This will minimize strain on your shoulders. Also, try not to sit for hours with your hand on the mouse; let go of the mouse when you're not using it. If you use the mouse even more than the keyboard, put the mouse directly in front of you and the keyboard slightly off to the side. If you do start developing strain in your mouse arm or shoulder, consider using a touch pad.

How-to Hint

Breaks Are Important

One of the best ways to baby your body while using a computer is to take frequent and regular breaks. At least once an hour, take a minute or two to stand up, stretch your arms, turn your head from side to side, roll your shoulders around, and flex and extend your wrists.

Using a Glare Screen

If you're suffering from eye strain, you might want to try a glare screen. These screens, which you can buy for about $20, are usually made of very fine wire mesh, to fit over the front of your monitor—cutting down on glare and, in many cases, sharpening the contrast between light and dark.

4 Proper Wrist Position

Oneof the worst things you can do to your wrists is lean the heel of your hand on the desk with your wrist flexed backward as you type. Train yourself to hold your wrists up while you're typing (like your piano teacher taught you) or rest them on a wrist rest. Some mice conform to the shape of your hand and can result in less strain. You can also alleviate wrist strain by adjusting the angle of your keyboard. You can angle most keyboards so the back is slightly higher than the front.

5 Ergonomic Keyboards

Part of the problem with most computer keyboards is that they force you to hold your hands at an unnatural angle to your arms; your hands are both more horizontal to the desk than they'd like to be and rotated slightly outward at the wrist. Microsoft makes an ergonomic keyboard in which the left-hand and right-hand keys are slightly separated and angled outwards. (The angle between the keys cannot be adjusted.) There are similar keyboards available from third-party vendors.

6 Rest Your Eyes

Many people also experience some eye strain after staring at a computer screen for a few hours. The best approach here is to rest your eyes periodically by focusing on a distant object once in awhile, and blinking often. Also make sure you have proper lighting. Avoid overhead lights; they almost always reflect off your screen. The best source of lighting is probably a desk or floor lamp or track lights that are not directly aimed at your screen. Beautiful as it is, sunlight streaming in the windows usually leads to glare as well.

7 Find a Good Chair

Finally, if you have back problems (or want to avoid them), a good chair is essential. Look for one that provides support for your lower back and is fully adjustable. (You should be able to change both the height of the seat and the angle of the seat and the back.)

(1) How to Log On to Windows XP 50

(2) How to Use Your Mouse 52

(3) How to Display Icons on Your Desktop 54

(4) How to Start a Program 56

(5) How to Arrange Windows on the Desktop 58

(6) How to Switch Between Programs 60

(7) How to Use the Notification Area 62

(8) How to Browse Your Disk Drives 64

(9) How to Get Help 66

(10) How to Use the Recycle Bin 68

(11) How to Log Off Windows XP 70

(12) How to Turn Off Your Computer 72

Task

Using the Windows XP Desktop

The Windows desktop works much like its real-world counterpart; it is a place where you organize files, run programs, and coordinate your work. When you run a program or open a folder, these items open in a window on the desktop. You can keep multiple windows open at once, arrange them how you like, and switch between them easily.

In the following tasks, you will explore some of the basic features of the Windows desktop—features that you will use daily. You will learn how to log in and out of Windows, how to use a mouse, how to run a program, and how to get help when you need it. You will also learn techniques for arranging windows and switching between open programs. Finally, you will learn the proper way to shut down your computer.

How to Log On to Windows XP

Windows XP is a secure system. If more than one user account is configured on your computer, or if your computer is on a network, you must log on so that Windows knows who you are and what you are allowed to do on the computer and network. If your computer is on a network, your logon information is supplied by your network administrator. When you install Windows XP on your own computer, you supply the information during setup. Depending on how your computer is set up, you may see the new Windows XP logon screen (steps 1–3) or the traditional logon screen (steps 4–7).

1 Select the User Account

From the list of available users, click the user account with which you want to log on. If a password is not assigned to the account (that is, if the password field was left blank when Windows was installed), you will enter directly into Windows. Otherwise, you'll be asked for a password.

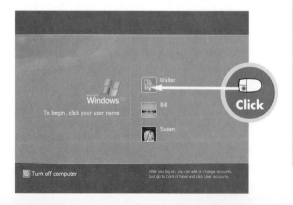

2 Enter Your Password

Type your password in the box that appears. As you type, the characters appear as dots. This prevents people looking over your shoulder from discovering your password. Note that the password is case-sensitive.

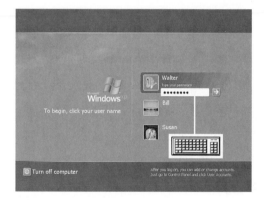

3 Log On

Click the arrow next to the password box (or press the Enter key on your keyboard) to submit the password and log on to Windows.

4 Press Ctrl+Alt+Del

An alternative way to log on to Windows is to use the traditional logon screen. To get to the main logon screen, you must press the **Ctrl**, **Alt**, and **Del** keys all at once. This special key combination informs Windows that you want to enter a username and password.

5 Enter Your Username and Password

Type your username and password into the appropriate boxes. As you type the password, the characters you enter appear on the screen only as dots. Passwords are case-sensitive. You must enter the correct combination of uppercase and lowercase characters and numbers.

6 Show Extra Login Options

Most of the time, a username and password are enough for you to log on to Windows XP. However, you can click the **Options** button for more choices, including choosing a different domain and logging on to just the computer instead of a network. For more information on domains and networking, see Chapter 6, "Working on a Network."

7 Shut Down

You can also shut down your computer from the logon screen. Clicking the **Shutdown** button opens a dialog box from which you can choose to shut down or restart the computer. These options are great when you need to shut down the system but don't want to wait through the logon process.

How to Use Your Mouse

Your mouse allows you to get tasks done quicker than with the keyboard. Sliding the mouse on your desk moves the pointer on the screen. The pointer usually appears as an arrow pointing up and to the left—just point it to the item you want to use. The pointer shape changes as you move over different areas of the screen— a vertical bar shows where you can enter text, for example. The shape also changes to indicate system status. An hourglass means that Windows is busy. An hourglass with an arrow means that Windows is working on something but that you can continue to do other things in the meantime.

① Point to an Object

An object refers to an item on your screen, usually an icon, that represents a program, file, or folder. You can point to an object by sliding the mouse so that the tip of the mouse pointer arrow is over that object.

② Click an Object

Clicking your left mouse button one time selects an object. When you select the object, its icon and text become highlighted with a dark blue background. Then you can perform another action on the object, such as deleting it.

③ Double-Click an Object

Double-clicking means to move the mouse pointer over an object and click the left mouse button twice in quick succession. Double-click an object to launch it. Double-click a folder to open it; double-click a program to run it.

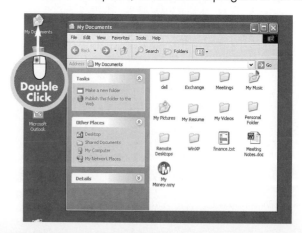

④ Right-Click an Object

When you click once on an object with the right mouse button, a shortcut menu pops up that lets you perform various actions associated with the object. The command in boldface is the action that would be performed by double-clicking the object.

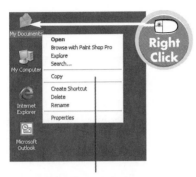

The shortcut menu

⑤ Drag an Object

To drag an object, point to the item, click and hold the left mouse button, and move the mouse to reposition the item. Release the mouse button to drop the object. The drag-and-drop approach is the way to move files to new folders and to move whole windows on your desktop.

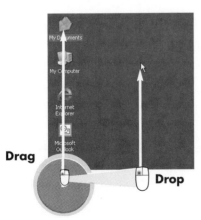

Drag

Drop

⑥ Open a Menu

Many windows, such as open folders and programs, have menus that provide access to different commands for working in the window. To open a menu, click the menu's name once.

⑦ Select a Menu Command

After a menu is open, you can click any command on the menu to have Windows perform that action.

How to Display Icons on Your Desktop

In previous versions of Windows, icons representing important parts of your system were always shown on your desktop. This may or may not be the case with Windows XP. If you buy a copy of Windows XP and install it yourself (see the Appendix), your desktop will be empty except for the Recycle Bin. If you buy your computer with Windows XP already installed, the icons may or may not be on the desktop, depending on the manufacturer of your computer. Throughout this book, many tasks assume that these icons are displayed on the desktop. If you don't see them on your desktop, you can find them on the Start menu. You can also tell Windows to show the icons on the desktop using the following steps.

❶ Open the Start Menu

The **Start** menu lets you access all your programs and most of the Windows settings available for configuration. The first time you start a computer with Windows XP, the **Start** menu opens automatically. After that, you must open it yourself by clicking its button once.

❷ Find the Icon You're Looking For

The icons that used to appear on the Windows desktop now appear in the upper-right part of the **Start** menu.

❸ Click an Icon to Open Its Window

To open the window for any of the icons in the **Start** menu, click the icon once with the left mouse button. The **Start** menu closes and a window opens on your desktop.

4 Open an Icon's Shortcut Menu

Right-click any icon to open a shortcut menu with special commands for working with that icon.

5 Show the Icon on the Desktop

Click the **Show on Desktop** command in the shortcut menu to have that icon appear on the Windows desktop. (The icon will still appear on the **Start** menu, as well.) If you decide you don't want the icon on your desktop after all, open the **Start** menu, right-click the icon in the menu, and choose **Show on Desktop** again to remove the icon from the desktop.

6 Open the Desktop Icon

After the icon is shown on your desktop, double-click it to open it.

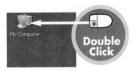

7 Turn on Other Icons

Each of the icons shown in the upper-right portion of the **Start** menu can appear as icons on your desktop. Just right-click each one in turn and choose the **Show on Desktop** command from the shortcut menu.

How to Start a Program

Windows XP provides several ways to run your programs. To begin with, all your programs are conveniently located on the Start menu. This menu includes some simple programs that come with Windows (such as a calculator and a notepad) and any other programs you have installed.

❶ Click the Start Button

Click the **Start** button to open the **Start** menu. Directly under your logon name, you'll find shortcuts to your Web browser and email program (Internet Explorer and Outlook Express, by default). Under these short-cuts, you'll find shortcuts to any programs you've run recently. On the right side of the **Start** menu, you'll find shortcuts to various important folders on your system and access to the help and search features.

❷ Click the More Programs Button

If you don't see the program you are looking for on the **Start** menu, click the **All Programs** button to see a list of all the programs installed on your computer. Some might be listed in folders within the **All Programs** folder; just point to a subfolder to open it. Programs that have recently been installed are highlighted. When you find a program you want, click the shortcut to run it.

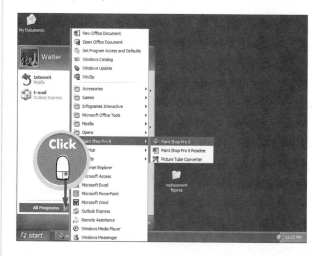

❸ Click a Quick Launch Shortcut

Some programs have shortcuts on the **Quick Launch** toolbar, just to the right of the **Start** button. Click any of these shortcut buttons to launch the program. The program opens in a new window on the desktop.

4   Maximize a Program Window

Click the **Maximize** button to make the program window take up the whole screen (except for the space occupied by the taskbar).

6   Minimize a Program Window

Click the **Minimize** button to remove the window from the desktop but leave the program running. You can tell the program is still running because its button remains in the taskbar at the bottom of the screen. Click the taskbar button to restore the window to the desktop.

5   Restore a Program Window

After a window is maximized, the **Maximize** button turns into a **Restore** button. Click the **Restore** button to shrink the window back to its previous size.

7   Close a Program Window

Click the **Close** button to end the program and remove its window from the desktop. The program displays a dialog box asking you to save any unsaved work before it closes. You can also close a program by choosing the **Exit** command from the **File** menu.

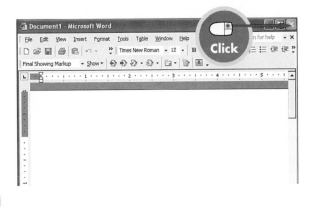

How to Arrange Windows on the Desktop

Windows offers the ability to keep many windows open at the same time. Although having multiple windows open at the same time provides the ability to easily move between tasks, using multiple windows can become confusing. Fortunately, Windows offers some clever tools for working with and arranging the windows on your desktop.

1 Resize a Window

When you move your pointer to the outer edge or corner of a window, the pointer changes into a double-headed arrow. When the pointer changes, click and drag the edge of the window to change its size.

2 Move a Window

You can move an entire window to a different location on the desktop by dragging its title bar. You can even move the window off the edges of your screen.

3 Cascade Windows

You can line up Windows in a cascade by right-clicking the taskbar and choosing **Cascade Windows** from the shortcut menu.

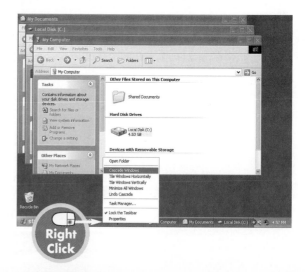

4 Tile Windows Vertically

Another way to arrange multiple windows on your desktop is to tile them. Right-click the taskbar and choose **Tile Windows Vertically** to arrange them from left to right on your screen.

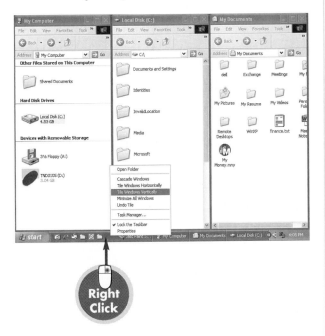

6 Minimize All Windows

You can minimize all open windows on your desktop at once (and thus clear them from your desktop) by right-clicking the taskbar and choosing **Minimize All Windows**. This is a great way to get to your desktop quickly.

5 Tile Windows Horizontally

You can also tile windows horizontally. Right-click the taskbar and choose **Tile Windows Horizontally**.

How-to Hint

Showing the Desktop

A better way to get to your desktop quickly instead of using the **Minimize All Windows** command is to use the **Show Desktop** button on the **Quick Launch** toolbar. This button effectively minimizes all windows, even if some windows are showing dialog boxes (something the **Minimize All Windows** command can't do). Click **Show Desktop** again to reverse the action and return all the minimized windows to their previous states.

How to Switch Between Programs

When you run several programs at once, you must be able to switch between these programs easily. Windows offers three great methods for switching between open applications—two using the mouse and one using the keyboard.

1 Click the Program's Window

The easiest way to switch to an open program is simply to click the program's window, if some portion of the window is visible. Inactive windows have a slightly dimmer title bar than the active window. Clicking anywhere on an inactive window brings it to the front and makes it active.

Click to make the inactive window active

The active window

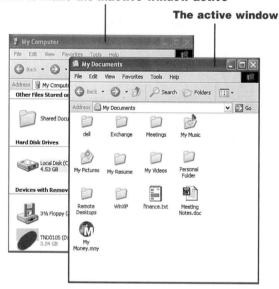

2 Click the Taskbar Button

When you can't see the window you want, the simplest way to switch to it is to click that window's button on the taskbar. This action brings that window to the front of the desktop in whatever size and position you left it.

3 Resize the Taskbar

When there are a lot of open windows, the buttons on the taskbar might get too small to be of much value in determining which window is which. You can hold your pointer over a button to see its full description, or you can drag the top edge of the taskbar up to make it bigger.

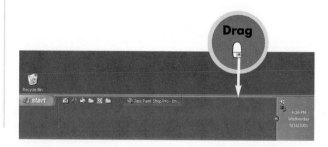

④ Use Grouped Taskbar Buttons

When more than one window is open for a single program, Windows XP groups those windows using a single taskbar button instead of multiple taskbar buttons. For example, you may be looking at a few different Web sites in different windows using Internet Explorer. A single taskbar button for Internet Explorer is displayed and the number of active Internet Explorer windows (five in the example shown here) is shown on the button. Click the button once to open a menu from which you can choose a specific window to activate.

⑤ Press Alt+Tab

You can also switch between open windows using your keyboard. Press and hold the **Alt** key and then press the **Tab** key once (without letting go of the **Alt** key). A box appears, displaying icons for each window. Press the **Tab** key to cycle through the windows. When you get to the window you want, release the Alt key to switch to it.

How-to Hint

Getting Out of Alt+Tab

If you use **Alt+Tab** to open the box that lets you switch between windows and then decide that you don't want to switch, just press **Esc** while you're still holding down the **Alt** key. The box disappears and puts you right back where you were.

Unlocking the Taskbar

If you find that you cannot resize the taskbar, it is probably locked. A locked taskbar cannot be resized or moved. Some people prefer to keep their taskbar locked so that no accidental changes are made to it. Others prefer to leave it unlocked so that they can easily resize it. Right-click anywhere on the taskbar and click the **Lock the Taskbar** command to deselect that command and unlock the bar.

How to Use the Notification Area

The notification area is the part of the taskbar at the far right side that holds your clock and probably several other small icons. These icons show information about programs that are running in the background on your computer. Some of the icons provide access to certain functions of the programs they represent. For example, the speaker icon lets you set your system's volume and configure audio properties.

1 Expand the Notification Area

The notification area collapses automatically to show only the clock and any recently used icons. To view the entire notification area, click the button with the double-left arrow at the left side of the notification area. A few seconds after you move your pointer away from the area, the notification area collapses again.

2 Viewing the Date

Hold the mouse pointer over the clock for a moment to view a pop-up balloon with the current date.

3 Setting the Clock

Double-click the clock to open a dialog box that lets you set the current date and time, as well as configure time-zone settings.

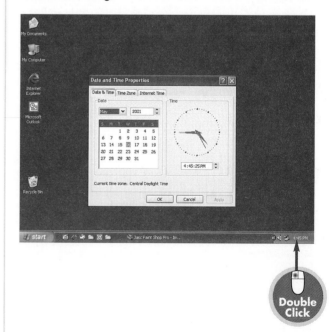

④ Setting the Volume

Click the speaker icon in the notification area to open the volume control. Slide the control up or down to change the volume of your system. A beep sounds to let you know how loud the volume is set.

⑤ Using Other Notification Area Icons

Unfortunately, the notification area icons for different programs behave in different manners. Sometimes, right-clicking or left-clicking the icon once opens a dialog box for configuration of some sort (as was the case with the volume control). Sometimes, right-clicking the icon opens a shortcut menu with program options. You'll have to experiment or read the documentation for the appropriate program.

Keeping the Notification Area Open

To keep the notification area open and showing all its icons all the time, right-click the taskbar and choose **Properties**. On the **Taskbar** tab of the dialog box that opens, disable (that is, remove the check mark next to) the **Hide inactive icons** option.

Turning Off Icons

You can turn off some icons in the notification area by right-clicking the icon and choosing the **Exit** command, if one exists. There also might be a command for setting options or preferences. Sometimes these settings contain an option for permanently turning off the icon. Another place you might look is in the **Startup** folder on your **Start** menu. Often, programs that are configured to start with Windows place icons on the notification area. For more about using the Startup folder, see Chapter 5, "Changing Windows XP Settings."

Updating the Clock Automatically

If you have Internet access and are not behind a firewall, Windows XP can update your clock automatically. Double-click the clock. In the dialog box that opens, select the **Internet Time** tab. Select the **Automatically synchronize with an Internet time server** option and then choose an available server.

How to Browse Your Disk Drives

Your disk drives hold all the information on your computer: all the files, folders, and programs, as well as all your documents. The My Computer window gives you access to these drives, whether they are hard drives, floppy drives, CD-ROM drives, or something else. My Computer also provides a shortcut to the Windows Control Panel, which is discussed more in Chapter 9, "Changing Windows XP Settings."

❶ Open My Computer

Double-click the **My Computer** icon on the desktop or Start menu to open the **My Computer** window.

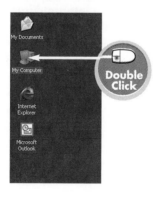

❷ Select a Disk Drive

The **My Computer** window shows any drives present on your computer. Click the icon for the drive you want to investigate to select it. Your floppy drive is usually named **A:** and your main hard drive is usually named **C:**. Information about the capacity and free space on any selected drive is shown in the **Details** pane to the left.

③ Open a Drive

Double-click the drive icon to open that drive.

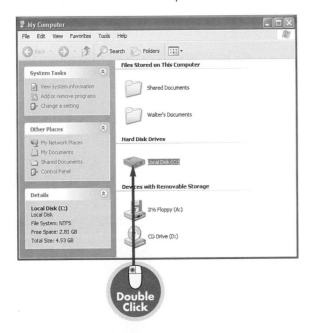

④ Open a Folder

Objects on a drive are organized into folders. *Folders* can contain both files and other folders. Double-click a folder to open it.

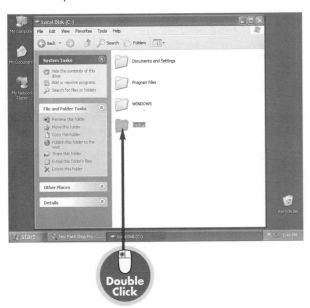

⑤ Open a File

When you select a file, a description of that file appears on the left side of the window. Double-click a file to launch the program that created the file (that is, the program *associated* with the file) and open that file within the program.

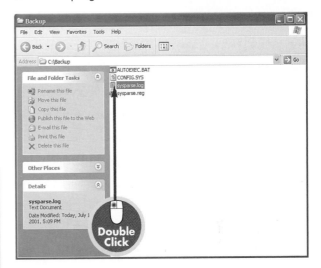

⑥ Navigate Folders

Click the **Back** button in the toolbar at the top of the folder window to go back to the folder you just came from. Click the down arrow next to the **Back** button to view a list of previous locations you can jump back to.

How to Get Help

Windows XP boasts a comprehensive Help system that lets you get details on Windows concepts and performing specific tasks. You can browse the contents of Windows Help, search for specific terms, or even ask questions in plain English.

1 Open Help

To open the Windows Help system, click the **Start** button and then choose **Help and Support**. The **Help and Support Center** window opens.

2 Enter a Search Term

If you know what topic you are looking for, type a word, phrase, or question in the **Search** box and click the **Search** button.

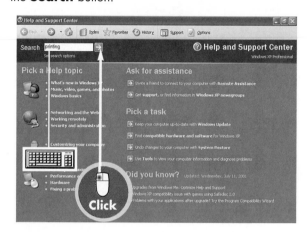

3 Select a Result

Windows shows a list of articles that match your search. Click one of the results in the left pane to view the article in the right pane. Buttons above the article let you print the article or add it to a list of favorites.

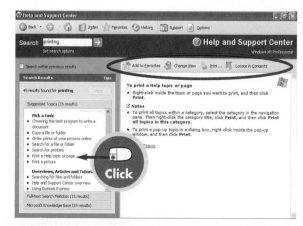

4 Pick a Help Topic

If you are not sure what the name of the topic you're looking for is, or if you just want to browse the Help system, click the link for a help topic on the main **Help and Support Center** page.

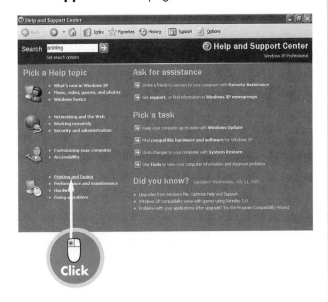

5 Pick a Category

In the left pane, Windows displays the categories for the topic you selected in step 4. Click a category to display a list of help articles related to that category in the right pane.

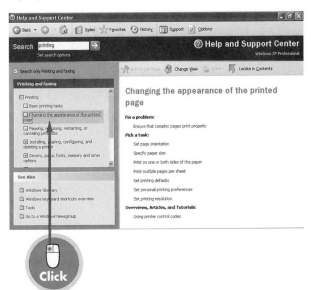

6 Pick an Article

Click the article in the list you want to view. Windows opens the selected article in a new window. When you're done reading the article, click the window's **Close** button to close the window and return to the **Help and Support Center** window.

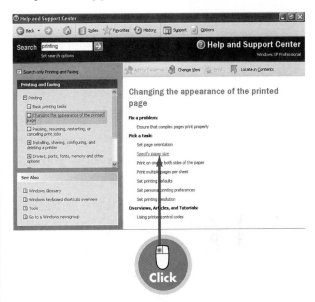

How-to Hint

Using the F1 Key

Press the **F1** key at any time while using Windows to open a help page related to your current activity. Many programs also support the F1/Help feature.

Using the Index

Click the **Index** button on the help window's toolbar to view a searchable index of all help articles. Some people find it easier to browse the Help system this way.

How to Use the Recycle Bin

You can delete files, folders, and programs from your computer at any time. However, when you delete an item, Windows does not immediately remove it from your computer. Instead, the item is placed into the **Recycle Bin**. You can restore an item from the **Recycle Bin** later if you decide you would rather not delete it. When the **Recycle Bin** becomes full (depending on the amount of disk space allocated to it), Windows deletes older items permanently to make room for newer items. You can think of the **Recycle Bin** as sort of a buffer between your files and oblivion.

❶ Drag an Object to the Recycle Bin

The easiest way to delete an object is to drag it to the **Recycle Bin**. You can drag an item from the desktop or from any open folder. You can also delete a file by selecting it and pressing the **Delete** key on your keyboard.

❷ Confirm the Deletion

When you try to delete an object, Windows asks you to confirm that you really want to delete it. Click **Yes** if you're sure; click **No** if you made a mistake and don't want to delete the object.

❸ Open the Recycle Bin

Double-click the **Recycle Bin** icon on the desktop to open it. All files in the **Recycle Bin** are listed with their original locations and the date on which they were deleted.

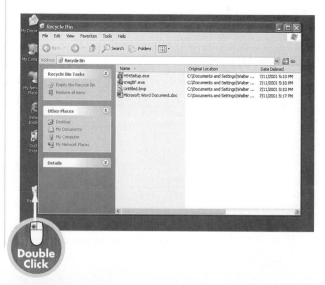

④ Restore Files

To remove a file from the **Recycle Bin** and restore it to its original location, select the file and click the **Restore this item** link that appears on the left.

⑤ Delete Files

Right-click a file in the **Recycle Bin** list and choose **Delete** from the shortcut menu to permanently delete that file from your hard disk.

⑥ Empty the Recycle Bin

To permanently delete all the files from the Recycle Bin (which you might want to do to regain some disk space), make sure that no files are selected and click the **Empty Recycle Bin** link on the left.

How-to Hint

Another Way to Empty the Bin

You can empty the **Recycle Bin** without opening it by right-clicking its icon on the desktop and choosing **Empty Recycle Bin** from the shortcut menu.

Allocating Recycle Bin Space

By default, 10% of your hard drive space is reserved for use by the **Recycle Bin**. You can change the amount of space used by right-clicking the **Recycle Bin** and selecting the **Properties** command from the shortcut menu. On the Global tab of the Recycle Bin Properties dialog box, drag the slider to change the maximum size of the **Recycle Bin**.

How to Log Off Windows XP

As you learned earlier in this chapter, logging on (providing Windows with your username and maybe a password) tells Windows who is using the computer. Logging off tells Windows that you are finished with your computer session. You should log off whenever you plan to be away from the computer for a length of time (such as for lunch or at the end of the day).

1 **Click Log Off**

Click the **Start** button and then choose **Log Off**.

2 **Switch User**

If you are not finished using Windows and just want to let someone else use the computer for a short time, you can simply switch users. Click the **Switch User** button if you want to leave all your programs running and your documents open while the other person uses the computer. The logon window (shown in Task 1) opens so that the other person can log on. When that person logs off, you can switch back to your account and continue working.

3 **Log Off**

Logging off closes any running programs. Although Windows usually gives you the chance to save any unsaved documents before it actually logs off, you should save your files manually before you log off to make sure that your data is safe.

④ Log On Another User

As soon as you log off, Windows presents the logon screen. You can now log back on as described in Task 1.

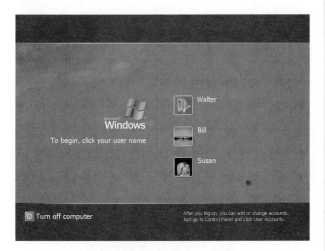

How-to Hint

Using a Screen Saver Password

Screen saver passwords let your computer automatically lock itself whenever the screen saver activates. To access the computer again, you'll have to type the password to deactivate the screen saver.

How to Turn Off Your Computer

While running, Windows keeps a lot of its information in system memory—memory that is not sustained when the computer is turned off. For this reason, you should never simply turn your computer off using the power button. You should always use the **Turn Off Computer** command to allow Windows to gracefully shut itself down.

➊ Click Turn Off Computer

Click the **Start** button and then choose **Turn off Computer**. The **Turn Off Computer** window opens.

➋ Choose the Turn Off Option

Click the **Turn Off** button. Windows closes all open programs (giving you the opportunity to save unsaved documents) and tells you when it is safe to turn off the power. This is the option you will likely choose at the end of the day or when the computer will be unused for a lengthy period.

➌ Choose the Restart Option

Click the **Restart** button to have Windows shut itself down and then automatically restart the computer. After the computer is restarted, you can log on to Windows again. Restarting your computer is the first thing you should try if you find that Windows, another program, or a hardware component isn't working as you think it should.

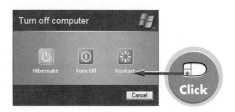

④ Choose Hibernate or Standby

Some computers offer additional logoff options, including **Hibernate** and **Standby**. The **Hibernate** option saves all the information in your computer's memory to hard disk and then shuts the computer down. When you restart the computer, all your programs and windows are restored to the same state in which you left them. The **Standby** option turns off the power to most of the components of your computer, but keeps enough power going to your computer's memory that it can remember its current state. When you restore a computer from **Standby** (usually by pressing the power button, but different computers can vary in the method), the computer returns to the state in which you left it.

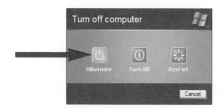

⑤ Save Any Open Files

If you attempt to shut down Windows while programs are running with unsaved documents, you are given the chance to save those documents before shut-down proceeds. Choose **Yes** if you want to save the changes to the named document; choose **No** if you don't want to save the changes; choose **Cancel** if you want to abort the shut-down process altogether.

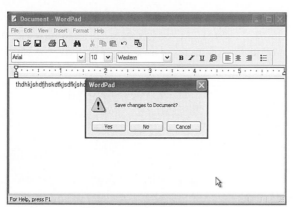

How-to Hint

Other Active Users

Because Windows XP now allows multiple user accounts to be logged on at the same time, you may find that when you try to shut down or restart the computer, other user accounts are still logged on. Windows XP informs you that the accounts are still active and gives you a chance to cancel your request to shut down. You should log off the other accounts (or have the people to whom the accounts belong log off); if you don't, any documents open in those accounts will be lost. Windows does not give you the option of saving other people's files the way it lets you save your own when shutting down or restarting.

1. How to Use Windows Explorer 76

2. How to Search for a File or Folder 78

3. How to Create a Folder 80

4. How to View Items in a Folder 82

5. How to Create a File .84

6. How to Open a File .86

7. How to Save a File .88

8. How to Create a Shortcut to a File or Folder 90

9. How to Rename a File or Folder 92

10. How to Delete a File or Folder 94

11. How to Move or Copy a File or Folder 96

12. How to Format a Floppy Disk 98

13. How to Send a File to the Floppy Drive 100

14. How to Open a File with a Different Program 102

Working with Files and Folders

Everything on your computer is made up of files on your hard drive. Windows itself is just thousands of different files that interact with one another. Your programs are also collections of files that interact with one another and with Windows files. Finally, all the documents you create are themselves files.

Files are organized into folders that can hold both files and other folders. For example, suppose your C: drive contains a folder named Backup, which in turn holds a folder named July, which in turn holds a file named smith.jpg. The full description of the location of a file on a drive is called a path and includes the name of the disk drive, the names of each folder, and the name of the file—each name separated by a backslash (\). For the smith.jpg document mentioned earlier, the path would be C:\Backup\July\smith.jpg.

The name of a file can be 256 characters long and has a three-character extension (the three characters after the dot) that identifies the type of file it is. By default, extensions are not shown for file types that your system knows about.

How to Use Windows Explorer

Chapter 3, "Using the Windows XP Desktop," explained how to use the **My Computer** window to browse through the folders and files on a disk drive. In truth, you can use the **My Computer** window to get to any file on your computer and do anything you want with it. However, Windows offers another utility, **Windows Explorer**, that you might find more useful for working with the files and folders on your computer. It's really a matter of personal style.

❶ Open Explorer

You run Windows Explorer just like you do any other program. Click the **Start** button and select **All Programs**, **Accessories**, **Windows Explorer**.

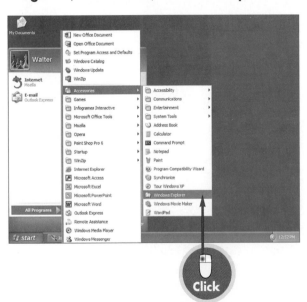

❷ Browse Folders

The left pane of the Explorer window shows a hierarchy of all the drives, folders, and desktop items on your computer. A drive or folder that contains other folders has a plus sign to the left of the icon. Click the **plus sign** to expand it and see the folders inside.

❸ Open a Folder

Click any folder in the list in the left pane; all the files and folders in that folder are shown in the right pane.

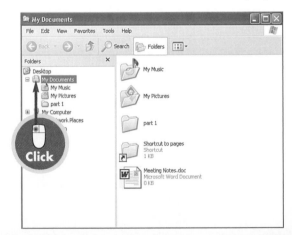

④ Open a File

The right pane works the same way as the **My Computer** window. You can double-click any file or folder in this pane to open it.

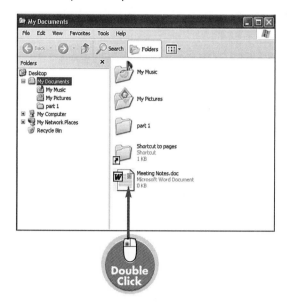

⑤ Move a File to Another Folder

One of the advantages of using Windows Explorer is that you can easily move a file to any other folder on your computer. Drag a file from the right pane and drop it on any folder icon in the left pane to move the file there.

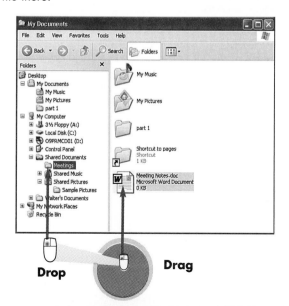

⑥ Copy a File to Another Drive

Copying a file to another drive is as easy as moving it. Just drag a file from the right pane to another disk drive (or a folder on another drive) to copy it there. Notice that the icon you are dragging takes on a small plus sign to let you know that the file will be copied, but not moved.

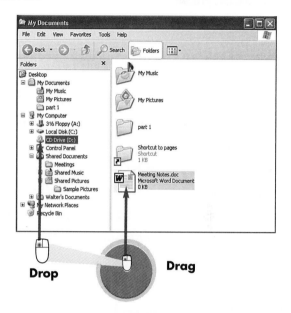

How-to Hint

Auto-Expanding

When you move a file to another folder in Windows Explorer, the folder doesn't have to be visible already. While dragging the file, hold the mouse pointer over a folder's plus sign for two seconds to automatically expand that folder.

Auto-Scrolling

While dragging a file, hold the mouse pointer at the top or bottom of the left pane for two seconds to automatically scroll up or down.

Copying or Moving to Other Locations

For more on how to move or copy files between folders and drives, see Task 11, "How to Move or Copy a File or Folder," later in this chapter.

How to Search for a File or Folder

Using Windows Explorer is great if you know where the file or folder you want is located. Sometimes, however, it's hard to remember just where you put something. Fortunately, Windows has a great search function built right in that helps you find files and folders. You can search for folders by all or part of their names, by text they might contain, or by their location. You can even search using all three of these criteria at once.

❶ Open the Search Window

Click the **Start** button and select **Search**. You'll also find a **Search** button on the toolbar of most windows that performs the same function. A search window opens.

❷ Select the Type of Document

The left pane holds the interface you will use for searching. Results of any search you perform are displayed in the right pane. Choose the type of document you want to search for from the list in the left pane. The pane changes to show additional search questions based on the type of file you choose.

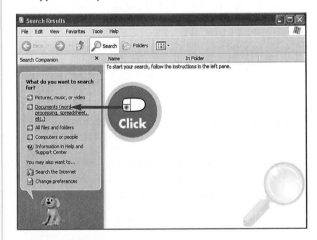

③ Type the Document Name

Type all or part of the name of the file or folder you want to search for in the text box. When you search, Windows shows all of the file and folder names that contain the text you enter.

④ Select a Time Frame

If you know approximately when the document was last modified, select one of the time options. If you don't remember, just leave the **Don't remember** option selected.

⑤ Click Search

After you have entered your search criteria, click **Search** to have Windows begin the search.

⑥ View the Results

The results of your search are displayed in the right pane. You can double-click a file to open it right from the search window.

Quickly Open a File's Folder

How-to Hint

You can quickly open the parent folder of a file you've found by right-clicking the file in the results pane and choosing **Open Containing Folder** from the shortcut menu.

How to Create a Folder

Folders help you organize your files. You create a folder using the **My Computer** window or **Windows Explorer**. You can create a folder in any existing disk drive or folder or on the Windows desktop itself.

❶ Find the Place to Make the Folder

The first step in creating a folder is to decide where you want to create it. Use the **My Computer** window or **Windows Explorer** to find the place you want to be.

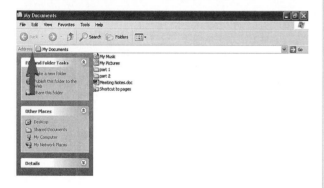

❷ Create the New Folder

In the **Tasks** list, select **Make a new folder**. Alternatively, pull down the **File** menu and select **New, Folder**.

❸ Rename the Folder

The new folder appears in the current location with the default name **New Folder**. The name is already highlighted; you can rename it by typing the name you want and pressing **Enter** or clicking somewhere outside the name field (here I've named the folder **Personal Folder**). You can also rename the folder later by selecting it and choosing **File**, **Rename** and then typing the new folder name. Note that renaming the folder does not affect any files contained in that folder.

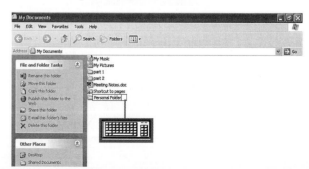

④ Create a Folder on the Desktop

To create a new folder directly on your desktop, right-click any empty area of the desktop. Point to **New** on the shortcut menu and then choose **Folder**.

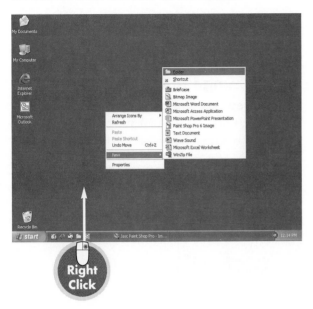

Right Click

⑤ Name the New Folder

As you did in Step 3, type a new name for the folder (its default name is **New Folder**) and press **Enter**.

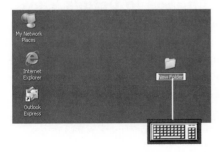

How-to Hint

Saving a Document

Some programs let you create a new folder from the same dialog box you use to save a document. There is usually a button named **Create New Folder**. Just click the button, name the new folder, and open it to save your document there.

Creating a Folder in the Start Menu

The Start menu is really a folder on your hard disk; you can create new folders in it to help organize your files. Right-click the **Start** button, choose **Open** from the shortcut menu, and create the folder in the window that opens using the methods described in this task. The new folder appears on your Start menu. For more on customizing your Start menu, see Chapter 9, "Changing Windows XP Settings."

How to View Items in a Folder

Normally, both the My Computer window and Windows Explorer show you the contents of a folder as large icons that represent other folders and files. This is a friendly way to view folders, but not always the most useful, especially if a folder contains large numbers of files or many files with similar names. You can also view the contents of a folder as small icons, as a list, as a list with file details, or even as thumbnails.

1 Open a Folder

First, you need to find a folder to view. You can do this in either the **My Computer** window or in **Windows Explorer**. In this **Windows Explorer** example, notice that the regular large icon view looks pretty cluttered.

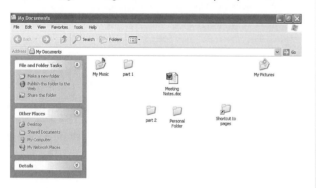

2 Change to List View

Choose **View**, **List** to view the folder contents as a list. The contents are listed in alphabetical order. You can also use the **View** button on the toolbar to change views.

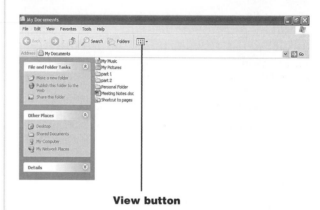

View button

3 Change to Details View

The **Detail** view is perhaps the most useful way to view the contents of a folder. Choose **View**, **Details**. Contents are presented in a list with columns that include file details, such as the size and type of the file and when the file was last modified.

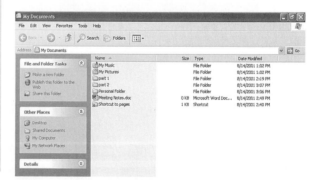

④ Change to Thumbnail View

Thumbnail view presents the contents of a folder as small thumbnails, or previews, of the actual documents. Only certain file types, such as JPEG images, support this type of viewing. Choose **View**, **Thumbnail** to display the folder contents as thumbnails. Other types of documents are displayed as larger versions of their normal icons.

⑤ Arrange Icons

In addition to choosing how to view the contents of a folder, you can also choose how those contents are arranged. Choose **View**, **Arrange Icons By** and then choose **Name**, **Type**, **Size**, or **Modified** (the date the files were last modified) to order the contents of the folder. You can also have the folder arrange the icons automatically.

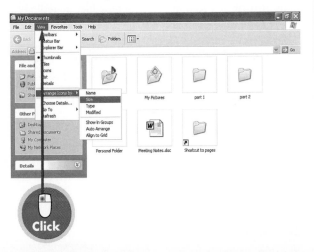

Click

How-to Hint

Arranging in Details View

You can easily arrange the contents of a folder in the Details view by clicking the column heading by which you want to order the contents. For example, click the **Type** column heading to group the files in the current folder by type. You can choose the columns that are shown in Details view by choosing **View**, **Choose Columns** from the menu bar. A window opens with lots of different choices for columns to display. Just select the ones you want.

Other Arrangements

Select **View**, **Arrange Icons By**, **Show in Groups** to divide a folder's window into different sections that show different types of items, such as folders, drives, and files. Within each group, icons are arranged according to your other settings on the View menu. The Auto Arrange option on the same menu automatically arranges the icons in a window by alphabetic and numerical order and groups them together at the beginning of a window. The Align to Grid option gives you the freedom to arrange your icons as you like, while making sure that they all uniformly align to an invisible grid in the window.

Cleaning Up Your Windows

Many users find that the common tasks shown on the left side of most windows take up too much space and really aren't that useful anyway. You can turn the task list off for all folders by going to **Start**, **Control Panel**, **Folder Options**. On the **General** tab of the **Folder Options** dialog box, choose the **Use Windows classic folders** option. To turn the task list back on, come back to the **Folder Options** dialog box and choose the **Show common tasks in folder** option. Unfortunately, you cannot enable the list for some folders and disable it for others.

How to Create a File

Most of the time, you will create new documents from within a particular program. For example, you usually use Microsoft Word to create a new Word document. However, Windows does offer the ability to quickly create certain types of documents without opening the associated program at all. This can be quite useful when you are creating a large number of new documents that will be edited later.

① Locate the Parent Folder

First, you must find the folder in which you want to create the new file. You can create a file directly in any folder on your computer. Here I used **Windows Explorer** to navigate to the new **Personal Folder** folder I created in Task 3, "How to Create a Folder."

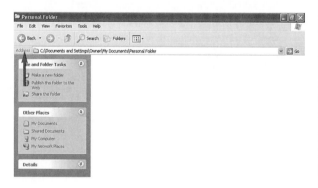

② Create the File

Choose **File**, **New**, and then select the type of file you want to create. Note that the list of file types presented in the submenu covers basic Windows objects (such as folders, shortcuts, and text files) and objects that depend on additional software you have installed (such as Microsoft Word documents).

③ Locate the New Document

The new document appears in the selected folder with a generic name, such as **New Microsoft Word Document**. If you don't see the new file immediately, use the window's scrollbars to find it.

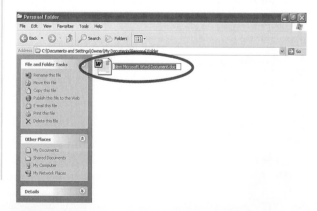

④ Rename the File

The new file appears with the name already high-lighted. Just start typing to enter a new name for the file. When you're done, press Enter or click somewhere outside the text box.

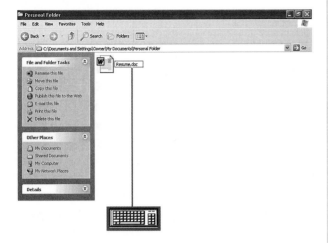

⑤ Open the File to Edit

After you have created and renamed your new file, double-click it to launch the appropriate program and open the new file with it. Now that the file is open in the appropriate application, you can work with it just as you would any other file created in that application.

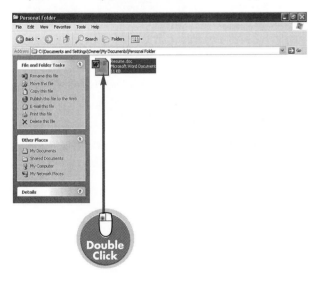

Renaming Files

Files can have names of up to 256 characters, including spaces. There are several special characters you cannot use in your file's name, including \ / : * ? " < >

Preserving the File Type

When you create a new file, Windows automatically gives it the right three-letter file extension (the three letters after the dot) to indicate the file type. If your Windows settings allow you to see the file extension (by default, they don't), be sure that you don't change the extension when you rename the file. If you do, the file won't open with the right program. Windows warns you if you try to change the file extension.

Populating a Folder Quickly

In Windows Explorer or My Computer, you can create as many new documents as you need and then go back and rename them later. To create files even more quickly, create one file, copy it by selecting it and pressing **Ctrl+C**, and then paste as many new files in the same folder as you need by pressing **Ctrl+V**. Each new file has the text **Copy of** and a number prepended to the filename to distinguish it from its siblings (for example, if the original file is named **resume.doc**, the first copy is named **Copy of resume.doc**; the second copy is named **Copy [2] of resume.doc**, and so on).

How to Open a File

There are several different ways to open a file in Windows. One way is to locate the file in the **My Computer** window or **Windows Explorer** and open it from there. You can also open a file from within the program that created it. Windows even keeps track of the files you have opened recently so that you can reopen these in one simple step using the **Start** menu.

❶ Double-Click the File

Find the file you want to open by using the **My Computer** window or **Windows Explorer**. Double-click the file to launch the file's program and open the file with it. Here, the file **Resume.doc** will open in Microsoft Word.

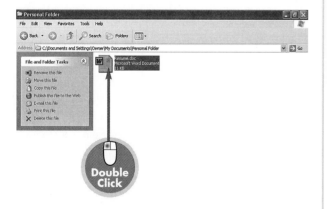

❷ Open a Recently Used File

Windows keeps track of the most recent 15 documents you have opened. To open any of these documents, click the **Start** button and point to the **My Recent Documents** option to see a list of the documents most recently opened on your computer. Select the document you want to open. If the My Recent Documents option does not show up on your **Start** menu, see Chapter 9, "Changing Windows XP Settings," for details on how to add it.

3 Run a Program

Yet another way to open a file is from within the program that created it. The first step is to run the program. Click the **Start** button, point to **More Programs**, and find the program you want to run in the submenus that appear.

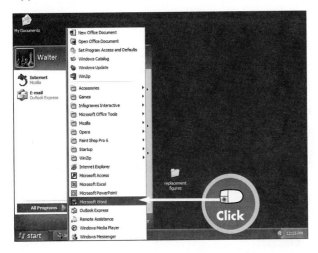

5 Find the File to Open

For most programs, the **Open** dialog box works a lot like the **My Computer** window. Navigate through the folders on your computer system to find the file you want to open, select it, and click **Open**.

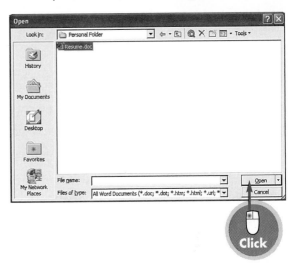

4 Choose Open from the File Menu

After the selected program opens, choose **File**, **Open** from the menu bar. The **Open** dialog box appears.

How-to Hint

Removing Recently Used Files

You can clear the list of recently used files from the **Recent Documents** folder by right-clicking the taskbar and choosing **Properties** from the shortcut menu. In the **Properties** dialog box that opens, click the **Start Menu** tab and then click **Customize**. In the dialog box that opens, click the **Advanced** tab and then click **Clear List**.

Searching for Files

When you search for files using the **Search** command on the **Start** menu, you can open any of the files you find just by double-clicking them. For more information about searching for files, see Task 2, "How to Search for a File or Folder," earlier in this chapter.

How to Save a File

Saving your work is one of the most important things you'll do. After all, if you don't save your work, what's the point of doing it in the first place? Saving a file is always done while you are working on it within a program. There are two save commands in most programs. **Save As** lets you choose a location and name for your file. **Save** simply updates the file using its current location and name. The first time you save a new file, the program uses the **Save As** function no matter which command you choose.

1 Open the Save As Dialog Box

If you want to save a file using a particular name or to a particular location, click the **File** menu and then choose **Save As**. Note that you can use this command to save a copy of the file you are working on with a new name or to save versions of a file. The **Save As** dialog box opens.

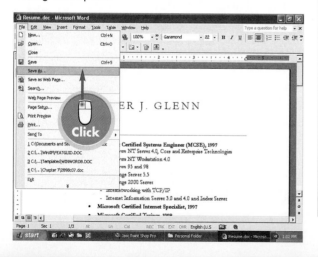

2 Choose a Location

The **Save As** dialog box works just like the **My Computer** window. Choose the disk drive to which you want to save the file using the **Save in** drop-down list. After you choose the drive, navigate to the desired folder.

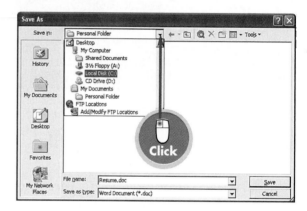

3 Choose a Favorite Place

Instead of using the drop-down list, you can choose a favorite place by clicking the icon for a folder in the bar on the left of the dialog box. You can then save your file in that folder or browse to another folder inside the folder.

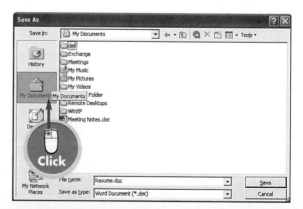

④ Create a New Folder

If you want to save the file you're working on in a new folder, navigate to the folder in which you want to store the new file, then click the **Create New Folder** button in the **Save As** dialog box toolbar. Type a name for the new folder and press **Enter**. Open the new folder by double-clicking it.

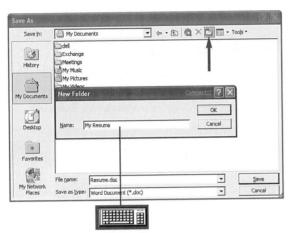

⑤ Name the File

Type the name for the document in the **File name** box. Note that, in most applications, you do not have to include the file extension when you type the filename. The application supplies the extension for you. If you do include an extension, the application accepts it.

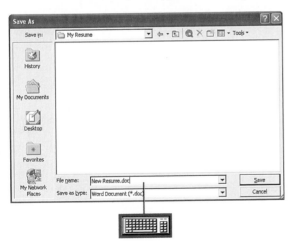

⑥ Save the File

Click **Save** to save the new file in the selected folder with the name you specified.

⑦ Save the File as You Work

Periodically as you work, save any changes to your document using the **Save** button on the program's main toolbar (or the **Save** command on the **File** menu). If you click **Save** and it is the first time you are saving a new document, the **Save As** dialog box opens and prompts you for a filename. Otherwise, the file is saved in the current location with the current filename, overwriting the last version of the file you had saved.

How to Create a Shortcut to a File or Folder

A shortcut is an icon that points to a file or folder somewhere on your computer. The shortcut is merely a reference to the actual object and is used to access the object without having to go to the object's location. For example, on your desktop you could place a shortcut to a frequently used document. You could then double-click the shortcut to open the file without having to go to the folder where the actual file is stored.

1 Open Windows Explorer

The first step in creating a new shortcut is to use the **My Computer** window or **Windows Explorer** to find the file or folder to which you want to make a shortcut. To open Windows Explorer, click **Start** and select **All Programs**, **Accessories**, **Windows Explorer**.

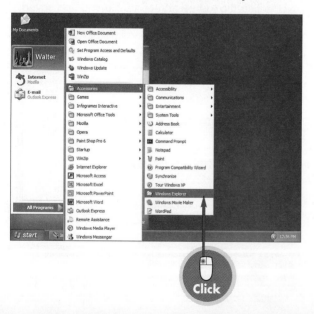

2 Select a File or Folder

In Windows Explorer, navigate to the object to which you want to make a shortcut. In this example, I want to create a shortcut to my new **Personal Folder** folder.

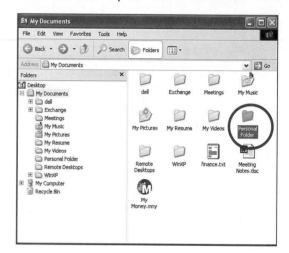

③ Drag the File to Your Desktop

Click and hold the *right* mouse button and drag the object to a blank space on the desktop. Release the right mouse button to drop the icon on the desktop.

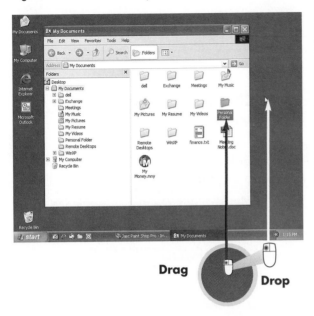

Drag **Drop**

④ Choose Create Shortcuts Here

When you release the right mouse button, a shortcut menu appears. Choose **Create Shortcuts Here**.

Click

⑤ Rename the Shortcut

Notice that the shortcut icon has a small arrow on it, indicating that it is a shortcut. You can rename the shortcut to anything you like by right-clicking the shortcut icon and choosing **Rename** from the shortcut menu.

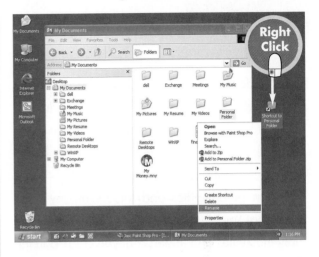

Right Click

⑥ Double-Click the Shortcut

To open the original object to which you made the shortcut, double-click the shortcut icon. In this example, double-clicking the **Shortcut to Personal Folder** shortcut opens the **Personal Folder** folder in Windows Explorer.

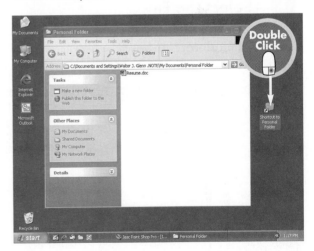

Double Click

How to Rename a File or Folder

In Windows XP, you can name files or folders just about anything you want. Names are limited to 256 characters, including spaces, but there are a few special characters you are not allowed to use, including the following: \ / : * ? " < >. You can rename files and folders at any time. Note that you should be very careful to rename only those files and folders that you created in the first place. Windows and Windows programs are composed of many folders and files that have special names. Changing the names of these files can often cause a program, or even Windows itself, to malfunction.

❶ Select the File

To rename a file in the **My Computer** window or **Windows Explorer**, first select the file with a single click.

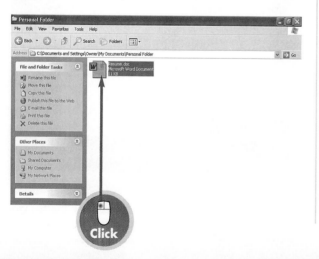

❷ Choose Rename from the File Menu

From the menu bar, choose **File**, **Rename**. A box appears around the name of the file or folder you selected in step 1 and the filename itself is highlighted.

❸ Type a New Name

Type a new name for the selected file. Note that as you type, the highlighted filename is replaced by the text you type. If you want to edit (and not replace) the current filename, use the arrow keys or mouse pointer to position the insertion point, then add and delete characters from the filename as desired. When you're done with the filename, press **Enter**.

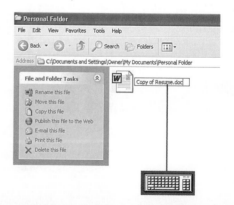

④ Click the Name Twice Slowly

A quicker way to rename a file (and one that also works on files on the desktop) is to first select the file with a single click and then click the name of the file a second later—not so fast as to suggest a double-click. You can also select the file and press the **F2** key. When the filename is highlighted, you can then type a new name.

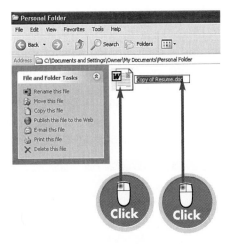

Keeping Names Simple

Although you can create very long filenames in Windows, it is usually better to keep them short and simple. The reason for this is that when you view the contents of a folder, filenames are often cut off after the first 15–20 characters so that you can view more files in the folder. Keep the filenames short so that you can view the contents of a folder without having to switch to details view and adjust the default column size to see the entire filename. For more on adjusting window views, see Task 4, "How to View Items in a Folder."

⑤ Right-Click the File

Yet another way to rename a file is to right-click the file and choose **Rename** from the shortcut menu. You can then type a new name as explained in step 3.

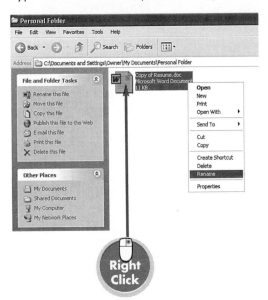

How to Delete a File or Folder

When you delete a file or folder in Windows, the object is not immediately removed from your computer. It is first placed into the **Recycle Bin**, where it is kept temporarily before being permanently deleted. The **Recycle Bin** gives you the chance to recover files you might have accidentally deleted. For more information about the **Recycle Bin**, see Chapter 3, Task 10, "How to Use the Recycle Bin." There are a few ways to delete objects in Windows, including dragging them to the **Recycle Bin** or deleting them directly using the keyboard or Windows Explorer.

1 Select a Group of Files

Place the mouse pointer in a blank spot near a group of objects you want to delete. Click and hold the left mouse button and drag the pointer toward the objects. A dotted rectangle (named the lasso) appears behind the pointer. Drag the lasso over all the objects to select them all at once.

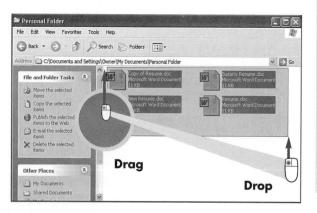

2 Drag to the Recycle Bin

After you have selected a group of files, drag them to the **Recycle Bin** by clicking any single selected file and holding the mouse button while you drag the pointer over the **Recycle Bin**. Release the mouse button when the **Recycle Bin** icon becomes highlighted to drop the selected files into the **Recycle Bin**.

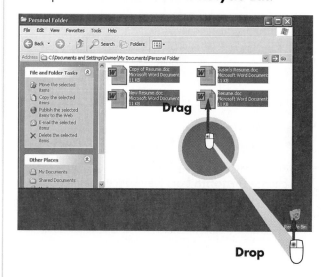

③ Select a File

It is also easy to delete files without using the **Recycle Bin**, which is helpful when you can't see your desktop. First, select the file you want to delete by clicking it once.

④ Use the Delete Key

Press the **Delete** key on your keyboard to send the selected file (or files) to the **Recycle Bin**.

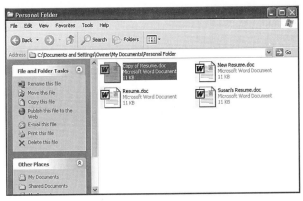

⑤ Choose Delete from the File Menu

After a file is selected, you can also open the **File** menu and choose **Delete** to send the file to the **Recycle Bin**.

Disabling the Recycle Bin

If you would rather not use the **Recycle Bin**, right-click the **Recycle Bin** icon on the desktop and choose **Properties** from the shortcut menu. Select the **Do not move files to the Recycle Bin** option. Be careful, though. When this option is selected, files that you delete are permanently removed from your system, giving you no chance to recover them.

Changing the Recycle Bin Settings

There are several ways you can customize the operation of your **Recycle Bin**. For more information on this, see Chapter 3, "Using the Windows XP Desktop."

How to Move or Copy a File or Folder

Most people move objects around from folder to folder by simply dragging them using the left mouse button. This usually works fine, but it might not provide the exact results you want. Depending on where you drag an object, you can move the object or you can copy it to the new location. For better results, try using the right mouse button instead of the left when you drag files to a new location.

① Find the Parent Folder

Use the **My Computer** window or **Windows Explorer** to find the folder that contains the object you want to move or copy.

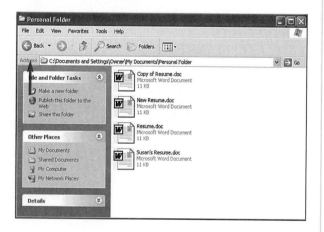

② Locate an Object

Locate an object you want to move. The object can be a file or a folder. Note that if you move a folder, you move the contents (all the files and folders contained in that folder) as well. If you copy a folder, you copy the contents of the folder as well.

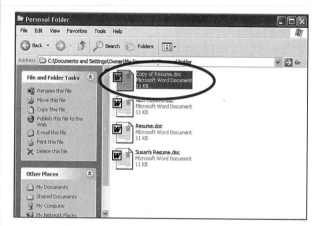

③ Drag the File to a New Location

Place the mouse pointer over the object, click and hold the right mouse button, and drag the object to the target location. In this example, I am dragging the document file to the desktop. Release the right mouse button to drop the object in its new location.

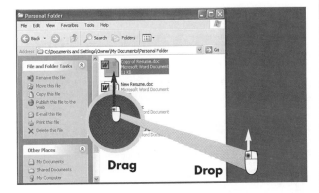

④ Choose Copy Here

When you release the right mouse button, a shortcut menu appears. Choose **Copy Here** to place an exact copy of the selected item in the new location and keep the original object in the old location.

⑤ Choose Move Here

Choose **Move Here** from the shortcut menu to move the object to the new location and remove it from the old location.

How-to Hint

Left-Dragging

When you use the left mouse button to drag a file, the icon you drag changes to reflect what action will be performed. If the icon has a small plus sign on it, the file will be copied when you release the mouse button. If the icon has a small arrow, a shortcut will be created. If the icon has nothing extra on it, the object will be moved.

Right-Dragging

A better way to move files is to drag them using the right mouse button (instead of the left). When you release a file or folder you have dragged with the right button, a menu pops up asking whether you want to copy, move, or create a shortcut.

Dragging with Keys

When you drag using the left mouse button, you can hold down the **Shift** and **Ctrl** keys to get different effects. For example, hold down the **Shift** key while dragging a file to move the file instead of copying it. Hold down the **Ctrl** key while dragging a file to copy the file instead of moving it.

How to Format a Floppy Disk

When you buy floppy disks from a store, they are usually formatted. Make sure that you buy disks formatted for your system. The package should read "**IBM Formatted**" if the floppy disks are to work with Windows. If you have an unformatted disk, it is easy enough to format in Windows. Formatting is also a quick way to erase all the files that you don't need anymore from a disk. Before you start the steps in this task, insert the floppy disk to be formatted in your floppy drive.

1 Open My Computer
Double-click the **My Computer** icon on your desktop to open the **My Computer** folder.

2 Right-Click the Floppy Drive
Right-click the drive labeled **3½ Floppy (A:)** and select the **Format** command from the shortcut menu. The **Format** dialog box opens.

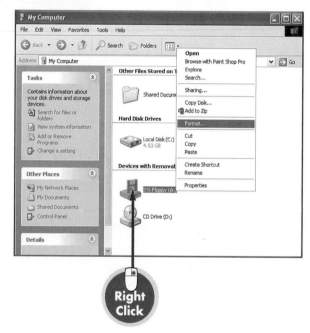

③ Choose a Capacity

Almost all computers today use 1.44MB floppy drives, which is the default choice in this dialog box. If you are formatting an older floppy (or one for an older computer), choose the 720K size from the **Capacity** drop-down list.

⑤ Perform a Quick Format

If you are formatting a disk that has been previously formatted by Windows (as you would do when erasing a disk), choose the **Quick Format** option to significantly shorten the time needed to format the disk.

④ Enter a Volume Label

Type a label into the **Volume Label** box. The volume label is the name of the floppy disk. You can leave this blank if you do not want a label (most people do leave this field blank).

⑥ Format the Disk

Click **Start** to begin formatting the disk. A progress indicator at the bottom of the dialog box shows the formatting progress. Another dialog box opens to inform you when the format is done.

How-to Hint

Be Careful When Selecting a Drive

The **Format** dialog box lets you select any drive on your system to format. Be sure that the correct drive is selected before formatting. Formatting a hard drive erases all its contents!

How to Send a File to the Floppy Drive

Floppy disks are often used to back up files or transfer files to another computer. In Windows, the floppy drive is always labeled A: in the **My Computer** window and **Windows Explorer**. As with most other tasks, Windows offers a couple different ways to send files to a floppy disk. Before you begin this task, make sure that a properly formatted floppy disk is in the floppy disk drive.

❶ Open My Documents

Double-click the **My Documents** icon on your desktop to open the **My Documents** folder. If you don't see the **My Documents** icon on your desktop, you can find it on the **Start** menu or add it to your desktop as explained in Chapter 3, "Using the Windows XP Desktop."

❷ Open My Computer

Double-click the **My Computer** icon on your desktop to open the **My Computer** window.

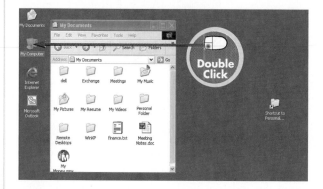

❸ Tile Your Windows

Right-click the taskbar and choose **Tile Windows Vertically** so that you can see both the **My Computer** and the **My Documents** windows at the same time.

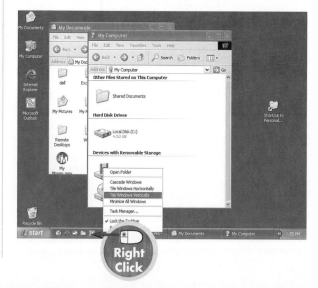

4 Drag the File to the Floppy Drive

Place the mouse pointer over the file in the **My Documents** window that you want to copy. Click and hold the left mouse button while dragging the file to the floppy drive icon in the **My Computer** window.

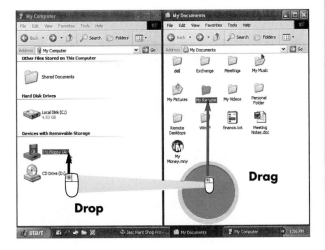

5 Copy the File

Release the left mouse button to drop the file on the floppy drive icon. A dialog box appears to track the progress of the copy operation.

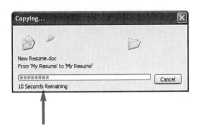

6 Select a File

Another way to send a file to the floppy drive is to choose a command rather than dragging and dropping the file. Start by selecting the file (click it once).

7 Choose Send to Floppy Drive

Right-click the selected file, point to the **Send To** command on the shortcut menu, then choose the floppy drive option. Windows copies the file to the floppy disk in the drive.

How to Open a File with a Different Program

Files usually have a certain program associated with them, normally the program that created them. A text file, for example, is associated with Notepad. Windows knows what program to use to open a file because of the three-character extension following the file's name. For example, a text file might be named Groceries.txt. Windows knows that files with the .txt extension should be opened in Notepad. Sometimes, however, you might want to open a file with a different program or even change the program associated with the file altogether.

1 Right-Click the File

Right-click the file you want to open with a special program and choose **Open With** from the shortcut menu. The **Open With** dialog box opens.

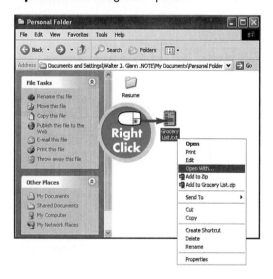

2 Choose the Program

Select the program you want to use to open the file.

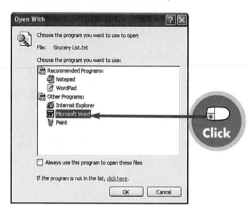

3 Find Another Program

If the program you want to use does not appear in the list, click the **Click Here** link to find the program file on your computer yourself. Most of the programs installed on your computer are located in the **Program Files** folder on your C: drive. If you don't find the program there, consult the documentation for the program to get more information.

4 Make It the Default Choice

If you want to change an extension's association (that is, to make all files of that type open with the new program you've selected from now on), enable the **Always use this program to open these files** option.

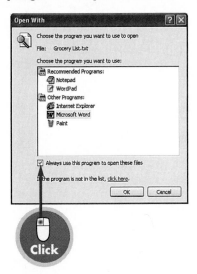

5 Open the File

Click **OK** to open the file in the selected program.

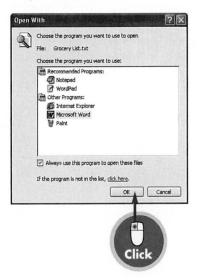

Viewing File Associations

You can view a complete list of file associations in Windows. Click **Start** and choose **Control Panel**. In the **Control Panel** window, double-click **Folder Options**. In the dialog box that appears, click the **File Types** tab. All associations are listed here. You can create new associations and change existing ones.

How-to Hint

Task

1   How to Print a Document from a Program 106

2   How to Print a Document from Windows 108

3   How to Manage Documents Waiting to Print 110

4   How to Change Printer Settings 112

5   How to Share a Printer with Others 114

6   How to Install a Local Printer 116

7   How to Set Up Your Computer to Use a Network Printer 120

5

Printing

Printing is one the basic functions you will perform with your computer. Windows XP makes printing as easy as it has ever been, coordinating all the mechanics in the background so that you can focus on your work.

In the tasks in this chapter, you learn how to print a document from within the program that created it and also from the Windows XP desktop. You also learn how to manage various printer settings, such as how to set your default printer, paper source, and paper size. You learn how to install a printer attached to your own computer and how to set up your computer to use a shared printer—one that's available on the network. Finally, you learn how to share your own printer with others on the network.

How to Print a Document from a Program

Most of the time, you print documents directly from the program you used to create them. Because most programs designed for Windows follow similar guidelines, you will find that the process of printing from any Windows program is very similar to the following steps. Many Windows programs also offer a **Print** button on the main toolbar. This button usually prints one copy of the document using all the default printer settings. If you print this way, you bypass the **Print** dialog box described in this task altogether.

1 Open the File

Open the file you want to print using the **File**, **Open** command of the program used to create the file. In the program's **Open** dialog box, navigate to the folder where the file is stored, select the file, and click **Open**.

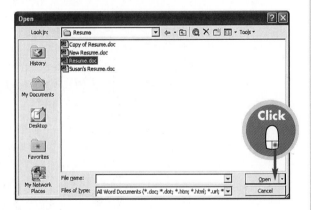

2 Choose the Print Command

When you are ready to print the open document, choose **File**, **Print** from the program's menu bar. The **Print** dialog box opens, which allows you to specify which pages of the document as well as how many copies you want to print.

3 Choose the Printer to Use

If you have access to more than one printer, use the **Printer** drop-down menu to select a printer.

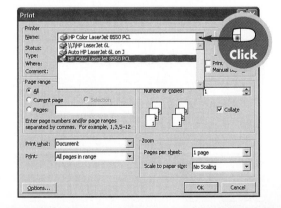

❹ Choose Printing Options

Some programs let you set special printing options that are specific to that program. This is usually done by clicking an **Options** button in the **Print** dialog box. For example, some programs allow you to print a document in draft mode, which can save a lot of time and printer ink because it prints characters in a lighter text.

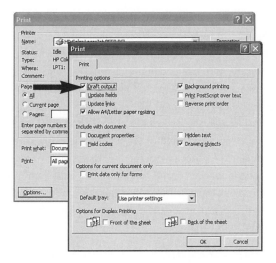

❺ Choose Pages and Number of Copies

Almost every Windows program lets you specify the range of pages you want to print. You can use the program's **File**, **Print Preview** command to see a preview of what the document will look like when printed so that you can determine which pages of a lengthy document you want to print. In the **Number of copies** box, type the number of copies of the document you want to print.

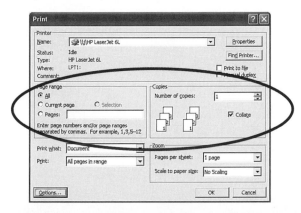

❻ Print the Document

After you have selected your printer, specified the pages and number of copies you want to print, set any extra options, and click **OK** to print. Most programs allow you to continue working while your document is being printed.

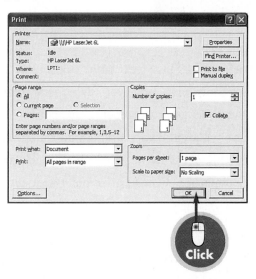

How-to Hint

Setting Printer Properties

The Print dialog boxes for most programs include a **Properties** button. This button gives you quick access to system-wide properties for your printer—the same properties you can set from within Windows, as described in Task 4, "How to Change Printer Settings."

Previewing Before You Print

Some programs offer a feature named **Print Preview**, usually available from the **File** menu, that lets you see your document onscreen as it will look when it is printed. This can be a handy way of making sure that your document looks the way you think it should before using up paper and ink to print it.

How to Print a Document from Windows

Most of the time, you print documents from within programs. However, Windows offers a few ways to print documents straight from the desktop without first opening the document's program. This is a great way to dash off quick copies of documents, or even to print multiple documents at once.

① Find the Document You Print

The first step to printing a document in Windows is to find the document. You can use the **My Computer** folder, the **My Documents** folder, or **Windows Explorer**—whichever you prefer. Here, a document named **Resume** is selected in a folder named **Personal Folder**. You learn more about navigating in Windows in Chapter 4, "Working with Files and Folders."

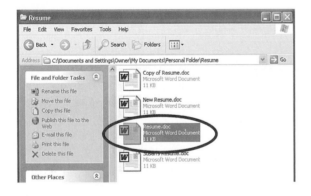

② Right-Click and Choose Print

To quickly print the document using your default printer and the default settings of the document's program, right-click the document (or select multiple documents and right-click any one of them) and choose **Print** from the shortcut menu. Windows prints one copy of each document. Windows opens the associated program just long enough to print the document and then closes the program again. Note that this trick does not work with all programs—just with programs that have included this feature.

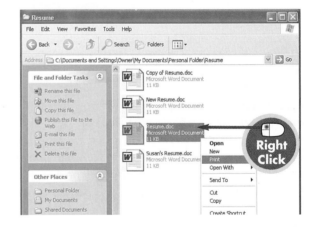

③ Open Your Printers Folder

Another way to print a document in Windows is to drag the document onto a printer icon. To perform this action, both the folder holding the document you want to print and your **Printers** folder must be open. To open the Printers folder, click **Start** and select **Printers and Faxes**.

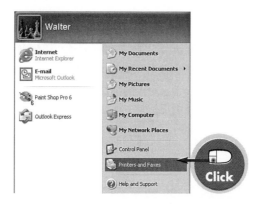

④ Select Documents to Print

Using **My Computer** or **Windows Explorer**, find the folder with the document or documents you want to print and select those document icons.

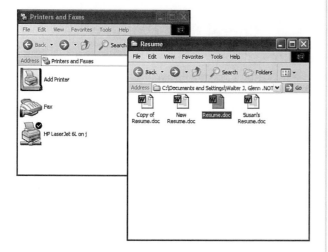

⑤ Drag a Document to a Printer Icon

Drag any document (or group of documents) from the folder and release it on the icon for the printer you want to use. Windows prints the documents using the default settings for the program that created the documents. This method is the same as using the **Print** toolbar button mentioned in Task 1, but lets you choose the printer you want to use.

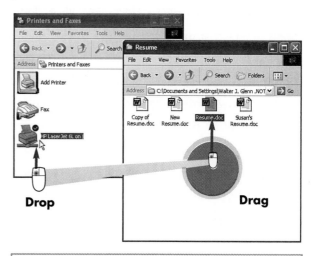

Drop   **Drag**

How-to Hint

Don't See Printers and Faxes on the Start Menu?

If you don't see the **Printers and Faxes** shortcut on the **Start** menu, open the **Control Panel** instead. You'll find the Printers and Faxes folder inside. You can add the **Printer and Fax** shortcut to your **Start** menu by right-clicking the taskbar and choosing **Properties**.

Dragging Multiple Files

You can drag multiple documents to a printer icon in one step: Hold down the **Ctrl** key while you left-click documents in the **My Computer** window.

Creating a Printer Shortcut on Your Desktop

If you frequently drag files to a printer icon and don't want to keep your **Printers** folder open all the time, drag the desired printer icon to your desktop and release it. When Windows offers to create a shortcut for you, click **OK**.

How to Manage Documents Waiting to Print

Whenever you print a document, that document enters a print queue, a line of documents waiting for their turn at the printer. A printer icon appears in your system tray next to the clock to let you know that the queue is active. You can open the print queue and do some document management. Some of the things you can do in the print queue depend on whether you are using a printer hooked up directly to your computer or a network printer. Network printers are usually shared by many users; you can manage only the documents that belong to you. You cannot affect other user's documents or the print queue itself, unless you are the administrator of the printer.

1 Open the Print Queue

To open the print queue, double-click the printer icon in the notification area when it appears. Right-clicking the printer icon opens a shortcut menu that lets you open the print queue for any printer on your system, not just the actively printing one.

2 View Documents Waiting to Print

The print queue shows a list of documents waiting to print in the order in which they are to be printed. For each document, details such as owner, number of pages, document size, and time of submission are also shown.

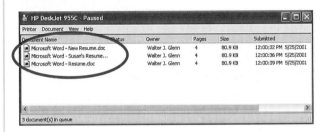

3 Cancel the Printing of a Document

To remove a document from the print queue—that is, to stop it from being printed—right-click the document and choose **Cancel** from the shortcut menu. Be sure that you choose the correct document because Windows does not ask whether you are sure that you want to remove the document.

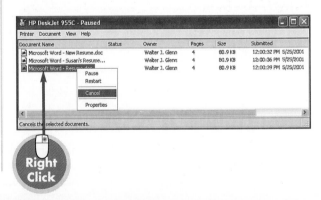

④ Pause the Printing of a Document

If you pause a document, it remains in the print queue but does not print until you choose to resume printing. Other documents waiting in the queue continue to print. To pause a document, right-click the document and choose **Pause** from the shortcut menu; the status of the document in the print queue window changes to **Paused**. Choose **Resume** from the document's shortcut menu when you are ready for the document to continue printing.

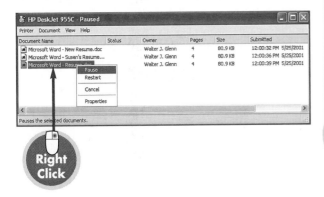

⑤ Restart the Printing of a Document

When you *restart* a paused document, it begins printing again from the beginning. This can be useful if, for example, you start to print a document and then realize the wrong paper is loaded in the printer. You can pause the document, change the paper, and then restart the document. To restart a document, right-click the document and choose **Restart** from the context menu.

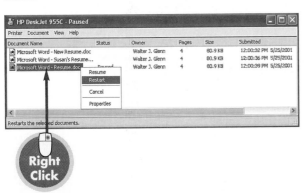

⑥ Change a Document's Priority

A document's *priority* governs when it prints in relation to other documents in the print queue. By default, all documents are given a priority of 1, the lowest priority available. The highest priority is 99. Increasing a document's priority causes it to print before other waiting documents. Double-click the document to open its **Properties** dialog box. Then drag the **Priority** slider to set a higher priority.

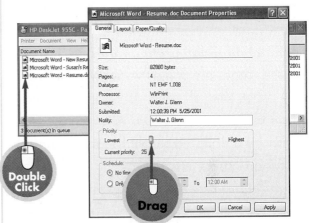

⑦ Pause the Whole Print Queue

Pausing the entire print queue keeps *all* documents from printing. This can be useful if you suspect a problem with your printer (perhaps it's low on toner). You can pause the queue, fix the problem, and then restart the queue. To pause the queue, open the **Printer** menu and choose **Pause Printing**. The title bar for the print queue window changes to indicate that the printer is paused. To resume printing, choose the **Pause Printing** command again.

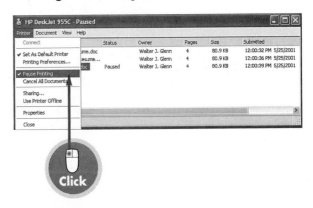

How to Change Printer Settings

When you first install a printer in Windows XP, common settings are configured for you. The settings include which printer is used by default, whether pages are printed vertically or horizontally, what kind of paper is being used, and where that paper comes from. After you use your printer for a while, you might find that you need to change those printer settings.

① Open the Printers Folder

Click the **Start** button and select **Printers and Faxes**. The **Printer and Faxes** window opens.

② Set the Default Printer

In the **Printers and Faxes** window, the default printer has a small check by it. To set a different printer as the default, right-click its icon and choose **Set as Default Printer** from the shortcut menu.

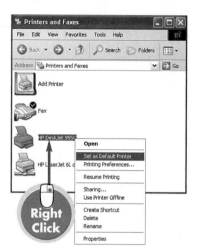

③ Open Printer Preferences

To specify your preferences for the printing options that a particular printer uses, open its **Printing Preferences** dialog box. Right-click a printer and choose **Printing Preferences** from the shortcut menu.

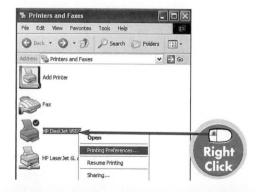

4 Change the Page Layout

Select the orientation of the pages to be printed. You can choose to print the pages in **Portrait** format (normal vertical orientation) or **Landscape** (horizontal orientation).

6 Change the Media Type

Click the **Media** drop-down list to choose the type of paper you want to print to. Some printers can use special kinds of paper (such as glossy paper for photos or presentation graphics, transparencies, and even slides). Those printers print differently depending on the kind of paper being used.

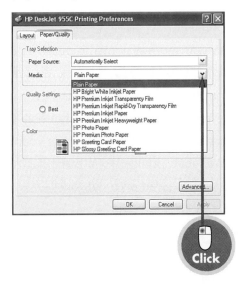

5 Change the Paper Source

Click the **Paper/Quality** tab to see more preferences. Click the **Paper Source** drop-down list to choose a different tray on your printer. The options you see in this list vary based on the printer you are configuring.

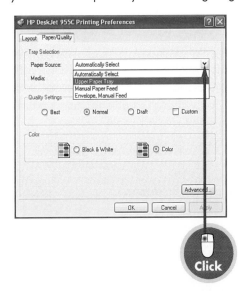

7 Change the Print Quality

Choose the quality of print you want. Better quality uses up more ink and takes more time. Draft quality prints quickly and uses less ink. When you're done setting preferences for this printer, click **OK** to close the dialog box and put these options into effect.

How to Share a Printer with Others

When you share a printer, it becomes accessible to other users on your network. By default, all users on the network can see and print to your printer. You can change this so that only particular users or groups of users can use your printer. To share your printer, your computer must be properly configured on a network.

① Open the Sharing Dialog Box

In the **Printers and Faxes** window, right-click the printer you want to share and choose **Sharing** from the shortcut menu. The **Properties** dialog box for the selected printer opens.

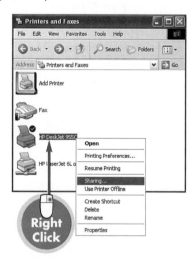

② Share the Printer

On the **Sharing** tab, enable the **Share Name** option and type a name for the shared printer. This is the name others will see when they look for a printer.

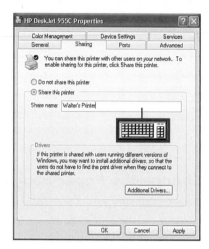

③ Click the Security Tab

If you are using Windows XP Professional on a domain-based network, Windows also provides a **Security** tab that lets you limit the users who can access your printer. You will only be able to access this tab if you have administrative privileges.

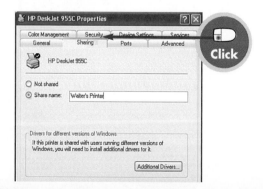

④ Remove the Everyone Group

Select the group named **Everyone** and click **Remove**. This action removes the permissions for all users to access the printer.

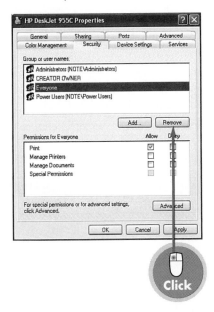

⑤ Add New Users

Click **Add** to give a new user or group of users permission to access the printer. The **Select Users or Groups** dialog box opens.

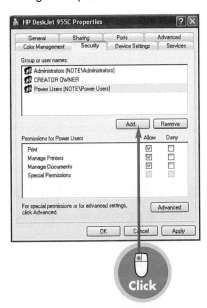

⑥ Select a User to Add

Select a user from the list at the bottom of the dialog box and click **OK** to add that person or group to the list of users who can use the printer. You return to the printer's **Properties** dialog box.

⑦ Apply the New Permissions

Select the exact permissions each user should have using the check boxes. The **Print** permission allows the user to print to the printer. **Manage Printers** allows the user to change printer settings. **Manage Documents** allows the user to move, pause, and delete documents waiting to print. Click **OK** to grant the new users you have added access to your printer.

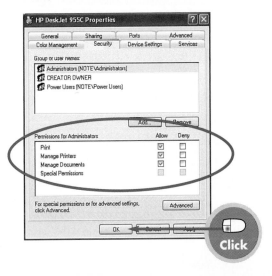

How to Install a Local Printer

6

In Windows lingo, the actual piece of hardware you usually think of as the printer is called the *print device*. The *printer* is the icon you install in the **Printers and Faxes** folder that represents the print device. After you have attached the print device to a computer, it is relatively easy to install the printer to the **Printers and Faxes** folder. In fact, Windows will normally find the print device automatically and configure a printer icon for you. If Windows doesn't find it, use the steps in this task to add the printer yourself.

1 Run the Add Printer Wizard

In the **Printers and Faxes** folder, click the **Add a Printer** link to launch the **Add Printer Wizard**. When you see the Welcome screen, click **Next**.

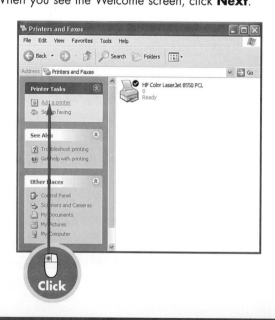

2 Choose Local Printer

On the first page of the wizard, enable the **Local printer** option. A *local printer* is attached directly to your computer.

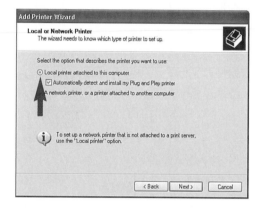

3 Don't Detect the Printer Automatically

Disable the option to automatically detect the printer. If Windows didn't find it automatically already, it probably won't now. If you leave this option selected, Windows will attempt to find the printer itself and figure out what kind it is. If Windows does not find the printer, the wizard will continue as described in this task. If Windows does find the printer, it will set it up for you.

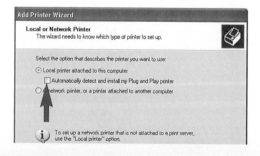

④ Go to the Next Page

Whenever you finish with the options on one wizard page, just click **Next** to go to the next page.

⑤ Choose a Port

Choose the port on your computer to which the print device is attached. The first print device on a computer is usually on the LPT1 port (the first parallel port). The second print device is usually on the LPT2 port (the second parallel port). Newer printers may be installed on a USB port. When you've selected the port, click **Next** to go on.

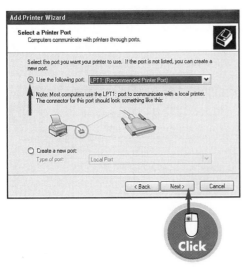

⑥ Choose a Manufacturer

On the left side of this page is a list of common printer manufacturers. Choose the manufacturer for the print device you are installing.

⑦ Choose a Model

After you choose a manufacturer from the left side of the page, the list on the right changes to display printer models made by the selected manufacturer. Choose the model of the print device you are installing. Click **Next** to go on.

8 Name the Printer

By default, Windows creates a name for your printer based on its manufacturer and model number (for example, **HP DeskJet 855C**). If you want the printer icon to have a different name, type a new name in the **Printer name** text box.

9 Make It the Default Printer

If you want your new printer to be the default printer used by programs on your computer, click **Yes**. If you prefer to preserve an existing default printer, click **No**. Click **Next** to go on.

10 Share the Printer

To share the new printer with other users on the network, select the **Share name** option. Windows creates a share name for you based on the printer name you selected in Step 8 of this task, although you can type a different share name. For more on sharing a printer, see Task 5, "How to Share a Printer with Others." Click **Next** to go on.

11 Enter a Location and Description

Optionally, you can enter a location and description for the printer to help identify it to others who may use it. You won't see this screen if you did not choose to share the printer in Step 10. Whether you fill in these fields or not, click **Next** to go on.

⑫ Print a Test Page

Click **Yes** if you want Windows to print a test page to ensure that your new printer is working properly. If the test doesn't work, you are shown how to troubleshoot the installation. Click **Next** to go on.

⑬ Finish the Installation

Review the configuration of your new printer. If you discover any problems or errors in this information, click **Back** to go back through the steps of the installation. If you are satisfied with the information displayed here, click **Finish**.

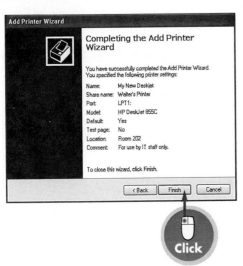

How-to Hint

Creating a Share Name

When you create a share name for your printer, it is best to keep the name under eight characters in length. Older programs (those created for use with pre-Windows 95) can recognize only eight-character names. If you are at all unsure whether any users of older programs will print to your printer, keep the name short.

Installing a Printer More Than Once

Each icon in the **Printers and Faxes** folder represents a real printer. You can install more than one icon for a single printer by running the **Add Printer Wizard** again, choosing the same printer and port during setup, and giving the new icon a new name. You may want to do this to configure each icon with different settings. For example, your printer may have two paper trays: one for letter-size paper and one for legal-size paper. You could name one icon **Letter Printer** and configure it to use paper from the letter-size paper tray. You could name the other icon **Legal Printer** and configure it to use the legal-size paper tray. You can also set up additional printer icons to use different print quality, paper types, or whatever other configurations you desire.

How to Set Up Your Computer to Use a Network Printer

A *network printer* is often one that is attached to another computer on the network; that computer's user has shared the printer with other users on the network. Some network printers are attached directly to the network and are not on a computer. Either way, setting up your computer to print to a network printer requires that you know where on your network the printer is located. This means knowing the name of the computer the printer is attached to (if it is attached to a computer) or the name of the printer itself (if it is attached directly to a network) and maybe the workgroup that the computer or printer is part of.

❶ Run the Add Printer Wizard

In the **Printers and Faxes** window, click the **Add a Printer** link to launch the Add Printer Wizard. Click **Next** to skip the Welcome page.

❷ Choose Network Printer

On the first page of the wizard, enable the **A network printer, or a printer attached to another computer** option.

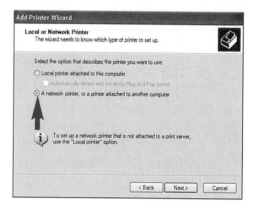

❸ Go to the Next Page

When you finish with the options on one wizard page, just click **Next** to go to the next page.

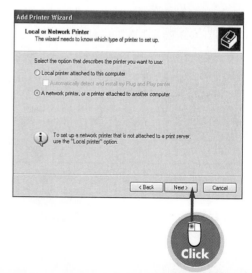

④ Find the Printer

If you know the exact name of the printer you want to connect to (including the network path to that printer), you can enter it in the **Name** text box. You can also connect to an Internet-based printer by entering its address in the **URL** box. If you don't know the name or address (which is usually the case), leave the **Find a printer in the directory** option selected and click **Next** to browse the network for the computer.

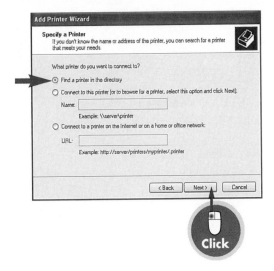

⑤ Choose the Printer

The **Browse for Printer** page of the wizard shows a hierarchical view of the workgroups and computers on your network. All shared printers are listed at the top. Choose the printer you want to set up and click **Next**.

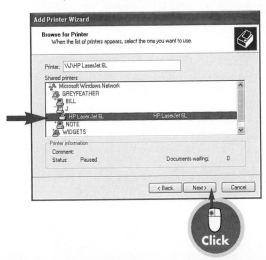

⑥ Make It the Default Printer

If you want this new printer to be the default printer used by programs on your computer, click **Yes**. If you prefer to preserve an existing default printer, click **No**. Click **Next** to go on.

⑦ Finish the Installation

Review the configuration of your new printer. If you discover any problems or errors in the information shown here, click **Back** to go back through the steps of the installation. If you are satisfied with the information displayed, click **Finish**.

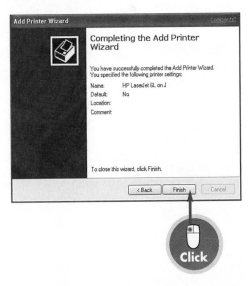

① How to Set Up a Small Network 124

② How to Set Up Additional User Accounts 128

③ How to Share an Internet Connection 130

④ How to Use My Network Places 132

⑤ How to Add a Network Place 134

⑥ How to Find a Computer on the Network 136

⑦ How to Find a File on the Network 138

⑧ How to Share a File or Folder with Others 140

⑨ How to Map a Network Drive 142

Working on a Network

A network is really just a bunch of computers (and sometimes other devices) that are connected together—a setup often referred to as a local area network, or LAN. Sometimes these LANs are connected together over different types of telephone lines to form one large network—often called a wide area network, or WAN.

When your computer is part of a network, you can share files, folders, and printers on one computer with other computers on the network. On a Windows network, computers and users are grouped together in one of two ways: domains or workgroups. Domains are fairly complicated networks, often used by large companies. Powerful computers called servers provide security, Internet access, file storage, and much more to less powerful computers called workstations. Workgroups are used on smaller networks and are usually groups of workstations networked together with no servers. Each of the workstations takes an equal part in the network and is often called a peer. If you are setting up your own network, you'll almost certainly use a workgroup.

How to Set Up a Small Network

Windows XP makes it easy to configure a small network after all the networking hardware is in place and the computers are physically connected. The installation instructions that come with the hardware you're using to create the network will help you physically connect your computers. Windows XP is all you need to handle the communications between the connected devices. This task provides an overview of setting up your network.

1 Buy Your Networking Hardware

The majority of networks installed today use a type of cable called *twisted pair*. Twisted pair cable looks like a thick phone cable with jacks on the ends that are slightly wider than normal phone jacks. Cables and hardware are rated based on industry standards. As of the publication of this book, the highest standard officially available is Category 5e, although standards for Category 6 are in the works. Make sure that all the hardware and cables you use are rated at least Category 5e.

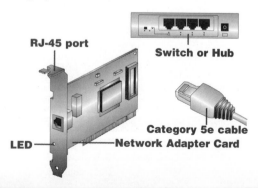

RJ-45 port

Switch or Hub

Category 5e cable

LED — Network Adapter Card

2 Install Network Cards

A network adapter card must be installed into each computer that will be on the network. The card translates information back and forth between your computer and the network cable attached to the card.

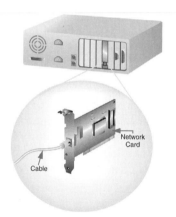

Network Card

Cable

3 Set Up a Hub or Switch

If you have only two computers to network, you can connect them directly together using a crossover cable (a cable in which some of the wires are switched). Connect one end of the cable to each computer and that's it. If you have more than two computers, each computer must be connected to a central hub or switch with a normal cable (that is, not a crossover cable). Switches offer some advantages over hubs (including speed and ease of configuration), and are only about 15–20% more expensive. Use a switch when possible.

Switch

Crossover Cable

Computer   Computer   Computer   Computer   Computer

④ Set Up a Router

If you have a broadband Internet connection, such as a cable modem or DSL line, routers are available that can connect directly to your cable or DSL modem and then share your Internet connection automatically with the rest of your network. Many of these routers contain a built-in switch so that you can simply connect your computers right to it without using a separate hub or switch. Some routers even contain built-in firewalls that protect your computers from the Internet. If you don't want to use a router, you can still share an Internet connection with other computers on the network using Windows XP.

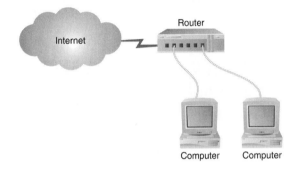

⑤ Set Up Other Networking Devices

Devices such as printers and fax machines can connect directly to the network cable in the same way that a computer with a network card does. These devices can then be shared by all computers on the network. On a small network, you probably won't use such devices. Instead, you might want to share the printer (or other device) attached to one of your computers with the rest of the network. For now, just make sure that the device is hooked up to the computer in the location you desire. You'll configure it later.

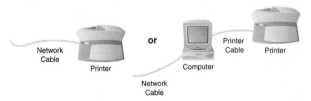

⑥ Connect Cables

After you've decided where the computers (and other network hardware) will be located, it's time to hook up the cables. Just plug one end of a cable into each computer and plug the other end into one of the jacks on your switch or hub. When the cables are connected, the physical part of setting up the network is finished. Next, you'll be working with Windows.

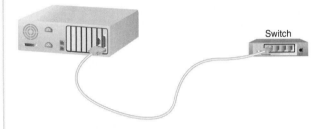

⑦ Install Windows XP

You'll have to install Windows XP on each of the computers on the network. It doesn't matter which edition of Windows XP you use—Home Edition or Professional. You can even use one edition on some computers and the other edition on other computers. In fact, you can even use previous versions of Windows on some of the computers (although you might have to do a little more configuring than with Windows XP). All editions and versions of Windows will talk to one another on the network. For details on installing Windows XP, see the Appendix.

8 Name the Computers

During the installation of Windows XP, you will be asked to provide a name for your computer. The setup program suggests one for you, but it is usually a somewhat convoluted name with lots of numbers in it. The name of the computer distinguishes it from the other computers on the network. For this reason, it is best to use simple names that help you identify each computer. For example, you might want to name the computers after the people who use them.

9 Join the Same Workgroup

During the installation of Windows XP, you will be asked to make the computer a member of either a domain or workgroup. For a small network, you will want to choose the **Workgroup** option and type in the name of the workgroup. It doesn't matter what workgroup name you use, as long as all the computers on the network use the same workgroup name.

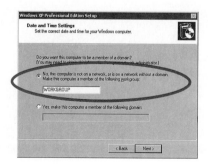

10 Set Up Network Cards

After you have installed Windows on each computer, turn on the computers. It is likely that Windows XP figured out what type of network adapter card you are using and configured it for you during installation. If Windows could not determine the network card, you will be asked the first time you start Windows after the installation to insert the disk that came with your network adapter card. Windows then finishes configuring your card.

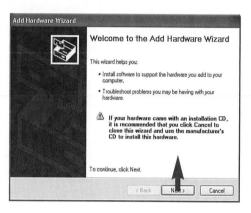

11 Make Sure the Network Works

Double-click the **My Network Places** icon on your desktop and then click the **View workgroup computers** link on the left side of the window. The resulting window should show a list of computers on the network. If no computers are shown, try another computer on the network. If none of the computers show any other computers, something is probably wrong with your switch or hub. If some computers show up and some don't, something is probably wrong with those computers. Double-check your installation.

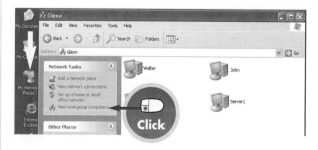

⑫ Share Folders and Files

When you know that the network is working, it's time to set up a few things. The first thing you'll want to do is go to each computer and share the folders and files you want other computers to be able to access. You learn how to do this in Task 8, "How to Share a File or Folder with Others."

⑬ Share Printers

You'll also want to share any printers that you want other computers to use. This process is covered in Chapter 5, "Printing."

⑭ Share an Internet Connection

If one of your computers has an Internet connection (whether it be a dial-up modem connection or a broadband connection such as cable or DSL), you can share the connection with all the computers on the network. Sharing an Internet connection is covered in Task 3, "How to Share an Internet Connection."

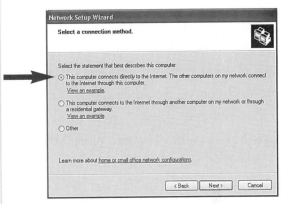

⑮ Get to Work

Your network should now be ready to use. Remember to check the rest of this chapter and the other chapters of this book (particularly Chapter 16, "Protecting Yourself on the Web") for more on using your network.

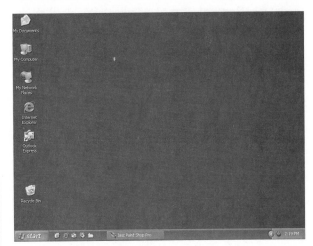

How to Set Up Additional User Accounts

User accounts provide an easy and secure way to share a single computer with more than one person. Although you could let different people share the same user account, creating different accounts has some advantages. When you first install Windows, two accounts are created. One is named by whatever name you provide to Windows during installation. The other is called a **Guest** account. This task shows you how to set up additional user accounts.

1 Open User Accounts

Click the **Start** button and choose **Control Panel** to open the **Control Panel** window. Double-click the **User Accounts** icon to open the **User Accounts** window. It's possible that your **Control Panel** window will open in category view, which groups the various icons in the **Control Panel** according to their use and even hides some of the more useful ones. If your **Control Panel** is in category view, click the **Switch to Classic View** link.

2 Create a New Account

The **User Accounts** window shows the accounts currently configured on the computer. Click **Create a new account**.

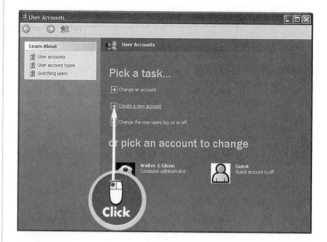

3 Name the New Account

Type a name for the new account. With a small number of users, it is usually best to use the first name of the person for whom you are creating the account. If two people have the same first name, you might want to use a last initial or some other variation of the name.

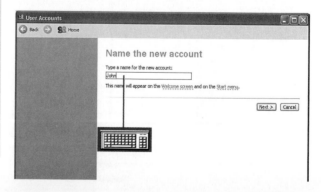

④ Choose the Type of Account

Each user account you create can be one of two types. A person with a **Computer Administrator** account can add, change, and delete other user accounts. That user can also install and remove software and make changes that affect all users of the computer. A person with a **Limited** account can change his own password, work with programs already installed by a **Computer Administrator**, and make limited configuration changes. After you choose the type of account you want to create, click **Create Account**.

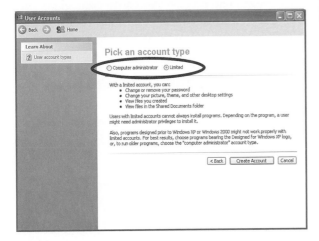

⑤ Change an Account

From the main **User Accounts** window, you can also change existing user accounts if you are allowed to do so (you must be using an account of the **Computer Administrator** type to make these kinds of changes). Click the **Change an account** link.

⑥ Choose an Account to Change

Click the account to which you want to make changes.

⑦ Select Changes to Make

Click the link for the change you want to make. You can change the name of the account, the picture that appears beside it, the type of account, and the password. You can also delete the account altogether.

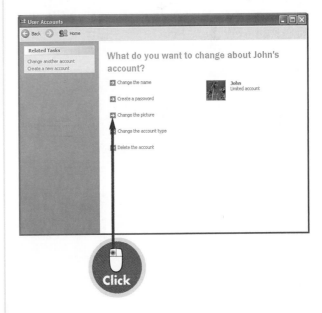

How to Share an Internet Connection

One of the biggest advantages of a home network (aside from playing games together and transferring large files easily) is the ability to share a single Internet connection among several computers. This task explains how to set up the computer that has the Internet connection so that the connection is shared with the other computers on the home network.

① Start the Home Networking Wizard

These steps should be performed on the computer that has the Internet connection. Refer to the How-To Hints at the end of this task for instructions on setting up the other computers in your network. Click **Start** and choose **All Programs**, **Accessories**, **Communications**, **Network Setup Wizard**.

② Click Next Twice

Click **Next** to go past the **Welcome** page of the wizard. Click **Next** again to go past the page that tells you that your computers must be connected together before starting the wizard.

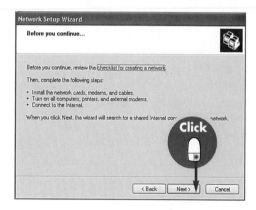

③ Select the Connection Method

Select the first listed option—**This computer connects directly to the Internet**. When you set up the other computers on your home network (as explained in the How-To Hints at the end of this task), you'll select one of the other options in this list. Click **Next** to go on.

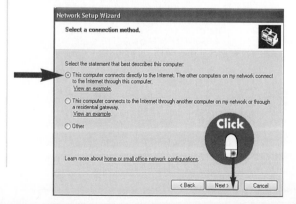

④ Choose the Internet Connection

Choose the specific connection that your computer uses to connect to the Internet. This connection could be a modem or it might be a networking card if you are directly connected. Click **Next** to continue.

⑤ Enter a Description for the Computer

Optionally, you can type a description for the computer that makes it easier for others on the network to identify it as the computer sharing an Internet connection. Click **Next** to go on.

⑥ Apply Network Settings

The wizard presents a summary of the settings you have chosen. When you have reviewed them and are sure that you want to apply them, click **Next**. When you are done, the wizard will let you know that the process has been successful; click **Finish** to exit the wizard.

<table>
<tr><td>How-to Hint</td></tr>
</table>

Setting Up Other Computers on the Network

After you have set up the computer with the Internet connection, run the **Home Networking Wizard** from each of the other computers on the network. On those computers, select the **This computer connects to the Internet through another computer on my network** option when asked for a connection method in Step 3.

Configuring a Firewall

When you set up a network connection that Windows recognizes as an Internet connection Windows automatically configures firewall software on the connection. For the most part, this software requires no configuration on your part. If you suspect that the firewall is not active for a connection, click the **Start** button and choose **Network Connections**. Right-click the connection that is used for the Internet, choose **Properties**, and select the **Advanced** tab. You can enable or disable the firewall for the connection on this tab.

④

How to Use My Network Places

Most of what you do on the network is done using the **My Network Places** icon on your desktop. If you do not see the **My Network Places** icon on your desktop, you can find it on your **Start** menu or add it to your desktop using the procedure described in Chapter 3. With it, you can access all the shared resources your network has to offer, add new network places of your own, and even search for computers and documents on the network.

❶ Open My Network Places

Double-click the **My Network Places** icon on your desktop to open the **My Network Places** window.

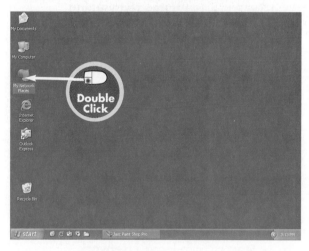

❷ View Workgroup Computers

The **My Network Places** window shows a list of all the shared folders on the local network. You can double-click any of them to open the folder and look for files. If you are in a workgroup, you'll also see a **View workgroup computers** link in the left column; if you are in a domain, you'll see an **Entire Network** link. Both links work the same way and let you further browse the resources on a network. Click the appropriate link or icon to begin browsing.

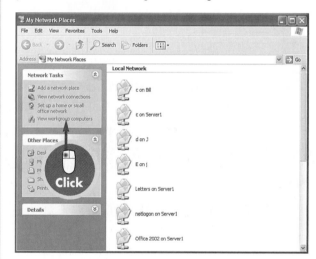

③ Open a Computer

The workgroup window shows all the other computers in your workgroup. Double-click a computer to open its window.

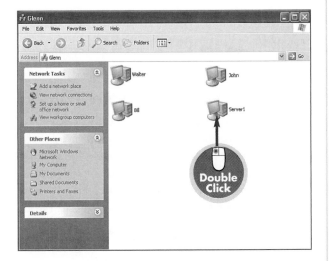

⑤ Open a File

You can use items in a shared folder just as you use items on your own computer. Double-click a file to open it.

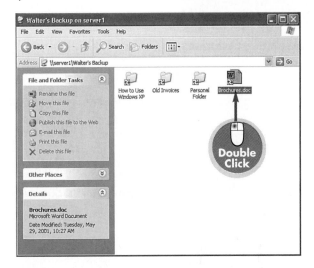

④ Open a Shared Folder

When you open a particular computer, all the resources shared on that computer are listed in this window. The computer's "resources" include shared folders, files, and printers. Double-click any shared object to open it.

⑥ Copy a File to Your Computer

Instead of just opening and modifying a file on someone else's computer, you might want to copy it to your computer. To do that, just drag the file directly onto your desktop or into any open folder.

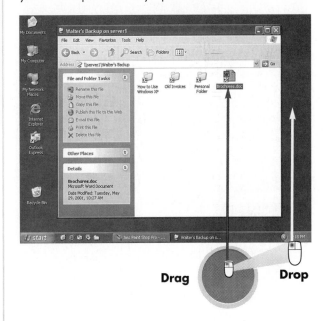

How to Add a Network Place

Although you can use **My Network Places** to browse the network looking for the right folder, you might want to add frequently used shared folders on your network, Web sites, or even FTP sites directly to the My **Network Places** window. Doing so lets you quickly get to files you use often.

1 Add a Network Place

In the **My Network Places** window, click the **Add a network place** link to launch the **Add Network Place Wizard**. On the welcome page of the wizard, click **Next** to continue.

2 Select Other Location

You can configure a remote storage location on the Microsoft Network if you have an account there, or you can configure a shortcut to a place on your local network. In this example, you'll create a shortcut to a place on your local network. Select the **Choose another network location** option and click **Next**.

3 Browse for a Computer

If you know the exact path to the network resource you want, enter it in the text box. Don't be concerned that the text asks for the "name of a server." Type the path of any resource for which you are creating a network place. If you don't know the exact path, click the **Browse** button.

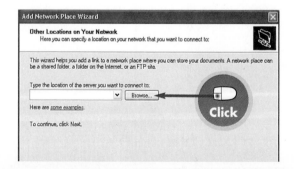

④ Select the Network Resource You Want

The **Browse** window lists all the computers in your domain or workgroup. Select the computer that contains the shared resource you want from the list, select the folder in that computer, and click **OK**. Note that you can select an entire computer if you want to make a network shortcut.

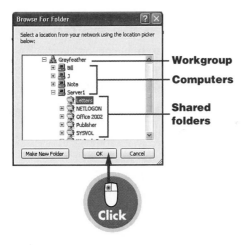

⑤ Click Next

The path for the resource you've chosen appears in the **Type the location** text box on the wizard page. Click **Next** to go on.

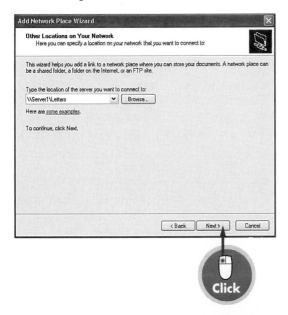

⑥ Enter a Name for the Network Place

A name for the new shortcut is suggested for you. If you want to name it something different, type the new name in the **Enter a name for this network place** box and click **Next**.

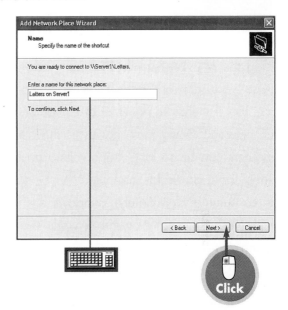

⑦ Finish

Click **Finish**. When you are done, the new shortcut is available in the **My Network Places** window.

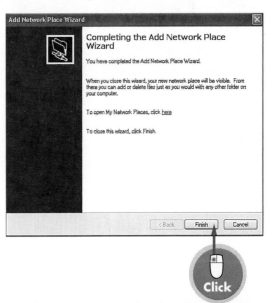

How to Find a Computer on the Network

Using the **My Network Places** window to browse your network and locate a computer works fine if there are not a lot of computers on your network. Sometimes, however, the list of computers can be so long that scrolling around looking for a particular computer can be quite time consuming. Fortunately, Windows lets you quickly find a computer on the network, even if you know only part of its name.

① Open My Network Places

Double-click the **My Network Places** icon on your desktop to open the **My Network Places** window.

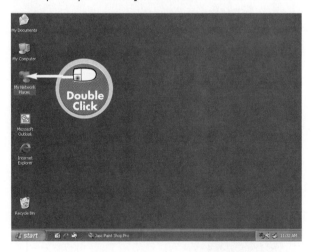

② Open the Search Pane

Click the **Search** button on the toolbar to open the **Search Companion** pane on the left side of the **My Network Places** window.

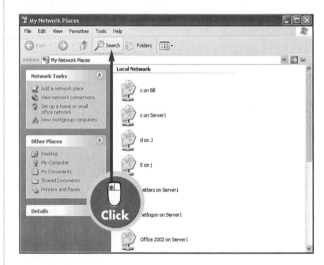

How-to Hint

Auto-filling

As it does in many other places throughout the system, Windows remembers searches you have performed in the past. As you type your search term, Windows will try to fill in the rest of the search term for you based on what it remembers.

3 Enter a Computer Name

Type the name of the computer you are looking for in the **Computer name** text box. You can type just part of a name if you don't remember the whole thing.

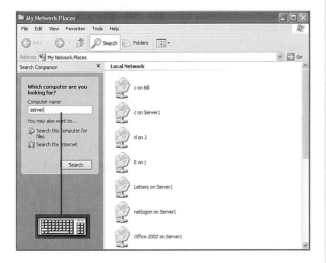

4 Search for the Computer

Click the **Search** button or press Enter to begin the search. Results of your search are displayed in the right pane of the **My Network Places** window.

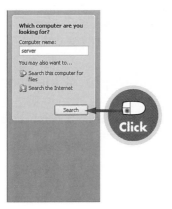

5 Open the Computer

You can open any computer displayed in the search results list simply by double-clicking it. In this example, my search for a computer with the partial name "**server**" turned up only one match: **Server1**.

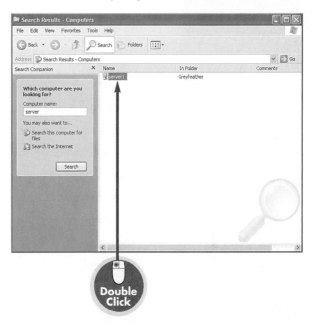

6 Close the Search Pane

Click the **Search** button on the toolbar again to close the **Search Companion** pane and get back to work.

How to Find a File on the Network

7

Windows does not really have the built-in capability to search an entire network full of computers for a particular file. However, it is easy enough to perform a regular search on a shared folder. This, at least, saves you from having to rummage through the shared folder and its sub-folders yourself. The trick is to know at least the names of the computer and shared folder holding the document for which you are looking.

1 Open Computers Near Me

In the **My Network Places** window, click the **View workgroup computers** link to open the workgroup window. If you are on a domain, click the **Entire Network** link instead. Both links work the same way.

2 Open a Computer

Double-click the computer on which you want to search for a file.

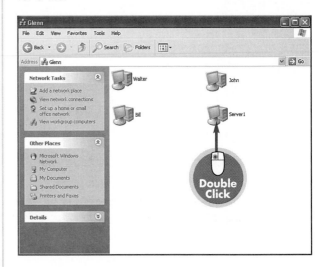

Searching from the Start Menu

You can also get to the **Search Results** window by choosing **Search** from the **Start** menu. When the Search Results window appears, select the type of file for which you want to search. Next, enter the filename and use the **Look In** drop-down list to browse to the shared folder you want to search. Learn more about the windows search feature in Chapter 4, "Working with Files and Folders."

③ Search a Shared Folder

Find the shared folder in which you want to search for a file. Right-click the folder and choose **Search** from the shortcut menu that appears. The **Search Results** window opens with the **Search Companion** pane on the left.

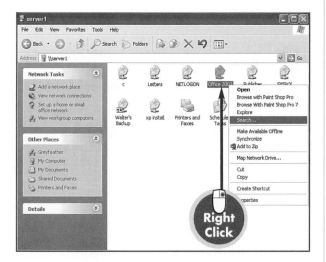

④ Enter the Name of a File

Type the name of a file for which you want to search in the text box. You can also enter part of a name if you don't remember the whole thing.

⑤ Search for the File

Click the **Search** button or press Enter to begin the search. Results are displayed in the right pane of the Search Results window.

⑥ Open the File

After you find the file for which you are looking, double-click it to open it, or drag it to your desktop to copy it from the shared folder to your computer.

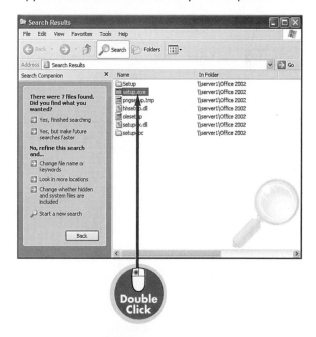

How to Share a File or Folder with Others

In addition to giving you access to other user's files, folders, and printers, networks allow you to share your resources with other users. To share resources, your computer must be on a network and your network administrator must have already set up your computer so that you can share items with others.

① Open the Sharing Dialog Box

Using the **My Computer** or **My Documents** window, find the folder or file you want to share. Right-click it and choose **Sharing and Security** from the shortcut menu to open the **Sharing** tab of the item's **Properties** dialog box. This task focuses on sharing a folder, but the process of sharing a file is the same.

② Share the Folder

Click the **Share this folder on the network** option to enable sharing of the folder.

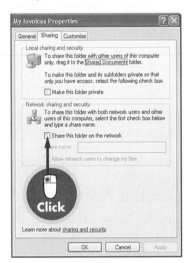

How Do You Know It's Shared?

A shared file or folder shows up on your computer as a standard icon with a hand underneath the icon.

③ Change the Share Name

Windows names the shared folder the same as the original name of the folder. If you want, type a new share name in the text box for the folder you are sharing.

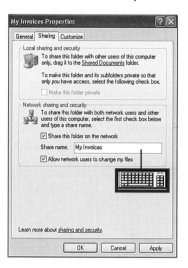

④ Allow Network Users to Change Files

When you share the file, Windows automatically turns on the **Allow network users to change my files** option. If you would rather other people be able to view your files, but not change them, disable this option.

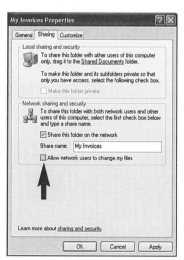

⑤ Learn More

The Windows XP Help system contains a large amount of useful information on sharing files. To access this information quickly, click the **sharing and security** link at the bottom of the tab.

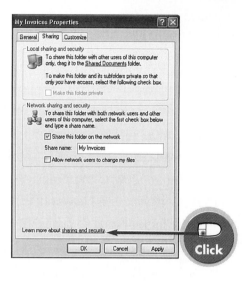

⑥ Close the Properties Dialog Box

Click **OK** to close the **Properties** dialog box. Users can now access the folder you just shared.

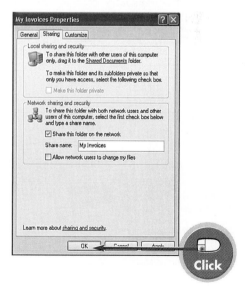

How to Map a Network Drive

When you map a network drive, you essentially tell your computer to treat a shared resource as a drive on your computer—the resource even gets its own drive letter and shows up in the **My Computer** window. Older programs sometimes don't know how to use Network Places and can only open files on real disk drives. By mapping a network drive, you can fool these programs into thinking that a shared folder is a real disk drive.

❶ Open Computers Near Me

In the **My Network Places** window, click the **View workgroup computers** link. If you are on a domain, click the **Entire Network** link instead. Both links work the same way.

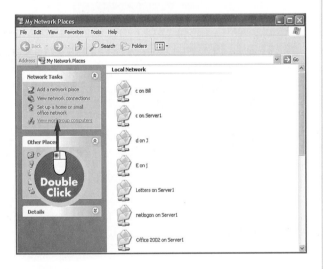

❷ Open a Computer

Find the computer that contains the shared folder you want to map as a network drive and double-click it.

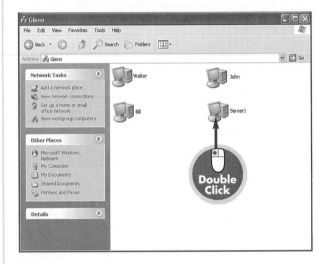

❸ Select a Shared Folder

Find the shared folder you want to map and select it by clicking it once.

④ Choose Map Network Drive

From the File menu, choose the **Map Network Drive** command. The **Map Network Drive** dialog box opens.

⑤ Select a Drive Letter

Select a drive letter using the **Drive** drop-down menu. Only letters that are not already used on your computer are listed here, so you don't have to worry about conflicts.

⑥ Reconnect at Logon

If you want the network drive to be remapped to the same drive letter each time you log on to your computer, click the **Reconnect at logon** option. When you're done, click **Finish**.

⑦ View the New Drive

In the **My Computer** window, the new network drive appears using the drive letter you assigned it in Step 5. Network drives look like a regular disk drive with a network cable attached.

Task

1. How to Create and Fill a Briefcase 146

2. How to Take a Briefcase with You 148

3. How to Update Files in a Briefcase 150

4. How to Make Items Available Offline 152

5. How to Use Offline Items 154

6. How to Synchronize Offline Items 156

7. How to Change Offline Settings 158

Working Away from the Network

Many people work when away from the network by connecting to the network over a modem or by taking work home with them on a disk. Some even take their computers off the network and on the road with them. Windows XP offers two ways to work when you are away from the network.

The Windows briefcase is a special folder designed for users to take work home with them on a removable disk, work on the files, and then synchronize the updated files with the originals on the hard drive back at work.

Offline folders are for users who take their computers away from the network, as with a notebook, or who dial into the network with a modem. You can mark any shared folder on a network to be available offline. The contents of the folders are copied to the hard drive on your computer. Once disconnected from the network, you can still work on these files. When reconnected, the files are synchronized with the originals.

How to Create and Fill a Briefcase

Creating a briefcase in Windows is pretty easy. After it is created, you can move files into and out of it the same way you move other folders on your computer. You can create a briefcase directly on the desktop or in any folder using the method described in this task.

1 Create the New Briefcase

Right-click any empty space on your desktop, point to **New** on the shortcut menu, and then choose **Briefcase**. A new icon with the label **New Briefcase** appears on the desktop.

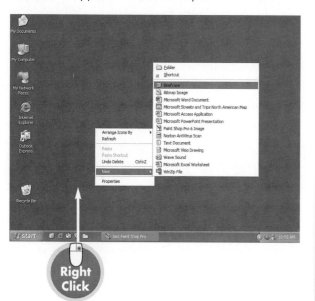

2 Open the New Briefcase

Double-click the **New Briefcase** icon to open it. The first time you open any new briefcase, you are shown a welcome screen that gives you a brief introduction to using it.

3 Open My Documents

To place objects in the briefcase, you must first locate those objects. Double-click the **My Documents** icon on the desktop to open the **My Documents** window.

④ Tile Windows Vertically

Right-click a blank space on the taskbar and choose **Tile Windows Vertically** so that you can see both the **My Documents** and the **New Briefcase** windows side by side.

⑤ Drag a File to the Briefcase

Copy any file or folder to your briefcase by simply dragging it to the **New Briefcase** window. You can copy as many files and folders as you want to the briefcase.

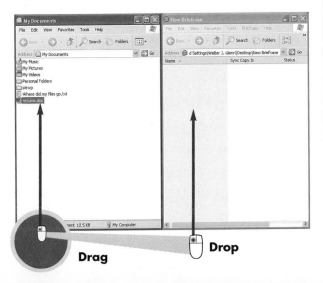

Drag **Drop**

How-to Hint

Watch Your Disk Space

If you are using a floppy disk to carry your briefcase, do not copy more files to your briefcase than the disk can hold. Find out how big a briefcase is by right-clicking it and choosing **Properties** from the shortcut menu. If you routinely place more files in the briefcase than will fit on a typical 1.44MB floppy disk, consider investing in a Zip disk drive. Zip disks hold 100MB or 250MB of data (depending on which drive you buy). You'll need a Zip drive at home and at work.

Renaming Your Briefcase

Rename your briefcase the same way you do any folder. Right-click its icon and choose **Rename** from the shortcut menu. See Chapter 4, "Working with Files and Folders," for more on renaming folders.

How to Take a Briefcase with You

Taking a briefcase with you is as simple as copying it to a floppy disk (or other removable disk). Any computer running Windows 95/98/Me, Windows NT 4.0, Windows 2000, or Windows XP will recognize the briefcase for what it is.

① Open My Computer

Double-click the **My Computer** icon on your desktop to open the **My Computer** window.

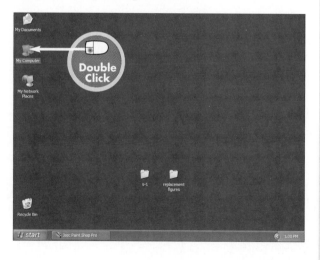

② Move the Briefcase to Your Floppy Drive

Move the mouse pointer over the briefcase icon. Click and hold the left mouse button, then drag the briefcase over the floppy drive icon in the **My Computer** window. Release the mouse button to move the briefcase. You can also right-click the briefcase and choose the **Send To, 3-½" floppy A**: command from the shortcut menu.

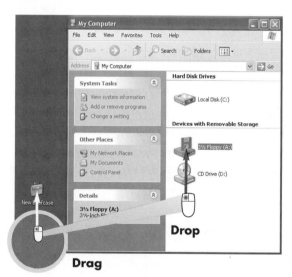

③ Open the Briefcase on Your Home Computer

When you're at the computer away from the network, pop the floppy disk into the computer. Open the **My Computer** window, open the floppy drive, and double-click the **New Briefcase** icon to open the briefcase.

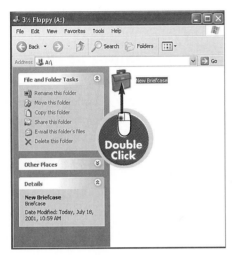

④ Open a File from the Briefcase

In the briefcase, find the file you want to work on and double-click to open it.

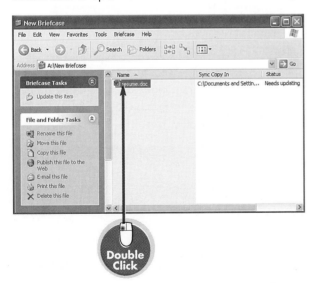

⑤ Save the File

The file opens in whatever application was used to create it. To open a Word file from the briefcase, for example, you must have Microsoft Word installed on your home computer. When you're done working, save the file. The file is updated in the briefcase on the floppy disk.

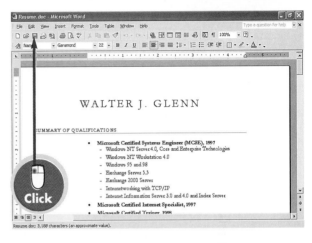

⑥ Move the Briefcase to Your Work Computer

When you get back to your main computer, insert the floppy disk in the drive, open the **My Computer** window, open the floppy drive, and drag the briefcase onto your desktop. In Task 3, you'll see how to update the files on your main computer with the files in the briefcase.

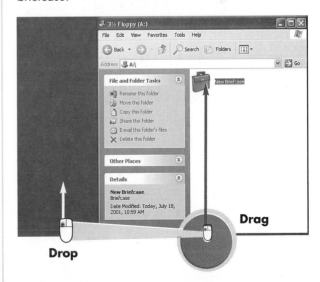

How to Update Files in a Briefcase

Now that you are back at work, you have files in your briefcase that have changed from the originals that are still on your work computer. The next step is to update the original files. You do this from within your briefcase.

1 Open Your Briefcase

Double-click the **New Briefcase** icon to open the **New Briefcase** window. If the briefcase is still on a floppy disk, you should move it back to your desktop first for quicker access.

2 Note the Status of Files

In the **New Briefcase** window, choose **View**, **Details** from the menu bar to switch to **Details** view. The **Status** column tells you which files on your work computer's hard disk need to be updated.

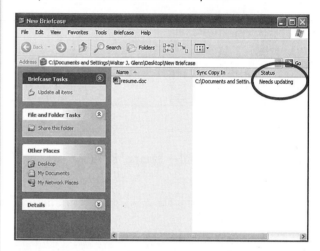

3 Select a File to Update

Select any file you want to update by clicking it once. You can select additional files by holding down the **Ctrl** key while you click other files.

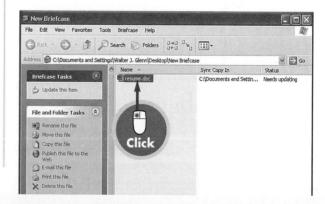

④ Update Selection

From the **Briefcase Tasks** list on the left side of the window, choose the **Update this item** link to update the selected files.

⑤ Review the Update

After you choose the **Update** this item link, you are given the chance to review the updates in the **Update** window. The version of the file in the briefcase is shown on the left. The original file on your hard disk is shown on the right. The arrow in between indicates which version should be updated.

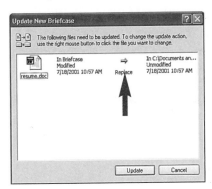

⑥ Update the File

When you are ready to begin the update, just click the **Update** button. Windows replaces the file on the hard disk with the file in the briefcase. Now both files are identical.

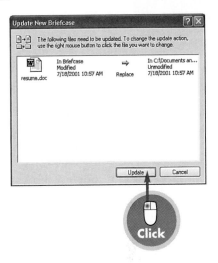

Updating All

Use the **Update All** button on the toolbar in the **New Briefcase** window to update all the files in the briefcase that need to be updated. A link of the same name is available on the left side of the window if no files are selected.

Resolving Conflicts

If the **Update** window shows a red arrow pointing down between the two versions of a file, it means that both versions have been updated since the original was copied to the briefcase. When this happens, you should open both versions of the file and figure out for yourself which is the most recent.

How to Make Items Available Offline

If you are running Windows XP Professional, you can make any shared folder on the network available as an offline folder so that you can use those files when you disconnect from the network. Windows does this by copying the files in the shared folder to a temporary location on your computer's hard disk. When you are connected to the network, you can work on the original files. When you disconnect from the network, you work on the temporary copies. When you connect again, any temporary files you worked on are copied back to the original location and replace the older originals.

❶ Open My Network Places

While still connected to the network (either through a direct cable connection or remotely with a dial-up connection), double-click the **My Network Places** icon to open the **My Network Places** window.

❷ Open Computers Near Me

Browse for a shared folder on the network using the techniques in Chapter 6, "Working on a Network." If you don't see the shared folder that contains the files you want make available offline in the **My Network Places** window, click the **View workgroup computers** link to browse all the computers on your network for the shared folder. If you are in a domain instead of a workgroup (such as on a large corporate network), you'll see a link named **Entire Network** instead of **View workgroup computers**. Both links work the same way.

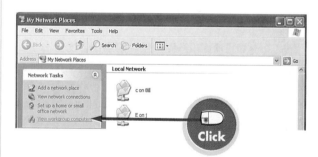

How-to Hint

Making an Item Unavailable

After you make a folder available offline, you can make it unavailable again by right-clicking the folder and choosing the **Make Available Offline** command from the shortcut menu. The temporary files are removed from your hard drive. When you no longer need offline access to a folder, you should make the folder unavailable to reclaim the disk space taken up by the temporary files.

③ Open a Computer

When you find the computer on the network that holds the shared folder you want to change into an offline folder, double-click to open its window.

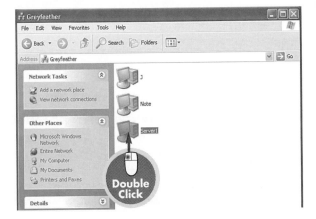

④ Locate a Shared Folder

Scroll through the computer window to find the shared folder you want to make available offline. Click once to select it.

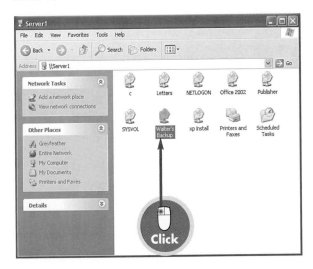

⑤ Make It Available Offline

Right-click the folder you want to make available offline and choose **Make Available Offline** from the short-cut menu.

⑥ Make Subfolders Available

You can decide whether to make just the folder you selected available offline or all of its subfolders available, as well. Choose the appropriate option and click **OK**. Files from the network folder are copied as temporary files to your computer's hard disk. Should you disconnect from the network, you can work on these temporary files until you reconnect. To use the folder offline, refer to the next task.

How to Use Offline Items

After you set up a folder to be available offline, that folder is surprisingly easy to use. All you have to do is open **My Network Places** and browse to the folder the same way you do when you are connected to the network. When you are offline, only the folders configured for offline use are visible.

❶ Open My Network Places

On the computer that you have taken off the network (your laptop or the remote computer that is no longer connected to the workplace through a telephone connection), double-click the **My Network Places** icon to open the **My Network Places** window. Note that you cannot access items offline unless you have first made those items available as described in the preceding task.

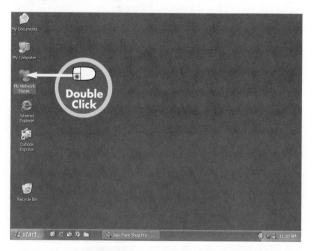

❷ Open Computers Near Me

Click the **View workgroup computers or Entire Network** link (depending on the type of network you're on) to browse for the computer that contains the offline folders you want to access.

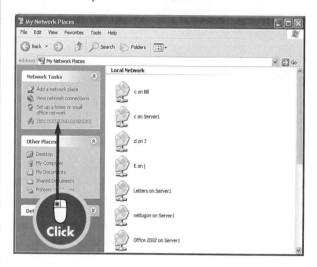

③ Open a Computer

When you are disconnected from the network, only computers that have shared folders configured for offline use are visible in the window. Double-click the computer's icon to open it.

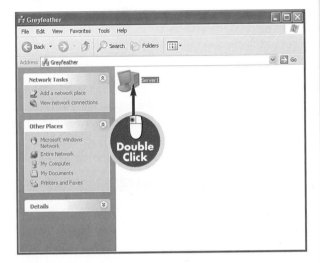

④ Open an Offline Folder

When you open a computer, only the shared folders configured for offline use show up in the computer's window—these folders are called, appropriately enough, *offline folders*. Double-click any offline folder to open it.

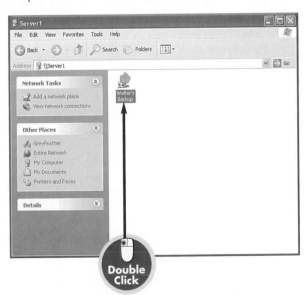

⑤ Open a File

Folders and files in an offline folder have two small arrows at the bottom left of their icons to show that they are offline copies of original files on the network. Double-click any file or folder to open it, just as you would with any regular file or folder.

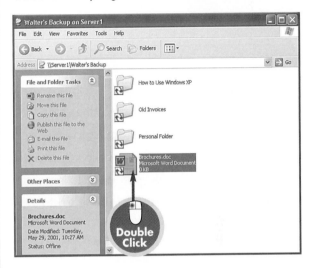

How-to Hint

Offline Permissions

When you are using offline folders and files, the same permissions (such as only being able to read and not change a file) apply to you that would apply if you were using the actual shared folders or files on the network. So don't think that you can bypass security just by using offline folders.

Your Network Places

If you have added any of your own Network Places that point to a shared folder (see Chapter 6, "Working on a Network," for more on this), you might notice that there is no **Make Available Offline** command on the **Network Places** shortcut menu. To make that shared folder available offline, you actually have to browse to the real shared folder the Network Place represents.

How to Synchronize Offline Items

When you have been working on files offline, all you have to do is log back on to the network to automatically synchronize all the files you worked on while you were disconnected. If you are working with offline folders while you are still connected to the network, you have to synchronize files manually. In this task, you learn to synchronize files manually.

1 Synchronize a Specific Folder

Use the **My Network Places** icon on your desktop to browse to the offline folder or file you want to synchronize. Right-click the folder or file and choose **Synchronize** from the shortcut menu. The item is automatically synchronized with the original shared item on the network.

2 Synchronize Multiple Folders

To synchronize multiple folders, open the **Tools** menu of any open folder and choose **Synchronize**. This method also gives you more control over synchronization by opening an **Items to Synchronize** dialog box.

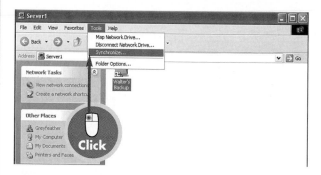

3 Choose Items to Synchronize

The **Items to Synchronize** dialog box shows a list of offline items you can synchronize with their online versions. Select the items you want to synchronize and click **Synchronize**. Remember, when you synchronize an offline item, newer versions of files replace older versions of files.

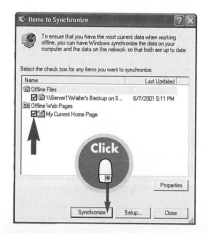

④ Set Up Automatic Synchronization

There are a few ways in which you can configure the automatic synchronization of your files. In the **Items to Synchronize** dialog box, click the **Setup** button to open the **Synchronization Settings** dialog box.

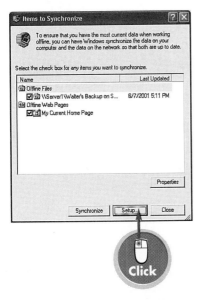

⑤ Set Up Logon/Logoff Synchronization

From the list, select the items you want to be automatically synchronized when you log on or log off the network. Then choose whether you want the selected items to synchronize during logon, logoff, or both. You can also have Windows ask you before synchronizing any items.

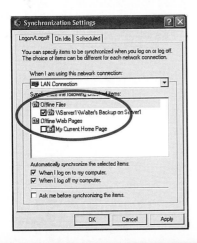

⑥ Switch to On Idle Tab

In the **Synchronization Settings** dialog box, click the **On Idle** tab to configure your computer to synchronize offline files during idle time—when your computer is connected to the network but is not being used.

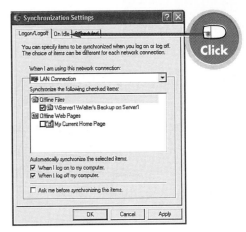

⑦ Set Up Idle Synchronization

Choose the folders you want to be synchronized during idle time from the list and enable the **Synchronize while my computer is idle** option. You can also click the **Advanced** button to specify how many minutes should pass before your computer is considered idle.

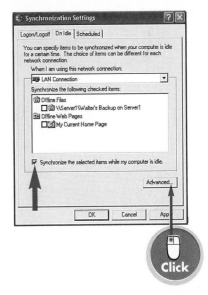

How to Change Offline Settings

For the most part, the default settings for offline folders should work pretty well. However, there are a few settings that might be useful to you. For example, you can change when files are synchronized, how much disk space offline files can use, and whether Windows continuously reminds you when you are using offline instead of online files.

➊ Open the Control Panel

Click the **Start** button and then click **Control Panel**. The Control Panel window opens.

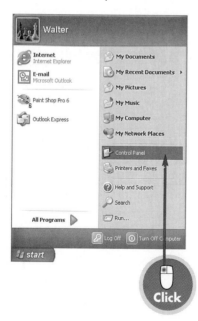

➋ Open Folder Options

Double-click the **Folder Options** icon to open the **Folder Options** dialog box.

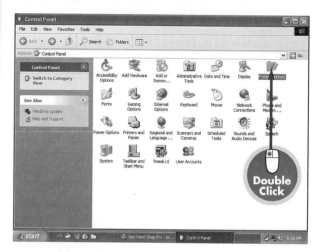

➌ Open Offline Files Tab

In the **Folder Options** dialog box, click the **Offline Files** tab.

④ Synchronize at Log Off/On

By default, the **Synchronize all offline files when logging on** and **Synchronize all offline files before logging off** options are enabled. If you prefer not to wait through this process each time you log off and on, disable these options. If you disable these options, remember to synchronize your files for offline use (as explained in Task 4, "How to Make Items Available Offline," before disconnecting from the network.

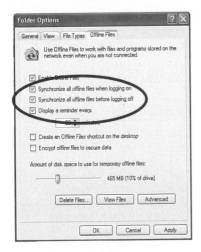

⑤ Enable Reminders

When the **Display a Reminder every** option is enabled, a small icon appears in the notification area next to your clock to indicate that offline files are being used. In addition, a text bubble appears once in a while as yet another reminder. You can specify the interval at which this reminder appears.

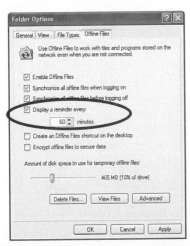

⑥ Place a Shortcut on the Desktop

When you enable the **Create an Offline File shortcut on the desktop** option, a shortcut named **Shortcut to Offline Files** appears on the desktop. Double-clicking this shortcut opens a window that displays all the files you have configured for offline use.

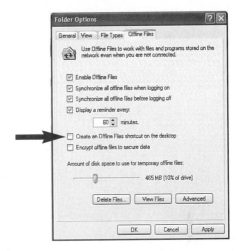

⑦ Choose Amount of Disk Space to Use

By default, offline folders are allowed to use 10% of the space on your hard drive. You can change this to any amount you like by simply dragging the slider to adjust the percentage. When you're done changing the settings for the offline folder, click **OK** to close the dialog box.

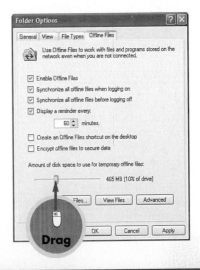

Drag

Task

(1) How to Play Music and Movies 162

(2) How to Record Music 164

(3) How to Find Music Online 166

(4) How to Make Movies 168

(5) How to Work with Pictures 172

(6) How to Play Games 174

8

Having Fun with Windows XP

You can't work all the time, and when you want to have some fun with your computer, Windows XP is ready for you with several built-in "fun" programs.

Windows Media Player can play audio CDs, MP3 music files, and movies in a variety of formats. You can use Windows Media Player to search for music on the Internet and even record your own CDs.

With Windows Movie Maker, you can take still pictures, movie files, home movies, and even music and put them all together to create your own movie. You can edit and play that movie at any time and even send it to friends.

Windows also includes a number of great games, from the classic Solitaire and Hearts to fast-action Pinball. With the variety of Internet games that are available at sites all over the world, you'll never be without a gaming partner again.

How to Play Music and Movies

Unless you have set up a different player program as your default player, Windows plays music and video files using the Windows Media Player. When you insert an audio CD, video CD, or DVD into your disc drive or double-click a music or movie file stored on your computer, Windows Media Player opens automatically and begins playing. To start this task, use Windows Explorer or the My Documents window to browse to a music file (a file with the extension .mp3, .wav, and so on) or a video file (a file with the extension .mpg, .avi, .asf, and so on); double-click it to launch the Windows Media Player.

1 Pause

You can pause the playback of the audio or video file by clicking the **Pause** button once. While playback is paused, the **Pause** button changes to a **Play** button; click the **Play** button to start playback where you left off.

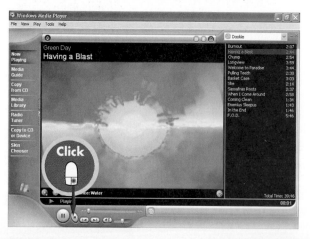

2 Stop

You can stop playback by clicking the **Stop** button. When playback is stopped, the **Pause** button turns into a **Play** button.

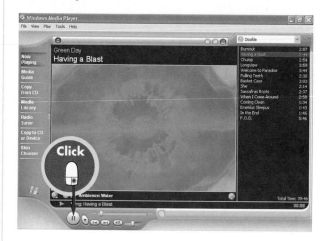

3 Play

When no music or movie is being played or when the movie or audio file is paused, a **Play** button appears. Click it once to start playback.

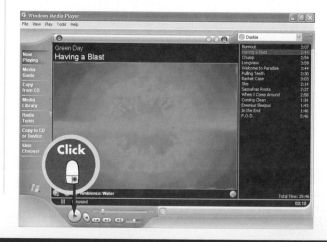

4 Change Volume

Change the volume for the music or video being played by dragging the **Volume** slider to the right (for louder) or to the left (for softer).

5 Go Backward and Forward

During playback, you can skip to the previous or next tracks by clicking the single arrows with lines next to them. During playback of some sorts of media (such as movies), you might also see rewind and fast-forward buttons which are small left and right-facing double arrows.

6 Pick a Track

If you are playing a CD or DVD with multiple tracks, each track is shown in the playlist on the right side of the player screen. Click any track to begin playing it.

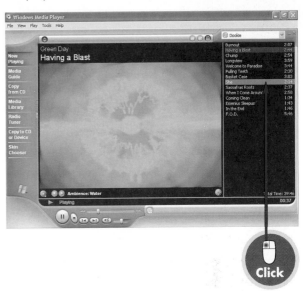

7 Select a Visualization

Visualizations are graphics that move along with the music file as it plays. Windows Media Player includes a number of interesting visualizations. Click the left and right arrows under the visualization window to browse through the available visualizations one at a time; alternatively, click the button with an asterisk to choose a particular visualization from a drop-down list.

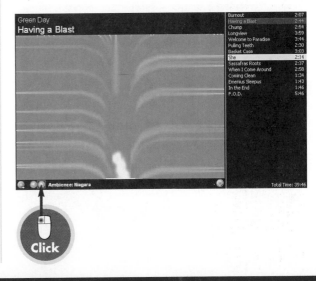

How to Record Music

Windows Media Player makes copying tracks from audio CDs easy. You can record songs from an existing audio CD to a file on your hard disk or to another CD if you have a recordable CD drive. You can also convert songs to the popular MP3 format. You can even listen to songs as they're being copied. Copying music for anything other than strictly personal use is a violation of copyright laws. If you want to copy a song to a CD that you can play in your car, you're probably okay. If you want to use a song in a presentation at the office, you're on shaky legal ground.

❶ Start Windows Media Player

Click **Start**, point to **All Programs**, point to **Accessories**, point to **Entertainment**, and then click **Windows Media Player**.

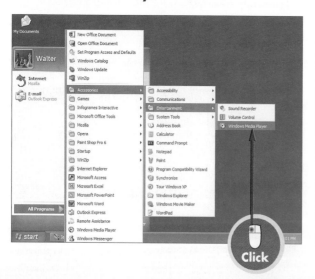

❷ Switch to Copy from CD

Click the **Copy from CD** button. If your CD is not in the computer's CD-ROM drive, insert it now. If the music begins playing, click the **Stop** button to stop playback.

❸ Find Album Information

If **Windows Media Player** does not display the album and track information for your CD, click the **Get Names** button. A wizard opens, asks a few questions, and helps you search the Internet for album information.

4 Select Tracks to Copy

By default, all the tracks on the CD are selected to be copied. Deselect a track by clearing the check from the box next to the track (click the box once). Only tracks with check marks will be copied.

5 Open the Options Dialog Box

By default, tracks are copied to the **My Music** folder inside your **My Documents** folder. You can change this location and specify some additional settings from the **Options** dialog box. Open it by choosing **Tools**, **Options**.

6 Set Options

On the **Copy Music** tab, you can change where the tracks are copied, the file format (such as MP3 and several others) in which the tracks are copied, whether content copy protection is enabled (which basically means that the recording you make can't be further copied and shared), and the quality of the recording (higher quality takes up more disk space). When you've made your selections, click **OK**.

7 Copy the Music

Click the **Copy Music** button to begin copying the selected tracks to the location specified in the Options dialog box, with the selected options.

How to Find Music Online

Windows Media Player provides two ways to find music on the Internet. The **Media Guide** feature lets you browse for downloadable music and video files. The **Radio Tuner** lets you tune in to streaming Internet audio in dozens of different formats.

1 Start Windows Media Player

Click **Start**, point to **All Programs**, point to **Accessories**, point to **Entertainment**, and then click **Windows Media Player**.

2 Switch to Media Guide

Click the **Media Guide** button to open an Internet connection and jump to the WindowsMedia.com Web site.

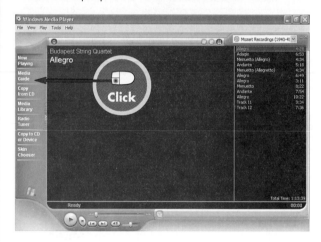

3 Browse the Web Site

Use the WindowsMedia.com Web site to browse for all kinds of files you can play in Windows Media Player.

④ Switch to Radio Tuner

If you want to listen to a radio station across town or across the globe, switch to the **Radio Tuner** feature. Many radio stations around the world (but not all) broadcast over the Internet. Click the **Radio Tuner** button.

⑤ Start a Preset List

Just as you can with the radio in your car, Windows Media Player lets you create preset lists of stations. Unlike your car radio (which has a limited number of preset buttons), you can create any number of lists and fill each list with as many stations as you want. A list named **My Stations** is created for you. Switch to it by clicking its link.

⑥ Find a Station

To find stations to add to your list, use the list of categories on the right side of the window to browse for stations. You can also search for stations by keyword or click the **Find More Stations** link to browse a complete list of radio stations available on the Web.

⑦ Listen

After you have displayed a list of stations, select a station and then click the **Play** link to begin listening. Click the **Add to My Stations** link to add the selected station to your list.

How to Make Movies

Windows XP includes a program named **Windows Movie Maker** that lets you import pictures and movies, edit them, and put them together as a movie. Movie Maker is complex enough that an entire book could be written about it, but this task should give you an idea of what it can do.

① Start Movie Maker

Click **Start**, point to **All Programs**, point to **Accessories**, and then click **Windows Movie Maker** to launch the program.

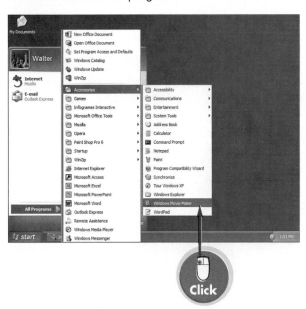

② Import Files

To import picture or movie files already on your computer into Movie Maker, select **File**, **Import** from the menu bar.

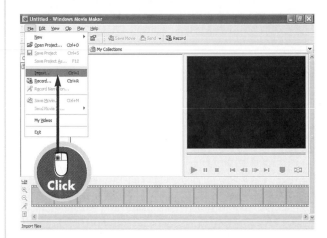

③ Record Video

To record video from a VCR or camcorder, select the **Record** command from the **File** menu. To use this feature, you must have a video card that supports recording from an external device, and the device must be hooked up correctly to this video card.

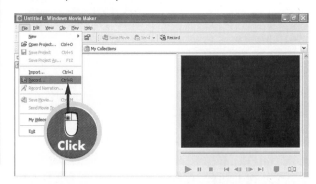

4 View a Collection

When you import pictures or record video into Movie Maker, the files are displayed as part of a collection. By default, the media files are placed into a collection named **My Collection**. When you select a collection from the **Collections** list on the left side of the screen, the files in that collection are displayed as thumbnails on the right side of the screen.

5 Create a New Collection

To organize the files you access in Movie Maker, you can create new collections. Right-click anywhere in the **Collections** list and choose **New Collection** from the shortcut menu.

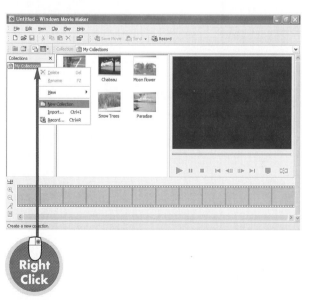

6 Name the New Collection

As soon as you create a new collection, you are given the chance to rename it. Type a name for the new collection.

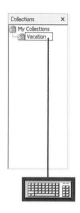

7 Move Files to the New Collection

To move files between collections, select the thumbnails of the files you want to move (the same way you do in Windows), drag them to the new collection in the **Collections** list, and drop the files.

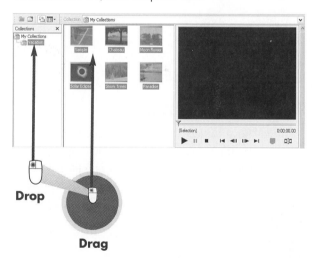

8 Move Pictures to the Storyboard

The storyboard is the filmstrip at the bottom of the Movie Maker window. It represents the movie you are currently creating. Each frame of the filmstrip is a picture in the movie. Drag each picture individually to a frame on the storyboard. This task shows the steps to make a slideshow movie out of still pictures.

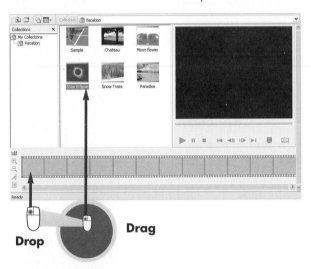

Drop　　**Drag**

9 Show the Timeline

After you have moved all the pictures to the storyboard, you can display the timeline for the movie. The timeline helps you adjust the length of each frame (just slide the divider between frames to adjust the size) and position an audio soundtrack should you decide to include one.

10 Select All Clips on Storyboard

After you have adjusted the lengths of your frames and are ready to make your movie, select all the clips on the storyboard (hold down the **Ctrl** key and click each of the clips in turn).

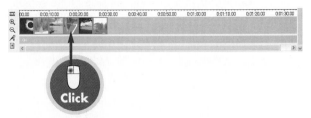

11 Combine the Clips

Combining the clips tells Movie Maker that you want each picture to play in succession when you play the movie. With all clips selected, choose **Clip**, **Combine** from the menu bar.

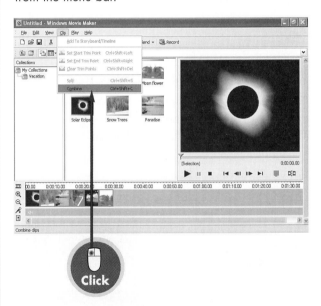

⑫ Play the Movie

To see what your movie looks like at any time, click the Play button. All the frames shown in the storyboard play in sequence. You can assess the flow of the scenes and adjust the duration of the frames in the storyboard.

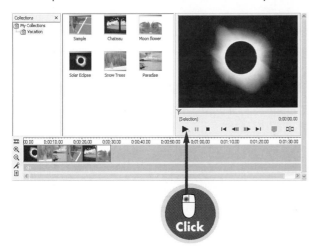

⑬ Save the Movie

When you are satisfied with your movie, choose **File**, **Save Movie** from the menu bar. This command opens the **Save Movie** dialog box.

⑭ Click OK

Use the **Save Movie** dialog box to adjust the quality of the saved movie. Higher-quality movies take up more disk space. When you have made your selection from the **Setting** drop-down list and provided any labeling information, click **OK** to save the movie. Movie Maker converts all the clips and individual pictures files in the storyboard into a single movie file. After the movie is saved, you are given the chance to watch it in Windows Media Player.

Recording Audio

You can record your own narration or even include a music soundtrack for your movie. To record narration, just click the button that looks like a microphone to open the **Record Narration Track** dialog box. Click the **Record** button and speak into your computer's microphone to narrate your movie. To add music, click the **Change** button on the **Record Narration Track** and choose a source for the audio. You can record audio from a music CD or another audio device (such as digital tape) that you have hooked up to your computer's sound card.

How to Work with Pictures

Most Windows applications store picture files in a folder named My Pictures, which you'll find inside the My Documents folder. This folder was created to include tools that are specific to working with picture files.

1 Open My Documents

Double-click the **My Documents** icon on your desktop to open the **My Documents** window. If you don't see the **My Documents** icon on your desktop, you can find it on your **Start** menu, and you can add it to your desktop using the procedure covered in Part1.

2 Open My Pictures

Double-click the **My Pictures** icon to open the My Pictures folder.

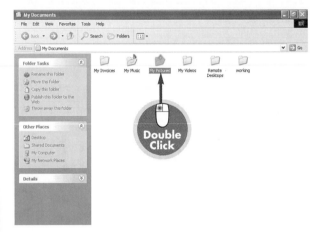

3 Select a Picture

Select any picture in the **My Pictures** folder by clicking it once.

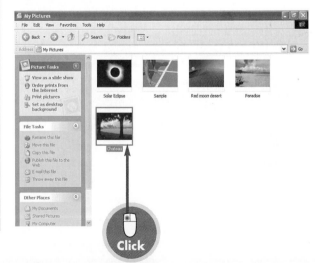

4 Print Pictures

To print the selected picture or pictures, click the **Print Pictures** link in the **Picture Tasks** list on the left side of the window.

5 View as Slideshow

If no pictures are selected or if multiple pictures are selected, click the **View as a slide show** link in the **Picture Tasks** list. Windows shows the selected pictures one by one in full-screen mode. You are given controls to advance, rewind, and stop the slide show.

6 View as Filmstrip

Select the **Filmstrip** command from the **View** menu.

7 Work with the Picture

In filmstrip view, the selected picture is shown enlarged. Use the tools under the enlarged picture to zoom in and out on, resize, and rotate the picture. These adjustments affect only the display of the picture and not the picture file itself. In filmstrip view, you can use the **Next** and **Previous** buttons to move through the slides one at a time.

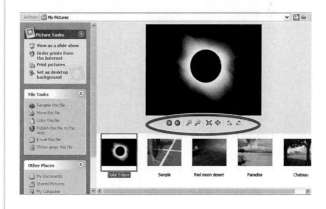

How to Play Games

Windows XP includes a number of games that you can play when you get tired of working. Some games you can play by yourself (such as the classic Solitaire); other games require you to sign on to the Internet to find other online gamers you can challenge to rounds of checkers, spades, and backgammon.

1 Start Solitaire

Click Start, point to **All Programs**, point to **Games**, and click **Solitaire**. The game opens in a new window.

2 Move Cards

To move a card, click it with the left mouse button and drag it to its new location on the seven row stacks. Double-click a card to move it directly to one of the four suit stacks in the top-right corner of the board.

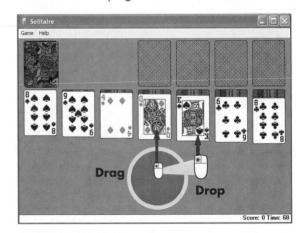

3 Get Help

To learn about the rules of the game and how to play the game, choose **Help**, **Contents** from the menu bar.

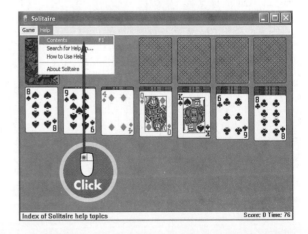

④ Start an Internet Game

Several Internet games are included with Windows. Start one the same way you would a game that can be played from your computer's hard disk: Click **Start** and choose **All Programs**, **Games**; then choose the name of the Internet game you want to play.

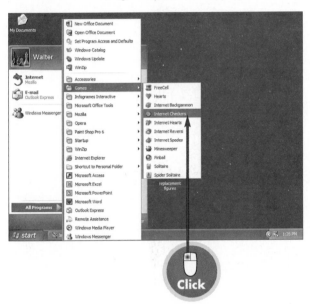

⑤ Enter Zone.com

To play on the Internet, you must connect to Microsoft's **Zone.com** Web site by clicking **Play**. You do not have to register or give any personal information. An opponent of your skill level will be selected for you, and the game will begin immediately. Set your skill level using the **File** menu of any open game.

⑥ Play

Play the game the way you would play a normal "non-computer" game. In checkers, for example, just drag a checker where you want it to go.

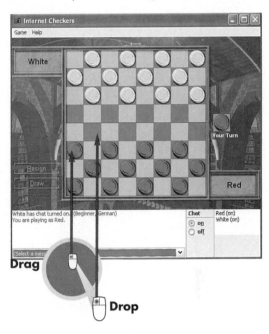

⑦ Send a Message

During play, you can send any of a number of preset messages to your opponent. Select one from the drop-down list at the bottom of the screen. Unfortunately, you cannot type your own messages.

1 How to Change the Volume 178

2 How to Set Up a Screensaver 180

3 How to Change Your Desktop Theme 182

4 How to Change Your Wallpaper 184

5 How to Change Desktop Appearance 186

6 How to Change Display Settings 188

7 How to Change Mouse Settings 190

8 How to Change Keyboard Settings 192

9 How to Customize the Taskbar 194

10 How to Change Folder Options 196

11 How to Change Power Options 198

12 How to Change System Sounds 200

13 How to Add an Item to the Start Menu 202

14 How to Add an Item to the Quick Launch Bar 204

15 How to Start a Program When Windows Starts . . .206

16 How to Set Accessibility Options 208

9

Changing Windows XP Settings

After you have worked with Windows XP for a while and gotten used to the way things work, you might find that there are changes you would like to make. Windows XP is wonderfully customizable and provides many options for changing its interface to suit the way you work.

Most of the changes you will make take place using the Windows Control Panel, which is a special folder that contains many small programs that adjust settings for a particular part of your system. For example, Display lets you change display settings such as background color, window colors, screensaver, and screen size. You can access the Control Panel through either the Start menu or the My Computer window, as you will see in the tasks in this chapter.

You'll also find that many of the Control Panel settings are also directly available from the shortcut menu of various desktop items. For example, right-clicking the desktop and choosing Properties from the shortcut menu that opens is exactly the same as opening the Display applet from the Control Panel. You'll see several such ways for accessing common controls in the following tasks.

How to Change the Volume

If you have speakers hooked up to your computer, you've probably noticed that some programs and certain things that Windows does (called events) make sounds. Many speakers have physical volume control knobs on them, but there is also a convenient way to change the volume from within Windows itself.

1 Click the Volume Icon

A small volume icon that looks like a speaker appears in the system tray next to your clock to indicate that sound is configured on your computer. Click the icon once with your left mouse button to open the **Volume** dialog box.

2 Change the Volume Setting

Click and drag the slider with your left mouse button to adjust the volume. Your computer beeps when you release the slider to give you an idea of the volume you've set.

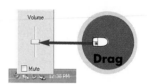

3 Mute Your Speakers

Click the **Mute** option to silence your speakers. While your speakers are muted, the volume icon is overlaid with a red circle and slash. When you want the speakers to play again, open the **Volume** dialog box again and deselect the **Mute** option.

④ Close the Dialog Box

Click anywhere out on your desktop once to close the **Volume** dialog box.

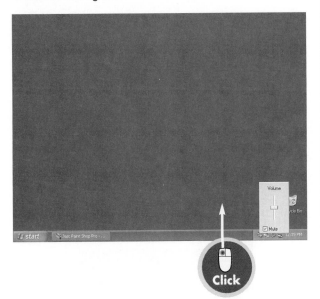

Double-Clicking

The main volume control adjusts the volume for all the sounds on your computer, no matter where that sound comes from. Double-click the **Volume** dialog box to open a more sophisticated volume control that lets you adjust the volume for each audio device configured on your system. For example, you might want to lower the volume for CD-ROMs but leave the volume for Wave files (which are used for Windows system events) alone.

Where's My Volume Icon?

On some computers, the volume icon on the system tray may be disabled. If you don't see one, but would like to, first open the **Start** menu and click **Control Panel**. In the **Control Panel** window, double-click the **Sounds and Audio Devices** icon. On the **Volume** tab of the **Sounds and Audio Devices Properties** dialog box that opens, select the **Place Volume icon in the taskbar** option.

How to Set Up a Screensaver

On older monitors (those more than ten years old), screensavers help prevent a phenomenon called *burn-in*, where items on your display can actually be permanently burned in to your monitor if left for a long time. Newer monitors don't really have a problem with this, but screensavers are still kind of fun and do help prevent passers-by from seeing what's on your computer when you're away. Windows XP provides a number of built-in screensavers.

① Open the Display Properties

Right-click any open space on your desktop and choose the **Properties** command from the shortcut menu. The **Display Properties** dialog box opens.

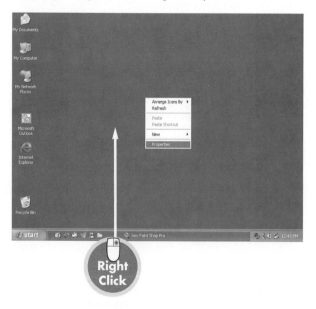

② Switch to the Screensaver Tab

Switch to the **Screen Saver** tab by clicking it once.

③ Choose a Screensaver

By default, Windows comes with no screensaver active. Click the arrow next to the **Screen saver** drop-down list to choose from the available screensavers.

4 Preview the Screensaver

When you choose a screensaver, Windows displays a small preview of it right on the picture of a monitor in the dialog box. To see how the screensaver will look when it's actually working, click the **Preview** button. Move the mouse or press a key during the preview to get back to the dialog box.

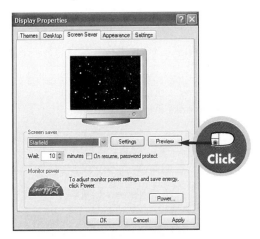

5 Adjust Settings

Each screensaver has its own specific settings so that you can change how the screensaver behaves. Settings for the **Starfield** screensaver, for example, let you control how many stars are displayed and how fast they move. Click the **Settings** button to experiment with options for any screensaver.

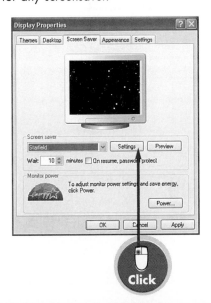

6 Adjust Wait Time

The **Wait** field specifies how long your computer must be idle before the screensaver kicks in. By default, this value is 15 minutes, but you can change it to whatever you want by using the scroll buttons. You can make a screensaver password protected by clicking the **password protect** option on the **Screen Saver** tab. Click **OK** when you're done setting up the screensaver.

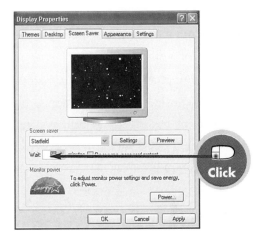

Getting Back to Work

After the screensaver kicks in, you won't be able to see the work that was on your screen because the screensaver "takes over." To get back to work, banish the screensaver simply by moving the mouse or pressing any key on the keyboard. The screen saver will come back on after the next lull in your activity.

Getting New Screensavers

New screensavers are available for purchase at most software stores; many are available free on the Internet. When you download a screensaver, it usually appears as a file with the extension .scr. Just copy the file to the **System32** folder inside your **Windows** folder to have it show up on the list in step 3.

How to Change Your Desktop Theme

A desktop theme determines the overall look and feel of your desktop. A theme includes a background picture, a set of desktop icons, a color scheme for window elements, a predetermined set of sounds for Windows events, and a set of display fonts. All these aspects of the theme are customizable.

1 Open Display Properties

Right-click any open space on your desktop and choose the **Properties** command from the shortcut menu. The **Display Properties** dialog box opens.

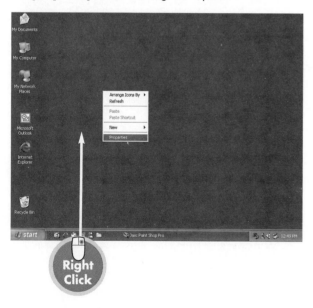

2 View the Current Theme

On the **Themes** tab of the dialog box, the name of the current theme is displayed along with a sample of what the theme looks like on your desktop.

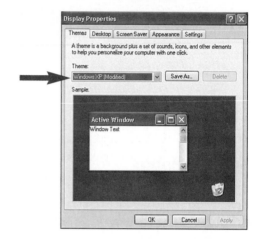

3 Select a Theme

Click the arrow next to the **Theme** drop-down list and choose a different theme.

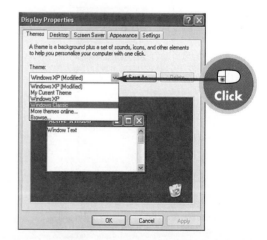

④ Sample the New Theme

A sample of the selected theme is displayed in the **Sample** window so that you can see what the theme will look like before actually applying it to your desktop.

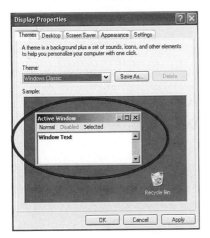

⑤ Set the New Theme

To apply the new theme to your desktop and close the **Display Properties** window, click **OK**. To apply the theme and keep the dialog box open, click **Apply**.

How-to Hint

Finding More Themes

Use the **More themes online** selection from the **Theme** drop-down list to go to the Windows Media Web site. There, you'll find a number of desktop themes you can download. After you download them, they will appear in your **Theme** list.

Browsing for Themes

If you downloaded a theme from a Web site other than the Windows Media site, it may be saved somewhere on your hard disk and not show up in your **Theme** list. Select the **Browse** option from the **Theme** drop-down list to open a standard dialog box that lets you find the theme on your hard disk. Theme files have a .theme extension.

How to Change Your Wallpaper

Wallpaper is a pattern or picture that is displayed on your desktop just to make things a bit more fun. By default, Windows uses no wallpaper; you see only the standard blue desktop color. Windows XP includes a number of interesting wallpapers you can use to spruce up your display.

① Open Display Properties

Right-click any open space on your desktop and choose the **Properties** command from the shortcut menu. The **Display Properties** dialog box opens.

② Switch to the Desktop Tab

Click the **Desktop** tab once to bring that page to the front.

③ Choose a Wallpaper

Choose any wallpaper from the **Background** list by clicking it once. Whatever wallpaper you choose is displayed in the picture of a monitor in the dialog box.

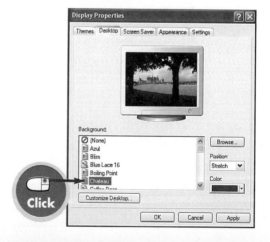

4 Use Your Own Picture

If you have a picture file on your computer that you want to use as wallpaper, click the **Browse** button to open a dialog box that lets you locate the file. Background pictures can have the following extensions: .bmp, .gif, .jpg, .dib, and .htm.

5 Adjust the Picture Display

You can display background pictures in one of three ways. You can **Center** a picture on the screen, **Stretch** a picture so that it fills the screen, or **Tile** a small picture so that it appears multiple times to fill the screen. Click the **Position** drop-down list to experiment with these options.

6 Set a Color

If you would rather not use a picture, but are tired of staring at a blue desktop, try setting a different color. Click the down-arrow next to the current color to open a palette for choosing a new color.

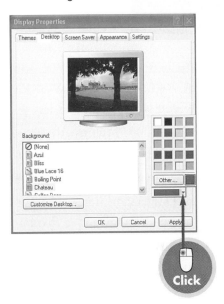

7 Apply the Settings

Click the **Apply** button to apply any new wallpaper to your desktop and keep the **Display Properties** dialog box open so that you can more easily experiment with backgrounds. After you find a background you like, click the **OK** button to get back to work.

How to Change Desktop Appearance

Changing your desktop appearance can really affect how you work. Windows lets you change the colors used on your desktop background, parts of windows, and even menus. For example, if you find yourself squinting at the text on the monitor, you can adjust the point size of the display font. If you don't like blue title bars on dialog boxes, you can change the color of that element, too.

① Open Display Properties

Right-click any open space on your desktop and choose the **Properties** command from the shortcut menu. The **Display Properties** dialog box opens.

② Switch to the Appearance Tab

Switch to the **Appearance** tab by clicking it once.

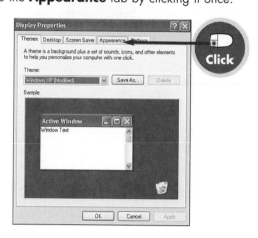

③ Choose a Style

The Windows XP style uses the new rounded windows and stylized buttons. **Windows Classic** uses windows and buttons that look like previous versions of Windows. In **Windows Classic** style, the **Advanced** button (not available in the Windows XP style) lets you set colors for the different window elements.

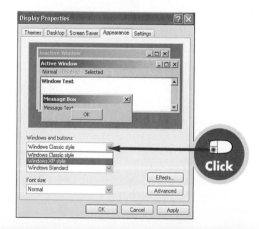

④ Choose a New Color Scheme

If you're using the **Windows XP** style, you have only a few choices for the color scheme, including blue (the default), olive, and silver. If you're using the **Windows Classic** style, you can choose from many predefined color schemes. Choose a scheme using the **Color scheme** drop-down list. The sample window in the dialog box changes to show you what a color scheme will look like.

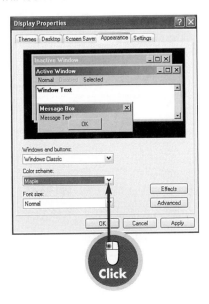

⑤ Adjust Font Size

Some of the color schemes allow for more than one font size to be used when displaying menus, window text, and dialog boxes. Use the **Font size** drop-down list to choose a **Normal**, **Large**, or **Extra Large** display font.

⑥ Open the Effects Dialog Box

Click the **Effects** button to open a separate dialog box for adjusting special desktop settings.

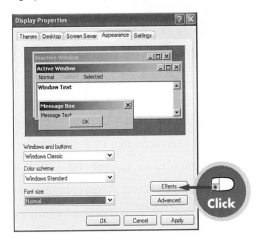

⑦ Adjust Effects

Many of the effects you can choose in this dialog box affect the speed with which windows are displayed on your computer. Using transition effects for menus, showing window contents while dragging the windows, and showing shadows under menus all make displaying windows on the desktop take just a little longer. Consider turning them off if you have a slower computer. Click **OK** twice to close both dialog boxes and apply the settings.

How to Change Display Settings

Display settings control various aspects of your video adapter and monitor. You can change the display settings to control the screen resolution (how many pixels are shown on your screen) and the color quality (how many colors are available for the display to use). Using a higher resolution lets you fit more on your desktop. Using better color quality makes things look better. However, both options depend on the quality of your video card and monitor, and using higher settings can slow down your system a bit.

① Open Display Properties

Right-click any open space on your desktop and choose the **Properties** command from the shortcut menu. The **Display Properties** dialog box opens.

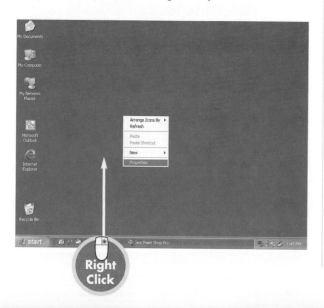

② Switch to the Settings Tab

Switch to the **Settings** tab by clicking it once.

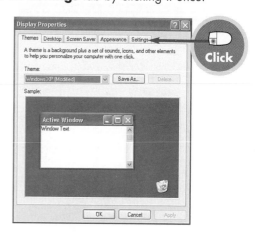

③ Choose a New Color Depth

Color depth refers to the number of colors your screen can display. Click the **Color quality** drop-down list to choose a new color setting. And although using the highest available color quality is usually the better choice, it can slow down your system just a bit. You'll have to play with the settings to find what you like best.

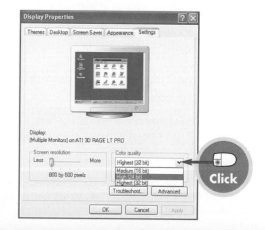

④ Choose a New Screen Resolution

Screen resolution refers to the size of items displayed on your screen. Increasing the area means that you can see more items on your screen at once, but also means that those items will appear smaller. Adjust the screen area by dragging the **Screen resolution** slider.

⑥ Open Advanced Properties

Click the **Advanced** button to open a separate dialog box with controls for changing the video adapter and monitor drivers your computer is using, along with other advanced display settings.

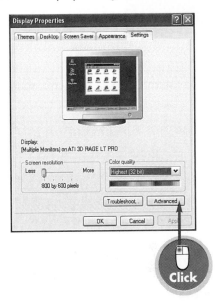

⑤ Start the Display Troubleshooter

If you are having display problems, click the **Troubleshoot** button to open the Windows Help system and go directly to the display troubleshooter.

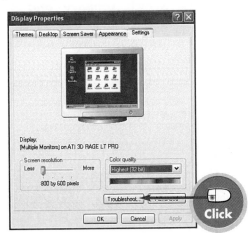

How-to Hint

Using Advanced Settings

Be careful when changing the advanced display settings. Although these setting can be useful, they can also cause problems. Incorrectly changing the drivers for your adapter or monitor can cause your display to stop working. Changing the refresh rate on your monitor can result in a more stable image, but changing it to a rate your monitor doesn't support can damage the monitor. In general, you should probably leave these settings alone if your display is working fine.

How to Change Mouse Settings

Because the mouse will likely be your main tool for getting around in Windows, it should come as no surprise that Windows allows you to change the way your mouse works. Among other things, you can change the clicking speed that makes for a successful double-click and the speed at which the pointer moves across the screen.

1 Open the Control Panel

Click **Start** and then select **Control Panel** to open the **Control Panel** window.

2 Open the Mouse Icon

Double-click the **Mouse** icon to open the **Mouse Properties** dialog box.

3 Change Button Configuration

Choose the **Switch primary and secondary buttons** option to swap the functions of the left and right buttons. This option is useful if you use your mouse with your left hand.

④ Adjust Double-Click Speed

The **Double-click speed** option refers to how close together two clicks of the mouse button must be for Windows to consider them a double-click rather than two single clicks. Drag the slider with your left mouse button to adjust the speed and then test it by double-clicking the folder icon in the test area.

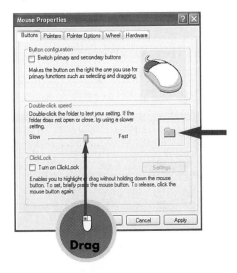

⑤ Adjust the Pointer Speed

Click the **Pointer Options** tab to switch to that page. Here you can set several options relating to how the mouse pointer moves. Drag the **Motion** slider to set how fast the pointer moves across the screen when you move the mouse. Click the **Apply** button to experiment with any settings you make while keeping the **Mouse Properties** dialog box open.

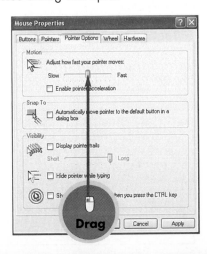

⑥ Enable Acceleration

Acceleration refers to whether the movement of your pointer accelerates if you begin moving your mouse more quickly. Without this option, the pointer keeps moving at a single speed no matter how quickly you move your mouse. Usually, you want this option enabled so that the speed you move the mouse on the table top is mimicked in the speed at which the mouse pointer moves onscreen. However, you sometimes may find that the mouse pointer moves too quickly or acts erratically with this option enabled.

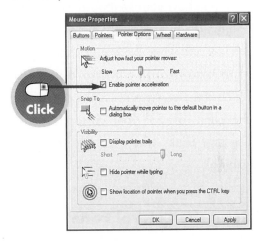

⑦ Snap to Default

Normally, when a new dialog box opens, the mouse pointer stays right where it is; you must move it to the buttons on the dialog box to do anything. With the **Snap To** option enabled, the mouse pointer automatically jumps to whatever the default button is.

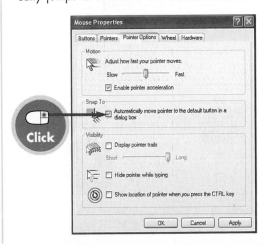

How to Change Keyboard Settings

Windows allows you to change a number of settings related to how your keyboard works. You can change the delay that occurs between when you press a key and when the key starts to repeat from holding it down. You can also change the rate at which the key repeats. Finally, you can change the blink rate for your cursor (the little vertical line that blinks where you are about to type something).

❶ Open the Control Panel

Click **Start** and then choose **Control Panel** to open the **Control Panel** window.

❷ Open the Keyboard Icon

Double-click the **Keyboard** icon to open the **Keyboard Properties** dialog box.

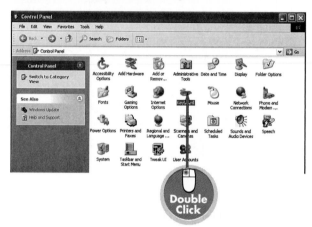

❸ Change the Repeat Delay

The **Repeat delay** option specifies the delay that occurs between when you press a key and when the key starts to repeat from holding it down. Drag the slider to change the rate.

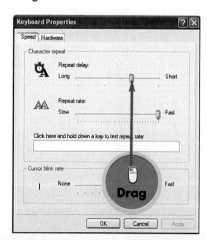

④ Change the Repeat Rate

When you hold a key down longer than the repeat delay you specified in the previous step, the key begins to repeat. Drag the **Repeat rate** slider to change the repeat rate.

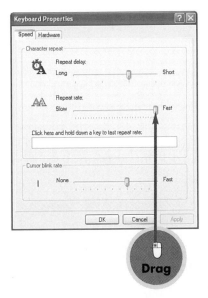

⑤ Test Your Settings

Click in the test box and then press and hold any key to test your repeat delay and repeat rate settings.

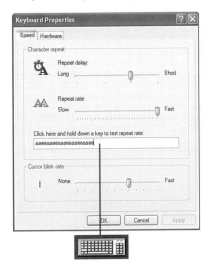

⑥ Change the Cursor Blink Rate

Whenever you click in a text box to type a value or to type a document, a little vertical line called a cursor blinks to let you know where the characters you type will appear. The cursor is sometimes also called the insertion point. Drag the **Cursor blink rate** slider to change the rate at which the cursor blinks. A sample cursor to the left of the slider blinks according to your settings.

How to Customize the Taskbar

The taskbar is one of the more important tools you use when working in Windows XP. There are several ways you can customize its use, as you will see in the following steps.

1 Open Taskbar Properties

Right-click anywhere on the taskbar and click **Properties**. The **Taskbar and Start Menu Properties** dialog box opens.

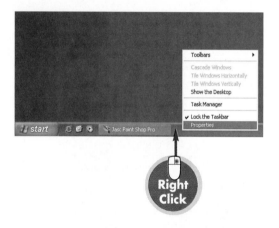

2 Lock the Taskbar

By default, you can drag the taskbar to other edges of the screen, resize the taskbar, and adjust the size of the system tray and Quick Launch portions of the taskbar. Enable the **Lock the taskbar** option to prevent this from happening.

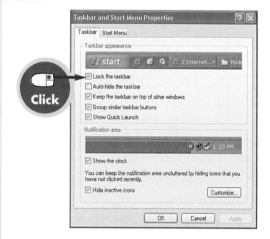

3 Make the Taskbar Autohide

Enable the **Auto-hide the taskbar** option to have the taskbar automatically scroll off the edge of the screen when it's not in use. Move your pointer to the edge of the screen to make the taskbar scroll back into view. This option cannot be used when the taskbar is locked.

4 Keep the Taskbar on Top

By default, the taskbar is always on the top of your display. Thus, when you move a window into the same space occupied by the taskbar, the taskbar still appears in front of the window. Disable the **Keep the taskbar on top of other windows** option so that other items can appear in front of the taskbar.

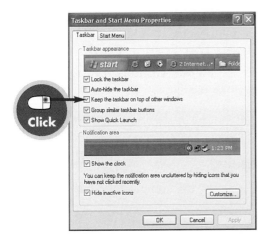

6 Show the Clock

The **Show the clock** option causes Windows to display the clock in the system tray at the far right of your taskbar. Disable this option to hide the clock. Double-click the clock to open a dialog box that lets you set the time and date.

5 Group Similar Buttons

When you start a program (such as Internet Explorer) more than once, a separate button appears on the taskbar for each instance of the program. When you enable the **Group similar taskbar buttons**, only one button appears for each program and a number to the side indicates how many documents for that program are open.

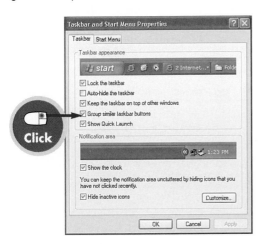

7 Hide Inactive Icons

By default, the system tray is collapsed so that only the most frequently used icons are shown. If you don't like this space-saving feature, turn it off by disabling the **Hide inactive icons** check box.

How to Change Folder Options

Windows XP handles folders in much the same way as previous versions of Windows. You have the option of viewing a folder as a Web page, in which a pane on the left side of the folder view gives you information about any selected item. You also have the option of having Windows open a new window for each folder you want to open. The following steps explain how to access these options using the **Control Panel**. You can also access the **Folder Options** dialog box from the **View** menu at the top of any open folder.

① Open the Control Panel

Click the **Start** button and then choose **Control Panel**. The **Control Panel** window opens.

② Open the Folder Options Icon

Double-click the **Folder Options** icon to open the **Folder Options** dialog box.

③ Use Web View

Web View is an option that shows Web content in folders. Normally, this just means that a pane at the left of a folder window shows information about selected items in that folder. Some folders, however, might have more specialized content. Enable the **Use Windows classic folders** option to disable this feature.

④ Change Folder Browsing

Normally when you open a folder, that folder opens in whatever window you are using at the time. If you would rather Windows open a whole new window for each folder you open, select the **Open each folder in its own window** option here.

⑤ Change Click Settings

By default, you single-click items to select them and double-click items to open them. If you prefer, enable the **Single-click to open an item (point to select)** option so that you only have to single-click items to open them, much like you do in Internet Explorer. With this option enabled, holding the mouse pointer over an item for a second selects the item.

⑥ Restore Defaults

If you find that you don't like the folder settings you have already made, click the **Restore Defaults** button to change the settings back to their original configuration.

How-to Hint

Advanced Options

The **View** tab of the **Folder Options** dialog box features a long list of specific settings relating to how folders work, such as whether hidden system files should be displayed, whether file extensions should be displayed or hidden, and whether Windows should remember the view for each folder you open. After you are familiar with using Windows, you may want to check the options on this list and see whether any appeal to you.

How to Change Power Options

You might find it useful to adjust the way Windows handles your power settings. To save energy, Windows can automatically turn off parts of your computer, such as the hard drive and monitor, after a certain amount of time. The next time you try to access these devices, the power is immediately restored and you can proceed with your tasks without delay.

1 Open Control Panel

Click **Start** and then choose **Control Panel**. The **Control Panel** window opens.

2 Open the Power Options Icon

Double-click the **Power Options** icon to open the **Power Options Properties** dialog box.

3 Choose a Power Scheme

The easiest way to configure power settings is to choose a custom scheme designed to fit the way you use your computer. Click the **Power schemes** drop-down list to choose from a number of schemes.

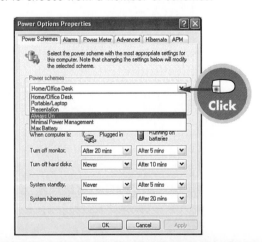

4 Turn Off Monitor

If you want to customize power settings beyond just choosing a scheme, you can choose how long the computer should be idle before certain devices are turned off. Click the **Turn off monitor** drop-down menu to specify how long the computer should be idle before your monitor is turned off. Note that you can specify a different delay time if your computer is running on batteries.

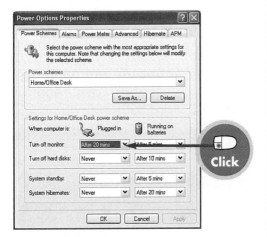

5 Turn Off Hard Disks

Click the **Turn off hard disks** drop-down menu to specify how long the computer should be idle before your hard drive is turned off. Note that you can specify a different delay time if your computer is running on batteries.

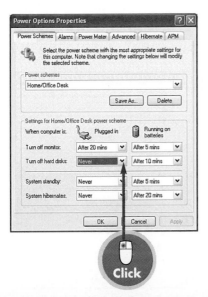

6 Send System to Standby

Some computers have the capability to go into standby, where only a trickle of power is used to keep track of what's in your computer's memory. When you come back from standby, everything should be as you left it. Use the drop-down menu to specify how long the computer should be idle before it goes into standby. Note that you can specify a different delay time if your computer is running on batteries.

Where Are All Those Options?

Depending on the type of computer and type of hardware installed, the **Power Options Properties** dialog box you see may be different than the one shown in this task. Notebook computers, for example, have settings both for when the computer is plugged in and when it is running on batteries. Notebooks also boast several more tabs on the dialog box to configure such things as advanced standby and hibernation modes. The best place to find out information about these advanced options is in the documentation for the computer itself.

How to Change System Sounds

If you have speakers on your computer, you might have noticed that certain things you do in Windows (such as emptying the Recycle Bin, starting Windows, and logging off) make certain sounds. These things are called *events*. Windows events also include things you don't do yourself, such as when an error dialog box is displayed or when email is received. You can easily change the sounds associated with Windows events by using the following steps.

① Open the Control Panel

Click **Start** and then choose **Control Panel**. The **Control Panel** window opens.

② Open the Sounds and Audio Devices Icon

Double-click the **Sounds and Audio Devices** icon to open the **Sounds and Audio Devices Properties** dialog box.

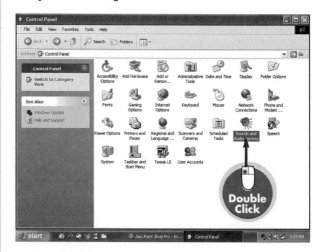

③ Switch to the Sounds Tab

Click the **Sounds** tab to bring it to the front.

④ Choose an Event

From the **Program** events list, select any system event, such as **Default Beep**.

⑤ Choose a Sound File

Click the arrow next to the **Sounds** drop-down list to select a sound to associate with the selected event. You can also use your own sound file (any .wav file) by clicking the **Browse** button.

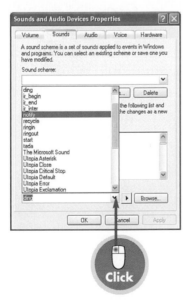

⑥ Play the Sound

Click the **Play** button to hear the selected sound.

⑦ Choose a Sound Scheme

Windows comes with a couple of different sound schemes, which are sets of sounds similar in effect that are applied to all the major system events at once. Use the **Sound Scheme** drop-down list to choose a scheme.

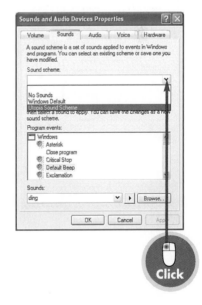

How to Add an Item to the Start Menu

The *Start* menu is loaded with shortcuts to various programs and folders on your computer. Whenever you install a new program, that program usually adds a shortcut of its own to the **Start** menu automatically. You can also add items of your own. You can add shortcuts to programs, documents, or even folders.

① Find the Item You Want to Add

Use the **My Computer** or **My Documents** window to find the item you want to add to the **Start** menu. This item can be a document, a program, or even a folder.

② Drag the Item over the Start Menu

Using the left mouse button, click and drag the item over the **Start** button, but *do not* release the mouse button yet.

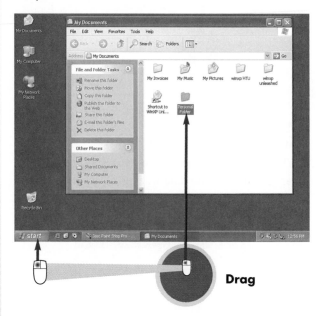

Drag

③ Place the Item in the More Programs Folder

After holding the item over the **Start** button for about two seconds, the **Start** menu opens. Continue dragging the item over the **All Programs** folder and then onto the **All Programs** menu that appears. When you find where you want to place the item (a horizontal line appears to guide placement), let go of the mouse button. After you have placed the shortcut, just click it to launch the original program.

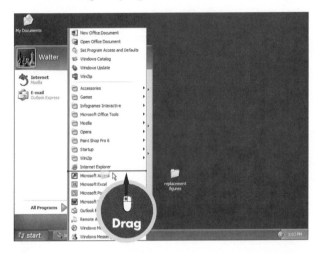

④ Rename the Shortcut

Right-click the new shortcut and choose **Rename** from the shortcut menu to give the shortcut a new name. This name appears in a pop-up window when you hold your pointer over the shortcut for a second.

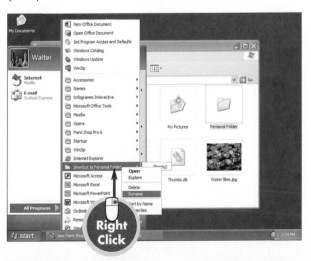

⑤ Delete the Shortcut

Right-click the shortcut in the **Start** menu and choose **Delete** from the shortcut menu to remove the shortcut from the **Start** menu.

How to Hint

Adding Shortcuts

Unfortunately, you can only add shortcuts to the **All Programs** menu and not to the main **Start** menu itself, as you could in previous versions of Windows. Still, this does provide an easier way to open programs, folders, and files than by browsing for them on your hard drive.

How to Add an Item to the Quick Launch Bar

The **Quick Launch** bar is handy feature located in the task bar next to the **Start** button. You can use it to open certain programs with a single click. Only three shortcuts appear by default on the **Quick Launch** bar: one to launch Internet Explorer, one to launch Outlook Express, and one to show your desktop when there are windows in the way. Fortunately, it's pretty easy to add new shortcuts for programs, documents, and folders. In fact, many programs (such as Microsoft Outlook) add their own shortcuts during installation.

❶ Find the Item You Want to Add

Use the **My Computer** or **My Documents** window to find the item to which you want to make a Quick Launch shortcut.

❷ Drag the Item to the Quick Launch Bar

Click the item with your left mouse button and, while holding the button down, drag the item into a blank space on the **Quick Launch** bar. You can even drag the item between two existing shortcuts to put it exactly where you want.

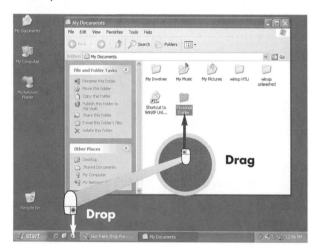

❸ Rename the Shortcut

Right-click the new shortcut and choose **Rename** from the shortcut menu to give the shortcut a new name. This name appears in a pop-up window when you hold the mouse pointer over the shortcut icon for a second.

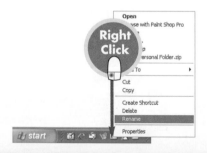

Delete the Shortcut

Right-click the shortcut and choose **Delete** from the shortcut menu to remove the shortcut from the **Quick Launch** bar and place it in the **Recycle Bin**. Hold the **Shift** key down when selecting **Delete** to permanently delete the shortcut without sending it to the **Recycle Bin**.

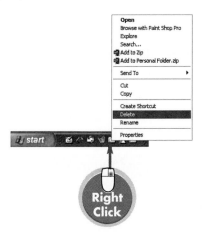

How-to Hint

Rearranging Shortcuts

You can rearrange existing shortcuts in the **Quick Launch** bar by simply dragging them to new locations on the **Quick Launch** bar.

Moving the Quick Launch Bar

You can move the **Quick Launch** bar separately from the taskbar by clicking at the leftmost edge of the **Quick Launch** bar (marked by two rows of small, dimpled dots) and dragging it. You can move the bar to one of the other edges of your display or into the center of the window.

Don't See a Quick Launch Bar?

On some computers, the **Quick Launch** bar may be disabled. If you don't see the **Quick Launch** bar and want to add it, right-click anywhere on your taskbar and choose **Properties**. On the **Taskbar** tab of the **Taskbar and Start Menu Properties** dialog box that opens, choose the **Show Quick Launch** option.

How to Start a Program When Windows Starts

Windows maintains a special folder named **Startup** that lets you specify programs, folders, and even documents that open every time Windows starts. You can see the **Startup** folder and what's in it by selecting **Start**, **All Programs**, and **Startup**. The following steps show you how to add shortcuts to that folder.

① Find the Item You Want to Add

Use the **My Computer** or **My Documents** window to find the item you want to add to the Startup folder menu. This item can be a document, program, or even a folder.

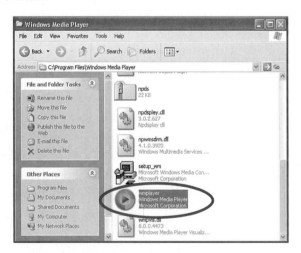

② Drag the Item over the Start Menu

Using the left mouse button, click and drag the item over the **Start** button, but *do not* release the mouse button yet.

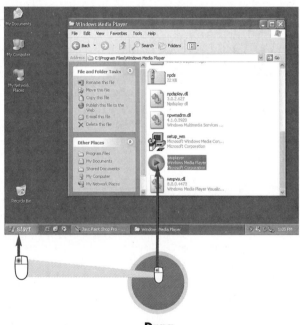

Drag

③ Drag the Item over the All Programs Folder

Continue dragging the item and hold it over the **All Programs** option on the **Start** menu. Do not release the mouse button yet.

④ Place the Item in the Startup Folder

When the **All Programs** folder opens, drag the item to the **Startup** folder and drop it there.

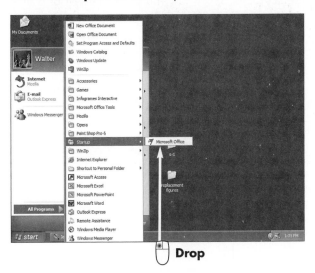

How-to Hint

Removing Startup Programs

Many of the programs you install (and even Windows itself) have small associated programs that are configured to start when your computer starts. For example, Windows Messenger starts automatically and so does the AOL Instant Messenger when you install AOL. You can usually tell these programs have started because you can see icons representing them in the system tray at the right side of the taskbar. If you have programs starting automatically that you would rather did not, try checking the **Startup** folder first. If there is a shortcut in there for the program, you can delete it and the program will not start automatically anymore. If you're not sure whether it's necessary that the program start when Windows starts, try moving the shortcut to your desktop and restarting Windows to see what happens. You can always move the shortcut back into the **Startup** folder if you decide you need it. If a program is starting and you don't see a shortcut for it in the **Startup** folder, try clicking or right-clicking the icon in the system tray. Sometimes you will find an option to exit the program or even prevent it from starting with Windows.

How to Set Accessibility Options

Windows includes a number of accessibility options intended for people with disabilities (some people without disabilities find these settings useful, as well). These options include a small window that magnifies whatever part of the screen your mouse pointer is on and the ability to make Windows flash the display instead of making sounds. All these options are available through the Windows **Control Panel**.

① Open the Control Panel

Click the **Start** button and then choose **Control Panel**. The **Control Panel** window opens.

② Open Accessibility Options

Double-click the **Accessibility Options** icon. The **Accessibility Options** dialog box opens.

③ Set Keyboard Options

Switch to the **Keyboard** tab to set various accessibility options for working with the keyboard. The **StickyKeys** option lets you press one key at a time (**Ctrl** and then **Shift**, for example) instead of having to press them simultaneously. The **FilterKeys** option tells Windows to ignore brief or quickly repeated keystrokes that may be caused by unsteady hands on the keyboard. The **ToggleKeys** option plays sounds to indicate when the **Caps Lock**, **Num Lock**, and **Scroll Lock** keys are turned on or off.

4 Set Sound Options

Switch to the **Sound** tab to set options for using sound in addition to the visual feedback your computer gives you in certain circumstances. The **SoundSentry** option generates visual warnings (such as flashes) when your system would otherwise just play a sound. The **ShowSounds** option generates captions for the speech and sounds made by certain programs.

5 Set Display Options

Switch to the **Display** tab to find settings that make it easier to read the screen. The **High Contrast** option causes Windows to display the desktop using colors and fonts that are easier to read. The **Cursor Options** adjust the size and blink rate of the cursor that appears where text is about to be typed.

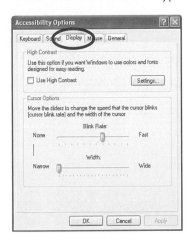

6 Set Mouse Options

Switch to the **Mouse** tab to enable **MouseKeys**, a feature that lets you use your keyboard's number pad to control the mouse pointer. Click the **Settings** button to open a dialog box that lets you control the pointer speed and turn on and off the **MouseKeys** feature using the **Num Lock** key on your keyboard.

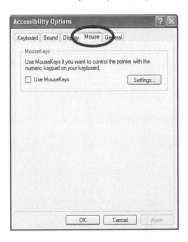

7 Set General Options

Switch to the **General** tab to set options that pertain to all accessibility features, such as when they are used and whether they are automatically turned off after a period of time. When you have specified all the options you want, click **OK** to apply the settings and close the dialog box.

(1) How to Free Up Space on Your Hard Disk 212

(2) How to Defragment Your Hard Disk 214

(3) How to Schedule a Task to Occur Automatically . .216

(4) How to Use the Windows Troubleshooters 218

(5) How to Get System Information 220

(6) How to Use System Restore 222

(7) How to Compress Files and Folders 224

Task

10

Optimizing Your Computer

Computers are pretty complicated. A lot of things can happen during the course of normal use that can slow a computer down or keep certain things from working as they should. If you are connected to a network, the chances are that you have a network administrator to rely on for fixing problems when they occur. If you don't have an administrator, you'll have to take things into your own hands. There are a few things you can do to help make sure that your computer is performing well and your work is not lost if something does go wrong. Windows XP provides a number of important system tools to help you protect your files and maintain your computer.

How to Free Up Space on Your Hard Disk

Even with the size of today's large hard drives, you might still find conservation of disk space an issue. During normal operation, Windows and the programs you run on it create temporary and backup files. Unfortunately, these programs (Windows included) are sometimes not very good at cleaning up after themselves. Windows includes a tool named *Disk Cleanup* that you can use to search for and delete unnecessary files.

1 Run Disk Cleanup

Click the **Start** button and choose **All Programs**, **Accessories**, **System Tools**, and **Disk Cleanup**.

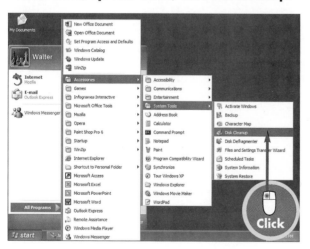

2 Select the Drive to Clean Up

Use the drop-down list to select the hard drive on which you want to free up space. Click the **OK** button after you have chosen your drive. **Disk Cleanup** scans the specified drive for files. This process might take a few minutes.

3 Select the Items to Remove

After **Disk Cleanup** has finished scanning your drive, it presents a list of categories for files it has found. Next to each category, Windows shows how much drive space all the files in that category take up. You can mark categories for deletion by clicking the check boxes next to them.

④ View Files

Categories that are already checked, such as Downloaded Program Files, are always safe to delete. Other categories might contain important files, and it is up to you to decide whether they should be deleted. Select a category by clicking its name once and click the **View Files** button to see what's contained in that category.

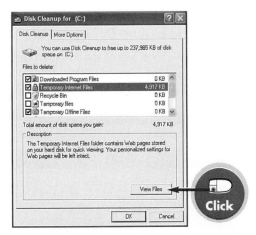

⑤ Click OK

When you have selected all the categories for files you want to delete, click the **OK** button to proceed. Windows asks whether you are sure you want to delete the files. If you are, click the **Yes** button.

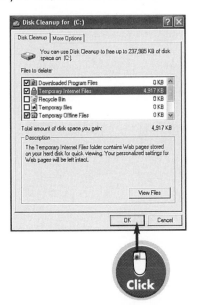

How-to Hint

Taking Out the Trash

One way to keep space free on your hard drive is to regularly empty your Recycle Bin. Right-click the bin and choose **Empty Recycle Bin** from the shortcut menu to delete all the files it holds. You can also double-click the **Recycle Bin** to display a list of the files it contains and then delete individual files.

Deleting Only Certain Files

When you click the **View Files** button (as described in step 4), a standard window opens showing the files in that location. If you want to delete only some of the files, select them in this window and delete them by pressing the **Delete** key. Make sure that you deselect the folder when you return to the **Disk Cleanup Wizard** or you'll end up deleting all the files anyway. Also, when you delete selected files using the View Files method, the files are moved to the Recycle Bin. You must empty the Recycle Bin to finish freeing the disk space. When you remove files using the **Disk Cleanup Wizard**, the files are permanently deleted.

How to Defragment Your Hard Disk

When you delete a file on your computer, Windows doesn't really remove it. It just marks that space as available for new information to be written. When a new file is written to disk, part of the file might be written to one available section of disk space, part might be written to another, and part to yet another space. This process fitting files in pieces on the disk is called *fragmentation*. It is a normal process, and Windows keeps track of files just fine. The problem is that when a drive has a lot of fragmentation, it can take Windows longer to find the information it is looking for. You can speed up drive access significantly by periodically defragmenting your drive.

❶ Run Disk Defragmenter

Click the **Start** button and choose **All Programs**, **Accessories**, **System Tools**, and **Disk Defragmenter**.

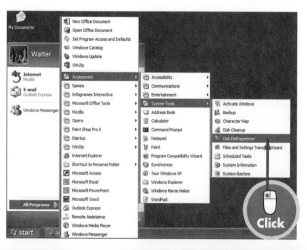

❷ Choose a Drive

The window at the top of the screen lists all the hard drives on your computer. Select the drive you want to defragment by clicking it once.

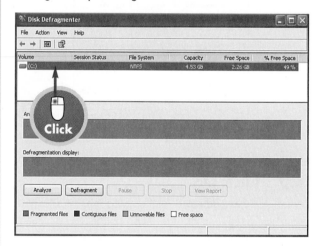

③ Analyze Drive

Click the **Analyze** button to have Disk Defragmenter analyze the selected drive for the amount of fragmentation on it. This process might take a few minutes, and the process is depicted graphically for you while you wait.

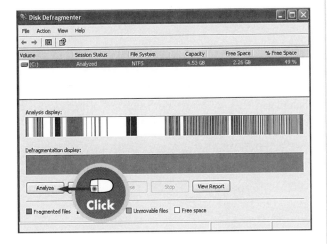

⑤ Defragment Drive

Should the analysis and report prove that your drive needs to be defragmented, you can start the procedure by clicking the **Defragment** button. This process can take a while—even an hour or so—depending on the size of your hard drive and how fragmented it is.

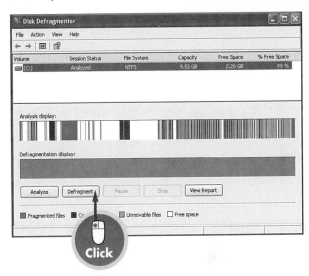

④ View Report

When the analysis is done, a dialog box appears that lets you view a report or go ahead with defragmentation. You can also perform these actions from the main program window itself. Click the **View Report** button to view a detailed report of the fragmented files that the analysis has discovered.

—How-to Hint

Some Helpful Tips

Make sure that you close all programs before beginning the defragmentation process. Also make sure that all documents are finished printing, scanning, downloading, and so on. In other words, your computer should not be busy doing anything else. During the defragmentation process, you will not be able to run any other programs. Unless you enjoy watching the defragmentation process, take a coffee break.

How to Schedule a Task to Occur Automatically

Windows XP includes a task scheduler that lets you schedule certain programs to run automatically. This can be particularly useful with programs such as Disk Cleanup and Disk Defragmenter, although you can schedule virtually any program. You might, for example, schedule Disk Cleanup to run automatically every Friday night after work and Disk Defragmenter to run once a month or so, saving you the time of running these programs when you have better things to do.

① Start Scheduled Tasks

Click the **Start** button and choose **All Programs**, **Accessories**, **System Tools**, and **Scheduled Tasks**.

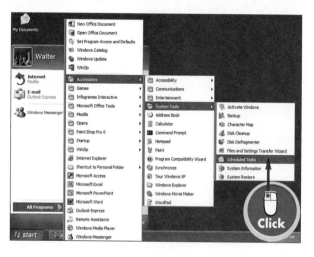

② Add a Scheduled Task

Double-click the **Add Scheduled Task** icon to start the Scheduled Task Wizard. The first page of the wizard is just a welcome page. Click the **Next** button to go on.

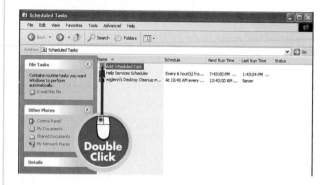

③ Choose a Program to Run

Select the program you want to schedule from the list by clicking it once. If you don't see the program on the list, you can try to locate it by clicking the **Browse** button. After you've selected the program, click the **Next** button to go on.

④ Choose When to Run the Program

If you want to change the default name of the task, type a new name in the text box. Choose when you want to perform the task by enabling that option. When you're done, click the **Next** button to go on.

⑤ Choose a Time and Day

If you choose to run the program daily, weekly, or monthly, you must also specify the time of day to run the program. Type in a time or use the scroll buttons. You must also select the day or days you want the program to run by clicking the appropriate check boxes. Click the **Next** button to go on.

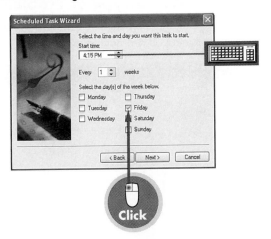

⑥ Enter a Username and Password

To run a program in Windows, Task Scheduler must have your username and password. Type this information into the boxes on this page, and then click the **Next** button to go on.

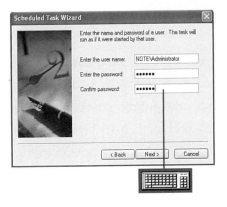

⑦ Finish

Click the **Finish** button to schedule your new task. When the specified day and time roll around, the selected program starts and runs with the default settings. If you want the selected program to start using any other settings, you'll have to consult the Help file for the program to see whether it supports changing settings in a scheduled task.

How to Use the Windows Troubleshooters

If your computer is on a corporate office network, you are probably fortunate enough to have a network administrator to call when your computer has problems. In a home office situation where you are the network administrator, or for a standalone installation, you will be relieved to know that Windows includes a few useful troubleshooters that can help you diagnose and repair problems.

① Start Help

Click the **Start** button and then choose **Help and Support**.

② Open Fixing a Problem Category

Click the **Fixing a problem** subject once to expand it.

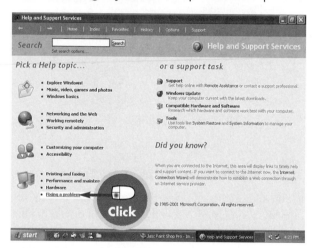

③ Choose a Type of Problem

From the list on the left side of the window, choose the type of problem you are having by clicking it once.

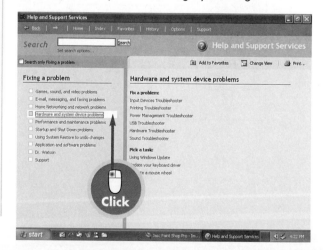

④ Choose a Troubleshooter

From the window on the right, locate the troubleshooter you want to run. After you find the troubleshooter you want, **Printing** for example, click it once to start it.

⑤ Work Through the Steps

Troubleshooters work just like wizards. Each page asks a question. Choose the answer by clicking it once, and then click the **Next** button to go on. Some pages offer steps for you to try to fix your problem. If the steps work, you're done. If the steps don't work, the troubleshooter continues. If the troubleshooter can't fix your problem, it recommends where you should go (Web sites and Microsoft technical support) for more information.

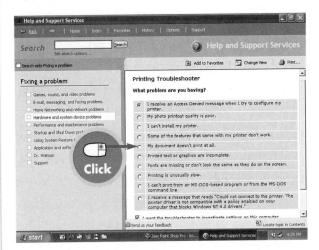

How to Get System Information

Often, fixing a problem requires that you find more information about your computer or your installation of Windows than is normally necessary. Fortunately, Windows includes a useful tool named System Information that lets you browse all kinds of useful information. Some of this information can be useful to you in determining why something is not working. For example, you can determine whether an existing piece of hardware is conflicting with the new piece you just installed. Much of the information is technical and will be useful when you're speaking with a technical support person.

1 Start System Information

Click the **Start** button and choose **More Programs**, **Accessories**, **System Tools**, and **System Information**.

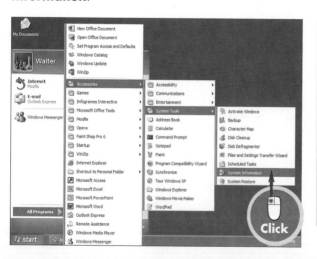

2 View System Summary

The right side of the Help and Support Services window that opens contains a brief summary of your system, including the exact version of Windows installed and a snapshot of your basic hardware.

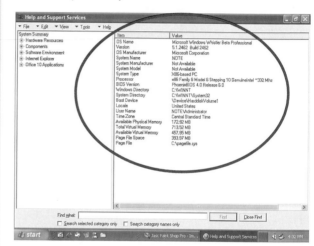

③ View Hardware Resources

Expand the **Hardware Resources** item in the left side of the window by clicking the plus sign next to it. Inside, you'll find various types of resources you can check on. Click any of these resources, such as **IRQs**, to view details on that resource.

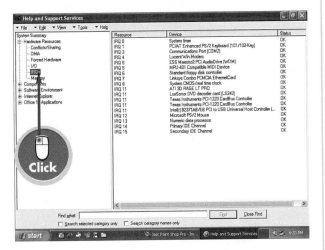

⑤ Access Tools

Many useful tools are available on the Tools menu in the Help and Support Services window. Some of the tools are not available anywhere else in Windows. A good example is the DirectX Diagnostic Tool, which can help you diagnose video problems related to the Windows DirectX drivers.

How-to Hint

Printing and Exporting System Information

The File menu of the Help and Support Services window offers the capability to print and export your system information. When exporting, a text file is created. The entire set of system information (not just the page you're looking at) is printed or exported.

④ View Components

Expand the **Components** item to view details about many of the hardware components on your system. Click any subcategory, such as **CD-ROM**, to view details about that particular component.

How to Use System Restore

Windows XP automatically creates system restore points at regular intervals. These restore points are basically backups of vital system settings and information. If you make a major change to your system, such as installing a new application or hardware driver, and then discover that the change has caused unwanted side effects, you can return to a previous restore point. The System Restore tool is used both to restore the computer to a previous point and to manually create a restore point.

❶ Start System Restore

Click the **Start** button and choose **All Programs**, **Accessories**, **System Tools**, and **System Restore**.

❷ Create a Restore Point

Although Windows creates restore points automatically, you can manually set a restore point before you make some change to your system that you think might adversely affect system performance. In the System Restore window that opens, select the **Create a restore point** option and then click **Next**.

③ Name the Restore Point

Type a name for the restore point that describes it well enough to help you remember it. For example, you might name the restore point after the date, an action you just performed (or are about to perform), or after the fact that you have installed Windows and have everything working the way you want.

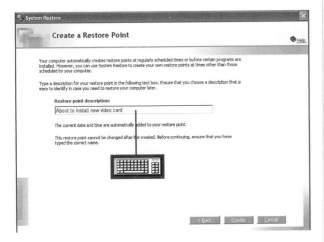

④ Create the Restore Point

When you have named the new restore point, click **Create**.

⑤ Close System Restore

When Windows has successfully created the restore point, it displays a message to that effect. To return to the Welcome to System Restore screen shown in Step 2, click **Home**. Otherwise, click **Close**.

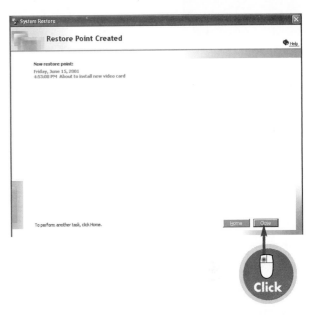

How-to Hint

Restoring a Restore Point

Returning your computer to a restore point is just as easy as setting one. On the initial page of the System Restore Wizard, select the **Restore my computer to an earlier time** option. The wizard will guide you through choosing the restore point to which you want to return your system. The necessary files will be restored, your computer will be restarted, and you'll be back in business in no time. If you use System Restore to return your computer settings to a point before a software installation that went bad, note that System Restore just returns your Windows settings to the restore point—it does not remove the software from your computer.

How to Compress Files and Folders

Windows XP includes a built-in compression tool. You can compress files and folders to help save hard disk space. While compressed, the items are still accessible. In fact, you probably won't notice any difference between files you've compressed and those you haven't. On large files, however, you might notice that access is a bit slower than normal because of the compression. But if disk space is an issue, you might decide that it's better to have the large file and wait through the file-access hesitation.

❶ Open an Item's Properties

In the My Documents or My Computer window, right-click the file or folder you want to compress and choose the **Properties** command from the shortcut menu.

❷ Open Advanced Options

On the General tab of the Properties dialog box, click the **Advanced** button to open the Advanced Attributes dialog box.

❸ Compress the Item

Select the **Compress contents to save disk space** option. Note that there is also an option here that lets you encrypt the item. You cannot use both compression and encryption at the same time.

④ Close the Dialog Boxes

Click the **OK** button to close the Advanced Attributes dialog box. Click the **OK** button on the General tab of the folder's Properties dialog box to close it.

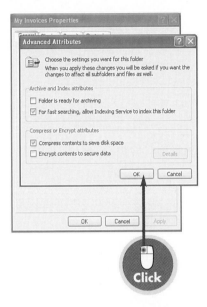

⑤ Compress Files and Subfolders

A dialog box appears that lets you choose whether to compress only the selected folder or also to compress the files and subfolders within that folder. Choose the option you want and click the **OK** button. The file or folder is compressed.

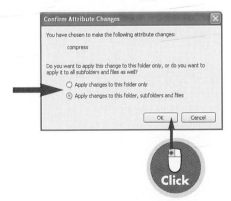

How-to Hint

Decompressing a Folder

To decompress a folder, simply follow the preceding steps and disable the Compress Contents to Save Disk Space option on the Advanced Attributes dialog box in Step 3.

Visual Indicator

When you compress a file or folder, by default Windows gives no visual indicator that compression is present. To see whether an item is compressed, you must open its Properties dialog box and see whether the Compress contents to Save Disk Space option is enabled. However, you can tell Windows to display compressed files in a different color: Open the Control Panel and double-click **Folder Options**. On the View tab of the dialog box that opens, enable the **Display compressed files and folder in alternate color** option.

Sending Compressed Files

If you send a compressed file as an e-mail attachment or transfer a compressed file or folder to another computer using a network or a removable disk, the compression is removed on the copy that is sent. For example, if you email a compressed file to a friend, the file remains compressed on your drive but the attachment is not compressed when your friend receives it.

1. How to Add a Program to Your Computer 228

2. How to Change or Remove a Program 230

3. How to Add Windows Components from the CD ..232

4. How to Add Windows Components from the Internet 234

5. How to Find Out About Your Installed Hardware 236

6. How to Tell Whether a Windows Service Pack is Installed 238

7. How to Install Windows XP Service Pack 1 240

8. How to Set Program Access and Defaults 242

Task

11

Installing New Software and Hardware

If your computer is connected to your company's network, a network administrator is probably responsible for adding and removing hardware and software on your computer and for keeping Windows up-to-date. If so, you should take advantage of his or her expertise. However, with Windows XP, adding components to your system has never been easier. If you are administering your own computer or network, this part shows how to install your own hardware and software and how to update Windows XP. This part also covers the installation of Windows XP Service Pack 1 and shows the major changes this service pack makes to your system.

How to Add a Program to Your Computer

Programs are the reason you use your computer. Almost all new programs today come on CD-ROM. When you insert the CD-ROM into your drive, Windows should automatically run the setup program for you. If this is the case, you won't need to follow the procedure in this task. If the setup process does not start automatically, or if your program is on floppy disk, the following steps show you how to start the installation yourself. If you download a program from the Internet, the setup process is much the same. You'll just have to tell Windows where the files are located. If the program is compressed (such as in a ZIP file), you'll have to expand it before installing.

1 Open the Control Panel

Click the **Start** button and choose **Control Panel**. The **Control Panel** window opens.

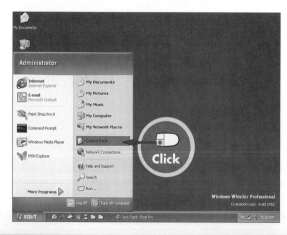

2 Open Add/Remove Programs

Double-click the **Add/Remove Programs** icon to open it.

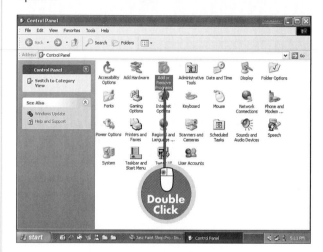

3 Add New Programs

Click the Add New Programs button to install a new program.

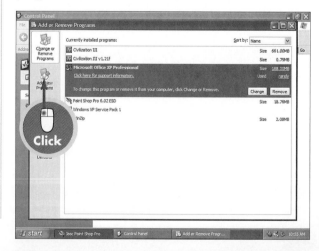

④ Choose CD or Floppy

If programs are available for installation on your network, they are shown in the window. Click the **CD or Floppy** button to install a program from disk. Click **Next** to skip the initial welcome page of the wizard that appears.

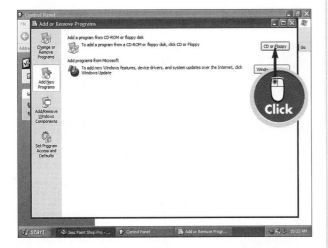

⑤ Finish

Windows searches both your floppy and CD-ROM drives for a setup program. If it finds one, the path to the program is displayed for your approval. If you think Windows found the right one, click the **Finish** button to launch the setup program. You can also click the **Browse** button to locate a setup program yourself.

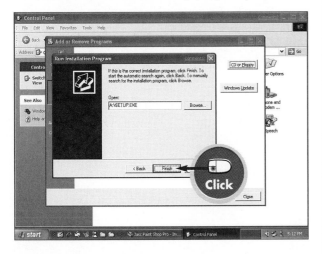

How-to Hint

Installing from the My Computer Window

You can also run a setup program manually without using the **Add/Remove Programs** applet. Just open the **My Computer** window and locate the setup program yourself on the floppy or CD-ROM drive. It is almost always a program named setup.exe. If it is not named setup.exe, it will be another program with the .exe extension. If you can't figure out which program is used to start the installation, check whether the folder has a text file that explains the installation process (This file is often named readme.txt or setup.txt). When you determine the setup program, double-click it to start.

The Program Files Folder

Your **C:** drive has a folder on it named **Program Files**. Most new programs that you install create a folder for themselves inside this folder that is used to store the program's files.

Restarting

Different programs have different installation routines. Some require that you restart your computer after the program has been installed. This is one reason why it is best to save any work and exit any running programs before you install new software.

How to Change or Remove a Program

Some programs, such as Microsoft Office, let you customize the installation of the program to include only the components that you want in the installation. You can then add new components later if you want. The **Add/Remove Programs** applet lets you change the installation of a program, and it lets you remove the installation altogether (a process sometimes called *uninstalling* a program).

① Open the Control Panel

Select the **Start** button and then choose **Control Panel**. The **Control Panel** window opens.

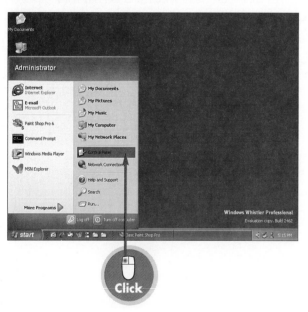

② Open Add/Remove Programs

Double-click the **Add/Remove Programs** icon to open it.

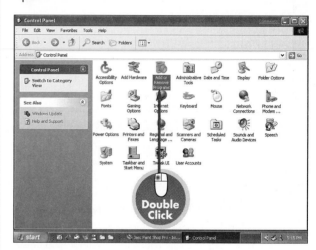

③ Select a Program

Choose a program from the list of currently installed programs by clicking it once. Notice that Windows lets you know how much disk space each program takes up and how often you use the program.

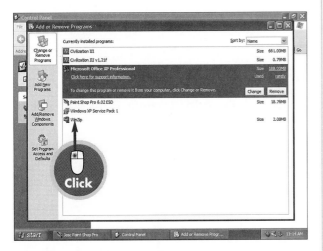

⑤ Follow the Program's Instructions

Every program has a slightly different routine for changing or removing the installation. Follow the onscreen instructions for the program you are using.

④ Click Change/Remove

Programs that do not let you change the installation show only a **Change/Remove** button. Programs that do let you change the installation show both a **Change** button and a **Remove** button. Click whatever button provides the action you want.

How-to Hint

Be Careful

Some programs automatically go forward with a removal without giving you a chance to confirm as soon as you click the **Change/Remove** or **Remove** button. Be sure you want to remove a program before clicking either of these buttons.

Task

How to Add Windows Components from the CD

Windows XP comes with literally hundreds of components—and not all of them are installed during a normal installation of the operating system. You can add components from the Windows XP CD-ROM at any time after installation.

1 Open the Control Panel

Click the **Start** button and then choose **Control Panel**. The **Control Panel** window opens.

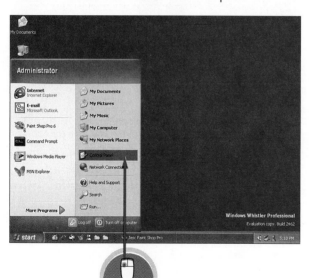

2 Open Add/Remove Programs

Double-click the **Add/Remove Programs** icon to open it.

3 Choose Add/Remove Windows Components

Click the **Add/Remove Windows Components** button to display a list of the components you can install from the original Windows installation CD-ROM.

④ Select a Component

Select a component from the list of available components by enabling the check box next to it. Some components have subcomponents that you can choose from. If so, the **Details** button becomes active, and you can click it to see a list of subcomponents to choose from.

⑤ Next

After you have selected all the components you want to install, click the **Next** button. Windows builds a list of files that must be installed and copies them to your drive. Windows might prompt you to insert your Windows CD-ROM during this process.

⑥ Finish

After Windows has installed the components, it lets you know that the process has been completed successfully. Click the **Finish** button to finish. Depending on the components you added, Windows might need to restart your computer.

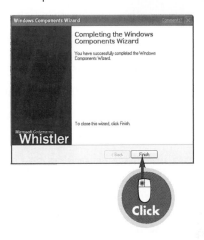

How to Hint

Installing Windows

Many components are installed when you initially set up Windows. When you finish installing Windows, you should always check the installed components using the procedure described in this task to see what goodies you might be missing.

How to Add Windows Components from the Internet

Microsoft maintains a Web site named **Windows Update** that contains the newest versions of Windows components that you can download and add to your system. These components are updated versions of the components that come with Windows as well as new components and updates that Microsoft makes available. If, for some reason, the shortcut to the Windows update site does not work, you can also get there using the address http://windowsupdate.microsoft.com/.

1 Start Windows Update

Click the **Start** button, point to **More Programs**, and select **Windows Update**. This command launches the **Windows Update** Web site in Internet Explorer.

2 Scan for Updates

Click the **Scan for Updates** link. The Windows Update site seaches for components that you can download.

How to Hint

Automatic Updating

Windows can automatically download and install updates when it detects that they are available—provided that you have Internet access. Turn on this feature by opening the **System Control Panel** applet (open the **Control Panel** window and double-click the **System** icon) and switching to the **Automatic Updates** tab. You can have Windows download updates and install them automatically, notify you when updates are available so that you can choose the update time, or disable the service. When automatic updating is active, an icon appears in the system tray to let you know the status.

③ Review and Install Updates

Critical updates (bug fixes and security patches) are automatically selected for download. If that's all you want, click the **Review and Install Critical Updates** link. Additional non-critical updates are available in the Windows Update section on the left. Click the **Review and Install Critical Updates** link when you are ready to continue.

⑤ Install the Updates

When you are satisfied with the list of updates, click the **Install Now** button to download *and* install the components.

④ Choose Components to Update

Scroll down the **Update Basket** window to review the list of updates selected for download. Click the **Remove** button next to any update to remove it from the download list.

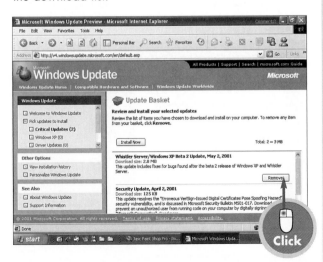

⑥ Accept the Licensing Agreement

Before you can download the updates, you must accept the Microsoft licensing agreement. Click **Accept** to continue. The files are then downloaded and installed to your computer. Windows will let you know when the process is finished and whether you have to restart your computer.

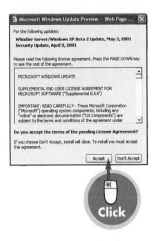

How to Find Out About Your Installed Hardware

Windows uses a tool named the **Device Manager** to help you find out about the hardware on your system. You can see what is installed, what resources are used, and what devices might be having or causing problems.

1 Open System Properties

Right-click the **My Computer** icon on your desktop and choose the **Properties** command from the shortcut menu. The **Systems Properties** dialog box opens.

2 Switch to Hardware Tab

Switch to the **Hardware** tab by clicking it once.

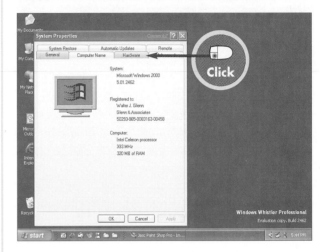

3 Open the Device Manager

Click the **Device Manager** button to open the **Device Manager** window.

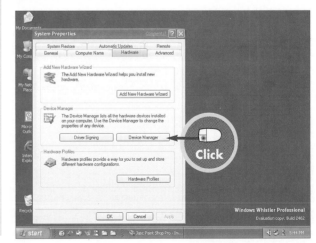

④ Expand a Category

The **Device Manager** window lists hardware categories for the hardware installed on your computer. Click the plus sign next to a category to expand that category and show the actual devices attached to your computer.

⑤ Identify Problem Hardware

Devices having problems are identified with a little yellow exclamation point. Another type of symbol you might see is a red X, which indicates a device that is turned off.

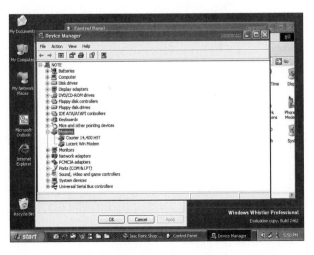

⑥ Open Hardware Properties

You can open a detailed **Properties** dialog box for any device by double-clicking the device's icon. The dialog box tells you whether the device is working properly and lets you disable the device. Other tabs let you reinstall software drivers for the device and view the resources it uses.

How-to Hint

Reinstalling a Device

If you see a device that isn't working, try running the **Add Hardware** applet (You'll find it in the **Control Panel** window). Windows scans your system for devices and presents a list of what it finds. The malfunctioning device should show up in the list, and you can try to reinstall it.

How to Tell Whether a Windows Service Pack is Installed

Microsoft occasionally releases collections of updates to Windows in the form of a service pack. Service packs are numbered because more than one is normally released over the years that an operating system is in production. At the time of this writing, Windows XP Service Pack 1 is the only one that has been released for Windows XP. This task shows how to tell whether a service pack has already been applied to Windows or whether you will need to install one yourself.

① Open the Start Menu

Click **Start** to open the **Start** menu.

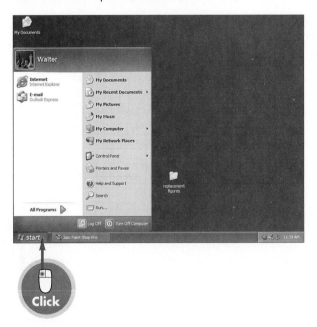

② Right-Click the My Computer Icon

Right-click the **My Computer** icon on your **Start** menu. If a **My Computer** icon is on your desktop, you can right-click that one instead.

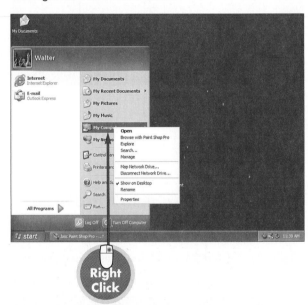

③ Open the Properties Dialog Box

Choose the **Properties** command on the **My Computer** icon's shortcut menu to open the **System Properties** dialog box.

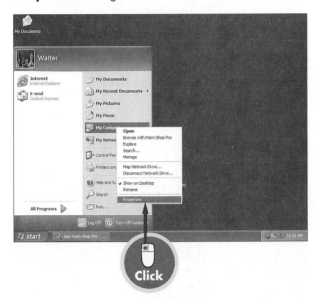

④ Determine Your Version of Windows

The **General** tab of the **System Properties** dialog box displays information about Windows and about the basic hardware on your computer. Look in the **System** section to find out if a service pack has been installed on your computer. If a service pack has not been installed, you will not see this line at all.

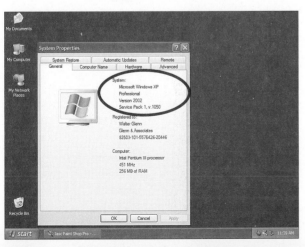

How-to Hint

Service Packs are Cumulative

When more service packs are released in the future, you can add them to your computer with no problem. Service packs are cumulative, in that each new service pack issued contains all the features included in previous service packs. So, if you have a computer with no service pack installed, you should only apply the latest service pack available.

How to Install Windows XP Service Pack 1

You can obtain a service pack in a few ways. If you are part of a corporate network, your administrator might make the service pack available for you on the network (and in fact, will probably install it for you). If you are installing it yourself, you will either download Service Pack 1 (SP1) from the Windows Update site or install it from a CD-ROM. Use the steps in Task 4 of this part to find and start the download of SP1 from the Internet, or insert your CD and run the program **XPSP1.EXE** on the CD. Whichever method you choose, the steps for the installation are the same.

❶ Read the Welcome Page

The welcome page of the Windows XP Service Pack 1 Setup Wizard has some good advice. Before installing, you should update your system repair disk and back up your computer. If you have done this, click **Next** to continue installation.

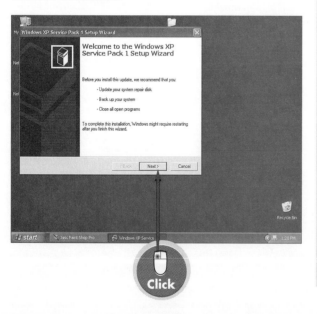

❷ Accept the Licensing Agreement

Read the licensing agreement for Service Pack 1. Select the **I Agree** option and click **Next** to continue installation. If you select the **I Do Not Agree** option, the setup program ends.

③ Choose Whether to Archive Old Files

If you want to uninstall Service Pack 1 at a later date, you must archive the current Windows files in a backup location on your computer. Archiving files takes a large amount of disk space but ensures that you can return your computer to its previous state if Service Pack 1 causes you any problems. Make your choice and click **Next**.

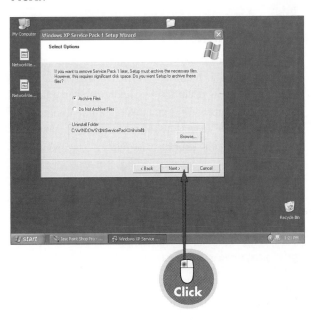

④ Finish the Installation

At this point, Windows begins to copy files. When it is done, you are shown the final page of the Setup Wizard. Click **Finish** to complete the installation and restart your computer. You can select the **Do Not Restart Now** option to finish the wizard without restarting, but you must restart your computer before the Service Pack 1 installation is complete.

How to Set Program Access and Defaults

Service Pack 1 includes security updates and support for new hardware devices, such as the tablet PC. The other big addition is a simple interface for letting Windows know whether you want to use built-in Microsoft programs (such as Internet Explorer and Outlook Express) or other programs installed on your computer. This is done using a feature named **Set Program Access and Defaults**, which is part of the **Add/Remove Programs Control Panel** utility.

① Open the Set Program Access and Defaults Tool

Click **Start**, point to **All Programs**, and select **Set Program Access and Defaults**. You can also get to this tool by opening the **Add/Remove Programs** utility from the **Control Panel** window.

② Use the Microsoft Windows Option

You have three choices for setting program defaults. The first is the **Microsoft Windows** option. When this option is set, Windows uses the built-in Microsoft programs for familiar functions: Internet Explorer for Web pages, Outlook Express for email, Windows Media Player for sounds and video, and Windows Messaging for instant messaging. There is also a setting for controlling what application loads Java applets on the Internet, but Microsoft does not provide a program for that. Click the **Microsoft Windows** option to use this setting.

③ Use the Non-Microsoft Option

Another choice you have is the **Non-Microsoft** option. This option uses whatever programs are currently set as your default programs for the listed functions. Whenever you install a new program (such as Netscape Navigator for browsing the Web), that program makes itself the default. Click the **Non-Microsoft** option to retain the default programs the way you have them set and to hide the icons for the Microsoft applications from your desktop and **Start** menu.

④ Use the Custom Option

Click the **Custom** option to exert a little more control over your default program settings. A section for each type of program (Web browser, email, and so on) lets you select whether to use the current default program or the Microsoft program, and whether the Microsoft program should be displayed on your desktop and **Start** menu.

How-to Hint

Why Is This Feature Here?

The **Set Program Access and Defaults** feature was really added to satisfy requirements set by the Department of Justice. It provides computer manufacturers a way to install programs that they choose to bundle with their computers and to hide the Microsoft equivalents from the casual Windows user. Interestingly, the program also provides an easy way for users who don't like the alternate programs that might come with a new computer to switch back to the Microsoft alternatives.

Task

① How to Clean Up the System Tray 246

② How to Boot Selectively 248

③ How to Stop a Service 250

④ How to Uninstall a Program 252

⑤ How to Use the Event Viewer 254

12

Troubleshooting Your Computer

Every so often, believe it or not, Windows XP will act up. You will see error messages, and programs might close down unexpectedly. Or, software and hardware you have installed will malfunction. Sometimes this is a matter of incompatibility—you should make sure that anything you install in Windows XP is supposed to run under this operating system.

Sometimes the manufacturer will tell you that although a product is not *certified*, it has been tested and will still run. Go ahead and use such a product, but take precautions that we cover here.

How to Clean Up the System Tray

Your **System Tray** is at the bottom right of your **Task Bar**. It consists of icons representing programs that are loaded into memory automatically on startup. Sometimes you have given permission to an item to inhabit the **System Tray**—and sometimes it has taken it upon itself to set itself up there. In any case, closing down a **System Tray** item can free up memory, and also eliminate a conflict between itself and another program. For example, let's temporarily close down our antivirus program.

1 Expand the System Tray

If you don't immediately see the icon representing the offending program, click the left double arrow to expand the **System Tray**.

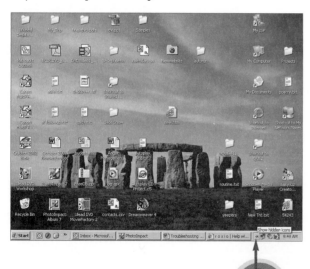

2 Locate the Icon

Moving your mouse over the icons should give a clue as to which program each represents. For example, if your virus checker has automatic scheduling, it might be enabled.

3 Open the Option Panel

A **System Tray** program should open an options panel when right-clicked.

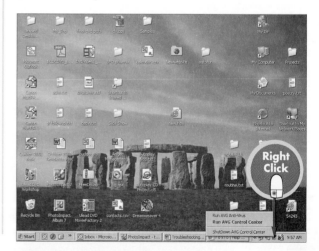

4 Disable the Program

Click the **Disable** option if it appears. If you don't see it, you might have to actually open the program itself, and look under **Tools**, **Options** for a **System Tray**-disabling option. (It might say something like **Run on Startup**, with a check box you need to clear).

Many **System Tray** programs will ask you again whether you *really* want to disable them.

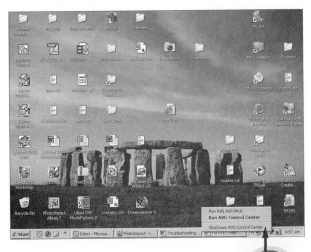

6 Reload the Program

After you have checked whether this was a problem by running another set of tests or programs, you can generally restart the removed application from the **Start Menu**. (In many cases, it will reload again automatically if you restart Windows).

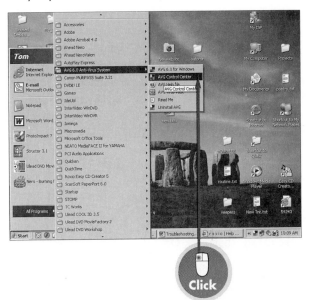

How-to Hint

Remember that most **System Tray** items are only temporarily disabled with this method. To permanently stop them from appearing, you need to go into the actual program options (usually **Tools**, **Options**) or, as we'll see in the next task, troubleshoot the startup routine of Windows.

5 Check the System Tray

Expand your **System Tray** again and make sure the program is really gone.

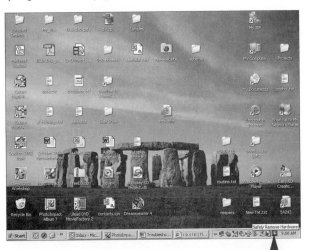

How to Boot Selectively

Many problems begin at startup, when all of your system device drivers and *services* are loaded together. A lot of these are Windows programs, but others represent the software choices you have made in your various installations. If a later installation is causing problems, it can be helpful to boot up selectively, either with no other programs, or only those you know you want.

1 Open MSCONFIG

On the **Start Menu**, click on **Run**, and type in `msconfig`. Then click **OK**.

2 Choose Selective Startup

Your **Normal** startup is automatic. Click **Selective Startup** to make some modifications.

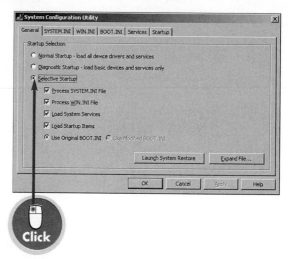

3 Open the Services Panel

The **Services Panel** shows all the services that begin each time Windows loads. Click the tab to reveal its contents.

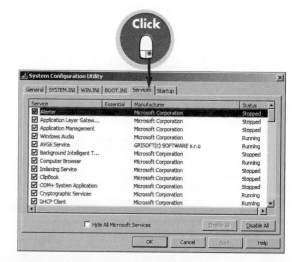

4 Hide the Microsoft Services

Because we don't want to mess with anything that actually affects Windows itself, we'll click to **Hide All Microsoft Services**.

5 Select and Disable Services

Now you can *uncheck* services that you suspect might be in conflict or potential conflict with an impending installation. Then click **Apply** and **OK**.

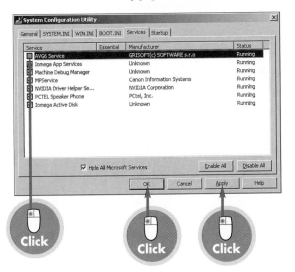

6 Reboot the Computer

To implement the changes you made, you must accept the prompt to reboot. When Windows restarts, click **OK** in the default windows (informing you that you have loaded selectively). Now try an offending program, or do an installation that previously failed. If things work smoothly, return to MSCONFIG and reselect a **Normal** startup.

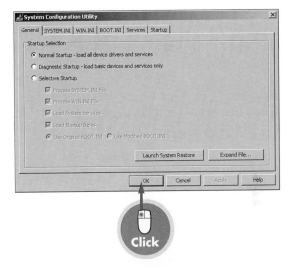

How-to Hint

Besides not disabling Windows services, *you don't want to disable anything that is critical to your entire system*. For example, the NVidia service is for the graphics card—you should know that by the manufacturer name—and disabling it will lead to driver complications on the reboot.

How to Stop a Service

Now that we've seen how Windows services load on startup, let's see how we can close one any time we want (or dare). We'll also see how we can shut down any program that is giving us trouble, or is showing an error.

① Open the Windows Task Manager

On your keyboard, press **CTRL+ALT+DEL**. This used to reboot your system, but now it gives you more options.

② Look at What's Running

Sometimes programs you thought were shut down are running. If a program is showing an error message, you can shut it down by clicking **End Task**. (Sometimes this takes several attempts.)

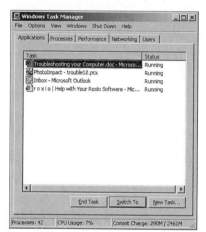

③ Open the Processes Panel

The **Processes** panel shows everything that is running—all services and programs. Click the tab to reveal its contents.

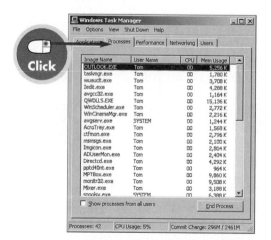

Click

4 Scroll Through the Processes

Scroll through to review and locate any processes that might be interfering with something you are trying to do, or otherwise causing trouble. Some are identified by the username that is currently logged in, and others are **System** or **Network** processes.

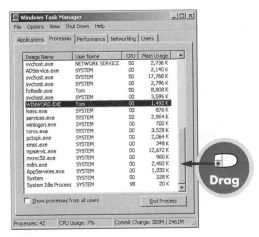

5 Shut Down a Process

Now you can click to select a process that you suspect might be in conflict, or potential conflict with another process or task. Then click **End Process**.

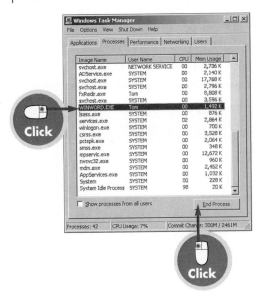

6 Check the Other Options

Clicking **Performance** can show you how efficiently your CPU is handling all your tasks. The other tabs relate to networking and user functions.

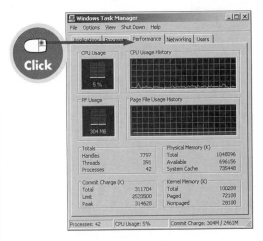

How-to Hint

Needless to say, *you don't want to end a process that is critical to your entire system.* Only attempt to shut down a process or task that you know is operating in error, or in potential error, with another program or task.

You can also *carefully* monitor and adjust services in the **Control Panel** by clicking **Administrative Tools** and then **Services**. You can click on a service to learn more about it, and start or stop it from the controller at the top of the panel.

How to Uninstall a Program

Sometimes you don't want to just stop a program, you want to get rid of it altogether. Although some programs will provide an Uninstall program in their folders, you can get rid of most programs in **Control Panel**.

1 Open the Control Panel

Click **Start**, and click the **Control Panel**.

2 Go to the Programs Category

Click Add or Remove Programs—if you're in the Category view.

3 Look at What's Loaded

All the programs that you have installed will momentarily appear. Drag through the list.

4 Sort by Frequency

To find programs that you rarely even use, click the drop-down arrow by **Sort** and select by **Frequency**.

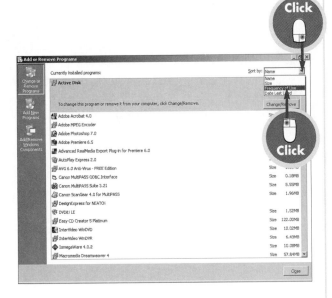

5 Uninstall a Program

Now you can click to select a program that is causing trouble or that you no longer need. Then click **Change/Remove**.

6 Clean Out the Program Folder

To free up disk space, you sometimes still need to go to the actual program folder under **Program Files** with the C: drive to locate subfolders that have not been deleted. Click to select them, and click **DEL** on your keyboard to get rid of them.

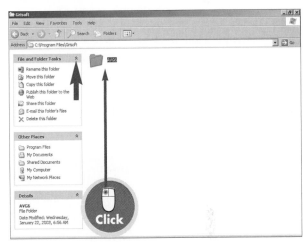

How-to Hint

You can't uninstall a program that is currently running, and in some cases, you need to reboot to complete an uninstallation.

If the **Category** view confuses you, you can modify the look of **Control Panel** to what you were used to in the past by clicking **Switch to Classic View**.

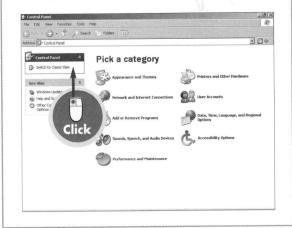

How to Use the Event Viewer

Windows XP lets you dig way down and find out a lot about what might have gone wrong with your system. You can do this with the **Event Viewer**.

1 Open the Control Panel

Click **Start**, and click the **Control Panel**.

2 Go to Administrative Tools

If you're in **Category** view, click **Performance and Maintenance**, and then click **Administrative Tools**. If you've switched to **Classic** view, you can go there directly.

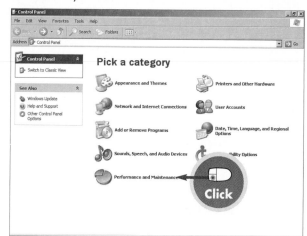

3 Open the Event Viewer

The **Event Viewer** is now available—double-click its icon.

④ Look at What's Available

The **Event Viewer** can tell you about errors with regard to applications, security, or the system itself. Double-click **Application**.

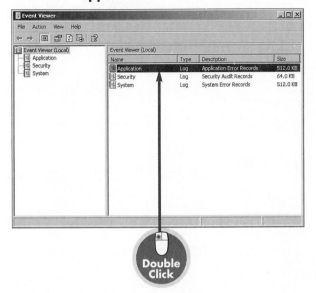

⑤ Analyze the Results

Notice the icons for errors, warnings, and general information. Double-click the latest error.

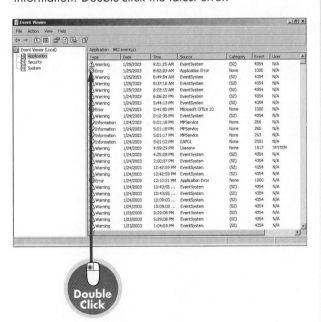

⑥ Get Help

Although this information might be gibberish to you, notice that it does reference a specific *DLL file*, and you have a link to go online to find out more. With the events sorted by time and other parameters, you should be able to eventually get to the root of problems in your system.

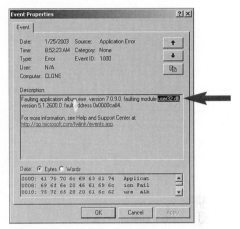

How-to Hint

To save the information in the **Event Properties** window, hold down the **ALT** key and press **PrtScn** on your keyboard. Then open Microsoft Word and hit **CTRL+V** to paste it into a Word document that you can fax to your IT department or other tech support resource.

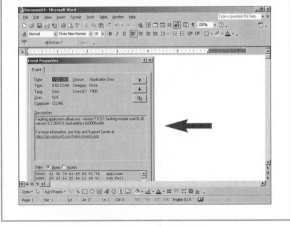

Task

1 How to Back Up Your Files 258

2 How to Restore Files from a Backup 260

3 How to Use Automated System Recovery 262

4 How to Upgrade to Windows XP 264

5 How to Install Windows XP on a Blank
Hard Drive 266

6 How to Activate Windows XP 270

7 How to Create Setup Floppy Disks 272

13

Back Up and Restore Your Computer

There may come a time when you need to backup, install or reinstall Windows. Even though the product itself is far more complex than previous versions of Windows, the installation of Windows XP is much simpler than the installation of previous versions of the program. This is, in part, because the setup routine is smarter and can detect and configure more types of hardware for you. It is also because Microsoft has taken a lot of the decisions out of the setup process.

The installation of the Home and Professional versions of Windows XP do not differ significantly, except that the Professional version offers a few more networking choices. The tasks in this appendix focus on the Professional version, but are virtually identical for the Home version. There are several ways to install Windows XP. The simplest method is to upgrade from another operating system, such as Windows 98/Me, Windows NT, or Windows 2000. In this case, Windows XP takes the place of the old operating system. You can also install Windows XP while keeping an old operating system, such as Windows 98. This is known as a *dual-boot configuration*. When you turn on your computer, you are given the choice of booting to Windows XP or booting to your old operating system. Yet another way to install Windows XP is to install it on a *clean system*—one that has no operating system at all. This is the method you should choose if you build your own computer or if you decide to clear off or format your hard drive before installation. You might also use this method if you put a new hard drive in your computer.

In this chapter, you are introduced to each of these methods of installing Windows XP. You are also shown how to create a set of setup floppy disks to use when installing Windows XP on a clean system. Finally, you are shown how to activate Windows XP and register the software after it is installed.

How to Back Up Your Files

The single most important thing you can do to prevent loss of work should your computer fail is to back up your files. Many companies have automated routines for backing up users' files, and you should check with your administrator to see what the policy is at your company. Windows XP comes with a program named Backup, which lets you back up files on your computer to floppy disks, a Zip drive, a recordable CD-ROM drive, or even another computer on your network. Even if your network has backup routines in place, you might also want to use the Backup program on your more important files.

❶ Start Backup

Click the **Start** button and select **All Programs**, **Accessories**, **System Tools**, and **Backup**.

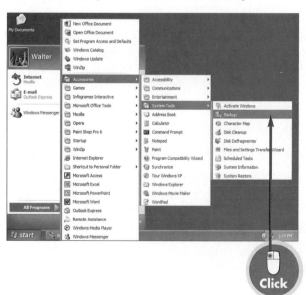

❷ Start the Backup Wizard

Click the **Backup Wizard** button to start the **Backup Wizard**. The first page of the wizard is a welcome page. Just click the **Next** button when you see the welcome page.

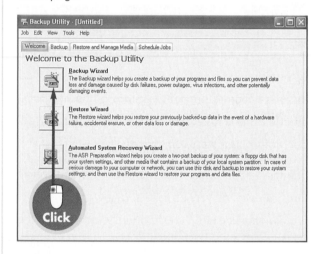

❸ Choose What to Back Up

Choose what you want to back up on your computer. Unless your backup media (floppy, tape drive, and so on) is very fast, it is usually best to back up only selected files.

4️⃣ Choose the Files to Back Up

This page of the Backup Wizard works just like Windows Explorer. In the left pane, select a folder you want to browse. Files in that folder appear in the right pane. Click the boxes next to the files to indicate that you want to include those files in the backup. You can also select whole folders. When you have selected all the files you want to back up, click the **Next** button to go on.

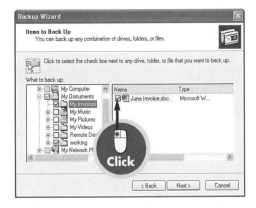

5️⃣ Choose Where to Back It Up

No matter how many files you back up, the whole backup is saved as a single file with a .bkf extension. Type the path for the drive and folder where you want to save the backup. If you don't know the exact path, click the **Browse** button to locate it. Using the **Browse** button also lets you locate drives on other computers on the network. Click the **Next** button to go on.

6️⃣ Finish

The last page of the **Backup Wizard** gives you a second look at all the settings you've made. Click the **Back** button to go back and change settings. Make sure that your backup media (floppy disk, CD-ROM, tape, Zip disk, and so on) are inserted in the appropriate drive. Click the **Finish** button to go on with the backup.

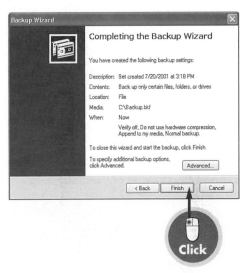

7️⃣ View the Report

While the backup is in progress, a dialog box appears that shows you how things are going. When the backup is finished, Windows lets you know that it was completed successfully. Click the **Report** button to view a detailed report on the backup. Click **Close** to finish up.

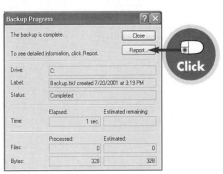

How to Restore Files from a Backup

Whether you are restoring files from a backup following a computer failure or you just want to dig up an old file you deleted, Windows makes the process pretty easy. Before you get started, make sure that the disk you backed up to (Zip disk, CD-ROM, or whatever) is inserted in your drive.

① Start Backup

Click the **Start** button and choose **All Programs**, **Accessories**, **System Tools**, and **Backup**.

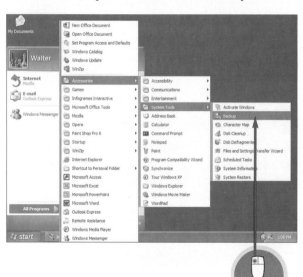

② Start the Restore Wizard

Click the **Restore Wizard** button to start the **Restore Wizard**. The first page of the wizard is a welcome page. To continue, just click the **Next** button when you see the welcome page.

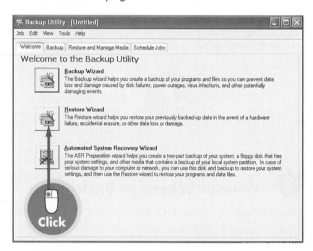

③ Choose What to Restore

A list of backup sessions on your backup media is displayed. Choose the backup session you want to restore by clicking the check box next to it. Sessions are listed by date. If you want to know exactly what is in a session, right-click it and choose **Catalog** from the shortcut menu. When you're done, click the **Next** button.

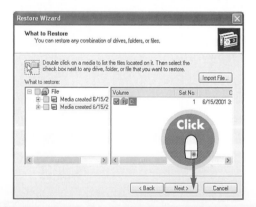

4 Finish

The last page of the **Restore Wizard** gives you a second look at all the selections you've made. Click the **Back** button to go back and change settings. Click the **Finish** button to go on with the restore process.

5 Enter the Backup Filename

Type the path and name of the backup file you want to restore from. If you don't know the exact path or name, click the **Browse** button to locate the file. When you're ready to start, click the **OK** button.

6 View the Report

While the restore is in progress, a dialog box appears that shows you how things are going. When the restore is finished, Windows lets you know that it was completed successfully. Click the **Report** button to view a detailed report on the backup. Click **Close** to finish up.

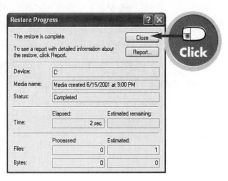

How-to Hint

Choosing a Backup Session

If you are using a large backup media, such as CD-ROM, you may have a number of backup sessions available from which to restore. Sessions are listed by date and by the name you gave them during the backup. This is why it is important to give your backup sessions names that mean something to you. You can also right-click any session and choose **Catalog** from the shortcut menu to browse the actual files contained in the backup.

How to Use Automated System Recovery

Automated System Recovery is a two-part backup process. First, a snapshot of your vital system settings and files is taken and backed up to the backup media of your choice. Second, an Emergency Recovery Disk is created that you can use to boot your system and recover the saved system settings in the event of failure.

1 Start Backup

Click the **Start** button and choose **All Programs**, **Accessories**, **System Tools**, and **Backup**.

2 Start the Automated System Recovery Wizard

Click the **Automated System Recovery Wizard** button to start the **Automated System Recovery Wizard**. On the welcome page of the wizard that opens, click **Next** to go on.

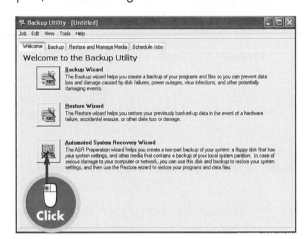

3 Enter a Backup Destination

Type the path for the location where selected files should be backed up. The files will probably consume a good amount of disk space, so you will need to select a location on your hard disk or use a large backup medium, such as a tape, a Zip drive, or a CD-RW. Click **Next** to go on.

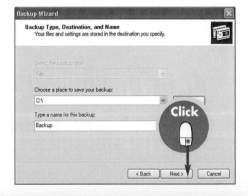

④ Click Finish

Click the **Finish** button to begin the backup.

⑤ Insert a Disk

After Windows backs up certain vital system information to the location you specified, it will prompt you to insert a floppy disk in the **A:** drive. This floppy disk will become your Automated System Recovery disk (also known as the Emergency Repair Disk). Insert a blank, formatted floppy disk into your **A:** drive and click the **OK** button.

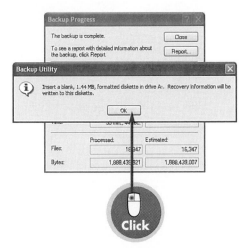

⑥ Finish and Label the Disk

When the Automated System Recovery disk has been created, a dialog box lets you know the process was successful. Click the **OK** button to finish. Be sure to label the disk and keep it in a safe place.

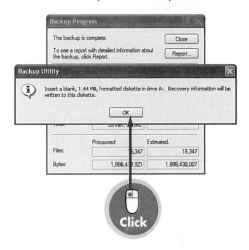

How-to Hint

Using the ASR Disk

If your computer experiences a major system failure (for example, it cannot finish booting), you will have to repair the operating system. If you suffer a hardware failure (such as a crashed hard disk), you can run this process after repairing the hardware to restore your system. To start the emergency repair process, start your computer using the original Windows XP setup disks or CD-ROM. During setup process, you are given the option of performing setup or performing a repair. Choose to repair the system; the setup program prompts you to insert the ASR disk.

(4) How to Upgrade to Windows XP

Upgrading is the easiest way to install Windows XP. You can upgrade to Windows XP from Windows 95, Windows 98, Windows Me, Windows NT Workstation 3.5 or 4.0, and Windows 2000 Professional. To get started with the upgrade, all you have to do is insert the Windows XP CD-ROM in your computer's CD-ROM drive.

(1) Upgrade

When you insert the Windows XP CD-ROM into your drive, a splash screen automatically appears along with a dialog box that asks what you want to do. Click the **Install Windows XP** button to start the upgrade. If the splash screen does not appear, you must open the CD-ROM and run the **Setup** program yourself.

(2) Choose Upgrade or Clean

If you choose **Upgrade**, your old operating system is overwritten. Settings you have made in the previous version of Windows and all your software are preserved. If you choose **Clean installation**, Windows XP is installed in addition to your old operating system. You can choose which OS to boot into whenever you start your computer. Click the **Next** button to go on.

(3) Accept the License Agreement

You must accept Microsoft's licensing agreement by clicking the **I accept this agreement** option.

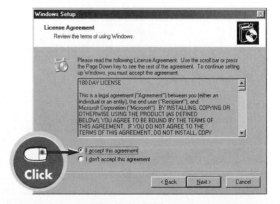

④ Enter the Product Key

Type the 25-digit product identification key from the back of your CD-ROM case and click **Next** to go on.

⑤ Perform Dynamic Update

Microsoft often updates the setup files used to install Windows XP. If your computer has Internet access, the Setup program can download any available updates. Make sure that the **Yes, download the latest Setup files** option is selected and click **Next**.

⑥ Download Updates

From this point on, the upgrade is mostly an automatic process. After the updated files are downloaded, the Setup program will begin examining your system and copying files. During this process, your computer might restart once or twice.

⑦ Finish the Upgrade

You can watch the progress of the upgrade. Depending on the speed of your computer, the process could take a good bit of time. If it ever seems that nothing is happening, you can verify that the upgrade is still working by watching the progress indicator in the lower-right corner of the screen. If this indicator stops flashing for a long period of time, you should turn your computer off and turn it back on to resume the upgrade process.

How to Install Windows XP on a Blank Hard Drive

Installing Windows XP on a blank hard drive is a bit more complicated than upgrading from an existing version of Windows. It requires that you have a bootable CD-ROM drive or a set of five setup floppy disks. The procedure for creating the floppy disks is discussed in Task 7, "How to Create Setup Floppy Disks." To begin, insert the CD-ROM or the first of the five floppy disks into your floppy drive and start your computer. If you are using floppy disks, setup asks you for the second, third, fourth, and fifth disks before you can make any other setup decisions.

1 Choose Setup or Repair

The first decision you are asked to make is whether you want to set up Windows XP or whether you want to repair an existing installation. To continue with setup, press the **Enter** key.

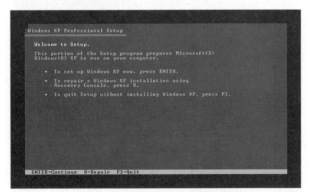

⏎Enter

2 Agree to Licensing

To continue setup, you must agree to Microsoft's licensing agreement. Press the **F8** key to continue.

F8

3 Choose a Partition

You must choose the disk partition on which to install Windows XP. Highlight a partition using the up and down arrow keys (in this example, only one disk partition is available). Select the highlighted drive by pressing the **Enter** key. You can also create and delete drive partitions.

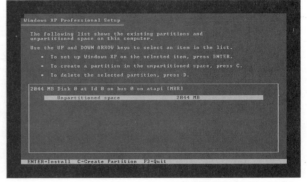

⏎Enter

4 Format Your Drive

Use the arrow keys to choose whether to format your drive with the NTFS or FAT32 file system. NTFS is more secure, but only Windows XP, Windows 2000, and Windows NT recognize it. Windows 95 and 98 can recognize the FAT system. If your computer will only run Windows XP, you should use NTFS. If your computer will dual-boot Windows XP and Windows 95/98/Me, you should choose FAT32. Other users on the network will be able to access shared files no matter what file system you choose. If your drive is already formatted, you also have the option of saving the existing format or doing a quick format. Press **Enter** when you have made your selection. On the next setup screen, you'll be asked to confirm the format option. Depending on the size of your drive, formatting can take a few minutes.

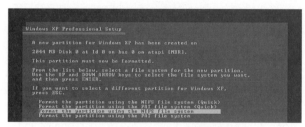

╝Enter

5 Copy Files to Your Disk

The Setup program then copies files to your hard drive. This process can take several minutes.

6 Restart Your Computer

After all files are copied to your disk, your computer must restart. This happens automatically after 15 seconds, but you can also press the **Enter** key as soon as you see this screen. Make sure that you remove any floppy disks before you restart the computer. When the computer starts back up, the Setup program continues in a more familiar graphical interface.

╝Enter

7 Look for Hardware Devices

After your computer restarts, the Setup program initially spends several minutes looking for hardware devices attached to your computer and preparing the installation. It is normal for your screen to flicker during this process. It is also possible that the Setup program might have to restart your computer a few times. All this happens automatically. You can watch the progress indicator in the lower-right corner of the screen to make sure that the installation is proceeding.

Continued ⑤

⑧ Customize Your Locale

When all the hardware devices on your system have been identified, you are given the chance to customize your locale and keyboard input. The default is for the English language. Click the **Customize** button to change this locale. When you're done, click the **Next** button to go on.

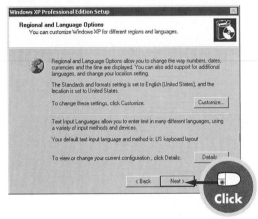

⑨ Enter Your Name and Organization

Type your name and the name of your company. If you want, you can leave the company name blank. When you're done, click the **Next** button to go on.

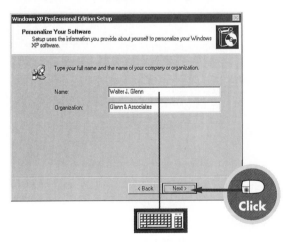

⑩ Enter Your Product Key

Type the 25-digit product identification number from the back of your CD-ROM case and click **Next** to go on.

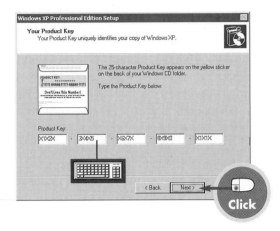

⑪ Enter a Computer Name and Password

When you install Windows XP on any computer, that computer must be given a name. If you are going to be on a network, this name distinguishes your computer from other computers. Even if you're not planning to put your computer on a network, you must still give the computer a name. A primary user account for your computer is created during installation. This account is given the name **Administrator**. This account is used to change basic computer settings. You can also create additional accounts that other people can use to log in. On this screen, you should create and confirm a password for the **Administrator** account.

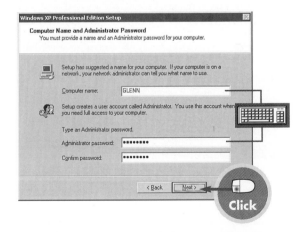

12 Enter the Date and Time

Enter the correct date and time if the Setup program is not reporting it correctly. Select the correct time zone from the drop-down list box. If you want Windows to automatically adjust the system time for daylight savings time, enable that option. Click the **Next** button to go on.

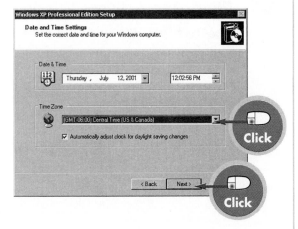

13 Choose Network Settings

The Setup program then installs networking components for your computer. When it's done, you must choose your network settings. Unless you know that custom settings are required for your computer (such as a specific IP address or the names of specific servers on your network), choose the **Typical** option. When you're setting up a home network, you should choose the **Typical** option. You can always change the settings after installation if needed. Click the **Next** button to go on.

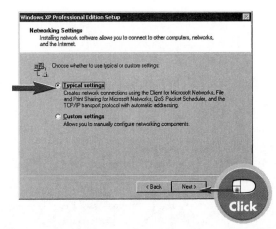

14 Join a Workgroup or Domain

If your computer will be part of a Windows networking domain, choose the **Yes** option. If instead your computer will be part of a workgroup (or will be a standalone computer), choose **No**. Either way, type the name of the domain or workgroup with which this computer is to be associated into the appropriate text box. After you enter this information, the setup program will copy the needed files to your computer, finalize the installation, and restart one more time. You'll then be ready to start using Windows.

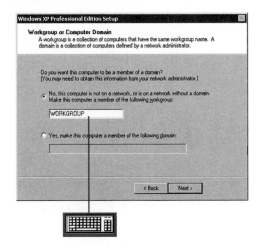

How to Activate Windows XP

Windows XP is the first version of Windows that requires *activation*. You must register your copy of Windows over the Internet or by phone if you want to use it for more than about 14 days. The **Activation Wizard** will start immediately the first time you start Windows if you upgraded from a previous version of Windows that had Internet access. Otherwise, you might have to run the **Activate Windows** shortcut located on the **Start** menu to launch the wizard.

❶ Welcome to Windows

The welcome page of the wizard presents an opportunity to run a short tutorial on using the mouse. After you watch it (or if you choose not to watch it), click **Next** to continue.

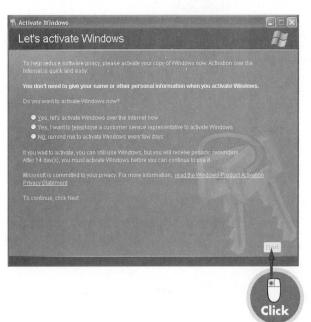

❷ Choose to Activate Windows

Make sure that the **Yes, activate Windows over the Internet now** option is selected and click **Next**.

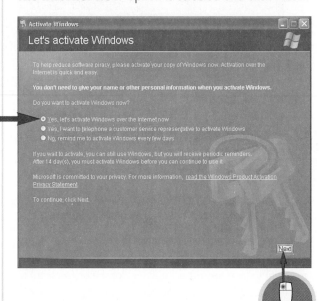

③ Register Windows

During the activation process, you also have the option of *registering* Windows with Microsoft. When you register, you are registering for a warranty; Microsoft will email or mail you information about itsproducts. If you want to do so, choose **Yes, I'd like to register with Microsoft now** and click **Next**.

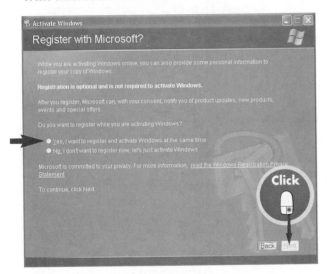

④ Enter Registration Information

If you chose to register, enter the appropriate information in the text boxes. Disable the two check boxes near the bottom of the screen if you don't want to receive advertisements from Microsoft or its partners. Click **Next** to continue.

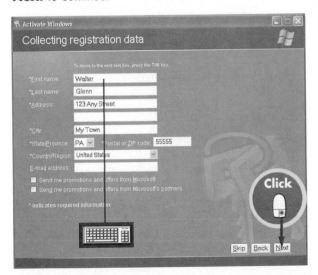

⑤ Finish

When the activation process is finished, click **Finish**. You'll be returned to the Windows desktop.

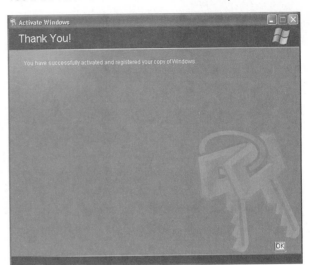

How to Create Setup Floppy Disks

If you plan to install Windows XP on a clean system (one without an operating system on it already), you first must create a set of five setup floppy disks. These disks are used to start your computer so that it can recognize your CD-ROM drive and other hardware and install Windows XP. To make these disks, you must perform this task on a computer that has some version of Windows already installed. Insert the Windows XP CD-ROM into that computer's CD-ROM drive and follow these steps.

① Browse This CD

When you insert the Windows XP CD-ROM, a splash screen should appear automatically, presenting you with several choices. Click the **Browse This CD** link.

② Open the BOOTDISK Folder

Double-click the **BOOTDISK** folder to open it.

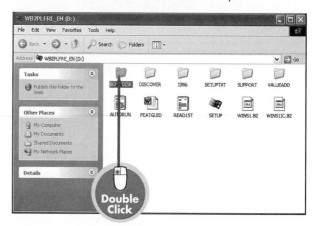

③ Start MAKEBT32

From the list of files in the **BOOTDISK** folder, double-click the **MAKEBT32** program icon to start it. A DOS window from which the boot disks will be created opens.

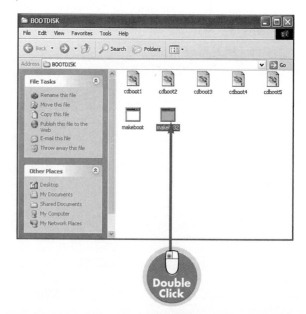

④ Type the Floppy Drive Letter

Type the letter of the floppy drive you want to use to make the setup floppies. This is usually drive **A**.

⑤ Insert Floppy and Press Enter

Insert a blank, formatted floppy disk into the selected drive and press the **Enter** key. The program begins copying files to the disk, which becomes the first disk in the set. When finished copying, the program prompts you for the next disk and then the next. When the last disk is done, the DOS program window closes automatically.

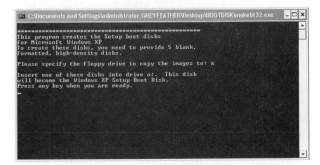

⏎Enter

⑥ Label the Disks

It is important that you label the disks in the order in which they were made. Use a felt-tip marker to write the disk numbers on the disk labels.

II

Using the Internet

14 Connecting to the Internet **277**

15 Browsing and Searching the World Wide Web **293**

16 Protecting Yourself on the Web **329**

17 Communicating with Electronic Mail **349**

18 Sending and Receiving Instant Messages **377**

19 Participating in Chat and Online Communities **387**

20 Participating in Usenet Discussion Groups **399**

Task

① How to Set Up an Internet Connection 278

② How to Choose an Internet Service Provider 282

③ How to Connect to the Internet 286

④ How to Connect to the Internet Through a
Proxy Server 288

⑤ How to Load a Web Page 290

14

Connecting to the Internet

Every day, millions of people use a worldwide network of computers called the *Internet*. This network, once the province of scholars, students, and the military, has changed the way many of us communicate, shop, work, and play.

The Windows operating system includes software to connect to the Internet and its most popular services. One of these services is the *World Wide Web*. Exploring the Web requires software called a *Web browser*; one of the most popular browsers is installed along with Windows: Microsoft Internet Explorer.

Before you can use the Web or any other Internet service, you must establish a connection between your computer and the Internet. That connection will be used automatically by each program designed to send and receive information using the Internet.

How to Set Up an Internet Connection

Before you can connect to the Internet, you must have an account with an *Internet service provider* (also called an *ISP*). An ISP offers access to the Internet through your computer's modem. Most cities have local companies that offer Internet service. To find them, look in the Yellow Pages under "Internet" or "Internet Services." These companies often offer a local access number to call, meaning that when your computer dials in to the Internet, no long-distance fees apply. Windows also can help you find an ISP and set up a connection. To do this, skip ahead to Task 2, "How to Choose an Internet Service Provider."

① Open the Control Panel

To begin setting up a new Internet connection, click the **Start** button and choose **Control Panel**. The **Control Panel** window opens.

② Choose a Category

The **Control Panel** window displays a list of categories that can be used to set up your computer and change existing settings. Click the **Network and Internet Connections** link. The **Network and Internet Connections** window opens.

③ Begin a New Setup

To set up Internet service for the first time, click the **Set up or change your Internet connection** link. The **Internet Properties** dialog box opens.

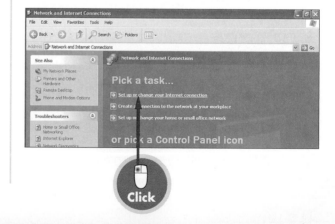

④ Set Up a Connection

When the **Internet Properties** dialog box opens, the **Connections** tab is displayed on top. To start a wizard that helps you create a new Internet connection, click the **Setup** button. The **New Connection Wizard** appears.

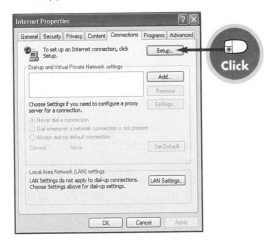

⑥ Choose a Connection Type

This wizard can be used for several kinds of network connections. For the Internet, choose the **Connect to the Internet** option and click **Next** to continue.

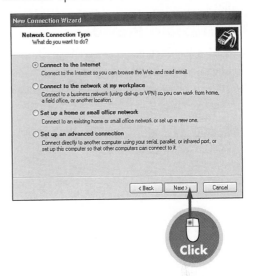

⑤ Start the Wizard

Wizards are programs that make complex tasks easier by breaking them down into a series of simple questions for which you select responses. The **New Connection Wizard** helps you connect to the Internet and other networks. Click **Next** to begin.

How to Hint

Choosing an ISP

In addition to the local companies listed in your Yellow Pages, there are several dozen national ISPs. Some of the most popular are America Online, AT&T WorldNet, BellSouth, and EarthLink. To find out how to join the others, call their customer-service numbers or use someone else's computer to visit their Web sites:

- **AT&T WorldNet**: Call (800) 967-5363 or visit http://www.att.net
- **BellSouth**: Call (800) 436-8638 or visit http://www.bellsouth.net
- **EarthLink**: Call (800) 395-8425 or visit http://www.earthlink.net

After you have subscribed to an ISP and received an access number, username, and password, you can begin this task and set up an Internet connection on your computer.

7 Choose a Provider

The wizard asks whether you need help choosing an ISP. Because you already have subscribed to one, choose the **Set up my connection manually** option and click **Next**.

Click

8 Choose a Connection Type

Choose the option that describes your Internet connection. If you don't know, you're probably using a *dial-up connection* and should choose **Connect using a dial-up modem**. After you choose the appropriate option for your computer, click **Next**.

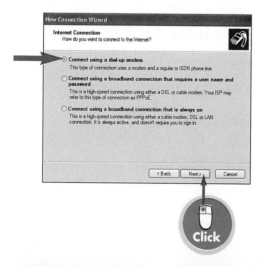

Click

9 Name the Connection

Type the name of your ISP in the **ISP Name** text box (the name *BellSouth.Net* was used in this example) and click **Next** to continue.

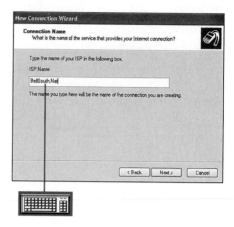

10 Enter Your Access Number

Your ISP should have provided the phone number you need to connect to the Internet. Type the access number in the **Phone number** text box, including an area code if it is required. If you have to dial long distance to connect (which can be extremely expensive), include a **1** before the access number. Click **Next** to continue.

⑪ Connect to the Internet

Your ISP also should have provided a username and password for your account. Type your username in the **User name** text box and your password in the **Password** and **Confirm Password** boxes. If you are setting up your computer's main (or only) Internet connection, enable the **Make this the default Internet connection** check box. Don't click **Next** yet.

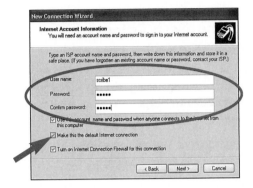

⑫ Enable a Firewall

Windows XP can make your Internet connection safer by using a *firewall*—a security measure described in detail in Chapter 6, Task 6, "How to Make Your Internet Connection More Secure." To turn this feature on, enable the **Turn on Internet Connection Firewall for this connection** check box. Click **Next** to continue.

⑬ Finish the Wizard

The **New Connection Wizard** describes your new Internet connection; click **Finish** to set it up. You'll learn how to connect to the Internet and begin using it in Task 3, "How to Connect to the Internet."

How to Hint

Choosing an Internet Subscription

Most national Internet service providers offer two kinds of monthly subscriptions, depending on how much you want to use the service.

One subscription plan limits the number of hours you can use the service per month. If you exceed that number, you must pay an extra per-hour fee. For example, AT&T WorldNet currently offers 150 hours a month for $16.95 and 99 cents for each extra hour.

A more expensive subscription plan offers unlimited hours, so you never pay a per-hour cost. AT&T WorldNet's unlimited plan sells for $21.95 per month.

Although 150 hours is a lot—around five hours a day—it can be expensive to use an Internet service with per-hour charges if you forget about the limit.

Installing a Broadband Connection

A broadband Internet connection, which is generally 10–20 times faster than a dial-up connection, uses a cable modem or DSL modem. These high-speed connections usually require special installation—a service provided by an Internet service provider—and cost from $40 to $60 a month.

② How to Choose an Internet Service Provider

Before you can connect to the Internet, you must obtain an account with an *Internet service provider (ISP)*. Windows XP can help you set up an account with one of several national ISPs, such as AT&T WorldNet, EarthLink, or Prodigy. To use this feature, you must live in an area where one of these providers offers service. Most cities, suburbs, and large towns fit this description. If you'd like to use an ISP that isn't offered in Windows XP, set up your Internet service using Task 1, "How to Set Up an Internet Connection."

❶ Open the Control Panel

To begin choosing an Internet service provider, click the **Start** button and choose **Control Panel**. The **Control Panel** window opens.

❷ Choose a Category

The **Control Panel** window displays a list of categories that can be used to set up your computer and change existing settings. Click the **Network and Internet Connections** link. The **Network and Internet Connections** window opens.

❸ Begin a New Setup

To begin setting up Internet service, click the **Set up or change your Internet connection** link. The **Internet Properties** dialog box opens.

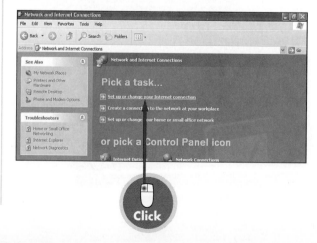

④ Set Up a Connection

The **Connections** tab is displayed on top of the **Internet Properties** dialog box. To start a wizard that helps you find an Internet service provider, click the **Setup** button. The **New Connection Wizard** appears.

⑤ Start the Wizard

Wizards are programs that make complex tasks easier by dividing them into a series of simple questions, for which you select responses. The New Connection Wizard helps you connect to the Internet and other networks. Click **Next** to begin.

⑥ Choose a Connection Type

The New Connection Wizard can be used for several kinds of network connections. Choose the **Connect to the Internet** option and click **Next** to continue.

⑦ Find a Provider

The wizard asks how you want to connect to the Internet. Because you do not yet have an ISP, select the **Choose from a list of Internet service providers (ISPs)** option and click **Next**.

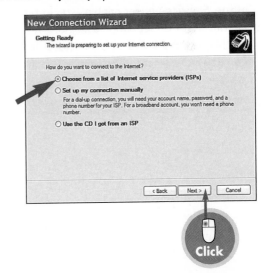

⑧ Close the Wizard

Because you don't have an account with an ISP at this point, the New Connection Wizard can't finish the job. Choose the **Select from a list of other ISPs** option and click **Finish**. The **Online Services** folder opens.

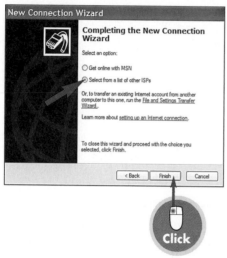

⑨ Look for an ISP

The **Online Services** folder enables you to set up an account with MSN or see what other ISPs are available. Double-click the **Refer me to more Internet Service Providers** icon. The Internet Connection Wizard starts.

⑩ Choose an ISP

The Internet Connection Wizard dials a toll-free number to retrieve a list of ISPs you can join. When it's done, click a provider's name to find out more about it in the Provider information box. If you're ready to join one, select its name and click **Next**.

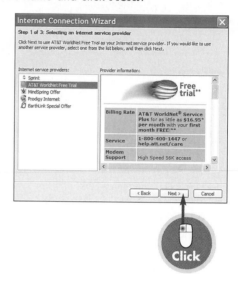

⑪ Identify Yourself

All ISPs require your name, mailing address, and phone number to join. Type these things in the text fields and click **Next**. The wizard might ask you to select a subscription plan. If so, choose one and click **Next** again.

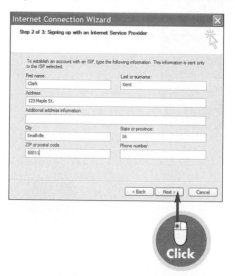

⑫ Pay the ISP

You must have a credit card to subscribe to an ISP. Type your credit card information in the text fields and choose the card type in the **Select a method of payment** drop-down box. Click **Next** when you're finished.

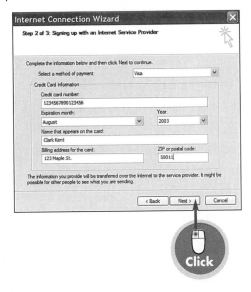

⑬ Pick a Service Number

In the drop-down box, pick the *access number* (the number your modem will dial to connect to the Internet) that's closest to you. Be warned that if the access number you pick is a long-distance call, you'll run up long-distance charges every time you connect to the Internet. Click **Next**.

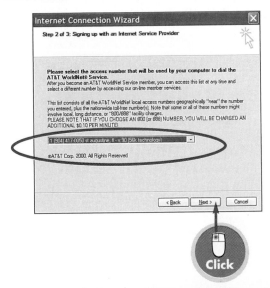

⑭ Choose an Address

The wizard suggests an email address for you. Use this or type your own in the **E-mail Address** field and click **Next**. If your preferred address is not available, you'll be asked to pick again; do so until you hit upon an available valid address. You will be shown the ISP's terms of service. If you agree to them, choose **I accept the agreement** and then click **Next**.

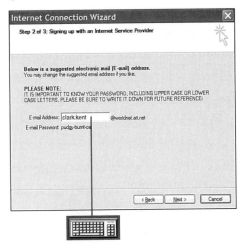

⑮ Finish the Wizard

After the terms of service, the wizard displays your email address and password. Write these down and click **Next**. Your Internet connection will be set up with your new username and password. You're done; click **Finish**. The next task covers how to begin using your new ISP subscription to access the Internet.

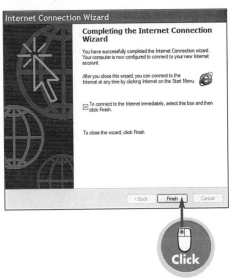

How to Connect to the Internet

Before you can surf the World Wide Web, check your email, or do anything else involving the Internet, you must establish a connection between your computer and the Internet. Some programs such as Microsoft Internet Explorer will try to connect to the Internet when you begin using them. Other programs will display an error message if you haven't connected first. This task explains what to do when you see the instruction to "connect to the Internet."

1 List Your Internet Connections

To see what Internet connections are available on your computer, click the **Start** button, choose **Connect To**, and choose **Show all connections**. The **Network Connections** folder opens with the connections you can use.

2 Dial Your Access Number

Double-click the icon that represents the Internet connection you want to use. The **Connect** dialog box opens.

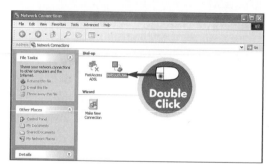

3 Review Your Settings

Make sure that your username and access number are correct, and then click the **Dial** button to make a connection. Note that if you are using a DSL connection, the procedure for connecting is exactly the same as that for a dial-up connection (except that the "access number" isn't really a phone number).

4 Connect to the Internet

If your computer can't connect because of a busy signal or another problem, you'll get the chance to try again or to adjust your Internet settings. When you successfully connect, the **Connecting** dialog box disappears.

6 Stay Connected

In this example, the connection speed is 49.2Kbps. Even if you have a 56Kbps modem, you may connect at slower speeds such as 28Kbps or 35Kbps—the speed depends on phone line quality and other factors. To close the **Status** dialog box and remain connected to the Internet, click the **Close** button.

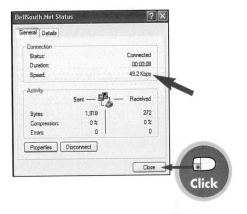

5 Check Your Connection Speed

While you're connected, a connection icon appears on your Windows taskbar in the system tray (near the current time). Double-click this icon to open the **Status** dialog box to check the speed of your connection.

7 Disconnect from the Internet

When you're finished using the Internet and want to disconnect, double-click the connection icon in the system tray. Then, when the **Status** dialog box opens, click the **Disconnect** button.

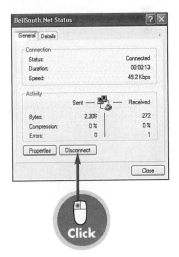

How to Connect to the Internet Through a Proxy Server

If you're using the Internet at work, you might not be able to connect directly to the Internet with your Web browser. For security reasons, a *proxy server* (or *firewall*) is sometimes used as an intermediary between your computer and the Internet. They make it much more difficult for outsiders to access your computer system or your company's files illegally over the Internet. You can set up Internet Explorer to connect through a proxy server when loading Web pages.

1 Start Internet Explorer

Before you can set up Internet Explorer to connect to the Internet through a proxy server, you must have the proxy server's address and port number (check with your network administrator). When you have that information, click the **Start** button and choose **Internet**. The **Internet Explorer** window opens and displays a default Web page.

2 Set Your Internet Options

From the **Tools** menu at the top of the **Internet Explorer** window, choose **Internet Options**. The **Internet Options** dialog box opens; you can use this dialog box to customize Internet Explorer.

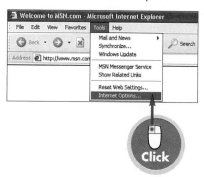

3 Configure Your Connection

Click the **Connections** tab to bring all the settings related to your Internet connection to the front. This window shows how your browser connects to the Internet.

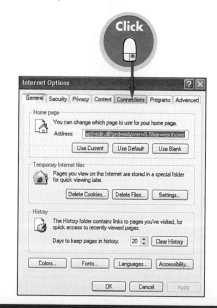

4 Change Dial-Up Settings

A proxy server is associated with a specific Internet connection. Choose the appropriate connection in the **Dial-up settings** list box and click the **Settings** button. The **Settings** dialog box opens.

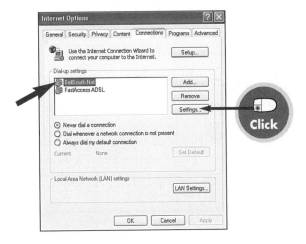

6 Save the New Settings

Click the **OK** button to save your new Internet Explorer settings and close the dialog box, and then click **OK** to close the **Internet Settings** dialog box. (The **Apply** button also saves your settings, but it doesn't close the dialog box.) After you save the settings, all attempts to connect to Web pages with your browser will now be routed through the proxy server.

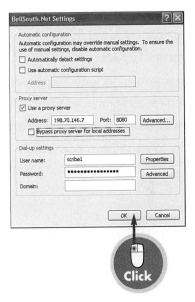

5 Set Up a Proxy Server

Enable the **Use a proxy server** check box and type the address and port number of the server in the **Address** and **Port** text boxes. (You can obtain this information from a computer administrator at the place where you're accessing the Internet.)

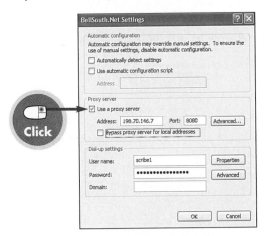

How to Hint

Bypassing the Proxy Server

If you're using a proxy server in a corporate setting, you might not need it when you're visiting Web pages on your company's intranet. If so, you can bypass the proxy server for those pages. In the **Settings** dialog box for the connection you're setting up (shown in step 5 of this task), enable the **Bypass proxy server for local addresses** check box.

How to Load a Web Page

After you connect to the Internet, you are ready to use Internet Explorer, the World Wide Web browsing software included with Windows. If you're not already connected to the Internet when you run Internet Explorer, Windows gives you the opportunity to establish a connection.

1 Run Internet Explorer

To run Internet Explorer and open a Web page, click the **Start** button and choose **Internet**. The browser opens and displays a starting page. This page is called the browser's *home page*, and it can be set to any page on the Internet or your own computer.

2 Explore the Browser

The Internet Explorer window includes a menu bar, toolbar buttons along the top edge of the window, and an Address bar. You'll use all three as you visit different World Wide Web sites. Click the **Search** button in the toolbar at the top of the screen to open a pane from which you can search the Web.

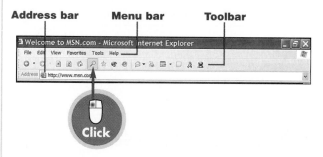

3 Search the Web

Internet Explorer works with MSN's *search engine*, a database containing the text of millions of Web pages. You use a search engine to find Web pages that contain text such as a phrase or company name. Type the text you want to look for and click the **Search** button.

4 View Search Results

The results of your search are presented as a list of Web-page titles and descriptions on the right side of the window. Each of these results is a *hyperlink*—text or a graphic you can click to load a new page in your browser. Click one of these hyperlinks to open the linked page.

5 Load a Web Page

The Web page associated with the hyperlink is loaded in the window to the right of the search-results list. Click the **Search** button along the top of the Internet Explorer window to close the search pane so that the Web page you've loaded can take up the entire window.

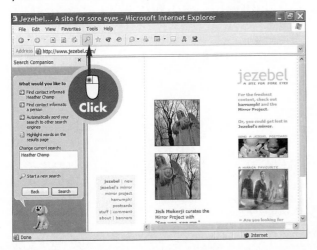

6 View a Page's Address

Every Web page has a unique address called a *uniform resource locator* (or *URL*), which is displayed in the Address bar at the top of the Internet Explorer window. You can type URLs into the Address bar to load pages in the browser. For example, type `http://www.yahoo.com` in the **Address bar** and press **Enter** to visit the Yahoo! Web site.

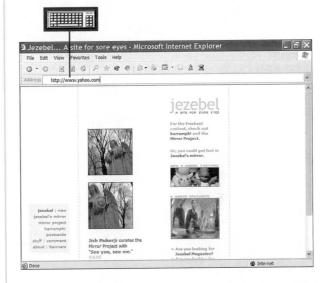

How to Hint

Returning to Your Home Page

The first page your Web browser displays when you open the program is its **home page**. Click the browser's **Home** button (in the toolbar at the top of the window) at any time to return to this page.

Visiting an Interesting Site

If you're curious about Heather Champ, the person I used MSN's search engine to find in this task, she's a talented Web designer and writer whose sites include Jezebel, Harrumph!, and the Mirror Project. To visit her personal Web site and see some of her work, type `http://www.jezebel.com` in Internet Explorer's **Address bar** and press **Enter**.

① How to Use a Web Site 294

② How to Visit a Web Site When You Know
Its Address 296

③ How to Revisit Your Favorite Web Pages 298

④ How to Load a Web Page for Faster Viewing 300

⑤ How to Pick a New Home Page for Your
Browser 302

⑥ How to Change Internet Explorer's Settings 304

⑦ How to Print a Web Page 306

⑧ How to Save a Web Page to Your Computer 308

⑨ How to Find a Site When You Don't Know Its
Address 310

⑩ How to See Pages You Have Recently Visited 312

⑪ How to Search for a Specific Topic on the Web . . . 314

⑫ How to Search Through Millions of Web Pages . . . 316

⑬ How to Find Software on the Web 318

⑭ How to Find a Company on the Web 320

⑮ How to Find a Person on the Web 322

⑯ How to Find a Job on the Web 324

⑰ How to Find Your Ancestors on the Web 326

15

Browsing the World Wide Web

Although the Internet dates back to 1969, for most of its existence the network had been used primarily by scholars, students, and the U.S. military.

This changed with the popularization of a new Internet information service: the World Wide Web. The Web, which was invented by Tim Berners-Lee of the European Laboratory for Particle Physics in 1989, was designed to be an easy way to publish and share information. It also became the simplest way for millions of people to receive information over the Internet.

The World Wide Web uses *hypertext*—a way of publishing information so that documents can be linked to relevant places in other documents. Everything that's on the Web can be connected together, creating the largest database of knowledge in human history.

A *Web browser* such as Internet Explorer enables you to visit sites on the Web.

How to Use a Web Site

The easiest way to navigate the World Wide Web is to use *hyperlinks*—text or images on a Web page that can be clicked to load another document in your browser. Hyperlinks can connect to anything on the Web, such as pages, graphics files, and programs you can download. Although Internet Explorer 6 has a toolbar with useful buttons that you can use as you're visiting Web pages, you'll likely use hyperlinks most often to move from one Web page to another.

❶ Load Internet Explorer

To run Internet Explorer, click the **Start** button and choose **Internet**. When started, the first Web page that Internet Explorer loads is its *home page*—often a page on MSN or one hosted by your computer's manufacturer. Click the **Home** button in Internet Explorer to go to your browser's home page.

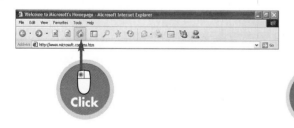

❷ Click a Hyperlink

Web pages often contain hyperlinks that make it easy to visit other pages. Your mouse pointer changes to a hand when it's over a hyperlink. Click a hyperlink to load the Web page or other document associated with the link.

❸ Go Back to the Last Page

If you have viewed multiple Web pages, you can click the **Back** button on the Internet Explorer toolbar to return to the previous page that was displayed in your browser.

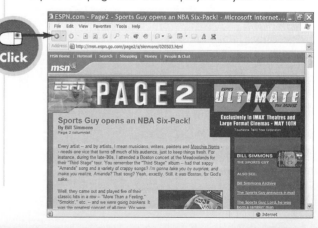

4 Move Forward Again

After you have clicked the Back button, you can click the **Forward** button on the toolbar to see the page you displayed before clicking **Back**. Click the **Back** and **Forward** buttons to cycle through all the pages you've looked at while Internet Explorer has been running.

5 Reload the Current Page

Click the **Refresh** button on the toolbar to reload the current page. When Web pages are updated frequently, you can click **Refresh** to make sure that you are viewing the most current version of a page. This is especially useful on news and financial sites, which are often updated several times an hour.

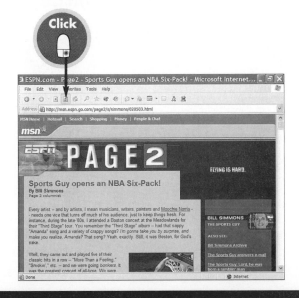

6 Stop Loading a Page

If you decide not to wait for a Web page to finish loading, click the **Stop** button. Your Web browser displays everything that was loaded up to that point, as if it were the entire document.

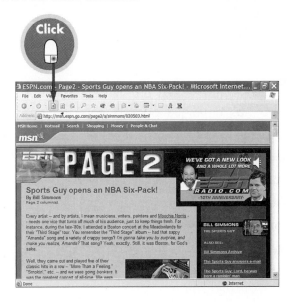

How to Hint

Opening Pages in a New Window

You can instruct Internet Explorer to open Web pages in a new window, leaving the current page on display. To do so, hold the **Shift** key down and click a hyperlink to open the linked page in a new window.

Closing a Pop-Up Window

Some Web sites open additional pages in their own browser windows. These are called *pop-ups* because they pop up on the screen in front of other pages, usually to display advertising.

Often, pop-up windows do not include a title bar, so you can't close them by clicking the **X** button found on that bar. To close one, press **Ctrl+W** on your keyboard.

② How to Visit a Web Site When You Know Its Address

Every page you can view on the World Wide Web has a unique address called a *uniform resource locator* (*URL*). Internet Explorer 6's **Address bar** normally shows the URL of the document currently being displayed (some Web sites, however, display their main URLs even if you load a different page on the site). If you know a Web page's URL, you can view it without using hyperlinks.

① Enter a URL

To go directly to a Web page, type its URL in the **Address bar** and press **Enter**. Internet Explorer attempts to load the document associated with that URL, if one exists. Try this: type `http://www.yahoo.com` in the **Address bar** and press **Enter**.

② Use a Shortcut

Internet Explorer can find many popular Web sites even if you only know a site's name or its subject matter. To see this feature in action, type `Excel` in the **Address bar** and press **Enter**. The browser's Autosearch feature loads Microsoft's official Excel site, the best match for the topic keyword *Excel*.

③ Find the Best Sites

If Autosearch cannot match a URL, Internet Explorer loads a Web page on the MSN Web site that lists popular sites matching the topic. Use the scrollbar to view the list of sites and click a hyperlink to visit that site. Here you see the results of a search for the word `Journalism`.

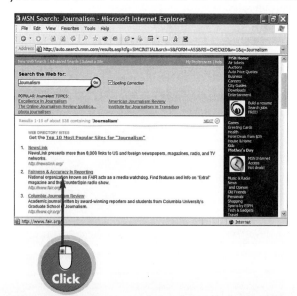

4 Select an Address Again

Click the arrow next to the **Address bar** to see a list of entries you have recently typed into the bar, including URLs and Autosearch shortcuts. Click an item in the list to load that page again.

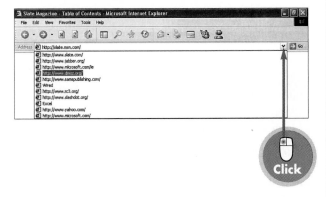

5 Remove Address Bar Requests

Internet Explorer automatically deletes past **Address bar** requests after a designated number of days. You also can delete all the entries manually. Open the **Tools** menu and choose **Internet Options**. The **Internet Options** dialog box opens.

6 Clear the History Folder

Internet Explorer saves all **Address bar** requests you make in a **History** folder. Click the **Clear History** button in the **Internet Options** dialog box to delete all the entries from the **History** folder *and* from the **Address bar** drop-down list.

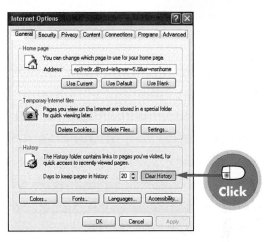

How to Hint

Displaying the Address Bar

If the **Address bar** is not visible, choose **View, Toolbars, Address Bar**. The Internet Explorer toolbar expands to show an **Address** combo box.

How to Revisit Your Favorite Web Pages

One of the biggest timesavers Internet Explorer 6 provides is the **Favorites** list, which can be used to hold shortcuts to Web pages you visit frequently. (In contrast, the **History** list simply tracks the last sites you've visited, whether you liked them or not.) Internet Explorer comes with a default list of favorites when it is installed, which may have been customized by your computer manufacturer. You can easily edit the **Favorites** list by adding your own shortcuts and removing any you don't want.

1 Visit Your Favorite Sites

In Internet Explorer, click the **Favorites** button to open the **Favorites** list along the left side of the browser window. The list is organized like a file folder, and it can contain both Internet shortcuts and subfolders. (Note that you don't have to be connected to the Internet to edit your list of favorites.)

2 Select an Internet Shortcut

To load a Web page from the **Favorites** list, click its Internet shortcut (the entries in the **Favorites** list are really just links to Web pages). If you are not connected to the Internet, a dialog box opens that enables you to establish an Internet connection.

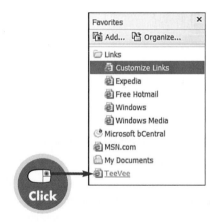

3 Add the Current Site to the List

If you'd like to add the currently displayed Web document to your **Favorites** list, click the **Add** button. The **Add Favorite** dialog box opens.

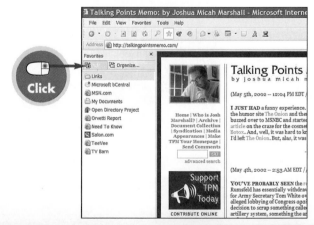

4 Save Your New Favorite

The **Add Favorite** dialog box displays a name for the site in the **Name** text box. You can use this name or change it—the name will appear in your **Favorites** list. Click **OK** to continue.

5 Delete a Site from the List

You might want to delete entries from your **Favorites** list if your interests change or if the link to the site breaks. To remove a shortcut from the **Favorites** list, right-click the entry and select **Delete** from the shortcut menu that appears.

6 Move a Site to a New Folder

You can move shortcuts to different folders in the **Favorites** list. You might want to do this to group your favorites in a more logical manner. Drag the shortcut from its present location to a new folder; release the mouse button to make the change.

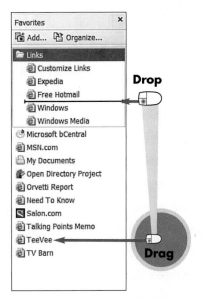

How to Hint

Renaming an Internet Shortcut

You can change the name of any shortcut in your **Favorites** list. To do so, right-click the shortcut, select the **Rename** command from the shortcut menu, type the new name, and press **Enter**.

Adding New Favorites Quickly

You can add favorites in Internet Explorer even if the **Favorites** list is not visible. With the Web page you want to add displayed in the browser, open the **Favorites** menu and choose the **Add to Favorites** command to open the **Add Favorite** dialog box described in step 4. The **Favorites** menu also contains all the shortcuts in your **Favorites** list, so you can access your favorite Web pages without devoting a portion of the screen to the **Favorites** list pane.

How to Load a Web Page for Faster Viewing

Internet Explorer 6 can speed up your use of the World Wide Web by downloading your favorite sites ahead of time—especially if you use a dial-up connection. These sites can then be viewed while you're *offline*—that is, disconnected from the Internet. Because the files have already been downloaded to your computer, they load more quickly into your browser. You can set up a Web page for offline viewing as you're adding it to your **Favorites** list. You view the page by clicking its link in the list.

2 Use the Offline Wizard

Click the **Customize** button. The **Offline Favorite Wizard** opens with an explanation of what the wizard does. Click **Next** to continue.

1 Select Offline Browsing

To select a page for offline browsing, you must first add it to your **Favorites** list. With the page open in your browser, open the **Favorites** menu and choose **Add to Favorites**. In the **Add Favorite** dialog box that appears, choose the folder in which you want to store your new favorite and select the **Make available offline** option. Don't click the **OK** button yet.

3 Save Linked Pages

You can retrieve pages that are linked to your new favorite, even if they're not part of the same Web site. To save linked pages, click the **Yes** radio button.

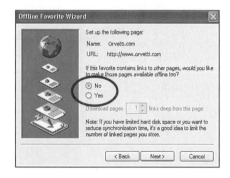

④ Choose How Much to Retrieve

If you clicked **Yes** in step 3, use the **Download pages** text box to specify how many links Internet Explorer should follow as it retrieves documents. Higher values save more pages for offline browsing, but they also take more time and disk space—3 is probably as high as you need. Click the **Next** button to continue.

⑤ Choose When to Retrieve Pages

You can retrieve a favorite for offline viewing in two ways: manually or at a scheduled time each day. For the latter approach, click the **I would like to create a new schedule** radio button. Then, click the **Next** button to continue.

⑥ Set Up a Schedule

Choose the time and days on which pages should be retrieved. There's also an option to connect to the Internet automatically at the scheduled time, in case you're not already connected. Click the **Next** button, answer the wizard's remaining questions, and click the **Finish** button to add this new shortcut to the Favorites list. Click **OK** to close the **Add Favorite** dialog box.

⑦ Download Offline Pages Manually

To immediately retrieve all pages set up for offline browsing without waiting for a scheduled time, open the **Tools** menu and choose the **Synchronize** command. To view a page after it has been retrieved, click its link in your **Favorites** list.

How to Pick a New Home Page for Your Browser

A term you'll see often on the World Wide Web is *home page*—the main page of a Web site. There's another kind of home page: the one loaded by a Web browser when it first starts. Internet Explorer 6 includes a **Home** button on its main toolbar, which you can click to quickly return to the browser's home page. The browser's default home page is usually MSN, although some computer manufacturers change this setting. You may, however, prefer to use a home page of your own choosing.

① Set Up a New Home Page

Your Internet Explorer home page can be any page on the World Wide Web or even a page stored on your own system. When you have found a page you want to use as the browser's home page, load it into your browser.

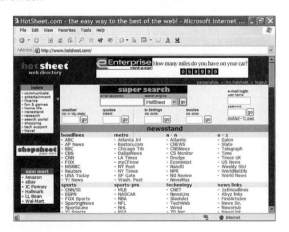

② Adjust Your Browser Settings

With your prospective home page loaded, open the **Tools** menu and choose **Internet Options**. The **Internet Options** dialog box opens. (You were introduced to this dialog box in Task 2, "How to Visit a Site When You Know Its Address," when you cleared the **History** folder.)

③ Display the General Settings

The **Internet Options** dialog box has seven tabs that display different settings you can adjust. If the **General** tab is hidden behind another tab, click the **General** tab to bring it to the front.

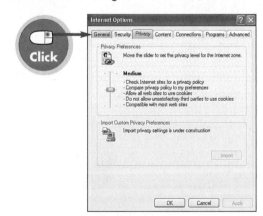

Change Your Home Page

4 The Address text box identifies your browser's home page. Click the **Use Current** button to change your browser's home page to the page currently displayed in the browser. If you decide to restore Internet Explorer's original home page, click the **Use Default** button. To save any changes you've made and close the dialog box, click the **OK** button.

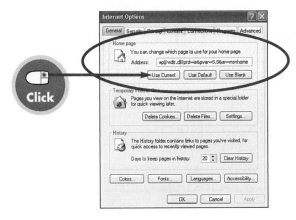

5 Load Your Home Page

Click the **Home** button in the browser's toolbar to return to your browser's home page at any time. When the home page loads in the browser, it will be the page you specified in step 4.

How to Hint

Using a Blank Home Page

You can make your Internet Explorer home page an empty one that loads faster than the other alternatives. To set this up, choose **Tools**, **Internet Options**; click the **General** tab in the **Internet Options** dialog box; and then click the **Use Blank** button. Click **OK** to exit the dialog box.

Using a Page Stored on Your Computer

Any page that Internet Explorer can display is suitable for use as the browser's home page. To open a Web page stored on your computer, choose **File**, **Open**; in the **Open** dialog box, click the **Browse** button. Browse to find any document on your system and click **OK** to open that document in the browser. The document then can be set as your home page using steps 2–5 of this task.

Choosing a Useful Home Page

The MSN homepage contains interesting content from Microsoft Web sites but doesn't offer much from other publishers. HotSheet.com, the site shown in this task, contains links to more than 150 sites in categories such as news, finance, travel, shopping, and tech support. To visit the site, type **http://www. hotsheet.com** in the **Address bar** and press **Enter**.

How to Change Internet Explorer's Settings

While using Internet Explorer 6, you can customize the way the browser looks, displays information, and operates. You've already used some of the software's customization features to set up a new home page and clear out past Address bar requests. There are more than 100 other settings you can adjust with the **Internet Options** dialog box, which is accessible from the **Tools** menu.

❶ Configure Your Browser

You can change Internet Explorer's settings whether you're online or offline. To get started, open the **Tools** menu and choose the **Internet Options** command. The **Internet Options** dialog box opens.

❷ Set Your Internet Options

To see groups of related settings, click the tabs along the top edge of the **Internet Options** dialog box. For example, click the **General** tab to display some of the browser's main settings.

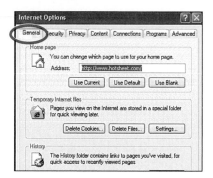

❸ Clean Out Temporary Files

As you use Internet Explorer, Web pages you view are saved along with graphics and other files included on these pages. Your browser eventually deletes these files, but you can do so immediately to make room on your hard disk; simply click the **Delete Files** button in the **General** tab. You'll be asked to confirm by clicking **OK** before any files are deleted.

4 Resize the Temporary Folder

Internet Explorer deletes temporary files when the folder they are stored in exceeds a maximum size. To increase this maximum (which enables more to be stored in your **History** folder), click the **Settings** button on the **General** tab to open the **Settings** dialog box. Drag the **Amount of disk space to use** slider, releasing it where you want the new maximum to be. Click **OK**.

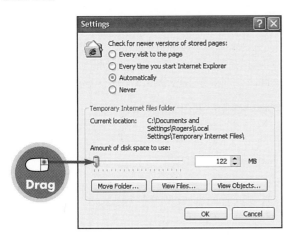

5 Change the Default Font

You can make many Web pages more readable by choosing different fonts for the text they display. Click the **Fonts** button on the **General** tab to open the **Fonts** dialog box. Select a default font for Web pages and a default font for plain text. Click **OK** to save your changes.

6 Close the Dialog Box

When you have finished changing the settings in the **Internet Options** dialog box, click **OK** to save your settings and close the dialog box. The next time you start your browser, all your new settings will be active.

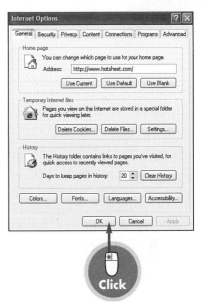

How to Hint

Making Your Font Selections Take Precedence

Normally, if a Web page is designed to use a specific font, that font is used for text instead of the one you specified for the browser in Step 5. You can change this functionality in the **Internet Options** dialog box: On the **General** tab, click the **Accessibility** button, and then select the **Ignore font styles specified on Web pages** option. This may make some pages look terrible, but it's useful if you want to make text larger or improve readability by using your own chosen font.

How to Print a Web Page

Internet Explorer 6, like many Windows programs, offers the capability to print documents. You can print the current Web page as it appears in the browser, print all the hyperlinks on the page, and even follow those hyperlinks and print every one of those pages at the same time. Web pages can be sent to a printer, sent out using a fax modem, and saved as a disk file optimized for printing.

① Choose the Print Command

To print the Web page that's currently displayed in the browser window, open the **File** menu and choose the **Print** command. The **Print** dialog box opens.

② Choose a Printer

You can send Web pages to any printer that has been installed on your system. To print the page, choose a printer from the **Select Printer** pane and click **Print**.

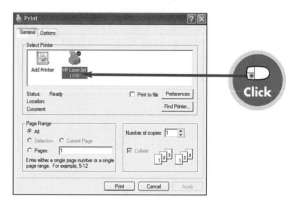

③ Customize How a Page Is Printed

You can make changes to how Internet Explorer 6 prints hyperlinks and *frames*—separate sections of a Web page that can have their own scrollbars and borders. To determine how these elements of a Web page will be printed, start by opening the **Print** dialog box and clicking the **Options** tab to bring it to the front.

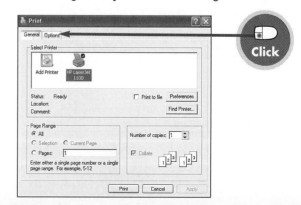

4 Print Associated Web Pages

Internet Explorer can look at all the hyperlinks on the current page and print the pages associated with those links, enabling you to print related pages on a Web site. Select the **Print all linked documents** option to print these linked pages.

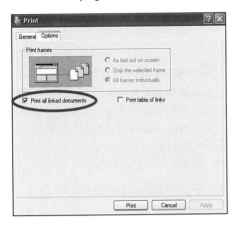

6 Print the Selected Frame

Click the **Print** button to print the Web page according to the options you have selected. A dialog box appears briefly as the page is sent to the printer. You should soon hear the printer working on the page.

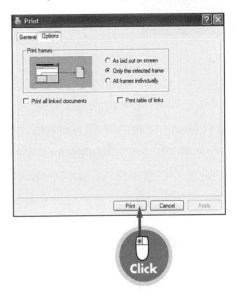

5 Print a Framed Web Page

Some World Wide Web sites divide the browser window into frames. You have three options when printing a page that uses frames: Print each frame individually, print the page as it looks in the browser, or print only the selected frame. To select a frame, click your mouse in that section of the Web page before printing the page and then select the **Only the selected frame** option.

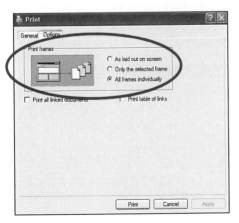

How to Hint

Printing News and Magazine Articles

When you print a Web page, you sometimes end up with a lot of stuff you don't need, such as large advertisements and a menu of other parts of the site. Some newspaper and magazine sites offer a different version of an article that's simplified for printing. Look for a **Print Page** link, **Printer-Friendly** link, or **Printer** icon at the top or bottom of the article. Two media sites that offer this feature are *Slate* at the address http://www.slate.com and the *International Herald Tribune* at the address http://www.iht.com.

How to Save a Web Page to Your Computer

One of the ways the World Wide Web is different from other media is in how quickly it changes. Sites are updated constantly, new sites appear, and old sites disappear. If you see a page on the Web you'd like to keep around for a while, no matter what happens to the company or individual hosting it, you can save it to your computer. Internet Explorer 6 can save the text of the page or save everything on a page in a single file, including the graphics and other content. You can later open the file in Internet Explorer, even if you are not connected to the Internet.

1 Save a Page

To save the Web page that's currently open in Internet Explorer, open the **File** menu and choose the **Save As** command. The **Save Web Page** dialog box opens.

2 Choose the Format

Use the **Save Web Page** dialog box to choose a folder where the page will be saved. Type a name for the file in the **File name** text field, click the arrow next to the **Save as type** list box, and then choose **Web Archive single file (*.mht)**.

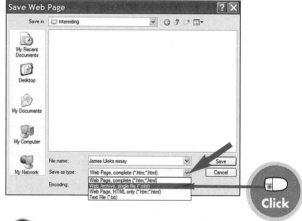

3 Store the Page

Click the **Save** button to save the page. If you chose the Web Archive format, the page and all its contents will be saved as a single file with the name you specified followed by **.mht**.

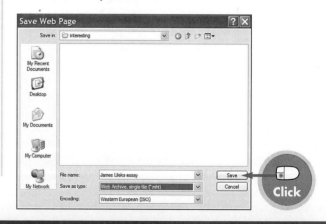

4 Open a Page

After you have saved a page, you can open it at any time with Internet Explorer, whether or not you are connected to the Internet. Open the **File** menu and choose the **Open** command. The **Open** dialog box opens.

6 Choose the File

Use the Microsoft Internet Explorer dialog box to find the page you saved. It will have the **.mht** extension if it was stored in Web Archive format. Choose the file and click **Open**. The **Open** dialog box reappears.

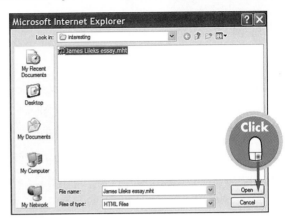

5 Find the Page

Click the **Browse** button in the **Open** dialog box. The Microsoft Internet Explorer dialog box opens.

7 Open the Page

Click the **OK** button. The page opens in Internet Explorer and can be used like any other page you view in the browser.

How to Find a Site When You Don't Know Its Address

Every document on the World Wide Web has a unique address called a *URL*, which is short for *uniform resource locator*. A site's address can take many forms, but most of the largest Web sites have similar-looking and simple URLs, such as `http://www.yahoo.com`, `http://www.microsoft.com`, `http://www.internic.net`, `http://www.slashdot.org`, `http://www.nasa.gov`, and `http://www.unt.edu`. By learning a few things about these addresses, you can make an educated guess about the addresses of some of the Web sites you're looking for. Subsequent tasks cover how to use search engines and directories to find a site.

1 Look for a Company's Address

The most popular ending used in a Web address is `.com`. If you know the name of a company or publication, you can try to find its Web site by typing `http://www.companyname.com` in the **Address bar**, where `companyname` is the name of the company. Press **Enter** to see whether the browser can find a site at that address. One example: Dell Computer Corporation's URL is `http://www.dell.com`.

2 Try a Shorter Address

Some sites with addresses ending in `.com` don't start with the `www.` prefix. You can also look for a company or publication's address by typing the company's name followed by `.com` in the **Address bar** and then pressing **Enter**. One example: `http://monster.com`.

3 Look for an Organization

Many Web addresses that end in `.org` are for not-for-profit organizations (although this is not a requirement). Look for an organization by typing `http://www.organizationname.org` in the **Address bar**, where `organizationname` is the name of the organization. Press **Enter** after typing the full address. One example is `http://www.unicef.org`.

④ Look for a Government Site

All Web addresses that end in **.gov** are affiliated with the United States government. One of the most popular is `http://www.whitehouse.gov`, the White House site. To look for a government agency or similar entity, type `http://www.groupname.gov` in the **Address bar** (where `groupname` is the name of the government entity), and press **Enter**.

⑤ Search for the Name

Internet Explorer 6 has an Autosearch feature that searches the World Wide Web for pages containing keywords you type in the **Address bar**. Type the name of the entity you're looking for in the **Address bar**. As you are typing, a text box appears below the **Address bar**, describing what you are looking for. Press **Enter** to begin the search.

How to Hint

Finding Universities and Colleges

Using another type of Web address can help you locate the sites of colleges, universities, and advanced research institutions. These institutions almost always have Web sites with URLs that end with **.edu**; in the **Address bar**, type `http://www.institutionname.edu` (where `institutionname` is the name of the institution), and press **Enter**. For example, `http://www.unt.edu` is the home page of the University of North Texas.

Shortening Web Addresses

The URL associated with a Web page is usually prefaced with **http://** (which indicates the protocol used to send the page to your browser). Another common prefix is **ftp://**. The current crop of browsers (including Internet Explorer 6) will add **http://** automatically if you forget to include **http://** or **ftp://** in a URL. For this reason, you can type a shorter version of a site's URL, such as `www.dell.com` instead of `http://www.dell.com`.

Getting Your Own Address

Anyone can buy an address on the Web; it isn't restricted to companies, schools, and other large organizations. You can use your personalized address, which is called a *domain name*, in email, on your own World Wide Web site, and with instant messaging.

To find out how to register and purchase a domain name, visit the InterNIC Web site: Type `http://www.internic.net` into your browser's Address bar and press **Enter**. The site's Registrar Directory lists dozens of companies that sell domains, usually for about $15 to $25 per year.

How to See Pages You Have Recently Visited

Internet Explorer 6 can keep track of the sites you've visited in recent days. This information is stored in the **History** list, which is presented in a manner similar to the browser's Favorites list. By default, Internet Explorer keeps track of all the sites visited in the past 20 days. If you're searching for something you have recently viewed, the place to start looking for it is your browser's **History** list.

① Open the History List

Click the **History** button in the browser's toolbar to open a window containing the **History** list.

② Open a Site's Hyperlinks

Each folder in the **History** list is devoted to a Web site you visited on a specific day or week. Open a folder by clicking it. You'll see Internet shortcuts for every page on that site you visited at that time.

③ Revisit a Web Site

To revisit a Web page, double-click its Internet shortcut in the **History** list. The page is loaded in a browser window.

4 · Search for a Shortcut

Looking through the **History** list by hand can be time consuming if you have visited a large number of Web sites. To search through the entire list, click the **Search** button in the bar above the **History** list.

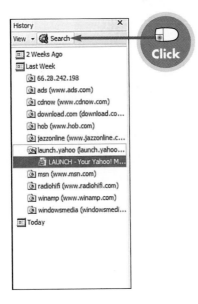

5 · Conduct the Search

Type the text you're looking for in the **Search for** box and click the **Search Now** button. All items in the **History** list that match the search text will be displayed.

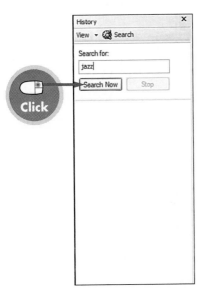

6 · Delete History Items

To remove a folder or shortcut from the **History** list, right-click the item and choose **Delete** from the pop-up menu. (You also can delete all shortcuts in the entire **History** list: Pull down the **Tools** menu, choose **Internet Options**, and click the **Clear History** button to delete them.)

7 · Rearrange History Items

Normally, items in the **History** list are organized by date. To arrange the list according to how often you visit pages, click the **View** button in the bar above the **History** list and choose the **By Most Visited** command.

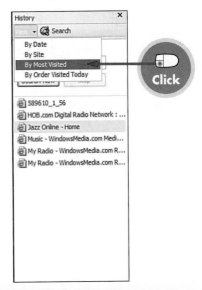

How to Search for a Specific Topic on the Web

There are several ways to search for sites related to a specific topic on the World Wide Web. Task 9, "How to Find a Site When You Don't Know Its Address," describes how to use Internet Explorer 6's **Autosearch** feature to search for sites by entering a topic in the browser's **Address bar**. Another way to search by topic is to use the World Wide Web directories published by Yahoo!, Excite, the Open Directory Project, and others.

① Visit a Directory

Most Web directories function in a similar manner. The Open Directory Project is a volunteer effort coordinated by AOL that organizes more than 3.4 million sites into categories. To visit the site, type `http://www.dmoz.org` into Internet Explorer's **Address bar** and press **Enter**.

② Search for a Topic

Type the topic you're looking for in the site's search box and click the **Search** button.

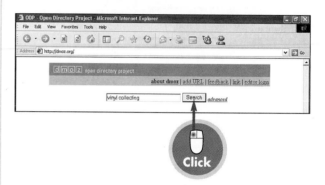

③ View the Results

Web directories are organized into categories—pages that contain Web sites and links to subcategories. Categories that match your topic are listed first in the search-results page and are usually the best place to find what you're looking for. To view a category, click its hyperlink in the results page.

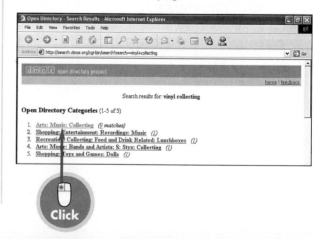

4 Scan a Category

Category pages display all subcategories and Web sites that match a given topic. Click a hyperlink to visit the associated site.

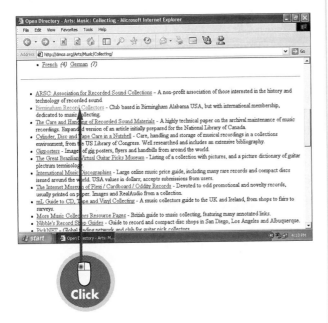

6 Begin a New Search

To begin a new search on the Open Directory Project home page, click the **dmoz** graphic ("DMoz" is short for "Directory Mozilla," an early name for the project).

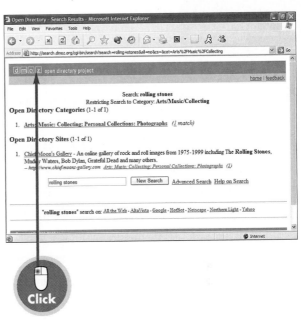

5 Search Within a Category

When you're viewing a page, you can conduct a new search that is confined to the portion of the directory related to the category. Type a topic in the search box, click the down-arrow button to the right of the drop-down menu, and select the **only in category** option, where **category** is the name of the category you're searching in; then click the **Search** button.

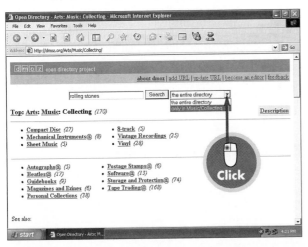

How to Hint

Using Other Web Directories

Each Web directory includes a different selection of Web sites, so you might want to try several directories in your search. Use the following URLs to visit some of the other popular services:

- **Yahoo!**: http://www.yahoo.com
- **Google Directory**:
  http://directory.google.com
- **Excite**: http://www.excite.com

Broadening Your Search

In the Open Directory Project and other directories, every category name includes hyperlinks to broader categories with which it is associated. For example, the **Top:Arts:Music:Collecting** category is a sub-category of the more general **Top:Arts:Music** category. Use these links to make your search *less* specific.

How to Search Through Millions of Web Pages

The World Wide Web grows at a speed much faster than any human-compiled directory can possibly match. To find sites the directories overlook, you can search through millions of machine-compiled pages by visiting a *search engine*. Search engines are massive databases containing the text of documents available on the Web. These engines continuously traverse links on the World Wide Web, adding new documents and deleting those that have been taken offline. Some of the most popular search engines are AltaVista, HotBot, Northern Light, and Google.

② Conduct a Search

To search Google, type a keyword, question, sentence, or phrase describing what you're looking for into the search box. Be as specific as possible. Click the **Google Search** button to begin looking.

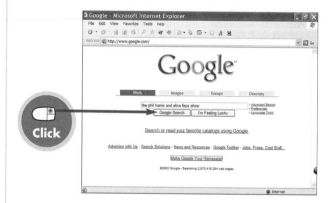

③ View the Search Results

Search engines rank the best-matching pages first. The engine ignores all common words you use (such as *the* or *and*) and ranks pages according to the number of other search words that were found. You can use the **Next** hyperlink at the bottom of a page to view more results. Click a page's title to visit that page.

① Visit a Search Engine

Currently, the most popular search engine is Google. To visit this engine, type `http://www.google.com` into the **Address bar** and press **Enter**.

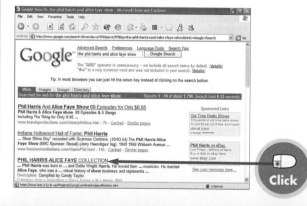

4 Conduct an Advanced Search

Google puts its advanced search features on a separate page. Click the **Advanced Search** hyperlink on the site's home page to conduct more complex searches.

5 Search for a Specific Phrase

To look for a specific phrase, type it in the **exact phrase** box and then click the **Google Search** button. The search results include only those pages that contain this exact phrase.

6 Search for Text in a Page Title

A Web page's title often contains a succinct description of its contents. To search through page titles, in the **exact phrase** box type the text you're looking for and then choose **in the title of the page** from the **Occurrences** drop-down list. Click the **Google Search** button to view results.

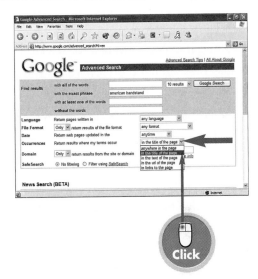

How to Hint

Visiting Other Search Engines

Even the best search engines can't keep up with how fast the World Wide Web is growing. For this reason, you might need to use more than one search engine to find Web pages with the information you need. Here are a few other search engines you can use:

- **HotBot**: http://hotbot.lycos.com
- **Google**: http://www.google.com
- **Northern Light**: http://www.northernlight.com
- **MetaCrawler**: http://www.metacrawler.com
- **WebCrawler**: http://www.webcrawler.com
- **Lycos**: www.lycos.com

How to Find Software on the Web

As you might expect, many World Wide Web users do their computer-software shopping online. You can use the Web to purchase software, receive and install demo versions of software, and choose from thousands of useful free computer programs. One site that offers each of these services is Download.com. The name comes from the term *download*, which means to transmit a file from another network to your system.

❷ Search for Software

Programs you can try before you buy are called *shareware*, and Download.com offers thousands of shareware items you can download. To search for a program, type its name in the **Search** box, choose **In Downloads** from the drop-down list, and click the **Go!** button.

❸ Explore Search Results

Download.com lists all programs that match the name you entered. To find out more about a specific program, click its hyperlink.

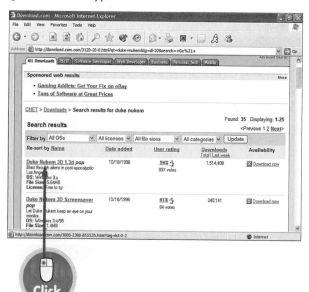

❶ Visit the Site

To get started, type http://www.download.com in Internet Explorer 6's **Address bar** and press **Enter**. The Download.com home page opens in your browser window.

4 Download a Program

If you decide that you want to download the program whose description you have been reading, click the **Download Now** hyperlink. The **File Download** dialog box opens.

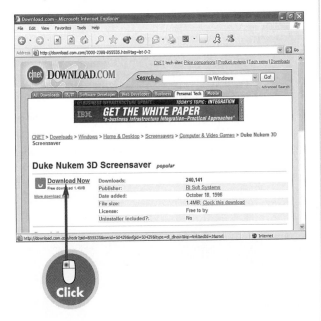

5 Choose a Download Method

Click the **Save** button to save the program in a folder on your system or the **Open** button to install the program immediately. If you save a program to a folder on your system, wait for the download to finish, then open the folder and double-click the program's icon to install it. After installation, use the **Start** menu to find and run the program.

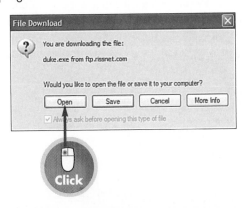

6 Look for Retail Software

To find commercial software—such as the software sold at computer superstores—click the **Price comparisons** hyperlink on the Download.com menu at the top of the home page.

7 Begin a Search

Type the name of the software in which you're interested in the **Find Pricing and Availability** box, choose **In Shopping** from the drop-down list, and click the **Go!** button. Download.com will compare prices on that commercial-software product at several different online software stores, displaying the results in tabular form on a new Web page.

How to Find a Company on the Web

Most companies that do business on a national or international scale have a World Wide Web site. Thousands of smaller local companies also are online, making the Web a great place to look up companies, buy their products, and seek customer support. You can find a company using the techniques introduced in Task 9, "How to Find a Site When You Don't Know Its Address," earlier in this part. There are, however, a few ways to speed up your search, as discussed here.

1 Use Autosearch

As you learned in Task 9, Internet Explorer 6's **Autosearch** feature can direct you to many sites. Type the company's name in the **Address bar** and press **Enter**.

2 Find the Company Site

If Autosearch recognizes the company name, its home page opens. Otherwise, a page opens on MSN containing a list of possible sites that match the text you typed. Click a hyperlink to load that site.

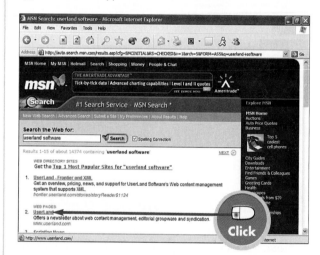

3 Search Yahoo!

Another good source for company sites is Yahoo!. Type http://www.yahoo.com in the browser's **Address bar** and press **Enter**. When the home page opens, type the name of the company you are looking for in the search box and click the **Search** button.

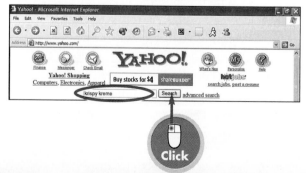

④ View Yahoo! Results

Yahoo! lists all categories and Web sites that match the name you typed, with the best matches displayed first. Click a hyperlink to visit the associated Web site.

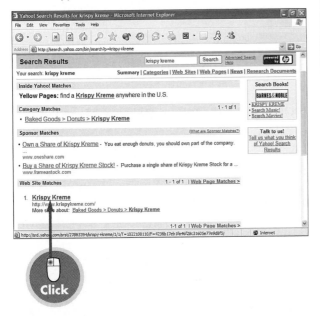

⑤ Use Google

The Google search engine is useful for company searches because of the unusual way it ranks Web sites. Type **http://www.google.com** in the **Address bar** and press **Enter** to go to the Google home page. When you're there, type the company name in the search box and click the **Google Search** button.

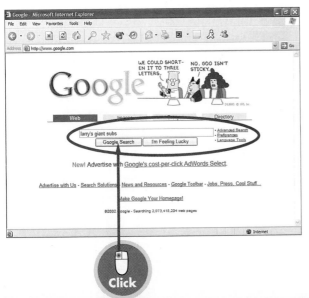

⑥ Visit a Site

When you use Google to search for a company, the first item listed on the search-results page is often a hyperlink to the company's official Web site. Click the link to visit that site.

How to Hint

Getting Lucky on a Google Search

Because Google is so good at finding the best-matching Web sites in a search, it offers a feature to automatically look for the best possible match and load it. To use this feature, type a company's name in the search box and click the **I'm Feeling Lucky** button.

Using a Business Search Engine

Another useful resource when looking for a company is Business.com, a directory, search engine, and news site for employers and employment-related information. To visit the site, type the URL **http://www.business.com** in your browser's **Address bar** and press **Enter**.

How to Find a Person on the Web

You can search for people just as you do any other subject on the World Wide Web: using Web directories such as Yahoo! and search engines such as AltaVista and Google. A more focused search is available using directories such as Yahoo! People Search, a mailing address and email directory. People Search scans a collection of public databases for matching names and can be narrowed to specific states or provinces. People Search also links to other public directories, such as 1800USSearch.com.

❶ Visit Yahoo!

Most of the special features on Yahoo! have a short, easy-to-remember address. To visit Yahoo! People Search, type **http://people.yahoo.com** in your browser's **Address bar** and press **Enter**.

❷ Search for a Phone Number

To search the entire database for someone's phone number, type the person's first and last names in the **Telephone Search** boxes and then click the **Search** button. You can omit the first name to see all matches for a surname. (Note that only publicly accessible phone numbers are returned by this search; private numbers are not returned.)

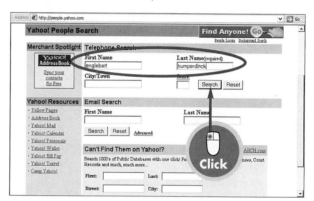

❸ Narrow Your Search

If you want to narrow your search to a single state, type the state's postal abbreviation in the **State** box. Click **Search** to look for a match.

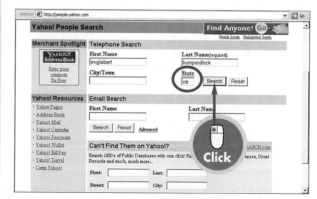

4 Search for an Email Address

To look for someone's email address, type the person's first and last names in the **Email Search** boxes and then click the adjacent **Search** button. Some of the addresses that are found are likely to be outdated, especially if the person has changed email addresses frequently.

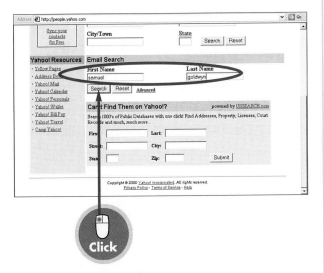

6 Fill Out the Search Form

Most fields in the **Advanced Search** page can be used to narrow a search. You can specify the state or province, country, former email address, and organization type. Enable the **SmartNames** check box to treat related first names (such as *Bill*, *Billy*, and *William*) as the same name. Click the **Search** button when you're ready to search.

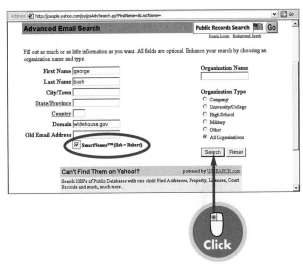

5 Make an Advanced Email Search

Yahoo! People Search offers even more options for email searches. If necessary, click the **Back** button in your browser's toolbar to return to the original search page. Then click the **Advanced** hyperlink to load the more sophisticated search page.

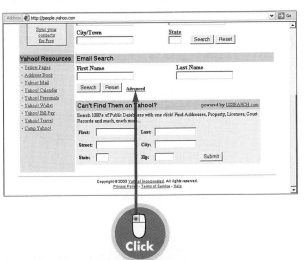

Finding Email Addresses on Usenet

How to Hint

Usenet (a collection of discussion forums on more than 20,000 topics) attracts thousands of Internet users who post messages that contain their email addresses. You can search Google Groups, an archive of Usenet messages, for a specific person. To visit the database, type **http://groups.google.com** into your browser's **Address bar** and press **Enter**.

How to Find a Job on the Web

The World Wide Web has hundreds of different resources for job seekers. One of the most popular is CareerBuilder, a database of help-wanted classified ads compiled from hundreds of newspapers, Web sites, and employment services. CareerBuilder, formerly known as CareerPath.com, also offers a place to post your résumé, save job searches you conduct frequently, and receive help-wanted ads by email.

❶ Visit the Site

Visit Career Builder by typing `http://www.headhunter.net` in your browser's **Address bar** and pressing **Enter**. When the site loads, click the **Advanced Job Search!** link. A job-search page opens.

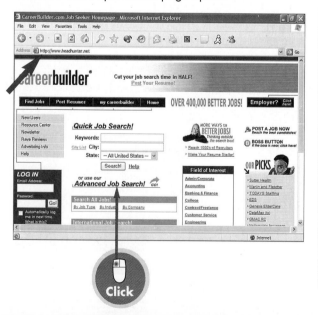

❷ Narrow Your Job Search

If you are looking for specific words in job postings, type them in the **Keywords** text box. Choose the type of search you want to conduct in the **Using** drop-down list.

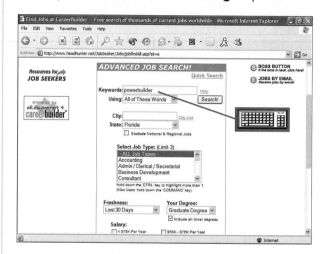

❸ Select an Industry

You can narrow your search to a specific industry, or you can search all industry categories. From the **Select Job Type** list box, select the industry you're interested in.

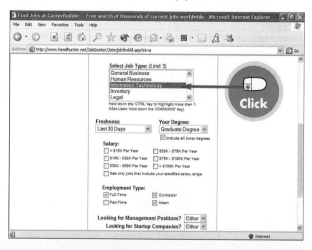

④ Indicate Your Degree

You can exclude postings based on your level of education. Select it in the **Degree** drop-down list and enable the **Include all lower degrees** check box if you want to include jobs looking for other levels of education.

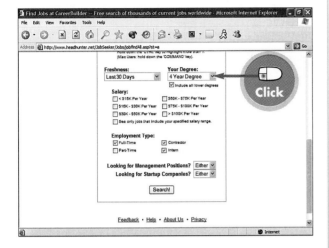

⑤ Indicate Your Desired Salary

You can exclude postings that don't meet your minimum-salary requirements by enabling one of the salary check boxes in the **Salary** section.

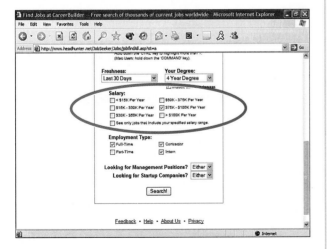

⑥ Search for a Job

After choosing one of the **Employment Type** check boxes, click **Search!**.

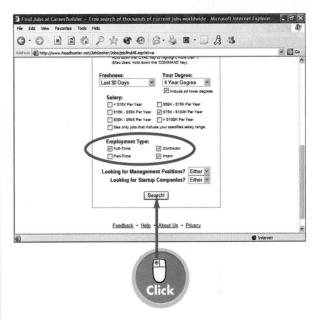

⑦ Read a Listing

CareerBuilder displays all the help-wanted ads matching your criteria. To read a job listing, click its entry in the **Title** column. If you're interested in a job, you can apply for it on the site.

How to Find Your Ancestors on the Web

The World Wide Web has become a boon for people conducting genealogy research. Before the Web, genealogy research took place mostly through visits to libraries and cemeteries or personal contact with distant relatives. Today, on the RootsWeb site, genealogists can pore over databases containing 200 million ancestor names, view the work of more than 225,000 other genealogists, and exchange information on thousands of mailing lists and message boards. Many of these services are free, although you also can buy some information from a related site, Ancestry.com.

➋ Look for a Name

In the **Search RootsWeb.com** section, type the name of an ancestor in the **First Name** and **Last Name** boxes and click the **Search** button.

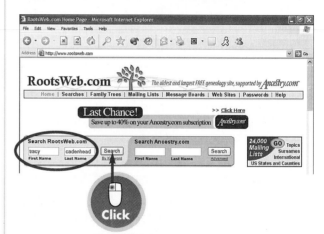

➌ Choose a Database

RootsWeb searches 43 databases for your ancestor's name and displays a list of places where it was found. To view a database, click its name.

➊ Visit the Site

Visit RootsWeb: Type `http://www.rootsweb.com` in your browser's **Address bar** and press **Enter**.

4 Exit the Database

When you're finished viewing the data, click your browser's **Back** button to return to the list of databases.

6 View a Page

The pages that come up in a search are published by RootsWeb members. To view a page, click its title.

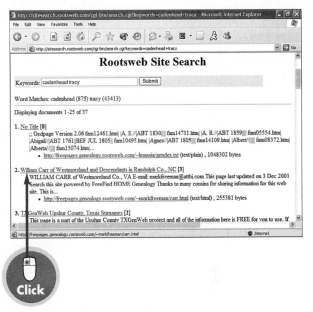

5 Search the Site

One of the databases you can search is the RootsWeb site, which contains pages submitted by thousands of genealogists. To see this data, click the **Web Site Search** link.

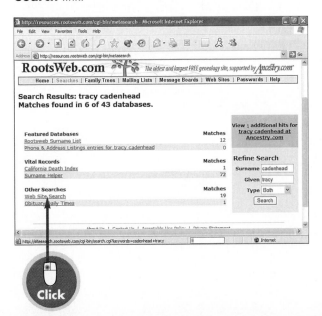

7 Try Ancestry.com

There may be records matching your ancestor's name on Ancestry.com, which charges for access. To see what's available before making a purchase, click the **Ancestry.com** link.

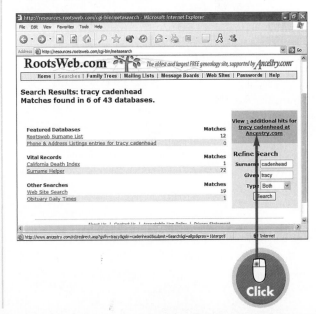

Task

1 How to Choose a Security Setting 330

2 How to Customize Your Security Setting 332

3 How to Block Objectionable Content from
   Being Viewed 334

4 How to Use Security Certificates 336

5 How to Disable Cookies in a Web Browser 338

6 How to Make Your Internet Connection
   More Secure 340

7 How to Install Antivirus Software 342

8 How to Check Your Computer for Viruses 346

16

Protecting Yourself on the Web

Part of the World Wide Web's appeal is its wide-open nature. Anyone can put a site on the Web and reach people all over the world.

This has its advantages—free speech is exercised on the Internet with great success. This also has its disadvantages—content that some people find objectionable is available in great quantity.

Another disadvantage of the Internet is that Web pages can contain interactive programs that can sometimes expose security holes that put your own computer at risk.

When you run a program in a Web browser, the program runs on *your* computer just like any other software you use. For this reason, browsers such as Internet Explorer 6 have security settings that restrict the ways a page can interact with your system.

Another way to reduce your risk is to install an antivirus program such as Norton AntiVirus 2002 and use it to scan all files you receive.

How to Choose a Security Setting

Although security risks are extremely small on the World Wide Web, you might encounter sites that try to damage files on your computer or steal confidential data. Internet Explorer 6's security settings can restrict or disable browser features that are most susceptible to abuse, such as JavaScript, Active Scripting, Java, and cookies. Restricting these features can limit your enjoyment of the Web because many popular sites rely on them, but you might feel it's a fair trade-off for a more secure computer system.

➊ Configure Your Browser

Pull down the Internet Explorer **Tools** menu and select the **Internet Options** command. The **Internet Options** dialog box opens.

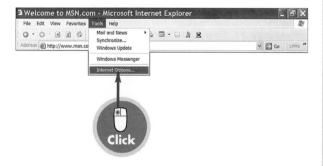

➋ View Security Settings

Click the **Security** tab to view your current security settings and to make changes to those settings.

➌ Set Your Internet Security

Internet Explorer enables different levels of security for sites on the Internet as well as sites on a local *intranet*—a private network of documents shared by people in a company, school, or organization. To change your Internet settings, click the **Internet** icon from the **Select a Web content zone to specify its security settings** list box.

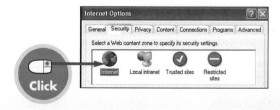

④ Pick a Security Level

There are four basic security levels: **High**, **Medium**, **Medium-Low**, and **Low**. These levels determine the kind of content Internet Explorer will load and the tasks it will restrict. To choose a security level, click the **Default Level** button and drag the slider toward the **High**, **Medium**, or **Low** setting, and release it. (The How-To Hints box at the end of this task provides some guidelines for setting a security level.)

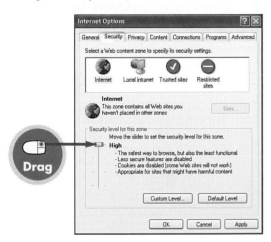

⑤ Oppose a Recommendation

Microsoft recommends that you use **High** or **Medium** security level while browsing the Internet. If you choose lower security level, a dialog box appears, asking you to confirm this choice. Click **Yes** if you want to disregard Microsoft's recommendation and choose a lower security level.

⑥ Restore the Default Level

If you want to restore your browser security to the level recommended by Microsoft, click the **Default Level** button.

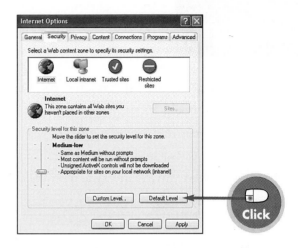

Deciding on a Security Level

Unless you're a Web-site developer, you probably won't have much to go on when choosing a security level. To help guide your decision, we suggest you try **High** security first. Afterward, as you're visiting Web sites, your browser and some sites will often tell you what you're missing out on because of your chosen security level. You can repeat the steps in this task to select a slightly lower security level if you want to access some of the features you've been missing.

How to Customize Your Security Setting

For most people, Internet Explorer 6's basic security levels should be sufficient. If you want more control over your browser's security, however, you can customize each of its security settings. This enables you to turn on and off specific features such as cookies, Java, JavaScript, file downloading, and some browser security warnings. Doing this can increase security risks, so you should be cautious about making drastic changes.

① Change Your Settings

Pull down the **Tools** menu and select the **Internet Options** command to open the **Internet Options** dialog box and view your Internet Explorer settings.

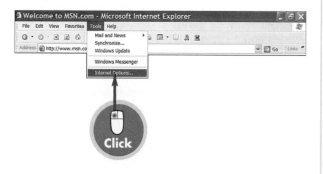

② Choose a Custom Level

Click to see your current security settings. To change how your browser handles specific security issues, click the **Custom Level** button.

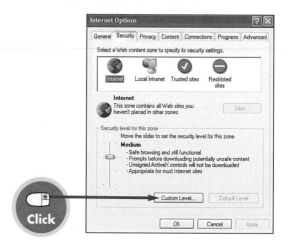

③ Set Up a Custom Level

By default, custom settings are identical to those specified by the **Medium** security level. To make them identical to a different level, click the down arrow next to the **Reset to** box and select the level you want to use as a starting point.

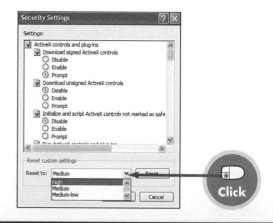

④ Reset All Settings

Click the **Reset** button to make all the custom settings the same as the level shown in the **Reset to** box.

⑥ Undo Customization

To remove a custom security level and undo all the changes you have made since opening the **Internet Options** dialog box, return to the **Security** tab of the **Internet Options** dialog box and click the **Default Level** button.

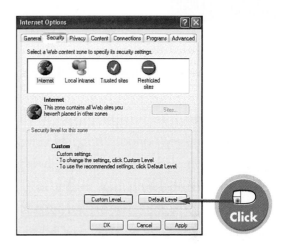

⑤ Customize Your Settings

Scroll through the **Settings** list box to see the various settings you can affect. To change a specific setting, click the appropriate radio button. Click **Disable** to turn off a feature, **Enable** to turn on a feature, and **Prompt** if you want the browser to ask whether a feature should be used each time it is encountered on a Web page. Click **OK** to save all your changes.

Turning Off Form Warnings

By default, Internet Explorer warns you before it sends data you've entered on a form that's located on an unencrypted Web server. This feature keeps you from sending private information (such as your credit-card number) without *encryption*—a way to encode data so that it remains confidential. This warning is cumbersome if you're one of those people who never reveals personal data on the Web. To turn off this warning, find the **Submit nonencrypted form data** setting in your custom settings (see step 5) and click the **Disable** radio button.

How to Block Objectionable Content from Being Viewed

To place restrictions on the material that can be viewed with Internet Explorer 6, use the browser's *Content Advisor*. The Advisor relies on RSACi ratings—an industry standard adopted voluntarily by some Web publishers to indicate their site's level of objectionable language, nudity, sex, and violence. Although the Content Advisor is far from foolproof—it relies on Web sites to honestly assess their own content—you might find it useful in conjunction with other methods of filtering the Web.

① View Content Settings

The Content Advisor is configured with all other browser settings. Choose **Tools**, **Internet Options** from the menu bar to open the **Internet Options** dialog box. Then click the **Content** tab to view the browser's content settings. To set up the Content Advisor, first click the **Enable** button.

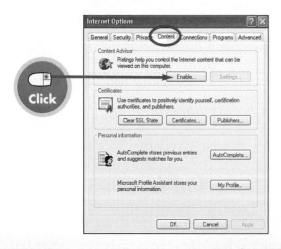

② Set Your Content Ratings

The **Content Advisor** dialog box opens to the **Ratings** tab, ready for you to set your browser's acceptable RSACi rating. Click the RSACi category you want to set, then drag the slider to a content setting. A site must have content rated at or below all four settings to pass the Content Advisor. Pages that don't pass are not displayed.

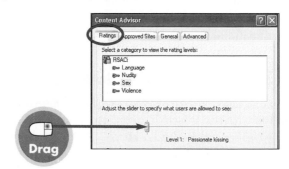

③ View Unrated Sites

By default, Web pages without RSACi ratings cannot be viewed. This keeps out unrated sites that contain objectionable material, along with thousands of sites that don't participate in RSACi. To allow unrated sites to be viewed, click the **General** tab of the **Content Advisor** dialog box and enable the **Users can see sites that have no rating** check box.

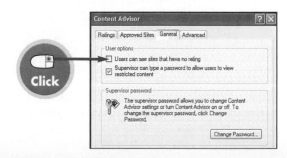

④ Approve Individual Sites

To allow individual sites to bypass the Content Advisor, click the **Approved Sites** tab, type the site's main address in the **Allow this Web site** text box, and click the **Always** button. Alternatively, you can completely restrict access to the specified site by clicking the **Never** button instead.

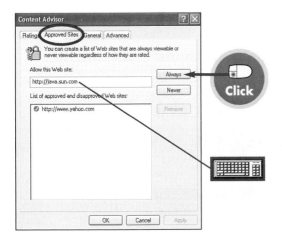

⑤ Save Your Changes

Click the **OK** button to save your new settings and close the **Content Advisor** dialog box. If you have imposed content restrictions, you should close Internet Explorer and launch it again. This action keeps recently visited sites from being reloaded without first being checked by the Content Advisor.

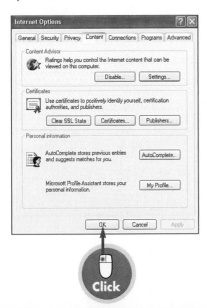

⑥ Choose a Password

When you save your content settings for the first time, you will be asked to select a supervisor password. This password can be used to change Content Advisor settings or turn it off completely. After you set one up, you can't modify the Content Advisor without it. Enter your password in both text boxes and click **OK** to return to the **Internet Options** dialog box.

⑦ Turn Off the Content Advisor

To turn off the Content Advisor completely, choose **Tools**, **Internet Options** to open the **Internet Options** dialog box. Click the **Content** tab, and then click the **Disable** button. You must type the supervisor password in order to disable the Content Advisor feature.

How to Use Security Certificates

As you are visiting Web sites, you might come across pages that contain interactive programs. These small programs are downloaded to your computer and run as if you installed them from a CD-ROM, but they must be approved before your Web browser runs them. Internet Explorer 6 presents a *security certificate*—a window vouching for the authenticity of the program's author. Examine this certificate and decide whether to let the program run.

① Inspect a Certificate

When you load a page that contains an interactive program, Internet Explorer presents a dialog box asking whether the control should be installed. The author of the program is presented as a hyperlink. Click this hyperlink to find out more about the author.

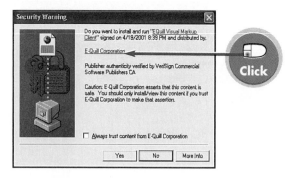

② Determine Authenticity

The link opens a security certificate associated with the program's author. Companies such as VeriSign and Thawte create these certificates after verifying the program's authorship. Click the tabs to find out more about the certificate and the author. Click **OK** to close the window.

③ Always Trust an Author

If you are comfortable with the program's author, you can automatically approve the download of any programs that author creates in the future. To do so, enable the **Always trust content** check box. (You should note, however, that it's safer to approve programs individually than to issue blanket approval with this check box.)

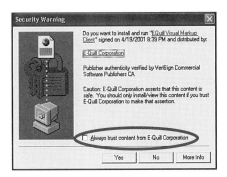

④ Reject an Author

To prevent a program from being installed, click the **No** button in the **Security Warning** dialog box. You can still use anything on the current Web page that doesn't rely on the program.

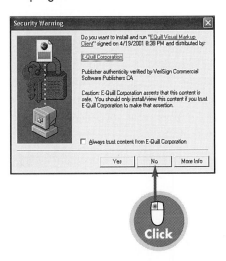

⑤ Approve an Author

To approve a program and run it in your browser, click the **Yes** button. The program will be saved on your system in the `Windows/Downloaded Program Files` folder so that it doesn't have to be installed again every time you visit the page.

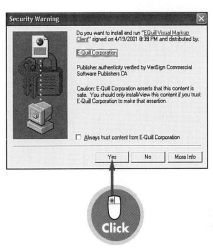

How-to Hint

Restricting Programs on Your Browser

If you are never asked whether a program should be installed before it starts running on a Web page, your browser may be configured with a low security level. To check your security settings, select **Tools**, **Internet Options** to open the **Internet Options** dialog box and click the **Security** tab. Refer to Tasks 1 and 2 in this chapter of the book for instructions on setting and customizing a security level in Internet Explorer.

How to Disable Cookies
in a Web Browser

Web sites can keep track of visitors by using *cookies*—small files that contain information collected by a site. Internet Explorer 6 saves cookie files for Web sites on your computer; when you revisit a site for which you have a cookie, Internet Explorer 6 sends the cookie file back to the site. The cookie can be used to store personal information such as your name, billing information, and similar data. By design, Internet Explorer sends a cookie file that exists on your computer only to the site that created it. Some Web sites require cookie files, but you can turn them off entirely by adjusting the browser's privacy settings.

1 Change Your Settings

Select **Tools**, **Internet Options**. The **Internet Options** dialog box opens to the **General** tab, displaying how your browser is configured.

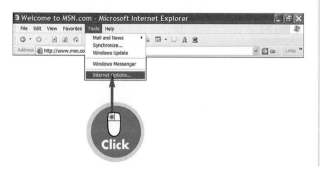

2 View Privacy Settings

Click the **Privacy** tab to bring its settings to the front of the dialog box.

3 Block All Cookies

To block all cookies from being stored on your computer, drag the slider up to the **Block All Cookies** setting. You should note, however, that this is the strictest setting and may prevent you from using some popular sites.

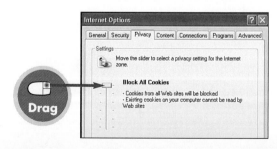

④ Block Most Cookies

To block most cookies (except for those already on your computer), drag the slider to the **High** setting. Cookies that store information related to your identity will not be stored without your consent.

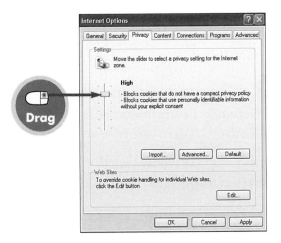

⑤ Block Advertiser Cookies

To block most cookies from advertisers and some others, drag the slider to the **Medium** setting. Ad cookies and cookies that identify you will not be stored unless you consent.

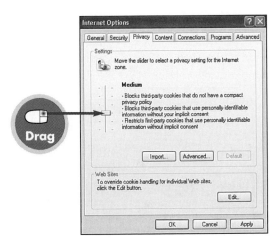

⑥ Save Your New Settings

To make your privacy changes take effect, click the **OK** button. Your cookie privacy settings will be in force until you change them or return to the **Privacy** tab and click the **Default Level** button.

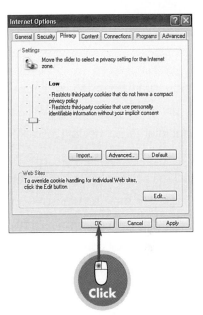

How-to Hint

Approving Cookies on a Case-by-Case Basis

As you will discover after changing your privacy settings to block cookies, many of the sites you use will no longer be fully functional—especially if they offer features that are personalized specifically for you. To allow a specific site to store cookies on your computer, return to the **Privacy** tab and click the **Edit** button. The **Per Site Privacy Actions** dialog box opens. Type the main URL of the site in the **Address of Web Site** text box and click the **Allow** button. When you have finished adding sites, click the **OK** button to close the dialog box.

How to Make Your Internet Connection More Secure

When you are connected to the Internet, the Internet is also connected to you. Malicious people can use that Internet connection to look for ways to access your computer's files, programs, and devices such as printers. Although problems of this kind are relatively rare, several software developers now offer *firewalls*—programs that restrict the kind of information that can be exchanged over an Internet connection. Windows XP comes with its own protection against unwelcome intruders: the Internet Connection Firewall.

① View Your Connections

In order to work, an Internet Connection Firewall must be associated with a network connection on your computer. (Note that the Internet Connection Firewall is available only with Windows XP.) To view your network connections, click the **Start** button, choose **Connect To**, and choose **Network Connections**.

② Choose a Connection

The **Network Connections** folder lists the connections you have set up to the Internet and other networks. To begin adding a firewall to an Internet connection, right-click the desired connection icon and choose **Properties** from the shortcut menu that opens.

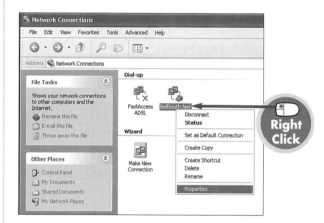

③ View Advanced Settings

The **Properties** dialog box includes five tabs that can be used to modify its settings. Click the **Advanced** tab to bring it to the front.

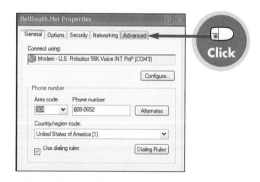

④ Turn On the Firewall

To turn on a firewall, enable the **Protect my computer and network by limiting or preventing access to this computer from the Internet** check box. To learn more about the Internet Connection Firewall, click the link of the same name.

⑤ Save Your Settings

Click the **OK** button to save the changes you have made to your Internet connection. If you are connected to the Internet when the firewall is set up, the current connection is not protected by the firewall. Disconnect and reconnect to the Internet so that the new connection will be protected by the firewall.

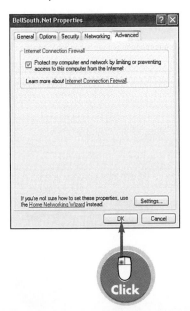

⑥ Connect Through the Firewall

After you have turned on the firewall, your Internet connection icon will change to show that a firewall is in place. Nothing else changes; double-click the connection icon to connect to the Internet as you normally would.

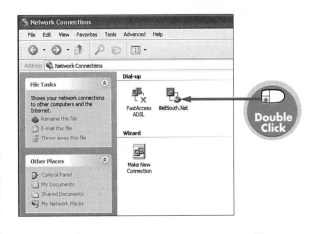

How-to Hint

Choosing a Different Internet Firewall

The Internet Connection Firewall is available only on Windows XP and does not protect against some security risks. If you don't use Windows XP or want a more full-featured firewall, you might be interested in the ZoneAlarm firewall. ZoneAlarm is available in free and pay versions from Zone Labs for Windows 95, 98, Me, XP, NT, and 2000. To find out more, type the URL http://www.zonealarm.com in your Web browser and press **Enter**; you can then download the free version of the software if desired.

How to Install Antivirus Software

It's only a matter of time before your computer is exposed to its first *virus*—a harmful program that runs without permission, tries to spread itself to other computers, and may damage or delete your files. Viruses infect millions of computers each day on the Internet. To avoid them, you should buy an antivirus program that can check files for viruses before you open them, even as they arrive in email. One of the best is Norton AntiVirus 2002, which sells for $39 at many software retailers. Most computer and office superstores sell the software, including Office Max, Staples, and CompUSA.

❶ Load the Wizard

When you place the Norton AntiVirus 2002 CD in your CD drive, it loads automatically. To begin installing the program, click the **Install Norton AntiVirus** link. An installation wizard starts.

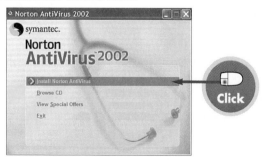

❷ Run the Wizard

If possible, you should close all other programs before installing Norton AntiVirus 2002. After you have done so, click **Next** to run the installation wizard.

❸ Review the License

The wizard presents the software's license agreement. If you agree to its terms, select the **I accept the license agreement** radio button and click **Next**.

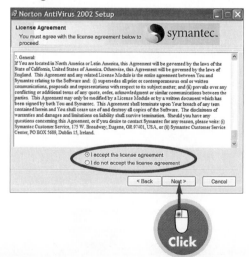

④ Choose a Folder

The wizard recommends a folder for the software: **\Program Files\Norton AntiVirus**. Click **Next** to accept this. (To pick a different folder, click the **Browse** button, use the **File** dialog box to choose a folder, and click **OK**, then click **Next**.)

⑤ Confirm Your Choice

The wizard displays the folders where Norton AntiVirus 2002 and related files will be installed. Click **Next**. Some last-minute information is displayed. After reading it, click **Next**.

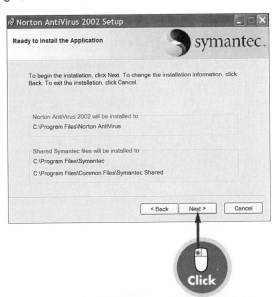

⑥ Begin Registration

The software will be installed. Click **Finish**. An information wizard opens; use it to register your name, email address, and mailing address with Norton, and then click **Next**.

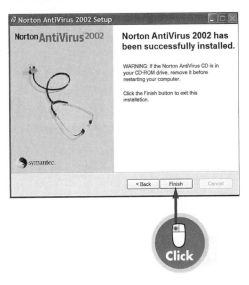

How-to Hint

Avoiding Virus Infection on Your Computer

If you install antivirus software such as Norton AntiVirus 2002 or McAfee VirusScan 6.0 and keep its virus database current, you should be able to avoid any problems with viruses on your computer. That said, you always should be careful about the programs you install and the files you open while using the Internet. Don't open files sent to you via email by people you don't know—even if the files appear to be something innocuous such as a digital photograph. Also, if an email from someone you know contains a file and seems a little suspicious, don't open it until checking with the person. If that person's computer is infected with an email virus, it may have sent the mail to you. Virus programmers count on tricks like this to spread viruses around the world.

7 Use LiveUpdate

Norton AntiVirus 2002 includes a free one-year sub-scription to LiveUpdate, a service that keeps your computer up-to-date on new virus threats and keeps the program current. After reviewing the dates of your subscription, click **Next**.

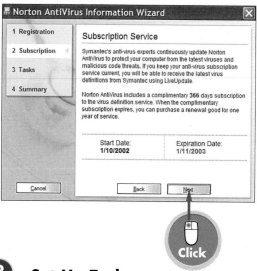

8 Set Up Tasks

Enable the check boxes for tasks you want Norton AntiVirus 2002 to undertake. (Choosing all three is a good idea.) When you're finished, click **Next**.

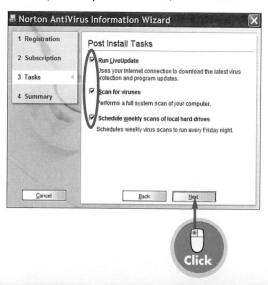

9 Review the Tasks

Review the tasks you have enabled and click **Finish**. Norton AntiVirus 2002 does a lot of the work automatically, including a Friday-evening scan of your entire computer.

10 Look for Updates

If you chose to run LiveUpdate, it begins immediately. Connect to the Internet (if you aren't already online) and click **Next**.

⑪ Select Updates

LiveUpdate connects to Symantec's Internet site and lists the things that need to be updated on your computer, with check marks next to each one. To install them, click **Next**.

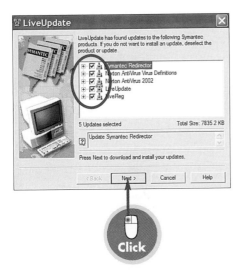

⑬ Run LiveUpdate Again

You are encouraged to run LiveUpdate several times when you first install Norton AntiVirus, just to make sure you get everything up to date (including LiveUpdate itself). To run the program, click **Start**, choose **All Programs**, choose **Norton AntiVirus**, and click **LiveUpdate—Norton AntiVirus**.

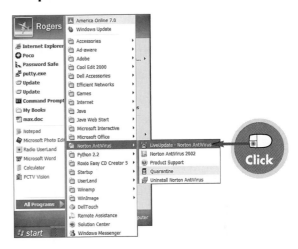

⑫ Close LiveUpdate

LiveUpdate downloads and installs each selected update and presents a status report. (You might also see a dialog box telling you to run LiveUpdate several times, as discussed in the next step.) Click **Finish** to close the program.

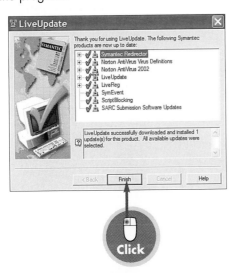

⑭ Look for Updates

The process of running LiveUpdate is the same as before; connect to the Internet and click **Next** to begin. Keep running LiveUpdate until you are told that no more updates are available. After that, LiveUpdate will run automatically while you are subscribed.

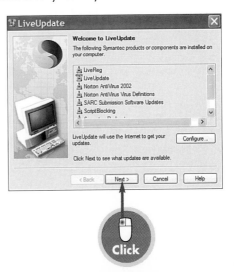

How to Check Your Computer for Viruses

After you install antivirus software such as Norton AntiVirus 2002 (described in Task 7), you should immediately use the software to look for viruses on your computer. This is called a *scan*. Norton AntiVirus 2002 conducts its own scan automatically every Friday evening if your computer is on during that time. The software also scans all incoming email, reporting immediately if any file that arrives is infected with a virus.

❶ Run the Program

Click the **Start** button, choose **All Programs**, choose **Norton AntiVirus**, then click **Norton AntiVirus 2002**.

❷ Begin a Scan

Norton AntiVirus 2002 presents a status report, which may contain items you need to handle. To scan your computer, click the **Scan for Viruses** link.

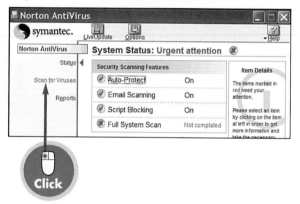

❸ Choose What to Scan

You can scan your entire computer, or scan specific parts of it such as a drive, folder, or file. For a full scan of your entire computer, click the **Scan my computer** link.

④ View the Summary

A complete scan can take an hour or more. If any viruses are found, a dialog box opens, advising you to either delete the file or put it in quarantine—a special folder with files that can't be opened. Click **Finished** to close the program.

⑤ Deal with a Virus

If a virus is emailed to you in a file, Norton AntiVirus 2002 opens automatically and asks you to deal with it immediately. Click **Quarantine** to put the file in the quarantine folder (or **Delete**, if that option is offered).

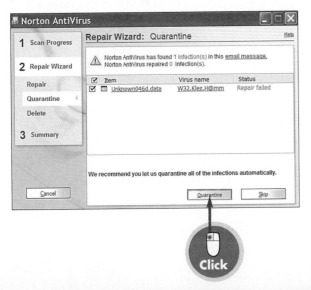

⑥ Close the Program

After Norton AntiVirus 2002 deals with the virus according to your instructions, click **Finished** to close the program.

How-to Hint

Scan a File for a Virus

Because a full scan of your computer can take an hour or longer, you will probably be reluctant to do one when you are concerned about an individual file and want to check it out before opening it. To scan a single file quickly, open the folder that contains the file, right-click its icon, and select **Scan with Norton AntiVirus** from the pop-up menu that appears. A quick scan will be performed of only that file.

1 How to Set Up Outlook Express for Email 350

2 How to Send Email 352

3 How to Receive Email 354

4 How to Send a Web Page Using Email 356

5 How to Send an Attached File 358

6 How to Receive an Attached File 360

7 How to Find Someone's Email Address 362

8 How to Subscribe to a Mailing List 364

9 How to Set Up a Free Web-Based Email Account . . 366

10 How to Set Up Hotmail in Outlook Express 370

11 How to Use Your Free Web-Based Email Account . . 372

12 How to Print an Email Message 374

17

Communicating with Electronic Mail

Electronic mail, more commonly called *email*, enables you to send messages to anyone who has an Internet email address. These messages, which are free to send and to receive, usually arrive within minutes of being sent.

Using email, you can communicate directly with friends, family members, and colleagues. You can send messages to your elected leaders, request customer support from a business, and exchange pictures with friends and family. You also can receive advertisements, although unfortunately many of these arrive unsolicited—a type of Internet marketing called *spam*.

Most Internet service providers offer an email account as part of your subscription. (One of the things you must obtain from your provider is the information necessary to use your new email account: your username and password, the name of your provider's mail servers, and other setup details.) In addition, many Web sites offer free lifetime email accounts, such as Microsoft Hotmail and Prontomail.

How to Set Up Outlook Express for Email

Windows XP includes Microsoft Outlook Express, a popular email program that can send and deliver email and manage an email address book. Before you can set up Outlook Express, you must have the following information from your Internet service provider: your username and password, the incoming mail server's name, the outgoing mail server's name, and the type of incoming mail server you'll be accessing (POP3, IMAP, or HTTP). Most incoming servers use a protocol called *POP3*.

❶ Run Outlook Express

To begin, click the **Start** menu and choose **Email**. Alternatively, there might be an **Outlook Express** icon on your desktop; if there is, double-click this icon to start Outlook Express.

❷ Identify Yourself

If Outlook Express has not been set up already, the **Internet Connection Wizard** opens. In the **Display name** text box, type a name (also called a *handle*) that will identify you on all outgoing mail. This name is displayed in addition to your email address on all email that you send. Most people use their full name. Click **Next** to continue.

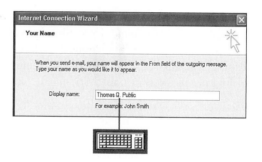

❸ Set Up an Email Address

If you have a new email address provided by your Internet service (or an existing email address you'd like to continue using), type it into the **Email address** text box and click the **Next** button.

4 Identify Your Servers

If your Internet service provider supports email, you should have been given the names of its mail servers when you joined the service. Type the names of its mail servers in the **Incoming mail** and **Outgoing mail** text boxes. Use the drop-down list to indicate the kind of incoming server being used (most services use POP3). Click **Next** to continue.

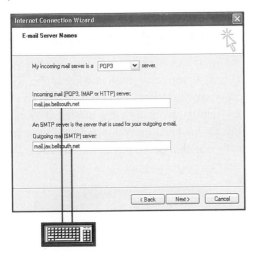

5 Enter Your Account Info

You must have a username and password to make use of Internet email servers. (You get this information from your Internet service provider.) Type these into the **Account name** and **Password** text boxes, checking the **Remember password** box if you want Outlook Express to log into your account automatically.

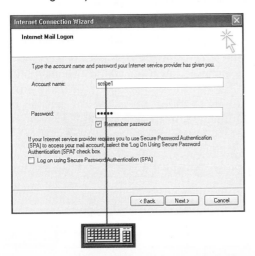

6 Set Up Authentication

If your Internet service requires it, check the **Log on using Secure Password Authentication (SPA)** option. To finish setting up Outlook Express to work with your email address, click the **Next** button and then click the **Finish** button.

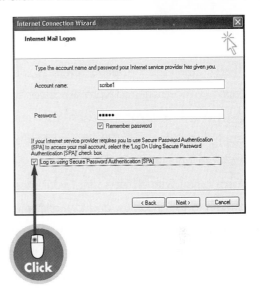

Click

How to Hint

Using Different Versions of Outlook

The Microsoft Office software suite includes an expanded version of Outlook Express called *Outlook 2002*. Outlook 2002 can be used for other things in addition to email. For example, there's a task-management feature for keeping a to-do list, a calendar, a contact book, and a place to keep notes. For more information, visit Microsoft's Outlook Web site: Type the URL http://www.microsoft.com/office/outlook in Internet Explorer's Address bar and press **Enter**.

How to Send Email

Writing a message in Outlook Express is similar to creating a document in a word processor such as Microsoft Word. You type the text of your message and apply formatting with familiar toolbar buttons such as Bold and Italic. Outlook Express normally composes email with HTML so that your messages can contain fonts, graphics, and formatting just like World Wide Web pages. Because your recipient must be able to read HTML mail to see all these features, you also can turn off HTML and send a message as text without any formatting.

❶ Create a New Message

Click the **Start** menu and choose **Email** to launch Outlook Express. To begin writing a new message, click the **new Mail message** hyperlink. (If you don't see this link, click the **Outlook Express** icon in the **Folders** pane.) The **New Message** window opens.

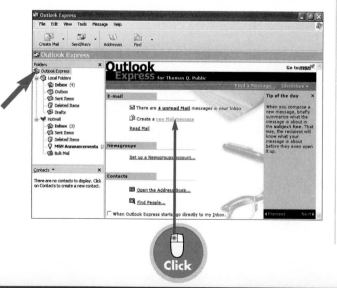

Click

❷ Address the Message

Type the email address of the message's recipient in the **To** text box. If you're sending a copy of this message to another email address, type that address in the **Cc** text box. Finish addressing the message by typing a short title for the message in the **Subject** box. The window's title bar changes to match the text you type in the **Subject** box.

❸ Write the Message

Type the text of your message in the edit pane. If you're sending a message that should not contain any HTML formatting, pull down the **Format** menu (located at the top of the message window) and choose the **Plain Text** option.

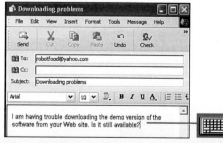

4 Format the Message

Messages you send with HTML formatting can contain different fonts, bold text, a graphical background, and other visual touches. These features are available on the toolbar above the edit pane. To make text bold, for example, select the text by dragging your mouse over it and then click the **Bold** button in the toolbar.

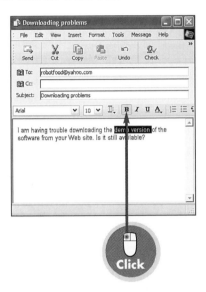

5 Set a Priority

To assign a priority to your message, choose **Message**, **Set Priority**, and then choose **High**, **Normal**, or **Low**. The priority setting does not cause the message to be delivered any differently, but the priority rating may be noted by the recipient's email program when the message is displayed in his or her inbox.

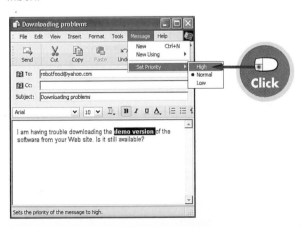

6 Send the Message

When your message has been addressed, typed, and formatted the way you want it, connect to the Internet and click the **Send** button to deliver the email message. A copy of the message is stored in the **Sent Items** folder of Outlook Express. (If you aren't connected, a copy is saved in the Outbox folder until it can be delivered.)

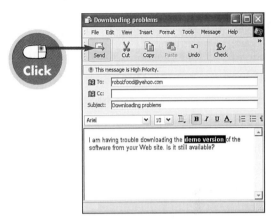

How to Hint

Applying HTML Formatting

Outlook Express, Hotmail, and other email services support email that contains HTML—the same kind of formatting used to create Web pages. To add images, colors, or sound to the background of your email message in Outlook Express, choose **Format**, **Background**, and select the **Picture**, **Color**, or **Sound** command. This special formatting, however, may make your message unreadable if your recipient's email program can't handle HTML-formatted email. For this reason, use special formatting only if you know that the recipient's email program supports it.

How to Receive Email

Outlook Express is organized like a file folder, and it contains subfolders for **Inbox**, **Outbox**, **Sent Items**, **Deleted Items**, and **Drafts**. New messages are placed in your **Inbox**, where they stay until you move them to a new folder or delete them. If you are also using Hotmail, an extra set of folders exists for mail received with that service. (You learn more about Hotmail in Task 9, "How to Set Up a Free Web-Based Email Account.")

1   Read Unread Mail

Click the **Start** menu and choose **Email** to launch Outlook Express. If any new email has been received, click the **unread Mail** hyperlink to see the messages you have. Alternatively, you can click the **Inbox** icon in the **Local Folders** list to see your new messages as well as any messages you have read previously.

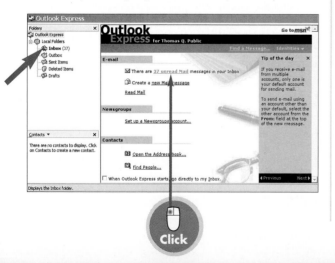

2   View Messages

The top-right pane of the **Inbox** window lists all the messages in the folder—new unread messages, and messages you've read previously. Use the scrollbar to move through this list. Click a message's icon to view the contents of that message in the bottom-right pane. To delete a message, click its icon in the top-right pane and then click the **Delete** button.

3   View a Message in a New Window

The bottom-right pane of the **Inbox** window doesn't have a lot of room to display a message. To view a message in a larger window, double-click the message's icon in the top-right pane of the **Inbox** window. A new window appears, with the selected message displayed.

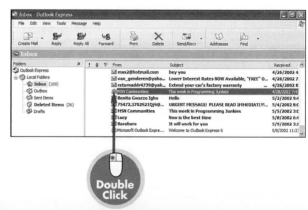

④ View Other Messages

As you're viewing a message in its own window, you can use the **Previous** and **Next** buttons in the toolbar at the top of the window to see other messages in the same folder. Click the **Next** button to view the next message in your Outlook Express Inbox window.

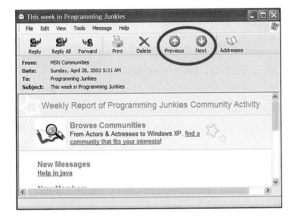

⑤ Reply to a Message

To reply to the message you're reading, click the **Reply** button. The **New Message** window opens with the text of the original message in the edit pane. If the message was sent to multiple addresses (as listed in the **To** and **Cc** text boxes), you can send your reply to all the addressees by clicking **Reply All** instead. Type your reply to the original message and click **Send**.

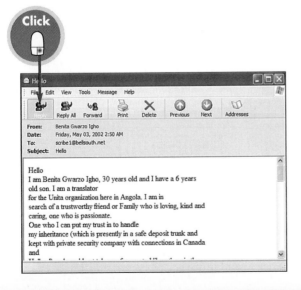

⑥ Forward a Message

To send a copy of a message to another email address, click the **Forward** button. You can send the forwarded message without changes, or you can add your own comments to it. (You also can forward a message while viewing your **Inbox** list: Click the message and then click the **Forward** button.) Type any additional comments you want to make to the message you're forwarding and click **Send**.

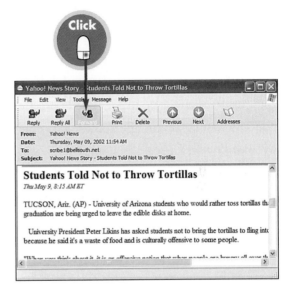

How to Hint

Choosing Between Forward and Reply

Because the **Forward** and **Reply** features both open a **New Message** window, you might be confused about the difference between the two features. **Reply** is used to respond directly to the person who sent you an email message. **Forward** is used to send a copy of an email message to someone who hasn't seen it—thousands of jokes, inspirational sayings, and safety warnings are forwarded around the Internet each day because people receive email messages, like them, and send them to friends and relatives.

How to Send a Web Page Using Email

As you're visiting sites on the World Wide Web, you might run across something that's worth telling a friend or colleague about. Internet Explorer 6 can send hyperlinks and full Web pages using your preferred email program. When you first set up the IE browser, it is configured to work with Outlook Express. This is easy to change if you use Eudora, Hotmail, or another popular email service. (One program you *can't* use is America Online—its email program is incompatible with this browser feature.)

① Choose a Hyperlink

To mail a hyperlink to someone from within Internet Explorer, load the page you want to recommend to someone else and choose **File**, **Send**, **Link by Email**. A new message is opened in your preferred email program.

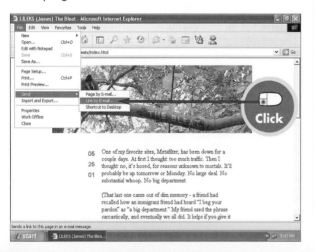

② Write the Email

The new email message includes the hyperlink to the current page in Internet Explorer. You can add comments of your own to go with it. Type the email address of the recipient in the **To** text box and a subject in the **Subject** box, and any comments you want to send.

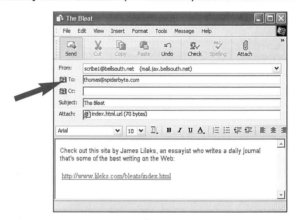

③ Send the Link

When you're ready to send the link and its accompanying message, click the **Send** button. If the recipient's email program supports hyperlinks, the recipient can click the link in your message to visit the page.

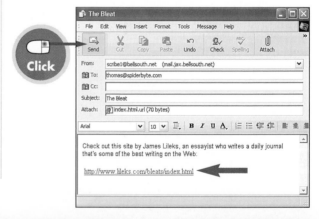

4 Choose a Page

To send an entire Web page using email, open the page in Internet Explorer and then choose **File**, **Send**, **Page by Email**. A new message is opened in your preferred email program containing a copy of the entire Web page.

6 Send the Page

To send the page with any changes you made, click the **Send** button. If the recipient is using an email program that can display Web pages, the page will be displayed by the email program's built-in browser.

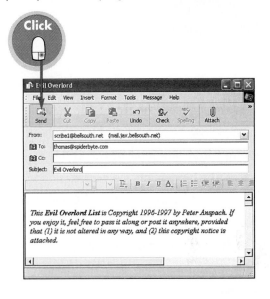

5 Write the Email

You can make changes to the copy of the Web page in the edit pane before sending it. When you're done, type the recipient's address in the **To** text box and a subject in the **Subject** text box.

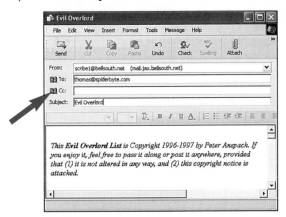

How to Hint

Sending a Link to Your Desktop

As you know, you can send to a friend the hyperlink to a particular Web page. You can also place a shortcut icon on your desktop that acts as a hyperlink to the Web page: Choose **File**, **Send**, **Shortcut to Desktop**. An Internet shortcut to the current Web page appears on your desktop. Connect to the Internet and double-click the shortcut to load the page in Internet Explorer.

How to Send an Attached File

Any file that's stored on your computer can be sent through email. Before the file can be opened by the recipient, however, it must be *downloaded*—transferred from the mail server to the recipient's computer. The amount of time this takes depends on the Internet connection speed and the file's size. A 200KB file takes more than five minutes to download at the most common Internet speed (56Kbps) and usually prevents the recipient from receiving other mail during the transfer. For this reason, you should send large files only to people who are expecting them.

1 Start Outlook Express

You send a file by attaching it to any email message you're sending out. Open Outlook Express (click the **Start** button and choose **Email**). Click the **new Mail message** hyperlink to begin writing a new message.

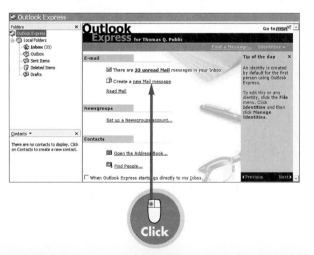

2 Attach a File

After writing and addressing the message, click the **Attach** button in the toolbar at the top of the window. The **Insert Attachment** dialog box opens; you use this dialog box to locate the file you want to attach to the message.

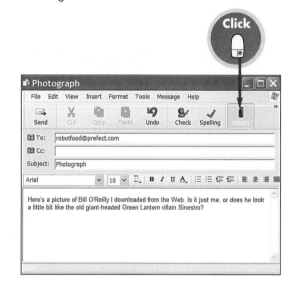

3 Choose the File

Use the **Insert Attachment** dialog box to find and open the folder that contains the file you want to send. Select the filename and then click the **Attach** button.

4 Send the Email and Its Attachment

The name of the file you've chosen is displayed in the **Attach** text box at the top of the message window. Click the **Send** button to deliver the message and its attached file. The file is uploaded to your mail server, so the time it takes to send the message depends on the speed of your Internet connection and the size of the file.

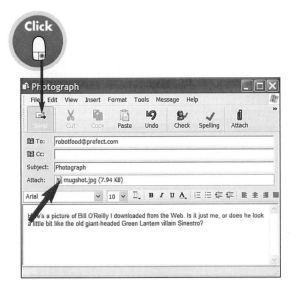

6 Send the Files

The name of each attached file appears in the **Attach** text box of the message window. Click the **Attach** button again if you want to choose another file to attach to the message. Click **Send** to send the message and its attached files.

5 Choose Multiple Files

You can attach more than one file to a single email message. In the message window, click the **Attach** button to open the **Insert Attachment** dialog box. Hold down the **Ctrl** key as you click to select individual files. When all the desired files are highlighted, click the **Attach** button.

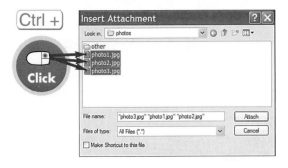

How to Hint

Sending a Shortcut Instead of a File

If you are sending an attached file to someone on the same *intranet*—computers networked together at a business, school, or other institution—you might be able to send a shortcut instead of the entire file. If the file you are sending is in a public folder on your intranet, open the **Insert Attachment** window, pick the file, and enable the **Make Shortcut to this file** check box before clicking the **Attach** button.

How to Receive an Attached File

You deliver files through Internet email by attaching them to normal email messages. To receive an attached file in Outlook Express, you must first open the message associated with the file. You can open files directly from Outlook Express or save them to a folder on your system. Be aware, however, that attached files can contain viruses that execute damaging code on your computer—even in documents created with Microsoft Word. Although some antivirus programs can scan incoming files as they are received through email, you should be cautious before opening files sent to you.

① Read Your Mail

Open Outlook Express (click the **Start** button and choose **Email**). If you have new mail, click the **unread Mail** hyperlink to open your Outlook Express **Inbox**.

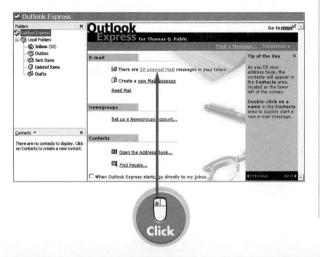

② Check for Attachments

Mail that has attached files is displayed with a paper clip icon. Open the mail message (click the message in the top-right pane to view it in the bottom-right pane). To open the file attached to the mail message, click the paper clip button and select the name of the file attached to the mail message.

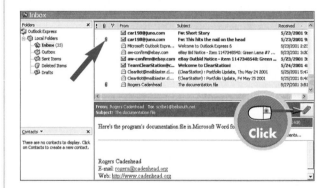

③ Open the File

Outlook Express might warn you before opening an attached file. If you decide to open the file in Outlook Express, click the **Open it** radio button in the **Open Attachment Warning** dialog box, and then click **OK**. The file is opened by the program associated with it (if there is one). If no program is associated with the file type, you'll be asked to pick one.

4 Save an Attachment

To save attached files to your system's hard drive instead of opening them in Outlook Express, click the paper clip button in the message window and choose **Save Attachments**. The **Save Attachments** dialog box opens.

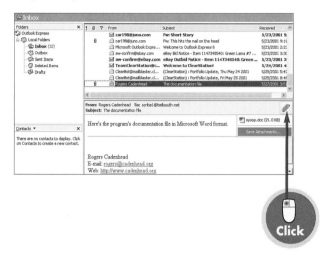

5 Choose a Location

Click the **Browse** button next to the **Save To** text box to choose the folder in which you want to save the attached file. Then click the **Save** button.

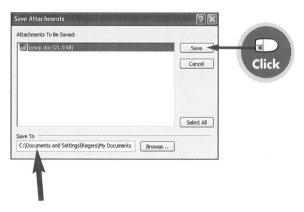

6 View Attachments

When you're reading mail in a separate window, Outlook Express does not display a paper clip icon. Instead, the name of the attached file is displayed in the **Attach** text box at the top of the window. Double-click the filename to see the **Open Attachment** dialog box, which you can use to open or save the attached file.

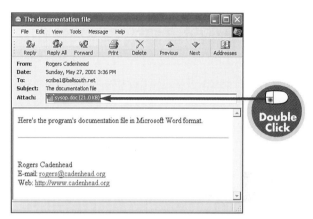

How to Find Someone's Email Address

Several sites on the World Wide Web (including Bigfoot and InfoSpace) offer huge directories of email addresses. If you want to contact a person, company, or other organization but don't know the contact's email address, you can use Outlook Express to search through each of these directories. You can use these same steps to quickly search your own *address book* (a personal database of your email correspondents you can create in Outlook Express).

① Find People

To begin looking for the email address of a person or company in Outlook Express, click the arrow next to the **Find** button and select the **People** option. The **Find People** dialog box opens.

② Search Your Address Book

To search through your personal address book in Outlook Express, choose **Address Book** from the **Look in** drop-down list at the top of the dialog box. Type information about the person you're looking for in at least one of the text boxes—**Name**, **Email**, **Address**, **Phone**, or **Other**. Click the **Find Now** button to start the search.

③ Send Someone a Message

The **Find People** dialog box expands to display the results of the search. To begin a new email message addressed to one of the people you find, right-click the name and choose **Action**, **Send Mail** from the pop-up menus that appear.

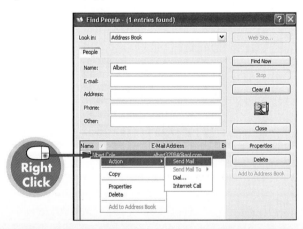

④ Search a Web Directory

You also can look for email addresses in several Web directories. In the **Find People** dialog box, in the **Look in** drop-down list, choose one of the directory services (for example, choose **Bigfoot** or **InfoSpace**). Type the name you want to look for in the **Name** text box and click the **Find Now** button.

⑥ Visit a Directory Site

Each of the address directories that you can access from Outlook Express has a related Web site that offers additional features and more sophisticated search tools. From the **Look in** list box, select the name of the directory you want to use and then click the **Web Site** button to visit that directory's site with your Web browser.

⑤ Add to Your Address Book

If you find the person or company you are looking for, you can copy the information from the Web directory to your personal address book. Click the name in the results pane and then click the **Add to Address Book** button.

How to Hint

Adding Someone to Your Address Book

You can add a person to your Outlook Express address book as you are reading a message from him or her in its own window. Double-click the name or email address you want to add, and then click the **Add to Address Book** button.

How to Subscribe to a Mailing List

A popular way to use email is to communicate with a group of people on a shared topic of interest. You can do this by joining an *electronic mailing list*, a discussion that takes place entirely with email. Lists are categorized by topic; people who are interested in a list's topic send an email message to subscribe. If the list allows public participation (as many do), you can use a special email address to send a message to all members of the list. Any message sent by another member of the list of subscribers winds up in your Inbox.

① Run Outlook Express

To begin, click the **Start** menu and choose **Email**. Alternatively, there might be an **Outlook Express** icon on your desktop; if there is, double-click this icon to start Outlook Express.

② Create a New Message

Before you can subscribe to a mailing list, you must know its subscription address and the command used to subscribe (see the "How-To Hints" section on the next page for information about finding mailing lists). When you have that information, begin a new email message in Outlook Express by clicking the **new Mail message** hyperlink.

③ Subscribe to a List

Address the message by typing the list's subscription address in the **To** text box. Type the subscription command in the body of the message or in the **Subject** text box—whichever the mailing list requires you to do.

④ Send the Message

Click the **Send** button to deliver your subscription request. You'll receive a confirmation message when you have been added to the mailing list; the confirmation message usually contains helpful information about how to use the list.

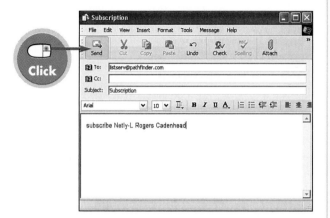

⑤ Contribute to the List

If the mailing list allows public participation, you can send a message to all list members using a special email address—probably not the same as the one you used to subscribe to the list. Usually, this address includes the name of the list—see your confirmation message for more information. Click **Send** to deliver the message.

⑥ Unsubscribe from a List

When you subscribe to a mailing list, you should save the confirmation message you received. This message usually contains instructions on how to quit the list. The address to which you mail your request to be removed from the list is often the same as the one you used to subscribe, but the command will be slightly different. Click **Send** to deliver the request.

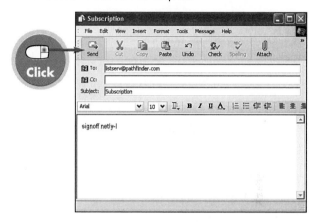

Finding Mailing Lists on Any Topic

There are thousands of mailing lists on topics related to technology, entertainment, hobbies, and more. To search a database of lists you can join, visit the Topica World Wide Web site at **http://www.topica.com.**

Joining the Netly-L Mailing List

One longtime general-interest mailing list is Netly-L, a place to discuss the Internet, online media, and technology. To subscribe, send an email message to **listserv@pathfinder.com**. In the body of the message, type **subscribe Netly-L** followed by your name (for example, if your name is Ulysses S Grant, type **subscribe Netly-L Ulysses S Grant** in the body of the message).

How to Set Up a Free Web-Based Email Account

Although you receive an email account when you subscribe to most Internet service providers, you might want to set up an account with a World Wide Web site that provides free lifetime email. These sites normally offer mail you can access by visiting the site with your Web browser. However, some services can work in conjunction with Outlook Express and other mail software. In this task, you set up Microsoft Hotmail, a free email service you can use in your browser or in Outlook Express.

❶ Run Your Browser

You set up Microsoft Hotmail by visiting the service's Web site. Click the **Start** button and choose **Internet**. Internet Explorer opens and displays your home page.

❷ Visit Hotmail

To visit Hotmail, type the URL http://www.hotmail.com in the browser's **Address bar** and press **Enter**. The main page of the Hotmail service loads.

❸ Begin Signing Up

Hotmail email accounts are completely free. To join, click the **Sign Up** hyperlink. A page opens with a form asking for information about you.

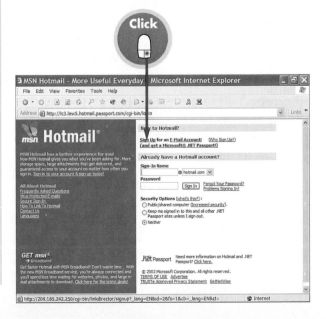

④ Identify Yourself

Type your name in the **First Name** and **Last Name** text boxes and fill out the rest of the fields in the **Profile Information** section. Your name will appear on all mail you send using Hotmail. Scroll down the page when you're done.

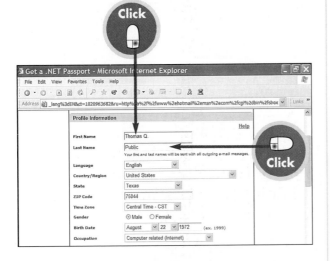

⑤ Choose an Address

Type the username you want to use in the **Email Address** text box and the password you want to use in the **Password** and **Retype Password** text boxes. Your email address will be your username followed by **@hotmail.com**. Your username must begin with a letter and contain only letters, numbers, or underscore characters (_).

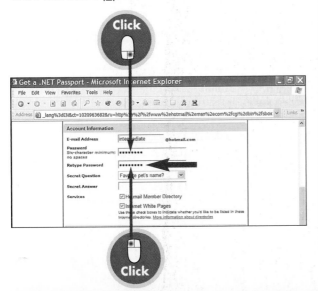

⑥ Pick a Secret Question

Choose a question in the **Secret Question** box and type an answer in the **Secret Answer** box. Only you should know the answer—Hotmail will ask the question if you forget your password and want to set up a new one.

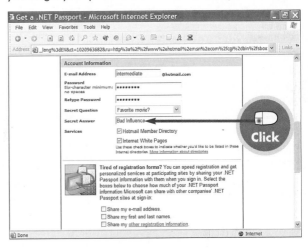

⑦ Go Public or Private

By default, Hotmail adds your name and email address to its public member directory and the Internet White Pages. To stay out of these directories, click to disable the check boxes next to the directory names.

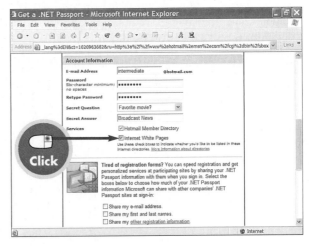

8 Review the Terms of Use

Microsoft displays the terms of use to which you must agree before an account will be created. If you agree, scroll to the bottom of the page and click the **I Agree** button to join Hotmail.

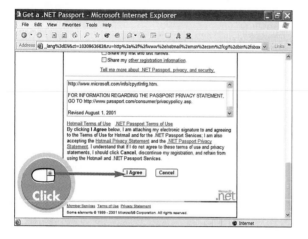

9 Choose Another Username

Because millions use Hotmail, you might find it difficult to find a unique username. If your choice is taken, you'll see a list of suggestions for alternative usernames. Click a radio button to choose that suggestion, or click the last radio button and type another username in the adjacent text box. When you're done, scroll down and click **I Agree** again.

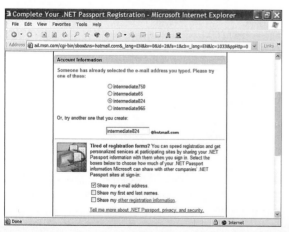

10 Continue Sign-Up

After you have found a username, Hotmail displays a page indicating that you have successfully signed up for a Microsoft .NET Passport. Your Hotmail username and password can be used at any site that supports Passport. Click the **Continue** button.

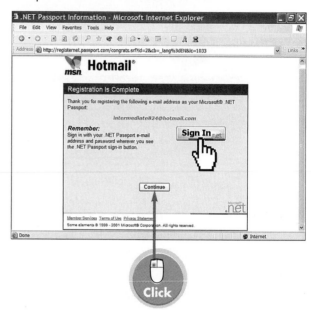

11 Choose a Subscription

Although Hotmail is free, there's also an expanded account available for $19.95 a year that offers more storage space for your mail and other benefits. If you want to join, click the **Continue to Billing Information** button. To stick with the free account, don't click anything yet.

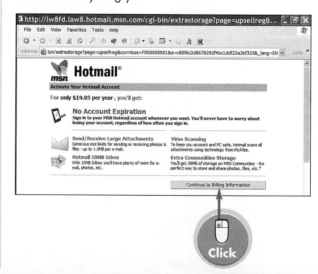

⑫ Use the Free Service

At the bottom of the page, Microsoft describes the pay and free Hotmail subscriptions. To choose the free option, click the **Click here** hyperlink.

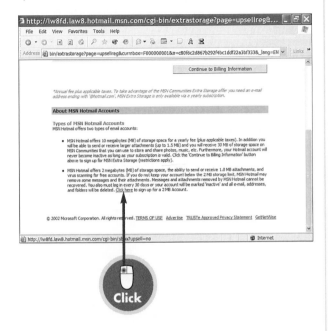

⑬ Pick WebCourier Services

After you pick a subscription (and pay for it, if necessary), Hotmail enables you to sign up to receive free WebCourier email newsletters. Hover your mouse over a newsletter's check box to read about the service in an adjacent area of the page. To subscribe to the service, enable the check box.

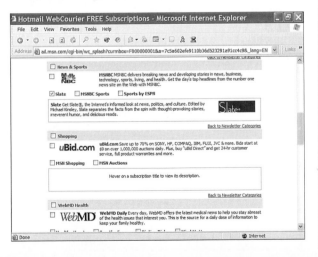

⑭ Complete Sign-Up

After you have decided whether to join any of the WebCourier email newsletters, scroll to the bottom of the page and click the **Continue** button.

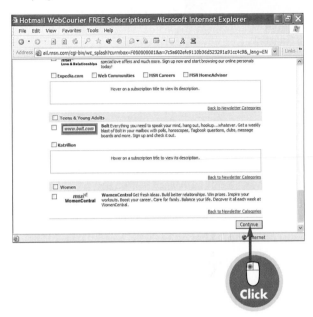

⑮ Choose Special Offers

To receive email offers on topics in entertainment, shopping, and other categories, enable the check boxes for the desired categories. When you're done, click **Continue to Email**. You can start using your new Hotmail account immediately in Internet Explorer or set it up in Outlook Express.

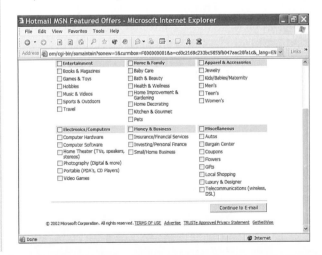

How to Set Up Hotmail in Outlook Express

You can use Hotmail to send and read your email can be in two different ways. One is to use Internet Explorer or another Web browser by visiting the URL http://www.hotmail.com and logging in with your username; you can employ this method regardless of where you are or whose computer you're using. Alternatively, you can use Outlook Express on your own computer to send and read your Hotmail email without ever running your browser. After you sign up for a Hotmail account (as explained in the preceding task), you can set up Outlook Express to work with this account. Hotmail won't interfere with any other email accounts that already use Outlook Express.

1 Run Outlook Express

To get started, run Outlook Express. Click the **Start** button and choose **Email**. When Outlook Express is running, open the **Tools** menu and choose **Accounts**. The **Internet Accounts** dialog box opens.

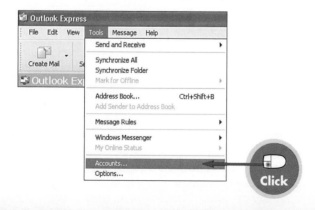

2 Add an Account

The **Internet Accounts** dialog box displays the accounts that currently are set up in Outlook Express. To add your Hotmail account, click the **Add** button and choose **Mail**. The **Internet Connection Wizard** starts.

3 Identify Yourself

Type the name you want to use on your outgoing mail in the **Display name** text box; most people use their real names, but that's not required. Click **Next** to continue.

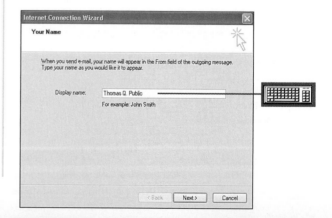

④ Provide Your Address

Type your Hotmail email address—which you set up in the previous task—in the **Email address** text box and click **Next**.

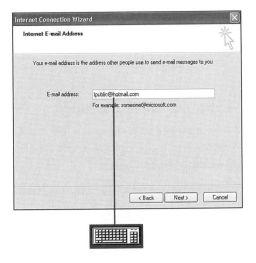

⑤ Confirm Your Settings

Because you entered a Hotmail address, the **Internet Connection Wizard** assumes that you are using an HTTP server with **Hotmail** as your provider. The wizard is correct—click the **Next** button without changing anything on this screen.

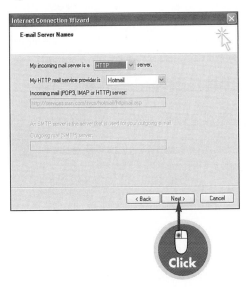

⑥ Provide Login Information

Outlook Express must log in to Hotmail. To make this possible, type your Hotmail email address again in the **Account name** text box and your password in the **Password** box. Then click **Next**. The wizard informs you that the account is ready to set up—click **Finish**.

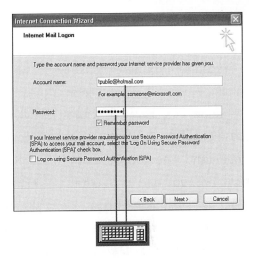

⑦ Close Your Settings

Your Hotmail account will be displayed in the list of accounts that are set up in Outlook Express. Click the **Close** button. A dialog box appears asking whether you want to download folders from Hotmail. Click the **Yes** button. Now you'll have a new set of folders in which you can store Hotmail mail, separate from any other mail.

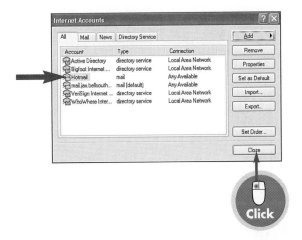

How to Use Your Free Web-Based Email Account

11

The preceding task described how to set up a free Hotmail account with Outlook Express. After you've done this, Hotmail service is fully integrated into all the features of Outlook Express. You can send and receive email through your Hotmail account and any other accounts you have set up. Hotmail messages are stored apart from your other Outlook Express mail in separate **Inbox**, **Sent Items**, **Deleted Items**, **MSN Announcements**, and **Bulk Mail** folders.

① Check Your Hotmail Account

Start Outlook Express: Click **Start** and choose **Email**. To check for messages sent to your Hotmail account, click the Hotmail **Inbox** folder icon in the top-left pane of the window. (If you don't see this icon, click the **Hotmail** icon. A dialog box opens asking if you want to view available folders. Click **Yes**.)

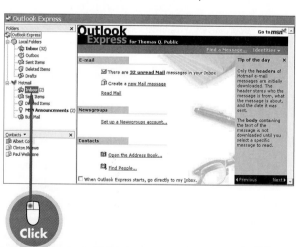

② Start a New Message

Start a new message with Hotmail: Click the **Create Mail** button in the toolbar at the top of the screen. A **New Message** window opens.

③ Choose an Account

Click the arrow to the right of the **From** drop-down list and select the address from which the message should be sent. (If your copy of Outlook Express is configured to use only one email account, the **From** list box will not appear in the **New Message** window.) The **From** list box contains your Hotmail account and any other email accounts you may have set up.

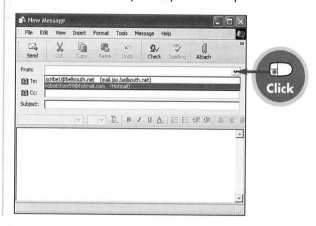

④ Send the Message

After you have specified the recipient of your message in the **To** text box and typed the body of your message, click the **Send** button to deliver the message using Hotmail. If the recipient replies to the message, the reply will be received in your Hotmail **Inbox** folder.

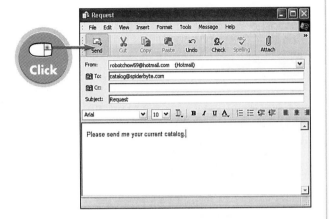

⑥ Choose a Default

Click the **Mail** tab to bring that screen to the front. All your mail accounts are listed. To make your Hotmail account the default, click the **Hotmail** list item and then click the **Set as Default** button.

⑤ Change Mail Settings

If you want Hotmail to be your primary mail service, you can change your Outlook Express settings to make that happen. From the **Tools** menu, choose **Accounts**. The **Internet Accounts** dialog box opens.

How to Print an Email Message

You can print email from Outlook Express using the standard Windows printing interface. Because email you receive from Outlook Express (and many other types of mail software) can contain the same kind of content as a Web page, printing a message is similar to printing a Web page. You can print the current message, print all the hyperlinks it contains, and print a collection of linked pages. Messages can be sent to a printer, sent out using a fax modem, or saved as a disk file.

1 Choose the Print Command

To print the message you're currently reading in Outlook Express, choose **File**, **Print**. The **Print** dialog box opens.

2 Choose a Printer

You can send Web pages to any printer or fax modem that has been installed on your system. To print the page, choose a printer from the **Select Printer** window and click **Print**.

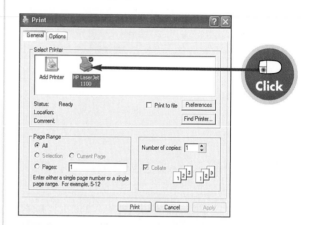

3 Customize the Print Job

You can make changes to how Outlook Express prints hyperlinks and frames (separate sections on a Web page that often have their own scrollbars and borders). To begin, click the **Options** tab to bring it to the front.

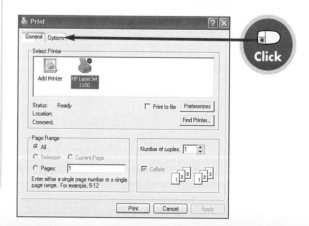

4   Print Associated Web Pages

Outlook Express can look at all hyperlinks in the current email message and print the Web pages associated with those links. Enable the **Print all linked documents** check box to print the pages that are linked to the email message.

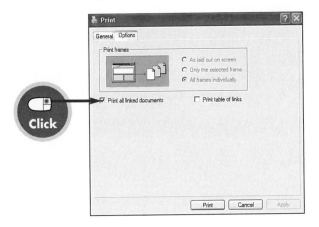

5   List All Hyperlinks

At the same time you print the email message, you can print a report listing all the hyperlinks in that message. Enable the **Print table of links** check box to print the list.

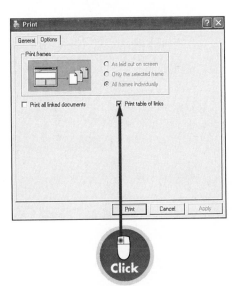

6   Print a Framed Message

Some email messages are divided into separate frames. If a message contains frames, three options will be available: Print each frame individually, print the message as it looks in Outlook Express, or print only the selected frame. To select a frame, click your mouse in that section of the message before printing the page and then select the **Only the selected frame** option.

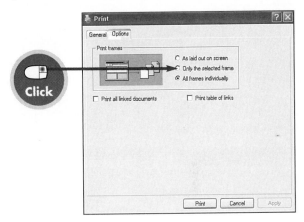

7   Print the Message

Click the **Print** button to print the email message according to the options you have selected. Your printer's dialog box opens, displaying the status of the printing operation. You should soon hear the printer working on the page.

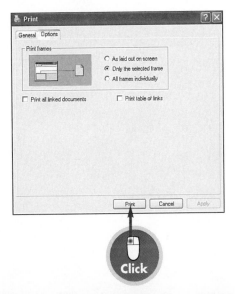

Task

(1) How to Add Someone to Your Contact List 378

(2) How to Invite Someone to Use Messenger 380

(3) How to Send Someone an Instant Message 382

(4) How to Prevent Someone from Sending
You Messages 384

18

Sending and Receiving Instant Messages

There are more than a dozen different ways to chat, including America Online's member-only chat rooms and World Wide Web chat pages. Some of these chat options are described in Chapter 19, "Participating in Chat and Online Communities." You also can use the free instant-messaging services offered by AOL, Microsoft, and others.

Instant messaging is a style of chat in which you can keep track of people you know who are using the same software. A server tells you when selected people are online and provides the same information about you to others. You can send private messages that are received instantly on another user's computer.

Windows XP includes Windows Messenger, instant-messaging software you can use to communicate with other people who employ the same software. Other Windows users can download the program free from Microsoft at the Web address `http://messenger.msn.com`.

How to Add Someone to Your Contact List

Before you run Windows Messenger, you must set up a Microsoft Passport. When Windows Messenger is running, it adds its icon to the *system tray*—the area of the Windows taskbar closest to the current time. You can display Messenger's main window by double-clicking the Messenger icon in the system tray. One of the ways to use the program is to keep in touch with people you know who are also Messenger users. You can track whether they are online by adding them to your contact list.

① Open Windows Messenger

To run Windows Messenger for the first time, click the Messenger icon in the Internet Explorer toolbar. The main Windows Messenger window opens.

② View Your Contacts

The main Windows Messenger window lists all the contacts you communicate with using the software (if you're just getting started, this window will contain no contacts). To begin setting up your contact list, click the **Add a Contact** link. The **Add a Contact Wizard** opens.

③ Add a New Contact

If you know the email address of someone you want to contact using instant messages, choose the **By email address or sign-in name** option and click the **Next** button. (The **Search for a contact** option is covered in the next task.)

4 Enter the Address

You can add people to your contact list whether or not they currently use Windows Messenger. To add a contact to your list, type the person's email address in the text box and click the **Next** button.

5 Notifying a Contact

Windows Messenger doesn't immediately recognize whether your contact uses Messenger or not. You have a chance to send an email message to the person about Messenger, even if it isn't necessary. Click the **Next** button to continue.

6 Add Another Contact

If you have another contact to add to your list, click the **Next** button. Otherwise, click the **Finish** button to return to the main **Windows Messenger** window.

How to Hint

Trying Other Instant-Messaging Software

Millions of people use other instant-messaging software from AOL, Yahoo!, and other companies. Note that you can't communicate with those people directly from Windows Messenger; to send instant messages, you must be using the same software as the person with whom you want to chat. To try these other instant-messaging programs, type one of these addresses in your browser's **Address bar** and press **Enter**:

- **Yahoo! Messenger**: http://messenger.yahoo.com
- **AOL Instant Messenger**: http://www.aim.com
- **ICQ**: http://www.icq.com/download
- **Jabber.com**: http://www.jabber.com/downloads

How to Invite Someone to Use Messenger

Although Windows Messenger has more than 25 million users, you're likely to find that many people you'd like to chat with aren't yet using the software. More than 50 million people use instant-messaging programs from AOL and Yahoo!, and many others don't use any messaging software at all. If you add someone to your contact list who does not use Messenger, the program makes it easy to send an email message telling that person how to get the appropriate software.

1 Open Windows Messenger

To open the Windows Messenger program, double-click the Windows Messenger icon in the system tray. The main **Windows Messenger** window opens.

2 Add the Person

To look for someone you'd like to contact using Messenger, click the **Add a Contact** link. The **Add a Contact Wizard** appears.

3 Search for a Contact

If you don't know the person's email address but do know that he or she uses Hotmail, you can search Hotmail's member directory. Choose the **Search for a contact** radio button and click the **Next** button.

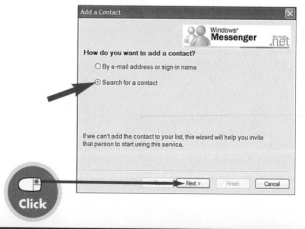

④ Look in Hotmail

Type the person's name in the **First Name** and **Last Name** text boxes. To narrow a search, fill out the **Country/Region**, **City**, and **State** boxes. Make sure that **Hotmail Member Directory** is selected in the **Search for this person at** drop-down list and click **Next**.

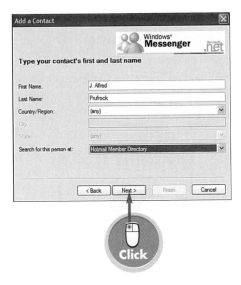

⑥ Notify the Person

Hotmail won't release a person's email address if you find it in the directory, but it can send an email to that person on your behalf describing Windows Messenger. If you'd like to do this, click the **Next** button.

⑤ Find the Right Person

The **Search Results** dialog box lists everyone who matches the fields in your search. If you think you have found the right person, choose his or her name from the results list and click the **Next** button.

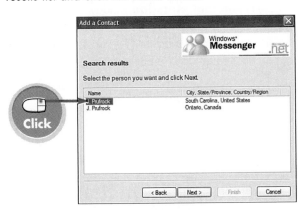

⑦ Send an Invitation

You can read the message that Microsoft will send on your behalf touting Windows Messenger and add a note of your own. Type your message in the top text box. When you're done, click **Next** to send it (or **Cancel** if you have decided not to send an email message). Click **Finish** to exit the wizard.

How to Send Someone an Instant Message

After you have added some people to your contact list, you can use Windows Messenger to send private messages to them. Messages are delivered instantly if the person is connected to Messenger. Two things happen when new messages arrive: A distinctive sound is played and the message appears briefly above the system tray. If you try to send a message to someone who isn't connected, Messenger asks whether you want to send an email message instead of an instant message.

❶ Run Windows Messenger

To run Windows Messenger, double-click the Windows Messenger icon in the system tray. (You also can run the program by clicking the Windows Messenger icon on the Internet Explorer toolbar.) The **Windows Messenger** main window opens.

❷ Choose a Contact

You can send an instant message to anyone in your contact list who is listed under the **Online** heading. To send a message, double-click the contact's name. If you double-click a contact in the **Not Online** list, a dialog box opens asking if you want to send an email message instead.

❸ Write a Message

You use the **Instant Message** window to compose an instant message. The recipient of the message is the person listed in the window's title bar. Type your message in the text box at the bottom of the window.

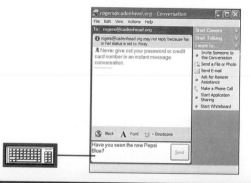

④ Send the Message

To send your message, click the **Send** button. If this button becomes grayed out before you can click it, that means the recipient has disconnected from Windows Messenger, making it impossible for you to send a message.

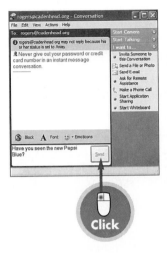

⑤ End the Chat

The top window displays your messages along with any replies that you receive. When you're finished chatting, close the window by clicking the **x** button in the window's title bar.

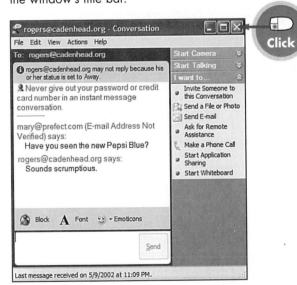

Sending Messages to Other People

You can send instant messages to people who are not on your contact list. Click the **Send an Instant Message** link on the main Windows Messenger window and choose the **Other** tab. A dialog box opens that can be used to enter the recipient's email address. The instant message can be delivered only if the recipient is online with Windows Messenger.

Sending Photos and Other Files

You also can send a file to someone on your contact list if they currently are online. Click the **Send a File or Photo** link. The **Send a File** dialog opens with a list of your contacts. Click the name of a contact and click **OK**. A dialog box opens that enables you to find a file on your computer. Click the name of the file to send it.

Asking for Remote Assistance

The Windows Messenger version on Windows XP has a feature called *Remote Assistance* that enables a person you're chatting with to control your computer over the Internet. One way to use this: Get a technically minded friend to help you fix something.

To use this feature, both of you must have Windows Messenger on Windows XP. Begin a chat with the person, and then click the **Ask for Remote Assistance** link in the Conversation window to request assistance.

How to Prevent Someone from Sending You Messages

As is true with email and other forms of communication on the Internet, instant messaging is open to abuse. There's nothing to prevent people from sending you unsolicited commercial advertisements (for scam products or worse), abusive comments, and other unwelcome messages. Windows Messenger can be set up to block specific users from ever contacting you again. You also can block all messages temporarily when you are too busy to chat or away from the computer.

1 View a Message

Windows Messenger can receive instant messages even when you're not actively using the program. When a message arrives, the first few lines are displayed briefly in a small window near the system tray. Click the message text to read it.

2 Open a Message

After an instant message arrives, if you don't open it right away, its window is minimized on the Windows taskbar. Click the message's taskbar button to read the message.

3 Block Someone

If you read an instant message and decide that you don't want to receive more messages from the sender, click the **Block** button. A dialog box may open asking you to confirm your decision to block messages from this sender.

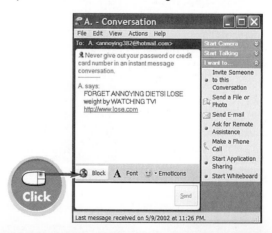

④ Confirm the Block

If you see a confirmation dialog box, click **OK** to block the sender. You will appear to be offline to that person at all times, and no more messages from him or her will be delivered to you. Windows Messenger does not inform the person that you are blocking messages.

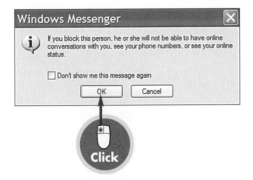

⑤ Discourage Messages

To let people know when you can't chat, open the main **Windows Messenger** window and click your email address. From the menu of options that appears, choose **Busy, Be Right Back**, **Away**, **On the Phone,** or **Out to Lunch**. This text and a special icon will appear next to your name on the contact list of people you chat with. Any messages that are sent to you while you are busy still come to you in the normal way; the sender just gets a message indicating that you can't respond immediately for the reason you specified.

⑥ Prevent All Messages

You still can receive messages if you have selected **Busy** or one of the other choices in Step 5. To stop receiving instant messages, click your email address in the main **Windows Messenger** window and choose **Appear Offline**. Now people on your contact list will think you are no longer connected to Messenger.

How to Hint

Letting People Know You Can Chat

After you choose **Busy**, **Be Right Back**, or one of the other message-discouraging options in Windows Messenger, you should let people know when you're back and available to talk again. To do so, click your email address in the main Windows Messenger window and choose **Online**.

Task

1 How to Create an Account to Chat on MSN 388

2 How to Chat for the First Time on MSN 390

3 How to Participate in a Chat on MSN 392

4 How to Join a Community on MSN 394

5 How to Read and Send Messages in an
MSN Community 396

19

Participating in Chat and Online Communities

There are thousands of World Wide Web sites where you can hold conversations with other people. Some of these sites are chat rooms, where people send and receive messages that are delivered immediately to each other. Everyone talks at once, several conversations can occur at the same time, and it can be hard to keep track of what's going on. After you become familiar with using chats, however, it will be easier for you to follow the many threads of conversation in a room.

Other sites are message boards, where people can post messages that are presented on a page for others to read and respond to by writing their own replies.

There are a variety of ways and places to chat on the Internet: Web sites, America Online, Internet Relay Chat (IRC), and instant-messaging services such as Windows Messenger and ICQ.

MSN, the Web portal offered by Microsoft, offers chat rooms and message boards for everyone with a Microsoft Passport.

How to Create an Account to Chat on MSN

On MSN Chat, a feature of Microsoft's MSN Web site, there are hundreds of chat rooms in which people gather to talk in groups of 2–35 people. You can hold conversations with people who share a common interest, age, city, or lifestyle. Topics include current events, politics, sports, dating, music, and software. These chats are informal and lively. Before you can set up an account on MSN Chat, however, you must have a Microsoft Passport.

1 Visit MSN Chat

To visit the Chat section of the MSN site, type the URL http://chat.msn.com into your browser's **Address bar** and press **Enter**. A page opens listing a directory of chat rooms and some upcoming chats with celebrities that will take place soon.

2 Present Your Passport

Before you chat, you should sign in to your Microsoft Passport account. If you haven't done so yet, click the **Sign In** button at the top of the page.

3 Provide Your Age

If this is one of the first times you have used your Microsoft Passport, you might be asked for your birth date. Use the drop-down boxes to choose your birth month and day then type your year in the adjacent text box. When you're finished, click **Continue**.

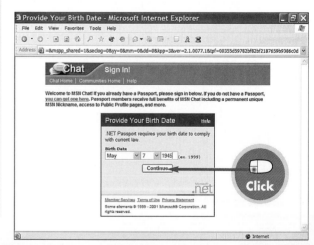

4 Choose a Nickname

MSN Chat identifies you using a nickname of your choosing rather than your email address or real name. Microsoft suggests several nicknames; click a name to use it or click the **More Suggested Names** link to see more suggestions. To choose your own nickname, type it in the text box and click **Register Nickname**.

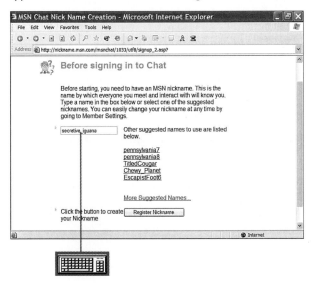

5 Create a Profile

Every participant in MSN Chat has a public profile that can be viewed by others. To make sure that you're revealing only the things you want to reveal, click the **Create a public profile** button.

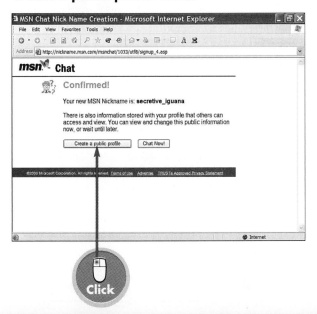

6 Identify Yourself

Fill out all the items in the **About Me** section (these items are required to set up an MSN Chat account). To protect your privacy, however, don't type your full name in the **Display name** text box. Scroll down to see the rest of the form.

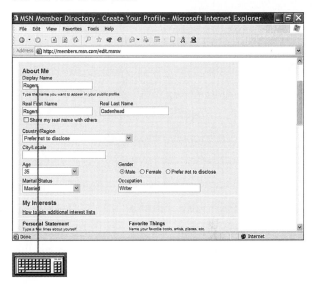

7 Complete Your Profile

Finish the form by filling out the **Permissions** section. Click the **Code of Conduct** link to review the site's rules; enable the **I accept** box if you agree. Finally, click the **Save** button to set up your MSN Chat account.

How to Chat for the First Time on MSN

As you will discover quickly when you participate in a chat room, chats are a part of the Internet that's susceptible to abuse. Although most chat users are friendly, you should be extremely cautious about what you reveal in any chat room. The term *phishing* refers to efforts to steal a password or credit-card information in a chat or instant message, and scams like that are relatively common. To be safe when chatting on the Internet, you should never reveal personal information such as your phone number, address, credit-card number, or passwords.

1 Visit MSN Chat

To visit the Chat section of the MSN site, type the URL `http://chat.msn.com` into your browser's **Address bar** and press **Enter**.

2 Sign In To Passport

You can't join a chat without signing in to MSN, which requires your Microsoft Passport. If you aren't signed in, click the **Sign In** button at the top of the page.

Click

3 Identify Yourself

You might be asked to sign in to your Passport account. Choose your email address from the drop-down box and type your password in the **Password** text box. When you're finished, click **OK**.

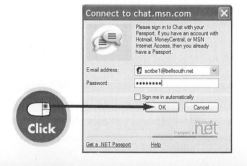

Click

④ Choose a Chat Category

MSN Chat organizes chat rooms by topic. To see the chat rooms in a specific category, click the hyperlink for a category (such as **News**). A page opens listing chat rooms that are currently open in that category.

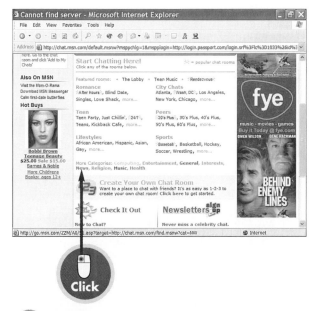

⑤ Choose a Chat Room

Rooms can be created by MSN or chat users. To visit one of the listed chat rooms, click its name. **Headlines** is one of the permanent rooms in the **News** category, as indicated by a MSN butterfly icon. Click the **Headlines** link to join an ongoing discussion of current news.

⑥ Download Software

If you have never participated in an MSN Chat, your browser might require special software that works with Internet Explorer. In that case, the **We are now downloading MSN Chat software** text appears. (If you're not using Internet Explorer, you'll be directed to a "this feature requires Internet Explorer" page.) A **Security Warning** dialog box appears after the download is finished.

⑦ Install Software

MSN Chat Control is software that works in conjunction with Internet Explorer to present chat rooms. To install the software, click the **Yes** button. To participate in your first chat, proceed to Task 3.

How to Participate in a Chat on MSN

If you have never participated in an MSN Chat, follow the instructions in the preceding task, "How to Chat for the First Time on MSN," before you start to chat. After MSN Chat Control is set up to work with Internet Explorer, it appears whenever you enter a chat room on MSN. To find a chat room, type the URL `http://chat.msn.com` in your browser's **Address bar** and press **Enter**, click the link of a chat category such as **News**, and then click the name of a room.

1 Write a Message

In an MSN chat room, all messages sent by people using the room appear in a large chat window along with the nickname of the sender. To write your own message, type it in the box at the bottom of the chat window.

2 Send a Message

To send your message to everyone in the chat room, click the **Send** button. Your message appears along with your nickname (also called your display name) at the bottom of the chat window.

3 Ignore a User

To ignore all messages sent by a particular user, click that user's nickname in the list of people in the room on the right side of the page, and then click the **Ignore** button.

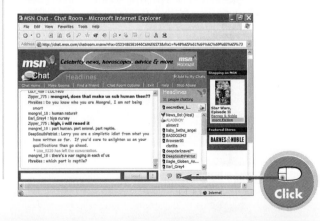

4 Begin a Private Chat

You can speak to a chat room participant privately while in MSN Chat. To begin a private conversation, double-click the person's nickname in the list of people in the room. A **whisper** window opens in which you can conduct a conversation away from the rest of the room.

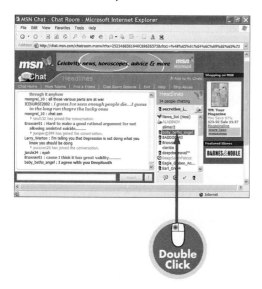

Double Click

5 Send a Private Message

In the **whisper** window, type the private message in the text box at the bottom of the window. When you're ready, click **Whisper** to send the message. The message does not appear in the chat room window; instead, it is sent only to the specified recipient.

6 Read a Response

Your private messages and the replies you receive will appear in the **whisper** window's top text box. To continue the private conversation, type text in the bottom box and click **Whisper**. When you're done chatting privately, click the **x** button on the **whisper** window's title bar to close the window and return to the main chat room.

Click

How to Hint

Chatting with People on Yahoo!

Yahoo! offers chat rooms that are similar to those featured on the MSN portal. You can participate in live chats with celebrities, join rooms created by Yahoo! and other users, and talk privately with other participants. To use a Yahoo! account to participate in these chats, type the URL **http://chat.yahoo.com** into your browser's **Address bar** and press **Enter**.

How to Join a Community on MSN

If the pace of a chat room is not to your liking or you'd like to participate in more formal discussions, you may be interested in message boards and other discussion Web sites. Message boards are Web pages where you can read messages posted by others and write your own responses. MSN offers this feature in its **Communities** section, where hundreds of people create and maintain boards on various topics. Joining an MSN community requires a Microsoft Passport account.

① View Your Communities

To see the communities associated with your Microsoft Passport account, type the URL **http://communities.msn.com** in the browser's **Address bar** and press **Enter**.

② Provide Your Passport

The **MSN Communities** home page highlights some of the coolest communities you can join. If you haven't yet signed in to your Microsoft Passport account, click the **Sign In** button at the top of the page.

③ Find a Community

MSN has a directory of communities, but the fastest way to find one of interest is to search for it. Type text to look for in the **Find a Community** text box and click the **Go** button. A page opens listing communities whose names match the text you typed.

④ Visit a Community

MSN offers public communities and private ones. Each community that turns up in a search is open for the public to visit. To take a look at one of these communities, click its hyperlink.

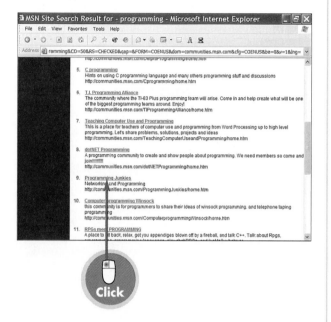

⑤ Join a Community

To join a community, click the **Join Now** hyperlink in the column along the left side of the page.

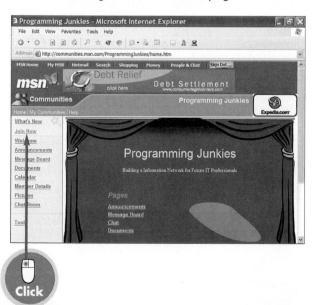

⑥ Identify Yourself

Type a nickname you would like to use in the community in the first text box and your email address in the second text box. Choose an option for how you would like to receive messages.

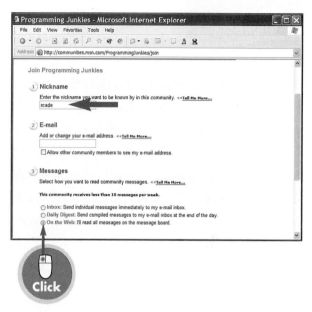

⑦ Send Your Application

Before joining a community, you must review the MSN conditions of membership by clicking the **Code of Conduct** hyperlink. If you accept the terms, enable the **I accept** check box. When you're finished, click the **Join Now** button. You'll be added to the community if it allows public membership.

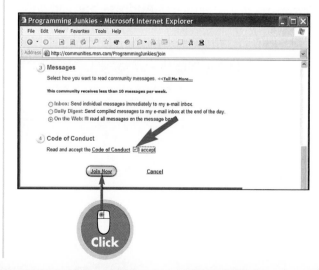

How to Read and Send Messages in an MSN Community

Because MSN Community message boards can be read and replied to at your leisure, the discussions are often more formal than those you find in a chat room. In some ways, a message board is like a discussion taking place in email, except that everything is published for others to read. On its community message boards, MSN publishes the messages you post with your chosen nickname rather than with your email address or any other identifying information.

② Visit a Community

To visit one of the communities you have joined, click its hyperlink. If you'd like to look for other communities instead, click the **Home** hyperlink at the top of the page.

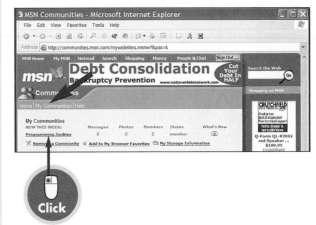

① View Your Communities

To see the communities you have joined (or created) on MSN, type the address **http://communities.msn.com/MyWebSites** in your browser's **Address bar** and press **Enter**. A page opens with links to each community.

③ View a Message Board

Click the **Message Board** hyperlink to see a community's message board. If a community has more than one message board, a page opens where you can choose a specific board by clicking its link.

4 Read Messages

Discussions are organized by subject. To read a discussion, click a link in the **Subject** list. You also can start a new discussion of your own: Click the **New Discussion** hyperlink.

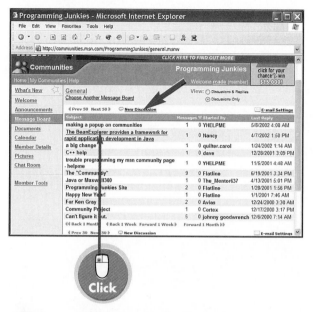

5 Reply to a Message

Every message you read has a **Reply** hyperlink you can use to post a public message in response to the original message. Click this link to reply to the message you are reading. A window opens where you can type your message and send it.

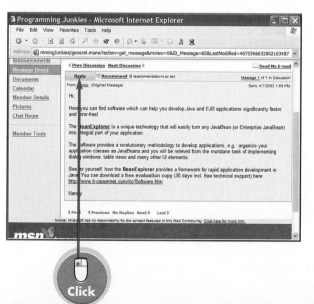

6 Compose a Reply

Type your message in the text box. When you're finished, click the **Send** button. Within a minute or two, your message should show up on the community's message board.

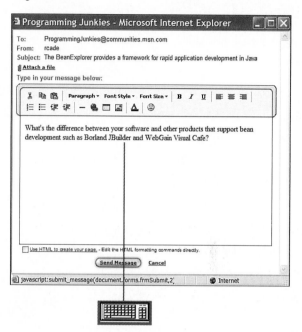

How to Hint

Creating Your Own Message Board

If you don't find an MSN community on a topic that interests you, you can build your own. Anyone with a Microsoft Passport account can create a community with a message board and other features and decide whether to make it available to the public or restrict its membership.

Visiting a Weblog Community

Some communities on the Web are organized to exchange links to interesting sites and news stories. These sites are called *weblogs* because they present a daily log of site links. One of the most popular is the 14,000-member MetaFilter, a weblog established by Matt Haughey that's frequented by Web developers, programmers, political aficionados, and others. To visit, type the URL **http://www.metafilter.com** in your browser's **Address bar** and press **Enter**.

1 How to Set Up Outlook Express for Usenet
   Newsgroups 400

2 How to Read a Newsgroup 402

3 How to Read Newsgroups You Have
   Subscribed To 404

4 How to Post a Message to a Newsgroup 406

5 How to Find a Newsgroup 408

6 How to Search an Archive of Past Newsgroup
   Discussions 410

7 How to Decrease the Junk Email You Receive 412

Task

20

Participating in Usenet Discussion Groups

One of the most popular communities on the Internet is Usenet, a collection of public discussion groups on a diverse range of topics. Usenet groups, which also are called *newsgroups*, are distributed by thousands of Internet sites around the world.

Newsgroups function in a manner similar to electronic mailing lists. Subscribers join a group in which they are interested, read the messages written by other subscribers, and contribute their own messages. When you post a message in a Usenet newsgroup, it is copied by all servers connected to Usenet that carry the newsgroup.

The decentralized design of Usenet gives it a unique personality. Messages can't be removed from all those servers after they are sent. Although a small number of Usenet newsgroups have a moderator who must approve messages before they are distributed, most newsgroups are unrestricted.

This freedom leads to many discussions that might never take place anywhere else but on Usenet. Of course, it also does little to discourage things that shouldn't be taking place at all.

How to Set Up Outlook Express for Usenet Newsgroups

Outlook Express supports Usenet newsgroups in addition to email. To participate in Usenet, you must have access to a *news server*—an Internet site that can send and receive newsgroup messages. Many Internet service providers offer Usenet as part of a subscription. If yours does, the provider must give you the name of its news server. You also can subscribe to Usenet with services such as Supernews and NewsGuy. Before you can set up Outlook Express to work with Usenet, you must have the name of your news server. If your server requires a username and password, you also must have this information to get started.

❶ Run Outlook Express

Launch Outlook Express: Click the **Start** button and choose **Email**.

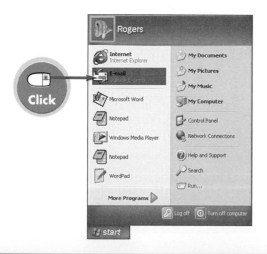

❷ Set Up Newsgroups

If Outlook Express has not already been set up to work with Usenet, a **Set up a Newsgroups account** hyperlink will be displayed. Click this hyperlink to start the **Internet Connection Wizard**.

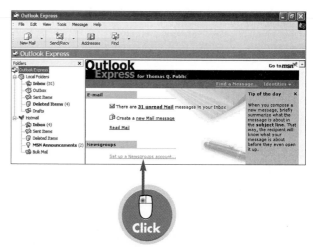

❸ Identify Yourself

A name will be displayed on all the messages you post in Usenet newsgroups. In the **Display name** text box, type the name, or *handle*, that will identify you. Unlike email, where real names are the norm, on Usenet it is commonplace for people to use a nickname or similar pseudonym when posting messages. Click **Next** to continue.

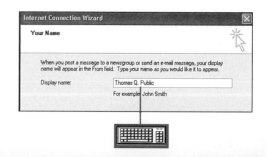

④ Identify Your Address

An email address also will be displayed on your Usenet messages. In the **Email address** text box, type your email address and click **Next** to continue.

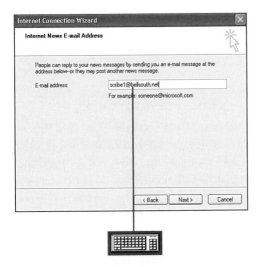

⑤ Identify Your Server

Type your server's name in the **News (NNTP) Server** text box. Most news servers do not require a username and password. If your server does not require you to log on, click **Next** to finish setting up your Usenet service. If your news server does require you to log on (your ISP will have told you so), check the **My news server requires me to log on** box. When you click **Next** to continue, you'll be asked for your username and password for the news server.

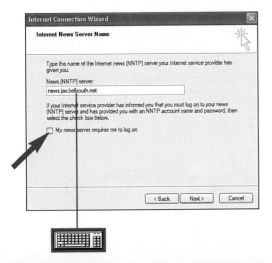

⑥ Set Up the Usenet Service

After you have created a Usenet account, you are asked whether you want to download newsgroups from your server. This step is needed so that you can find discussion groups on topics of interest. Click the **Yes** button to download them. Many servers offer more than 20,000 different newsgroups, so it might take five minutes or more to download the list of groups.

How to Read a Newsgroup

After you have set up Usenet service in Outlook Express, you're ready to read *news*—public messages contributed to the various newsgroups. There are more than 54,000 newsgroups on many Usenet servers, and some of the more popular groups receive more than 100 messages a day. If you find a newsgroup you'd like to read on a regular basis, you can subscribe to it and keep up with the group more easily.

1 Read Usenet Messages

To begin reading newsgroups in Outlook Express, click the **Start** button and choose **Email** to launch Outlook Express. Then, click the **Read News** hyperlink.

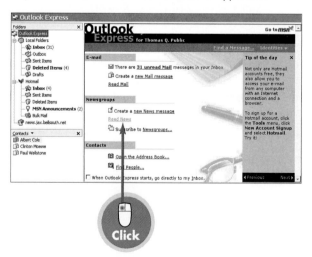

2 View Newsgroups

If you have not yet subscribed to any newsgroups, you'll be asked whether you want to see a list of available groups. Click the **Yes** button to display the **Newsgroup Subscriptions** dialog box. (If you have subscribed to any groups, you can view available groups by clicking the **Newsgroups** button in the news window when it opens.)

3 Search Newsgroups

Usenet newsgroups are given names that describe their purpose. To search for groups on a topic, type the topic in the **Display newsgroups which contain** text box. As you type, matching groups will be listed in the bottom pane of the window.

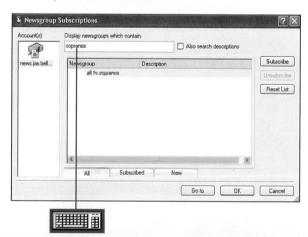

④ Choose a Group

If you want to read the messages in one of the newsgroups that is listed as a result of your search term, click the newsgroup name and then click the **Go to** button.

⑤ Read Messages

Outlook Express displays Usenet messages similarly to the way it displays email messages. Click the subject of a message to view that message in the Outlook Express window; alternatively, double-click the subject to view the message in a new window.

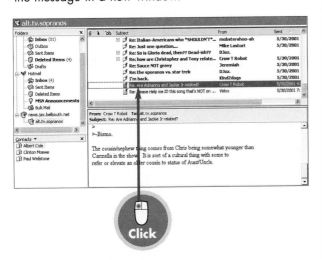

⑥ Subscribe to a Group

The easiest way to read Usenet newsgroups is to subscribe to the groups you frequent. To subscribe to a group while reading it, right-click the group name in the **Folders** pane and select **Subscribe** from the context menu that appears. The next task explains how to read news for newsgroups you've subscribed to.

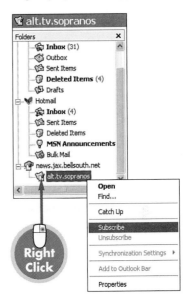

How to Hint

Finding Groups by Their Descriptions

Many newsgroups also have brief descriptions that provide more information about the group. To search through these descriptions as you're looking for newsgroups, enable the **Also search descriptions** check box in step 4. The first time you enable this option, descriptions must be downloaded, which may take five minutes or more depending on the speed of your Internet connection.

How to Read Newsgroups You Have Subscribed To

The most convenient way to read Usenet newsgroups is to subscribe to them. The preceding task explained how to subscribe to a newsgroup with Outlook Express. Outlook Express keeps track of your subscription internally and makes it easy to follow new discussions. After you have subscribed to a group, you can automatically download new subjects and messages with the synchronization feature.

1 View Newsgroups

After you have subscribed to a newsgroup, you can read the news for that group at any time. Click the **Start** button and choose **Email** to open Outlook Express; then click the **Read News** hyperlink to begin setting up synchronization. A new window opens; Outlook Express uses the name of your news server as the window's title when you read news.

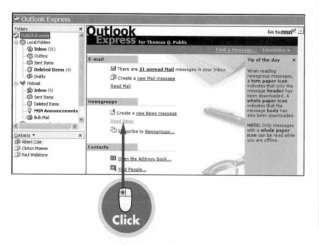

2 Set Up Newsgroups

The synchronization feature in Outlook Express determines how a subscribed newsgroup will be updated. To set up a group so that new subject headings are downloaded, click the name of the newsgroup in the right pane of the window, click the **Settings** button, and then choose **Headers Only** from the drop-down list.

3 Download All Messages

To set up a group so that all messages are downloaded automatically to a Usenet folder in Outlook Express, click the group name, click the **Settings** button, and then choose **All Messages**. This is the most time-consuming option, especially for a popular and active newsgroup.

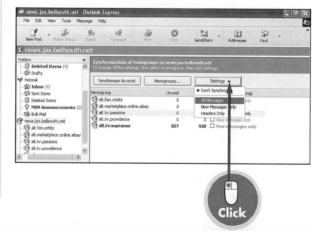

④ Download New Messages

To set up a group so that new messages are downloaded as they arrive, click the group name, click the **Settings** button, and then choose **New Messages Only**.

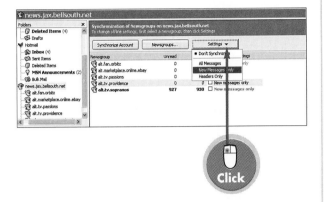

⑤ Synchronize Newsgroups

After you have specified how you want to synchronize your newsgroups, click the **Synchronize Account** button to retrieve messages based on the settings specified in the **Settings** column. Click this button every time you want to check your server for new Usenet messages in your subscribed groups.

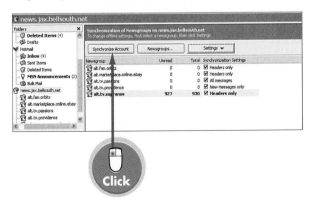

⑥ Retrieve Messages

As Outlook is synchronizing newsgroups and downloading messages, it displays a progress dialog box. Click the **Details** button to see more information on what Outlook Express is retrieving.

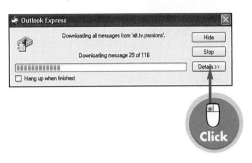

How to Hint

Stopping the Retrieval of Messages from a Group

If you want to put a Usenet subscription on hold for a while, choose the group, click the **Settings** button, and choose **Don't Synchronize**. You'll remain subscribed, but you won't retrieve any messages or subject headings until you change the **Settings** option for that group.

How to Post a Message to a Newsgroup

Anyone who reads a Usenet newsgroup can participate in its discussions by posting a message. Your message may be distributed to thousands of servers around the world, depending on the newsgroups you're posting to. One thing you'll become acquainted with as you post messages is the concept of *netiquette*—commonly accepted standards for behavior on the Internet. Although you can post a Usenet message to as many groups as you like, established netiquette says you should post to four groups or fewer.

1 Post a New Message

After you have decided which newsgroup(s) you want to post a message to, click the **new News message** hyperlink in Outlook Express. A **New Message** dialog box opens.

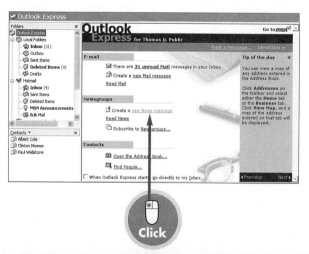

Click

2 Choose Newsgroups

In the **Newsgroups** text box, type the name of the group to which you want to post this message. You can specify more than one newsgroup if you separate the group names with commas.

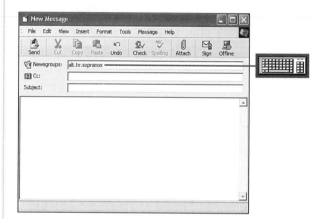

3 Send a Copy by Mail

You also can email a copy of your newsgroup posting to anyone who has an Internet email account—regardless of whether that person reads the newsgroup you're posting to. Type the recipient's email address in the **Cc** text box.

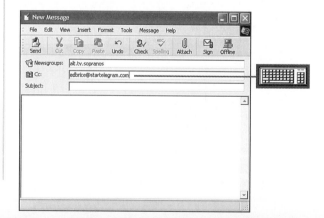

4   Describe Your Message

In the **Subject** text box, type a succinct description of your message. The subject helps Usenet news readers skim a Usenet newsgroup looking for topics that interest them.

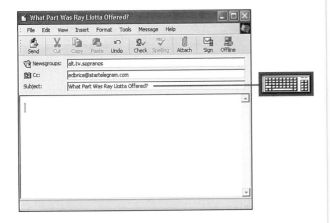

5   Send Your Message

Type the text of the message you want to post and then click the **Send** button. Your message will be submitted to the newsgroup on your news server and distributed to servers around the world.

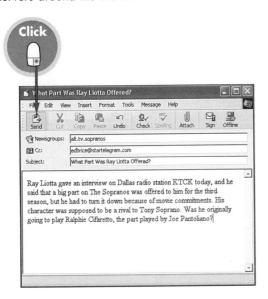

6   Reply to a Message

You also can post messages on Usenet by replying to a message you're reading. With the message selected and displayed in the message pane in the lower-right portion of the Outlook Express window, click the **Reply Group** button. A modified **New Message** window opens. (If you want to reply by email to the author of a Usenet message rather than replying to the entire newsgroup, click the **Reply** button.)

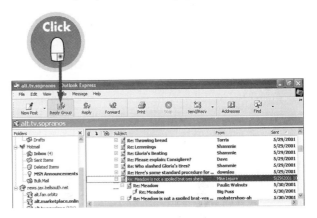

7   Send Your Reply

The text of your reply starts out with the name of the newsgroup you're responding to in the **Newsgroups** box, the **Subject** line filled in, and the text of the original message. If the original message is lengthy, netiquette dictates that you delete any text that is not relevant to your reply. Type your reply and click the **Send** button to distribute the message to the newsgroup.

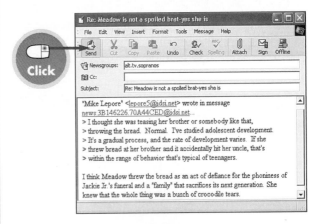

How to Find a Newsgroup

As you're searching for newsgroups in Outlook Express, you may be dismayed to find that there are no groups devoted to a topic you're interested in. There's a chance, however, that you can find a relevant newsgroup elsewhere, since no single Usenet server carries all newsgroups. Currently, there are more than 54,000 Usenet newsgroups; more than a dozen new ones are created every day. After you've searched for a group using Outlook Express, you can use sites on the World Wide Web such as Google to find other newsgroups.

1 Search in Outlook

Start by looking for newsgroups in Outlook Express. Click the **Start** button and choose **Email** to open Outlook Express; then click the **Newsgroups** hyperlink. The **Newsgroup Subscriptions** dialog box opens.

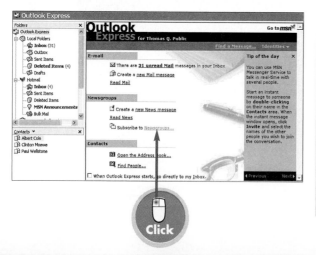

2 Search for Newsgroup Names

To search for specific text in a newsgroup name, type the text in the **Display newsgroups which contain** text box. Outlook Express displays results as you're entering text. To subscribe to a group, click its name, and then click the **Subscribe** button.

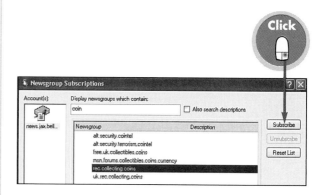

3 Search Descriptions

To search for text in both newsgroup names and descriptions, check the **Also search descriptions** box. The first time you select this option, descriptions are downloaded from your Usenet server to your local machine to speed up the search process.

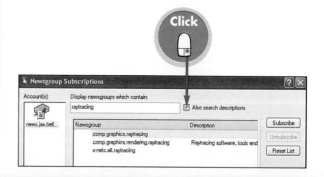

4 Find Other Groups

Several World Wide Web sites offer directories of Usenet groups. To use Google Groups Usenet directory, for example, launch your Web browser, type the URL `http://groups.google.com` in the browser's **Address bar**, and press **Enter**.

6 Read Newsgroups

If Google finds any groups that match the text you typed, they are listed above a list of Usenet messages that also contain that text. Click the newsgroup's name to use your browser to view a list of recent messages posted in the newsgroup.

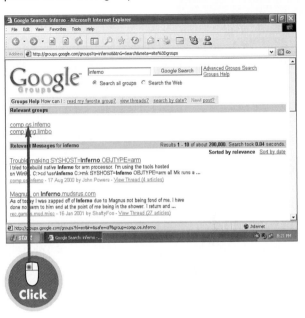

5 Search the Directory

When the Google Groups home page opens, type the text you're looking for in the search box and click the **Search** button.

Comparing Your Usenet Server to Others

One of the best reasons to search a Web directory of Usenet newsgroups is because many groups will be completely unknown to you. No single Usenet server offers a full assortment of the more than 54,000 newsgroups currently available, and many servers carry only those groups that have been specifically requested by users. For more information on how to search Google Groups for newsgroups and other information, see the next task, "How to Search an Archive of Past Newsgroup Discussions."

How to Search an Archive of Past Newsgroup Discussions

An important thing to note about Usenet is that it's routinely archived. Messages you post to newsgroups are saved by several Web sites that make their archives searchable by topic and by author. Google Groups, the most popular archive, has Usenet discussions that date back to 1981. The Google archive is a good place to find newsgroups you aren't familiar with. It's also a great research tool on many subjects—especially technical subjects related to the Internet and computers.

2 Search the Archive

Type the text you're looking for in the search box and click **Search** to begin a search.

1 Visit Google Groups

To visit the Google Groups home page, start your Web browser, type the URL **http://groups.google.com** into the **Address bar**, and press **Enter**. The Web page opens in your browser window.

3 Read Messages

In the results list, Google lists the subjects and some text of messages that match the text you are searching for. To read a message, click the appropriate hyperlink.

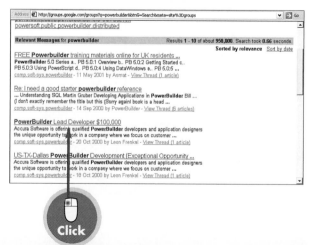

4 Conduct an Advanced Search

For a more advanced search, return to the main Google Groups page and click the **Advanced Groups Search** hyperlink next to the **Search** button.

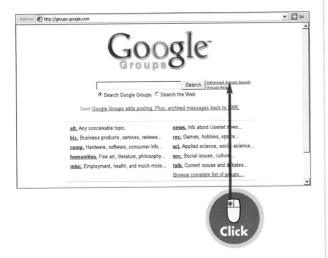

5 Conduct a Search

The Advanced Search feature supports some common searching techniques. Type your search text in one of four **Find messages** boxes and click the **Google Search** button.

6 Search for Recent Messages

Google Groups normally sorts messages based on how well they match the text you are searching for. To arrange messages by date, beginning with the most recent and going backwards, change the **Sort by relevance** drop-down menu selection to **Sort by date**.

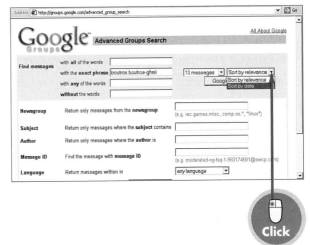

How to Hint

Reading Usenet on Google

Because Google has the most comprehensive archive of Usenet discussions, it's a convenient place to read newsgroups not available on your Usenet server. Simply load the Web site's home page and use the directory of newsgroups.

Keeping Posts Out of Google

All the Usenet messages you post are archived by Google—if its server receives them. To keep a message out of the archive, type the text **X-No-Archive: Yes** on a line of its own as the first line of your message.

How to Decrease the Junk Email You Receive

When you start contributing to Usenet, you can count on receiving more email as a result. Unfortunately, almost all of it will be *spam*—unsolicited advertising email. Marketers who rely on spam to promote their products often build their mailing lists by scanning Usenet messages. You can deter them by posting with a fake email address. Your real address can be placed in a *signature file*—text that is automatically appended to email, Usenet postings, and similar documents.

1 Set Up Options

Start by creating a signature file in Outlook Express. From any screen in Outlook Express, open the **Tools** menu and select the **Options** command. The **Options** dialog box opens.

2 Create a Signature

Click the **Signatures** tab to bring that screen to the front of the dialog box. Click the **New** button to create a new signature file. The default signature filename (**Signature #1**) appears in the **Signatures** list box.

3 Edit the Text

A signature file usually contains your name, email address, personal Web site, and similar personal information. In the **Text** box at the bottom of the dialog box, type the text for your signature file—including your real email address—and click the **Advanced** button. The **Advanced Signature Settings** dialog box opens.

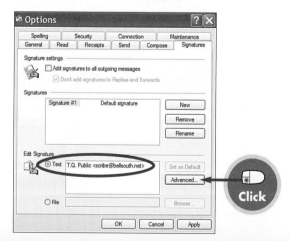

4 Use a Signature

In the list box, enable the check box in front of the Usenet account for which you want to use your new signature file. If you want to use the signature file with other Outlook Express accounts, enable those check boxes also. Then click the **OK** button. Next, close the **Options** dialog box by clicking the **OK** button.

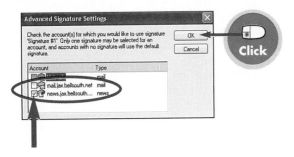

5 Change Your Address

After creating a signature file, you should remove your real email address from your Usenet account. To do so, open the **Tools** menu and choose the **Accounts** command to open the **Internet Accounts** dialog box.

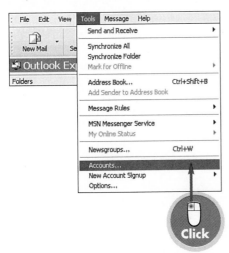

6 Adjust Your Account

Click the **News** tab to view your Usenet newsgroup accounts. Select the account you want to change and then click the **Properties** button. The **Properties** dialog box opens.

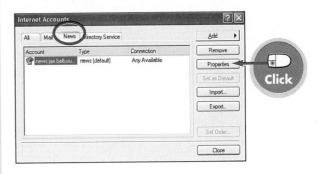

7 Falsify Your Address

In the **Email address** text box on the **General** tab, type an obviously false email address (the address see_my_sig@fake_address.com is suitable for this purpose). Click **OK**. Usenet participants who want to send you mail will know to look for a signature if they want to contact you personally. Spammers will add the fake address to their mailing lists, and you'll never get unsolicited mail from vendors who picked up your email address from the newsgroup.

III

Being Productive with Microsoft Office XP

21 Using Common Office Features **417**

22 Using Word to Create and Edit Documents **447**

23 Using Outlook for Email, Contacts, and Scheduling **507**

24 Using Excel Spreadsheets **539**

25 Creating Presentations with PowerPoint **601**

26 Making Databases with Access **643**

27 Working with Office's Graphics Tools **669**

1 How to Start and Exit Office Applications 418

2 How to Navigate Office Applications 420

3 How to Work with the Task Pane 422

4 How to Work with Menus and Toolbars 424

5 How to Customize Toolbars 426

6 How to Start a New File 428

7 How to Save Your Work 430

8 How to Open and Close Files 432

9 How to Print a File 434

10 How to Find Files 436

11 How to Use the Office Help Tools 438

12 How to Cut, Copy, and Paste Data 440

13 How to Link and Embed Data 442

14 How to Add and Remove Office Components 444

Task

21

Using Common Office Features

All the programs in the Microsoft Office suite have a common look and feel. They share plenty of features and procedures, such as saving and opening files. In the tasks in Part 3, you'll learn to use many of these shared features. For example, each program is opened and closed in the same way. As you use the programs, you'll notice similar dialog boxes for common tasks. This similarity allows you to apply the skills you've learned in one program to another program.

The Office programs share help features, including Office Assistant. You'll also encounter smaller applications that are shared across the Office programs, such as WordArt (a program for creating text-based graphic effects) and Smart Tags (shared buttons for options such as copying, pasting, and correcting errors). You'll learn more about the drawing and graphics tools in Chapter 27, "Working with Office's Graphics Tools."

How to Start and Exit Office Applications

You can start Office programs by using the Windows **Start** menu. When you install the programs, each application's name is added to the **Programs** menu list. If you install Outlook, a shortcut icon is added to the Windows desktop to give you quick access to your daily schedule and email. You can easily add shortcut icons for the other Office programs, but you can also access them quickly from the **Start** menu. After you finish using an application, use one of the several methods for closing the program window. Don't forget to save your work before exiting.

❶ Open the Start Menu

Click the **Start** button on the Windows taskbar. The Windows **Start** menu opens.

❷ Choose Programs

Click **Programs** to display the menu list.

❸ Choose an Application

Click the name of the Microsoft Office program you want to open. To open Excel, for example, select **Microsoft Excel**.

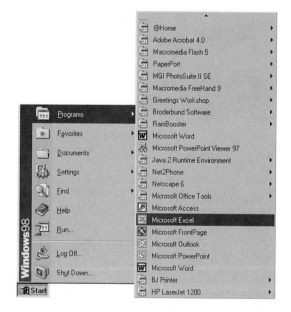

④ View the Program Window

Immediately, the program opens into its own window, with its name in the title bar. Depending on which program you open, you can begin working on a new file, such as a blank Word document, an Excel worksheet, a new PowerPoint presentation, or an Access database. In Outlook, you can check your calendar or view email. In this figure, the Excel program window is open.

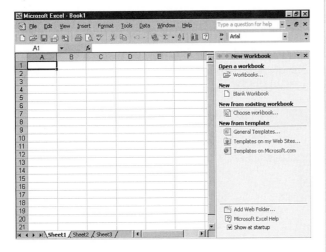

⑤ Quick Exit

The quickest way to close an Office program is to click the window's **Close** button, the one with an × symbol in the upper-right corner of the window. You can also choose **File, Exit** or press **Alt+F4** on the keyboard to close the application.

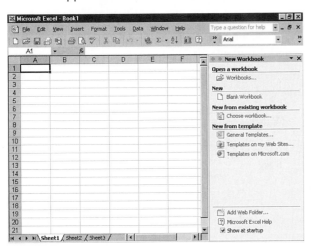

⑥ Save It

If you haven't saved your work yet, the program prompts you to do so before exiting. Click **Yes** to save, **No** to exit without saving, or **Cancel** to cancel the exit procedure. (Outlook doesn't work with files like the other programs, so you won't see this prompt box when exiting it.) To learn more about saving files, turn to Task 7, "How to Save Your Work."

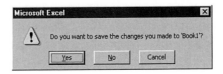

How-to Hint

Switching Between Programs

To switch between open program windows, use the Windows taskbar. Each open program is represented by an icon on the taskbar. Press **Ctrl+Esc** to display the taskbar, and then click the button for the program you want to see.

Creating a Shortcut Icon

You can easily create a shortcut icon for any Office program you want to access from the Windows desktop. Right-click over a blank area of the desktop and choose **New**, **Shortcut** from the pop-up menu. This opens the **Create Shortcut** Wizard. Use the **Browse** button to locate and select the Office program to which you want to create a shortcut, such as WINWORD.EXE for Word, and then click **Next** to continue. Type a name for the shortcut and click **Finish**. The next time you want to open the program, double-click its shortcut icon.

How to Navigate Office Applications

All the Office programs share a common look and feel. After you've learned your way around one program, you can easily recognize common elements in the other programs. When you first open a program (with the exception of Outlook and Access), a new file automatically appears onscreen, ready for you to start work. The document is surrounded by tools to help you work with the program. Many of the tools that appear onscreen in an Office program can be hidden to free up window workspace. If you're new to Office, take a few moments to familiarize yourself with the various window elements presented in this task.

❶ View the Window Controls

The program window opens along with a blank document window. Usually, both windows are *maximized*—the program window fills the whole screen, and the actual document window fills the program window. (When both are maximized, two **Restore** buttons—one for each window—are displayed in the upper-right corner.) If your program window isn't maximized, click its **Maximize** button.

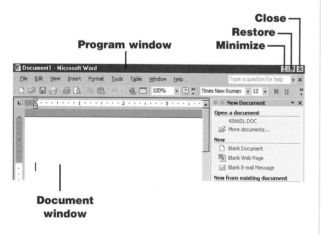

❷ View the Title and Status Bars

The *title bar* tells you what is in the window, the name of the program (such as Microsoft Word) and the filename. At the bottom of the program window, the *status bar* displays pertinent information about the file, such as the current page number.

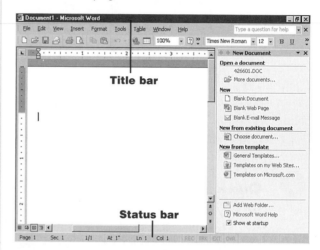

❸ View the Menu Bar

The *menu bar* contains all available commands. Click the menu's name to display it and then click the command you want.

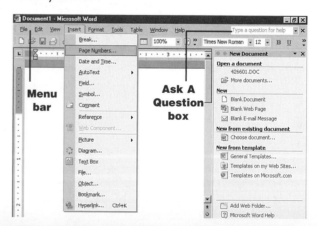

4 View the Toolbars

Every Office program displays at least one toolbar; several programs have two or more toolbars by default. Toolbars contain shortcut buttons for frequently used commands, such as open, save, print, and undo. To activate a toolbar button, click it. To see a button's name, hover the mouse pointer over the button for a moment and a *ScreenTip* appears. (Learn all about customizing toolbars in Task 5, "How to Customize Toolbars.")

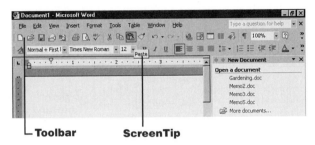

— **Toolbar**   **ScreenTip**

5 View the Work Area and Scrollbars

The work area is where you work with data in a file. Each program's work area varies, but typically it takes up the middle of the screen. This work area might include vertical and horizontal scrollbars, which allow you to view different portions of the file. Click the arrows on the scrollbars or drag the scroll box to move the file in the appropriate direction. Use the **Previous Page** and **Next Page** buttons at the bottom of the vertical scrollbar to jump quickly from one part of the file to the next.

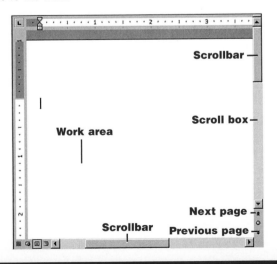

Scrollbar —

Scroll box —

Work area

Next page
Scrollbar   Previous page

6 View the Task Pane

A new feature in this version of Microsoft Office is the task pane (not used in Outlook). This pane appears as a separate window on the right side of the program window. It has links to common program tasks, such as opening an existing file or starting a new file, and it provides quick access to common commands. To learn more, see Task 3, "How to Work with the Task Pane."

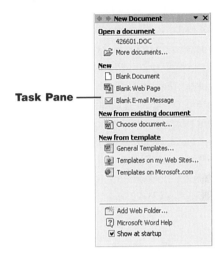

Task Pane —

How to Work with the Task Pane

The task pane is new to the Office suite of programs. When you start any program (with the exception of Outlook), the task pane is displayed on the right side of the program window by default. It offers users quick access to common commands and controls. You can have more than one pane displayed in the task pane, and you can use the navigation buttons to view open panes. The current pane's name appears at the top of the task pane. For example, in PowerPoint, you might have the **New Presentation** and **Slide Layout** panes open and switch between the two. You can also hide the pane to free up workspace onscreen.

① Navigate the Task Pane

When two or more task panes are open, you can navigate between them by using the arrow buttons at the top of each task pane. Click the **Back** arrow button to move back a pane, or click the **Forward** arrow button to move forward a pane.

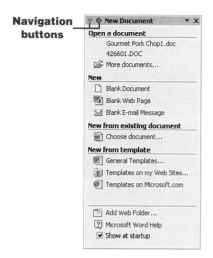

Navigation buttons

② Scroll the Task Pane

Use the pane's scroll buttons to view different areas of the task pane.

Scroll buttons

③ Activate a Feature

You can activate a feature by clicking its link or clicking the graphic icon representing the choice you want to select.

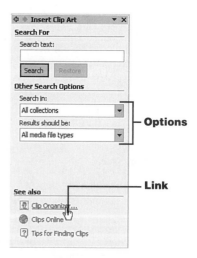

Options

Link

4 Switch Pane View

A quick way to switch between task panes is to click the **Other Task Panes** drop-down arrow button and select another pane from the list that opens. The current pane always has a check mark next to its name.

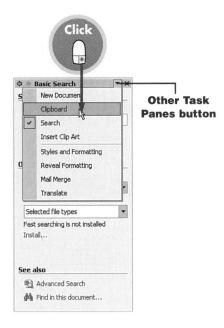

Other Task Panes button

5 Close the Task Pane

To free up workspace onscreen, you can close the task pane by clicking its **Close** button.

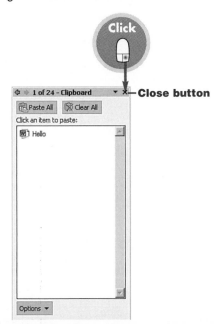

Close button

6 Redisplay the Task Pane

If you close the task pane, you can redisplay it again at any time. Open the program's **View** menu and choose **Task Pane**.

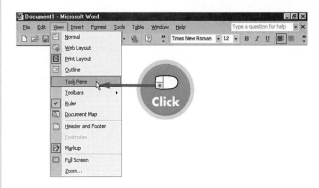

How-to Hint

Changing the Task Pane Startup Mode

The task pane is set up to appear as soon as you open an Office program. (This pane is not used in Outlook.) To keep the pane from appearing when you open the program, you need to turn off the pane's startup option. First, choose **Tools**, **Options**. In the **Options** dialog box, click the **View** tab and deselect the **Startup Task Pane** check box. Click **OK** to exit the dialog box. The task pane will not appear the next time you start the program. Follow these same steps to turn off the task pane for each Office program.

You can hide the task pane temporarily to free up onscreen workspace and then display it again when you need it. To hide the task pane, right-click it and select **Task Pane** from the shortcut menu.

How to Work with Menus and Toolbars

To help expedite your work, Office menus and tool-bars can display only the commands and buttons you use the most often. Simply put, this means a menu or toolbar doesn't have to show every available command unless you tell it to. In this task, you'll learn how to work with personalized menus and toolbars.

❶ Display a Full Menu

To open a menu, click its name. If your personalized menus are on, the menu displays the most recently used commands. To view the full menu, wait a few seconds. All the menu commands will appear. You can also click the double-arrow at the bottom of the menu list to view the full menu. If the personalized menus are off, you see the full menu automatically.

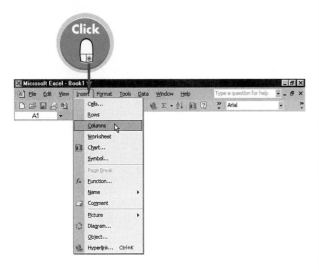

❷ Customize Your Menus

Open the **Tools** menu and select **Customize**. The **Customize** dialog box opens.

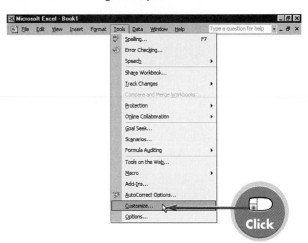

❸ Toggle Personalized Menus

Click the **Options** tab. Click the **Always show full menus** check box to toggle personalized menus. Click **Close** to exit the dialog box and apply the change.

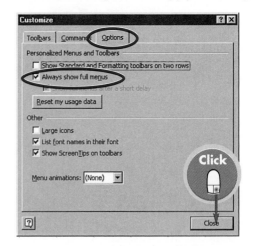

④ Display Hidden Toolbar Buttons

If the toolbar button you're looking for isn't onscreen, click the **More Buttons** icon on the toolbar to display a pop-up list of additional buttons.

⑤ Select a Toolbar Button

From the pop-up list, select the toolbar button you want to use. As soon as you make a selection, the command is activated, and the button is added to the visible display of buttons on the toolbar.

⑥ Hide or Display Toolbars

To display or hide a toolbar, open the **View** menu and select **Toolbars**. This opens a submenu that lists every available toolbar for the program. A check mark next to the toolbar name indicates that the toolbar is already being displayed.

Viewing Full Toolbars

Some Office programs, such as Word and Excel, show two toolbars in the same toolbar space onscreen, side by side: the **Standard** and **Formatting** toolbars. This arrangement enables users to see more of the work area. You can display the two toolbars in their entirety by deselecting the **Standard and Formatting toolbars share one row** check box in the **Customize** dialog box (refer to step 3 in this task).

Resetting the Commands

The **Customize** dialog box has an option for restoring the default set of visible commands displayed in the program's menus and toolbars. To activate the default settings, click the **Reset my usage** data button.

⑤

How to Customize Toolbars

Every Office toolbar has a default set of buttons. However, you can customize any toolbar to show only the buttons you want. For example, you might want to add a few Web buttons to the **Standard** toolbar to tailor it to the way you work. This task will show you how to customize Office toolbars.

① Open the Customize Dialog Box

To customize a toolbar, open the **View** menu and select **Toolbars**, **Customize**. (Depending on which Office program you're using, the **View** menu might differ slightly from what is shown here.) The **Customize** dialog box opens.

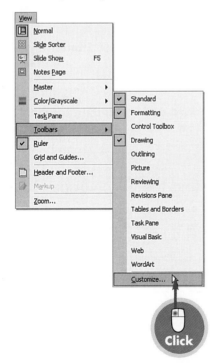

② Set Toolbar Options

Click the **Options** tab to view toolbar options. You can show the toolbars in full by clicking the **Show Standard and Formatting toolbars on two rows** check box. To show larger toolbar button icons, click the **Large icons** check box.

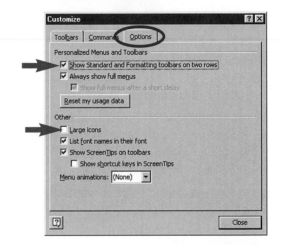

③ Choose a Toolbar to Edit

Click the **Toolbars** tab and select the toolbar you want to customize. For example, to customize the **Drawing** toolbar, click the **Drawing** check box.

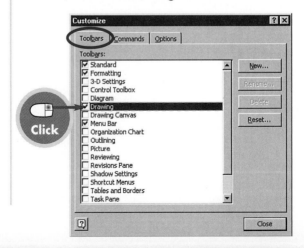

④ Choose a Command

Now click the **Commands** tab. To add a button to the toolbar, first select a command category from the **Categories** list. Then scroll through the **Commands** list box to find the icon you want to use.

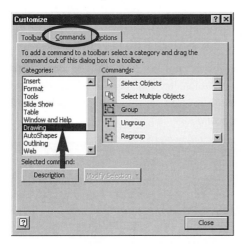

⑤ Add the Button to the Toolbar

In the **Commands** list, select the icon representing the button you want to add to the toolbar. Drag it from the list and drop it onto the toolbar where you want to insert it.

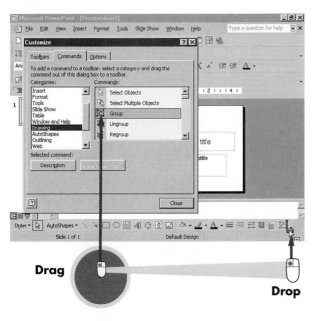

Drag

Drop

⑥ Close the Dialog Box

When you've finished adding or deleting buttons from the toolbar, click **Close** to close the **Customize** dialog box.

Click

How-to Hint

Removing Buttons

To remove a toolbar button, make sure that the **Customize** dialog box is open and then drag the button off the toolbar. Drop the button anywhere in the work area. The toolbar button is immediately removed, and the remaining buttons adjust to fill the space.

How to Start a New File

When you installed Office, two new items were added to the top of the **Start** menu. One is the **New Office Document** command. When you select this feature, the **New Office Document** dialog box opens. Here you can select the type of file you want to create (a Word document, an Excel spreadsheet, a PowerPoint slide, an Access database, and so on). You can also open new files within each Office program (with the exception of Outlook). Use the program window's **File** menu to start a new file based on a *template*, a prebuilt file that contains a layout and formatting. Use the **New** button on the **Standard** toolbar or the new file links on the task pane to open new, default documents.

1 Select New Office Document

One way to create a new file is with the **New Office Document** command. Click the **Start** menu and choose **New Office Document**. The **New Office Document** dialog box opens.

2 Select a File Type

Use the tabs at the top of the dialog box to locate the type of template for the new file. Then double-click to open the new file. The file type you select opens into the program.

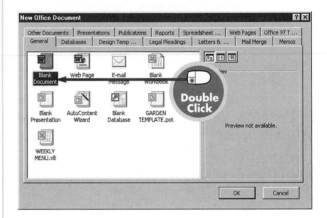

3 Open New Files

You can also start new files from within an open program. To open a file based on a template, choose **File**, **New**. The **New Document** task pane opens.

4 Use the New Document Pane

In the **New Document** task pane, click the link for the type of new file you want to create. A new file immediately opens in your program window.

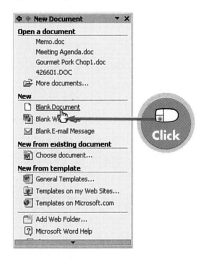

5 Use the New Button

You can also click the **New** button on the **Standard** toolbar to open a new file. In Word and Excel, a new file based on the default template opens immediately. In PowerPoint, a new slide opens. In Access, the **New File** task pane opens, from which you can choose a new file type.

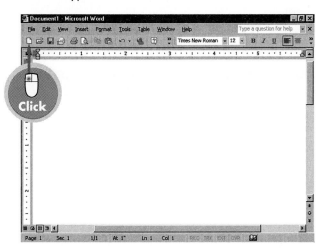

All Files Are Templates

Every file you open in Office starts from a *template*, which is a bare-bones, ready-made document, worksheet, presentation, or database. When you first open Word, for example, a blank document awaits you. Although this document is blank, it's actually based on the no-frills **Normal** template.

What's a Wizard?

Some of the file types listed in the **New Office Document** dialog box are *wizards*. A wizard helps you create a new document, step by step, based on choices you make in the wizard's dialog boxes. You start a wizard just as you start any other file—by double-clicking the icon.

Macro Warning

Depending on the template you choose, a warning might appear to tell you that the file you're about to open contains *macros* (automated commands for common tasks) that might have viruses. If you purchased your Office program from a reliable source, click the **Enable Macros** button in the warning box to continue. If you're not sure whether the macros are safe, click the **Disable Macros** button. If you disable macros, some of the template features might not work properly.

How to Save Your Work

Once you've started work on an Office file, you'll want to save it so that you can open it again later. It's a good idea to save your work often in case of power failures or computer glitches. When you save a file the first time, you must give it a name. You can use up to 256 characters in a filename, uppercase or lowercase letters. You can choose a specific folder or disk to save the file to, and you can save it in a specific file format. All the save options are found in the **Save As** dialog box, which looks pretty much the same in all Office programs. After you've saved a file, subsequent saves don't require renaming (unless you want to save a duplicate of the file under a different name). So you don't have to reopen the **Save As** dialog box. Instead, just click the **Save** button on the toolbar.

❶ Save a New File

To save a file for the first time, open the **File** menu and select **Save** or **Save As**. The **Save As** dialog box opens.

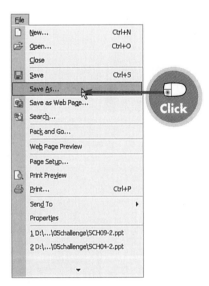

❷ Designate a Folder

Choose the folder where you want to save the file. Use the **Save in** drop-down list to locate the folder, if necessary. To open a folder, double-click the folder icon in the large center pane. You can also open any of the folders displayed along the left edge of the dialog box by clicking the folder icon.

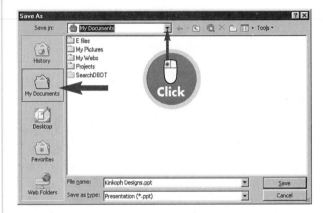

❸ Type a Filename

Type a name for the file in the **File name** text box.

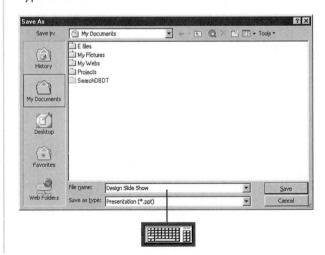

④ Click Save

Click the **Save** button to close the **Save As** dialog box. The file is saved with the filename you've specified and in the folder you've designated.

⑤ View the Title Bar Name

Notice that the program's title bar now reflects the name you assigned to the file in the **Save As** dialog box.

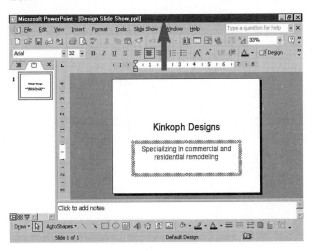

⑥ Use the Save Button

For subsequent saves of the same file, click the **Save** button on the **Standard** toolbar. All the changes you've made to the file will be saved. The program saves the current version of the file by overwriting the last version of the file. The filename doesn't change.

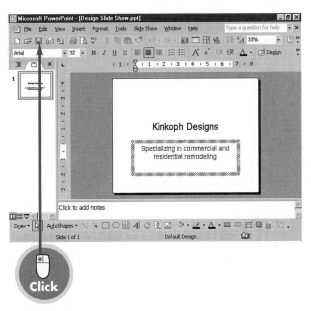

Changing the Format

To save a file in another format (for example, to save an Excel file as a Lotus 1-2-3 file), open the **Save As** dialog box. Click the **Save as type** drop-down arrow and choose a file type from the list of options.

Saving as a New File

To save an existing file under a new name, follow steps 1 through 4 in this task but type a different filename in step 3. A duplicate of the original file is saved under the new filename, and the original file remains intact.

Saving to a New Folder

Click the **Create New Folder** button in the **Save As** dialog box to create a new folder to save the file in. Type a folder name and click **OK**.

How to Open and Close Files

If the program window is already open, you can use the **Open** dialog box to quickly open existing files you've saved. If you haven't started the program yet, you can use the **Open Office Document command** on the **Start** menu to open both the file you want and the program in which it was created. If you finish working with a file but want to keep the program window open, select the **Close** command. This closes only the file, leaving the program window open so that you can work on other files or start new ones.

1 Use the Open Dialog Box

To open a file from within a program window, choose **File**, **Open**. The **Open File** dialog box appears. You can also click the **Open** button—the one that looks like an open file folder—on the **Standard** toolbar, or choose from the file options in the task pane if it's open.

2 Locate the File

Locate the file you want to open. The list box displays the files stored in the default folder. To open a different folder in the list box, double-click the folder icon. You might have to use the **Look in** drop-down list to find the folder, or click a folder along the left side of the dialog box.

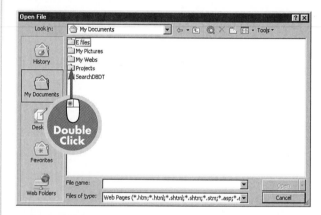

3 Select the File

When you find the file you want to open, double-click it or select it and click the **Open** button.

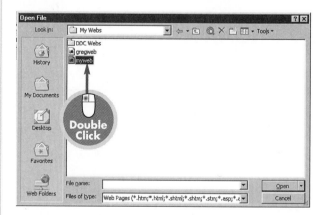

4 Choose Open Office Document

Another way to open files is with the **Open Office Document** command. This is a quick way to open both the file and the program window (if it's not already open). Click the **Start** button on the Windows taskbar and choose **Open Office Document**. The **Open Office Document** dialog box appears.

5 Choose a File

Locate the file you want to open. (Refer to step 2 for information about navigating the folders in this dialog box.) Double-click the filename to open both the file and the program, or select the file and click **Open**.

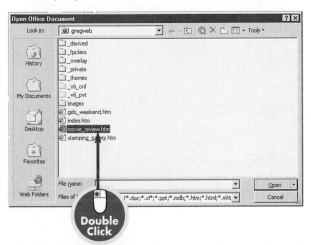

6 Close a File

To close a file—but not the program window—choose **File**, **Close**. If you haven't saved your work, you're prompted to do so before the file is closed. Another way to close the file but not the window is to click the file's **Close** button, which is located directly below the program window's **Close** button.

Previewing the File

If you're not sure about a file's contents, click the **View** button in the **Open File** dialog box's toolbar, and then select the **Preview** command to peek at the file before opening it.

Open Options

Notice that the **Open** button in the **Open File** dialog box has a drop-down arrow. Click this arrow to display a drop-down list of four commands: **Open**, **Open Read-Only**, **Open as Copy**, and **Open in Browser**. If you select the **Open Read-Only** command, you can view the file but can't make any changes to it. If you select **Open as Copy**, a copy of the file opens—not the original. If you select **Open in Browser**, the file opens in the Internet Explorer browser window.

How to Print a File

To print an Office file, you must have a printer connected to your computer, the appropriate printer driver installed, and the printer must be turned on and ready to print. You can send the file to the printer immediately, using the default printer settings, or you first can set specific printing options by using the **Print** dialog box. Depending on the program and your setup, the printer options you see might vary slightly from those shown here.

❶ Open the Print Dialog Box

To set printing options, choose **File**, **Print**. The **Print** dialog box opens. (The figures in this task show **Print** dialog boxes from Excel, Word, PowerPoint, and Access. Despite subtle differences, the **Print** dialog box works the same way for every Office file or Outlook item you print.)

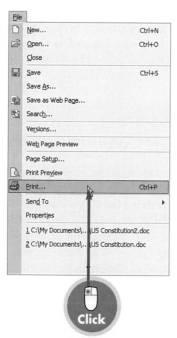

❷ Choose a Printer

If you have access to more than one printer, use the **Name** drop-down list to choose another printer.

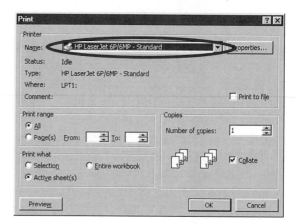

❸ Choose a Page Range

To designate specific pages or selected data to print, use the options in the **Page range** or **Print range** area of the dialog box. (The precise name of this option depends on what type of file you're trying to print.) To print every page, select the **All** option; or type a single page number or a range, such as **2–4**.

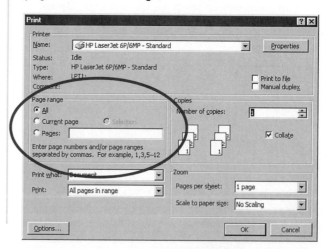

④ Number of Copies

To print multiple copies of the file, indicate a number in the **Number of copies** box. (The dialog box in this figure is from PowerPoint. Notice the numerous options for printing slides, which are more graphical in nature than other Office files.)

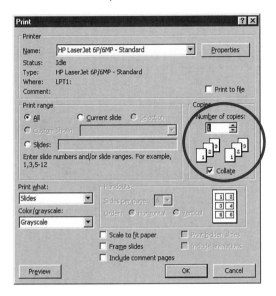

⑤ Print

Click **OK** to print the file using the options that you've specified in the dialog box. (The dialog box shown here is from Access.)

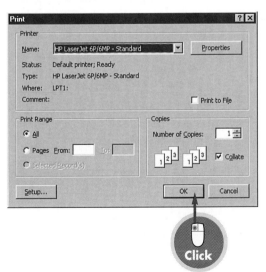

⑥ Use the Print Toolbar Button

To print the current file using the default printer settings without selecting any new options, click the **Print** button on the **Standard** toolbar.

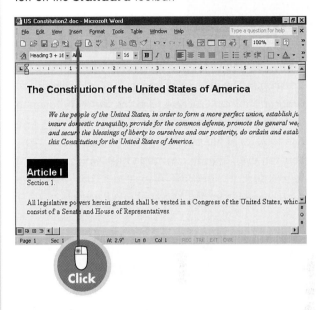

How-to Hint

Previewing a File

The **Print Preview** feature lets you see exactly how your file will look so you can make any last-minute changes before printing. The preview window has various tools for working with the file, depending on the program. Click the **Print Preview** button (the page with a magnifying glass) to open the preview window. Click the **Close** button to close the feature and return to the program window.

Printing in Outlook

In Outlook, use the **Print Style** area in the **Print** dialog box to choose a print style for the Outlook item you're printing. You can also edit the style by clicking the **Define Styles** button, or you can change the page setup settings by clicking the **Page Setup** button.

How to Find Files

Need to find a specific file you've saved? There's a **Search** button on every main toolbar in all the Office programs except Outlook. Click the **Search** button to open the **Basic Search** task pane. From here, you can look for a file based on the filename or file type. You can even specify a location from which you want to conduct the search. Also, there are advanced search options to assist you with your search.

① Click the Search Button

Click the **Search** button on the **Standard** toolbar. The **Basic Search** task pane opens.

② Enter the Search Text

Click inside the **Search text** field and type the name of the file you want to search for.

③ Search in a Specific Folder

In the **Other Search Options** area, specify how you want to conduct the search. Click the **Search in** drop-down arrow and select a drive or folder to search.

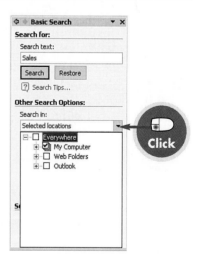

4 Search for a Specific File Type

To search for a specific file type, click the **Results should be** drop-down arrow and select a file type from the list.

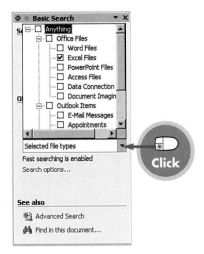

5 Start the Search

Click the **Search** button to begin searching for the file using the search criteria you've specified.

6 View the Search Results

The results of the search appear in the task pane. To open a file, double-click the filename or click the file's drop-down arrow and choose a program in which to edit the file. To see the file's drop-down arrow, just move the mouse pointer over the filename.

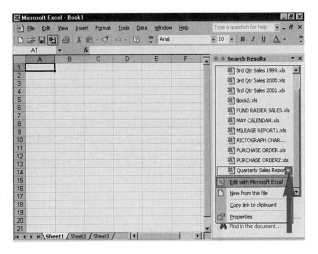

How-to Hint

Starting a New Search

To start a new search from the task pane, click the **Restore** button. All the fields and options are reset, and you can start a fresh search.

Task Pane Shortcut

If the task pane is open, you can quickly display the **Basic Search** task pane by clicking the **Other Task Panes** button and choosing **Search** from the drop-down list.

Searching from the **Open File** Dialog Box

Another way you can conduct a search is to use the **Open File** dialog box in Word, Excel, PowerPoint, or Access. Click the **Open** button in the **Standard** toolbar. Then, in the **Open File** dialog box, click the **Tools** drop-down button and choose **Search**.

How to Use the Office Help Tools

Regardless of your level of computer experience, you might need help from time to time, especially when you're learning a new software program. Help is always a click away in any Office program. You'll find the **Ask A Question** box on the title bar of any program. You can use it to find help with a particular task or feature. You can also open Microsoft's **Office Assistant**, an animated feature you can use to look up specific instructions or topics.

❶ Ask a Question

To quickly access help, click inside the **Ask A Question** box in the title bar and type a question, phrase, or word you want to find help with, and then press **Enter**.

❷ Choose a Match

A drop-down list of possible topic matches appears. Click the topic that most closely matches your question.

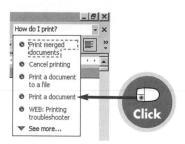

❸ Read the Help Window

A **Help** window appears with more information on the topic, or additional topics from which you can choose. Underlined words are links to related topics; click the text to follow the link. Use the **Back** and **Forward** buttons at the top of the **Help** window to navigate between topics. To exit the window when you're finished, click the window's **Close** button.

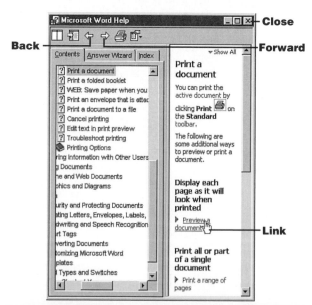

④ Open Office Assistant

Another way to seek help with the program you're using is to display the **Office Assistant**. Click the **Help** button on the **Standard** toolbar, press **F1**, or choose **Help**, **Show the Office Assistant**.

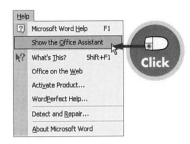

⑤ Ask a Question

In the **Office Assistant** balloon, you can type a question or select from the options listed. To type a question, click inside the text box and type it. Then click **Search** or press **Enter**. If the question text box doesn't appear, click the Office Assistant character to display the box.

⑥ Choose a Topic

The Office Assistant produces a list of possible topics. Click the topic that most closely matches the information you desire, and the Help window opens. (If the question you type doesn't produce the results you expect, enter a new question and try again.)

Working with the Assistant

To close the **Office Assistant**, open the **Help** menu and select **Hide the Office Assistant**, or right-click the Office Assistant character and select **Hide**.

If you don't like the default Clippit character (the animated paper clip), you can change it. Click the **Options** button in the **Office Assistant** balloon to open the Office Assistant dialog box. Click the **Gallery** tab and choose another character by using the **Back** or **Next** buttons. Then click **OK**.

Finding Help on the Web

You can log on to the Microsoft Web site to find more help with your program. Open the **Help** menu and choose **Office on the Web**. This opens your browser window and a connect box so you can log on to your Internet account. Click **Connect** and follow the Web page links to the information you're looking for. (Try starting from the Microsoft home page.)

How to Cut, Copy, and Paste Data

The easiest way to share data between programs is to use the **Cut**, **Copy**, and **Paste** commands, which are common to all the Office programs. Use the **Cut** command to move data from one area of your document to another, or from one program to another. Use the **Copy** command to duplicate the data and place it in a different area of the document or in another file entirely. When you cut or copy data, it's placed in the Windows Clipboard, a temporary storage area, until it's pasted into a new location. You can use the **Cut**, **Copy**, and **Paste** commands to move or duplicate text, pictures, formulas, or any type of data you place in a file. You can also use these commands to share data between non-Microsoft programs.

❶ Select the Data

Select the data you want to cut or copy.

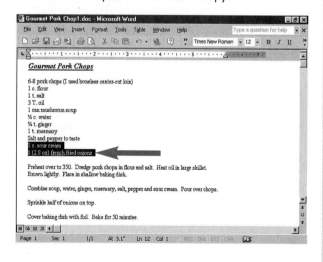

❷ Cut the Data

To move the data (that is, to delete it from its current location and insert it somewhere else), start by clicking the **Cut** button on the **Standard** toolbar or choosing **Edit**, **Cut**.

❸ Copy the Data

To copy the data while leaving the original in its current location, start by clicking the **Copy** button on the toolbar or choosing **Edit**, **Copy**. This places a duplicate of the data in the Windows Clipboard.

4 Choose an Area to Cut or Copy To

Whether you're moving or copying data, you must now place the cursor where you want to insert that data. If you're cutting or copying to another file, first open the file and then click where you want to paste the data.

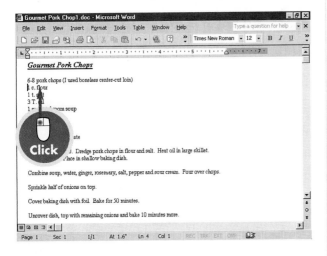

5 Use the Paste Command

Click the **Paste** button on the toolbar or choose **Edit**, **Paste**. The data on the Clipboard is immediately inserted into the designated area, and a **Paste Options** Smart Tag button appears. A Smart Tag indicates that the program has recognized data or an action that's commonly associated with other tasks, such as pasting text and formatting. Smart Tags are new in Office XP.

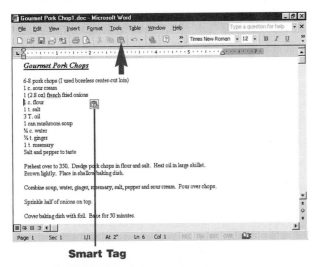

Smart Tag

6 View the Smart Tag

Click the Smart Tag to view a drop-down list of related options. Depending on the type of data you're pasting, the Smart Tag displays different options. To choose an option from the list, simply click the option you want to apply to the pasted data.

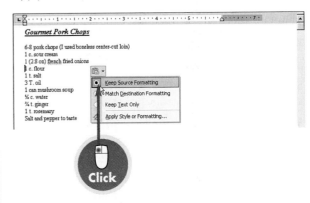

How-to Hint

Using the Office Clipboard

If you cut or copy multiple pieces of data, the **Office Clipboard** task pane opens. The Office Clipboard holds up to 24 items. To paste an item from the Clipboard task pane, first place the cursor in the document where you want to paste the item. To paste all the items at once, click the **Paste All** button in the Clipboard pane. Or, you can click the item you want to paste from the list of items. To keep the Clipboard task pane from appearing, click the **Options** button at the bottom of the task pane and deselect the **Show Office Clipboard Automatically** option.

Dragging and Dropping

You can also drag and drop data to move or copy it. Move the data by dragging it from one area to another and dropping it in place. To copy data with the drag-and-drop method, hold down the **Ctrl** key while you drag.

How to Link and Embed Data

Object linking and embedding, or *OLE*, enables Windows programs to share data transparently. The data maintains a relationship with the original program. When you *link* data, any changes made to the data in the source program (the program you originally used to create the data) are reflected in the destination program (the program receiving the shared data). When you *embed* data, the data isn't updated in the destination file when it's changed, but it does retain a relationship with the source file. Any time you want to edit the data in the destination file, double-click it to reopen the source file and make your changes. When you embed, you can access the source file directly (without opening the source program and file), make the changes, and copy and paste data into the destination file.

1 Copy to the Clipboard

The first step in linking or embedding is to copy the data to the Windows Clipboard. Open the source file containing the data you want to link or embed, select the data, and then choose **Edit**, **Copy** or click the **Copy** button.

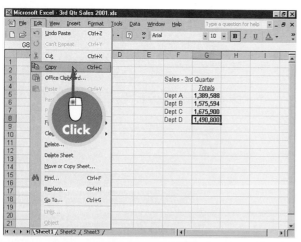

2 Open the Destination File

Next, open the file in which you want to link or embed the data. Click to position the cursor where you want the data to appear.

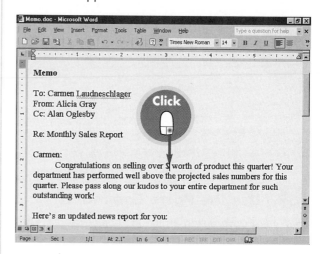

3 Open the Paste Special Dialog Box

Choose **Edit**, **Paste Special**. This opens the **Paste Special** dialog box, where you can link or embed data.

④ Link the Data

To link the data, enable the **Paste link** option and select a format to use from the As list box. The formats listed vary depending on the type of data you select. When you select a format, the **Result** area at the bottom of the dialog box displays notes about what will happen.

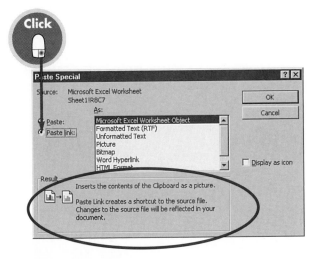

⑤ Embed the Data

To embed the data, choose the **Paste** option and select a format from the As list box. Notice that the **Result** area describes what will happen.

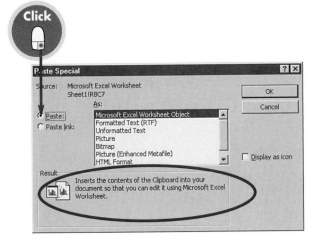

⑥ Click OK

Click **OK** to close the dialog box and link or embed the data.

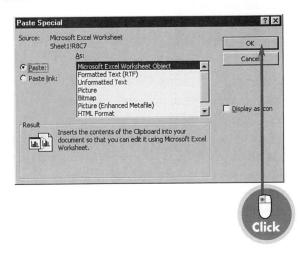

Linking Options

Use the **Display as Icon** check box in the **Paste Special** dialog box to display the pasted object as an icon. If you're linking sound clips to an Office file, for example, display the link as an icon. To play the sound clip, double-click the icon.

If you rename, delete, or move the source file, the link between the source and the destination file is broken and you get an error message in the destination file. To edit your links, use the **Edit**, **Links** command. In the **Links** dialog box, you can break the link, change its source, or apply other options.

Editing an Embedded Object

To edit data you've embedded, double-click the data to open the original program in which the data was created.

How to Add and Remove Office Components

If you install only certain Office components and later decide to add more components, or if you find you're not using a program and want to remove it from your hard drive, you can easily open the Microsoft Office Maintenance Mode program and make the necessary changes. To add or remove components, you'll need the Office CD-ROM. Be sure to close any open programs before installing or removing Office components.

1 Open Office Setup

Insert the Office CD and double-click **SETUP.EXE**. The first screen of the Office Setup program opens.

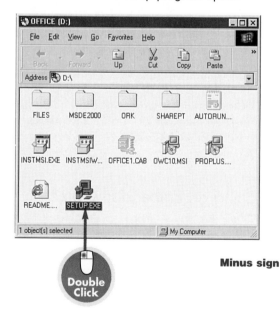

Double Click

2 Choose an Option

Select the **Add or Remove Features** option and click **Next** to continue.

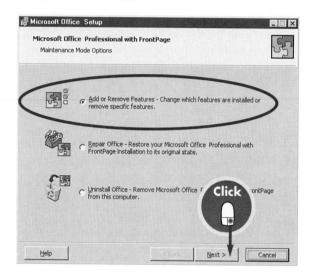

Click

3 View the Components List

The next screen lists the Office components. Click the plus sign to see all the features associated with the component.

Minus sign ———

Plus sign ———

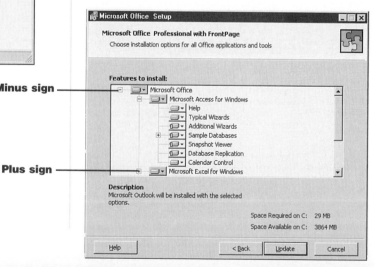

④ Add or Remove a Feature

Click the drop-down arrow next to the component or feature name to change the item's status. For example, to remove a component, click the drop-down arrow and click the **Not Available** icon. To add a feature that's currently not installed, click the drop-down arrow and select the **Run from My Computer** icon.

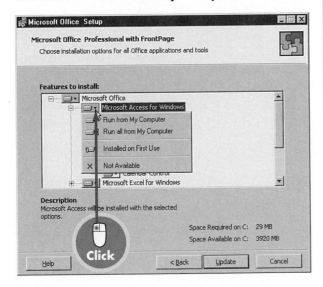

⑥ Confirm the Update

When the Setup program finishes installing or removing a feature, a confirmation box tells you that the procedure is complete. Click **OK**.

⑤ Update the Components

Continue selecting or deselecting the features you want to add or remove. When you're ready to proceed, click the **Update** button.

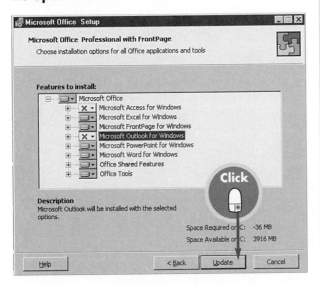

① How to Use Word's Views 448

② How to Enter and Edit Text 450

③ How to Select Text 452

④ How to Move and Copy Text 454

⑤ How to Use Templates 456

⑥ How to Work with AutoText 458

⑦ How to Format Text 460

⑧ How to Copy Text Formatting 462

⑨ How to Insert Symbols 464

⑩ How to Set Margins 466

⑪ How to Set the Line Spacing 468

⑫ How to Align and Indent Text 470

⑬ How to Work with Bulleted and Numbered Lists . . .472

⑭ How to Set Tabs 474

⑮ How to Create Columns 476

⑯ How to Insert a Table .478

⑰ How to Add Borders and Shading to Text 480

⑱ How to Use Headers and Footers 482

⑲ How to Insert Comments, Footnotes, and Endnotes .484

⑳ How to Insert Page Numbers and Page Breaks . . .486

㉑ How to Use Styles 488

㉒ How to Work with Drop Caps and Text Case 490

㉓ How to Add a Watermark 492

㉔ How to Find and Replace Text 494

㉕ How to Check Your Spelling and Grammar 496

㉖ How to Work with AutoCorrect 498

㉗ How to Track and Review Document Changes 500

㉘ How to Change Paper Size 502

㉙ How to Print an Envelope 504

Task

22

Using Word to Create and Edit Documents

Microsoft Word is one of the most popular, best-selling word processing programs ever created. With it, you can create all manner of documents, including letters, memos, reports, manuscripts, and newsletters. When it comes to working with text, Microsoft Word has no match. Out of all the programs that compose Office, Word will probably become your most-used application: It's so versatile that you will use it for just about anything involving text.

In this part of the book, you will learn how to get up and running with Word, including learning how to work with text and with the program's many formatting features to help make your own documents more professional-looking and polished. After you have created and formatted a Word document, you're ready to print it out or distribute it to others. Before you do, you need to proof it and make sure that everything is in order. Word has several proofing tools you can use to make sure that your documents are accurate and readable.

When you finally have the document the way you want it, use the **Print** command to create a hard copy of the file. Because some of your Word documents will present different printing needs, tasks in this part show you how to change the paper size and how to print envelopes in Word.

How to Use Word's Views

Word offers you several ways to view your document. For starters, you can use the **Zoom** tool to view your document in detail, or zoom out to see your document from a "bird's-eye view." You can also change the way you view a document page using four main view options: Use **Normal** view to see only the text area of the page; no graphics or special elements appear. Switch to **Print Layout** view to see graphics, page margins, and elements such as headers and footers. Use **Outline** view to help build and maintain outline levels in your document. **Web Layout** view takes its cue from Web pages, allowing you to take advantage of the full width of a Web page document.

1 Use the Zoom Tools

The quickest way to zoom your view of the document is to use the **Zoom** control on the **Standard** toolbar. Click the drop-down arrow to display the list of zoom percentages; choose a percentage (such as **75%** or **150%**) to zoom your view.

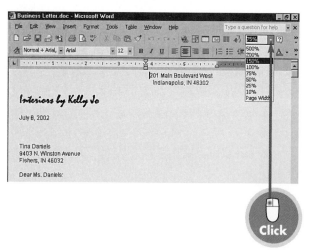

2 Assess the View

Word zooms your view of the document based on the selection you made in step 1 (in this case, **150%**).

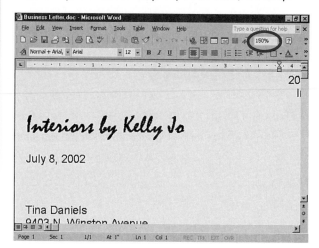

3 Open the Zoom Dialog Box

To specify an exact zoom percentage, open the **View** menu and select **Zoom**. The **Zoom** dialog box opens.

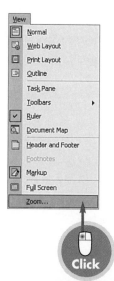

4 Specify a Zoom Percentage

In the **Zoom** dialog box, you can enter an exact zoom percentage in the **Percent** box (such as **50%**). The **Preview** area gives you an idea of how the zoomed text will look onscreen. Click **OK** to apply the new view.

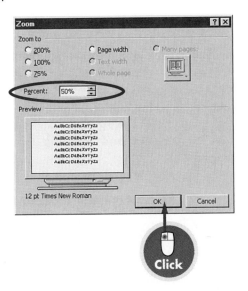

5 Use the View Buttons

Use the view buttons in the lower-left corner of the Word window to switch between **Normal**, **Web Layout**, **Print Layout**, and **Outline** views. You can also switch your document page views using options in the View menu.

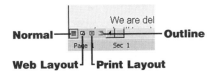

6 Change the View

If you clicked the **Print Layout** view button in step 5, Word displays the document just as it will print. Most users stick with **Normal** and **Print Layout** views to work with and view document pages. To change your view again, click the view button you want to use.

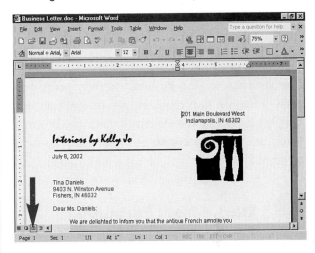

Using Outline View

Outline view is intended to help you modify the structure of your outline. In **Outline** view, you can move headings—and any body text or subheadings they contain——by dragging and dropping them. You can hide and display heading levels by clicking toolbar buttons. You can also apply heading styles or outline levels to your headings while you're using **Outline** view.

Accessing More Workspace

To get more room to work in your Word document, you can close program elements such as the **Task Pane** and the **Ruler**. Open the **View** menu and deselect **Task Pane** or **Ruler**. You can use the scroll arrows on the vertical and horizontal scrollbars to move your view of longer documents. Click the **Previous Page** and **Next Page** buttons on the scrollbar to navigate your document one page at a time.

How to Enter and Edit Text

Microsoft Word opens with a blank document window ready for you to begin typing text, whether it's in the form of a best-selling novel, a personal letter, or an interoffice memo. The flashing insertion point indicates where the next character you type will appear. Simply start typing to enter text. If you make any mistakes, use the **Backspace** or **Delete** key to delete unwanted characters.

❶ Start a New Paragraph

Each time you press **Enter**, you start a new paragraph. Press **Enter** to end short lines of text, to create blank lines, and to end paragraphs. Don't press **Enter** to start new lines within a paragraph: Word wraps the lines for you.

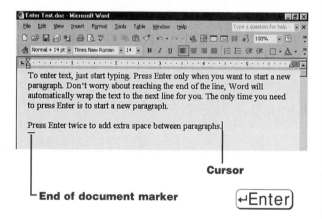

Cursor

└ End of document marker

⏎Enter

❷ Indent with the Tab Key

Press the **Tab** key to indent the first line of a paragraph. If you keep pressing **Tab**, you increase the indent one-half inch at a time. (To indent all the lines in the paragraph instead of just the first one, right-click in the paragraph and click **Paragraph** from the shortcut menu. On the **Indents and Spacing** tab of the **Paragraph** dialog box that opens, reset the indentation settings and click **OK** to apply them.)

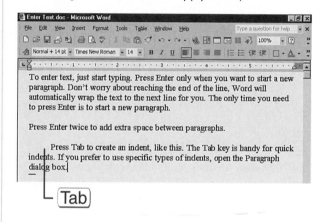

└ Tab

❸ Type Repeating Characters

To type the same character repeatedly, hold the key down. Word automatically converts some repeated characters into different types of lines, as shown here. If you type three or more asterisks (*) and press **Enter**, for example, Word replaces them with a dotted line. Do the same with the equal sign (=) for a double line, the tilde (~) for a wavy line, the pound symbol (#) for a thick decorative line, or the underscore (_) for a thick single line.

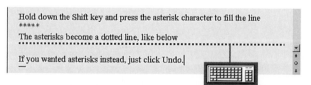

4 Type Uppercase Letters

To produce all uppercase letters without holding down the **Shift** key, press the **Caps Lock** key once before you begin typing. Press the **Caps Lock** key again when you're ready to switch caps off. The **Caps Lock** key affects only the letter keys, not the number and punctuation keys. Therefore, you always have to press **Shift** to type a character on the upper half of a number or punctuation key, such as @ or %.

Hold down the Shift key and press the asterisk character to fill the line
*****
The asterisks become a dotted line, like below
••
If you wanted asterisks instead, just click Undo.

CLICK THE CAPS LOCK KEY TO TYPE ALL CAPS.

Caps Lock

5 View Nonprinting Characters

Every time you press **Enter**, the **Spacebar**, or the **Tab** key, Word marks the spot in your document with a nonprinting character. You can't see these characters unless you click the **Show/Hide** button in the **Standard** toolbar. You can use this button to check whether you accidentally typed an extra space between two words or to see how many blank lines you have between paragraphs. To turn off **Show/Hide**, click the button again.

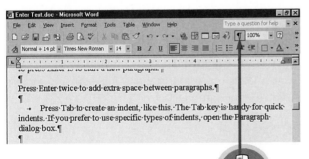

6 Fix Mistakes

Press the **Backspace** key to delete characters to the left of the cursor. You can also click inside a word and press the **Delete** key to remove characters to the right of the cursor.

Hold down the Shift key and press the asterisk character to fill the line
*****
The asterisks become a dotted line, like below
••
If you wanted asterisks instead, just click Undo.

CLICK THE CAPS LOCK KEY TO TYPE ALL C

Overtype and Insert Modes

By default, Word starts in **Insert** mode: Any time you click the cursor in the document and start typing, any existing text moves to the right to make room for new text you type. If you prefer to replace the existing text entirely, use **Overtype** mode. Press the **Insert** key to toggle **Overtype** mode on or off. You can also double-click the letters **OVR** on the status bar to toggle the feature on or off (the letters **OVR** appear in black when **Overtype** mode is on).

Need a New Page?

By default, Word starts a new page when the current page is filled with text. At times, you might want to start a new page without filling the current page (when you want a title page, for example). Press **Ctrl+Enter** to insert a manual page break. To remove a manual page break, click the page break line and press **Delete**.

How to Select Text

After entering text, you can do a variety of things with it, such as applying formatting or moving and copying the text. Before you can do any of these things, however, you must first learn to select text. *Selecting text* means to highlight the specific text you want to change or apply commands to. Selected text—whether it's a single character, a word, a paragraph, or an entire document—always appears highlighted onscreen with a black bar.

① Select Text with the Mouse

To select a character, word, or phrase, click at the beginning of the text you want to select, hold down the left mouse button, and drag to the end of the selection. Release the mouse button, and the text is selected.

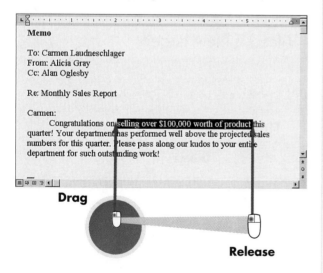

Drag

Release

② Select Text with the Keyboard

To select text using the keyboard, press the arrow keys to move the cursor to the beginning of the word or phrase you want to select. Hold down the **Shift** key and press the appropriate arrow keys to select the desired text. To select a word, for example, move the cursor to the beginning of the word, hold down the **Shift** key, and press the right arrow key until the text is selected.

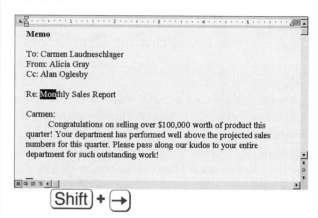

③ Use Mouse Shortcuts

To select a single word quickly, double-click inside the word. To select a paragraph, triple-click anywhere inside the paragraph.

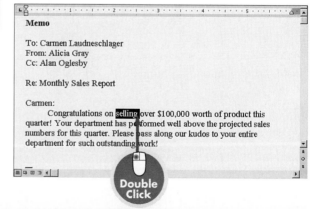

Double Click

4 Click Inside the Left Margin

You can also click inside the left margin to select lines of text. Hover your mouse pointer to the left of the line you want to highlight until it takes the shape of a north-east-pointing arrow. Click once to select the line.

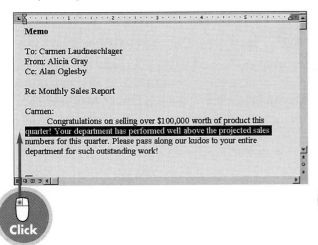

6 Select the Entire Document

Finally, you can use the left margin to select the entire document: Triple-click anywhere in the left margin to select the entire document.

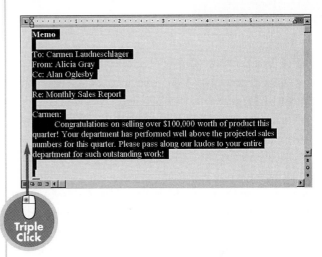

5 Select a Paragraph

You can also use the left margin to select a paragraph: Simply double-click next to the paragraph you want to select.

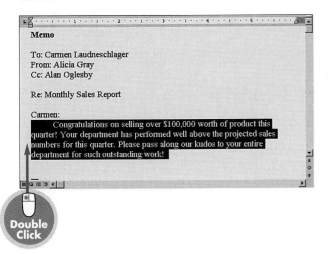

Deselecting Text

To deselect text quickly, click anywhere outside the text or press any arrow key.

Editing Selected Text

You can easily replace selected text with new text. Just start typing, and the selected text is deleted and replaced with any new text you type. To delete selected text without typing new text, press the **Delete** key.

Keyboard Shortcuts

To select one word at a time using the keyboard keys, press **Ctrl+Shift+Right Arrow** or **Ctrl+Shift+Left Arrow**. To select one paragraph at a time, press **Ctrl+Shift+Up Arrow** or **Ctrl+Shift+Down Arrow**. To select all the text from the insertion point onward, press **Ctrl+Shift+End**. To select all text above the insertion point, press **Ctrl+Shift+Home**. To select the entire document, press **Ctrl+A**.

How to Move and Copy Text

Use Word's **Cut**, **Copy**, and **Paste** functions to move and copy text from one location to another. Word makes it easy to pick up characters, words, sentences, paragraphs, and more and to move or copy them to a new location. You can even move and copy text between files. You can apply a variety of methods to move and copy text. You can use menu commands, shortcut menu commands, toolbar buttons, keyboard shortcuts, and drag-and-drop techniques. Everybody finds their favorite method. To move text, cut it from its position and paste it somewhere else; to copy text, make a copy of the text and paste it elsewhere.

① Select the Text

Select the text you want to cut or copy.

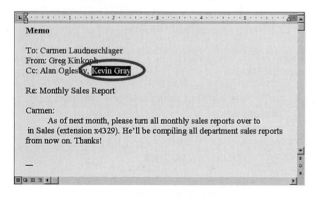

② Use the Cut and Copy Buttons

An easy way to cut and copy is to use the toolbar buttons. To move the text, click the **Cut** button in the **Standard** toolbar. The text is deleted from your document, but it remains in a special Windows storage area called the *Clipboard*. To copy the text, click the **Copy** button in the **Standard** toolbar. When you copy text, nothing appears to happen because the text remains in its original location, but a copy of the selected text is sent to the Clipboard.

Cut ⌐ └ Copy

③ Relocate the Cursor

Click to place the cursor in the document where you want to paste the cut or copied text. If necessary, you can open another document or switch to another already open document to paste text there.

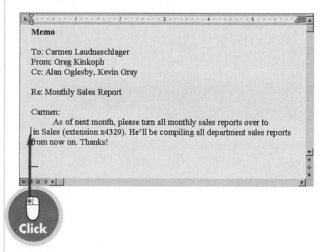

Click

4 Use the Paste Button

Click the **Paste** button in the **Standard** toolbar to paste the text. The text is pasted into the document beginning at the position of the insertion point.

Paste ⌐

5 Check the Smart Tag

As soon as the text is pasted, a Smart Tag icon appears. Click the icon to display a list of options pertaining to the pasted text. You can click an option or ignore the Smart Tag and continue working in the document.

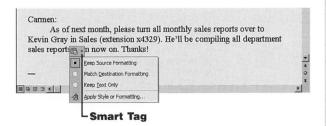

Carmen:
As of next month, please turn all monthly sales reports over to Kevin Gray in Sales (extension x4329). He'll be compiling all department sales reports n now on. Thanks!

Keep Source Formatting
Match Destination Formatting
Keep Text Only
Apply Style or Formatting...

└ **Smart Tag**

6 Use the Drag and Drop Method

Another easy method to move or copy text is to drag and drop it. To move text, click the selected text, hold down the mouse button, and drag the mouse to where you want to paste the text. Release the mouse button to drop, or paste, the cut text. To copy instead of cut, hold down the **Ctrl** key while dragging.

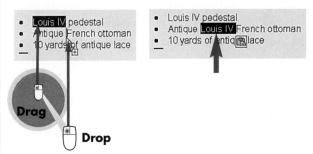

Drag

Drop

How-to Hint

Keyboard Shortcuts

If you prefer using the keyboard, try these shortcut commands: **Ctrl+X** for **Cut**, **Ctrl+C** for **Copy**, and **Ctrl+V** for **Paste**. These keyboard shortcuts are standard for all Windows-based programs.

Using the Office Clipboard

Office XP has a new and improved Clipboard feature that lets you cut or copy up to 24 items and paste them in any order you want. If you cut or copy multiple pieces of data, the Office **Clipboard** task pane opens. To paste an item from the **Clipboard** pane, first click in the file where you want to paste the item and then click the item you want to paste from the list of items in the task pane. To paste all the items at once, click the **Paste All** button in the **Clipboard** task pane.

To keep the **Clipboard** task pane from appearing, click the **Options** button at the bottom of the task pane and disable the **Show Office Clipboard Automatically** option. To open the **Clipboard** task pane again, open the task pane, click the **Other Task Panes** button, and choose **Clipboard**.

How to Use Templates

Use Word's templates to create documents quickly when you don't have time to format and design them yourself. A *template* is a ready-made document. Just fill in your own text. Word comes with numerous templates you can use. If you don't see a template that meets your specific needs, you can choose a template that is close, add your own design and formatting elements, and save the document as a new template. The next time you need the template, it's ready to go.

① Open the New Document Task Pane

Choose **File**, **New** to display the **New Document** task pane. (You can't use the **New** button on the **Standard** toolbar as a shortcut. If you click the **New** button, Word assumes that you want to start a new document based on the **Normal** template and doesn't give you the chance to choose a different template.)

② Click the Templates Link

Click the **General Templates** link in the **New Document** task pane.

③ Choose a Tab Category

The **Templates** dialog box has several tab categories to choose from, such as **Letters & Faxes**. Depending on the type of document you want to create, click the tabs and see what is available.

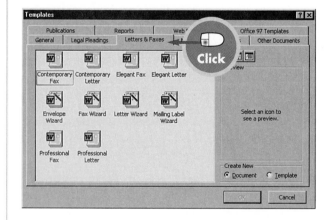

4 Choose a Template

When you locate a template you want to use, select it by clicking just once on the icon; the **Preview** area lets you see what the design looks like. If you decide you like the template, double-click its name or select it and choose **OK**.

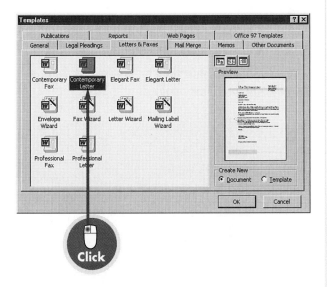

5 Fill It In

Word creates a new document based on the template you chose. Many templates, such as the one shown here, include placeholder text with instructions to **Click here and type** to help you fill in your text. You might also see some cross-hatched boxes. Word uses these for formatting purposes only: they won't print. Click the placeholder text and type your own text.

6 Save, Print, and Close

The text you typed replaces the **Click here** text. Continue replacing all the **Click here** instructions with the text you want in the document. When you have completed the document, use the regular methods to save, print, and close it.

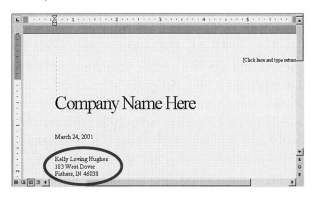

How-to Hint

Creating a Custom Template

You can save a Word template as your own personalized template without changing the built-in template. In the **Templates** dialog box, click the **Template** option in the lower-right corner before you open the template. This opens a copy of the built-in template that you can save as your own template with a different name. You can personalize the text and formatting in this template. After you save this template, its icon appears on the **General** tab the next time you open the **Templates** dialog box.

To delete a custom template, open the **Templates** dialog box, right-click the icon for the template you want to delete, and click **Delete**. Click **OK** to close the dialog box.

How to Work with AutoText

AutoText is a great tool that saves you time when entering text. If you find yourself repeatedly typing the same company name, phrase, or address, make that text an AutoText entry. Assign the entry a brief abbreviation, and the next time you enter the abbreviation, AutoText inserts the entire text entry for you. AutoText entries can be of any length—from a short sentence to an entire letter—and they are easy to save and use.

To turn on or off automatic AutoText entries, choose **Tools**, **AutoCorrect Options**. At the top of the **AutoText** tab, enable or disable the **Show AutoComplete** suggestions check box. Click **OK** to exit.

❶ Select the Text

Select the text you want to include in your AutoText entry (for example, **Human Resources Department**) and apply any formatting you want to that text.

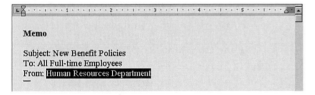

❷ Choose the AutoText Command

Choose **Insert**, **AutoText**, **New**. The **Create AutoText** dialog box opens.

❸ Enter a Name

Type a title for the entry in the **Please name your AutoText entry** field (such as **Human Resources** or use the default suggestion) and click **OK**. Although AutoText names can be more than one word long, you're better off using a title or abbreviation that's short and memorable.

4 Insert AutoText

The next time you're ready to use the entry, position the insertion point in the document where you want the entry to be inserted and type the first few letters of the AutoText entry's title. As you type, an AutoComplete tip containing the title might appear next to the characters you typed. If you press **Enter**, the AutoText entry is inserted at the current location.

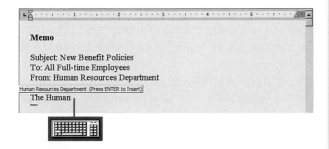

5 Open the AutoText Tab

You can also choose which AutoText entry you want to use by choosing **Insert**, **AutoText**, **AutoText**. The **AutoCorrect** dialog box opens with the **AutoText** tab selected.

6 Choose an Entry

In the list of **AutoText** categories, point to the category where your entry is stored and click the title of the entry. Click the **Insert** button, and the entry is pasted into your document.

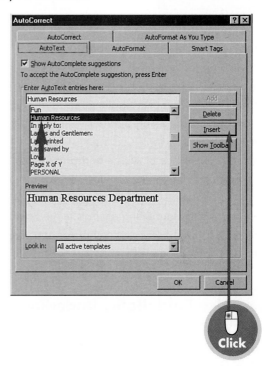

How-to Hint

Deleting Entries

To delete an AutoText entry, choose **Insert**, **AutoText**, **AutoText** to display the **AutoText** tab of the **AutoCorrect** dialog box. Click the entry you want to delete from the list, click the **Delete** button, and click **OK**.

Using the AutoText Toolbar

Another way to create and insert AutoText entries is with the **AutoText** toolbar. Display the toolbar by selecting **View**, **Toolbars**, **AutoText**, and use the **New** button to add new entries as you encounter them. To insert an entry, click the **AutoText** button, choose the entry from the list, and click **Insert**.

How to Format Text

You can find all kinds of formatting tools on the **Formatting** toolbar. By far the easiest formatting to apply is bold, italic, and underline. These are the most commonly used formatting commands. You can also find controls for applying different fonts and sizes to your text. Changing fonts and sizes is an easy way to alter the appearance of words and of the document. You can change the font or size for one word, a paragraph, or the entire document. In addition, you can also find all these formatting controls in the **Font** dialog box, a comprehensive dialog box for applying formatting options in one fell swoop.

❶ Use Bold, Italic, Underline Buttons

Select the text you want to format, or choose the formatting commands before you type the text. To boldface text, click the **Bold** button on the **Formatting** toolbar. To italicize text, click the **Italic** button. To underline text, click the **Underline** button.

Bold┘ └Underline

Italic

❷ Choose a Font

On the **Formatting** toolbar, click the down arrow on the **Font** drop-down list box to display a list of the fonts installed on your computer. Scroll through the list to find the font you want; click it to apply it to the selected text. (Word places the fonts you've used recently above a double line at the top of the list; below the double line is an alphabetical list of all the fonts.)

❸ Choose a Font Size

After you have chosen a font, you can make it larger or smaller by changing the font size. On the **Formatting** toolbar, click the down arrow on the **Font Size** box to display a list of sizes for the current font. Scroll, if necessary, to find the size you want; click it to apply it to the selected text.

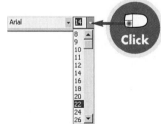

④ Open the Font Dialog Box

The quickest way to experiment with fonts, sizes, and other characteristics all at the same time is to use the **Font** dialog box. Select the text you want to format and choose **Format**, **Font** to open the dialog box.

⑤ Preview Formatting Selections

Use the **Font** tab to change the font and size, set font style, and check the results in the **Preview** area. Choose a font from the **Font** list, for example, to see what it looks like in the **Preview** area.

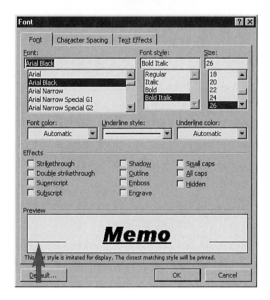

⑥ Apply the Formats

Click **OK** to close the **Font** dialog box and apply the new settings.

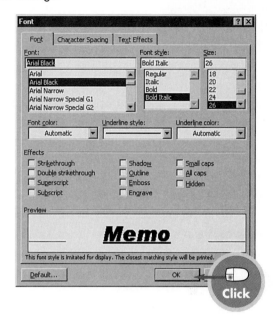

How-to Hint

Keyboard Shortcuts

To format text from the keyboard, select the text and use these keyboard shortcuts: **Ctrl+B** for boldface, **Ctrl+I** for italic, **Ctrl+U** for underline, or **Ctrl+Shift+D** for double underline.

Adding Color

To color text, click the **Font Color** drop-down arrow in the **Font** dialog box and click the color you want to use. You can also use the **Font Color** button on the **Formatting** toolbar: Click the button's arrow and choose a color from the palette that appears.

Changing the Default Font and Size

By default, Word uses the font **Times New Roman** and the font size **10**, which can be pretty hard to read. To change the default font or size, change it in the **Font** dialog box, and click the **Default** button. Click **Yes** to confirm.

How to Copy Text Formatting

If you have applied several character formats—such as a font, a font size, and a format (bold, italic, underline)—to a block of text in your document and later decide you want to apply the same formatting to another block of text, you don't have to apply those formats to the new location individually. Instead, you can use the **Format Painter** button to take all the formats from the original block of text and "paint" them across the new text.

1 Select the Text

Select the text that has the formatting you want to copy (characters, words, whole paragraphs, headings, and so on).

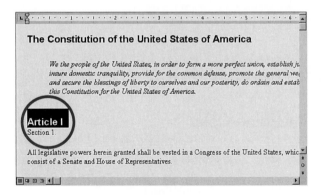

2 Choose Format Painter

Click the **Format Painter** button in the **Standard** toolbar.

Format Painter

3 The Mouse Pointer Changes

The mouse pointer changes to a paintbrush pointer.

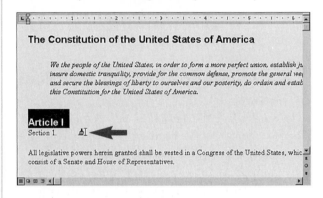

④ Drag to Copy Formatting

Drag the paintbrush pointer across the text where you want to paint the copied format.

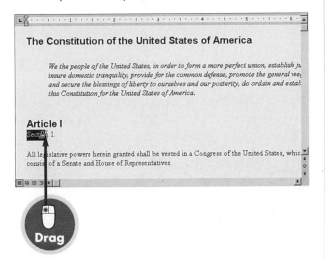

⑤ Formatting is Applied

Release the mouse button. The formatting is painted to the block of text (click anywhere to deselect the text).

How-to Hint

Keep Painting

To paint the same formatting to several blocks of text more quickly, double-click the **Format Painter** button. The **Format Painter** remains turned on so that you can paint the formatting repeatedly. For example, you could paint across all the headings in the document shown here. When you're finished painting the formatting, click the **Format Painter** button again to turn it off.

Another Route

Another way to copy formatting is to use the **Repeat** command. Apply formatting to a selection of text with the **Font** dialog box (by using the Font dialog box, you can apply several formatting characteristics at once) and click **OK**. To apply that same formatting to another section of text, don't bother opening the **Font** dialog box again. Just select the block of text where you want to copy the formatting, choose **Edit**, **Repeat Font Formatting**; the same formatting is applied to the new text. (This works only if your previous action was to assign formatting.)

Using AutoFormat

Don't like the pressures of coming up with formatting yourself? Use Word's **AutoFormat** feature to format your documents automatically. Choose **Format**, **AutoFormat**. In the **AutoFormat** dialog box, select the type of document you're creating and click **OK**.

How to Insert Symbols

Need to insert a special character or symbol not found on the keyboard? Tap into Word's collection of characters and symbols to find exactly what you seek. Symbols include fractions (3/4), trademarks (™), and other graphical elements; special characters include em dashes (—) and ellipses (…). You can insert a copyright © or trademark ™ symbol, for example, into your text for products you mention. Depending on what fonts you have installed, you might have access to additional symbols, such as mathematical or Greek symbols, architectural symbols, and more.

① Open the Symbol Dialog Box

Click the insertion point where you want to insert the symbol and choose **Insert**, **Symbol**. the **Symbol** dialog box opens.

② Choose a Symbol

On the **Symbols** tab, click a symbol. To change the symbols shown, click the **Font** drop-down arrow and choose another symbol font.

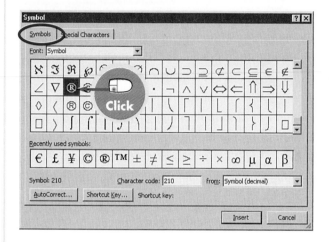

③ Insert the Symbol

After selecting the symbol you want to use, click the **Insert** button; the symbol is placed in your text. The **Symbol** dialog box remains open for your use.

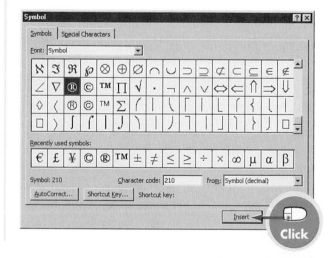

④ Choose a Special Character

If you want to insert a special character in your text, such as an em dash or special quote mark, click the **Special Character** tab in the **Symbol** dialog box to view what's available.

⑤ Insert the Special Character

Select the special character you want to insert and click the **Insert** button. The selected character is added to your text.

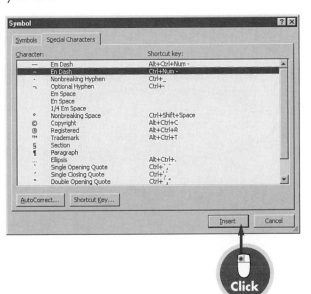

⑥ Close the Dialog Box

The **Symbol** dialog box remains open in case you want to add another symbol. Click the **Close** button to exit the dialog box.

How-to Hint

Customizing the Symbols

Use the **Font** drop-down list in the **Symbol** dialog box to change the font used for the symbols. Use the **Wingdings** font, for example, if you want to insert character icons such as clocks and telephones. Be sure to check out the symbols available for the fonts you have installed on your computer.

Symbols Ready to Go

Word's **AutoCorrect** feature watches out for common symbols you need to type, such as the copyright or trademark symbols, and automatically inserts them for you. For example, if you type **(c)**, **AutoCorrect** automatically replaces the keystrokes with the ©symbol. For more information about using the **AutoCorrect** feature, turn to Task 26, "How to Work with AutoCorrect."

How to Set Margins

The default margins in Word are 1 inch on the top and bottom of the page and 1.25 inches on the left and right sides of the page. These margins are fine for most documents, but like all features in Word, they can be changed. Wider margins can give the page a more spacious appearance, for example. You might find that you have just a line or two more than will fit on a page, but if you adjust the margins slightly, everything fits.

1 Open the Page Setup Dialog Box

Open the **File** menu and select **Page Setup**. The **Page Setup** dialog box opens.

2 View the Margins Tab

Click the **Margins** tab to edit margins.

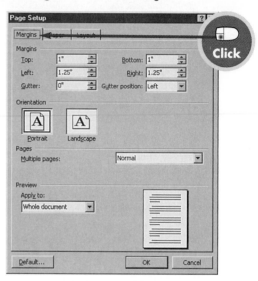

3 Change the Margins

Type new margin settings in the **Top**, **Bottom**, **Left**, and **Right** text boxes; the settings are measured in inches.

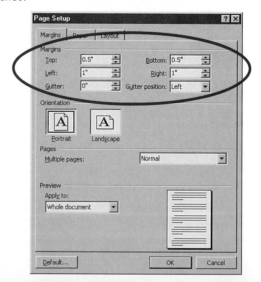

④ Apply the New Settings

The **Preview** area shows what the new margin settings look like. Click **OK** to apply the new margins to your document.

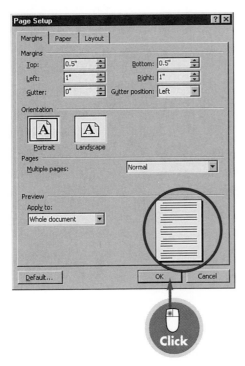

Click

⑤ View the New Margin Settings

On the **Standard** toolbar, click the **Print Preview** button to switch the document to **Print Preview** mode. In **Print Preview**, you see a whole-page view of your document, where it's easier to check the margin settings for a good visual appearance.

Print Preview

⑥ Change Margins Manually

Instead of setting inch measurements, you can manually change margins in either **Print Preview** or **Print Layout** view. The margins are displayed as gray bars at each end of the horizontal and vertical rulers. You can drag a margin to reset it. Click the **Close** button in the **Print Preview** toolbar to exit **Print Preview** mode.

Drag

How-to Hint

Caution!

Be careful about setting margins too narrow or wide—most printers have a minimum margin in which nothing can be printed. (Commonly, less than 0.25 of an inch is outside the printable area.)

Changing the Default Margins

If your company wants margin settings on all its documents that differ from Word's default margins, you can set the default margins to match those used in your company (so that you won't have to change the margins each time you start a new document). To set new default margins, follow steps 1 through 3 in this task, but before you click **OK** in step 4, click the **Default** button. When Word asks whether you want to change the default settings for page setup, choose **Yes** and click **OK**. You can change the default margins as often as you prefer.

How to Set the Line Spacing

Line spacing is the amount of space between lines within a paragraph. By default, Word starts each new document with single spacing, which provides just enough space between lines so that letters don't overlap. You might want to switch to double-spacing for rough drafts of documents so that you have extra room to write in edits by hand. Or try one-and-a-half spacing, which makes text easier to read by separating lines with an extra half-line of blank space. You can also control the amount of space between paragraphs. For example, documents with an extra half-line of space between paragraphs are easier to read, and you won't have to press **Enter** twice to end a paragraph and insert an extra blank line between paragraphs.

1 Select the Paragraph

To change the line spacing of only one paragraph, click anywhere in the paragraph. To change the line spacing of several paragraphs, select them first. To change the line spacing for the entire document, press **Ctrl+A** to select the entire document.

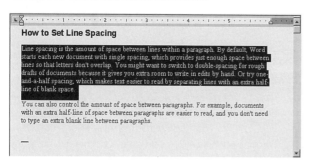

2 Use the Line Spacing Button

Click the **Line Spacing** drop-down button on the **Formatting** toolbar and choose a line spacing value from the list.

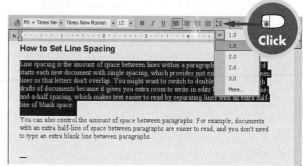

3 Open the Paragraph Dialog Box

Another way to set line spacing is using the **Paragraph** dialog box. You can display the dialog box by clicking **More** on the **Line Spacing** drop-down list or by choosing **Format**, **Paragraph**.

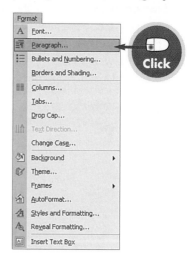

4 Choose a Line Spacing

At the top of the **Paragraph** dialog box, click the **Indents and Spacing** tab. Then click the drop-down arrow on the **Line spacing** list box. Select **Single**, **1.5 lines**, or **Double**.

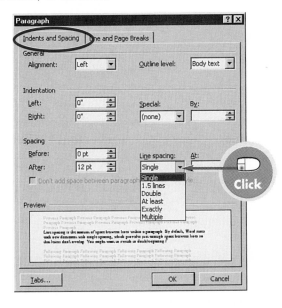

5 Change Paragraph Spacing

To change the spacing between paragraphs, designate a new setting in the **Before** and **After** boxes under **Spacing**. The **Before** box sets spacing at the top of the paragraph; the **After** box sets spacing at the bottom of the paragraph. Click **OK** to close the dialog box.

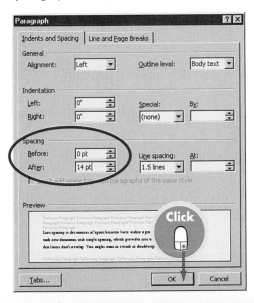

6 Apply Line Spacing

Any changes you made in the **Paragraph** dialog box are applied to the selected text.

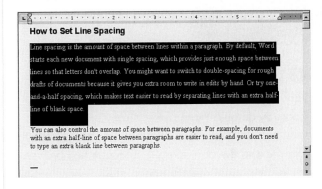

Previewing First

When changing the settings in the **Paragraph** dialog box, check out the effects in the **Preview** area to see how the selected effects will appear in your own text.

Made a Mistake?

If you do not like the effects of the new line spacing applied to your text, just click the **Undo** button and try another setting.

How to Align and Indent Text

Use Word's alignment commands to change the way your text is positioned horizontally on the document page. By default, Word automatically aligns your text with the left margin as you type. You can choose to align text to the right margin, to center text between the left and right margins, or to justify text so that it aligns at both the left and right margins. Indents also control the positioning of text horizontally. *Indents* are simply margins that affect individual paragraphs or lines. Indents can help make paragraphs easier to distinguish. The quickest way to indent a line of text is with the **Tab** key; however, there are other ways to indent text more precisely. You can set exact measurements for left and right indents, choose to indent only the first line of text, or create a *hanging indent* that leaves the first line intact but indents the rest of the paragraph.

① Use the Alignment Buttons

Select the text or paragraphs you want to align and click an alignment button on the **Formatting** toolbar. Click **Align Left** to left-align text, click **Center** to center text, or click **Align Right** to right-align text. Click **Justify** to justify text between the left and right margins.

To center text using only the keyboard, press **Ctrl+E**. Press **Ctrl+L** for left alignment, **Ctrl+R** for right alignment, and **Ctrl+J** for justified alignment.

Align Left — Justify
Center — Align Right

② Use the Indent Buttons

For quick indents, use the **Indent** buttons on the **Formatting** toolbar. To increase the indentation, click anywhere in the paragraph or sentence you want to indent, and click the **Increase Indent** button. To decrease the indentation, click **Decrease Indent**.

Decrease Indent ———
Increase Indent ———

③ View the Changes to Your Text

Depending on which alignment button or indent button you clicked, Word positions your text accordingly. Here you can see several alignment and indent examples in effect.

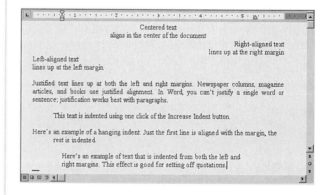

4️⃣ Use the Paragraph Dialog Box

Another way to apply alignment and indents is with the **Paragraph** dialog box: It's one-stop shopping for paragraph-formatting commands. Choose **Format**, **Paragraph** to open the dialog box.

5️⃣ Choose an Alignment

On the **Indents and Spacing** tab, click the **Alignment** drop-down arrow to display a list of alignment options. Click the one you want to use.

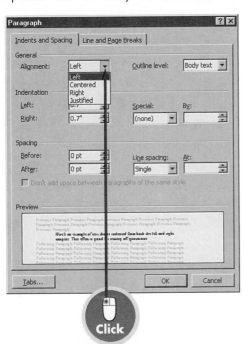

6️⃣ Set an Indent Measurement

Use the **Left** or **Right** indentation boxes to set a specific measurement for the indentation. You can type directly into the boxes or use the spin arrows to increase or decrease the settings. To set a **First Line** or a **Hanging** indentation, select the appropriate option from the **Special** drop-down list. Click **OK** to close the dialog box and apply the settings to your document.

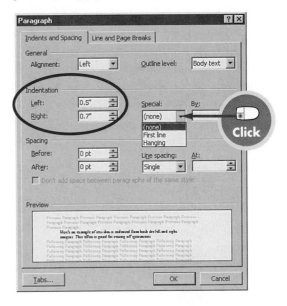

Vertical Alignment

To change your document's vertical alignment, use the **Page Setup** dialog box. Choose **File**, **Page Setup** and click the **Layout** tab. Use the **Vertical Alignment** drop-down list to choose a new alignment: **Top** (default), **Center**, or **Justified**. Click **OK** to close the dialog box and apply the alignment to the document.

Indentations on the Ruler

You can also set indents on the ruler, including **First Line** and **Hanging** indents. To set an indentation, drag the appropriate indent marker on the ruler bar. The indent markers are funny-looking triangle shapes on the left side of the ruler. If you hover your mouse pointer over an indent marker, a ScreenTip appears to identify the marker.

How to Work with Bulleted and Numbered Lists

Use Word's **Bullets** and **Numbering** list features to set off lists of information in your documents. For example, a bulleted list can make a list of related information easy to spot on a page, and a numbered list organizes items that must appear in a certain order. You can set the formatting for a bulleted or numbered list before typing the text of the list, or you can turn existing text into an organized list.

① Select Text

To turn existing text into a list, first select the text.

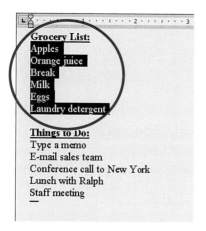

② Use the Formatting Buttons

To add bullets, click the **Bullets** button on the **Formatting** toolbar. To turn the text into a numbered list, click the **Numbering** button.

Numbering ——
Bullets ——

③ View the Formatting

If you clicked the **Bullets** button, the selected text is immediately indented with bullet points in front of each line. If you clicked **Numbering**, the list is numbered sequentially, as shown here.

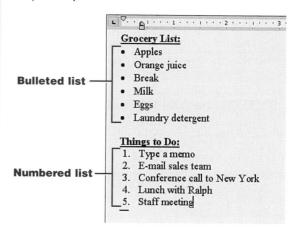

Bulleted list ——
Numbered list ——

4 Add to the List

To add more items to the list, click at the end of the line before the place where you want to add another item and press **Enter**. Word inserts a new bullet or numbered step for you; just type in the new text. After you type the last item in the list, press **Enter** twice to turn the numbered or bulleted list off, or click the **Numbering** or **Bullets** button on the toolbar to turn off the feature.

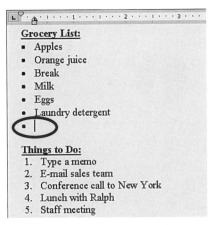

5 Change the Style

If you prefer to use a different bullet or numbering style in your list, open the **Bullets and Numbering** dialog box. Select the text of the list you want to format and choose **Format**, **Bullets and Numbering** to open the dialog box.

6 Apply the Style

To change the bullet style, click the **Bulleted** tab and choose another style. To change the number style, click the **Numbered** tab and select another style. Click **OK** to close the dialog box and apply the new style.

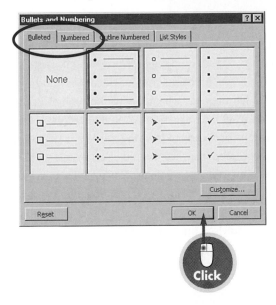

How-to Hint

Creating the List from Scratch

You can also create a bulleted or numbered list as you type. For a numbered list, type **1**. followed by a space, type the text for the first item, and press **Enter**. To create a bulleted list, type an asterisk (*) followed by a space, type the text for the first item, and press **Enter**. Continue entering list items as necessary. Press **Enter** twice after the last item to turn off the list feature.

Customizing Bullets or Numbers

Use the **Customize** button in the **Bullets and Numbering** dialog box to choose another font for the bullets or numbers you use, or to customize the way in which the numbers or bullets are positioned in the document. For example, you can specify exactly how your numbers and numbered text are indented on the page.

How to Set Tabs

Tabs are used to indent and create vertically aligned columns of text. By default, Word has tab stops set at every 0.5-inch interval in your document, and the tab text is left-aligned, which means that it lines up at the left edge of the tab column. You can create your own tab stops and change how the tab text is aligned at a tab stop. You can, for example, align tab text to the right edge of the tab column, center the text in the column, or use the decimal point tab to make the decimal points in your text line up in the tab column. You can even apply a bar tab, which sets a vertical bar between tab columns. You can use the ruler to set tabs, or open the **Tabs** dialog box.

❶ Set a Tab Stop on the Ruler

To set a tab stop on the ruler, first select the type of tab alignment you want to use. By default, **Left Tab** alignment is selected. To select another, you must cycle through the selections. Each click on the alignment button displays a different tab alignment symbol (hover the mouse pointer over the button to display the name of the currently selected tab alignment).

Tab alignment button

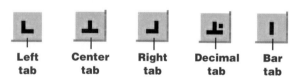

| Left tab | Center tab | Right tab | Decimal tab | Bar tab |

❷ Click in Place

On the ruler, click where you want the tab inserted; the selected tab symbol is added to the ruler at the location you clicked.

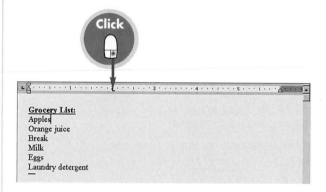

❸ Apply a Tab

To use the new tab stop, place the cursor at the beginning of the line and press **Tab**, or place your cursor in front of the text you want to reposition and then press **Tab**. The tab is in effect until you change it to another setting.

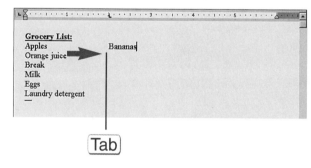

4 Open the Tabs Dialog Box

Another way to set tabs is to use the **Tabs** dialog box. Open the dialog box by choosing **Format**, **Tabs**.

5 Enter a Tab Stop

In the **Tab stop position** text box, type a new tab stop measurement. For example, if you want to create a tab stop at a position 1.5 inches in from the left margin, type **1.5**. Use the **Alignment** options to change the tab stop alignment. Click **Set** to set the new tab stop.

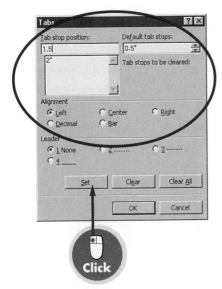

6 Close the Dialog Box

Repeat step 5 to set up additional tab stops. When you are done specifying tab stops, click **OK** to close the dialog box. The new tab stops are ready to go.

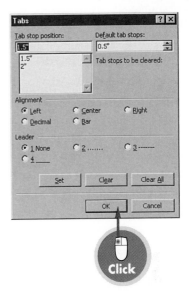

How-to Hint

Deleting Tabs

To delete a tab, drag it off the ruler, release the mouse button, and it's gone. To delete tabs from the **Tabs** dialog box, select the tab from the list box and click **Clear**.

Leader Tabs

Use the **Tabs** dialog box to set leader tabs. *Leader tabs* are tabs separated by dots or dashes. They're used to help the reader follow tabbed information from column to column.

Changing the Default Tab

If you prefer a default tab setting different from 0.5-inch intervals, set a new default tab measurement in the **Tabs** dialog box. Click inside the **Default tab stops** text box and type a new measurement, or use the spin arrows to change the existing setting. Click **OK** to apply the new default tab stop.

How to Create Columns

If you're creating a newsletter or brochure with Word, consider formatting the text into columns, similar to a newspaper or magazine. Word's columns are *newspaper-style columns*, which means that the text flows to the bottom of a column and then continues at the top of the next column. Newspaper columns are different than columns you create with tabs and tables; the text in newspaper columns flows from column to column without your having to adjust the tab settings.

1 Select Text

If you want a certain portion of your document treated as columnar text, you can first select the text you want to format into columns. Then choose **Format**, **Columns** to open the **Columns** dialog box.

2 Select a Column Type

In the **Presets** area, click the column style you want to use, such as **Two** or **Three**. Use the **Width and spacing** options to set an exact measurement for the columns and the space between them (or go with the default settings). The **Preview** area lets you see what the columns will look like.

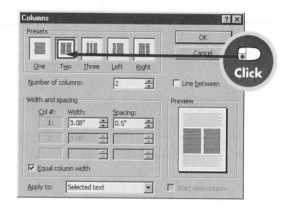

3 Apply To

To apply the column format to a specific area, click the **Apply To** drop-down arrow and choose the extent to which the columns should apply in the document. For example, choose **Whole Document** if you want the entire document to use columns.

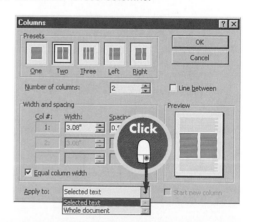

4 Close the Dialog Box

Click **OK** to close the dialog box and apply the column format to your text.

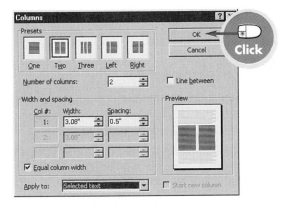

5 Make Quick Columns

Another way to set columns is with the **Columns** button on the **Standard** toolbar. Select the text you want to apply columns to, and then click the **Columns** button on the **Standard** toolbar and drag to select the number of columns you want to use.

6 View the Column Format

When you release the mouse button, the columns are assigned. Word displays the columns in **Print Layout** view, the best view for seeing columns in Word. In this figure, the view is zoomed to see the whole page onscreen; notice that only the text selected in step 1 is in columns.

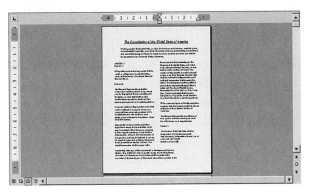

How-to Hint

Can't See Them?

The best view for columns is **Print Layout** view. You can see columns only in **Print Layout** view or in the **Print Preview** window. Click the **Print Layout** view button in the bottom-left corner of the screen to switch views as needed.

Setting Column Breaks

To make a break within a column and cause the text to flow to the next column, click where you want the break to occur, and then press **Ctrl+Shift+Enter**. To remove a column break, select it and press **Delete**.

To turn your column text back into normal text (which is really just one column anyway), select the text, click the **Columns** button on the **Standard** toolbar, and click a single column.

Inserting a Divider Line

One of the options in the **Columns** dialog box lets you add a divider line between columns, which defines the columns and gives a nice visual appeal. Enable the **Line between** check box to add such a line between your columns.

How to Insert a Table

If you want to create a complex list or chart, the best option is to use a Word table. A *table* is a grid of rows and columns; each box in a table is called a *cell*. You can use tables to create anything from simple charts to invoices and employee lists. Tables are useful for any kind of information that has to be organized in a row-and-column format. Tables are flexible; you can specify exactly how many rows or columns they have, control the size and formatting of each cell, and include anything from text to graphics.

1 Create a Quick Table

To quickly create a table, click in the document where you want to place the table; then click the **Insert Table** button on the **Standard** toolbar. A grid appears; use it to tell Word how many columns and rows you want in the initial table: Drag to select squares that represent cells in the table (for example, drag to select three columns by four rows).

2 Instant Table

When you release the mouse button, a table with the number of rows and columns you selected appears on the page. The table stretches across the width of the page; to make a column narrower, point to a vertical border and drag it to a new position (drag the right table border to narrow the entire table).

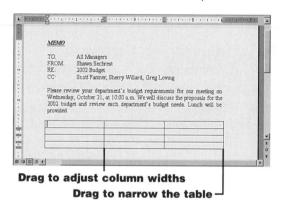

Drag to adjust column widths
Drag to narrow the table

3 Enter Table Text

Click in a cell and begin typing. The text in each cell behaves like a paragraph; if you press **Enter**, a new paragraph is started in the same cell. You can format the text in each cell the same way you format text in a normal paragraph.

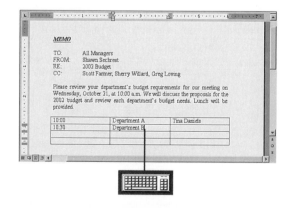

④ Draw Your Own Table

To draw an asymmetrical table, cell by cell, click the **Tables and Borders** button on the **Standard** toolbar. The floating **Tables and Borders** toolbar appears, the view changes to **Print Layout** view, and the mouse pointer becomes a pencil.

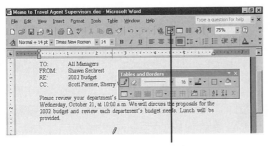

Tables and Borders

⑤ Choose Table Options

Click the **Draw Table** button if it isn't already selected, and then use the **Line Style**, **Line Weight**, and **Border Color** buttons on the **Tables and Borders** toolbar to specify the type and color of line you want for the outside border of your table. Drag the mouse to draw a rectangle for the outside border of the table.

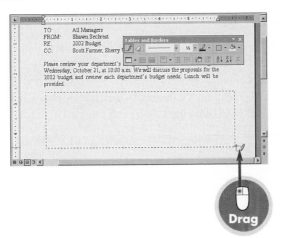

⑥ Draw the Table Lines

Select a different line type or color for the inside borders, if you want; then draw internal lines to delineate rows and columns. As you drag, a dashed line shows you where the line will be inserted. Release the mouse button when the line extends across the entire width or height of the table. You can draw a table as complex as you want with this method.

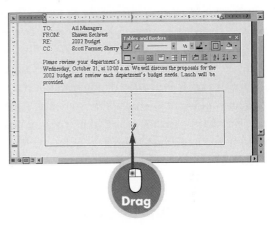

How-to Hint

Navigating a Table

Press **Tab** to move cell by cell to the right, and **Shift+Tab** to move cell by cell to the left. (To insert a tab character in a cell, press **Ctrl+Tab**.)

Adding and Deleting Rows

To insert a new row within a table, click in the row below where you want the new row inserted, and then click the **Insert Table** drop-down arrow on the **Tables and Borders** toolbar and choose **Insert Rows Above**; or choose **Table**, **Insert**, **Rows Above**. To delete a row, click anywhere in the row and choose **Table**, **Select**, **Row**; then choose **Table**, **Delete**, **Rows**.

Formatting Gridlines

You can show your table's gridlines and format them with the **Borders** formats or hide them (which makes the table resemble a neat list). To hide gridlines, click in the table and choose **Table**, **Hide Gridlines**; to show them again, click in the table and choose **Table**, **Show Gridlines**.

How to Add Borders and Shading to Text

You don't have to know anything about graphics to add attractive borders and shading to tables, headings, and paragraphs of text. You can even create a decorative border around the entire page. This task shows you how to work with the options available in the **Borders and Shading** dialog box, but you can also issue most of the commands with the **Tables and Borders** toolbar (click the **Tables and Borders** button on the **Standard** toolbar to display this toolbar).

① Choose Borders and Shading

Click anywhere within the paragraph or table cell to which you want to add borders and shading, or select adjacent paragraphs or table cells if you want to add borders and shading around the group of them. Choose **Format**, **Borders and Shading** to display the Borders and Shading dialog box.

② Apply a Border

Click the **Borders** tab if it isn't already in front. If you see an option under **Setting** that closely matches the type of border you want to add, click it.

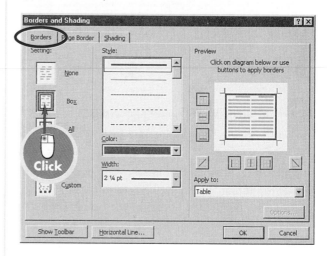

③ Select a Line Style

To customize the style of the lines in your border, scroll through the **Style** list and click the desired style. You can also use the **Color** and **Width** drop-down lists to change the color and width of the lines.

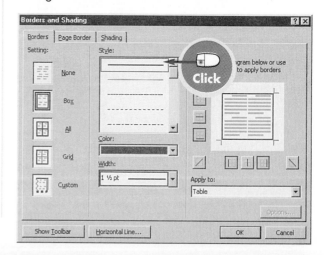

4 Add Shading

To add shading, click the **Shading** tab; then click the color you want to use from the **Fill** palette. To add a pattern, click the **Style** drop-down arrow and select a pattern. When you have made all your selections in the **Borders and Shading** dialog box, click **OK**.

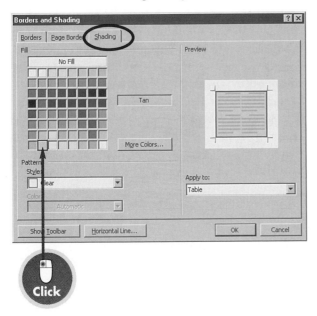

5 View the Settings

The table or paragraph you chose in step 1 reflects the new shading and border settings.

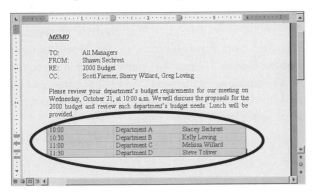

6 Create a Page Border

To create a border around your page, open the **Borders and Shading** dialog box and click the **Page Border** tab. Specify the type of border you want, and choose **OK**. Word creates the border around every page in your document.

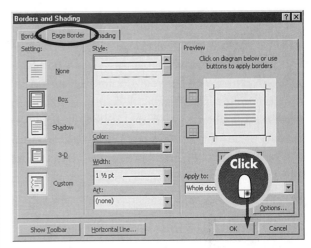

How-to Hint

Using the Outside Border Button

Another way to add a border to a paragraph is to click the **Outside Border** button on the **Formatting** toolbar. Click anywhere inside the paragraph; then click the **Outside Border** button's drop-down arrow and choose a border style.

Custom Borders

If you want to design a border from scratch, choose the **Custom** option from the **Borders** tab in the **Borders and Shading** dialog box, select the desired style, color, and width options for one of the lines, and then click the line in the sample box under **Preview**. Repeat this process to create the remaining three lines.

Quick Borders

To quickly add a single-line horizontal border, click the line where you want the border to go, type - - - (three hyphens, no spaces) and press **Enter**. To create a double-line border, type === (three equal signs) and press **Enter**.

How to Use Headers and Footers

A *header* is text that appears at the top of every page; a *footer* is text that appears at the bottom of every page. You might want to use headers and footers to display the title of your document, your name, the name of your organization, and so on. You can also insert *fields* in headers and footers—a field is a holding place for information that Word updates automatically, such as the current date or the page number of a multipage document.

1 Choose Header and Footer

To add a header or a footer to a document, open the **View** menu and select **Header and Footer**.

2 Enter Header Text

Word switches to **Print Layout** view, places the insertion point in the header area, and displays the **Header and Footer** toolbar. You type and format text in a header or footer just as you would normal text. By default, Word places the cursor in the header section. Type any header text. (You might have to zoom your view with the **Zoom** percentage button on the **Standard** toolbar.)

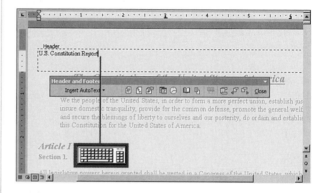

3 Enter Footer Text

To create a footer, click the **Switch Between Header and Footer** button on the **Header and Footer** toolbar to place the insertion point in the footer area. You can switch between the header and footer by clicking this button. In the footer area, type the text you want to see at the bottom of every page.

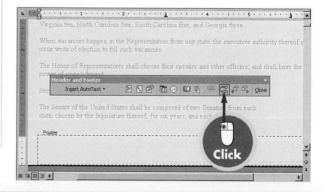

④ Insert Fields

You can select built-in header and footer entries from the **AutoText** button on the **Header and Footer** toolbar, or you can insert fields. For example, click the **Insert Date** button to insert a field for the current date. Click the **Insert Time** button to insert the current time. To add both to a single header line, press the **Tab** key to space out the entries, as shown here.

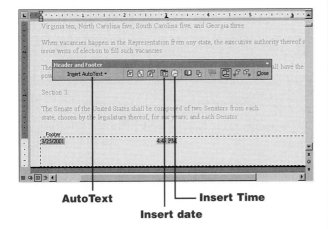

AutoText   **Insert Time**

Insert date

⑤ Close Header and Footer

Click the **Close** button in the **Header and Footer** toolbar to return to the body of the document.

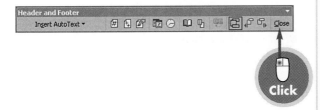

Click

⑥ View Headers and Footers

Headers and footers aren't visible in **Normal** view, but you can see them in both **Print Layout** view and in **Print Preview**.

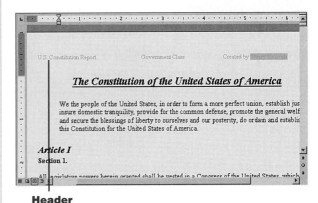

Header

How to Insert Comments, Footnotes, and Endnotes

Comments, footnotes, and endnotes can help you add additional material to your Word documents. Comments can help you identify various users who work on a document. If your office situation requires you to pass along reports for feedback from various department heads, you can use comments to add text to the document. Some documents you create in Word might require footnotes or endnotes to identify the source of your text or to reference other materials. You can easily add such notes to your document pages using the **Footnote and Endnote** dialog box. Footnotes appear at the bottom of each page; endnotes appear at the end of the document.

1 Start a Comment

Click in the document where you want to insert a comment and then choose **Insert**, **Comment**.

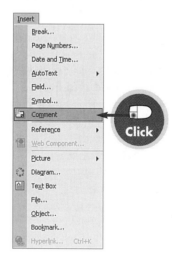

2 Enter a Comment

A comment balloon opens with space for entering your own comment along with the **Reviewing** toolbar. Type the comment text just as you do any other text in Word.

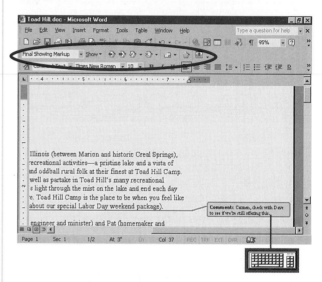

3 View the Comment

To see the author of any comment in a document, simply hover the mouse pointer over the comment. A ScreenTip box appears, revealing the name of the person who wrote the comment.

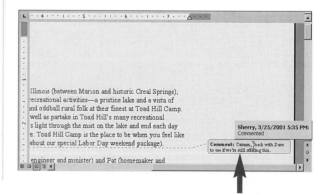

④ Add a Footnote or Endnote

Click in the document where you want to add a reference number. Choose **Insert**, **Reference**, **Footnote** to open the **Footnote and Endnote** dialog box.

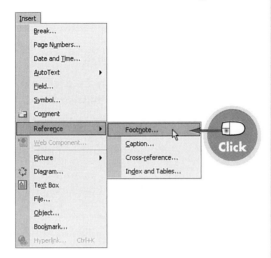

⑤ Choose an Option

In the Location area of the dialog box, select either **Footnotes** or **Endnotes**, depending on the kind of notes you want to add. Click **Insert** to close the dialog box and return to the document page.

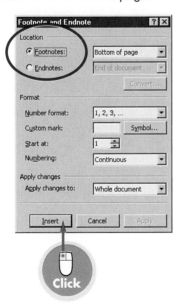

⑥ Add a Reference

Word adds a superscript reference number to the text in **Print Layout** view; a footnote or endnote area opens at the bottom of the window in which you should enter the reference text. When you're done typing the text of the note, click the **Close** button at the top of the footnote area.

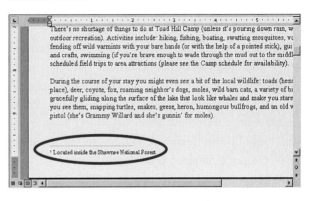

How-to Hint

Reviewer Options

If your workplace requires frequent document sharing, you'll be pleased to note the numerous reviewing tools offered in Word for tracking changes, saving versions, and more. You'll find all the options available from a single toolbar, the **Reviewing** toolbar. To access this toolbar, choose **View**, **Toolbars**, **Reviewing**.

Using the Reviewing Pane

You can also type comments into the **Reviewing** pane. Click the **Reviewing Pane** button on the **Reviewing** toolbar. Click in the pane and type your comment.

Deleting a Comment

To delete a comment, click the comment to select it. Then click the **Reject Change/Delete Comment** button on the **Reviewing** toolbar.

How to Insert Page Numbers and Page Breaks

By default, Word keeps track of how much text can fit onto a document page and makes page breaks automatically for you. However, you will encounter times when you want to insert a page break yourself. If you're creating a document with two or more pages, you should consider adding page numbers. Word inserts them and adjusts them according to changes you make to the document. When you're ready to print, the page numbers print, too.

❶ Insert a Manual Page Break

To insert a manual page break, click in the document where you want the break to occur and press **Ctrl+Enter**.

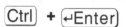

Ctrl + ↵Enter

❷ View the Break

Word inserts a dotted line in the document that represents a page break (seen in **Normal** view here).

❸ Open the Page Break Dialog Box

For a greater variety of page breaks, column breaks, and section breaks, open the **Break** dialog box by choosing **Insert**, **Break**.

4 Select an Option

To set a page break, click the **Page Break** option. If you're setting a column or section break, select the appropriate options. Click **OK** to close the dialog box and apply the break.

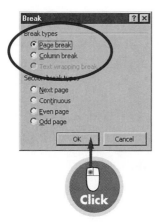

5 Open the Page Numbers Dialog Box

To add page numbers to your document, choose **Insert**, **Page Numbers** to open the **Page Numbers** dialog box.

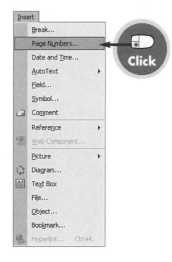

6 Choose Position and Alignment

Click the **Position** drop-down arrow to change whether your page numbers appear at the top of the page or at the bottom. Click the **Alignment** drop-down arrow to change how the numbers are aligned on the page. Click **OK** to close the dialog box and apply the page numbers.

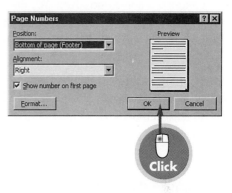

Viewing Page Numbers

You won't be able to view page numbers in **Normal** view. Switch to **Print Layout** view to see page numbers, headers and footers, columns, and other special formatting options.

First Page Numbers

If you prefer to print the first page in your document without a page number, be sure to disable the **Show number on first page** check box in the **Page Numbers** dialog box.

Formatting Page Numbers

To change the number format of your page numbers, click the **Format** button in the **Page Numbers** dialog box to open the **Page Number Format** dialog box. Use this box to specify a number style and control page numbering and chapter numbering.

How to Use Styles

A *style* is a collection of formatting specifications that has been assigned a name and saved. You might have a report, for example, that uses specific formatting for every heading. Rather than reapply the formatting for every heading, you can assign the formatting to a style. You can then quickly apply the style whenever you need it. Word comes with a few predefined styles, but you can easily create your own and use them over and over.

① Format the Text

Format the text as desired. You can apply any of Word's formatting commands, including character, paragraph, and page formatting. Then select the text or click anywhere in the formatted text.

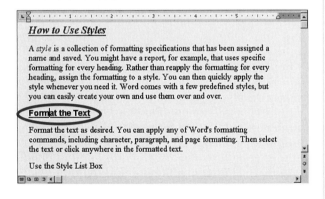

② Use the Style List Box

Click inside the **Style** list box on the **Formatting** toolbar. Type a name for the new style. Be careful not to use any of the existing style names. Press **Enter** when finished. The style is added to the list and is ready to assign. In this example, I gave the assortment of formatting features in the text I selected in step 1 the name **Paragraph Title**.

Click

③ Assign a Style

To assign the new style to another block of text, first select the text.

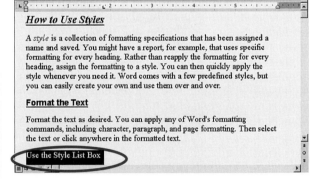

④ Open the Style List

Click the **Style** drop-down arrow and select the style you want to apply from the list of named styles. The chosen style is immediately applied to the selected text. Continue applying the style to other text in your document as needed.

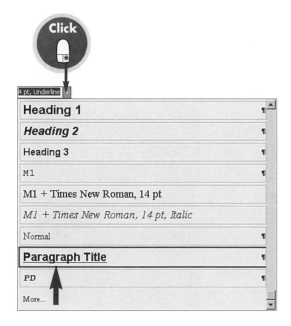

⑤ Create Keyboard Shortcut for the Style

An easy way to apply styles to text is to assign a keystroke combination to the style. Choose **Format**, **Style** to open the **Styles and Formatting** task pane. Select the style to which you want to add a keyboard shortcut, click the **Style** drop-down arrow, and choose the **Modify** option. The **Modify Style** dialog box opens.

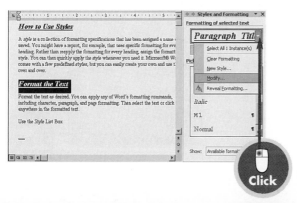

⑥ Add a Shortcut Key

Click the **Format** button and choose **Shortcut Key**. Assign a keystroke combination to the style in the **Press new shortcut key** text box. For example, press **Ctrl+Shift+P+T** to assign these four keys to the **Paragraph Title** style you created in steps 1 through 4. If the keystroke combination is already in use by another feature, the dialog box will tell you, and you can try another combination. When you find an available keystroke combination, click **Assign** and close the open dialog boxes. To apply this style, select the text and press **Ctrl+Shft+P+T**.

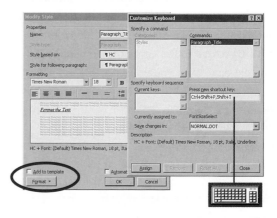

How-to Hint

Using the Styles Task Pane

Another way to assign styles is with the **Styles and Formatting** task pane. Choose **Format**, **Style** or click the **Styles and Formatting** button on the Formatting toolbar to open the **Styles and Formatting** task pane. You can select a new style and formatting to apply from the task pane.

How to Work with Drop Caps and Text Case

In some documents you create, you might want the first letter of the first word in a paragraph to stand out—perhaps you want it larger than the rest of the letters or in a different font. Use Word's **Drop Cap** command to format the letter. In other documents, you might decide to use all capital letters, or turn an all-caps title into uppercase and lowercase letters. Use Word's **Change Case** command to change the case of the text exactly as you want it.

1 Select the Text

Select the letter you want to change to a drop cap character.

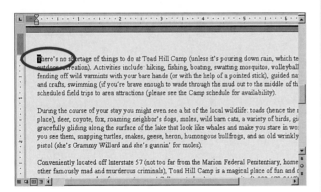

2 Open the Drop Cap Dialog Box

Choose **Format**, **Drop Cap** to display the **Drop Cap** dialog box.

3 Choose a Drop Cap

Choose a position for the drop cap: **Dropped** or **In Margin**. Then assign any formatting, such as a new font or a change in the positioning. Click **OK** to close the dialog box and apply the new settings.

④ View the Settings

Word immediately switches to **Print Layout** view if you aren't already using the view so that you can see the drop cap character in your paragraph.

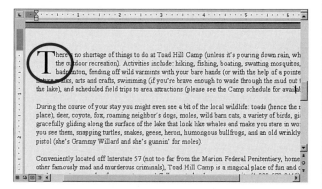

⑤ Change Text Case

If you want to change the case of text in your document, select the text and choose **Format**, **Change Case**. The **Change Case** dialog box opens.

⑥ Select a Case Option

Choose a case option from those available. To make lowercase letters all caps, for example, enable the **UPPERCASE** option. To make capital letters all lowercase, enable the **lowercase** option. Click OK to close the dialog box and apply the new case.

How-to Hint

Which Is Which?

The way the options are written in the **Change Case** dialog box shows how the text will appear. For example, the **Sentence case** option capitalizes the *S* in *sentence* and ends the phrase with a period. The lowercase option is written in all **lowercase** letters.

How to Add a Watermark

A new feature to Word is the ability to add watermarks to your documents. A *watermark* is a picture or text image that appears in the background of your document. Watermarks are designed especially for printed documents; the watermark image—whether it's a company logo or a word such as *CONFIDENTIAL* or *DRAFT*—appears behind the document text.

1 Choose Printed Watermark

Open the **Format** menu and select **Background**, **Printed Watermark**. Word opens the **Printed Watermark** dialog box.

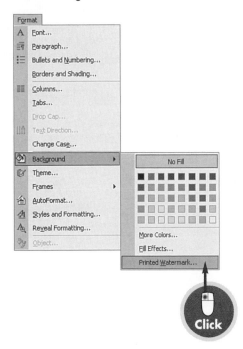

2 Assign a Picture Watermark

To assign a picture as your watermark, enable the **Picture watermark** option and click the **Select Picture** button. Word opens the **Insert Picture** dialog box. If you want to use text as a watermark instead, skip to step 4.

3 Choose a Picture

From the list of image files, select the picture you want to use for your watermark. Click a filename and observe the thumbnail image that opens on the right side of the dialog box. When you have located the image you want to use, click **Insert**. You return to the **Printed Watermark** dialog box.

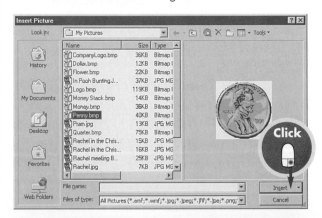

④ Assign a Text Watermark

To assign text as your watermark instead of a picture, enable the **Text watermark** option. Click the **Text** drop-down arrow and choose the word or words you want to use. You can also type your own watermark text in the **Text** box.

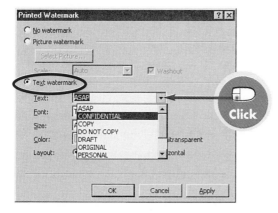

⑤ Assign Additional Options

You can specify a particular font, size, color, or layout as necessary. You can disable the **Semitransparent** check box if you want to make the watermark bold (you cannot see any text you type over a bold watermark). Click **Apply** to apply the effect to the document page. As soon as you click **Apply**, the **Cancel** button in the dialog box is replaced with a Close button. Click **Close** to close the dialog box and view the results onscreen.

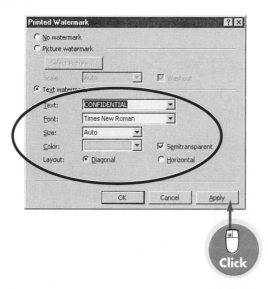

⑥ View the Watermark

To view the watermark, you must switch to **Print Layout** view. The watermark appears on every page in your document file. In this example, you can see a picture watermark applied to the document.

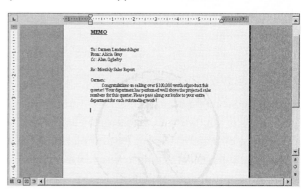

How to Find and Replace Text

When you need to search your document for a particular word or phrase, don't bother scrolling and reading; use Word's **Find** command. This feature searches your entire document for the word or phrase you want. If you want to locate and change every occurrence of a word, use the **Replace** command. If you misspelled a client's name throughout a report, for example, you can quickly fix the mistake by using the **Find and Replace** feature.

1 Find a Word or Phrase

To perform a quick search of your document for a particular word or phrase, choose **Edit**, **Find**. This command opens the **Find and Replace** dialog box, with the **Find** tab displayed.

2 Enter the Text

In the **Find what** text box, type the text you want to search for (for example, type **impeachment**). If you want to specify search criteria, such as matching case or finding whole words only, click the **More** button to reveal search options you can choose. Select the options you want from the expanded dialog box.

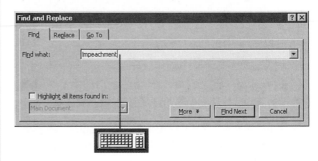

3 Conduct the Search

Click the **Find Next** button to locate the first occurrence of the word or phrase. Word highlights the text in your document, and the **Find and Replace** dialog box remains open on your screen. Click **Find Next** again to search for the next occurrence, or click **Cancel** to close the dialog box.

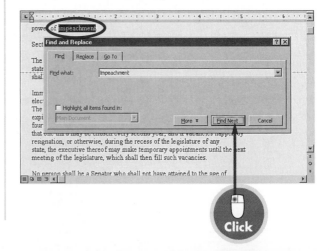

4 Find and Replace Text

To find the text and replace it with new text, use the **Replace** command. Choose **Edit, Replace** to open the **Find and Replace** dialog box with the **Replace** tab up front.

5 Enter the Text

Type the word or words you're looking for in the **Find what** text box (such as **shall**), and type the replacement text in the **Replace with** text box (such as `will`). If you want to specify any search criteria, click the **More** button and select from the available options.

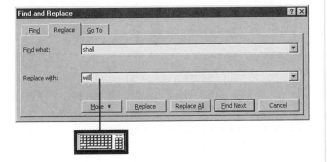

6 Search and Replace

Click the **Find Next** button to locate the first occurrence. Word highlights the text in the document. Click the **Replace** button to replace the highlighted text with the new text. Click **Replace All** to replace every occurrence in the document, or click **Find Next** to ignore the first occurrence and move on to the next.

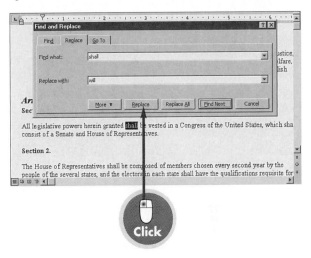

How-to Hint

Search Complete

When Word completes a search, it displays a prompt box telling you that the search is complete. Click **OK**. If the search didn't reveal any occurrences of the text, a prompt box alerts you; click **OK** and try another search.

Searching and Deleting

Use the **Find and Replace** tools to delete text from your document. Open the **Find and Replace** dialog box and type the word you're looking for in the **Find what** text box, but leave the **Replace with** box empty. Word searches for the text and deletes it from your document without replacing it with new text.

How to Check Your Spelling and Grammar

The Spelling and Grammar Checker enables you to check the spelling and grammar of a document as you type or to check the entire document all at once. Because most of us tend to forget about running the Spelling Checker when we finish typing, the Automatic Spelling Checker can save errors by pointing them out as we type and making them difficult to ignore. If the Automatic Spelling Checker is not on, choose **Tools**, **Options**, and select the **Spelling and Grammar** tab. Enable the **Check spelling as you type** check box to turn it on (enable the **Check grammar as you type** check box if you want to turn on Automatic Grammar Checking). Disable these options to turn off the automatic checking features.

❶ Look for the Red Wavy Line

As you type, any word that Word can't find in its dictionary gets a red wavy line under it to tell you that it might be misspelled (in this example, Word points out **vacencies** as a possible misspelling).

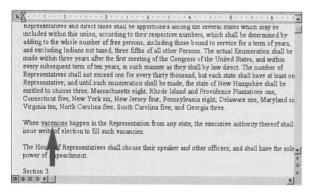

❷ Display the Shortcut Menu

Right-click the word to open a shortcut menu displaying possible alternative spellings (at the top) and a few additional commands. Click an alternative spelling to choose it from the shortcut menu. If your spelling is correct (for example, someone's last name), click **Add**; the word is added to Word's dictionary and won't be picked up by the Spelling Checker ever again.

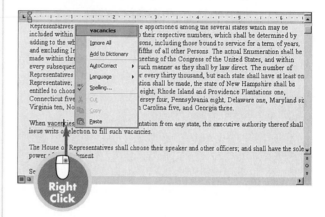

❸ Ignore the Spelling

If you don't want to add the word to the dictionary but want to leave the word the way you spelled it in the current document, click **Ignore All**. To add the correct spelling to your AutoCorrect list so that future misspellings will be corrected automatically as you type, click **AutoCorrect** (see Task 26, "How to Work with AutoCorrect"). To open the **Spelling** dialog box, click **Spelling**.

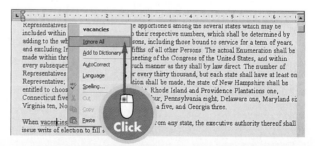

4 Look for the Green Wavy Line

If the wavy line under the text is green, Word detects a possible grammatical error. Right-click the underlined word and choose a correction at the top of the shortcut menu, or click **Ignore Once** to ignore the error.

5 Spell Check the Document

To run the Spelling and Grammar Checker for the whole document at one time, click the **Spelling and Grammar** button on the **Standard** toolbar, or choose **Tools**, **Spelling and Grammar**.

6 Correct Errors

Word checks every word in your document against its dictionary and list of grammatical rules; it presents the **Spelling and Grammar** dialog box when it encounters a word that is not in its dictionary or a sentence that does not conform to a grammatical rule. You can choose to ignore the problem, change it, or select from other options in the dialog box.

How-to Hint

Checking a Section

To check the spelling and grammar of only a portion of the document, select that portion before starting the check. When Word finishes checking the selection, it asks whether you want to check the rest of the document. Click **No** to end the check.

Checking the Writing Style

To modify what Word looks for in a grammar check, choose **Tools**, **Options**, and click the **Spelling & Grammar** tab. In the **Writing Style** drop-down list, select a style that best describes your document. You can choose which items Word checks by clicking the **Settings** button. Enable or disable check boxes for items such as wordiness or passive sentences. Click **OK**.

How to Work with AutoCorrect

Word's **AutoCorrect** feature can save you time by automatically correcting misspelled words as you type. AutoCorrect comes with a list of common misspellings, but the list isn't comprehensive; you can add your own common misspellings to the list to personalize it to your work habits.

1 Try It Out

To see how AutoCorrect performs, type **teh** and press the spacebar, or type a punctuation mark, such as a comma or a period. Because **teh** is a common misspelling, AutoCorrect corrects it to **the** before you realize you mistyped it.

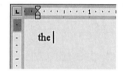

2 Undo AutoCorrect

If you type something you don't want corrected (for example, **Mr. Edmund Teh**), press **Ctrl+Z** to undo the correction before you type any other characters. The AutoCorrection is undone, and you can continue typing; the "misspelling" is left uncorrected.

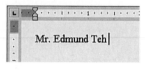

3 Remove a Word from AutoCorrect

If you no longer have to worry about correcting a word, you can remove it from the AutoCorrect list. For example, perhaps your company name has changed and you no longer have to worry about misspelling the old name. To remove a word from the AutoCorrect list, choose **Tools**, **AutoCorrect Options**. The **AutoCorrect** dialog box opens.

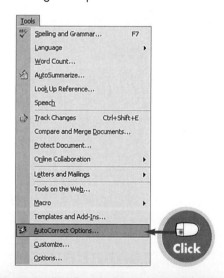

④ Delete the Word

Click the **AutoCorrect** tab. In the **Replace** box, type the first few letters of the word you want to delete from AutoCorrect; the list of words and replacements scrolls to the point where you can find your word. Select your word in the list and then click **Delete**. Click **OK** to close the dialog box.

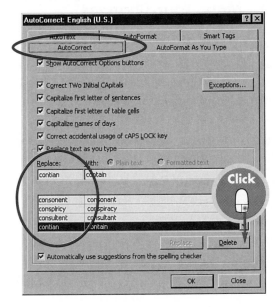

⑤ Add a Misspelling

To add a word you frequently misspell to the AutoCorrect list, open a document and type the correct spelling. (Alternatively, type a long phrase, including any special capitalization, for which you want to create a shortcut.) Select the word or phrase and choose **Tools**, **AutoCorrect Options**.

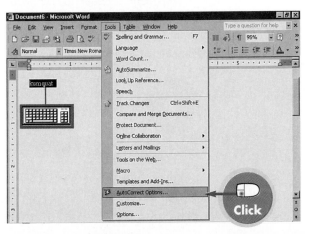

⑥ Click Add

Click the **AutoCorrect** tab. Your word or phrase appears in the **With** box. In the **Replace** box, type the incorrect word or the acronym you want to replace. If you want to add only a single item, click **OK** to close the dialog box; if you want to add more words to the AutoCorrect list, click **Add** to add each word and click **OK** when you finish.

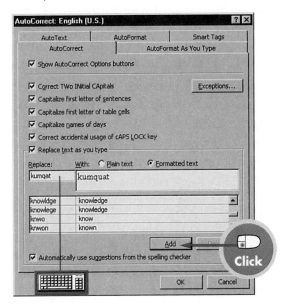

How to Track and Review Document Changes

If you are sharing your documents with others, as you would in a workgroup situation, you can use Word's markup features to keep track of changes others make to a document. For example, you can see what edits others have made to a document, including formatting changes and text deletions and insertions. You can even print out the markups so that you can keep a copy of the changes applied to documents. Markup elements appear in balloon boxes that appear in the margins. When you review the changes, you can choose to accept or reject the markup suggestions.

❶ Turn Tracking On

Open the document you want to set up to track changes and choose **Tools**, **Track Changes**.

❷ Mark Your Changes

Word displays the **Reviewing** toolbar and makes bold the letters **TRK** in the status bar to indicate that the **Track Changes** feature is on. Edit the document. Additions appear underlined in another color, deletions and formatting changes are marked with markup balloons.

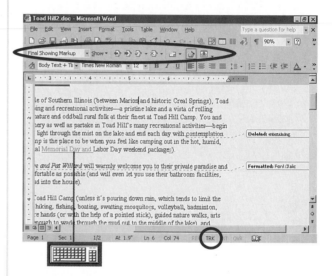

❸ Change Markup Item View

To change which markup items appear in the document, click the **Show** drop-down arrow on the **Reviewing** toolbar and choose the items you want to mark during the editing process.

4 Set Tracking Options

To change tracking options, such as the colors used and the specifics about the balloons, click the **Options** command in the **Show** drop-down list. The **Track Changes** dialog box opens.

5 Change Tracking Options

Specify any tracking options you want to set for the document. For example, you can change how insertions appear or set whether markup balloons are used. Make your changes and click **OK** to close the dialog box.

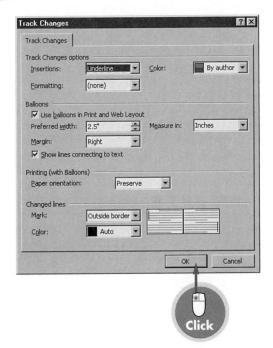

6 Review Changes

To review the changes that have been made to a document, make sure that the markup items are displayed (choose **View**, **Markup** if they are not). Use the buttons on the **Reviewing** toolbar to review the changes. Click **Next** to view the next change. Click **Accept Change** to accept the change and make it a part of the document or click **Reject Change** to refuse the change.

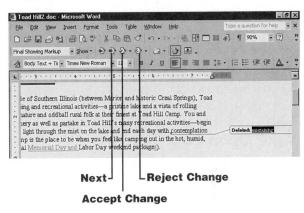

Next ⎯⎯⎯ ⎿Reject Change

Accept Change

How-to Hint

Accepting All Changes

Click the **Accept Change** button drop-down arrow on the **Reviewing** toolbar to see a list of other options, including the option to accept all changes in the document at once. You also can find a similar list by clicking the **Reject Change** button drop-down arrow.

Closing the Reviewing Toolbar

To close the **Reviewing** toolbar, right-click the toolbar and deselect the **Reviewing** toolbar name in the list.

Turning Off Track Changes

To turn off the **Track Changes** feature, choose **Tools**, **Track Changes** or click the **Track Changes** button on the **Reviewing** toolbar.

How to Change Paper Size

By default, Word assumes that your document is a standard 8 1/2" by 11" page. If you have to create a document that uses a different paper size, open the **Page Setup** dialog box and change the settings. From the **Paper Size** tab, you can change the paper size and orientation or specify the measurements for a custom paper size.

1 Open Page Setup

If you want to change the size of the paper on which Word is formatting your document, choose **File**, **Page Setup**. This command opens the **Page Setup** dialog box.

2 Select the Paper Tab

Click the **Paper** tab to view the associated options.

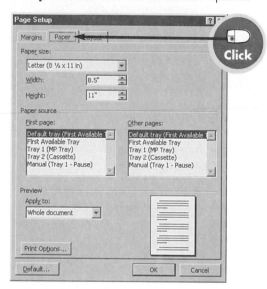

3 Change the Paper Size

Use the **Paper Size** drop-down list to select another paper size.

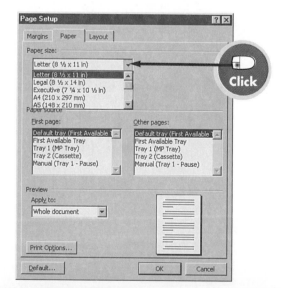

④ Change the Paper Source

You might have to change the paper source option before printing. Select the appropriate trays from the **First Page** and **Other Page** lists in the **Paper Source** area of the tab.

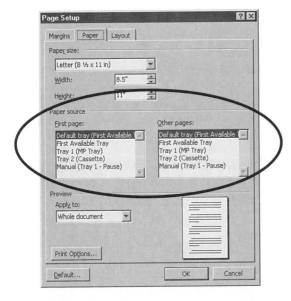

⑤ Change the Page Orientation

By default, Word prints the document "shortways" across the 8 1/2" page. This orientation is called **Portrait**. You can switch to **Landscape** orientation to print across the length of the page ("longways" across the 11" page).

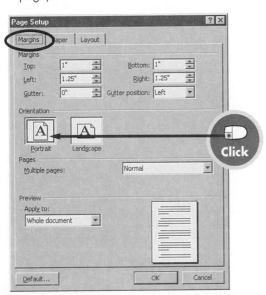

⑥ Close the Dialog Box

After you have set your paper size and source options, click **OK** to close the **Page Setup** dialog box and start creating the document. When you're ready to print, click the **Print** button on the **Standard** toolbar.

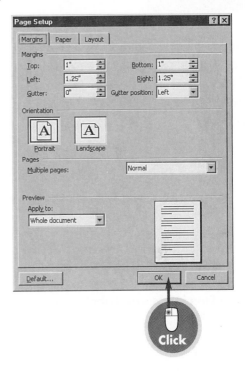

Caution!

If you choose to set a new paper size after you have already designed and created the document, you might have to make a few adjustments. Be sure to check the document in **Print Preview** (click the **Print Preview** button on the **Standard** toolbar) to see whether everything still fits properly or needs adjusting.

Changing the Default

If you find yourself using a different paper size over and over, you can select it from the **Paper Size** tab and click the **Default** button to make it the new default paper size.

How to Print an Envelope

When you create letters in Word, you can create envelopes to go with them. Use Word's **Envelopes and Labels** dialog box to enter addresses and select from a variety of envelope sizes so that you can print your envelopes with style.

① Open the Dialog Box

If you have created a letter with an address you want to print on the envelope, open the letter document. If your document doesn't contain the address, don't worry; you can open the envelope feature from any document and create a quick envelope. Choose **Tools**, **Letters and Mailings**, **Envelopes and Labels** to open the **Envelopes and Labels** dialog box.

② Use the Envelopes Tab

Click the **Envelopes** tab. If needed, type the delivery address and the return address in the appropriate text boxes. If you're using this feature with a letter file, Word borrows the addresses you entered in the letter document.

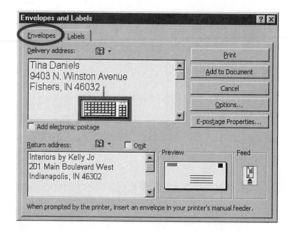

③ Open the Envelope Options

To choose an envelope size other than the default size, click the **Options** button to open the **Envelope Options** dialog box.

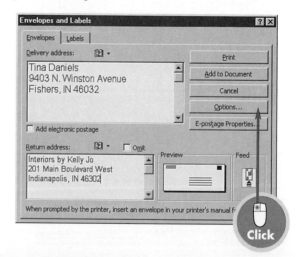

4 Choose an Envelope Size

Select another size from the **Envelope size** drop-down list.

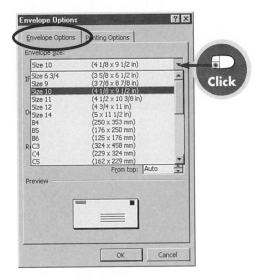

5 Close the Envelope Options

You also can change the font used for the addresses and control the spacing between the addresses and the edges of the envelope. Click **OK** to return to the **Envelopes and Labels** dialog box after you finish setting envelope options.

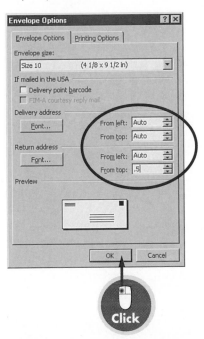

6 Print

To print the envelope, click the **Print** button. Be sure to feed the envelope into your printer correctly. Depending on your printer setup, the **Feed** area in the dialog box gives you a clue about how to feed the envelope into the printer.

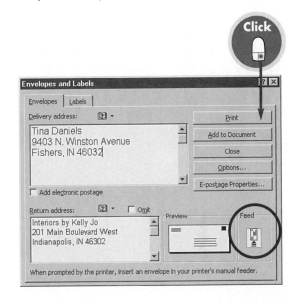

Omitting the Return Address

Enable the **Omit** check box in the **Envelopes and Labels** dialog box if you have preprinted envelopes that already have a return address or company logo.

Adding the Envelope to the Document

Click the **Add to Document** button in the **Envelopes and Labels** dialog box to add the envelope style and contents to the document to save them for later use.

① How to Get Around the Outlook Window 508

② How to Schedule an Appointment 510

③ How to Set a Recurring Appointment 512

④ How to Schedule an Event 514

⑤ How to Plan a Meeting 516

⑥ How to Create a New Task 518

⑦ How to Create a New Contact 520

⑧ How to Import Contact Data 522

⑨ How to Organize Items 524

⑩ How to Compose and Send a Message 526

⑪ How to Read an Incoming Message 528

⑫ How to Reply to or Forward a Message 530

⑬ How to Attach a File to a Message 532

⑭ How to Clean Up the Mailbox 534

⑮ How to Screen Junk Email 536

Task

23

Using Outlook for Email, Contacts, and Scheduling

Outlook is a desktop information manager you can use to organize and manage your daily activities at home or at the office. Outlook is extremely versatile; you can schedule and keep track of your daily appointments, build and maintain a database of people you contact the most, create "to do" lists for projects or events and track each item's status, jot down electronic notes, and more. In addition to managing your daily commitments, you can track and manage your email correspondence. You can send and receive email from the Outlook window, whether it's messages sent to Internet users or to colleagues on your company LAN, WAN, or intranet.

The tasks in this part cover the basic features of using Outlook, including how to manage appointments and tasks, send and receive email, and organize contact information.

If you use Outlook on a network that uses Microsoft Exchange Server, your Calendar might be available for others to view—ask your system administrator for details. If your Calendar is not available, you can publish it on the company intranet in a public folder, publish it on the Internet at Microsoft's Free/Busy service, or you can share the private folders that contain your Calendar information. In any case, you can mark particular appointments as Private so that their details cannot be viewed by others. No one can schedule anything in your Calendar unless you specifically set up Outlook to allow that interaction. Using Outlook on a network to access other's Calendars is not covered in these tasks—but you should know that Outlook can be expanded in this way.

How to Get Around the Outlook Window

The Outlook window is similar to other Windows programs, with a few unique exceptions, such as the **Outlook Bar** on the left side of the window. Use the **Outlook Bar** to access each Outlook component. Outlook's components are organized into folders, represented by icons on the **Outlook Bar**. When you click a component, such as **Inbox**, the appropriate folder opens in the work area. Take a few minutes to acclimate yourself to Outlook before you use it for the first time.

1 Use the Outlook Bar

To open an Outlook component, click the appropriate icon in the **Outlook Bar**. To open the **Contacts** feature, for example, click the **Contacts** icon. If necessary, use the scroll button at the end of the bar to view more icons.

2 Use Group Buttons

The **Outlook** Bar has two group buttons for organizing your folders and shortcuts: **Outlook Shortcuts** and **My Shortcuts**. To display the icons in a particular group, click its button.

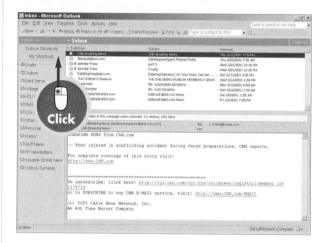

3 Display the Folder List

Choose **View, Folder List** from the menu bar, or click the **Folder List** drop-down arrow in the work area. (Click the **Pushpin** icon to keep the **Folder List** open.)

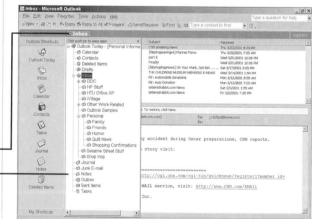

Pushpin ⎯⎯⎯

Folder List ⎯⎯⎯

④ Change Views

Some of the Outlook components enable you to change your view of the information presented. With the Calendar, for example, you can see your schedule by **Day**, **Work Week**, **Week**, and **Month**. To change a view, use the **View** menu or click the appropriate view button on the toolbar.

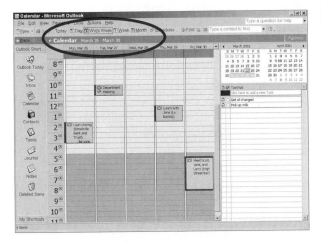

⑥ Find Outlook Contacts

Use the **Find a Contact** box in the toolbar to quickly look up a name in your **Contacts** database (learn more about adding contacts in Task 7, "How to Create a New Contact"). Click inside the text box and type the person's name, first or last. Press **Enter**, and Outlook displays the Contact form with details about the person.

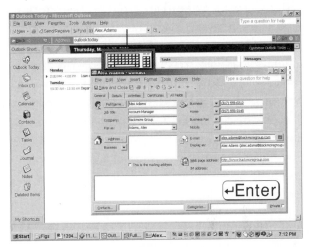

⑤ Use Outlook Today View

Click the **Outlook Today** icon on the **Outlook Bar** to see an overview of incoming and outgoing messages, appointments, meetings, and tasks. The items displayed are actually hyperlinks to other Outlook items. Click an appointment, for example, to view the details of the appointment.

Link

Click

How-to Hint

Customizing Outlook Today

By default, Outlook opens with the **Inbox** displayed; however, you might want to customize Outlook to start with the **Outlook Today** feature displayed so that you can always see your day's events and tasks at a glance. Click the **Customize Outlook Today** button on the Outlook Today screen. Enable the **When starting, go directly to Outlook Today** check box, and then click the **Save Changes** button.

Adding Shortcut Icons

To add icons to the **Outlook Bar**, right-click the bar and select **Outlook Bar Shortcut**. Select the folder you want to add and click **OK**. (See Task 9, "How to Organize Items" for help in adding your own folders as well.)

Dragging to Adjust

Drag the border of any area to adjust its size. For example, make the **Outlook Bar** skinnier (and the work area bigger) by dragging its border inward.

How to Schedule an Appointment

Use Outlook's **Calendar** feature to keep track of appointments, events, and any other special engagements. When you open the **Calendar** folder, Outlook displays your daily schedule in the appointment area, along with a **Date Navigator** and a miniaturized version of your **TaskPad**. (If not, you can change to this view by clicking the **1 Day** button.) You can easily add appointments to your calendar and set reminder alarms to let you know of imminent appointments. To open **Calendar**, click the **Calendar** icon on the Outlook Bar.

1 Choose a Date

In the **Date Navigator**, select the month and date for the appointment. When you click the date, the appointment area changes to display that date. Notice that the current date is always highlighted with a red border in the **Date Navigator**.

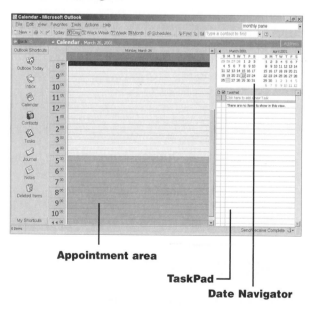

Appointment area

TaskPad

Date Navigator

2 Choose a Time

In the appointment area, double-click the time slot for which you want to schedule an appointment. This action opens the **Appointment** window.

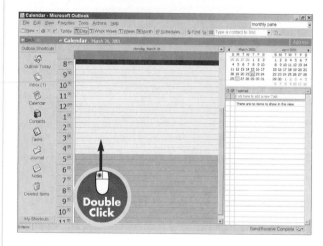

3 Fill Out the Form

The **Appointment** window is actually a form you can use to enter details about the appointment. Fill out the **Subject** and **Location** text boxes. For example, type the name of the person you're meeting with and the place where you're meeting. Click inside the text boxes or use the **Tab** key to move from field to field.

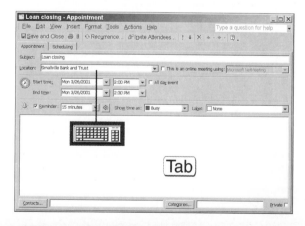

4 ⬛ Enter Appointment Details

Use the **Start time** and **End time** drop-down arrows to set or change the date and time of the appointment. By default, Outlook schedules your appointments in 30-minute increments, but you can easily set a longer time increment.

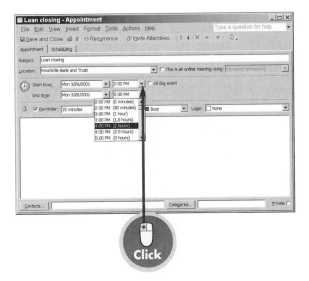

5 ⬛ Need a Reminder?

Enable the **Reminder** check box if you want Outlook to remind you about the appointment with a prompt box and an audible beep. (Outlook must be running for the beep to sound, but the program can be minimized.) Specify how long before the appointment you want to be reminded.

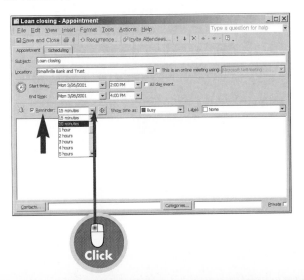

6 ⬛ Save and Close

To help organize your appointments, you can select a color to highlight the appointment with from the **Label** list. Type any notes in the large text box along with any other details you want to include with the appointment. Click the **Save and Close** button on the **Appointment** window's toolbar to close the form and return to Calendar. Note that any days on which you have scheduled appointments, meetings, or events appear in bold in the **Date Navigator**.

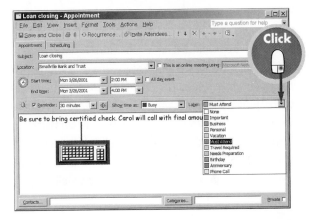

How-to Hint

Blocking Your Time

If you're using Outlook on a network, use the **Show time as** drop-down list on the **Appointment** form to determine how others see the appointment on your calendar. If you don't want others on the network to see the appointment details, enable the **Private** check box (people can still see that you're busy, but they can't see what the appointment is).

Making Contact

To create an appointment with someone in your **Contacts** list, drag the contact's name onto the **Calendar** icon on the **Outlook Bar** to open an **Appointment** window. You also can link a contact to an appointment by clicking the **Contact** button in the **Appointment** window and selecting a name. To display the contact information later, double-click the contact's name in the **Appointment** window.

How to Set a Recurring Appointment

If your schedule is prone to recurring appointments, Outlook's **Recurring Appointment** features can help. Perhaps you have a monthly hair appointment. Rather than schedule each appointment separately, you can set it up as a recurring appointment. Outlook adds the appointment to each month's calendar for you automatically. With the **Recurring Appointment** feature, you can specify the recurrence pattern to tell Outlook how often the appointment occurs (**Daily**, **Weekly**, **Monthly**, or **Yearly**), on which day of the week it falls, and other related options. You can use this same procedure to create recurring meetings and events as well.

❶ Schedule a Recurring Appointment

To schedule a recurring appointment from the **Appointment** window, click the **Recurrence** button. (To create a recurring appointment from within Calendar, choose **Actions, New Recurring Appointment**.) The **Appointment Recurrence** dialog box opens.

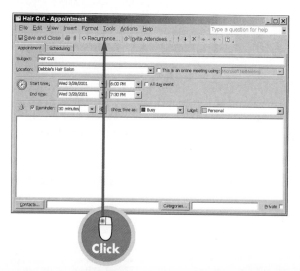

❷ Enter a Recurrence Pattern

In the **Recurrence pattern** area of the dialog box, enable the check boxes that identify the frequency of the appointment and the day on which the appointment falls: **Daily**, **Weekly**, **Monthly**, or **Yearly**.

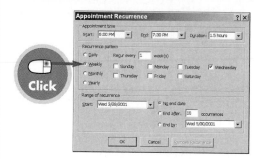

❸ Refine the Pattern

Depending on the selection you made in step 2, the remaining recurrence options will vary. If you select **Weekly**, for example, you can specify every week or every other week.

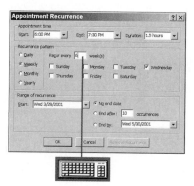

4 Range of Recurrence

Use the **Range of recurrence** options to enter any limits to the recurring appointment. Suppose that you have to schedule five doctor visits over the next five months but won't need the appointment after that. Use the **End after** option to set such a range. Click **OK**.

5 Save the Appointment

The **Appointment** window displays the recurrence pattern. Click the **Save and Close** button to save the appointment and all its occurrences.

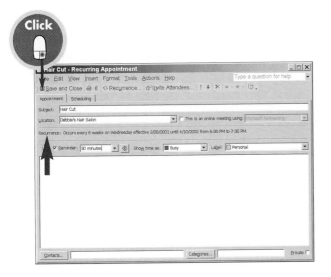

6 View the Appointment

The recurring appointment now appears on your calendar with a double-arrow icon to indicate that it's a recurring appointment.

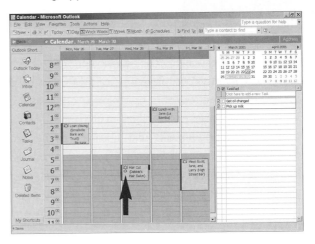

How-to Hint

Adding a Reminder

Click the **Reminder** check box in the **Appointment** window to add a reminder alarm to your recurring appointment. If you need a period of time not shown in the list (such as 45 minutes), just type it into the text box.

Editing Appointments

To edit a recurring or any other appointment, double-click the appointment in your schedule. Outlook asks if you want to edit just the one occurrence or the series. Select the appropriate option and click **OK**. This action opens the **Appointment** window, where you can make any changes.

Other Recurring Ideas

Recurring appointments are great for marking your kids' athletic practices throughout a season, personal tasks (such as haircuts), club meetings, church meetings, and so on.

How to Schedule an Event

An *event* is any activity that lasts the entire day, such as an anniversary, a conference, a trade show, or a birthday. An event appears as a banner at the top of the scheduled date, rather than in the appointment area. Unlike appointments and meetings, events are normally listed as "free" time when viewed by others. However, if an event (such as a conference) will keep you busy so that you shouldn't be scheduled for other things, change the event to "busy" time in the **Event** window.

1 Open the Event Window

To schedule an event, open the **Actions** menu and choose **New All Day Event**. The Event window opens.

2 Enter the Event Title

The **Event** window resembles the **Appointment** window. Start by filling in a title for the event in the **Subject** text box and entering a location (if applicable) in the **Location** text box.

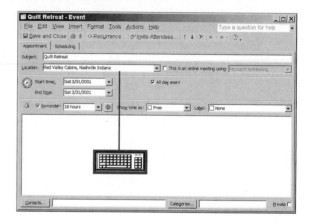

3 Enter Start and End Times

Use the **Start time** and **End time** drop-down lists to specify a time frame (the number of days) for the event.

4 Set Other Options

Set a **Reminder** if you like—if you want to be reminded at a time that isn't listed in the drop-down box, just type it in! If you want, use the **Show time as** list to display the time as "busy" on your schedule so that others can't schedule this time for you. Select a **Label** for the event and type any notes.

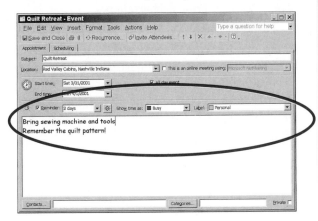

5 Save and Close

When you have finished filling in the event details, click the **Save and Close** button to close the **Event** window.

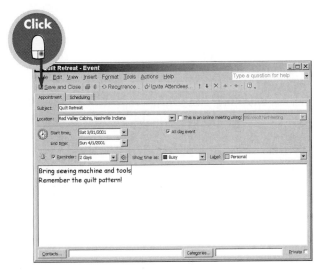

6 View the Event

The event now appears as a banner at the beginning of the day in the schedule pane (use Day view to see it clearly).

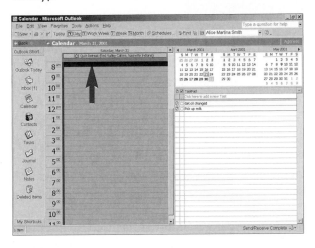

Editing Events

To edit an event, double-click the event on your calendar. This action reopens the **Event** window so that you can make the necessary changes.

Displaying More Months

To display more months in the **Date Navigator**, drag its border downward (making the **TaskPad** smaller) or outward (making the **Appointment** area smaller). You can then view a custom number of days (such as two weeks) in the **Appointment** area by dragging to select the days you want to view in the **Date Navigator**.

Turning an Appointment into an Event

If you started creating an appointment but meant to create an event, you can turn an appointment into an event by enabling the **All day event** check box in the **Appointment** window.

How to Plan a Meeting

If you're using Outlook on a network that uses Microsoft Exchange Server, or if you have access to other people's Calendars through the intranet or Internet, you can use the **Plan a Meeting** feature to schedule meetings with others. The feature also enables you to designate any resources needed for the meeting, such as a conference room or equipment. You can use the **Plan a Meeting** feature to send email messages to invite attendees and track their responses. To get started, open the **Calendar** folder by clicking the **Calendar** icon on the **Outlook Bar**.

❶ Open the Plan a Meeting Feature

From the **Calendar** folder, open the **Actions** menu and select **Plan a Meeting**. This action opens the **Plan a Meeting** window.

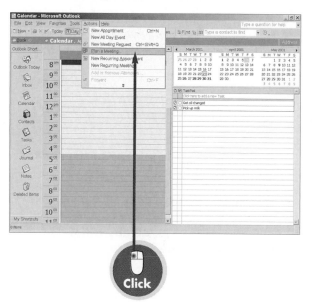

❷ Enter the Attendees

Click **Click here** to add a name and type a person's name. After you type a name and press **Tab** to enter the next person, Outlook automatically searches for the matching email address in the Contacts list and inserts it. Continue typing one name per line until all the attendees have been listed. (You can also click **Add Others** to insert names instead of typing them.)

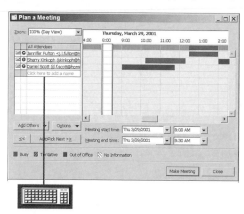

❸ Set a Date

Click the **Meeting start time** drop-down arrows and choose a date and time for the meeting. Click the **Meeting end time** drop-down arrows to specify an end date and time for the meeting.

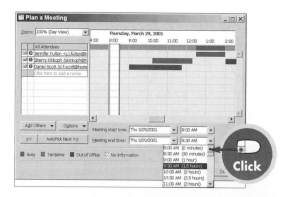

④ Use AutoPick to Set the Time

Alternatively, you can click **AutoPick Next** to find the next available free period for everyone in your list of attendees. (This option works only if the attendees' schedules are shared over a network or the Internet.) Outlook finds the next available time and date at which all the attendees are free. When you have finished specifying the meeting's attendees and times, click the **Make Meeting** button.

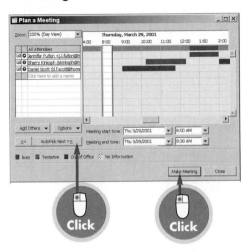

⑤ Fill In Meeting Details

The **Meeting** window, which resembles the **Appointment** window, opens. Refine the meeting details as needed.

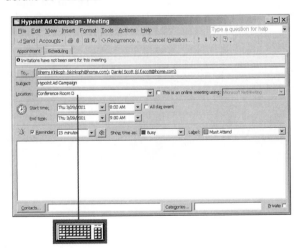

⑥ Send the Invitations

When you have finished filling out the meeting details, click **Send** to send email invitations to the attendees. Click the **Close** button to close the **Plan a Meeting** window.

Tracking Responses

To see how the attendees are responding to your meeting invitation, click the **Scheduling** tab of the **Meeting** window.

Publishing Your Schedule

If your company's network doesn't offer schedule sharing or you're out of the office a lot, you can share your schedule over the Internet. Choose **Tools, Options, Calendar Options, Free/Busy Options**. Enable **Publish and search using the Microsoft Office Internet Free/Busy Service** option. (If you select the **Request free/busy information in meeting invitations** option, you will automatically invite attendees to share their information with you, and to grant you the necessary permissions.) Click **Manage** to grant permissions to the people with whom you want to share your schedule.

How to Create a New Task

Use Outlook's **Tasks** folder to keep track of things you need to do, such as picking up your dry cleaning or writing a report. Tasks can be as complex as a year-long project, or as simple as a shopping list you need to fill on the way home. A task list can include such things as writing a letter, making a phone call, or distributing a memo. After you create a task list, you can keep track of the tasks and check them off as you complete them. Tasks appear on the **TaskPad** in the **Calendar** folder, on the **Outlook Today** page, and in the **Tasks** folder. To open the **Tasks** folder, click the **Tasks** icon in the **Outlook Bar**.

1 Open the Task Window

From the **Tasks** folder, click the **New Task** button on the toolbar. The **Task** window opens.

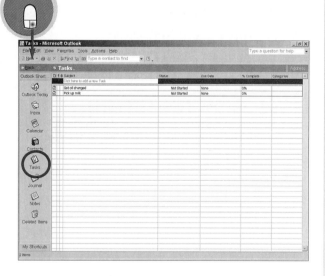

2 Enter a Title

The **Task** window, like the **Appointment** window, is a form you can fill out, detailing the task. With the **Task** tab displayed, type the subject or title of the task you are creating in the **Subject** text box.

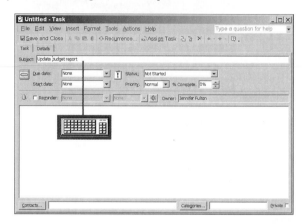

3 Enter a Due Date

If the task has a due date, click the **Due date** drop-down arrow and choose a due date from the calendar. You can also enter a start date for the task—either the date on which the task was already begun, or the future date on which you have to start working on the task.

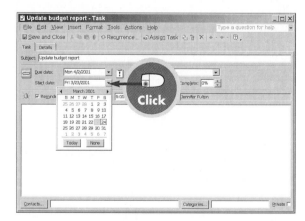

4 Select a Status Setting

Use the **Status** drop-down list to select a status setting for the project: **Not Started**, **In Progress**, **Completed**, **Waiting on someone else**, or **Deferred**. Change the **% Complete** field if it is applicable (you can type any percentage you want in the text box). As you manage your task list, you can update the **Status and Percent Complete** fields.

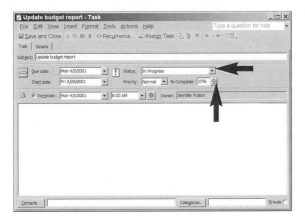

5 Set a Priority

Use the **Priority** drop-down list to give the task a priority level: **Normal**, **Low**, or **High**. Set a **Reminder** to complete the task if you want. Use the **Notes** box to enter any notes about the task. To record statistics about a task, such as billable time, contacts, or mileage, click the **Details** tab. When you have finished filling out the **Task** window, click the **Save and Close** button.

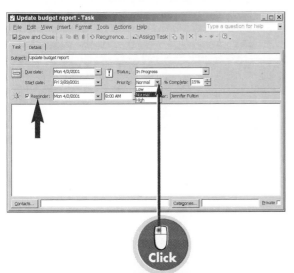

6 View the Task

The task is added to your **Tasks** folder's task list.

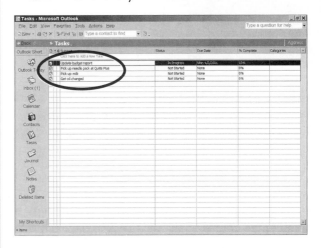

How-to Hint

Managing Tasks

To mark a task as complete, right-click the task and choose **Mark Complete**. The task appears in strikethrough on the task list. To edit a task, double-click the task in the task list; the **Task** window opens. To remove a task from the list, right-click the task and choose **Delete**.

Working with the TaskPad

The **TaskPad** in **Calendar** helps you manage tasks without changing to the **Tasks** folder. You can add a task by clicking **Click here to add a task** and typing a title. If you display other fields (such as **Date Due**), you can enter that information as well, without having to open a **Task** window. To display additional fields on the **TaskPad**, right-click the header and select **Field Chooser**. To mark a task as **Complete**, enable the check box. To display the details of a task, double-click it.

How to Create a New Contact

Use Outlook's **Contacts** folder to build a database of contacts such as co-workers, relatives, vendors, or clients. You can enter all kinds of information about your contacts, including addresses, phone numbers, email addresses, and so on. After you enter a contact, you can quickly fire off an email message, have your modem dial the phone number for you, or display a map to the address. You can associate any item with a contact—such as a task, appointment, or meeting—and then display a history of such activities. To begin entering contacts, click the **Contacts** icon on the **Outlook Bar**.

❶ Open the Contact Form

From the **Contacts** folder, click the **New Contact** button on the toolbar. The **Contact** window opens.

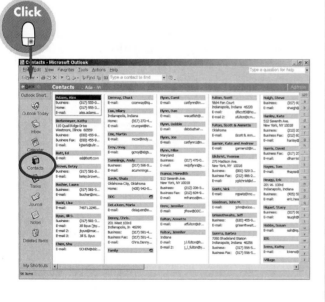

❷ Enter Contact Information

Click the **Full Name** box and type the contact's name; then enter other information about the contact.

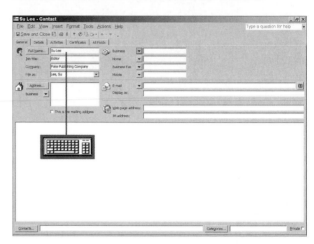

❸ Use the File As List

Click the **File as** drop-down arrow and choose how you want to file your contact—by last name or first name. This field helps you sort your **Contacts** list, so sorting by last name is usually best. If filing by a name isn't helpful, you can type a nickname or other identifier in this field, such as **dentist** or **plumber**.

④ Use Arrow Fields

Outlook provides multiple fields for entering numerous phone numbers for a contact. However, if you don't see what you need, click the down arrow next to a field and select an option such as **Business 2**. You can enter multiple items in one field and switch between them using the down-arrow list. You can enter a business and home address this way, as well.

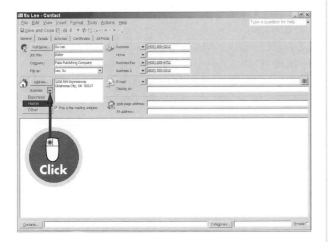

⑤ Enter Email Address

Enter the contact's email address. Use the drop-down arrow to enter any additional email addresses. Enter the contact's Web page address, which you can use to launch Internet Explorer. Enter an IM address, which you can use to send instant messages through the MSN Messenger service.

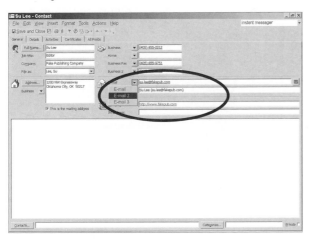

⑥ Save the Contact

After filling out all the pertinent information for this contact, click the **Save and Close** button to add the contact to your database. To enter another contact, click the **Save and New** button to open another **Contact** window.

Save and New

How-to Hint

More Details

Use the **Details** tab in the **Contact** window to enter information such as a spouse's name, birthdays, anniversaries, and other details about the contact.

To view activities related to a contact, such as email messages sent and received, appointments, meetings and tasks, click the **Activities** tab.

To display a map to a contact's address, double-click the contact's name and click the **Display Map of Address** button.

To make changes to the contact's information, double-click the contact's name in the **Contacts** folder. This action reopens the **Contact** window, where you can make changes to the data.

To create a quick email message to a contact, click the contact's name, and then click the **New Message to Contact** button.

How to Import Contact Data

If already have a database of contacts in another program—whether it's an Office program such as Excel or Access, or a non-Microsoft program such as Lotus Organizer—you can import the database into Outlook. You can import and export all sorts of data—contact lists, email messages, tasks, appointments, meetings, and events. For example, you might want to export your sales contact list into Excel to combine it with other sales data. Use Outlook's **Import and Export Wizard** to walk you through the steps of the process.

1 Open the Import and Export Wizard

Open the **File** menu and choose **Import and Export**. The first screen of the **Import and Export Wizard** opens.

2 Choose an Action

In the first wizard dialog box, choose an import or export action. Depending on the program from which you're importing data, you might have to choose **Import from another program or file** or **Import Internet Mail and Addresses**. To export data, click **Export to a file**. Click **Next** to continue.

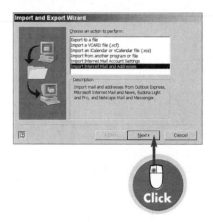

3 Choose a File Type

If you're importing data from an old email program (as shown here), in the next wizard dialog box, choose the type of address file you want to import. Disable any options for kinds of data you don't want to import (such as email messages). Click **Next**.

4 Choose a Destination Folder

Depending on the type of import you're performing, the remaining steps might differ from what is described here. The dialog box shown here asks you to select a destination folder to hold the imported data, such as the **Contacts** folder. You can also choose to replace duplicate items. Click **Finish**.

5 Select What to Import

When importing data from some programs, you'll be asked to confirm what's imported. Make your selections and click **Finish**.

6 Read the Import Summary

When the import is finished, a summary box appears, telling you how successful the import was; click **OK**. (If you want to save a copy of the summary, click the **Save in Inbox** button—you can then view the summary as an email message in your Inbox.)

How-to Hint

Copying and Pasting Outlook Items

Not only can you import and export with Outlook, you can also copy and paste Outlook items between the Office programs by using the **Copy** and **Paste** commands.

How to Organize Items

Outlook saves items you create in folders, such as the **Inbox**, **Contacts**, and **Task** folders. To organize items, you might want to create additional folders. For example, you could store all your personal email in a subfolder of the Inbox called **Personal**. You can easily move Outlook items into new folders as needed. In addition, you can delete from the folders items you no longer need. The simplest way to organize items is to use the **Folder List**. To display it, choose **View, Folder List**. Because you can use the **Folder List** to change between Outlook components, you might want to hide the **Outlook Bar** to give yourself more room to work.

1 Create a New Folder

Click the arrow on the **New** button and select **Folder**. The **New Folder** dialog box opens.

2 Enter a Folder Name

Type a name for the new folder in the **Name** box.

3 Select the Item Type

Use the **Folder contains** drop-down list to choose the type of items you want to store in the folder.

524 Chapter 23: Using Outlook for Email, Contacts, and Scheduling

4 Select a Parent Folder

Scroll through the **Select where to place the folder** list and select the folder into which you want to place your new folder. Click **OK** to close the dialog box, create the folder, and return to the **Folder List**.

5 Move Items to the Folder

Select the items you want to move to your new folder, drag them to the **Folder List**, and drop them on the new folder.

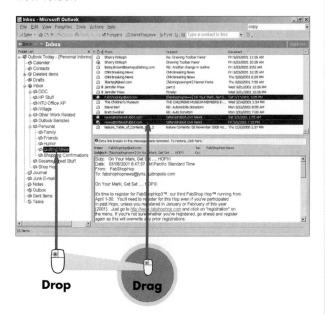

Drop   **Drag**

6 Delete Items

To remove items from a folder, select the items you want to delete and then click the **Delete** button. The items are moved to the **Deleted Items** folder. To empty that folder, right-click it and choose **Empty "Deleted Items" Folder**.

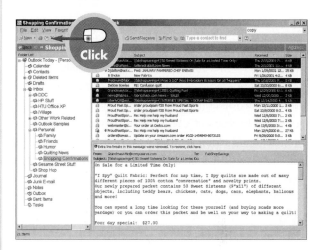

Click

More About Folders

To remove a folder you no longer need (and the items it contains), right-click the folder and choose **Delete** folder name.

You can create subfolders within subfolders. For example, you might have a subfolder in the **Inbox** folder named `Vendor Mail`, and additional folders within that folder named `Suppliers and Printers`.

You can set up Outlook so that it automatically deletes items from the **Deleted Items** folder whenever you exit the program. Open the **Tools** menu and select **Options**. Display the **Other** tab, select the **Empty the Deleted Items folder upon exiting** option, and click **OK**.

Click the **Organize** button while in any folder to discover unique ways in which you can organize items by adding colors, automatically moving them into particular folders based on their contents, and so on.

How to Compose and Send a Message

Providing that you have the correct email address, you can use Outlook to send a message to anyone with an email account. As do the other Outlook components, the email portion features a message form you fill out. You can even add formatting to your message. Before you can use Outlook's email options, you must set up Outlook to work with your email service—see the How-To Hints for help. Then click the **Inbox** icon on the **Outlook Bar** when you're ready to begin.

① Open a New Message Form

Click the **New Mail Message** button on the toolbar to open the **Message** window.

② Enter the Recipients

Click inside the **To** text box and type the recipient's name. Outlook will recognize the name and insert the appropriate email address. (If the person is not in your Contacts list, type that person's email address instead.) To send the message to multiple recipients, type a semicolon between each name.

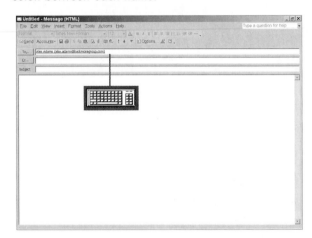

③ Send Someone a Carbon Copy

To send a carbon copy of the message to someone else, enter that person's name in the **Cc** text box.

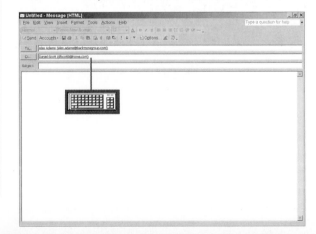

④ Enter the Subject

Click in the **Subject** text box and type a phrase to identify the content or purpose of your message. The recipients will see the **Subject** line in their Inboxes and have some idea what your message is about even before reading it.

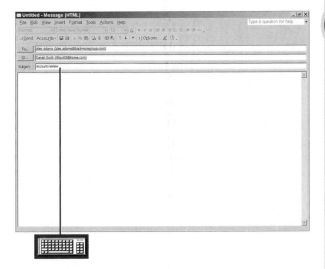

⑥ Send the Message

To send the message, click the **Send** button. If you're offline (that is, if you aren't connected to the Internet or network), the message waits in your Outbox until the next time you go online to collect your mail.

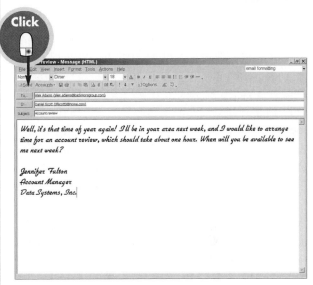

⑤ Type Your Message

Click in the large message text box and type your message text. When you type to the end of a line, Outlook automatically wraps the text to the next line for you. Use the **Delete** and **Backspace** keys to fix mistakes, just as you would in a Microsoft Word document. Use the **Formatting** toolbar to apply different fonts, sizes, and other attributes to your text.

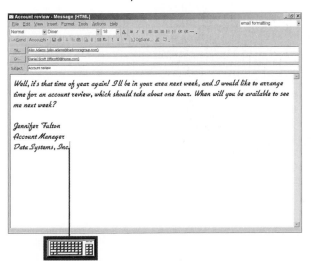

How-to Hint

More About Email

If you haven't set up Outlook to work with your Internet account, select **Tools**, **Email Accounts**. Select **Add a new email account** and click **Next**. A wizard walks you through the necessary steps to set up Outlook to use your Internet account.

If you use Microsoft Word, Outlook can use Word's spell checker to check your messages for errors before sending them. Choose **Tools, Options, Spelling** and then enable the **Always check spelling before sending** option.

Use the **Options** button on the **Message** window's toolbar to assign options such as priority levels or tracking options.

To use one of Outlook's stationery patterns for the current email message, choose **Actions, New Mail Message Using** from the menu on the Inbox screen. To use stationery with every message, choose **Tools, Options, Mail Format** and select a stationery from the **Use this stationery by default** list.

How to Read an Incoming Message

Use the **Inbox** to view the messages you receive in Outlook. The **Inbox** displays each message as a single line (called the message header) with a **From** field that tells you who sent it, a **Subject** field that gives you an idea about what's in the message, and a **Date** field that tells you when it was received. The symbol columns at the left provide important information about each message, such as priority level or whether it has a file attachment. Use the **Preview Pane** below the list of message headers to view message text. You also can open each message in its own window. To hide the **Preview Pane**, choose **View, Preview Pane**. You can then use **AutoPreview** to see the first three lines of a message in the list box before you open it. To turn on **AutoPreview**, choose **View, AutoPreview**.

❶ Check for New Mail

To check for new messages in the Inbox folder, click the **Send/Receive** button on the Outlook toolbar to pick up your mail. New messages appear in bold in your **Inbox**.

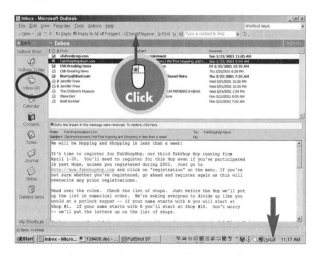

❷ View the Message

To view the contents of the message in the **Preview Pane**, click the message header in the list. To view the next message in your list of messages, click it or press the down-arrow key.

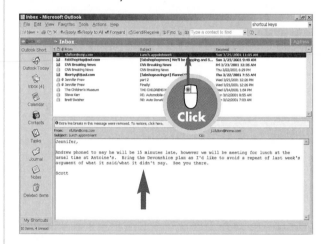

❸ Open a Message

If the message is long, open it in its own message window by double-clicking the message header. The message opens for you to read.

4 Read the Next Message

To continue reading new mail messages without return-ing to the **Inbox** list, click the **Next Item** button on the message toolbar. To return to the previous message, click the **Previous Item** button. To close the window, click its **Close** button.

Previous Item ┐ ┌ **Next Item**

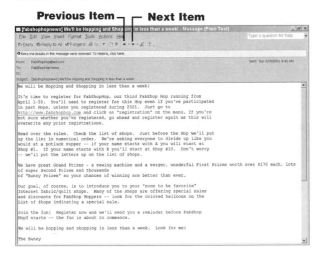

5 Perform Message Maintenance

Whether you're in a **Message** window or the **Inbox**, you can perform simple mail maintenance. To print a message, click the **Print** button. To delete a message, click **Delete**. If you want to reply to a message or for-ward it to someone else, see Task 12, "How to Reply to or Forward a Message."

┌ **Print button**
┌ **Delete button**

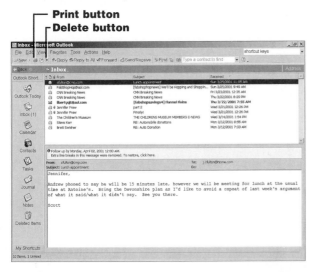

6 Move Messages

Keep on top of incoming messages by organizing them in folders—see Task 9, "How to Organize Items," for help. To move a message to a folder, click the **Move to Folder** button and select a folder from the drop-down list that appears.

How-to Hint

Automatic Send and Receive

You can set up Outlook to automatically check for new messages periodically. Choose **Tools, Options, Mail Setup**, click **Send/Receive**, enable the **Schedule an automatic send/receive every XX minutes** option, and click **OK**.

Receiving Message Headers

One way to protect yourself against email viruses is to download just the message headers and delete messages from people you don't know, without read-ing them. To do that, choose **Tools, Options, Mail Setup**, click **Send/Receive**, select a group, and click **Edit**. Select an **Account** and choose **Download item description only**.

Adding a Sender to Your Contacts List

When you receive a message, the sender's name and email address are always included in the **From** line of the message form. To transfer the name and address directly into your Contacts list, right-click the sender's name and choose **Add to Contacts**.

How to Reply to or Forward a Message

You can reply to or forward any message. A *reply*, of course, is an answer to a message sent to you, and a *forward* is a message you have received that you send on to others. Outlook creates a reply or forward message that includes all the original text, although you can delete that text. When you view the original message, its header displays your action (reply or forward) and the date/time you took that action. You can click the header to view related messages—the original, your reply, the response to your reply, and so on.

① Click Reply

To reply to a message, click the **Reply** button to open a **Reply Message** window. If the message you received contains names in the **Cc** box, you can send your reply to all the recipients by clicking **Reply to All** instead.

② Enter Your Reply

The **Reply Message** window includes the text of the original message with the sender's name in the **To** text box. Select and delete any text you don't need to include. Type your response to the message.

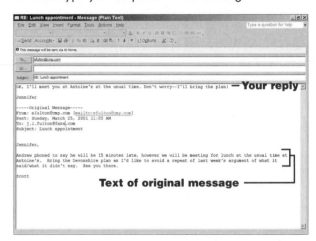

③ Send Your Reply

When your reply is ready, click the **Send** button on the message window's toolbar to send the email message on its way.

4 Forward a Message

To forward the open message to others, click **Forward** while viewing the message. The **Forward** window opens.

5 Enter the Forwardee's Address

In the **To** box, type the name of the person to whom you're forwarding the message. Add a note to the top of the message and select and delete any of the original text you don't want to include in the forwarded message.

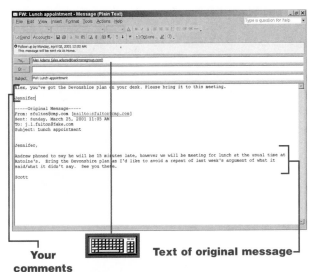

Your comments

Text of original message

6 Send It Forward

When the message is ready to be forwarded, click the **Send** button on the message window's toolbar.

What About Attachments?

When you forward a message, the attachments are also forwarded. If you want to delete the attachments, click each one and press **Delete**. When you reply to a message, the attachments automatically disappear because the person who sent you the original message doesn't need his attachments back! To keep the attachments in place, you must either forward the message instead of just replying to it, or you must reattach the attachment. Learn more about attaching files in the next task.

Oops!

If you send a message and then realize you left out a recipient, you don't have to retype another message. Instead, open the **My Shortcuts** folder group in the **Outlook Bar** and open the **Sent Items** folder. Select the message you just sent, click the **Forward** button, and address the message to the "forgotten" recipient. Click **Send** to email it.

How-to Hint

How to Attach a File to a Message

You can attach files of any type to Outlook messages. You can send your boss the latest sales figures from your Excel worksheet, for example, or pass along a Word report to your colleague on the Internet. You can also attach other Outlook items, such as a contact or note. When you attach a file to a message, its name appears in the message header. The recipient can open the file to view it, or save the file to open later. Keep in mind, however, that the recipient must have the appropriate program to view the file. If you send a PowerPoint presentation to a co-worker, for example, he must have PowerPoint (or its viewer) installed in order to view the file.

❶ Click Insert File

After you compose the message to which you want to attach a file, click the **Insert File** button on the message toolbar. The **Insert File** dialog box opens.

❷ Locate the File

Use the **Look in** drop-down list to locate the folder or drive in which the file you want to attach is stored.

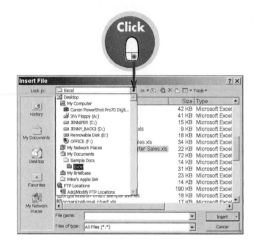

❸ Select the File

From the list box of files in the selected folder, select the file or files you want to attach to the message and click **Insert**.

④ The File Is Attached

The filename appears in the message header. You can now send the message—and the file attached to it.

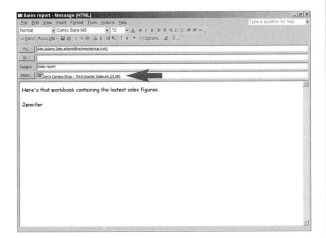

⑤ Attaching Outlook Items

To attach an Outlook item to a message, open the **Insert** menu and select **Item**. The **Insert Item** dialog box opens.

⑥ Locate the Item

Open the folder in which the item is stored and select the item. If you know that the recipient uses Outlook, choose **Attachment**. Otherwise, choose **Text** only. Click **OK** and send the message and its attachment.

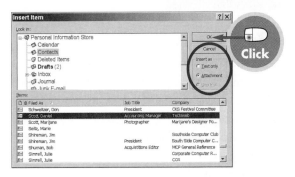

How-to Hint

Sending Pictures

You can send a picture embedded within your message, or as an attachment that must be opened to be viewed. To send a picture within the message, choose **Insert, Picture**, click **Browse**, select the picture you want to send, click **Open**, and then click **OK**. The picture appears within the text of your message. To attach a picture file instead, follow steps 1 through 4.

Receiving Attachments

Messages that contain attached files have a paperclip symbol in the message listing. The filenames appear in the message header. Double-click the filename and choose **Open it** to view the file; double-click the filename and choose **Save it to disk** to copy the file to your hard disk. If multiple files are attached to the message, choose **File, Save Attachments** to save all of them in one step. Do not open any attachment from a person you don't know! Better yet, run a virus scanner on all your attachments before opening them.

How to Clean Up the Mailbox

With as many email messages as most people receive, it's easy for your **Inbox** to become full very fast. Ordinarily, the process of managing email can be quite daunting, but Outlook makes the process easy. To help remove clutter and restore disk space, use the **Mailbox Cleanup** feature. With **Mailbox Cleanup**, you can view the current size of your Inbox, locate old or large files, archive old messages in a separate file that you can open later when needed, or delete old messages permanently.

1 Open Mailbox Cleanup

From the **Tools** menu, select **Mailbox Cleanup**. The **Mailbox Cleanup** dialog box opens.

2 Determine Inbox Size

Click the **Click here** button at the top of the dialog box to open the **Folder Size** dialog box, which displays the size of your Inbox folder and subfolders. Click **Close** when you're done scanning this information.

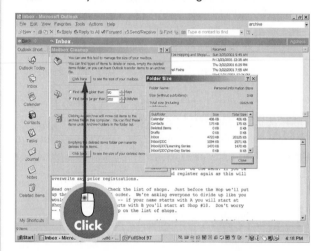

3 Locate Messages

To locate old messages, enable the **Find items older than 90 days** option. To locate large messages, click the **Find items larger than XXX kilobytes** option. (You can type a new time interval or file size as needed.) Click **Find**.

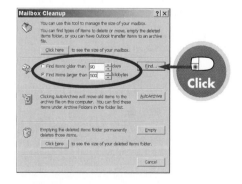

4 Delete Messages

Outlook locates message that meet the criteria you specified in step 3 and opens the **Advanced Find** dialog box to provide additional search options and a list of the matches. Select the messages you no longer need and press **Delete**. (Use the **More Choices** or **Advanced** tab to refine your search.) The items are moved to the **Deleted Items** folder. When you're through, click the window's **Close** button.

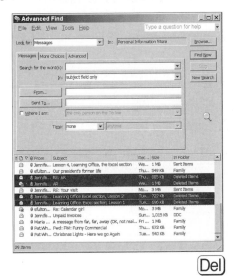

Del

5 Archive Messages

To archive messages and other Outlook items, click **AutoArchive**. Old items are placed in an archive file or deleted, based on the current archive settings.

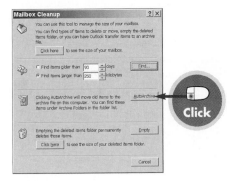

6 Empty the Deleted Items Folder

To permanently remove any items you have deleted recently, click **Empty**. (If you're wondering just how big your **Deleted Items** folder is, click the **Click here** button to see information about that folder before you continue.)

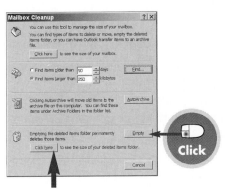

How-to Hint

Changing Archive Settings

To change the default archive settings, choose **Tools, Options, Other**. Click **AutoArchive**, select **Run AutoArchive every _n_ days**, change options as desired, and click **OK**. To change the settings for an individual folder, right-click its name in the **Folder List**, choose **Properties**, and click the **AutoArchive** tab.

Viewing Archived Items

After using AutoArchive, the archive folder is left open for you to review. To close it, right-click the folder and select **Close Archive Folders**. To open an archive file later on, choose **File, Open, Outlook Data File**, select the file, and click **OK**. You can then view, copy, move, or delete the archived items.

How to Screen Junk Email

Unfortunately, junk email is a fact of life. But that doesn't mean that you have to let junk email over-whelm your normal day-to-day activities. Outlook provides an easy mechanism for screening incoming messages: Based on the identity of the sender, you can move messages directly to the **Deleted Items** folder, the **Junk Items** folder (where you can review them before deleting them), or any other folder you designate.

❶ Display the Organize Pane

From the **Inbox**, click the **Organize** button. The **Ways to Organize** pane appears at the top of the **Inbox** screen.

❷ Display Junk Email Options

Click the **Junk Email** tab to display the options related to the management of junk email.

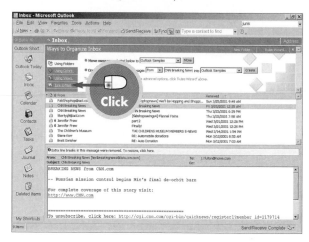

❸ Set Junk Message Options

From the first drop-down list, select how you want junk messages handled. You can highlight them with color or move them to another folder. After selecting **color** or **move** from the first list, further refine your choice with an option from the second drop-down list. Click the **Turn on** button to establish this filter. Repeat this step to set options for handling adult content messages.

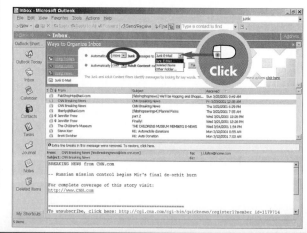

4 View Additional Options

To view additional options, click the **Click Here** link. The **Junk Email** tab changes to show additional options.

5 Edit Junk Senders List

To edit the list of addresses identified as junk senders, click the **Edit Junk Senders** link. The **Edit Junk Senders** dialog box opens.

6 Add a Name to the List

Click **Add** to open the **Sender** dialog box, type the email address you want to add to the **Junk Senders** list, and click **OK**. Repeat this step to add as many addresses as you want, and then click **OK** twice to close both dialog boxes. To close the **Ways to Organize** pane, click the **Organize** button in the main toolbar.

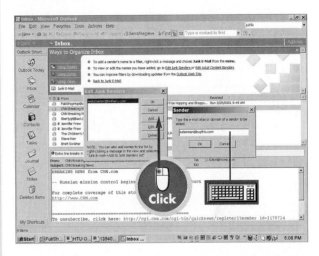

How-to Hint

Downloading a List

Updates to the **Junk Senders** list can be found on Microsoft's Web site by clicking the **Outlook Web Site** link in step 5.

Adding to the List

Another way to add a name to the **Junk Senders** list is to right-click an incoming message, select **Junk Email**, and then select either **Add to Junk Senders list** or **Add to Adult Content Senders** list.

Other Ways to Organize

The **Ways to Organize** pane contains other ways in which you can manage your mountain of email—such as colorizing message headers and moving email messages into specific folders automatically. Be sure that you return to that pane soon to explore this powerful tool.

① How to Enter and Edit Cell Data 540

② How to Navigate Worksheets 542

③ How to Select Cells .544

④ How to Use AutoFill .546

⑤ How to Move and Copy Data 548

⑥ How to Insert and Delete Columns and Rows 550

⑦ How to Remove Data or Cells 552

⑧ How to Set the Column Width and Row Height 554

⑨ How to Define a Range Name 556

⑩ How to Find and Replace Data 558

⑪ How to Sort Data 560

⑫ How to Filter Data 562

⑬ How to Work with Worksheets 564

⑭ How to Create Formulas 566

⑮ How to Use AutoSum 568

⑯ How to Enter Functions 570

⑰ How to Use Absolute and Relative Cell Addresses . .572

⑱ How to Fix Formula Errors 574

⑲ How to Change Number Formats 576

⑳ How to Adjust the Cell Alignment 578

㉑ How to Work with Borders and Patterns 580

㉒ How to Copy Cell Formatting 582

㉓ How to AutoFormat a Range 584

㉔ How to Add a Comment 586

㉕ How to Track Changes 588

㉖ How to Create a Chart with Chart Wizard 590

㉗ How to Move and Resize Charts 592

㉘ How to Change the Chart Type 594

㉙ How to Work with Chart and Axis Titles 596

㉚ How to Change the Chart Data 598

Task

24

Using Excel Spreadsheets

The second most popular program included in the Office suite is Excel. Excel is an excellent tool for keeping track of data and crunching numbers. With Excel, you can create worksheets to add up sales for your department or to track your personal expenses. You can use Excel to set up a budget or to create an invoice. You can even use Excel as a simple database program. With Excel, you can perform any kind of mathematical calculation, from the simplest to the most complex, and organize data so that it becomes meaningful and useful.

When you start Excel, the screen presents some familiar elements, such as a menu bar, toolbars, the status bar, and scrollbars. You'll also see some unfamiliar elements, such as the **Formula bar**, which allows you to view and edit data. The work area is divided into a grid called a *worksheet*. Initially, there are three worksheets in a *workbook* (which is the term for an Excel file). You organize data within this grid. In the tasks in this part, you learn how to enter and format data, add and delete rows and columns, and enter formulas. In addition, you'll learn some of Excel's more advanced features, such as sorting and filtering data and creating charts.

How to Enter and Edit Cell Data

When you first start Excel, a blank workbook opens. By default, each workbook contains three worksheets, which resemble an accountant's spreadsheet divided into a grid of columns and rows that intersect to form cells. Data in a worksheet is entered into these cells. Valid data falls into three categories: labels (text), values (numbers, dates, and times), or formulas (calculations). Text data always lines up to the left of the cell, and number data aligns to the right—unless you change the alignment. Based on the type of data you enter, Excel can perform various calculations. Study the worksheets shown in these tasks for more ideas on how to organize your data.

❶ Select a Cell

Click the cell in which you want to enter data. The cell you click becomes the active cell and a highlighted border surrounds the cell; the associated column/row header is also highlighted. The cell's address (its column and row number) appears in the **Name** box to the left of the **Formula** bar.

Name box   **Formula bar**

❷ Enter Data in the Selected Cell

Type your entry (numbers and/or letters) in the selected cell. As you type, data appears in the active cell and in the **Formula** bar. When you're finished, press **Enter** to move down one cell, **Tab** to move right one cell, or an **arrow key** to move in any direction.

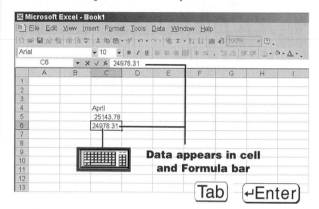

Data appears in cell and Formula bar

Tab   ↵Enter

❸ Enter a Multicolumn List

To enter a multicolumn list, begin at the top-left corner of the list. As you type the entries, press **Tab** to move to the right to enter the data for each cell in the row. After you type the last entry in the row, press **Enter** instead of **Tab**; the active cell moves to the beginning of the next row. This maneuver is called *AutoReturn*.

↵Enter

4 Copy the Cell Above

To copy the entry from the cell above the active cell, press **Ctrl+'** (press **Ctrl** and the apostrophe key simultaneously) and then press **Enter**.

Ctrl + '

5 AutoComplete an Entry

If you want to repeat an entry from anywhere in the same column (which not only saves time, but also prevents typing mistakes), type the first few letters of the entry. A possible match appears in the cell. This function is called *AutoComplete*. If the entry is correct, press **Enter**. If you don't want that entry, just continue typing.

6 Pick a Repeated Entry

If you want to repeat an entry that already exists in the column somewhere, you can select it from a list instead of retyping it. Right-click the active cell, and choose **Pick From List**. A list of all the entries in the column appears. Click the entry you want.

How-to Hint

Edit Data

You can edit data in the cell or in the **Formula** bar. Double-click a cell to edit its contents directly in the cell. To edit the cell data in the **Formula** bar, click the cell, and then click in the **Formula** bar and make your changes. You can use the **Backspace** and **Delete** keys to remove data, type over existing data, or enter new data.

Not a Good Fit?

If you enter data that's too big for a cell, that data is displayed in the next cell, provided that the next cell is blank. If the next cell contains data, the data that's too big is truncated. To fix this problem, widen the column. See Task 8, "How to Set Column Width and Row Height," for help.

Enter a Date

Use a slash or a hyphen to separate the parts of a date, as in 3/21/01 or 10-7-01.

How to Navigate Worksheets

Each worksheet comprises 256 columns and 65,536 rows. With so much space in a single worksheet, you can easily lose yourself in the vast forest of worksheet cells. You need to know how to read cell addresses. Each cell in the worksheet grid has an address, or reference, based on which row and column it's in. Excel labels columns with letters; it labels rows with numbers. Cell names always reference the column letter first, and then the row number. For example, the cell in the top-left corner of the worksheet is A1.

1 Use the Mouse

One way to navigate the worksheet is to use the mouse. To move to a particular cell, simply click the cell. This makes the cell active. If the cell is not in view, use the scrollbars to locate the cell.

2 Use the Keyboard

If you prefer using the keyboard to navigate, press the arrow keys to move around the worksheet. The active cell changes with each press of the arrow keys.

3 Double-Click a Cell Border

Double-click the border of an active cell to move around a *range* (a group of adjacent cells) of data quickly. For example, to jump to the bottom of a list of data, click a cell in the list and point to the bottom edge of the cell. When your mouse pointer becomes an arrow, double-click. Excel takes you to the bottom cell in the range.

④ Jump Home or to the End

To jump back to the first cell in the worksheet (cell A1), press **Ctrl+Home**. To jump to the lower-right corner of the working area of the worksheet (the area you've been working in, not cell IV35536), press **Ctrl+End**.

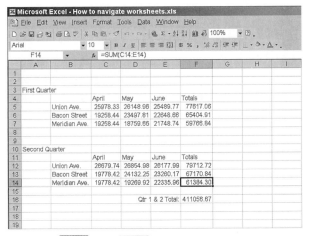

Ctrl + End

⑤ Jump Around Rows and Columns

To jump to the beginning of a row (column A), press **Home**. To jump to the rightmost cell in the row (within the data area of the worksheet), press **End** and then press **Enter**.

Home

⑥ Use the Go To Command

Yet another way to move to a particular cell in a worksheet is to use the **Go To** command: Open the **Edit** menu and select **Go To** to open the **Go To** dialog box. Type the cell address you want to reach in the **Reference** text box and click **OK**.

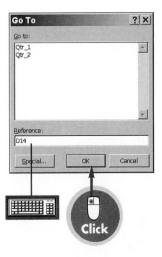

Click

Other Navigation Methods

How-to Hint

When you double-click the left, right, top, or bottom of a cell border, the active cell jumps to the end of a contiguous block of data. If you have a list of data, for example, double-clicking the edge of a cell in the list sends you to the end of the list and stops short of the first empty cell. If you double-click again, the active cell jumps to the end of the block of empty cells and stops short of the next block of data.

You can open the **Go To** dialog box by pressing **F5** or **Ctrl+G**. The **Go To** dialog box remembers the name of the reference you just came from, so to go back again quickly, press **F5** and press **Enter**.

Another way to make a particular cell active is to type the address or range name of the cell into the **Name** box and press **Enter**.

How to Select Cells

If cells are the building blocks of worksheets, ranges are the mortar for holding them together. A range is a rectangular group of adjacent cells. After you select a range of cells, you can perform a variety of tasks on them all in one simple step. You can format a group of cells all at once, for example, rather than one cell at a time. You can use a range to print a specific group of cells from your worksheet. You can also use ranges in formulas, which can really save you time. (Learn how to name ranges in Task 9, "How to Define a Range Name.")

1 Click the First Cell

To select a range, start by clicking the first cell in the range. Typically, this is the upper-left cell in the range you want to select.

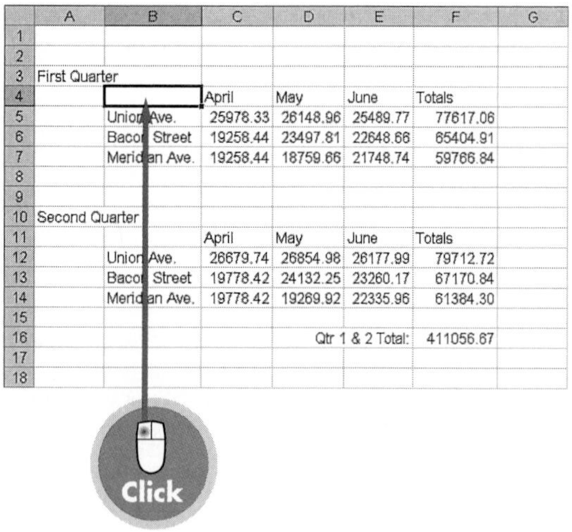

2 Drag to Select

Hold down the mouse button and drag across the cells you want to include in the range. (Drag downward and to the left, to the cell located in the bottom-right corner of the range.)

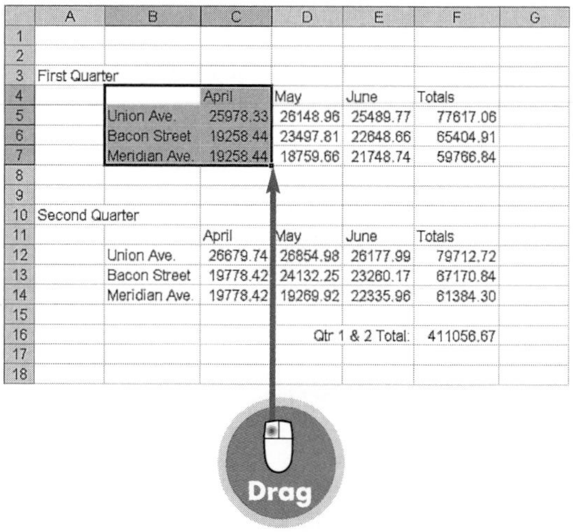

3 Release the Mouse Button

When you release the mouse button, the range is selected. (The active cell—the cell you clicked in step 1—is not highlighted, while the rest of the range is.) Ranges are referred to by their anchor points: the top-left corner and the bottom-right corner. For example, the range shown here is referred to as B4:F7.

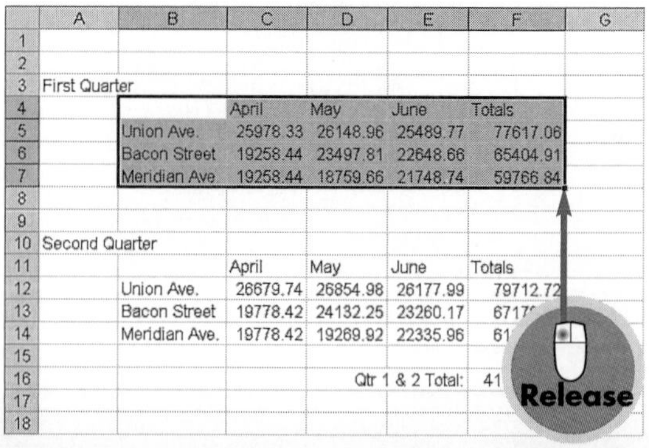

④ Select a Range with the Keyboard

To select a range using the keyboard, use the arrow keys to move to the first cell in the range.

	A	B	C	D	E	F	G
1							
2							
3	First Quarter						
4			April	May	June	Totals	
5		Union Ave.	25978.33	26148.96	25489.77	77617.06	
6		Bacon Street	19258.44	23497.81	22648.66	65404.91	
7		Meridian Ave.	19258.44	18759.66	21748.74	59766.84	
8							
9							
10	Second Quarter						
11			April	May	June	Totals	
12		Union Ave.	26679.74	26854.98	26177.99	79712.72	
13		Bacon Street	19778.42	24132.25	23260.17	67170.84	
14		Meridian Ave.	19778.42	19269.92	22335.96	61384.30	
15							
16					Qtr 1 & 2 Total:	411056.67	
17							
18							

⑤ Use the Shift Key

Press and hold the **Shift** key, and then use the arrow keys to select the range. The range selected here is A10:F16.

	A	B	C	D	E	F	G
1							
2							
3	First Quarter						
4			April	May	June	Totals	
5		Union Ave.	25978.33	26148.96	25489.77	77617.06	
6		Bacon Street	19258.44	23497.81	22648.66	65404.91	
7		Meridian Ave.	19258.44	18759.66	21748.74	59766.84	
8							
9							
10	Second Quarter						
11			April	May	June	Totals	
12		Union Ave.	26679.74	26854.98	26177.99	79712.72	
13		Bacon Street	19778.42	24132.25	23260.17	67170.84	
14		Meridian Ave	19778.42	19269.92	22335.96	61384.30	
15							
16					Qtr 1 & 2 Total:	411056.67	
17							
18							

⑥ Select the Entire Worksheet

To select the entire worksheet as a range, click the **Select All** button located at the top of the worksheet to the left of the column labels.

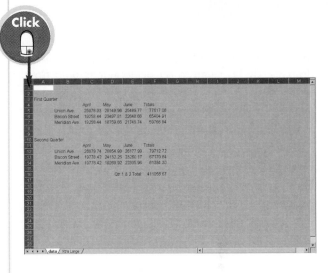

Selecting Cells

Remember: To select a cell, click the cell. A selector (a black outline around the cell) surrounds it. When you select a cell, its reference or address appears in the **Name** box in the **Formula** bar.

When selecting a large range, click the first cell, press and hold the **Shift** key, and then scroll to the last cell and click. To select multiple nonadjacent ranges, select the first range, press and hold **Ctrl**, and then select the next range. To deselect a range, click outside the range or press any arrow key.

Selecting a Row or Column

To quickly select an entire row, click the row's heading. For example, to select row 23, click the number **23** on the far left edge of the worksheet. To select a column, click the column's heading. To select multiple adjacent columns or rows, drag over their headings.

How to Use AutoFill

A feature called *AutoFill* can speed up data entry dramatically by filling in duplicate entries or a data series (such as the labels April, May, June) for you. With AutoFill, you can quickly create a list of day or month names, a series of numbers, or a list of identical text entries. Day and month names, and their standard three-letter abbreviations, are built-in lists in Excel. That's how AutoFill knows what to enter. You can create custom lists (of people or product names, for example), and AutoFill will fill them, as well.

❶ Start a Month List

To AutoFill a list of month names, type a single month name in a cell and then select that cell. You can enter an abbreviation or type the entire month name.

	A	B	C	D	E	F	G
1							
2							
3	First Quarter						
4			April	May	June	Totals	
5		Union Ave.	25978.33	26148.96	25489.77	77617.06	
6		Bacon Street	19258.44	23497.81	22648.66	65404.91	
7		Meridian Ave.	19258.44	18759.66	21748.74	59766.84	
8							
9							
10	Second Quarter						
11			April	May	June	Totals	
12		Union Ave.	26679.74	26854.98	26177.99	79712.72	
13		Bacon Street	19778.42	24132.25	23260.17	67170.84	
14		Meridian Ave.	19778.42	19269.92	22335.96	61384.30	
15							
16					Qtr 1 & 2 Total:	411056.67	
17							
18	Third Quarter		April				
19							
20							

❷ Drag the Fill Handle

Move the mouse pointer over the *fill handle* (the small black square in the bottom right corner of the cell) until it takes the shape of a crosshair. Click and hold the left mouse button while you drag across a row or column of cells. (You can fill cells in any direction.) A **ScreenTip** shows what's being filled in to each cell you drag so that you can tell when you've dragged far enough.

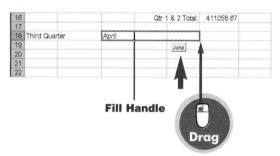

16			Qtr 1 & 2 Total:	411056.67
17				
18	Third Quarter	April		
19				
20			June	
21				
22				

Fill Handle

Drag

❸ Select AutoFill Options

Release the mouse button at the end of the row or column of cells you want to fill. The series is entered in the cells, in the proper order. An **AutoFill Options** button appears; click its down arrow to see a menu of options. Use this menu to select how the cells are filled—for example, you could tell Excel to create a series without copying the formatting as well.

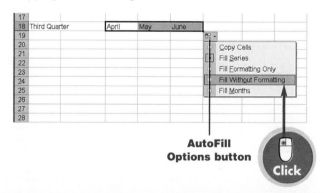

17					
18	Third Quarter	April	May	June	
19					
20					Copy Cells
21					Fill Series
22					Fill Formatting Only
23					Fill Without Formatting
24					Fill Months
25					
26					
27					
28					

AutoFill Options button

Click

④ Start a Text Series

To enter a text series, such as Division 1, Division 2, and so on, click inside the cell and type the first entry in the series. Select the cell and drag the fill handle in the direction you want to go.

⑤ Release the Fill Handle

Release the fill handle; the text series appears in the selected cells. If needed, click the arrow on the **AutoFill Options** button and select an option such as **Copy Cells**, which copies the data without creating a series.

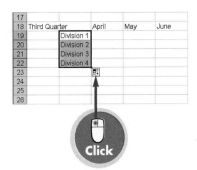

⑥ Start a Number Series

To create a number series, type the first two numbers in adjacent cells, select the two cells, and drag the fill handle to fill the series. AutoFill automatically fills in the rest of the series based on the first two cell entries. For example, if you type **5** in one cell and **10** in the other, you'll create a series that increases by five with each cell.

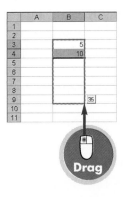
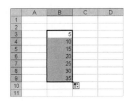

How-to Hint

Copying Data

To fill a list with a copied entry, type the entry, select it, and drag the fill handle to copy the entry repeatedly. If Excel creates a series instead, just click the **AutoFill Options** button and select **Copy Cells**.

Copying a Formula with AutoFill

You can use AutoFill to copy a formula down the side or across the bottom of a table. The cell references in the formula adjust so that the formula calculates the correct cells (see Task 17, "How to Use Absolute and Relative Cell Addresses," to learn how to use cell references).

Creating a Custom List

To create a custom list, type the whole list in any worksheet. Select the list and choose **Tools**, **Options**. On the **Custom Lists** tab, choose **Import** and click **OK**. The list is saved in the **Custom Lists** window. You can fill the list in any workbook by typing any entry in the list and then dragging with the fill handle.

How to Move and Copy Data

If you have to move or copy data to another location on a worksheet, and the new location is only a short distance from the original location, the easiest way to accomplish your goal is to drag the data and drop it with the mouse. Whether you're moving or copying a single cell or a range of cells, the drag-and-drop method makes it easy and fast.

1 Select Cells to Move

To move cells, first select the range of cells you want to move. Point to any border of the selected range so that the mouse pointer becomes an arrow with a cross-hair underneath.

	A	B	C	D	E	F	G	H	I	J
3			Auto Sales Contest							
6			Name	Week 1	Week 2	Week 3	Week 4	Total Sales	Sales Goal (Units)	
7			Joeline Waters	21	19	15	23	78	75	
8			Andrew Carter	9	15	18	17	59	65	
9			Michael Johnson	14	17	18	16	65	75	
10			Wu Ngyeun	6	7	11	13	37	65	
11			Hector Valdez	18	22	14	17	71	65	

2 Drop the Cells

Drag the range to a new location. While you drag, an outline of the range moves across the worksheet, and a **ScreenTip** tells you the reference of the current range location. When the range border is where you want it, drop the data by releasing the mouse button.

	A	B	C	D	E	F	G	H	I	J
3			Auto Sales Contest							
6			Name	Week 1	Week 2	Week 3	Week 4	Total Sales	Sales Goal (Units)	
7			Joeline Waters	21	19	15	23	78	75	
8			Andrew Carter	9	15	18	17	59	65	
9			Michael Johnson	14	17	18	16	65	75	
10			Wu Ngyeun	6	7	11	13	37	65	
11			Hector Valdez	18	22	14	17	71	65	
19				D13:E18						

Drag

3 The Range Moves

The range moves to its new location.

	A	B	C	D	E	F	G	H	I	J
3			Auto Sales Contest							
6			Name	Week 1	Week 2	Week 3	Week 4			
7			Joeline Waters	21	19	15	23			
8			Andrew Carter	9	15	18	17			
9			Michael Johnson	14	17	18	16			
10			Wu Ngyeun	6	7	11	13			
11			Hector Valdez			14	17			
13				Total Sale	Sales Goal (Units)					
14				78	75					
15				59	85					
16				65	75					
17				37	65					
18				71	65					

4 Select Cells to Copy

To copy cells, select the range of cells you want to copy and point to any border of the selected range so that the mouse pointer becomes an arrow. Drag the range to a new location.

Drag

5 Drag the Cells

While you drag, an outline of the range moves across the worksheet, and a **ScreenTip** tells you the reference of the range location.

6 Press Ctrl and Drop the Cells

When the range border is where you want it, press and hold the **Ctrl** key and drop the data by releasing the mouse button. When you press **Ctrl**, the mouse pointer acquires a small plus symbol that tells you it's copying. A copy of the data is dropped in the new location.

Ctrl + **Drop**

Copying or Moving Longer Distances

If you want to copy or move data greater distances (to another worksheet, workbook, or to an area far away), use the **Copy**, **Cut**, and **Paste** toolbar buttons.

Copying or Moving Multiple Items

You can collect multiple items to copy or move by displaying the **Office Clipboard** task pane (choose **Edit**, **Office Clipboard**), selecting the items one by one, and clicking the **Copy** or **Cut** toolbar button. After collecting the items, use the buttons on the **Office Clipboard** task pane to paste them in their new locations individually or as a group.

⑥ How to Insert and Delete Columns and Rows

You might find that you need to add or delete rows or columns after you've already entered data into your worksheet. You can easily insert rows or columns between existing data—the data is simply shifted over to make room for the new columns or rows you insert. You can delete rows or columns just as easily—regardless of whether they contain data. When you delete rows or columns, existing data is shifted back to fill the gap created by the deleted cells. If you have written formulas that calculate across the table, the formulas adjust themselves automatically after you add or delete rows or columns.

① Select the Row or Column

To insert a row, select the row under the location in which you want the inserted row to appear (click the row number to select it). The inserted row will appear *above* the row you select. To insert a column, select the column to the right of the place where you want the new column to appear (click the column letter to select it). The inserted column will appear to the *left* of the column you choose.

Click

② Choose Insert

Right-click the selected row or column and choose **Insert** from the shortcut menu.

Click

③ A New Row or Column Is Inserted

A new row is inserted above the row you selected. A new column is inserted to the left of the column you selected. To select whether formatting is applied to the row or column you inserted, click the arrow on the **Paste Options** button and make a selection.

Click

4 Select the Row or Column

To delete a row or column, select its heading.

Click

	A	B	C	D	E	F	G	H
1	Auto Sales Contest							
2								
3								
4		Name	EE ID#	Week 1	Week 2	Week 3	Week 4	
5		Joeline Waters	45789	21	19	15	23	
6		Andrew Carter	31528	9	15	18	17	
7		Michael Johnson	22174	14	17	18	18	
8		Wu Ngyuen	48971	6	7	11	13	
9		Hector Valdez	38447	18	22	14	17	
10								
11		Name		Total Sales	Goal (Units)			
12		Joeline Waters	45789	78	75			
13		Andrew Carter	31528	59	65			
14		Michael Johnson	22174	65	75			
15		Wu Ngyuun	48971	37	65			
16		Hector Valdez	38447	71	65			
17								
18								
19								

5 Delete the Row or Column

Right-click the selected column or row and choose **Delete** from the shortcut menu. As soon as you select the command, the column or row is immediately deleted. Adjacent data is shifted up or to the left to fill the gap.

Right Click

6 Select Adjacent Rows or Columns

To insert or delete several adjacent rows or columns at one time, drag over their headings to select the rows or columns. Right-click the selection and choose **Insert** or **Delete**. An equal number of rows or columns is inserted, or the selected rows or columns are deleted.

Right Click

Formulas Self-Adjust

If you have written formulas that calculate across a range of cells, the formulas adjust themselves automatically after you insert new rows or columns in that range.

Inserting a Cell

If you select a cell or cells and then choose **Insert**, an **Insert** dialog box appears for you to specify how you want the cells inserted—by shifting existing cells down or to the right. Make your selection and click **OK**.

How to Remove Data or Cells

It's easy to delete data from cells, but sometimes you will want to remove the cells themselves. You might also want to delete just the formatting from the cells. Excel has several delete options you can apply to your worksheets. You could remove some cells, for example, to shift the data up or to the left, without affecting surrounding data (such as a nearby table).

① Select the Cells

Select the cells whose data you want to delete.

	A	B	C	D	E	F	G	H
1	Auto Sales Contest							
2								
3								
4		Name	Week 1	Week 2	Week 3	Week 4		
5		Joeline Waters	21	19	15	23		
6		Andrew Carter	9	15	18	17		
7		Michael Johnson	14	17	18	16		
8		Wu Ngyuun	6	7	11	13		
9		Hector Valdez	18	22	14	17		
10								
11		Name	Total Sales	Goal (Units)				
12		Joeline Waters	78	75				
13		Andrew Carter	59	65				
14		Michael Johnson	65	75				
15		Wu Ngyuun	37	65				
16		Hector Valdez	71	65				
17								
18								

② Press Delete

Press the **Delete** key on the keyboard; the data in the selected cells is removed. Note, however, that the cells themselves remain; just the data is removed.

	A	B	C	D	E	F	G	H
1	Auto Sales Contest							
2								
3								
4		Name	Week 1	Week 2	Week 3	Week 4		
5		Joeline Waters	21	19	15			
6		Andrew Carter	9	15	18			
7		Michael Johnson	14	17	18			
8		Wu Ngyuen	6	7	11			
9		Hector Valdez	18	22	14			
10								
11		Name	Total Sales	Goal (Units)				
12		Joeline Waters	55	75				
13		Andrew Carter	42	65				
14		Michael Johnson	49	75				
15		Wu Ngyuun	24	65				
16		Hector Valdez	54	65				
17								
18								
19								

Del

③ Clear the Formatting Only

If you want to remove just the formatting of the cells (cell borders and colors) without affecting the data, select the cells and choose **Edit**, **Clear**, **Formats**.

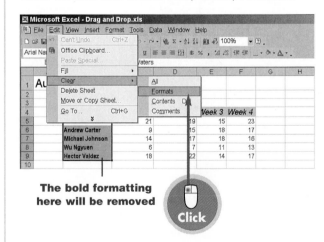

The bold formatting here will be removed

Click

4 Select Cells to Remove

If you want to remove cells (and shift surrounding cells to fill the gap left by the deleted cells), select the cells; then right-click them and select **Delete** from the shortcut menu.

6 Cells Are Removed

The cells are removed from the worksheet, and the cells to the right move over or the cells below move up to fill in the empty space. If you shift cells left, the cells above or below the selection are unaffected. If you shift cells up, the cells to the left or right are unchanged.

5 Shift Replacement Cells

In the **Delete** dialog box that opens, choose **Shift cells left** or **Shift cells up**, depending on how you want the data in the table to fill in the gap. Click **OK**.

How-to Hint

Clearing Versus Deleting

In Excel, removing data from a cell is called *clearing* the cell, even though you use the **Delete** key to do it. *Deleting* a cell means removing that cell from the worksheet, shifting surrounding data.

Wrong Formulas

If any remaining formulas reference the data in cells that you have removed or cleared, you'll get an error.

Oops!

If you make a mistake when deleting or removing cells, click the **Undo** button on the **Standard** toolbar.

How to Set Column Width and Row Height

In a new worksheet, all the columns and rows are the same size. However, it's quite common to exceed your column width when entering data. If it's a text entry, the text flows over into the cell to the right, until you enter data in that cell. Then, the wide entry is cut off at the cell border. (It's partially hidden.) If it's a number entry, it won't flow over. Instead it appears in scientific notation (1.23154E+10), or as ######## in the cell. You can quickly adjust the column width or row height in your worksheets. You can drag a row or column to a new size, or you can specify an exact size.

1 Drag a New Column Width

To adjust the column width, point at the right border of the heading for the column you want to widen. The mouse pointer becomes a two-headed arrow. Hold down the left mouse button and drag the border in either direction to adjust the width. A ScreenTip lets you know the width measurement. Release the mouse button when the column is the width you want.

2 Resize Multiple Columns

To make several columns the same width, select all the columns by dragging over their headings, and then adjust the width for any one of the columns while all the columns are selected. All the selected columns will adjust to the same width.

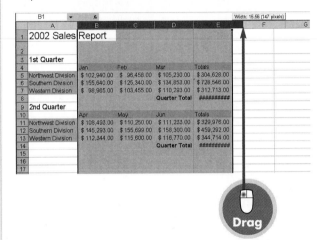

3 Open the Column Width Dialog Box

To enter an exact value for the width of a column, select the column and choose **Format**, **Column**, **Width**. The **Column Width** dialog box opens.

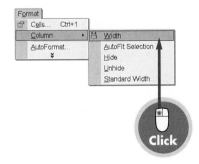

④ Specify an Exact Size

Type a measurement (in numbers of characters of the standard font width) for the column width and click **OK**.

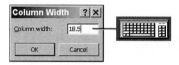

⑤ Drag a New Row Height

You can adjust the height of a row in the same way you adjust the width of a column. Point to the bottom border of the heading for the row you want to adjust. The mouse pointer becomes a two-headed arrow. Drag the border in either direction to adjust the row height. A ScreenTip lets you know the measurement. Release the mouse button when the row is the height you want.

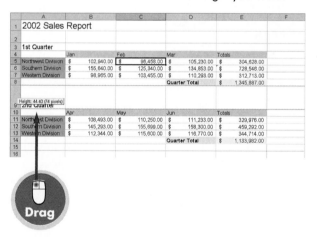

⑥ Open the Row Height Dialog Box

You can also specify an exact value for the row height. Select the row or rows to which you want to apply a new measurement and choose **Format**, **Row**, **Height**. Type a new value (in points—there are 72 points to an inch) and click **OK** to apply the change.

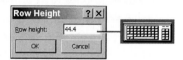

Best Fit

To make the column fit its widest entry, point at the right border of the column heading and double-click. This feature is called a *best fit*. You can do the same with a row; double-click the bottom border of the row heading.

Multiple Non-adjacent Columns

You can adjust non-adjacent columns to the same width the same way as you can adjust adjacent columns (as described in step 2). To select non-adjacent columns, select the first column, press and hold the **Ctrl** key, and then select the other columns.

Copying Column Widths

When pasting data, you might want to copy the widths of the original columns as well as the data. To do that, choose **Edit**, **Paste**, **Paste Special**; in the dialog box that opens, choose **Column widths** and click **OK**.

How to Define a Range Name

It's much easier to refer to your data by name than with a meaningless cell address. For example, a range named **Sales_Totals** is a lot easier to decipher than **F2:F14**. The formula **=INCOME-EXPENSE** is easier to understand than **=B24-C24**. Giving ranges (or single cells) recognizable names can make your formulas a lot easier to follow. Range names appear in the **Name** box at the top of your worksheet. When you have defined at least one range name in a worksheet, you can click the **Name** box drop-down list to see a list of the named ranges.

1 Select a Range

To name a range, first select the range in the worksheet. To name a single cell, click that cell to select it.

2 Click the Name Box

Click inside the **Name** box located at the far left end of the **Formula** bar.

3 Type a Name

Type a name for the range. Names must begin with a letter or an underscore (_); after that, you can use any other character you want. Don't use spaces in range names; instead, use the underscore (_) or a period (.). You can't use a name already defined in the workbook, even if it's on another worksheet.

④ Press Enter

Press **Enter** when you're finished typing the range name. The name appears in place of the cell reference in the **Name** box when the range is selected in the worksheet.

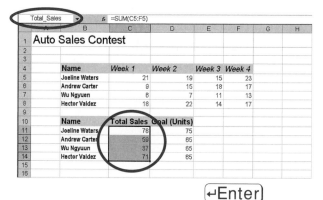

⏎Enter

⑤ Go to the Range

To jump to the named range from anywhere in the workbook, click the drop-down arrow next to the **Name** box and select the range name from the list.

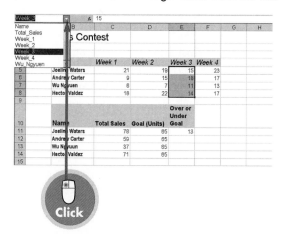

Click

⑥ Use the Define Name Dialog Box

Another way to name a range or edit an existing range name is to use the **Define Name** dialog box. Choose **Insert**, **Name**, **Define** to open the **Define Name** dialog box. Here you can enter a new range name, enter its cell references, and click the **Add** button, or edit an existing name. Click **OK** to exit the dialog box.

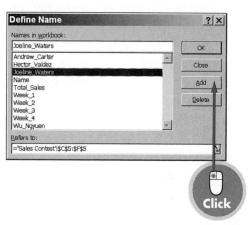

Click

How-to Hint

Deleting a Range Name

To delete a range name, open the worksheet that contains the named cell or range and choose **Insert**, **Name**, **Define**. In the **Define Name** dialog box, select the name from the list, click **Delete**, and then click **OK**.

Using Range Names in Formulas

To use the range name in a formula, write the formula and click the range to include it; the range name appears in the formula in place of cell references.

Automatic Range Names

To create range names using your row and column labels, select the range containing the labels and the data. (In the worksheet shown here, you might select B4:F8.) Then choose **Insert**, **Name**, **Create**. In the **Create Name** dialog box, choose the location of the labels you want to use as names and click **OK**.

How to Find and Replace Data

You can search for and replace any character in a worksheet or in the entire workbook. You can find or replace text strings, such as a company or employee name, and you can find or replace numbers, either single digits or strings of numbers. You can limit your search to only cells that contain formulas or comments, or you can search every cell. If you have used Microsoft Word, you will discover that the **Find and Replace** procedures are almost identical in the two programs, so there won't be much that's new for you to learn about this process in Excel.

❶ Use the Find Command

To search for a word or number in a worksheet, start by choosing **Edit**, **Find**.

❷ Enter the Search Data

In the **Find and Replace** dialog box, click inside the **Find what** text box and type the characters (numbers, text, and symbols) for which you want to search.

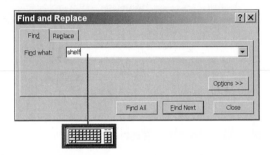

❸ Set Any Options

Click **Options**, and choose from options that limit your search: Click **Format** to find data with a particular format, use the **Within** list to search the entire workbook, use the **Search** list to control how the search is conducted, and use the **Look in** list to look *only* in formulas, comments, or the displayed values for a match. Use the **Match** check box options to limit how a match is found.

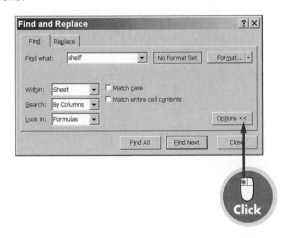

4 Start the Search

Click the **Find Next** button to start the search. Excel locates the first cell containing a match and highlights it in the worksheet. Click **Find Next** repeatedly to find each occurrence of the search string.

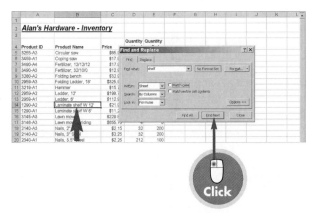

6 Replace the Data

Click **Find Next**, and Excel highlights the first match. Click the **Replace** button to replace the data; click **Replace All** to replace all occurrences in all selected worksheets in the workbook at once.

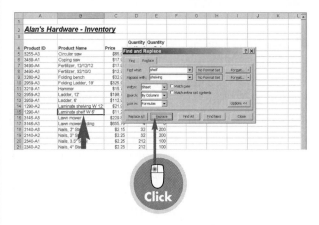

5 Use the Replace Command

To conduct a search and replace the matches with a specified set of characters or formatting, click the **Replace** tab. Type the replacement data in the **Replace with** text box; click the **Format** button to specify any formatting you want to apply to the replacement data.

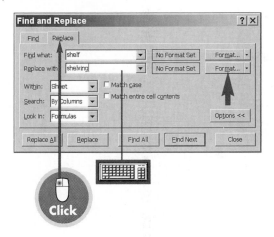

Filtering Data

Another way to locate specific data is to *filter* it, a process that hides the data you don't want to see. See Task 12, "How to Filter Data," for more help.

Narrowing Your Search

To limit your search to text with specific capitalization, enable the **Match case** check box. To limit your search to complete entries instead of including partial entries (if you want to search for 100, for example, and not find 1,000 or 20,100), enable the **Match entire cell contents** check box.

Speeding Up the Search

In a large table, sometimes the search is faster if you select **By Rows** or **By Columns** from the **Search** drop-down list, especially if you start by selecting a cell in the specific row or column you want to search. In a small table, it makes no difference what's selected in the **Search** list.

How-to Hint

How to Sort Data

Excel can be used as a *database*, a tool for organizing data. For example, an inventory database might contain fields (columns) for product name, product number, and price. A record (row) is a complete entry in the database with data recorded for each field. You can sort a data list to see product names in alphabetical order, for example, or product prices from highest to lowest. For Excel to sort data correctly, you must set up your table precisely. First, type a row of column labels (such as **Product ID**, **Product Name**, **Price**, and so on). In the row below that, type the data for your first product. Do not skip rows.

① Select a Field

To sort by a single key, or field (column), click any of the table data cells in that column (not the column label). For this example, I want to sort the data in the table by the **Product Name** column, so I click cell B5.

② Select a Sort Order

To sort the data in alphabetical order (A-to-Z) or in lowest-to-highest numerical order, click the **Sort Ascending** button on the **Standard** toolbar. To sort in reverse alphabetical order (Z-to-A) or in highest-to-lowest numerical order, click the **Sort Descending** button.

Sort Ascending ⌐ ⌐ **Sort Decending**

③ Sort by Multiple Fields

To sort the data by multiple fields (for example, by last name and then by first name)—a process called a *multikey sort*—click anywhere in the table data and choose **Data**, **Sort** to open the **Sort** dialog box.

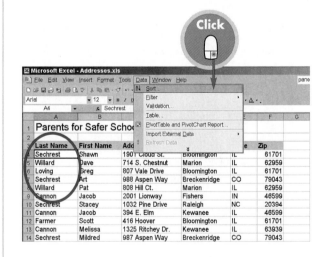

4 Set the First Field

From the **Sort by** drop-down list, select the field you want to use for your major sort. Then select the option button for the sort order you want (**Ascending** or **Descending**). In this example, I'm sorting an address table in A-to-Z order by the **Last Name** column.

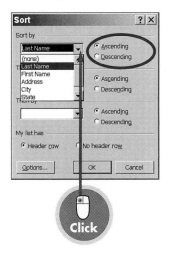

5 Set the Second Field

For the second key in the sort, click the **Then by** drop-down arrow and select the column you want to use for the secondary sort (in this example, my second key sort is the **First Name** column). Then choose the option button for a sort order. To sort by a third key within the second key (for example, to sort the first and last names by the **State** column), use the second **Then by** drop-down list. Click **OK** to run the sort.

6 Results of a Multikey Sort

Shown here is the result of the three-key sort: first by **Last Name**, and then by **First Name**, and then by **State**. If two people have the same last name, they are sorted by first name; if both the first and last names are the same, they are sorted by state.

	A	B	C	D	E	F	G
1	Parents for Safer Schools Membership List						
2							
3	**Last Name**	**First Name**	**Address**	**City**	**State**	**Zip**	
4	Allan	Carl	8012 Fen Court	Bloomington	IL	61701	
5	Alvarez	Martin	12 W. 89th	Marion	IL	62960	
6	Cannon	Doug	304 W. Chestnut	Vincennes	IN	47589	
7	Cannon	Jacob	394 E. Elm	Kewanee	IL	46599	
8	Cannon	Jacob	2001 Lionway	Fishers	IN	46599	
9	Cannon	Melissa	1325 Ritchey Dr.	Kewanee	IL	63939	
10	Crosson	Tim	4080 Music Blvd.	Kansas City	KS	32920	
11	Farmer	Bob	808 Toad Hill	Marion	IL	62959	
12	Farmer	Rita	808 Toad Hill	Marion	IL	62950	
13	Farmer	Scott	416 Hoover	Bloomington	IL	61701	
14	Howell	Teresa	715 Armadillo Ct.	Dallas	TX	79803	
15	Hu	Joi	225 Alan Street	Raleigh	NC	20394	
16	Janese	Jay	90 East Main	Mt. Vernon	IL	65940	
17	Loving	Greg	807 Vale Drive	Bloomington	IL	61701	
18	Loving	Kelly	30090 Jeremiah Dr.	Champaign	IL	63293	
19	Sechrest	Art	988 Aspen Way	Breckenridge	CO	79043	
20	Sechrest	Mildred	987 Aspen Way	Breckenridge	CO	79043	
21	Sechrest	Shawn	1901 Cloud St.	Bloomington	IL	61701	
22	Sechrest	Stacey	1032 Pine Drive	Raleigh	NC	20394	
23	Toliver	Steve	9490 Main, Apt. B	Pinedale	WY	80934	
24	Willard	Dave	714 S. Chestnut	Marion	IL	62959	

Unsorted / Sorted / Sheet7 / Sheet2 / Sheet3 /

How-to Hint

Undoing a Sort

To return your data list to its former, unsorted state, immediately click the **Undo** button on the **Standard** toolbar to undo the sort.

Lose Your Headings?

If your column headings are similar enough to the data in your list that Excel can't guess that they're headings, they might get sorted into the data. To fix that, click the **Undo** button to undo the sort. Then choose **Data**, **Sort**. In the **Sort** dialog box, enable the **Header row** option before you run the sort.

Sorting by Time and Customized Order

To sort by months or days of the week, click the Options button in the **Sort** dialog box and select the sort type you want. To use a custom list as the sort order, type the list and select it; then choose **Tools**, **Options**, click the **Custom Lists** tab, and click **Import**. Then use the **Options** button in the **Sort** dialog box to select the list.

How to Filter Data

Another activity you can do when using Excel as a database is to filter data. Filtering shows only the records you want to see and hides the rest. Records aren't removed, they're just hidden temporarily. Filtering is based on *criteria*: data that's shared by all the records you want to see. For example, in an inventory database, you might filter the data by price so that you can locate items within a certain price range. You don't have to sort a list before you filter, and you can have blank cells in the list. The top row, however, should contain column headings or labels, and the list should contain no completely blank rows.

❶ Click a Cell

To begin a filter, click any cell in the list or table.

	A	B	C	D	E	F	G
1	Parents for Safer Schools Membership List						
2							
3	Last Name	First Name	Address	City	State	Zip	
4	Allan	Carl	8012 Fen Court	Bloomington	IL	61701	
5	Alvarez	Martin	12 W. 89th	Marion	IL	62960	
6	Cannon	Doug	304 W. Chestnut	Vincennes	IN	47589	
7	Cannon	Jacob	2001 Lionway	Fishers	IN	46599	
8	Cannon	Joshua	394 E. Elm	Fishers	IN	46599	
9	Cannon	Melissa	1325 Ritchey Dr.	Kewanee	IL	63939	
10	Crosson	Tim	4080 Music Blvd.	Kansas City	KS	32920	
11	Farmer	Bob	808 Toad Hill	Marion	IL	62959	
12	Farmer	Rita	808 Toad Hill	Marion	IL	62950	
13	Farmer	Scott	416 Hoover	Bloomington	IL	61701	
14	Howell	Teresa	715 Armadillo Ct.	Dallas	TX	79803	
15	Hu	Joi	225 Alan Street	Raleigh	NC	20394	
16	Janese	Jay	90 East Main	Mt. Vernon	IL	65940	
17	Loving	Greg	807 Vale Drive	Bloomington	IL	61701	
18	Loving	Kelly	30090 Jeremiah Dr.	Champaign	IL	63293	
19	Sechres	Art	988 Aspen Way	Breckenridge	CO	79043	
20	Sechres	Mildred	987 Aspen Way	Breckenridge	CO	79043	
21	Sechres	Shawn	1901 Cloud St.	Bloomington	IL	61701	
22	Sechres	Stacey	1032 Pine Drive	Raleigh	NC	20394	
23	Toliver	Steve	9490 Main, Apt. B	Pinedale	WY	80934	
24	Willard	Dave	714 S. Chestnut	Marion	IL	62959	

❙◀ ◀ ▶ ▶❙ \ Unsorted \ Sorted / Sheet7 / Sheet2 / Sheet3 /

Click

❷ Click the Filter Command

Open the **Data** menu and select **Filter, AutoFilter**.

Click

❸ Open a Filter List

Filter arrows appear in the cell of each column label. In the column that contains the criteria you want to filter, click the filter arrow to drop down a list of all the values in the column. From the list, select the criteria you want.

Click

④ Matching Records Are Displayed

All records that don't meet the criteria you specified in step 3 are hidden. The filter arrow where you set the criteria turns blue, and the row numbers turn blue to remind you that some rows are hidden.

	A	B	C	D	E	F	G
1	Parents for Safer Schools Membership List						
2							
3	Last Name	First Name	Address	City	State	Zip	
4	Allan	Carl	8012 Fen Court	Bloomington	IL	61701	
5	Alvarez	Martin	12 W. 89th	Marion	IL	62960	
9	Cannon	Melissa	1325 Ritchey Dr.	Kewanee	IL	63939	
11	Farmer	Bob	808 Toad Hill	Marion	IL	62959	
12	Farmer	Rita	808 Toad Hill	Marion	IL	62950	
13	Farmer	Scott	416 Hoover	Bloomington	IL	61701	
16	Janese	Jay	90 East Main	Mt. Vernon	IL	65940	
17	Loving	Greg	807 Vale Drive	Bloomington	IL	61701	
18	Loving	Kelly	30090 Jeremiah Dr.	Champaign	IL	63293	
21	Sechrest	Shawn	1901 Cloud St.	Bloomington	IL	61701	
24	Willard	Dave	714 S. Chestnut	Marion	IL	62959	
25	Willard	Mima	2004 North View	Marion	IL	62959	
26	Willard	Pat	808 Hill Ct.	Marion	IL	62959	
27							
28							
29							

⑤ Set Multiple Criteria

To set multiple criteria to further filter the results of the first filter operation, click another filter arrow and select additional criteria. Here you see the list filtered to show all members living in Marion, Illinois.

	A	B	C	D	E	F	G
1	Parents for Safer Schools Membership List						
2							
3	Last Name	First Name	Address	City	State	Zip	
5	Alvarez	Martin	12 W. 89th	Marion	IL	62960	
11	Farmer	Bob	808 Toad Hill	Marion	IL	62959	
12	Farmer	Rita	808 Toad Hill	Marion	IL	62950	
24	Willard	Dave	714 S. Chestnut	Marion	IL	62959	
25	Willard	Mima	2004 North View	Marion	IL	62959	
26	Willard	Pat	808 Hill Ct.	Marion	IL	62959	
27							
28							
29							
30							

⑥ Remove the Filter

To remove the filter and show all the records in the list again, either click each filter arrow where you set criteria and click **(All)** or choose **Data**, **Filter**, **AutoFilter** to turn off AutoFilter.

Field or Column?

Excel (as well as Access, Word, and Outlook) uses the terms *column* and *field*, and *row* and *record* interchangeably. A *field* is a database term that refers to a column in a table. A *record* refers to a row in the database.

Top 10

To filter the top (or bottom) of a selected number (or selected percent) of numeric items in a list, select the **Top 10** filter criteria. Then choose **Top** or **Bottom**, select a number, select **Items** or **Percent**, and click **OK**.

Entering Comparison Criteria

To set complex criteria such as "prices greater than $4," click the filter arrow in the column in which you want to set the criteria and choose **(Custom)**. In the **Custom AutoFilter** dialog box, select comparison operators from the list box on the left, type or select criteria from the list box on the right, and click **OK**.

How to Work with Worksheets

By default, Excel opens every new workbook file with three worksheets. You can add or delete worksheets as needed. You can also rename worksheets to better describe their contents. For example, you might have a quarterly sales report workbook, with sales totals for each quarter on separate worksheets. You can name each sheet with distinctive names such as **Quarter 1**, **Quarter 2**, and so on. You can even move and copy sheets within a workbook, or from workbook to workbook. In this task, you'll learn the various ways you can work with worksheets.

1 Move from One Sheet to Another

To move from one sheet to another, click the tab for the sheet you want to view. The selected sheet, or *active* sheet, is the one with the bright white-and-black sheet tab.

2 Rename a Worksheet

You can rename any worksheet in the workbook. Double-click a sheet tab; the current name of the worksheet is highlighted. Type a new name and press **Enter**.

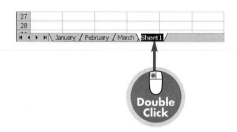

3 Delete a Worksheet

Deleting a worksheet is almost too easy: Right-click the sheet tab for the worksheet you want to delete and choose **Delete** from the context menu. When Excel prompts you for confirmation, click **Delete**.

4 Add Another Worksheet

You can also insert a new worksheet into the workbook. Right-click any existing sheet tab and choose **Insert** from the context menu. On the **General** tab of the **Insert** dialog box, double-click the **Worksheet** icon. The new worksheet is inserted to the left of the sheet tab you initially right-clicked.

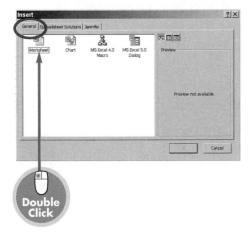

Double Click

5 Move a Worksheet

To move a worksheet within a workbook, drag its sheet tab. While you drag, the mouse pointer acquires a sheet-of-paper symbol, and a small black triangle points to the position where the sheet will be moved. Drop the sheet tab when the triangle points to the location to which you want to move the sheet.

	Household Budget				
16					
17					
18		Budget		Spent	Difference
19	Car Expense	$ 200.00	$ -	$ 200.00
20	Car Payment	$ 355.00	$ 355.00	$ -
21	Groceries	$ 300.00	$ 290.00	$ 10.00
22	Child Care	$ 400.00	$ 450.00	$ (50.00)
23	Utilities	$ 250.00	$ 327.00	$ (77.00)
24	Mortgage	$ 968.00	$ 968.00	$ -
25	Long Distance	$ 100.00	$ 97.00	$ 3.00
26	Internet	$ 55.00	$ 55.00	$ -
27	Miscellaneous	$ 350.00	$ 597.00	$ (247.00)

January March February

Ready

Drag   **Drop**

6 Copy a Worksheet

To make a copy of a worksheet within a workbook, press and hold the **Ctrl** key as you drag the sheet tab. While you drag, the mouse pointer acquires a sheet-of-paper symbol with a small plus sign, and a small black triangle points to the position to which the copied sheet will be inserted.

	Household Budget				
16					
17					
18		Budget	Spent	Difference
19	Car Expense	$ 200.00	$ 432.00	$ (232.00)
20	Car Payment	$ 355.00	$ 355.00	$ -
21	Groceries	$ 300.00	$ 334.00	$ (34.00)
22	Child Care	$ 400.00	$ 400.00	$ -
23	Utilities	$ 250.00	$ 244.00	$ 6.00
24	Mortgage	$ 968.00	$ 968.00	$ -
25	Long Distance	$ 100.00	$ 123.00	$ (23.00)
26	Internet	$ 55.00	$ 55.00	$ -
27	Miscellaneous	$ 350.00	$ 327.00	$ 23.00

January February March January (2)

Ready

Ctrl + **Drag**

Using the Context Menu

Right-click a sheet tab to display a context menu of commands that allow you to insert, delete, copy, move, and rename worksheets. You can also use the context menu to change the tab color: select **Tab Color** from the context menu and choose a color for the tab. The tab is displayed in that color until you select it (when it appears white). Use tab colors to organize the worksheets in a multisheet workbook.

Moving or Copying to Another Workbook

If you want to move or copy a worksheet from one workbook to another, right-click the sheet tab you want to move or copy and select **Move** or **Copy** from the context menu. In the dialog box that opens, choose the workbook to which you want to move or copy the worksheet and then choose where to place the sheet. Select **Create a copy** if you want to copy the sheet rather than move it, and click **OK**.

How to Create Formulas

On paper, formulas are written as follows:

2+2=4

In Excel, a formula takes a slightly different form:

=2+2

The answer, 4, is displayed in the cell. All formulas in a worksheet begin with an equal sign (=). In Excel, you aren't limited to writing **=2+2**; you can type **=C2+D14**, and the values entered in the cells you reference are added together. If you change the values in those cells, the formula continues to add together their current values. You can also use mathematical operators to perform other calculations, such as subtraction (–), multiplication (*), and division (/).

1 Select a Cell

Click the cell in which you want the result of the formula to show, and type an equal sign (=).

	A	B	C	D	E	F	G
	COUNTIF	▼ X ✓ ƒx	=				
1	Auto Sales Contest						
2							
3							
4		Name	Week 1	Week 2	Week 3	Week 4	
5		Joeline Waters	21	19	15	23	
6		Andrew Carter	9	15	18	17	
7		Wu Ngyuen	6	7	11	13	
8		Hector Valdez	18	22	14	17	
9							
10		Name	Total Sales	Goal (Units)	Over or Under Goal		
11		Joeline Waters	78	75	=		
12		Andrew Carter	59	65			
13		Wu Ngyuun	37	65			
14		Hector Valdez	71	65			
15							

2 Build the Formula

Click the first of the cells you want to add to the formula. The cell's reference is immediately added to the equation. Type an operator for the formula: add (+), subtract (–), multiply (*), or divide (/).

	A	B	C	D	E	F	G
	COUNTIF	▼ X ✓ ƒx	=C11				
1	Auto Sales Contest						
2							
3							
4		Name	Week 1	Week 2	Week 3	Week 4	
5		Joeline Waters	21	19	15	23	
6		Andrew Carter	9	15	18	17	
7		Wu Ngyuen	6	7	11	13	
8		Hector Valdez	18	22	14	17	
9							
10		Name	Total Sales	Goal (Units)	Over or Under Goal		
11		Joeline Waters	78	75	=C11		
12		Andrew Carter	59	65			
13		Wu Ngyuun	37	65			
14		Hector Valdez	71	65			
15							
16							
17							

Click

3 Finish the Formula

Click the next cell you want to add to the formula. As you click each cell, that cell's address, or *cell reference*, appears in the formula, and the cell is surrounded by a colored box. Continue typing operators and clicking cells as needed to create the formula.

	A	B	C	D	E	F	G
	COUNTIF	▼ X ✓ ƒx	=C11-D11				
1	Auto Sales Contest						
2							
3							
4		Name	Week 1	Week 2	Week 3	Week 4	
5		Joeline Waters	21	19	15	23	
6		Andrew Carter	9	15	18	17	
7		Wu Ngyuen	6	7	11	13	
8		Hector Valdez	18	22	14	17	
9							
10		Name	Total Sales	Goal (Units)	Over or Under Goal		
11		Joeline Waters	78	75	=C11-D11		
12		Andrew Carter	59	65			
13		Wu Ngyuun	37	65			
14		Hector Valdez	71				
15							

Click

4 Press Enter

Press **Enter** to complete the formula. The formula is entered into the cell, but only the result appears in the formula cell. The formula itself is displayed in the **Formula** bar. To view the formula, click the cell containing the formula results.

E11		fx	=C11-D11			
	A	B	C	D	E	F	G

Auto Sales Contest

	Name	Week 1	Week 2	Week 3	Week 4
Joeline Waters	21	19	15	23
Andrew Carter	9	15	18	17
Wu Ngyuen	6	7	11	13
Hector Valdez	18	22	14	17

Name	Total Sales	Goal (Units)	Over or Under Goal
Joeline Waters	78	75	3
Andrew Carter	59	65	
Wu Ngyuen	37	65	
Hector Valdez	71	65	

Click

5 Test the Formula

Now change the values in the cells you referenced in the formula; the formula result changes automatically because the formula adds whichever values are in the cells.

E11		fx	=C11-D11			
	A	B	C	D	E	F	G

Auto Sales Contest

	Name	Week 1	Week 2	Week 3	Week 4
Joeline Waters	21	19	15	23
Andrew Carter	9	15	18	17
Wu Ngyuen	6	7	11	13
Hector Valdez	18	22	14	17

Name	Total Sales	Goal (Units)	Over or Under Goal
Joeline Waters	78	65	13
Andrew Carter	59	65	
Wu Ngyuen	37	65	
Hector Valdez	71	65	

Totaling a Large Range

To total a large range of cells on a worksheet without entering each cell reference into the formula separately, use the SUM function (a pre-programmed calculation). For example, if you want to sum the values in cells A1, A2, A3, A4, and A5, you could type **=A1+A2+A3+A4+A5**. Instead, use the SUM function: **=SUM(A1:A5)**. This formula tells Excel to sum all the cells between A1 and A5. (You learn more about functions in Task 16, "How to Enter Functions.")

Keeping Things in Order

Excel calculates a formula from left to right, performing the operations of multiplication and division before addition and subtraction. To have certain operations performed first, use parentheses to divide the formula appropriately. If you want to add **4+6** and then divide the result by **2**, for example, the formula **=4+6/2** gives the wrong answer (**7**), but the formula **=(4+6)/2** gives the right answer (**5**). Operations within parentheses are performed first.

Using Range Names

You can use range names in formulas. For example, if you gave cell C23 on the August worksheet the name **Aug_Total** and cell C23 on the July worksheet **July_Total**, and you wanted to calculate the percentage of growth from last month, you could type the formula **=(Aug_Total/July_Total)-1**. If **Aug_Total** equals 1000, and **July_Total** equals 800, the result would be **(1000/800)-1**, or **25%**.

How to Use AutoSum

A *function* is a built-in formula. You give the function the required arguments (variables), and it computes the result. For the SUM function, all you have to specify is the range you want to total. The **Standard** toolbar provides quick access to SUM, as well as some other commonly used functions such as AVERAGE (calculates average of a range), MIN (finds the minimum), MAX (finds the maximum), and COUNT (counts the items in a range). You will learn how to enter other functions in Task 16, "How to Enter Functions."

❶ Select a Location for the Result

Select the cell in which you want the result of the function to appear (usually at the end of a row or column of numbers).

	A	B	C	D	E	F
1	Household Budget					
2						
3		Budget	January	February	March	
4	Car Expense	$ 200.00	$ 432.00	$ 120.00	$ -	
5	Car Payment	$ 355.00	$ 355.00	$ 355.00	$ 355.00	
6	Groceries	$ 300.00	$ 334.00	$ 270.00	$ 290.00	
7	Child Care	$ 400.00	$ 400.00	$ 385.00	$ 450.00	
8	Utilities	$ 250.00	$ 244.00	$ 346.00	$ 327.00	
9	Mortgage	$ 968.00	$ 968.00	$ 968.00	$ 968.00	
10	Long Distance	$ 100.00	$ 123.00	$ 218.00	$ 97.00	
11	Internet	$ 55.00	$ 55.00	$ 55.00	$ 55.00	
12	Miscellaneous	$ 350.00	$ 327.00	$ 458.00	$ 597.00	
13		Totals				
14						
15	Average spent per month					
16						

Click

❷ Click AutoSum

On the **Standard** toolbar, click the **AutoSum** button.

❸ The SUM Formula Is Entered

The **AutoSum** button inserts the SUM function formula for you, and surrounds the cells being summed with a flashing border. A yellow ScreenTip lists the arguments used in the SUM function.

COUNTIF	▼ X ✓ *fx*	=SUM(C4:C12)			
	A	B	C	D	E	F
1	Household Budget					
2						
3		Budget	January	February	March	
4	Car Expense	$ 200.00	$ 432.00	$ 120.00	$ -	
5	Car Payment	$ 355.00	$ 355.00	$ 355.00	$ 355.00	
6	Groceries	$ 300.00	$ 334.00	$ 270.00	$ 290.00	
7	Child Care	$ 400.00	$ 400.00	$ 385.00	$ 450.00	
8	Utilities	$ 250.00	$ 244.00	$ 346.00	$ 327.00	
9	Mortgage	$ 968.00	$ 968.00	$ 968.00	$ 968.00	
10	Long Distance	$ 100.00	$ 123.00	$ 218.00	$ 97.00	
11	Internet	$ 55.00	$ 55.00	$ 55.00	$ 55.00	
12	Miscellaneous	$ 350.00	$ 327.00	$ 458.00	$ 597.00	
13		Totals	=SUM(C4:C12)			
14			SUM(number1, [number2], ...)			
15	Average spent per month					
16						

4 Complete the Entry

If the flashing border is surrounding all the cells you want to sum, press **Enter** to complete the formula. If the surrounded cells are wrong, drag to select the cells you want summed (the flashing border surrounds the cells you drag); then press **Enter**. The result is displayed in the cell.

C13	▼	f_x =SUM(C4:C12)			
	A	B	C	D	E	F

	A	B	C	D	E
1	Household Budget				
2					
3		Budget	January	February	March
4	Car Expense	$ 200.00	$ 432.00	$ 120.00	$ -
5	Car Payment	$ 355.00	$ 355.00	$ 355.00	$ 355.00
6	Groceries	$ 300.00	$ 334.00	$ 270.00	$ 290.00
7	Child Care	$ 400.00	$ 400.00	$ 385.00	$ 450.00
8	Utilities	$ 250.00	$ 244.00	$ 346.00	$ 327.00
9	Mortgage	$ 968.00	$ 968.00	$ 968.00	$ 968.00
10	Long Distance	$ 100.00	$ 123.00	$ 218.00	$ 97.00
11	Internet	$ 55.00	$ 55.00	$ 55.00	$ 55.00
12	Miscellaneous	$ 350.00	$ 327.00	$ 458.00	$ 597.00
13		Totals	$ 3,238.00		
14					
15	Average spent per month				
16					
17					

⬆

⎆Enter

5 Create an Average with AutoSum

You can use a drop-down menu of function options available through the **AutoSum** button to quickly insert functions. To create a function that calculates averages, select the cell in which you want the result to appear and then click the arrow on the **AutoSum** button. From the drop-down list of options, select **Average**.

Arial	▼	10	▼	B I U	Σ ▼	100%	▼
C15	▼	f_x			Sum		

	A	B	C			
1	Household Budget			Average		F
2				Count		
3		Budget	January	Feb Max		
4	Car Expense	$ 200.00	$ 432.00	$ 120.00 Min	$ -	
5	Car Payment	$ 355.00	$ 355.00	$ 355.00 More Functions...	$ 355.00	
6	Groceries	$ 300.00	$ 334.00	$ 270.00	$ 290.00	
7	Child Care	$ 400.00	$ 400.00	$ 385.00	$ 450.00	
8	Utilities	$ 250.00	$ 244.00	$ 346.00	$ 327.00	
9	Mortgage	$ 968.00	$ 968.00	$ 968.00	$ 968.00	
10	Long Distance	$ 100.00	$ 123.00	$ 218.00	$ 97.00	
11	Internet	$ 55.00	$ 55.00	$ 55.00	$ 55.00	
12	Miscellaneous	$ 350.00	$ 327.00	$ 458.00	$ 597.00	
13		Totals	$ 3,238.00	,175.00	$ 3,139.00	
14						
15	Average spent per month					
16						
17						

⬆ Click

6 Complete the Entry

A flashing border surrounds the range Excel thinks you want to use in this function. Drag to select another range if needed, and then press **Enter** to complete the entry. The result is displayed in the cell; the formula used to calculate that result appears in the **Formula** bar.

C15	▼	f_x =AVERAGE(C13:E13)			
	A	B	C	D	E	F

	A	B	C	D	E
1	Household Budget				
2					
3		Budget	January	February	March
4	Car Expense	$ 200.00	$ 432.00	$ 120.00	$ -
5	Car Payment	$ 355.00	$ 355.00	$ 355.00	$ 355.00
6	Groceries	$ 300.00	$ 334.00	$ 270.00	$ 290.00
7	Child Care	$ 400.00	$ 400.00	$ 385.00	$ 450.00
8	Utilities	$ 250.00	$ 244.00	$ 346.00	$ 327.00
9	Mortgage	$ 968.00	$ 968.00	$ 968.00	$ 968.00
10	Long Distance	$ 100.00	$ 123.00	$ 218.00	$ 97.00
11	Internet	$ 55.00	$ 55.00	$ 55.00	$ 55.00
12	Miscellaneous	$ 350.00	$ 327.00	$ 458.00	$ 597.00
13		Totals	$ 3,238.00	$ 3,175.00	$ 3,139.00
14					
15	Average spent per month	$ 3,184.00			
16					
17					

⬆

How-to Hint

Summing a Whole Table at Once

To AutoSum all the columns in a table at once, select all the cells in the row under the last row of data in the table and click the **AutoSum** button. Each column is summed in the blank cell below that column. To sum all the rows in a table at once, select all the cells in the column next to the table and click the **AutoSum** button. Each row is summed in the cell at the end of the row.

Summing More Than One Range

To sum the values in more than one range, click **AutoSum**, select the first range, press comma (**,**), and then select the next range. You can select as many ranges as you want, provided that you type commas between them.

How to Enter Functions

As you learned in previous tasks, a function is a built-in formula. A function saves you from spending time setting up the math yourself. Excel has over 300 functions available, so you're sure to find one for the type of mathematical calculation you want to perform. To use a function in a formula, type =, the function name, and the arguments for that function surrounded by parentheses, like this: =SUM(C4:C22). Separate each pair of arguments with a comma. When you type a function name, its arguments appear in a ScreenTip to help you enter them in the correct order. If you need more help, the **Insert Functions** dialog box is one click away.

❶ Click Insert Function Button

Click the cell in which you want to result of the function to appear. Then click the **Insert Function** button on the **Formula** bar. The **Insert Function** dialog box opens.

	A	B	C	D	E	F	G	H
1	Auto Sales Contest							
2								
3								
4		Name	Week 1	Week 2	Week 3	Week 4		
5		Joeline Waters	21	19	15	23		
6		Andrew Carter	9	15	18	17		
7		Wu Ngyuen	6	7	11	13		
8		Hector Valdez	18	22	14	17		
9								
10		Name	Total Sales	Goal (Units)	Over/Under Goal			
11		Joeline Waters	78	65				
12		Andrew Carter	59	65				
13		Wu Ngyuun	37	65				
14		Hector Valdez	71	65				
15								

Click

❷ Select a Function

The dialog box offers two ways to find a particular function: Type a description of what you want to calculate and click **Go**. Possible matches are listed in the **Select a function** pane. Alternatively, select a category from the drop-down list; the list of functions in the bottom pane adjusts to show appropriate matches. Scroll through the list and click a function; a description of the selected function appears at the bottom of the dialog box. When you have located the function you want, click **OK**.

Click

❸ Enter the First Argument

A **Function Arguments** dialog box opens, optimized for the function you selected in step 2. The steps in this task demonstrate the IF function. The IF function requires three arguments: a statement to be evaluated, the action to take if the statement proves true, and the action to take if the statement is false. Type or click cells to enter the arguments. (Drag the dialog box out of the way if necessary to select cells.)

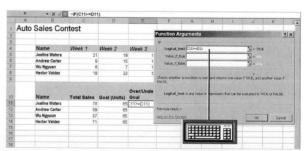

④ Enter Value if True

Click in the second argument box and type the value you want to appear if the test is true. I want the word Over to appear if the sales are equal or over the goal amount. Notice that the text must be contained in quotation marks: "Over".

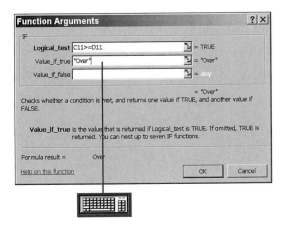

⑤ Enter Value if False

Click in the third argument box and type the value you want to appear if the test is false. I want the word Under to appear if the sales are under the goal amount. Notice that as you click in each argument text box, a description of that argument appears at the bottom of the dialog box.

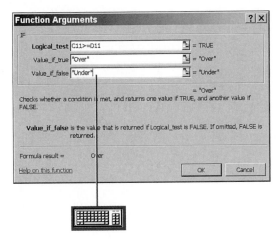

⑥ Complete the Formula

Click **OK** to close the **Function Arguments** dialog box and complete the formula. The formula result appears in the worksheet, and the formula itself, including the function, appears in the **Formula** bar.

How-to Hint

Logical Test

The logical test used by the IF function is basically a comparison between two values. You can compare two cells, or you can compare a cell to a value or formula result. Use operators such as > (greater than), < (less than), = (equal to), <> (not equal to), >= (greater than or equal to), and <= (less than or equal to) to make your comparisons.

Skipping the Dialog Boxes

If you're fairly familiar with a function, you don't have to use the dialog boxes shown here; you can simply type the function as you would any other formula. A ScreenTip appears below the result cell to remind you of any arguments you might have forgotten.

How to Use Absolute and Relative Cell Addresses

When you copy a formula to a new location, the formula is automatically adjusted using relative cell addresses. For example, if you copy the formula =C2+C3 from cell C4 to cell D4, the formula is changed to =D2+D3. The addresses are adjusted by one column because you copied the formula one column over. If you don't want a cell address to change (which is true when the address points to a value that the formula is required to use), use absolute cell addresses. To make an address absolute, precede it with a dollar sign ($), as in =$C$2+C3. If you copy this formula from cell C4 to cell D4, the formula changes to =$C$2+D3. The absolute address, $C$2, does not change.

❶ Enter a Relative Formula

To demonstrate the difference between relative and absolute references, we'll enter a formula that uses only relative addresses: =SUM(C7:F7).

G7		fx	=SUM(C7:F7)			

	A	B	C	D	E	F	G	H
1	Auto Sales Contest							
2								
3		Goal:	65					
4								
5								
6		Name	Week 1	Week 2	Week 3	Week 4	Totals	
7		Joeline Waters	21	19	15	23	78	
8		Andrew Carter	9	15	18	17		
9		Wu Ngyuen	6	7	11	13		
10		Hector Valdez	18	22	14	17		
11								
12								

❷ Copy the Formula

Copy the formula down the column using the AutoFill feature. The addresses used in the formula are adjusted to reflect the row number to which the formula was copied.

G10		fx	=SUM(C10:F10)			

	A	B	C	D	E	F	G	H
1	Auto Sales Contest							
2								
3		Goal:	65					
4								
5								
6		Name	Week 1	Week 2	Week 3	Week 4	Totals	
7		Joeline Waters	21	19	15	23	78	
8		Andrew Carter	9	15	18	17	59	
9		Wu Ngyuen	6	7	11	13	37	
10		Hector Valdez	18	22	14	17	71	
11								
12								

❸ Enter an Absolute Formula

Now we'll enter a formula that uses absolute addressing: =G7-$C$3. The absolute address $C$3 points to the sales goal value that all the formulas, regardless of which row they are in, must use. To enter the formula, type the first part of the formula (=G7-), click cell C3, and then press **F4**. Pressing **F4** makes the cell address to the left of the cursor absolute.

H7		fx	=G7-$C$3			

	A	B	C	D	E	F	G	H	I
1	Auto Sales Contest								
2									
3		Goal:	65						
4									
5									
6		Name	Week 1	Week 2	Week 3	Week 4	Totals	Under/Over Goal	
7		Joeline Waters	21	19	15	23	78	13	
8		Andrew Carter	9	15	18	17	59		
9		Wu Ngyuen	6	7	11	13	37		
10		Hector Valdez	18	22	14	17	71		
11									
12									

④ Copy the Formula

Use the **AutoFill** feature to copy the formula down the column again. This time, notice that the first address, G7, changes based on the row the formula is in. The second address, $C$3, does not change because it is absolute.

H10 ▾ ƒx =G10-$C$3

	A	B	C	D	E	F	G	H	I
1	Auto Sales Contest								
2									
3		Goal:	65						
4									
5								Under/Over	
6		Name	Week 1	Week 2	Week 3	Week 4	Totals	Goal	
7		Joeline Waters	21	19	15	23	78	13	
8		Andrew Carter	9	15	18	17	59	-6	
9		Wu Ngyuen	6	7	11	13	37	-28	
10		Hector Valdez	18	22	14	17	71	6	
11									
12									
13									

⑤ Enter a Mixed Formula

A *mixed reference* is one in which only the column or row number is absolute. This example uses a formula with a mixed reference. Type the first part of the formula (=C7 -), click cell C4, and press **F4** twice to make just the row number absolute: C$4.

C15 ▾ ƒx =C7-C$4

	A	B	C	D	E	F	G	H	I
1	Auto Sales Contest								
2									
3		Goal:	65						
4		Weekly Goal:	15		16	17	17		
5									
6		Name	Week 1	Week 2	Week 3	Week 4	Totals	Under/Over Goal	
7		Joeline Waters	21	19	15	23	78	13	
8		Andrew Carter	9	15	18	17	59	-6	
9		Wu Ngyuen	6	7	11	13	37	-28	
10		Hector Valdez	18	22	14	17	71	6	
11									
12									
13									
14		Under/Over Weekly Goal	Week 1	Week 2	Week 3	Week 4			
15		Joeline Waters	6						
16		Andrew Carter							
17		Wu Ngyuen							
18		Hector Valdez							
19									

⑥ AutoFill the Formula

Use the **AutoFill** feature to copy the formula down to row 18 and then across to column F. Notice that the mixed address changes to reflect the column to which it is copied, but not the row.

E17 ▾ ƒx =E9-E$4

	A	B	C	D	E	F	G	H	I
1	Auto Sales Contest								
2									
3		Goal:	65						
4		Weekly Goal:	15	16	17	17			
5									
6		Name	Week 1	Week 2	Week 3	Week 4	Totals	Under/Over Goal	
7		Joeline Waters	21	19	15	23	78	13	
8		Andrew Carter	9	15	18	17	59	-6	
9		Wu Ngyuen	6	7	11	13	37	-28	
10		Hector Valdez	18	22	14	17	71	6	
11									
12									
13									
14		Under/Over Weekly Goal	Week 1	Week 2	Week 3	Week 4			
15		Joeline Waters	6	3	-2	6			
16		Andrew Carter	-6	-1	1	0			
17		Wu Ngyuen	-9	-9	-6	-4			
18		Hector Valdez	3	6	-3	0			
19									
20									

How-to Hint

Editing References

To edit a reference in a formula, click in the **Formula** bar where you want to make your changes. Press **F4** to change the reference from relative, to absolute, to mixed. Press **Enter** when you're finished editing.

Referencing Other Sheets

You can reference cells from other worksheets in your workbook. Simply begin the formula, change to the other sheet when necessary, and click the cell you want. The address you enter will resemble this: Sheet2!B4. The sheet-name part of the address is absolute, even when the formula is copied to other sheets, but the cell address part of the formula is relative—unless you make it absolute or mixed.

How to Fix Formula Errors

Not all formulas are perfect, and when they aren't, Excel lets you know by displaying a green triangle in the upper-left corner of the formula's cell, along with an error message. For example, you might have entered an incorrect value or operator, the wrong cell reference, or function. The first thing to do when you see an error value is to recheck the formula and references used. For complex worksheets, it isn't always easy to see whether your formulas and data references are correct. Use Excel's auditing tools to help you find your mistakes. You can display tracer lines that locate *precedents* (cell references referred to in a formula) and *dependents* (cell references that are referenced in another cell, such as those used in a formula).

1 Display Formula Auditing Toolbar

When errors appear, one of your most powerful allies in correcting them is the **Formula Auditing** toolbar. Select **Tools**, **Formula Auditing**, **Show Formula Auditing Toolbar** to display it.

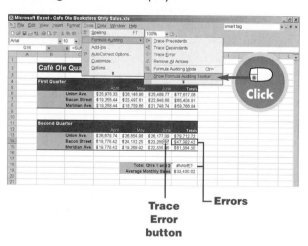

Trace
Error
button

Errors

2 Review Errors

To check each cell marked with an error triangle, click the **Error Checking** button in the **Formula Auditing** toolbar. Excel highlights the first cell with an error and provides you with options for fixing it.

3 Correct Error

This might or might not be an error. If this is a mistake, click **Copy Formula from Above**. You can change the formula yourself by clicking **Edit in Formula Bar**.

4 Correct Additional Errors

Excel highlights the next cell with an error. Select the option you want from the **Error Checking** dialog box; continue until all errors have been addressed. When it's through checking errors, Excel displays a message box; click **OK**.

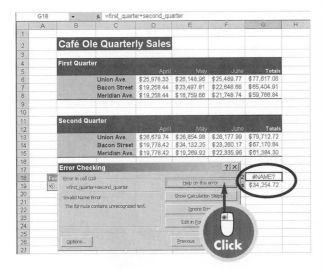

6 View the Trace

Excel displays trace arrows that point out the sources of the formula to help you track down the error. Here, I accidentally included the totals in column G in the ranges I used in the AVERAGE function! After locating your error, make the necessary corrections and turn off the trace arrows by clicking **Remove All Arrows**.

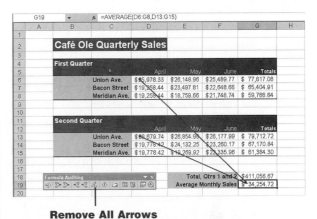

Remove All Arrows

5 Trace Precedents

Not all mistakes result in an error. If something doesn't look right, such as the average sales total shown here, you can trace the values used in the formula by displaying its precedents. Click the cell you want to evaluate and then click the **Trace Precedents** button. If necessary, click the **Trace Precedents** button again to trace the values for these cells.

Using the Trace Error Button

If a green triangle signals an error in a formula you've just typed, you can check it immediately by moving your pointer to the left of the cell to highlight the **Trace Error** button, clicking the down arrow that appears, and making a selection from the list of options.

Tracing Dependents

You can trace if and how the value in a cell is used in any formulas by clicking that cell and clicking the **Trace Dependents** button in the **Formula Auditing** toolbar.

Evaluating a Formula

To evaluate a formula, click the **Evaluate Formula** button on the **Formula Auditing** toolbar. A dialog box appears, allowing you to step through each portion of your formula. Click **Evaluate** to compute the underlined portion of the formula. Click **Evaluate** as many times as necessary.

How to Change Number Formats

Numeric values you enter into your worksheets are usually more than just numbers. They represent dollar values, dates, percentages, and other real values. By default, when you enter a number, it's displayed in **General** format, which is usually just the way you type it. But rather than typing $12.95, you can type just 12.95 and apply a number format to those characters, such as the **Currency** format. For example, the entry 5.05 can mean different things. If you apply the **Currency** format, the entry becomes $5.05; if you apply the **Percentage** format, the entry becomes 505%. In this task, you learn how to change the number format using toolbar buttons and the **Format Cells** dialog box.

1 Select the Cell or Range

Select the cell or range that contains numeric data for which you want to change the formatting.

2 Click Currency

To change a format to accounting format (which adds a $, rounds the number to two decimal places, and spaces the $ so that all the dollar signs in the column are aligned), click the **Currency Style** button on the **Formatting** toolbar.

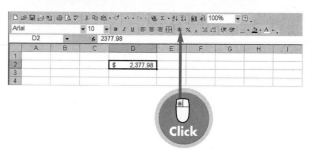

3 Click Percent

To change a format to percent format (which adds a % and changes the number from a fraction or integer to a percentage value), click the **Percent Style** button on the **Formatting** toolbar. (Remember that percent means hundredths, so 0.12 is displayed as 12%, but 12 is displayed as 1200%.)

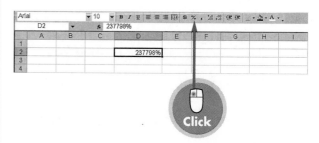

④ Click Comma

To apply comma format (which in the United States means to round the number to two decimal places and add a comma at each thousands mark), click the **Comma Style** button on the **Formatting** toolbar. To control the decimal point, you can also click the **Increase Decimal** or **Decrease Decimal** buttons on the **Formatting** toolbar.

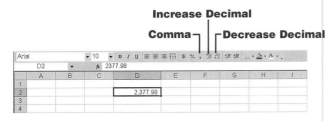

⑤ Use the Format Cells Dialog Box

To apply formats that aren't available from the **Formatting** toolbar, choose **Format**, **Cells** to open the **Format Cells** dialog box. Click the **Number** tab and choose a number format from the **Category** list. The value in the selected cell is displayed with that format in the **Sample** area.

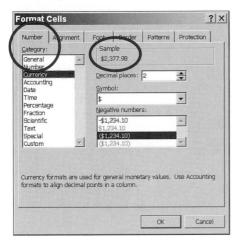

⑥ Set Format Options

Different formats in the **Format Cells** dialog box offer different options; select a **Category** and set the options for that format. A description of the selected category appears at the bottom of the dialog box. To close the dialog box and apply the new format, click **OK**.

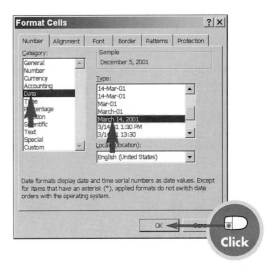

Copying Formatting

If you apply number formatting to a range of data and then add data in a cell adjacent to this range, Excel automatically applies the selected format to the new data.

Currency Isn't Really Currency

Although the toolbar button is named **Currency Style**, it doesn't apply the **Currency** format—it applies the **Accounting** format. In this format, dollar signs. To apply true **Currency** formatting (in which the dollar sign appears immediately to the left of the number, regardless of how wide the column is), use the **Format Cells** dialog box.

Removing Formatting

To remove all formatting (including number formats), without erasing the data from a cell, select the cell or range and then choose **Edit**, **Clear**, **Formats**.

How to Adjust the Cell Alignment

By default, Excel automatically aligns your entries based on their data type. Text entries always line up to the left of the cells. Number entries always align to the right. Both text and numbers align vertically at the bottom of the cells, but you can change the alignment of any entry, both horizontally and vertically. With Excel's alignment commands, you can angle the text, or you can rotate it to read from top to bottom instead of from left to right. You can also center text within several adjacent cells.

1 **Quick Cell Alignment**

For quick horizontal alignment changes, use the alignment buttons on the **Formatting** toolbar. Select the cell or range you want to align and click the appropriate button.

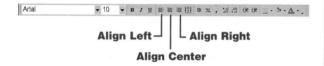

Align Left — | — Align Right
Align Center

2 **Center a Title Over a Range**

If you want to center text in a single row over a range of cells, select the entire range of blank cells you want to center the text within, including the cell containing the text you want centered.

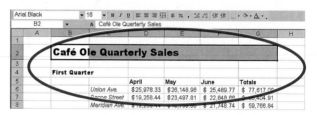

3 **Click the Merge and Center Button**

Click the **Merge** and **Center** button on the **Formatting** toolbar. Excel centers the title over the range, and maintains the center formatting, even if the cells are widened later on.

	A	B	C	D	E	F	G	H
1								
2			Café Ole Quarterly Sales					
3								
4		First Quarter						
5				April	May	June	Totals	
6			Union Ave.	$25,978.33	$26,148.96	$ 25,489.77	$ 77,617.06	
7			Bacon Street	$19,258.44	$23,497.81	$ 22,648.66	$ 65,404.91	
8			Meridian Ave.	$19,258.44	$18,759.66	$ 21,748.74	$ 59,766.84	
9								

Click

4 Unmerge the Text if Needed

If you want to remove the merge and center alignment, select the merged cell and click **Merge and Center** on the **Formatting** toolbar again.

5 Change Orientation

If you want to change the vertical alignment or flip or rotate your entry, use Excel's **Format Cells** dialog box. Choose **Format**, **Cells** to open the dialog box.

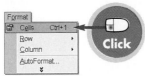

6 Select an Alignment or Orientation

On the **Alignment** tab, use the **Vertical** alignment drop-down list to align your entry between the top and bottom cell borders. Use the **Horizontal** list to align the entry between the left and right borders. To rotate text, click in the right **Orientation** pane to select a degree of rotation, or type one in the **Degrees** box. To rotate text to read from top to bottom, click the left **Orientation** pane. Click **OK**.

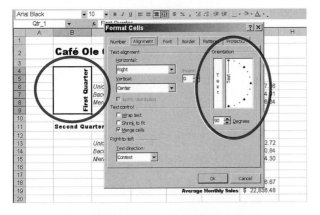

What About Fonts and Sizes?

You can format Excel data in the same way you format text in Word. You can use the **Font** and **Font Size** drop-down lists on the **Formatting** toolbar to change the font and size of your text. You also can apply bold, italic, or underline by clicking the appropriate toolbar button. To apply all these formatting options at once, choose **Format**, **Cells** to open the **Format Cells** dialog box; click the **Font** tab and select all your font options there.

Formatting with Indents

You can indent text within a cell using the **Increase Indent** button on the **Formatting** toolbar. This action moves the data away from the left or right border (or both), depending on the cell's alignment option.

Using Text Wrap

If you have a lot of text you're trying to fit into a single cell, consider using the **Wrap** text option in the **Alignment** tab in the **Format Cells** dialog box. When enabled, this option wraps text to the next line in the cell without expanding the cell width. Instead, the height of the cell is adjusted to display the wrapped text.

How to Work with Borders and Patterns

The gridlines you see in your Excel worksheets are a little misleading. Normally, these lines do not print, and if you do print them, they might appear faint. To give your cells well-defined lines, use Excel's **Border** options. You can choose to add a border to a single cell or to an entire range. You can specify a border on only one side of a cell or border the entire cell. If borders don't set off your cells to your satisfaction, try adding a background pattern, such as a color blend, a pattern effect, or a solid color fill. Keep in mind, however, that a background that's too busy will make it difficult for the reader to see your data.

1 Open the Format Cells Dialog Box

Select the cell or range to which you want to add a border or pattern, Choose **Format**, **Cells** to open the **Format Cells** dialog box.

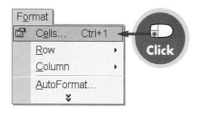

2 Set a Line Style

Click the **Border** tab. From the **Style** list, choose a border style. Use the **Color** drop-down list to select a border color.

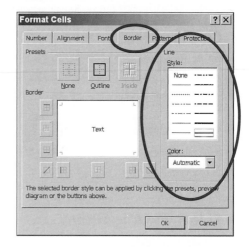

3 Use the Border Presets

With the line style set, select one of the border **Presets** that appear at the top of the tab. To set a border around the outer edges of the selected cell or range, click the **Outline** preset. To set gridlines within the range's inner cells, click **Inside**.

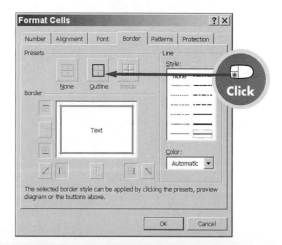

④ Set a Custom Border

To customize your border, use the **Border** buttons to select which sides of the selected cells you want to border. Click a button to add a border to that position; refer to the preview to see the results. Continue adding borders to the sides as needed.

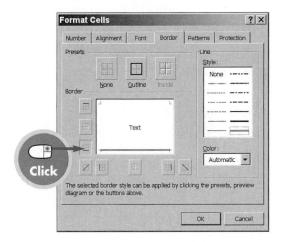

⑤ Use the Patterns Tab

To apply a pattern to the selected cells, click the **Patterns** tab. To fill the selection with a solid color, select a color from the **Color** palette. To blend two colors in a pattern, click the **Pattern** drop-down list button and select a second color. Open the list again to select a pattern to apply over the colors. Look in the **Sample** area to see the results of your choices.

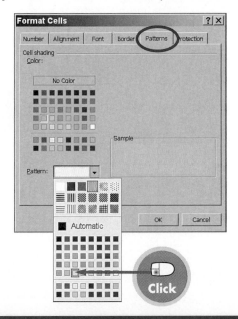

⑥ Apply the Formatting Selections

Click **OK** to close the **Format Cells** dialog box and apply the new settings to your worksheet, as shown here.

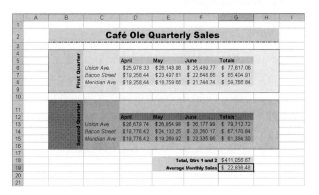

How-to Hint

Printing Gridlines

By default, Excel's gridlines don't print. To turn them on so that they do print, choose **File**, **Page Setup**. In the **Page Setup** dialog box, click the **Sheet** tab; in the **Print** area, enable the **Gridlines** check box and click **OK**. Now print the worksheet to see how your gridlines look.

Using the Formatting Buttons

To add a quick border to any cell or cells, select the cells, click the drop-down arrow next to the **Borders** button on the **Formatting** toolbar, and select a border style. To add color to your cell background, click the drop-down button next to the **Fill Color** button and choose a color from the palette. If you want to change the font color, click the drop-down button next to the **Font Color** button and choose another color.

How to Copy Cell Formatting

If you have applied several formatting attributes (such as font, size, color, and borders) to a cell or range of cells and then later decide you want to apply the same formatting to another range, you don't have to apply those formats one by one to the new location. Instead, you can use Excel's **Format Painter** button to take all the formats from the original range and "paint" them across the new range.

1 Click Format Painter

Select the cell or range that has the formatting you want to copy. Then click the **Format Painter** button in the **Standard** toolbar.

2 Mouse Pointer Changes

The mouse pointer changes to a paintbrush pointer.

3 Drag to Copy Formatting

Drag the paintbrush pointer across the range where you want to paint the formatting. Release the mouse. The formatting is painted to the range of cells.

4 Double-Click Format Painter

To copy formatting from one cell or range to multiple cells or ranges, select the cell or range whose formatting you want to copy, and then double-click the **Format Painter** button.

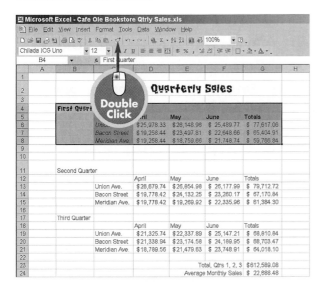

5 Drag Over the Ranges

Drag the paintbrush pointer over the first range to which you want to copy the formatting. Drag over additional ranges or click cells to copy the formatting there as well.

6 Turn Off Format Painter

After you're done copying the formatting, click the **Format Painter** button again to turn it off.

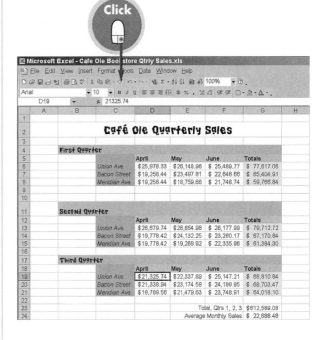

How-to Hint

Copying Column Widths

To copy the column width from one column to another, click the heading of the column whose width you want to copy and click the **Format Painter** button. Then drag across the column headings to which you want to copy that width.

Using AutoFormat

Don't like the pressure of coming up with formatting yourself? Use Excel's AutoFormat feature to format your worksheets automatically, as explained in Task 23, "How to AutoFormat a Range."

How to AutoFormat a Range

If formatting worksheets isn't your cup of tea, you will be happy to learn that Excel comes with predesigned formats you can apply to your worksheet data. The **AutoFormat** feature provides you with 16 table formats you can use to make your worksheet data look more presentable. Experiment with each format to see how it affects your data's presentation.

1 Select the Range

Select the range containing the data you want to format or click anywhere inside a range that is bordered by blank cells. For example, if you click one of your data cells, Excel will select the data, column, and row labels (but not the worksheet title) automatically.

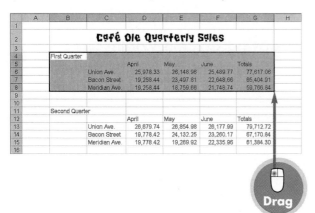

2 Open the AutoFormat Dialog Box

Choose **Format**, **AutoFormat** to open the **AutoFormat** dialog box.

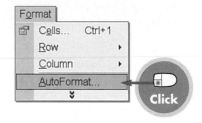

3 Choose a Table Format

Choose the format style you want to use. Click the scroll arrow buttons to move up and down the list. When you find a format you like, click it in the list box.

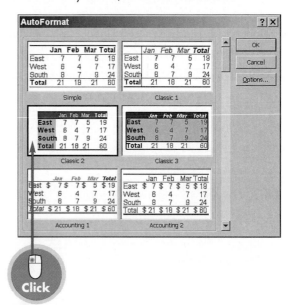

4 View Your Options

To exclude certain elements from the format set, click the **Options** button. The **AutoFormat** dialog box expands to include check boxes for options you might want to experiment with to fine-tune the format.

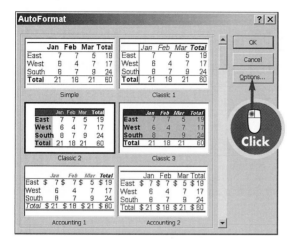

5 Turn Off Formatting Elements

Select or deselect the format options you want to turn on or off. The dialog box updates to show you the effects of enabling or disabling these options. When you are pleased with the customized formatting, click **OK** to close the dialog box.

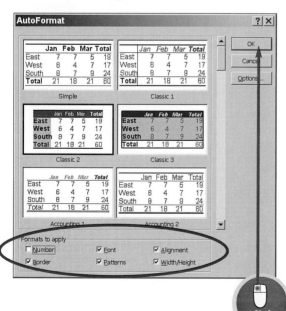

6 View the Results

The formatting is automatically applied to the selected cell or range. If needed, use the **Format Painter** button to copy the formats to additional ranges as we've done here. Note that the AutoFormatting you apply will overwrite any existing formatting the cells might already have.

	A	B	C	D	E	F	G	H
1								
2			Café Ole Quarterly Sales					
3								
4		First Quarter						
5				April	May	June	Totals	
6			Union Ave.	25,978.33	26,148.96	25,489.77	77,617.06	
7			Bacon Street	19,258.44	23,497.81	22,648.66	65,404.91	
8			Meridian Ave.	19,258.44	18,759.66	21,748.74	59,766.84	
9								
10								
11		Second Quarter						
12				April	May	June	Totals	
13			Union Ave.	26,679.74	26,854.98	26,177.99	79,712.72	
14			Bacon Street	19,778.42	24,132.25	23,260.17	67,170.84	
15			Meridian Ave.	19,778.42	19,269.92	22,335.96	61,384.30	
16								
17								
18		Third Quarter						
19				April	May	June	Totals	
20			Union Ave.	21,325.74	22,337.89	25,147.21	68,810.84	
21			Bacon Street	21,338.94	23,174.58	24,189.95	68,703.47	
22			Meridian Ave.	18,789.56	21,479.63	23,748.91	64,018.10	
23						Total, Qtrs 1, 2, 3	$612,589.08	
24						Average Monthly Sales	$ 22,688.48	
25								

How to Add a Comment

If you share your Excel workbooks with other people, you might want to add comments to the data from time to time, to explain a particular figure or to request that a change be made. Comments are not visible in a cell; instead, small red triangles mark the cells that contain comments. You can use the mouse pointer to display a comment, or you can display all comments in one step. You can print comments along with worksheet data when that kind of documentation is needed.

❶ Select a Cell

Select the cell to which you want to add a comment.

❷ Insert a Comment

Open the **Insert** menu and select **Comment**. A yellow box appears next to the cell you selected.

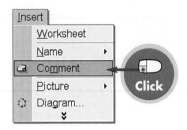

❸ Type the Comment Text

Type your comment into the yellow box.

④ Click Outside the Box

When you're through typing, click outside the comment box. The comment disappears, but a red triangle in the upper-right of the cell you selected in step 1 marks the presence of the comment.

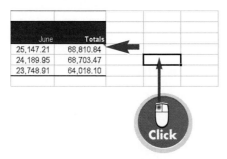

⑤ View a Comment

To view a comment, rest the mouse pointer over the cell containing the red triangle. The yellow box and its comment pop up for viewing.

⑥ View All Comments

To view all the comments that have been added to the worksheet at one time, choose **View**, **Comments**.

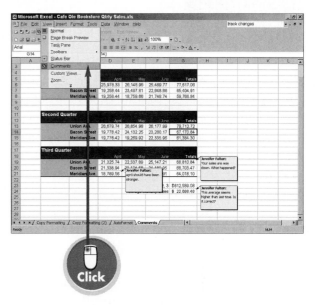

How-to Hint

Removing a Comment

To remove a comment, right-click the cell that contains the comment and choose **Delete Comment** from the context menu.

Editing a Comment

To edit a comment or to add a reply to a comment, right-click the cell that contains the comment and choose **Edit Comment** from the context menu. Make the changes or type your reply below the original comment; click outside the yellow comment box when you're done.

Printing Comments

Comments do not normally print with a worksheet. If you want a printed record of the comments, choose **File**, **Page Setup** to open the **Page Setup** dialog box. On the **Sheet** tab, select a printing option from the **Comments** drop-down list and click **OK**.

How to Track Changes

If you plan on sharing a workbook with a group of people, allowing each person to make changes (whether at the same time or one at a time), you might want a neat way of not only tracking the changes they make, but also of quickly reviewing and accepting or rejecting each change. It sounds like a big job, but Excel makes it easy to do.

1 Turn Track Changes On

Open the **Tools** menu and select **Track Changes**, **Highlight Changes**. The **Highlight Changes** dialog box opens.

2 Select Options

Enable the **Track changes while editing** option. Disable the **Highlight changes on screen** option if you don't want to see the colored changes while you work. Click **OK** to apply the change to the workbook.

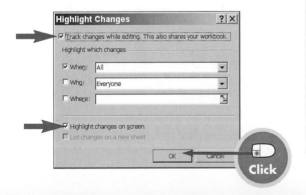

3 Make Changes

Make whatever changes you want to the worksheet; changed cells are marked with a triangle of a special color. Each person who makes changes to the worksheet has her changes marked in a different color. (Every Excel program has one user, who is listed on the **General** tab of the **Options** dialog box. If two people make changes using the same computer—without changing the username between users—their changes will be displayed in the same color.)

	A	B	C	D	E	F
1						
2	**Alan's Hardware - Inventory**					
3						
4	Product ID	Product Name	Price	Quantity on Hand	Quantity on Order	
5	3255-A3	Circular saw	$85.95	22	25	
6	3459-A1	Coping saw	$17.95	3	25	
7	3490-A4	Fertilizer, 12/12/12	$17.95	115	100	
8	3490-A3	Fertilizer, 32/10/0	$12.95	123	100	
9	3280-A2	Folding bench	$32.95	17	10	
10	2959-A3	Folding Ladder, 18'	$325.97	3	10	
11	3219-A1	Hammer	$15.75	89	25	
12	2959-A2	Ladder, 12'	$198.75	7	10	
13	2959-A1	Ladder, 6'	$111.95	4	10	
14	1290-A1	Laminate shelf W 6'	$11.25	47	100	
15	1290-A2	Laminate shelving W 12'	$21.95	57	100	
16	3145-A3	Lawn mower	$229.87	6	0	
17	3146-A3	Lawn mower, riding	$625.75	4	0	
18	2140-A3	Nails, 2" Steel	$2.15	42	200	
19	2140-A2	Nails, 3" Steel	$2.50	2	200	
20	2340-A1	Nails, 3.5" Steel	$2.25	2	100	
21	2340-A2	Nails, 4" Steel	$2.25	2	100	
22	2350-A2	Nails, 5" Steel	$3.00	4	25	
23	2350-A1	Nails, 6" Steel	$3.15	24	25	
24	3255-A2	Saw	$21.95	55	0	
25	3219-A2	Screw Driver Set	$9.95	26	150	
26	2650-A2	Screws, 2.5"	$2.95	2	25	
27	2650-A4	Screws, 3"	$3.55	12	25	

4 Review Changes

After all the changes have been made, you can review them one by one by choosing **Tools**, **Track Changes**, **Accept or Reject Changes**. If prompted, click **OK** to save the workbook before beginning the review process.

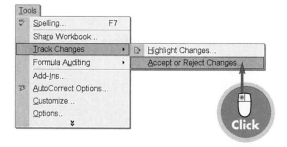

5 Select the Changes to Review

Choose the timeframe for the changes you want to review from the **When** list. Select the person whose changes you want to review from the **Who** list. Select the area of the workbook you want to review from the **Where** list. Click **OK** to begin reviewing the changes that match the criteria you have specified.

6 Reject or Accept Each Change

Excel highlights each change, one at a time. Click **Accept** to accept the highlighted change or **Reject** to undo the change. At any time, you can click **Accept All** or **Reject All** to accept or reject the rest of the changes without reviewing them individually.

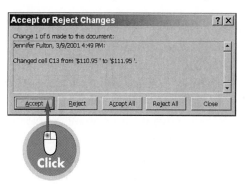

How-to Hint

Turning Off Track Changes

If, after you review changes, you continue to make more changes, the new changes will be highlighted—until you turn off the **Track Changes** feature by choosing **Tools**, **Highlight**, **Track Changes**. Disable the **Highlight** changes while editing option and click **OK**. When the confirmation box appears, click **Yes**.

What's Not Tracked

Some changes are not tracked by Excel, including formatting changes, inserted/deleted worksheets, new/edited comments, hidden/unhidden rows or columns, and cells that change because a value is changed in another cell.

History Worksheet

You can create a separate worksheet that lists the changes made to the workbook by choosing **Tools**, **Highlight**, **Track Changes**. Enable the **List changes on a new sheet** option and click **OK**.

How to Create a Chart with Chart Wizard

A chart turns boring numbers into an instantly accessible, persuasive visual presentation. This task explains how to create charts from your worksheet data. The **Chart Wizard** builds the chart for you as you make selections along the way. After the chart is built, you can resize it, rearrange it, recolor it, and personalize it so that it doesn't resemble every other Excel chart in the computer world. Chart data is organized by series. A series is a group of related cells (such as one row of data, or one column of data). Each series is assigned its own color on the chart. In the worksheet shown here, you could group the data by month, with each month assigned a unique color; you could also group the data by store.

① Select Data

Start by selecting the range of data you want to chart. Include headings and labels, but don't include subtotals or totals. Here you see the range C8:F11 selected. On the **Standard** toolbar, click the **Chart Wizard** button. The first of the series of **Chart Wizard** dialog boxes opens.

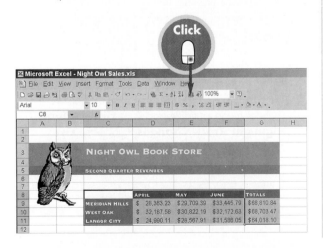

② Select a Chart Type

Select the **Chart** type and **Chart** subtype you want. Click **Next**.

③ Check the Data Range

Click each of the two **Series in** option buttons to see which layout is best. Click **Next**.

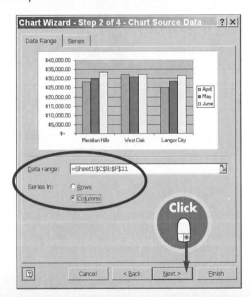

4 Set Chart Features

Click each tab and select the options you want for your chart. For example, enter a chart title on the **Titles** tab. Reposition or turn off the legend on the **Legend** tab, add labels to identify data on the **Data Labels** tab, and append a data table to the bottom of the chart on the **Data Table** tab. Click **Next**.

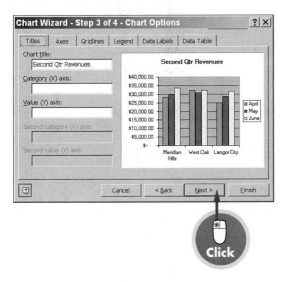

5 Choose a Location

Choose a location for the chart. The **As new sheet** option creates a separate chart sheet (similar to a worksheet, but it holds only a big chart), called CHART 1 (or whatever name you enter). The **As object in** option creates an embedded chart object on the worksheet you select from the **As object in** drop-down list. Click **Finish**.

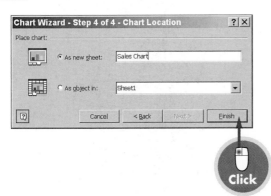

6 View the Chart

Depending on the option you chose in step 5, the chart appears in your worksheet or as a separate sheet in the workbook (as shown here). Notice that the **Chart** toolbar appears so that you can make changes to the chart as necessary.

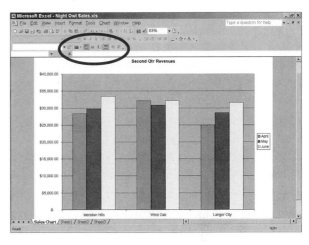

How-to Hint

Finishing Fast

To create a chart quickly using all the default chart settings, click **Finish** in the very first **Chart Wizard** dialog box.

Previewing Your Chart

To preview how your chart will appear, click the **Press and hold to view sample** button in the very first **Chart Wizard** dialog box. If you don't like the chart that appears, you can select another chart type right then and there.

Noncontiguous Ranges

The data you select for a chart does not have to be contiguous (adjacent to each other). To select noncontiguous ranges, select the first range, press **Ctrl**, and then select additional ranges.

How to Move and Resize Charts

If you created a chart as an embedded object on a worksheet (rather than on its own chart sheet), it probably won't be in the exact location you want it to be or the right size. For example, the chart might cover some of the existing data in the worksheet. You can move the chart out of the way and resize it to fit wherever you prefer. When you select a chart or any other graphic object, the object is surrounded by selection handles. You can use these handles to resize the object. When moving and resizing charts, you must click and hold the left mouse button and drag to move or resize. You learn how to accomplish both actions in this task.

1 Select the Chart

Start by selecting the chart you want to move or resize. Be sure that you click a blank area of the chart, or you might end up selecting an individual chart element. As soon as you click on the chart to select it, the chart is surrounded by tiny black boxes, called selection handles.

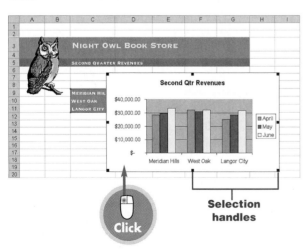

Selection handles

2 Move the Chart

To move the chart, hold down the left mouse button and drag the chart to a new location on the worksheet. As you drag, the outline of the chart is visible.

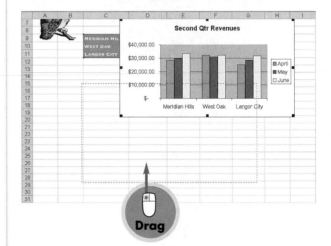

Drag

3 Drop the Chart

When the chart is at the location you want, release the mouse button to drop it in its new location.

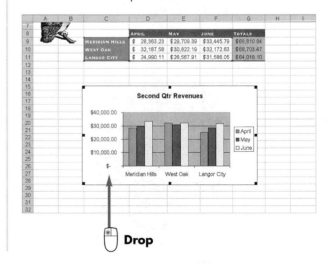

Drop

4 Change the Width or Height

To resize a chart, drag the selection handles. To change either the width or height of the chart, drag one of the side handles. Drag outward to make the chart bigger; drag inward to make the chart smaller.

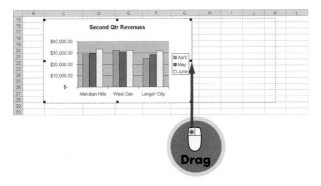

6 Release the Mouse Button

As you drag to resize the chart, an outline of the chart appears to guide you in your resizing efforts. When the chart is the size you want, release the mouse button. Click outside the chart to deselect it.

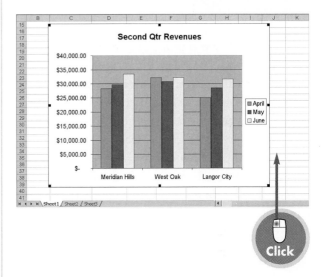

5 Change the Width and Height

To resize two sides at once (that is, to change the width and height), click and drag a corner selection handle. As you drag, both sides of the chart are resized.

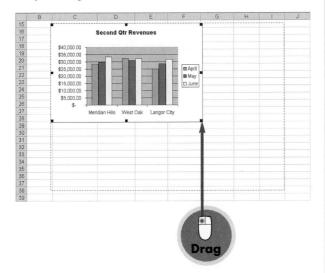

How-to Hint

Perfect Resizing

Press and hold the **Shift** key while dragging a corner of the chart object to resize the chart while maintaining its original proportions.

Changing Any Object

You can use these same techniques to resize or move any chart object. For example, you can drag to move the title or legend, or drag the selection handles to resize the plot area.

Deleting a Chart

To delete a chart from your worksheet, select it and press the **Delete** key.

Relocating a Chart

To move a chart from a chart sheet to a worksheet or vice versa, right-click the chart and select **Location** from the context menu; in the dialog box that opens, choose the location you prefer and click **OK**.

How to Change the Chart Type

When you create a chart, you have many options for the chart type. Standard chart types use columns or bars, lines and points, or a sliced-up pie. Your best bet is to probably stick to standard chart types. If you use a chart type that your audience isn't used to seeing, they might have difficulty deciphering it, and the data might lose its impact. After you have created a chart, you can easily change the chart type without having to re-create the chart, so you can try out different chart types to see which you like best.

1 Select the Chart

Click the chart to select it. If the chart is on a chart sheet, it is automatically selected when you click its sheet tab.

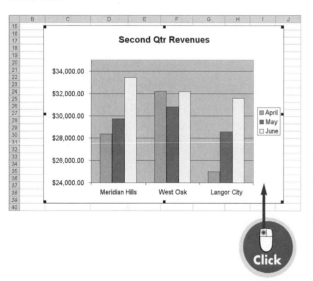

2 Click the Chart Type Button

On the **Chart** toolbar, click the down arrow on the **Chart Type** button. A drop-down list of chart types appears. Click the icon for the chart type you want to apply to the selected chart.

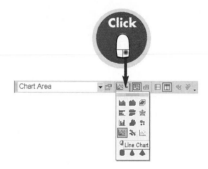

3 The New Chart Type Is Applied

The chart type changes to the type you select. Here you see the same column chart from step 1 changed to a line chart.

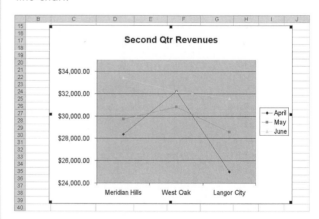

4. Use the Chart Type Command

You can also change the type of chart using the menus: Select the chart and choose **Chart**, **Chart Type**. From the **Chart Type** dialog box, select a **Chart** type and **Chart** subtype. To preview the chart, click and hold the **Click and Hold to View Sample** button (shown is the same chart changed to a 3D bar chart). When you find the chart type you want, click **OK**.

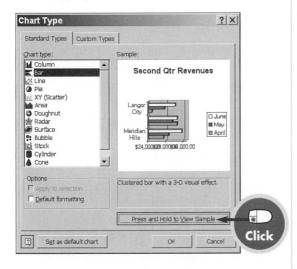

5. Change the Markers for a Data Series

To change the chart type for a single series in a multi-series chart, right-click one of the data markers (a data marker is one column, one row, one line, one pie slice, and so on) in the series and choose **Chart Type** from the context menu. The **Chart Type** dialog box opens.

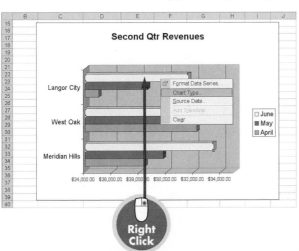

6. Select a Different Marker Type

Choose a new chart type for the selected series and click **OK** to close the dialog box and apply the change. Here you see that one series in the bar chart (June sales) has been changed to a pie chart type.

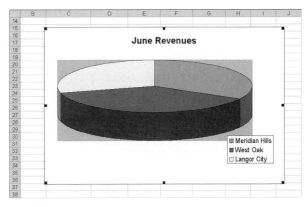

How-to Hint

Changing Colors

To change the color of any element in the chart (data series, gridlines, axes, plot area, chart background, and so on), first click the element to select it. Click the down arrow on the **Fill Color** button on the **Formatting** toolbar and select a different color.

Changing Font Size

When you resize a chart, the axis and title characters might be too big or too small for the chart's new size. To change the font size of any element in a chart (such as the chart title), click that element; to change the entire chart, click the chart. Select a new font size from the **Font Size** box on the **Formatting** toolbar.

How to Work with Chart and Axis Titles

You don't have to spend a lot of time deciding on titles for your chart when you first create it because you can add, change, move, and delete titles at any time. For example, you might decide that your chart needs a nice title centered above the chart data, or perhaps you want to rename the axes. You can easily make changes to the various chart elements until the chart looks just the way you want.

1 Move a Title

To ove a title, click to select it and then drag it to a new location.

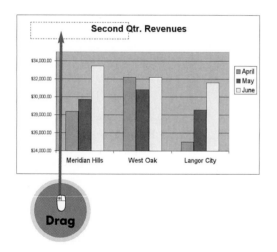

2 Change a Title's Text

To change the text of a title, click the title to select it; then click the text. The mouse pointer becomes a cursor. Drag to select the characters you want to change or delete, or click to place the insertion point within the title, and type the new characters. Press **Enter** to create a two-line title. Click anywhere outside the title when you're finished with your edits.

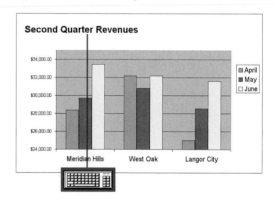

3 Delete a Title

To delete a title, click the title to select it, and then press **Delete**. You can also right-click the title and choose **Clear** from the context menu.

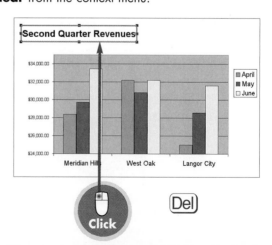

4 Add a Title

To add a new chart or axis title, choose **Chart, Chart Options** to open the **Chart Options** dialog box. On the **Titles** tab, type the title or titles you want to insert and click **OK** to add them to your chart.

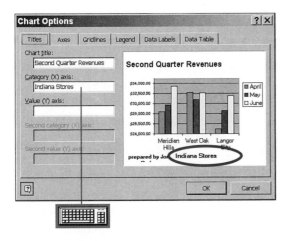

5 Add More Text

To add additional text to the chart, select the chart and start typing in your text. As you type, the text appears in the **Formula** bar. Press **Enter**, and a text box containing the text you just typed appears on the chart. Move the text box to the location you choose by dragging it there.

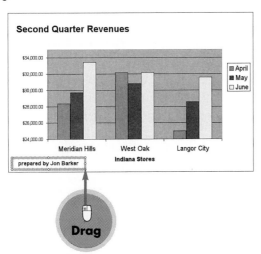

6 Add Colors

To add a background fill or font color to either a title or a text box, select that object and choose colors from the **Fill Color** and **Font Color** buttons on the **Formatting** toolbar.

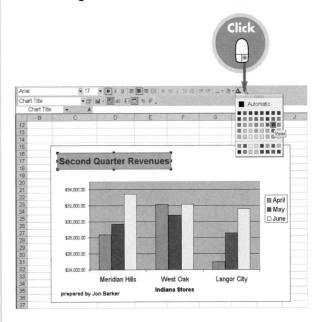

7 Change the Font or Font Size

To change the font or font size in either a title or a text box, select the text box and then select the characters you want to change. Make changes in the **Font** and **Font Size** boxes on the **Formatting** toolbar.

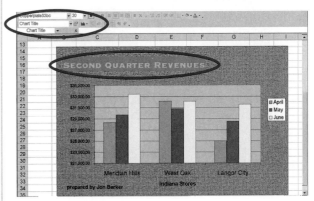

How to Change the Chart Data

If you delete a column or row of data from a chart's source data table, the chart adjusts automatically. Nevertheless, if you add data to the source table (for example, if you add another month's sales figures), you must add the new data to the chart manually. If you have already created a highly formatted chart, and you want to use that chart to display a different source data table (instead of creating a new chart), you can change the chart's source data range in one of several ways.

1 Select the Source Range

Click the chart to select it. A colored border surrounds the source data.

2 Drag the Border

Click and drag the corner handle of the colored border to expand (or reduce) the source data range. For example, in this figure, I'm expanding the data range to include the first quarter sales results from Carver City.

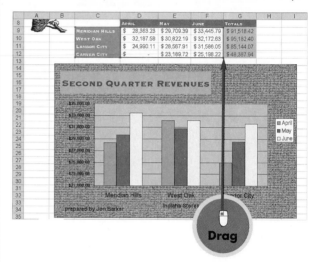

3 Release the Mouse Button

As soon as you release the mouse button, the source data range is redrawn, and the chart now reflects the new data. Notice that the colored border now surrounds a larger data range than it did in step 1.

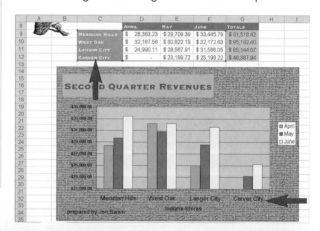

4 Use the Add Data Command

Another method of adding new data to the chart is to use the **Add Data** command. Choose **Chart**, **Add Data** to open the **Add Data** dialog box.

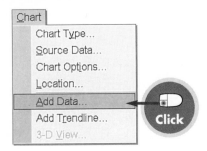

5 Select the New Data

With the **Add Data** dialog box open, highlight the data in the worksheet that you want to add to the chart. (You can drag the **Add Data** dialog box out of the way if you need to; just click and drag its title bar.) After you select the data you want to add to the chart, its range is inserted into the **Range** text box in the **Add Data** dialog box.

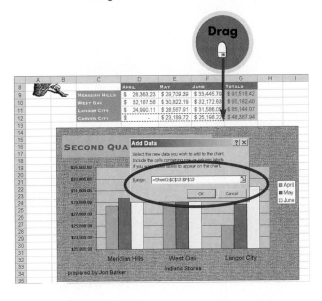

6 Add the Data

Click **OK** to close the **Add Data** dialog box and add the new data to your chart.

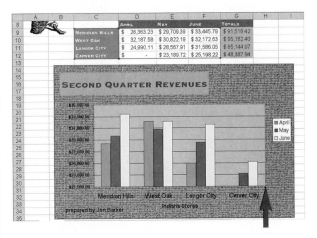

How-to Hint

Changes to the Source Data

You can make changes to the source data in your worksheet, and the changes are immediately reflected in the chart.

Changing the Source Data Range

If the range you originally selected for the chart is wrong, you can change it by reselecting it. Choose **Chart**, **Source Data** to open the **Source Data** dialog box. Type the new data range in the **Data Range** text box and click **OK**.

Printing Charts

To print only your chart and not the rest of the worksheet, first select the chart and then choose **File**, **Print**. In the **Print** dialog box, make sure that the **Selected Chart** option is selected and click **OK**.

① How to Use the AutoContent Wizard 602

② How to Start a New Presentation Based on a
Design Template 604

③ How to Build a Presentation from Scratch 606

④ How to Use PowerPoint's View Modes 608

⑤ How to Understand Slide Elements 610

⑥ How to Add and Edit Slide Text 612

⑦ How to Format and Align Slide Text 614

⑧ How to Add New Text Boxes 616

⑨ How to Add an Illustration to a Slide 618

⑩ How to Add a Chart to a Slide 620

⑪ How to Insert a Table in a Slide 622

⑫ How to Change the Slide Layout 624

⑬ How to Change the Slide Background 626

⑭ How to Insert and Delete Slides 628

⑮ How to Reorganize Slides 630

⑯ How to Define the Slide Transition 632

⑰ How to Add Animation Effects 634

⑱ How to Run the Slide Show 636

⑲ How to Create Speaker Notes and Handouts 638

⑳ How to Use Pack and Go 640

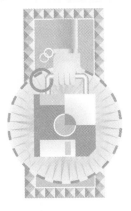

25

Creating Presentations with PowerPoint

PowerPoint is a presentation program designed to help you create visual presentations and slide shows for an audience, whether it's one person or a roomful of people. With PowerPoint, you can create and combine slides into a visual presentation that easily communicates your message with style and pizzazz.

You can create professional, self-running, or interactive slide shows to give a training presentation. You can present the quarterly sales review as a slide show to the sales staff, or present a new budget to your local civic organization. With PowerPoint, not only can you create visual presentations for any purpose, but you can also create speaker notes and audience handouts to go along with them.

In the tasks in this part, you will learn about PowerPoint's basic features, including how to begin creating your first slide show presentation, and how to use PowerPoint's specialized tools for adding text and graphics.

How to Use the AutoContent Wizard

The easiest way to create a new presentation is to use the AutoContent Wizard. This PowerPoint wizard walks you through each step in designing and creating a slide presentation. You can select a type of presentation, and PowerPoint builds an outline for it. It's up to you to fill in the text and choose graphics. AutoContent Wizard taps into the many presentation templates available. Presentation templates provide a color scheme, formatting, and a basic outline for the text of the slide.

① Start the AutoContent Wizard

From the **New Presentation** task pane, click the **From AutoContent Wizard** option link. If the task pane isn't onscreen, open the **File** menu and select **New**; PowerPoint displays the task pane again.

② Click Next

When the first **AutoContent Wizard** dialog box appears, click **Next** to begin.

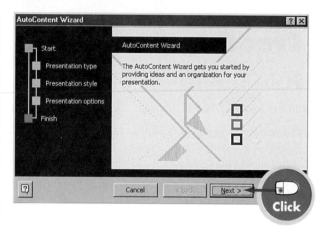

③ Choose a Presentation Type

From the next dialog box, click the button that best represents the type of presentation you want to build. For example, if you click the **Sales/Marketing** button, the list box displays several types of presentations geared toward this topic. Select a presentation type and click **Next**. (To see all the available presentation types, click the **All** button.)

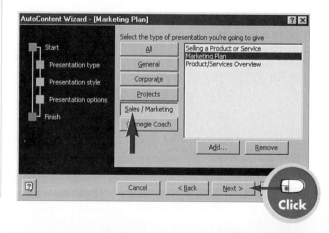

4 Choose a Method

Choose the method that best describes how you're going to give your presentation. For example, if you are giving the presentation on a computer, choose the **On-screen presentation** option; if you are using overhead transparencies, choose an overhead option (color or black and white). Click **Next** to continue.

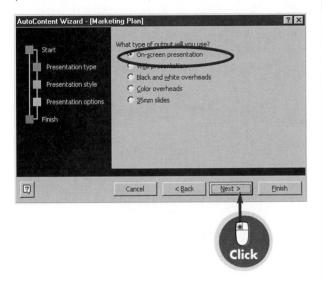

5 Enter a Title

Enter a title for the presentation and choose any footer items you'd like to appear at the bottom of each slide. Click **Next**.

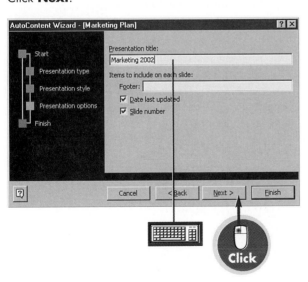

6 Click Finish

The last **AutoContent Wizard** dialog box appears. Click **Finish** to complete the procedure.

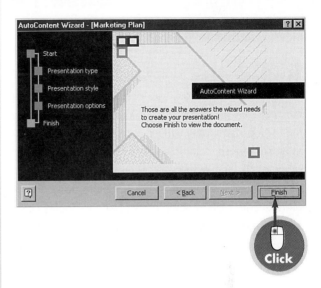

7 View the Presentation

PowerPoint opens the presentation in **Normal** view, which includes the outline for the entire presentation and displays the first slide in the presentation. The **Outline** pane shows the slides included with the template and the type of content on each slide. You should replace the content placeholder text throughout the presentation with your own text.

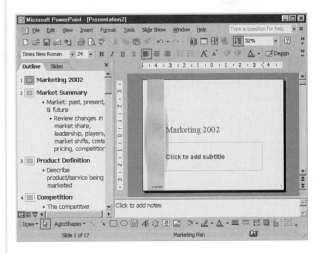

How to Start a New Presentation Based on a Design Template

In addition to using the AutoContent Wizard to create a new presentation, you can create a slide show by basing it on a PowerPoint template. You can use the same templates offered by the AutoContent Wizard (these templates provide a basic color scheme, as well as a basic outline for slide text), or you can use PowerPoint's presentation design templates. The design templates offer a single color scheme that you can use for each slide you create. A template gives the presentation a consistent look. You provide the slide content. Unlike the AutoContent Wizard (which walks you through the procedure for building a slide show), when you select a design template, PowerPoint immediately opens a new slide based on your selection.

1 Select the Template Option

From the PowerPoint **New Presentation** task pane, click the **From Design Template** option link. If the task pane isn't onscreen, open the **File** menu and select **New**; PowerPoint displays the task pane again.

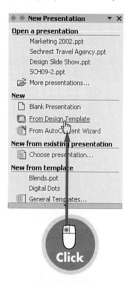

2 Preview a Design Template

PowerPoint opens the **Slide Design** task pane. Use the scrollbars to scroll through the list of slide design templates to view what's available.

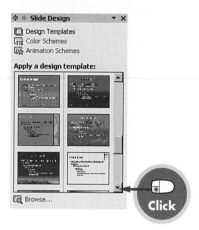

3 Select a Design Template

To choose a template, click the one you want to apply to the slide you're about to create.

④ View the Applied Design

PowerPoint opens the template design you selected. Now you're ready to fill in the text or graphics on the slide.

⑤ Close the Task Pane

Click the task pane's **Close** button to close the task pane and enlarge the slide work area.

Click

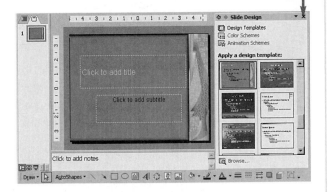

Customizing Templates

Create your own design template by making changes (color, font, and so on) to an existing template and saving the file as another template using the **File**, **Save As** command. In the **Save As** dialog box, name the new design and select **Design Template** from the **Save as type** drop-down list box. PowerPoint templates are saved with the .POT file extension.

Can't Find a Design You Like?

If you don't like any of the templates (including those used by the AutoContent Wizard), start with a blank slide and design your own presentation from scratch. Task 3, "How to Build a Presentation from Scratch," explains how to start a blank presentation.

More Templates on the Web

You can find additional PowerPoint design templates on the Web. Click the **Templates on Microsoft.com** option link in the **New Presentation** task pane. Log on to your Internet account, and your Web browser opens to the Microsoft Web site, where you can search for more templates and designs.

Filling in Placeholders

When you assign a template to a PowerPoint presentation, the template typically includes a preformatted layout, including text boxes for text. You can click inside a placeholder text box and enter your own text.

How to Build a Presentation from Scratch

If you're the adventurous type, you might prefer creating your own PowerPoint presentations and designs. Rather than relying on a preset color scheme or format, you can build a blank presentation and add your own touches. After you start a blank presentation, you can add text boxes, attach graphics, and set backgrounds and colors as needed.

① Start a Blank Presentation

From the PowerPoint **New Presentation** task pane, click the **Blank Presentation** option link. If the task pane isn't onscreen, open the **File** menu and select **New**; PowerPoint displays the task pane again.

② View Layouts

PowerPoint opens a blank slide in the work area, and the **Slide Layout** task pane appears. Use the scrollbars to scroll through and view the available layouts.

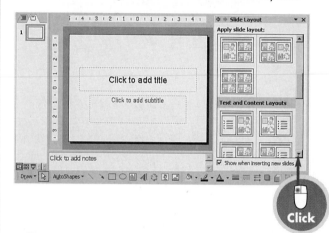

③ Select a Layout

Click to select the layout you want to assign to the blank slide. You can click the **Blank** layout to create a completely blank slide, or you can choose from layouts that already have text boxes and graphic boxes positioned and ready to be filled in.

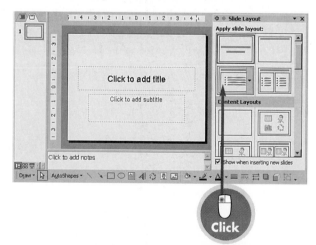

4 View the Applied Layout

PowerPoint applies the selected layout to the slide. Click the task pane's **Close** button to free up onscreen workspace.

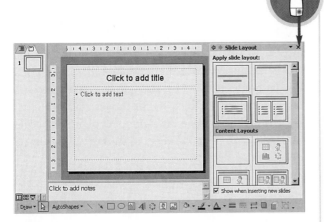

5 Replace Placeholder Text

To replace placeholder text with your own wording, click the text box you want to add text to and start typing.

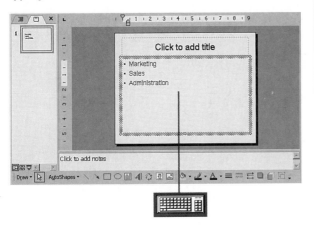

How-to Hint

Need Help?

For help with adding text boxes to your blank slide, see Task 8, "How to Add New Text Boxes." For help adding graphics to the slide, see Task 9, "How to Add an Illustration to a Slide."

Choosing a Color Scheme

To change the color scheme for your blank presentation, choose **Format**, **Slide Design**. The **Slide Design** task pane opens. Click the **Color Schemes** link to display a scrollable list of color schemes you can apply to the slide. To apply a color scheme, simply click it.

Customizing the Background

To change the background of your blank presentation, choose **Format**, **Background**. Click the **Background fill** drop-down list and select **Fill Effects**. The **Fill Effects** dialog box opens. Now you can set a gradient effect, add a pattern or texture background, or turn a picture into a background.

Adding a Slide Design

You can always add a slide design to your blank presentation if you decide you would rather not create your own. To do so, just open the **Slide Design** task pane and choose a design from the list. A quick way to open this task pane is to click the **Slide Design** button in the **Formatting** toolbar.

How to Use PowerPoint's View Modes

You can display your slide presentation in different views within PowerPoint to help you work with the slides. You can use the view buttons to change your view quickly, or you can open the **View** menu and select a view. In this task, you learn about available view modes.

Normal view —— Slide Show view

Slide
Sorter
view

1 Use the View Buttons

To change your view, click the appropriate view button located in the bottom-left corner of the PowerPoint window. Use **Normal** view to work on your slides, use **Slide Sorter** view to arrange slides in a presentation, and use **Slide Show** view to run your slide show.

2 Use the View Menu

You can also switch views using the **View** menu. Simply click the **View** menu and make your selection from the options at the top of the menu.

3 Switch to Normal View

In **Normal** view, you see a single slide in the right pane, tabs in the left pane, and the slide notes in the bottom pane. In this view, you can work with the various slide elements (such as text boxes and graphics) and move them around the slide, or change the outline and add slide notes as needed. **Normal** view is the default view.

Outline tab   Slides tab

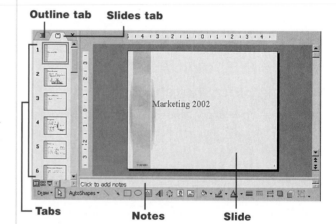

Tabs   Notes   Slide

4 Click the Outline Tab

Click the **Outline** tab to view your slide presentation in outline format, which allows you to see the organization of your presentation's contents.

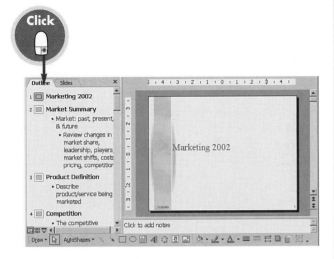

5 Click the Slides Tab

Click the **Slides** tab to view your slide presentation in thumbnail sizes, which allows you to see the slides in miniature.

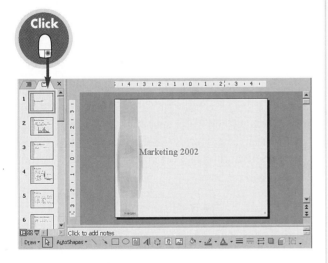

6 Close the Tabs Pane

You can close the tabs pane on the left side of the screen to free up workspace onscreen. Click the pane's **Close** button to close the pane. To bring back the pane, click the **Normal** view button or choose **View, Normal** from the menu bar.

How-to Hint

What About Slide Sorter and Slide Show Views?

In **Slide Sorter** view, you can see a *thumbnail* (or miniaturized version) of each slide in the presentation and the order in which the slides appear. You can easily rearrange the slide order and add or delete slides. See Task 14, "How to Insert and Delete Slides," to learn more about using this view. Use **Slide Show** view to run your show. See Task 18, "How to Run the Slide Show," to learn more about this view.

Resizing Panes

You can resize the tabs pane in **Normal** view. Move the mouse pointer over the pane's right border, and then click and drag to resize the pane.

Zooming Your View

You can use PowerPoint's **Zoom** controls to change your perspective in any view. To gain a closer look at a graphic object in **Slide Sorter** view, for example, click the **Zoom** drop-down list on the **Standard** toolbar and choose a zoom percentage.

How to Understand Slide Elements

Slide presentations can include a few slides or many slides, and each slide conveys particular information. Depending on the layout, whether the AutoContent Wizard assigned it or you added it, each slide can have one or more slide elements. Those elements include text boxes, clip art, bulleted lists, tables, charts, and more. The slide layout you select will indicate each element type you can use. Each slide element is treated as an object on the slide, which means that you can move or resize it as needed. Before you begin creating your own slide presentation, you should familiarize yourself with the types of slide elements you might encounter or want to include on your slides. To change a layout at any time, choose **Format**, **Slide Layout**.

1 Text Boxes

PowerPoint's text boxes let you enter slide text of your choice. Just about every slide you create in PowerPoint will require text. Here you see a common layout with a title text box and a subtitle text box. To enter text, click inside the text box and start typing.

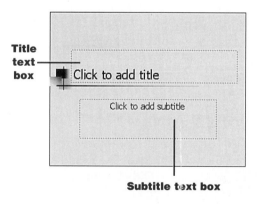

Title text box — Click to add title

Click to add subtitle

Subtitle text box

2 Bulleted Lists

Bulleted lists are quite common in slide presentations. They let you present data succinctly and focus the audience on the points you want to make. Here's an example of a bulleted list text box. To enter text, click inside the box and start typing. Press **Enter** to begin a new bulleted item automatically.

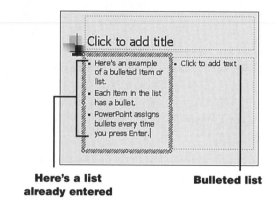

Click to add title

- Here's an example of a bulleted item or list.
- Each item in the list has a bullet.
- PowerPoint assigns bullets every time you press Enter.

Click to add text

Here's a list already entered   **Bulleted list**

3 Clip Art

Artwork can really spruce up your slide's message. You can choose many of the layouts from preset clip art boxes. To insert clip art, simply double-click the box and locate the clip art you want to use. Here you see a piece of clip art already selected and in place. Learn more about adding clip art in Task 9, "How to Add an Illustration to a Slide."

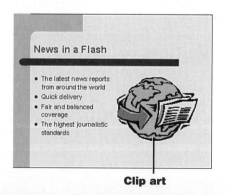

News in a Flash

- The latest news reports from around the world
- Quick delivery
- Fair and balanced coverage
- The highest journalistic standards

Clip art

4 Tables

If you've already worked with Word and Excel, you know how tables can help organize and present data. Use tables in PowerPoint to do the same. To insert text in a PowerPoint table, click inside the first cell and start typing. Use the **Tab** key to move from cell to cell. Here you see a table already filled in. If you have created a table in another program such as Word or Excel, you can insert the information into your PowerPoint slide. Learn how to insert tables in Task 11, "How to Add a Table to a Slide."

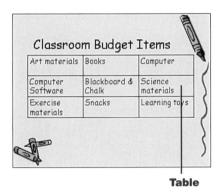

Table

5 Charts

Another way to present data is with charts. A few PowerPoint layouts let you insert charts such as organizational charts into your slides; you also can choose to add your own charts to any slide as necessary. Here's an example of a chart already inserted and sized to fit the slide. If you have created a chart in another program, such as Word or Excel, you can insert the information into your PowerPoint slide. Learn how to insert charts in Task 10, "How to Add a Chart to a Slide."

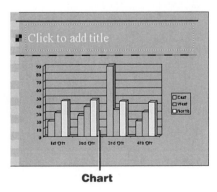

Chart

6 Objects

In addition to the slide elements already discussed, you can add other types of objects, such as graphic files created with other programs, media clips, or any other data object. Here's an example of a layout that lets you add a media clip. Double-click to open the Microsoft Media Clip Gallery so that you can add a sound or motion clip to the slide.

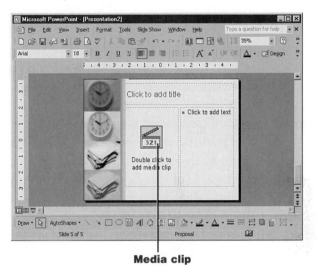

Media clip

How-to Hint

What's a Layout?

Each slide you add to your presentation needs a layout, a design that tells PowerPoint what goes where. If you create a presentation with the AutoContent Wizard, each slide has a preset layout. If you create a presentation using a design template or build the slide yourself, you choose a layout for each slide using the **Slide Layout** task pane. To learn more about changing slide layouts, see Task 12, "How to Change the Slide Layout," later in this chapter.

Working with Object Boxes

When you select an object, selection handles surround it. You can use the selection handles to resize and move the object box. See Chapter 27, "Working with Office's Graphics Tools," to learn more about working with graphic objects in Office.

How to Add and Edit Slide Text

After you have started a presentation, you're ready to start entering text. Your slides will have one or more text boxes; some of these text boxes might include placeholder text. Placeholder text is simply default text included to give you some ideas about content and the overall appearance of the slide. You can add and edit text in **Normal** view. This task shows you how to edit text in the **Outline** tab and directly on the slide. To learn how to add new text boxes, see Task 8, "How to Add New Text Boxes."

1 Select Outline Text

To edit text in the **Outline** tab, first click the slide number you want to edit. Next, select the placeholder text you want to replace. You select text in PowerPoint just as you do in Word or Excel: Click the mouse at the beginning of the text, hold down the left mouse button, and drag to select the text. You might have to resize the pane to see all the outline text.

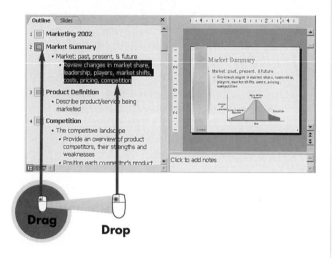

2 Enter Text in Outline View

Type your new text. The selected text is replaced by the text you type. Use the **Delete** key to delete characters to the right of the insertion point, or use the **Backspace** key to delete characters to the left.

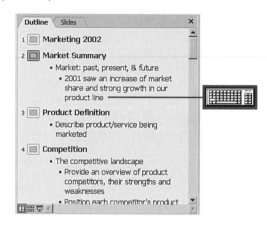

3 Use the Outlining Toolbar

You can use the **Outlining** toolbar to help you edit outline levels. To display the toolbar, choose **View**, click **Toolbars**, **Outlining**.

④ Change Outline Levels

The **Outlining** toolbar appears as a vertical toolbar to the left of the **Outline** tab. Use the buttons on the toolbar to change outline levels, such as demoting or promoting a level.

Outlining toolbar   **Slide icon**

⑤ Select Slide Text

You also can enter and edit text directly on the slide. Click the text box you want to edit; selection handles surround the text box.

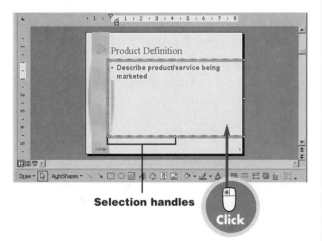

Selection handles

Click

⑥ Type New Slide Text

Select the placeholder text you want to replace and type the new text. The placeholder text is replaced with your new text. Use the **Delete** key to delete characters to the right of the insertion point, or use the **Backspace** key to delete characters to the left.

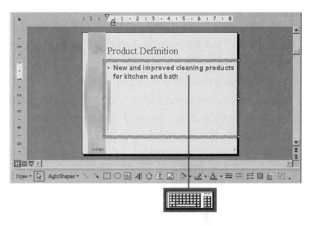

Adding Lots of Text?

If you want to add a lot of text, it's best to work directly on the slide so that you have a better sense of when the slide is getting too cluttered to be effective. To free up workspace onscreen, close the **Tabs** pane by clicking its **Close** button.

Moving Slides with the Outlining Toolbar

To move a slide up or down in the outline and rearrange the presentation order, click the **Move Up** or **Move Down** button on the **Outlining** toolbar. To quickly display the toolbar, right-click the **Drawing** toolbar and choose **Outlining**. Then select the outline text to move and click the **Move Up** button to move the text up in order; click **Move Down** to move the text down in order.

How to Format and Align Slide Text

You can quickly change the look of your slide text using PowerPoint's formatting commands. You can make text bold, italic, or underlined with a click of a button, or you can change the alignment to left, right, or center. You can even add a shadow effect to give text a three-dimensional look. If you learned how to use formatting commands in Word, those same commands come into play with text in PowerPoint. The easiest way to format text in PowerPoint is to use the available buttons on the **Formatting** toolbar.

1 Select the Text

Start by opening the slide that contains the text you want to format. Select the text. (It's easiest to format text directly on a slide in **Normal** view.) To quickly select a word to edit or format, double-click the word. To select a sentence, hold down the **Ctrl** key while you click anywhere in the sentence. To select all the text in the text box, press **Ctrl+A**.

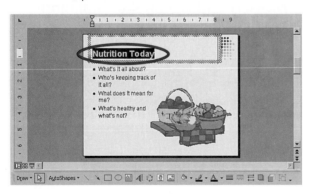

2 Use Bold, Italic, and Underline

To make text bold, click the **Bold** button on the **Formatting** toolbar. To italicize the text, click the **Italic** button. To add an underline to text, click the **Underline** button.

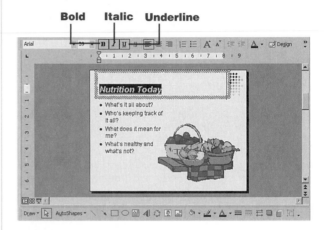

3 Change Font

Select the text you want to change, click the **Font** drop-down arrow on the **Formatting** toolbar, and choose a new font from the list.

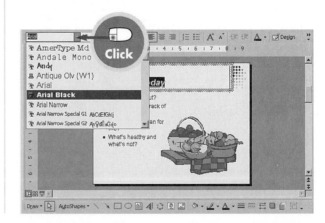

4 Change Font Size

To choose a specific font size, click the **Font Size** drop-down arrow and select a font size. If you would rather resize the text a little at a time until you reach the desired size, use the **Increase Font Size** and **Decrease Font Size** buttons. To nudge the selected text up a size, click the **Increase Font Size** button. To make the text smaller, click the **Decrease Font Size** button.

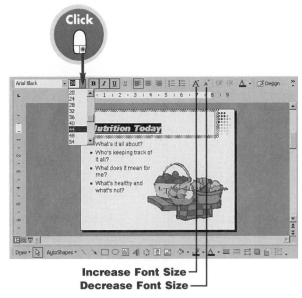

Increase Font Size
Decrease Font Size

5 Change the Alignment

To align text to the left in the text box, click the **Align Left** button on the **Formatting** toolbar. To center text, click the **Center** button. To align text to the right, click the **Align Right** button.

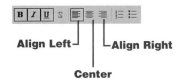

Align Left
Align Right
Center

6 View the Alignment

PowerPoint aligns your text in the text box as you specified. Here you can see samples of each of the alignment options as applied to slide text.

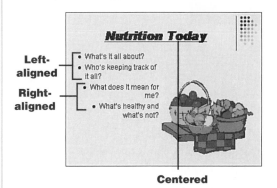

Left-aligned
Right-aligned
Centered

How to Add New Text Boxes

At times, you will want to add a new text box to a slide. You might have to add a text box for your corporate slogan, for example, or to add a caption text box to label a graphic. When you add a new text box, you can decide how large to make the box or let PowerPoint create a default size. In this task, you learn how to use a tool from the **Drawing** toolbar. Make sure that you're in **Normal** view. If the **Drawing** toolbar is not displayed, right-click any other toolbar and select **Drawing**.

➊ Select the Text Box Tool

From the **Drawing** toolbar (located at the bottom of the PowerPoint window), click the **Text Box** button.

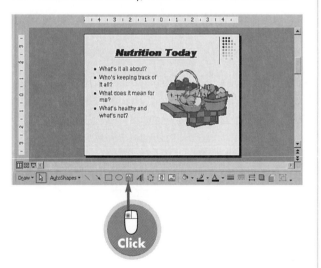

➋ Click in Place

Move the mouse pointer to the area on the slide where you want to insert the new text box and click the mouse button.

➌ Start Typing

A text box the size of one character appears where you clicked. Start typing the text you want to add.

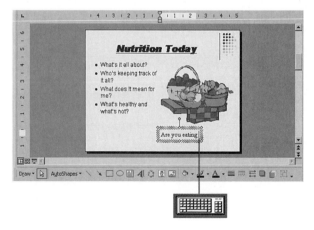

④ Watch the Box Expand

As you type, the size of the text box increases. To start a second line within the text box, press **Enter**. (Note that you can resize a text box at any time by dragging its selection handles: Select the box, position the pointer over a selection handle, hold down the left mouse button, and drag the box to a new size.)

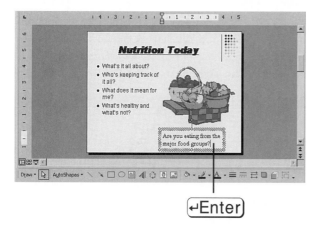

←Enter

⑤ Drag the Text Box

Another way to insert a text box after clicking the **Text Box** tool is to drag a rectangle that's the size of the text box you want to add to the slide. Click the top-left corner where you want the text box to start, drag to the desired size, and release the mouse button to set the size of the text box.

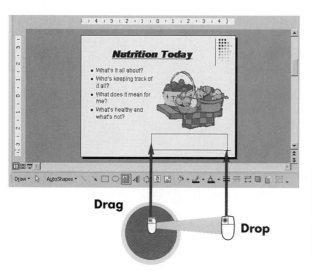

Drag

Drop

⑥ Type the Text

To enter text in the text box you just created, click inside the box and start typing.

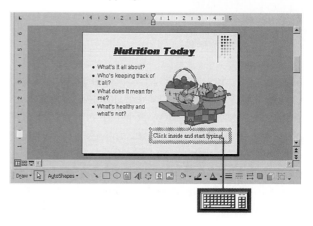

How to Add an Illustration to a Slide

Slide shows are meant to be visual, and part of their appeal is graphics—whether that graphic is clip art, a picture you create from a drawing program, or a photo found on the Internet. Illustrations, or graphics, can really spruce up your slides. For that reason, the presentations created with the AutoContent Wizard and the Slide Design templates have areas on the slides already designated for graphic elements. PowerPoint comes with a large collection of clip art you can use in your own slide shows, or you can use artwork from other files. After you insert a graphic, you can resize it, move it, rotate it, and more.

① Select a Graphic Placeholder

If your slide already has a placeholder for a graphic, double-click the placeholder to open the **Clip Gallery** (and skip to step 3). If the placeholder offers several content options, as is true in this example, click the **Insert Clip Art** button.

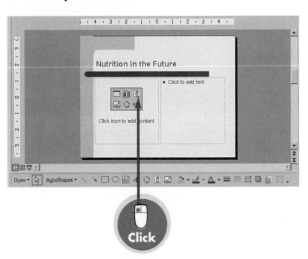

② Add a New Graphic Object

If your slide does not already have a placeholder box, or you want to add another picture to the slide, you must add a new object box to hold the graphic. Click the **Insert Clip Art** button on the **Drawing** toolbar.

③ Look for a Picture

In the **Select Picture** dialog box that opens, type a keyword or phrase for the type of graphic you want to use and click **Search**. You might be prompted to log on to your Internet connection and access clip art from the Microsoft Web site.

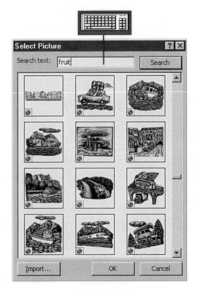

4 Select a Clip

Use the scrollbars to scroll through the catalog of available clip art. When you find a piece of clip art that you want to use, click it to select it and then click **OK**. The clip art is inserted into the slide.

5 Use an Image File

If you have a graphic image file stored elsewhere on your computer, you can insert it into a slide. Choose **Insert**, **Picture**, **From File** to open the **Insert Picture** dialog box.

6 Locate the Image

Locate the image file you want to use. When you find the file, double-click it to insert it into your slide.

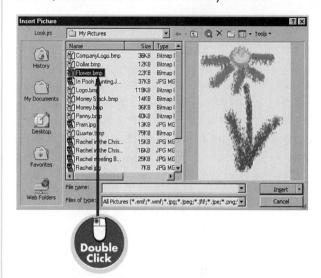

Graphics, Illustrations, or Pictures?

The terms *graphic*, *illustration*, and *picture* are used interchangeably to describe artwork that can be inserted into a slide.

Resizing Clip Art

Depending on the clip art you select, you might have to resize it to fit better on your slide. Select the object and drag a selection handle to resize it.

Working with Slide Objects

You can work with clip art and other objects on PowerPoint slides in a variety of ways. Chapter 27, "Working with Office's Graphics Tools," covers how to insert objects such as basic shapes and WordArt, how to add shadow effects, how to change the image formatting, and how to layer and group objects on top of each other. Check out Chapter 27 to learn more about these techniques.

How to Add a Chart to a Slide

In addition to adding text boxes and clip art to your slides, you can also add charts. Using the **Copy** and **Paste** commands, you can add a chart that you created with another program, such as Microsoft Excel, or you can create a chart from within PowerPoint. Charts go a long way in illustrating your data, and you can easily create a chart without leaving PowerPoint, as you'll see in this task. Start by displaying the slide in which you want to insert a chart.

1 Select the Insert Chart Command

To insert a chart, choose **Insert**, **Chart**, or click the **Insert Chart** button on the **Standard** toolbar. If your layout already has a box for a chart, double-click the box. If the placeholder offers several content options, click the **Insert Chart** button.

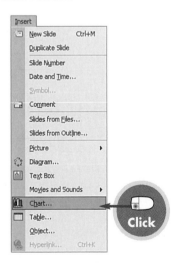

2 View the Generic Chart

A generic chart appears in your PowerPoint slide, along with a datasheet. The **Chart** menu option has commands to help you create or edit your chart.

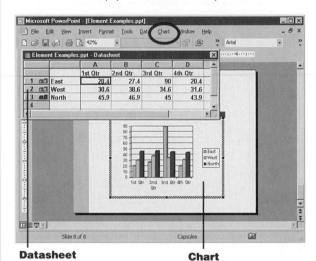

Datasheet **Chart**

3 Enter Your Chart Data

Use the datasheet to enter the data for your chart. Just replace the sample data with your own.

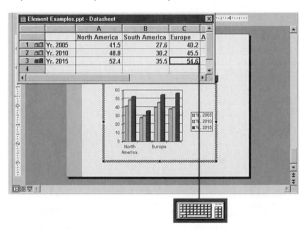

④ Change the Chart Type

By default, the charting tool displays a bar chart, but you can select another chart type. To do so, open the **Chart** menu and choose **Chart Type**. The **Chart Type** dialog box opens.

⑤ Select a Chart Type

From the **Chart Type** list, choose a new chart type and select a subtype from those available. Click **OK** to close the dialog box and apply the new chart type to your slide.

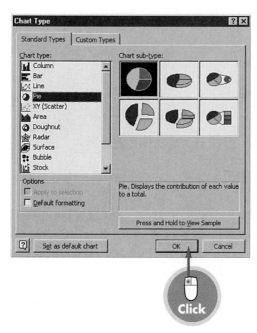

⑥ Insert the Chart

To insert the chart, updated with your data, into your slide, click the **Close** button on the datasheet. The chart is placed in your slide. You might want to resize or move it to fit properly. To edit the chart, double-click the chart object.

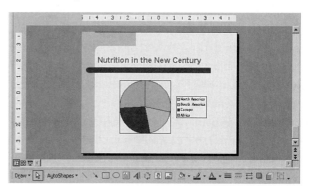

How-to Hint

Working with the Datasheet

You can move and resize the datasheet as necessary to create your chart. To move it, drag its title bar. To resize it, hover the mouse pointer over any border on the datasheet until the pointer becomes a double-sided arrow; drag to resize. Use the scroll-bars to move around the datasheet.

Inserting a Chart from Another Program

To insert a chart from Excel, open the Excel file containing the chart and select the chart. Click the **Copy** button or choose **Edit**, **Copy**. Switch back to the PowerPoint slide in which you want to insert the chart and click the **Paste** button or choose **Edit**, **Paste**. You might have to move or resize the chart to fit in the slide.

How to Insert a Table in a Slide

One way to organize and present information in a slide is to use a table. PowerPoint tables work similar to Word or Excel tables: Columns and rows intersect to form cells in which you can enter data. Depending on the presentation you're making, some layouts include tables automatically. Other times, you might want to insert a table yourself. In this task, you'll learn how to use both methods to add tables to your presentation.

① Use a Table Layout Object

If your slide layout has a preset table object box, double-click the box and skip to step 3. If the placeholder offers several content options, click the **Insert Table** button.

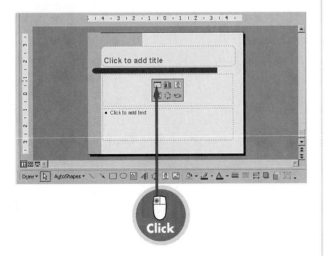

② Insert a New Table

To insert a new table object, choose **Insert**, **Table** or click the **Insert Table** button on the **Standard** toolbar. The **Insert Table** dialog box opens.

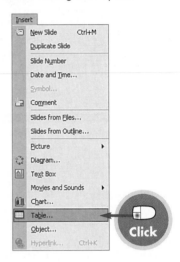

③ Define Columns and Rows

Enter the number of columns and rows you want for the table. Click inside each text box and type a number or use the spin arrows to select a number. Click **OK** to close the dialog box.

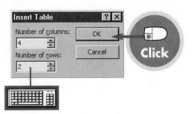

4 View the Table That Appears

A table with the number of columns and rows you specified in step 3 appears on the slide along with the **Table and Borders** toolbar. Here you see an example of a table with four columns and two rows.

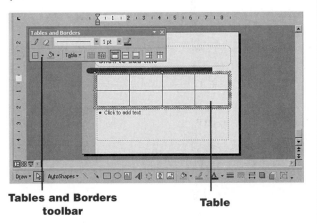

Tables and Borders toolbar   **Table**

5 Enter Table Text

By default, the cursor waits in the first empty cell, ready for you to enter data. Start typing to enter data in the first cell. Press **Tab** to move to the next adjacent cell on the right, or use the keyboard arrow keys to move around the table cells.

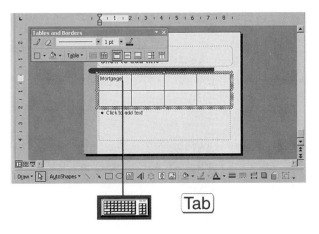

Tab

6 Finish the Table

When you've filled each cell of the table, click outside the table to see how it looks in the slide.

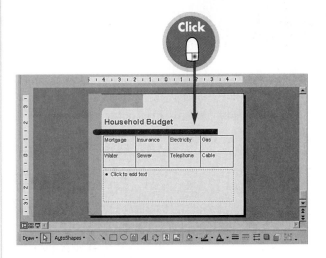

Click

Adding Rows or Columns

To insert a row, right-click inside a cell above which you want to add a row and choose **Insert**, **Rows**. To add a column, select the entire column to the left of which you want to insert a new column by clicking above the column. Right-click the column and choose **Insert**, **Columns** from the menu bar.

Moving or Resizing the Table

To resize the table, select it first so that it's surrounded by selection handles and drag a handle to resize. To move the table, select it and hover the mouse pointer over the table border until it takes the shape of a four-sided pointer. Then drag the table to a new location on the slide.

How to Change the Slide Layout

PowerPoint's **AutoLayouts** feature enables you to establish a structure for a slide. When you add a new slide, the **Slide Layout** task pane appears with a variety of layout options you can apply. You also can change the layout of an existing slide using the same pane. Applying a layout is much easier than adding your own text and graphic boxes. PowerPoint has layouts for just about any kind of slide you want. You will find layouts that offer a combination of title text, bulleted text, charts, and graphics. With the **AutoLayouts** feature, these slide elements are already positioned in place and ready to go. All you have to do is add your own text or choose a graphic element.

➊ Display the Slide

Display the slide you want to change. It's best to switch to **Normal** view so that you can clearly see the slide itself.

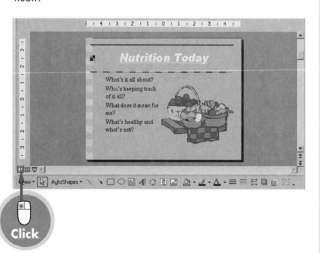

➋ Open the Slide Layout Task Pane

Right-click a blank area of the slide and choose **Slide Layout** from the pop-up menu to open the **Slide Layout** task pane.

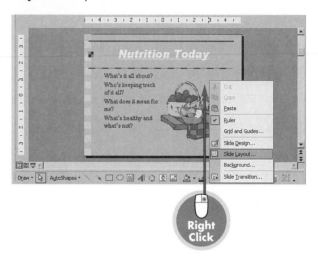

➌ View Available Layouts

In the task pane, use the scrollbar to scroll through and view the available layout options.

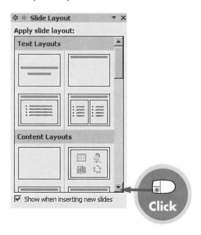

4 Select a Layout

When you find a layout you want to use, click to select it.

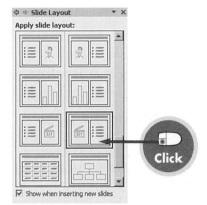

5 View the New Layout

PowerPoint applies the new layout. Depending on your slide's contents, you might have to resize or move some slide objects to fit the new layout. In this example, I applied a layout that switched the placement of the clip art and the bulleted text.

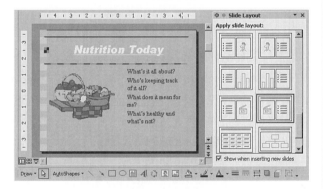

6 Close the Task Pane

To free up onscreen workspace, click the task pane's **Close** button.

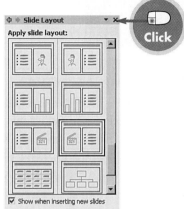

How-to Hint

Changing the Slide Design

You also can right-click any slide in your presentation and choose **Slide Design** from the shortcut menu to open the **Slide Design** task pane. You can choose a new design, and PowerPoint applies it to all the slides in the presentation.

Changing the Default Setting

The **Slide Layout** task pane is set up to appear whenever you insert a new slide into your presentation. To stop the pane from appearing by default, disable the **Show when inserting new slides** check box at the bottom of the task pane.

How to Change the Slide Background

You can change the background of every slide in your presentation. Changing the background will give your slides a new look. You'll find plenty of options: Backgrounds can include color, texture, or patterns. Be sure to explore the options available to find just the right look you need. The **Background** dialog box lets you change the color of the background or add a fill effect, such as a gradient, pattern, or texture.

1 Display the Shortcut Menu

Display the slide you want to change (switch to **Normal** view so that you can clearly see the slide), right-click a blank area on the slide (don't right-click a slide object), and choose **Background** from the context menu.

2 Open the Background Dialog Box

From the **Background** dialog box that opens, click the drop-down arrow to display a list of other colors. If the background color you want to use is displayed, click it. If not, click the **More Colors** option to open the **Colors** dialog box.

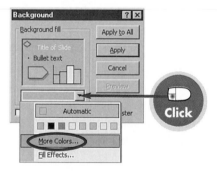

3 Choose a Color

On the **Standard** tab of the **Colors** dialog box, select a color by clicking the color you want to use from the palette and then clicking **OK**.

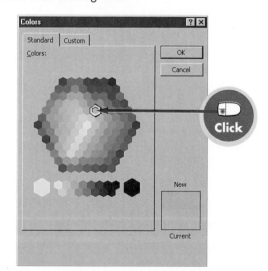

④ Apply the New Color

To apply the color to the background of the current slide, click **Apply** in the **Background** dialog box. To apply the color to every slide in the presentation, click **Apply to All**.

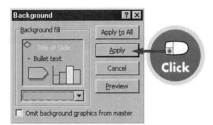

⑤ Choose Fill Effects

If you'd prefer a background other than a solid color, click the **Fill Effects** option in the **Background** dialog box instead of **More Colors** (as shown in step 2). The **Fill Effects** dialog box opens, where you can select from **Gradient**, **Texture**, **Pattern**, or **Picture** backgrounds. The **Texture** tab, shown here, contains quite a few interesting texture backgrounds you can apply. Select the fill effect you want to use and click **OK**.

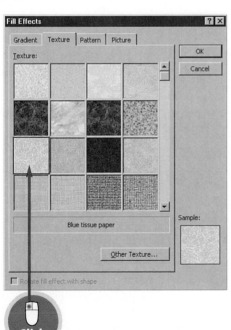

⑥ Apply a Texture

Click the **Apply** button in the **Background** dialog box to apply the fill effect to the current slide; click **Apply to All** to apply the effect to every slide in the presentation. Here you can see that a new background texture has been applied to the slide.

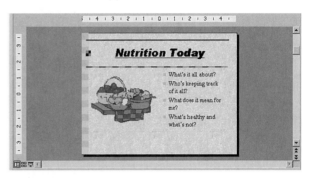

How-to Hint

Changing the Color Scheme

For a quick change of color in your slide presentation, consider changing the color scheme. Right-click the slide and select **Slide Design** to display the **Slide Design** task pane. Click the **Color Schemes** option link and choose another color scheme to apply.

Turning a Picture into a Background

If you have a picture that would make a good slide background, use the **Picture** tab in the **Fill Effects** dialog box to select and insert the picture. Be careful that you don't use a picture that competes too much with the message of your slide text!

How to Insert and Delete Slides

Do you need to add a new slide to your presentation? Perhaps you want to delete a slide that you no longer need. PowerPoint makes it easy to add and delete slides. You can add or delete slides in **Normal** view or in **Slide Sorter** view.

① Insert a New Slide

Display or select the slide that precedes the place where you want to add a new slide and click the **New Slide** button on the **Standard** toolbar.

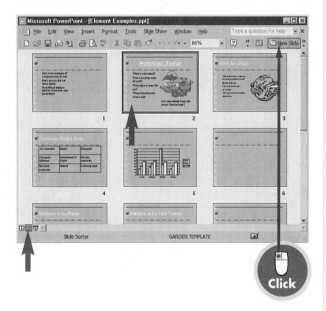

② Use the Slide Layout Task Pane

PowerPoint inserts the new slide following the selected slide and opens the **Slide Layout** task pane. Use the scroll arrows to view the various slide layouts.

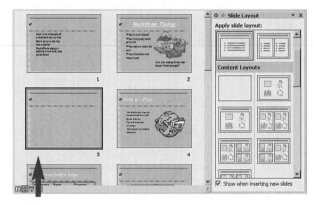

③ Apply a Layout

When you find a layout you want to apply to the new slide, select it. The layout is applied to the new slide. You can now fill the slide with text or graphics.

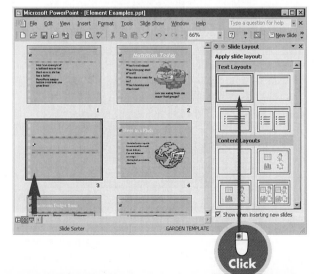

④ Delete a Slide

To delete a slide, select it in **Slide Sorter** view or display it in **Normal** view and choose **Edit**, **Delete Slide**.

⑤ Insert Slides from Other Presentations

Use PowerPoint's **Slide Finder** feature to insert slides from other presentations into the current slide show. Choose **Insert**, **Slides** from **Files** to open the **Slide Finder** dialog box.

⑥ Use the Slide Finder Dialog Box

Locate the presentation from which you want to borrow slides (use the **Browse** button, if necessary, to find the file). Click the **Display** button to view the slides in that presentation. Then select the slide or slides you want to insert and click the **Insert** button. The slides you selected are inserted in the current presentation. (Click **Close** to exit from the **Slide Finder** dialog box when you're finished.)

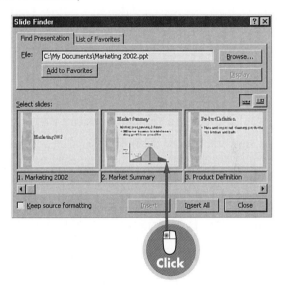

How-to Hint

Keyboard Shortcut

To insert a new slide using the keyboard, press **Ctrl+M**. This action opens the **Slide Layout** task pane, from which you can choose a layout.

Deleting Slides in Slide Sorter View

To remove a slide in **Slide Sorter** view, click the slide and press **Delete** on the keyboard.

Oops!

If you accidentally delete the wrong slide, click the **Undo** button on the **Standard** toolbar.

How to Reorganize Slides

Inevitably, you will need to rearrange the order of slides in your presentation. This is especially true after you have added new slides and deleted others. The easiest way to rearrange slides is in **Slide Sorter** view, where you can see all the slides at once. In **Slide Sorter** view, you easily can drag a slide from one location to another.

1 Switch to Slide Sorter View

Click the **Slide Sorter** button located in the bottom-left corner of the PowerPoint window to switch to **Slide Sorter** view.

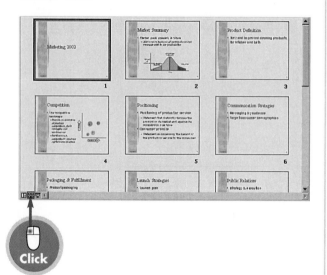

2 Select the Slide to Move

Click to select the slide you want to move to a new location.

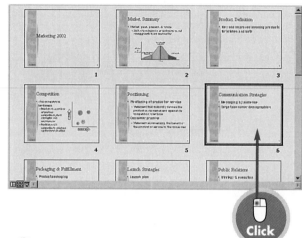

3 Drag the Slide

Hold down the left mouse button and drag the slide to its new location in the presentation order. As you drag, a line appears to show where you're moving the slide.

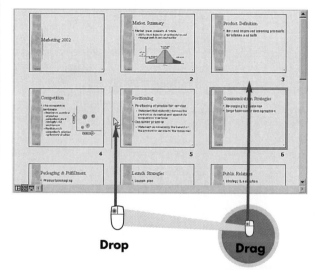

④ Release the Mouse Button

When the slide is positioned where you want it, release the mouse button. PowerPoint scoots the other slides over and places the moved slide in the new location.

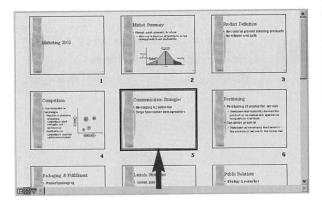

⑤ Scroll and Drag

Slide Sorter view only shows several slides at a time. If you want to move the selected slide beyond the slides in view, drag in the direction you want to go. The display scrolls in that direction.

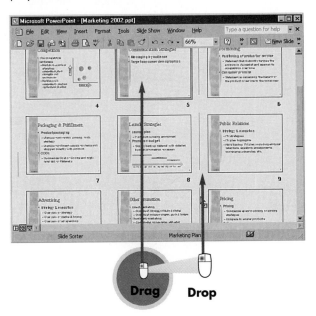

Quick Switch

To quickly view any slide in **Normal** view, double-click the slide in **Slide Sorter** view.

Slide Sorter Toolbar

When you switch to **Slide Sorter** view, the **Slide Sorter** toolbar appears at the top of the presentation window. The toolbar contains buttons for setting slide transitions, rehearsing timings, and setting other special effects.

Selecting Multiple Slides

To select two or more slides at the same time, press the **Shift** key while you click slides that are contiguous. To select slides that aren't next to each other, press the **Ctrl** key while clicking to select slides.

Copying a Slide

To quickly copy a slide, hold down the **Ctrl** key, drag the slide you want to copy, and release it in a new location. Now you have a copy of the original slide.

How to Define the Slide Transition

To make your slide show more professional, add slide transitions. Slide transitions determine how one slide advances to the next. PowerPoint includes numerous transition effects you can use, including dissolves, tiling effects, fades, and split screens. You can assign a different transition to each slide or use the same transitions throughout the entire slide show.

1 Switch to Slide Sorter View

Click the **Slide Sorter** view button to switch to **Slide Sorter** view and select the slide for which you want to set a transition. If you want to use the same transition for all the slides, select the first slide in the presentation.

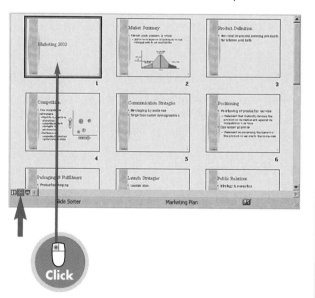

2 Click Slide Transition

From the **Slide Sorter** toolbar, click the **Transition** button. The **Slide Transition** task pane opens.

3 Choose an Effect

Scroll through the **Apply** to selected slides list and choose a transition effect. When you make a selection, AutoPreview plays the effect on the selected slide. If you don't like that effect, choose another one from the list.

4 Choose a Speed

Under the **Modify** transition heading in the task pane, click the **Speed** drop-down arrow and choose a speed option for the speed of the transition: **Slow**, **Medium**, or **Fast**.

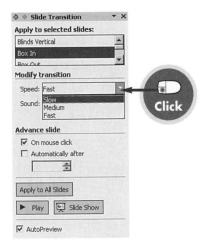

5 Add a Sound Effect

Also under the **Modify** transition heading, you can choose a sound effect to add to the transition. Click the **Sound** drop-down arrow and choose a sound effect.

6 Choose How to Advance

Use the **Advance** slide options to control how the slides will advance: either by mouse click or using automatic advance. If you select the **Automatically after** option, you must specify an amount of time, in seconds, for the advance. Enter a time, or use the spin arrows to set the time. You can set the advance at five seconds, for example, and PowerPoint automatically advances to the next slide in the presentation after the current slide has displayed for five seconds.

How-to Hint

Viewing Transition Icons

When you assign a transition, you will notice a transition icon under the slide (or slides) in **Slide Sorter** view. You can click any transition icon to see a demonstration of the transition effect.

Apply to All

To apply the slide transition effect to all the slides in your presentation, click the **Apply to All Slides** button in the **Slide Transition** task pane.

Advancing Tips

When setting a time for the automatic advance feature, practice viewing your slide show to make sure that you've allowed enough time to read everything in the slide. Learn how to run your slide show in Task 18, "How to Run the Slide Show."

How to Add Animation Effects

You can apply PowerPoint's animation effects to slide objects. You can make a bulleted list appear on the slide, for example, and add one bulleted item at a time during the presentation. You can control exactly when each item appears, which prevents your audience from reading ahead of you during the presentation. You can also make each list item fly in from the side of the screen or fade in slowly. Many effects are possible, so be sure to test each one to see what it does. You can apply animation effects to any slide object.

❶ Activate Animation Schemes

From **Slide Sorter** view, select the slide object you want to animate. Then choose **Slide Show**, **Animation Schemes**.

❷ View the Effects

PowerPoint opens the **Slide Design** task pane and displays the **Animation Schemes** options.

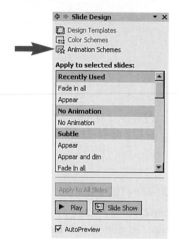

❸ Choose an Effect

Scroll through the list of effects. To select an effect, click the effect name. PowerPoint automatically demonstrates the effect in the selected slide.

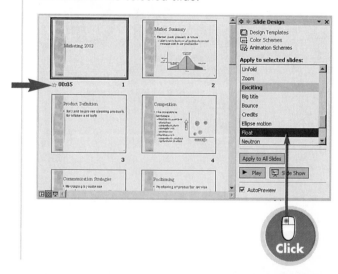

4 Activate Custom Animations

You can create your own custom animations in PowerPoint. In **Normal** view, select the slide object you want to animate, and then choose **Slide Show**, **Custom Animation**.

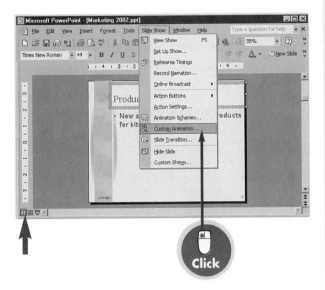

5 Assign an Animation Effect

PowerPoint opens the **Custom Animation** task pane. With the slide element selected, click the **Add Effect** button, select an effect category (such as **Entrance**), and click an effect type (such as **Checkerboard**).

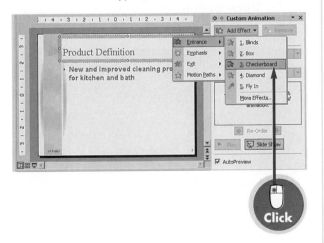

6 Modify the Effect

The task pane activates the various option settings you can adjust to control the effect. For example, to change the direction of the effect onscreen, click the **Direction** drop-down arrow and choose a direction. You also can adjust the speed and start mode for the effect.

7 Do More Customization

After you assign an effect, it is listed in the **Custom Animation** task pane list box. Click the effect to view a drop-down list of additional customizing options, several of which (such as the **Timing** option) open additional dialog boxes with controls you can set.

How to Run the Slide Show

After you finish building and preparing your presentation, you're ready to run the show. It's a good idea to run the show several times while preparing your presentation so that you have some idea of how the slides will look, how long you want each slide to display, and how transitions and animation effects will be used. You can set up a slide show to run manually so that you click the mouse or press a keyboard key to advance each slide; you can set up the slide show to run automatically, so that PowerPoint displays each slide for the amount of time you preset. You can even set the show to loop continuously.

❶ Choose Set Up Show

Open the presentation you want to view and choose **Slide Show**, **Set Up Show**. The **Set Up Show** dialog box opens.

❷ Choose Show Type Options

From the **Show type** options, select the option that best suits your situation.

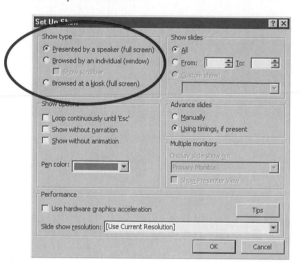

❸ Select Show Options

Use the **Show options** check boxes to indicate how the presentation should appear.

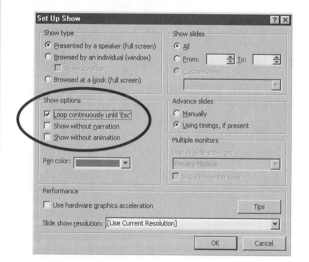

④ Choose Advance Options

From the **Advance slides** options, choose to advance your presentation manually or use preset timings. Click **OK** to close the **Set Up Show** dialog box.

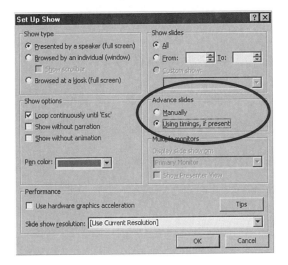

⑤ Run the Show

To start the slide show, display the first slide (or click the first slide in **Slide Sorter** view) and then click the **Slide Show** view button.

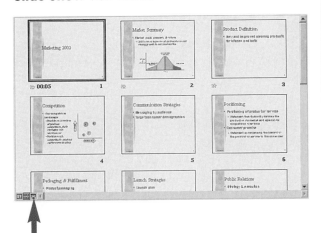

⑥ Stop the Show

PowerPoint starts your presentation. Each slide appears full screen, without toolbars or menu bars. To stop the show at any time, press **Esc**.

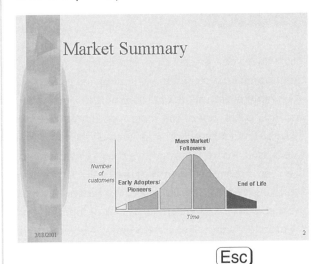

How-to Hint

Slide Show Controls

During the course of the slide show, you can use manual controls to advance slides, to return to previous slides, or to pause the show. Click the mouse or press the right arrow key on the keyboard to advance to the next slide. Press **Backspace** to return to the previous slide. Press the **S** key to pause or resume the show.

Rehearsing Your Timings

You can automate your slide show to advance each slide based on slide timings you set. One way to set timings is with the Rehearse Timings feature. Open the **Slide Show** menu and select **Rehearse Timings**. You can then time each slide. At the end, PowerPoint tells you the total time for the presentation.

How to Create Speaker Notes and Handouts

To make your presentation professional, polished, and organized, you can make speaker notes to assist you with the slide show and handouts for your audience. Speaker notes can help you organize your thoughts, make sure that you cover all the important points, and ensure that you have a cohesive presentation. You can add notes in **Normal** view, or you can switch to **Notes Pages** view. In **Notes Pages** view, speaker notes include a picture of the slide and an area for typing in your own notes. After you complete notes for the entire presentation, you can print them out along with audience handouts. In this task, you learn how to add notes in both views.

① Add Notes in Normal View

Click the **Normal** view button and display the first slide in your presentation. Click inside the **Notes** pane in the lower half of the window and start typing your notes for that particular slide. To print your notes, skip to step 6.

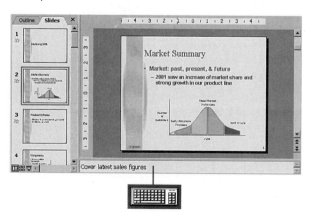

② Add Notes in Notes Page View

To switch to **Notes Page** view, choose **View**, **Notes Page**.

③ Enter Note Text

Click inside the **Notes** text box in the lower half of the window and start typing your notes for that particular slide.

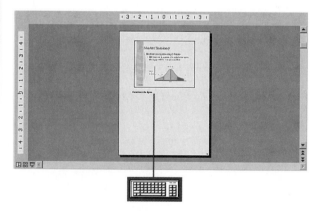

4 Use the Zoom Tools

If you're having trouble seeing what you type, use the **Zoom** drop-down list on the **Standard** toolbar to zoom in closer: try 100%.

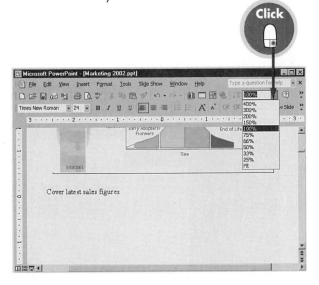

5 Click Next Slide

When you finish writing notes for the current slide, click the **Next Slide** button to continue to the next slide in the presentation.

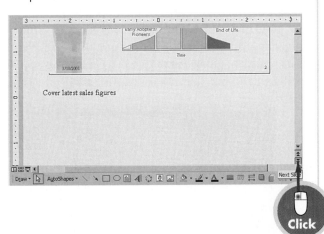

6 Prepare to Print

Continue entering notes for each slide in the presentation. When you're ready to print the notes, choose **File**, **Print**.

7 Select Notes Pages or Handouts

In the **Print** dialog box, click the **Print** what drop-down list box and choose **Notes Pages**. To print handouts instead, choose **Handouts**. Click **OK** to print your selection.

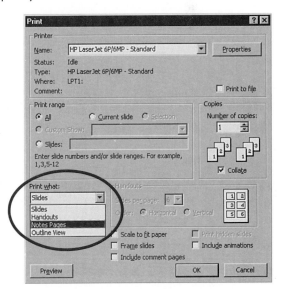

How to Use Pack and Go

To take your show on the road, you can package the presentation on disk or CD (if you have a read/write CD-ROM drive) to use at another computer. For example, you might have to take the presentation to a client across town or across the country. Use the Pack and Go Wizard to help you store the complete presentation on disk, including a PowerPoint viewer to use in case the client doesn't have PowerPoint.

❶ Open the File Menu

Start by opening the presentation you want to store on disk and insert an empty disk into your floppy disk drive or CD-ROM drive. Then choose **File**, **Pack and Go**.

❷ Start the Wizard

The first wizard dialog box appears. Click **Next** to continue.

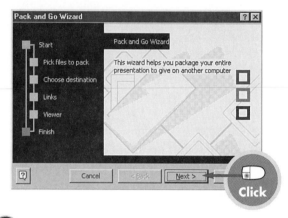

❸ Choose a Presentation

If you have already opened the presentation you want to pack, leave the **Active** presentation check box selected and click **Next**. If you want to pack a different presentation, click the **Other** presentation(s) check box and use the **Browse** button to locate the appropriate file.

4 Choose a Drive

In the next wizard dialog box, select the drive you want to save the presentation to and click **Next** to continue.

5 Choose Additional Options

The next wizard box presents you with options for saving linked files you might have used with the presentation as well as any fonts used exclusively in your presentation. The computer you use later to run the show might not have all the fonts you carefully selected, so enable the **Embed TrueType fonts** option to make sure that the same fonts are used wherever the presentation is run. Select the options you want and click **Next**.

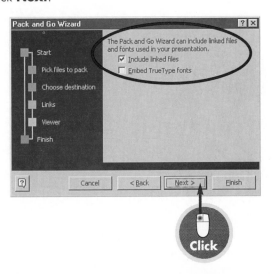

6 Pack the Viewer

If the computer on which you're going to run the slide show doesn't have PowerPoint installed, select the **Viewer for Windows 95 or NT** option. If you know that the computer has PowerPoint, select the **Don't include the viewer** option. Click **Next**.

7 Finish

In the final wizard box, click **Finish**. PowerPoint starts copying the files to the disk. If it's a particularly large presentation, you might need to use additional disks. A prompt box appears when the packing is complete; click **OK**.

(1) How to Understand Database Basics 644

(2) How to Use the Database Wizard 646

(3) How to Enter Data in the Database 648

(4) How to Add New Tables 650

(5) How to Modify a Table in Design View 652

(6) How to Create a New Form with the Form
Wizard 654

(7) How to Make Changes to a Form in Design
View 656

(8) How to Sort Records .658

(9) How to Filter Records 660

(10) How to Perform a Simple Query 662

(11) How to Create a Report 664

(12) How to Modify a Report in Design View 666

26

Making Databases with Access

Access is a database program that enables you to store, manipulate, manage, and retrieve data. If you're new to the world of databases, this might sound a bit intimidating. You work with databases each day, though, so you probably know more about them than you think. Your local telephone directory, for example, is a database. Do you have a Rolodex file on your desk? That's a database, too. And so is the card catalog at your nearby library. In its strictest sense, a database is simply a collection of information.

You can use an Access database to store information, just as directories or Rolodex cards do. In addition to storing the data, you can manipulate it in many ways. If you keep a database of your customers in Access, for example, you can sort them by ZIP Code, print out a list of all the customers who haven't ordered from you in the past six months, and create an order entry form your employees can use to process phone orders. That's only the tip of the iceberg: You can manage and manipulate your data for many purposes.

In the tasks in this part, you will learn the basics of using Access. After you master these fundamental skills, you can tap into the power of Access to work with your own computerized databases.

How to Understand Database Basics

The basic components of a database are tables, records, fields, forms, reports, and queries. All these components compose an Access database file. Before you can begin building your own databases, you must first understand these basic elements and how they fit together.

1 Tables

The root of any database is a series of one or more *tables*. Access tables are a lot like Excel spreadsheets. Information is organized into columns and rows. You can have many tables in each database file. You might have one table listing customers and addresses, for example, and another table listing products you sell.

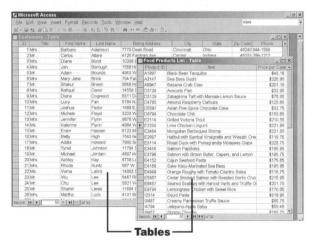

Tables

2 Records

Each entry in a database is called a *record*. Records appear as rows in a database table; each row represents one record.

Records

3 Fields

The detailed information that makes up a single record is broken into categories, called *fields*. When you're planning a database, think about what fields you need for each record. An address database, for example, needs fields for First Name, Last Name, Address, City, State, ZIP Code, and Phone number.

Fields

4 Forms

Entering data into tables can be awkward as you try to keep track of which column represents which field. To make things easier, use a form. A *form* is an onscreen fill-in-the-blanks sheet for completing a record. The form comprises each field needed to create a record. With forms, you enter data one record at a time.

5 Reports

After you build a database, you will probably want to organize certain aspects of the information and create specialized reports. *Reports* summarize and organize the data. Typically, reports are printed out. You might generate a report, for example, that lists your top 20 clients based on sales.

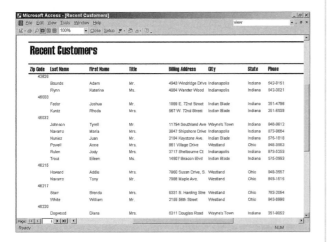

6 Queries

Queries are a formal way of sorting and filtering your data to produce specific results. With queries, you can specify which fields you want to see, the order in which you want to view them, filter criteria for each field, and more.

How-to Hint

Planning Is Everything

Before you build a database, spend a few minutes planning it. What kind of data do you want to store, and how should it be organized? Each table should have a topic, such as Customer Transactions. Determine what actions you want to perform on the data to help you know what kind of forms to create. Think about the information you want to extract from the data to help you know what kind of reports to generate. Try to break down your data as much as possible. For example, when compiling an address database, you need a field for each part. Don't combine fields, such as City and State, but instead break out the information into separate fields.

How to Use the Database Wizard

When you first open Access, you have the option of creating a blank database, using a database wizard, or opening an existing database. The easiest way to create a database is with a database wizard. Access includes several different database wizards that you can use to help you create the tables, forms, and reports you will need. Choose the kind of database you want to build and follow the wizard steps for completing the database structure. To begin, click the **General Templates** link in the **New File** task pane. (If the task pane is not visible, choose **File**, **New** from the menu bar.)

① Choose a Database

In the **Templates** dialog box, look through the wizards on the **Databases** tab to find the type of database you want to create and double-click the wizard name. To create a contact management database, for example, double-click **Contact Management**. The **File New Database** dialog box opens.

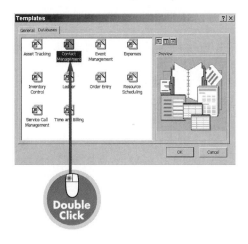

② Name the Database

Name your new database file. Either accept the name supplied by Access or type your own in the **File name** text box. Make the name something that will be easily identifiable the next time you want to use the database. Click **Create** to continue.

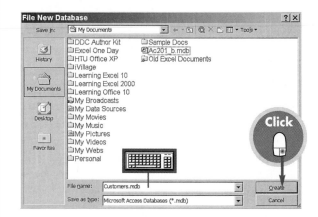

③ Determine the Structure

The first wizard dialog box tells you that you are creating a database. Click **Next**. The next dialog box has options for the actual structure of your database, including the tables that will be created and the fields to be included. Choose the table from the left pane and select any additional fields you want to use from the right pane. Click **Next**.

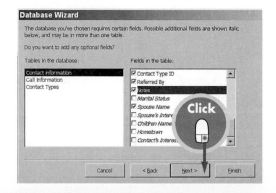

④ Choose a Screen Display

The next dialog box offers you several choices of backgrounds for screen displays and forms in the database. Click each name in the list to display the sample background. Choose a background and click **Next**.

⑥ Enter a Title

Enter a title for your database (the title can be the same or different from the filename used in step 2). Indicate whether to include a picture on all reports. (If you choose to include a picture, you must locate the picture file you want to use by selecting that option and clicking the **Picture** button.) Click **Next**.

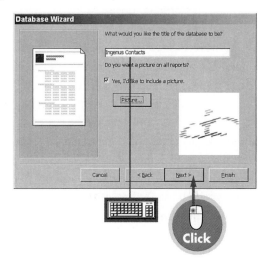

⑤ Choose a Style for Reports

From the next dialog box, choose the style for your printed reports and click **Next** to continue.

⑦ Finish the Wizard

In the final dialog box, you can choose to start the database immediately (note that "start the database" means to open it). Click **Finish** to create your new database.

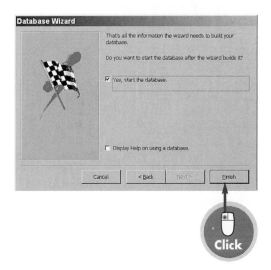

How to Enter Data in the Database

Access data is stored in tables. As long as you have created your new database using the wizard or a template, you have at least one table in which you can start entering your data. (If you need to create a table, see Task 4). Although you can enter data directly into a table, it's much easier to use a form. Forms are similar to dialog boxes; they contain text boxes with labels that identify where data for each field should be entered. If you prefer the plainness of a data sheet (similar to an Excel worksheet) with endless columns and rows, you can use **Datasheet** view to enter data into a table. This task shows you how to use both methods.

1 Open the Form

From the **Database** window, click the **Forms** object in the **Objects** bar and double-click the form you want to use in the list box. You can also select the form and click the **Open** button.

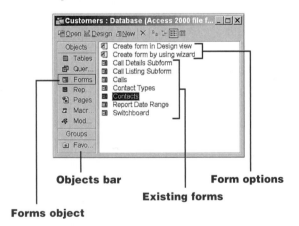

Objects bar

Form options

Existing forms

Forms object

2 Enter the Data

By default, you start out in **Form** view, in which data is entered into a dialog box-like form. (Later in this task, you'll switch to **Datasheet** view, in which you enter data in columns and rows.) Begin filling out a record. Click inside a field and start entering text; use the **Tab** key to move from field to field.

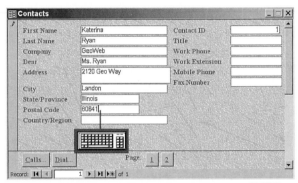

Tab

3 Start a New Record

After you complete a record, click the **New Record** button at the bottom of the form to open another record to fill out. The **New Record** button resembles a right-pointing arrow with an asterisk.

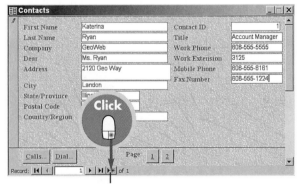

New Record button

4 Switch to Datasheet View

To enter data using **Datasheet** view, click the **View** drop-down arrow on the **Database** toolbar and choose **Datasheet View**. You can also open the **View** menu and select **Datasheet View**.

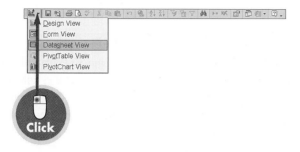

5 Enter the Data

Your form now appears as a table. Field names appear in the column headers, and each row represents a record. Click inside the first empty cell in the first column and type the data for that field. Press **Tab** to move from field to field.

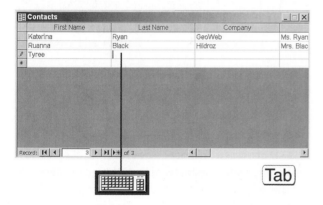

6 Close the Form

To close the form in **Form** view or **Datasheet** view, click the window's **Close** button. (Don't confuse the form window's **Close** button with the program window's **Close** button, or you will exit Access entirely.)

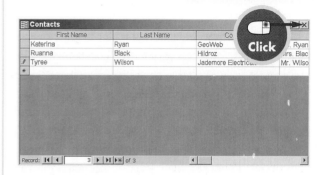

How-to Hint

I Don't Have a Form

If you don't have a form for entering data yet, use the **Create form by using wizard** option in the **Database** window list box (shown in step 1). Double-click the option and follow the wizard prompts for creating a form. When you're finished with the wizard, follow step 1 in this task to open and start using the new form.

Navigating Forms

Use the **Record** arrow buttons at the bottom of the form to navigate back and forth to view your records. Click the **New Record** button (the right-pointing arrow with an asterisk) to start a new record.

Repeating Your Entries

You can repeat an entry for a field in **Datasheet** view. Press **Ctrl+'** (apostrophe) to copy the contents of the cell above to the current cell. This shortcut works only in **Datasheet** view.

How to Add New Tables

You can create many different tables in each Access file, and each table can vary in its focus. For example, you might have one table consisting of customer data (such as names and addresses) and another table detailing your inventory (such as an item number and price). As long as you created your database using the wizard or a template, you have at least one table. For some databases, one Table is not enough. You have several ways of creating new tables. You can use the **Table Wizard**, you can design your own table from scratch, or you can use a default blank table and fill in your own fields. Regardless of how you create a table, all tables work the same way. Fields are listed in columns, and records are listed in rows.

❶ Select the Table Object

To work with database tables, click the **Tables** object in the **Objects** bar of the **Database** window. You'll see three options for working with tables: Use the **Create table in Design view** option to custom-design a table. Use the **Create table by using wizard** option to open the **Table Wizard** that walks you through steps for creating a table. To create a default blank table, use the **Create table by entering data** option.

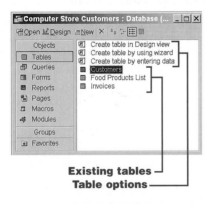

Existing tables
Table options

❷ Start a Blank Table

To start a blank table, double-click the **Create table by entering data** option. This action opens a default table in **Datasheet** view, as shown here. To rename the fields, double-click the field label and type your own text. To fill out a record, click the first empty cell in the first column and start entering data.

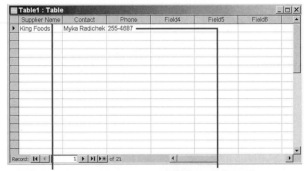

Double-click a field name to rename it

Click and type in a field to add data

❸ Use the Table Wizard

Another way to start a table is to use the **Table Wizard**, which does all the design work for you. From the **Database** window, double-click the **Create table by using wizard** option. This action opens the **Table Wizard**, as shown here. You can view two separate table lists, **Business** or **Personal**. Select the one you want.

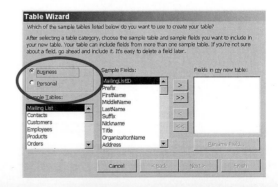

④ Add Fields

You can build your table using fields from different sample tables: just mix and match what you need from the samples. Select a table from the **Sample Tables** list; the **Sample Fields** list box displays the fields available for that table. To add a field, select the field and click the **>** button. When you have finished adding fields, click **Next** to continue.

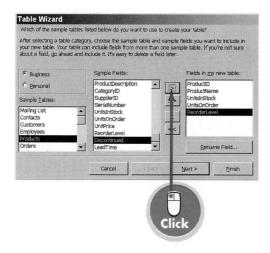

⑤ Assign a Name

In the next wizard dialog box, type a descriptive name for the table and let the wizard determine the primary key (a field that's unique for each record in the table—typically, it's just a number, starting with **1**). Click **Next** to continue.

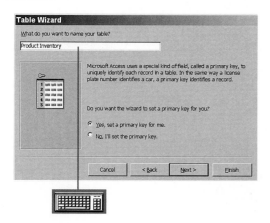

⑥ Create the Table

If your database already has at least one table, the next dialog box that appears asks about the relationship between tables. Ignore this dialog box for now and click **Next** to open the final dialog box. Indicate whether you want to change the table design, enter data directly, or have the wizard create a data entry form for you. When you're done selecting options, click **Finish**.

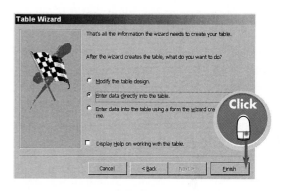

How-to Hint

Renaming Your Fields

You can select fields that are similar to ones you need and then rename them using the **Rename Field** button in the **Table Wizard** dialog box in step 4.

Entering Table Data

After you create a table, you can start entering data into it at any time. Open the table, click in the first empty cell in the first empty column, and type the data for that field. Be sure to use the correct data type. If it's a text field, use text; if it's a number field, use numbers. Press **Tab** to move to the next field and continue filling out a complete record for the table. When you get to the last field, press **Enter** to start a new record.

Designing a Table from Scratch

Use **Design** view to build a table from scratch. Learn more about using **Design** view in the next task, "How to Modify a Table in Design View."

How to Modify a Table in Design View

Access databases are flexible in their design. You might find that you have a field that is almost always blank, for example, indicating that it is unnecessary and should be removed. Or you might want to enter information for a field that you forgot to create. In either case, you can open the appropriate table and make the necessary change. Access makes it easy to change the various elements in your tables. You can change the look and design of any table, form, report, or query in **Design** view.

1 Open the Table

With the **Database** window open, click **Tables** on the **Objects** bar and select the table you want to change from the list box. Click the **Design** button to open the table in **Design** view.

2 Add a Field

Click inside the first blank line of the **Field Name** column and type the new field name.

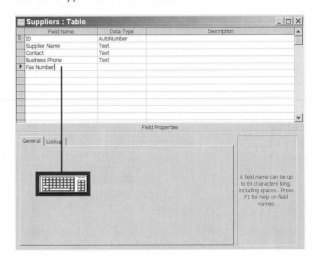

3 Select the Field Type

Press **Tab** to move to the **Data Type** column, click the **down arrow** to view the list of **Data Type** choices, and select a type.

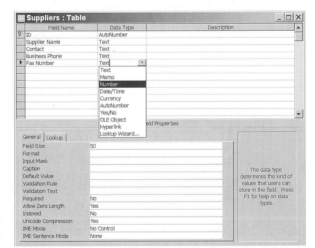

④ Remove a Field

To remove a field, click the row selector to the left of the field name to highlight the entire row. Click the **Delete Rows** button on the **Database** toolbar to remove the highlighted row. Click **Yes** when asked whether you want to delete the selected field permanently.

⑥ Close the Table

Click the **Close** button to close the table and return to the **Database** window. Click **Yes** in the dialog box that appears, asking whether you want to save your changes.

How-to Hint

Reordering Fields

To move the field to a new location in the table, select the field row in **Design** view and drag it to a new location in the table.

Using Field Properties

Use the **Field Properties** sheet at the bottom of the **Design** view to change things such as the default size of the field, whether the field can be left blank when entering data, how many decimal places you want (number fields only), and more. To change a property, click its line and make the necessary changes.

Quick Delete

You can also delete rows by highlighting them, right-clicking, and selecting **Delete Rows** from the shortcut menu that appears.

⑤ Edit a Field Name

To change a field name, click the field name and make your changes. You can edit existing text or enter a brand new name.

How to Create a New Form with the Form Wizard

To make data entry easy, use a form. You can use two types of forms: data entry forms or dialog box forms. Data entry forms are fairly self-explanatory: They're designed similar to a regular paper form, with empty boxes where you type in your data. Dialog box forms enable you to provide a vehicle for user input and a follow-up action based on the input. This task focuses on the data entry form, which can be produced using the **Form Wizard**. To begin, open the database you want to use.

1 Open the New Form Dialog Box

From the **Database** window, click **Forms**. Click the **New** button to open the **New Form** dialog box. Notice that the list box has several different form options you can pursue. In this task, we'll focus on the **Form Wizard**.

2 Start the Form Wizard

From the **New Form** dialog box, select **Form Wizard** from the list of form options and click **OK** to start the wizard.

3 Choose a Table

In the **Tables/Queries** drop-down list (the wizard's first dialog box), select the table that contains the fields you want to include on the form. Then select a field and click the **>** button to add the field to the new form. (To add all the fields at once, click the **>>** button.) When you're finished adding fields, click **Next**.

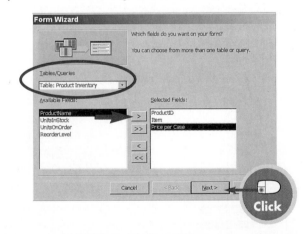

④ Choose a Layout

The next wizard dialog box asks you to choose a layout for the form. Select each option to see an example of each of the layouts. When you find the one you want, click **Next** to continue.

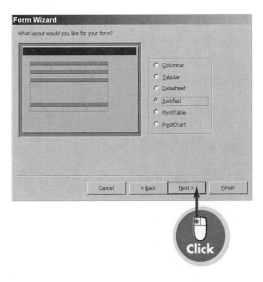

⑤ Select a Style

Choose a style to use for the form. When you select each style option, a sample appears to the left. Select the style you want to use for your form and click **Next** to continue.

⑥ Name the Form

The final Form Wizard dialog opens and asks for a title for the form. Type a descriptive name in the text box and click **Finish**.

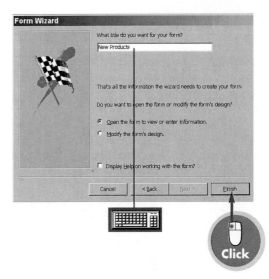

How-to Hint

Mixing and Matching Fields

If you have more than one table in your database, you can select fields from different tables to appear in a single form. In step 3, change the table that appears in the **Tables/Queries** drop-down list and add the required fields.

Using AutoForm

If you want a generic form based on the fields in your table, use AutoForm. From the **New Form** dialog box, select **AutoForm: Columnar** to create a single column of fields in a form; select **AutoForm: Tabular** to create a form that resembles a table; or select **AutoForm: Datasheet** to make a form that resembles a datasheet. Select **AutoForm: PivotTable** or **AutoForm: PivotChart** to create a re-arrangeable report with the table data. At the bottom of the **New Form** dialog box, click the drop-down arrow to select the table you want to associate with the form, and then click **OK**. A simple form is made.

How to Make Changes to a Form in Design View

The **Form Wizard** is great for producing a quick form (see Task 6, "How to Create a New Form with the Form Wizard"). You will frequently find that, after you have created a form, you want to change the layout or the fields. You can easily customize the form by using **Design** view. After you open a form in **Design** view, you can move the form elements around, add new titles, or change the field size. **Design** view is similar to an electronic paste-up board that enables you to move items around until they're exactly where you want them.

❶ Open the Form

Open the database you want to use if it isn't already open. In the **Database** window, click **Forms**. Select the form you want to modify from the list box and click the **Design** button.

❷ Use Form Design

The form opens in **Design** view, along with the floating **Field List** box. In **Design** view, you can place various elements into the form and move them around.

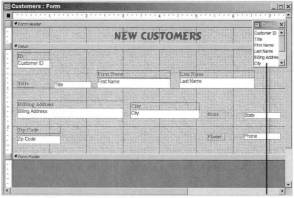

Field List

❸ Delete a Field

To remove a field and its label, click the field to select it and press **Delete**. Depending on the background design, it isn't always easy to tell what's a field and what's a label. In most instances, fields appear larger than text labels. When you click a field, its label is also selected. Selection handles appear around a selected item.

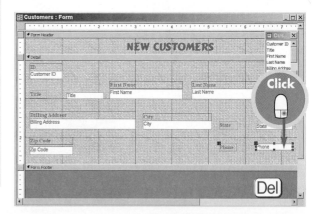

4 Add a Field

To add a field, drag a field from the **Field List** box onto the **Detail** area where you want to insert the new field. Release the mouse button, and the field and its text label are added to the form. Repeat this step to add as many fields as you want.

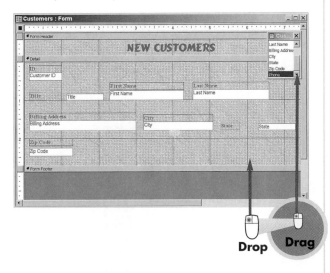

Drop Drag

5 Move a Field

To move a field, click the field to select it; selection handles surround the field. Position the mouse pointer over the field until the pointer takes the shape of a hand icon. Hold down the left mouse button and drag the field to a new position; release the mouse button. To resize a field, drag any of the field's selection handles.

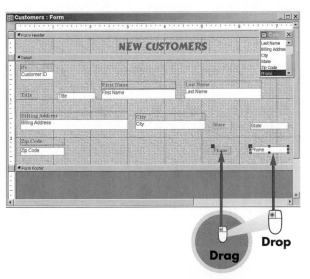

Drag Drop

6 Use the Toolbox

You can use all kinds of editing tools to change your form design. You'll find all the tools on the floating **Toolbox**. (If the **Toolbox** isn't displayed, click the **Toolbox** button on the **Form Design** toolbar.) Use the **Toolbox** buttons to add additional text to the form (such as subtitles or directions), to add pictures to the form, and more.

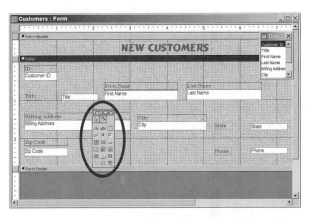

How-to Hint

No Field List?

If the **Field List** box doesn't appear on your screen, click the **Field List** button on the **Form Design** toolbar.

Saving Your Changes

After moving the form elements around and adding or deleting fields and labels, click the form's **Close** button or press **Ctrl+F4**. In the prompt box that appears, click **Yes** to save your changes.

Viewing Headers and Footers

To work with the header or footer area of your form, the **Form Header/Form Viewer** area must be visible. If it's not, open the **View** menu and select **Form Header/Footer**. You can add text to a header or footer area in the same way you add text to a form.

How to Sort Records

After you have entered data into a database, you're ready to start manipulating it. One of the most important ways in which a database manipulates data is by sorting it: putting it in a logical order according to criteria you specify. You might want to sort your address database, for example, by city, ZIP Code, or last name. The **Sort** command is the tool to use. You can sort by ascending order (from A to Z or 1 to 10) or descending order (from Z to A or 10 to 1). To begin, open the database you want to sort.

1 Open the Table

From the **Database** window, click **Tables** in the **Objects** bar and open the table you want to sort (double-click the table name or select it and click the **Open** button).

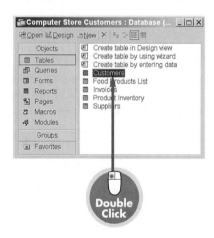

2 Choose the Sort Field

Click the column header for the field you want to sort, or place the insertion point anywhere in the column you want to use for the sort.

3 Use the Sort Buttons

To sort the table in ascending (A–Z) order, click the **Sort Ascending** button on the toolbar. To sort by descending order (Z–A), click the **Sort Descending** button.

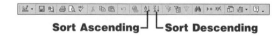

Sort Ascending ┘ └ Sort Descending

4 View the Sorted Data

The table is immediately sorted. Continue sorting the table fields as needed. When you exit the table after sorting, a prompt box asks whether you want to save the changes. Click **Yes** if you do, or **No** if you don't want the sort to be permanent.

5 Sort by Form Fields

You can also sort your records using a form. From the **Database** window, select **Forms** and open a form. Click to position the cursor in the field by which you want to sort.

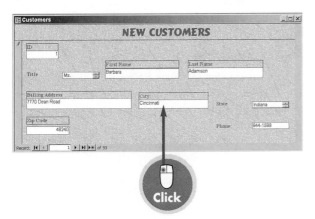

6 Select a Sort Order

Perform a sort in the same way you did in step 3—by clicking the **Sort Ascending** or **Sort Descending** buttons on the toolbar. As you cycle through the records using the arrow buttons at the bottom of the form, the records appear in the new sort order.

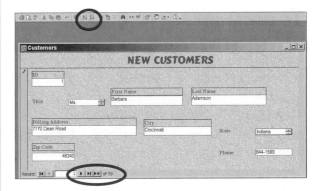

How-to Hint

What About Empty Records?

If you sort by a field that contains no information in some records, those records are automatically sorted first (in an ascending sort) or last (in a descending sort).

Sorting Tip

Changing the sort order of a table does not cause a related sort-order change in an existing form. If you create a form using a table with an established sort order, however, the form automatically takes on the sort order of the table.

Sorting in Datasheet View

You can also sort a form in the **Datasheet** view. Open the **View** menu and choose **Datasheet View**. The **Datasheet** view of the form not only looks the same as the table in step 2, but it also sorts the same. After you select the column to sort by, you can click the **Sort Ascending** or **Sort Descending** button to perform the sort.

How to Filter Records

You can filter out specific records in your database. Perhaps you want to see information only on a certain vendor or group of vendors, or you might want to find everyone in your address book whose birthday is in the month of May. You can temporarily filter out all the records except those you need to see. Access enables you to apply a filter in three ways: **Filter by Selection**, **Filter by Form**, and **Advanced Filters**. You can apply all the filters in a form, datasheet, or query. This task explains the first two methods.

❶ Filter by Selection

Open the form on which you want to perform the filter operation and click the field that contains the criteria you want to filter. If you want to search for all the records that have the same ZIP Code, for example, first locate a record containing that ZIP Code and click the ZIP Code field. To begin the filter, click the **Filter By Selection** button on the toolbar.

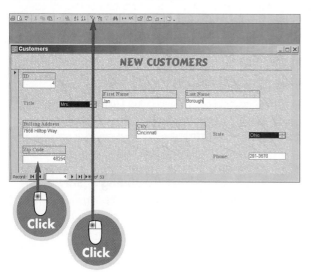

❷ View the Filtered Records

Any records with matching information in the field selected have been retained, but all other records have been hidden (filtered out). Use the form's arrow buttons to view the filtered records.

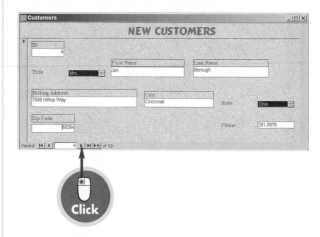

❸ Remove a Filter

To remove the filter, click the **Remove Filter** button on the toolbar. (When no filter has been applied, the **Remove Filter** button does double duty as the **Apply Filter** button.)

4 Filter by Form

Click the **Filter by Form** button on the toolbar to enter your own criteria for the filter. A blank form appears. (Note that fields which use list boxes will not be blank.)

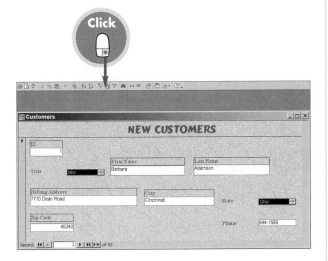

5 Enter Your Filter Criteria

Type your search criteria in the field of your choice or use the field's drop-down arrow to select a value. To search for all customers in Indianapolis, for example, select Indianapolis from the City list. You can enter criteria in more than one field, but Access will find only records that match all entries. To enter a second criteria—to also search for customers in the city of Carmel, for example—click the **Or** tab and enter the data for the second filter criteria.

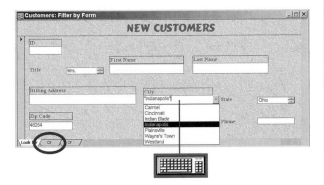

6 Filter the Records

Click the **Apply Filter** button on the toolbar; Access filters your database and displays any records matching your criteria. Use the arrow buttons to scroll through each record in the filtered database. To remove the filter and return the database to its "unfiltered" presentation, click the **Remove Filter** button.

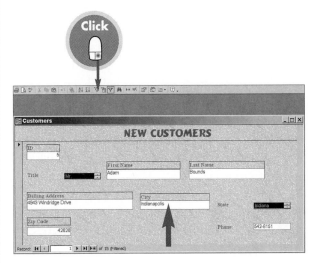

How-to Hint

Filtering by Exclusion

You can also filter out records that contain certain criteria. The regular filter finds records that contain the search criteria and filters out those that don't. The **Filter by Excluding Selection** on the **Records**, **Filter** menu returns all records that do not contain the search criteria you specify.

Advanced Filtering and Sorting

You can sort by multiple fields (such as city within state) and apply advanced filters using the **Records**, **Filter**, **Advanced Filter/Sort** command. Enter the primary sort field (such as State) in the first column of the datasheet that appears, and select ascending/descending from the row below it. Enter filter data (such as **Indiana**) in the next row. Enter a secondary sort field (such as City) in the second column, select ascending/descending, and enter filter data. Click the **Apply Filter** button to apply your selections.

How to Perform a Simple Query

Queries are a cross between filters and tables. With a query, you can quickly display a mix of fields from various tables and filter the list to display only the records you want to see. Queries can be used to edit and view your data as well as to furnish the material for forms and reports. The easiest way to create a query is to use the **Simple Query Wizard**. It enables you to select which fields you want to display. You can weed out fields you don't need and still see every record.

❶ Open the New Query Dialog Box

From the **Database** window, select **Queries** in the **Objects** bar and double-click **Create query by using wizard** to open the **Simple Query Wizard** dialog box.

❷ Select Fields

From the **Tables/Queries** drop-down list, select the table. Select a field you want included in the query table results and click the **>** button to add it to your query. Select as many fields from as many different tables as you want and click **Next**. In this example, I want to create a simple query that lists customers in Indiana—their names and phone numbers—which are fields in my **Customers** table.

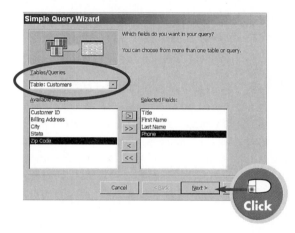

❸ Give the Query a Name

Type a name for the query and click **Finish** to create your query, which appears in table form.

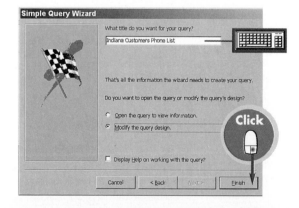

662 Chapter 26: Making Databases with Access

4 Filter the Query

If you decided to filter the query (to display only customers from Indiana, for example), enter the criteria you want in the datasheet that appears. To filter on a field that isn't in the query, select the field from an empty column's drop-down list (click in the **Field** box, and the drop-down list button appears), enter the criteria, and remove its check mark.

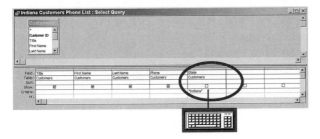

5 Run the Query

To display the results of your query, click the **Run Query** button on the toolbar.

Run Query button

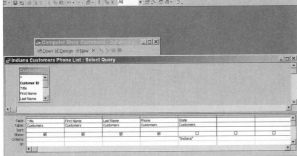

6 Query Results

Access displays the records, showing only the fields you specified. To close the query, click the window's **Close** button.

Searching for Blanks

In addition to finding records that contain fields with information, you can also use a query to find records that contain blank fields. To search for blank numeric fields, use `is null` for the search criteria. For blank text fields, use double quotation marks (`" "`).

Searching for Wildcards

Another way to conduct a search is to use *wildcards*—symbols that stand for other characters (* for multiple characters, ? for single characters). For example, to search for all the last names in your address database that start with CAN, you might enter CAN* and the results would produce names such as CANNON and CANTON.

How-to Hint

How to Create a Report

You can choose to print any table, form, or query at any time; however, using the **Report** tool can make the data appear more professional and polished. With the **Report Wizard**, the task of creating a meaningful report becomes simple and effortless.

1 Open the Report Wizard

Open the database you want to use and click **Reports** in the **Objects** bar of the **Database** window. Double-click **Create report by using wizard** to open the **Report Wizard** dialog box.

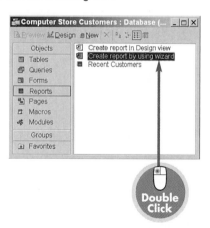

2 Choose a Table or Query

From the **Tables/Queries** drop-down list, select the table or query to use in your report. Select a field and click the **>** button to add it to your list of selected fields. Select as many fields from as many different tables or queries as you want and click **Next** when you're ready to continue. In this example, I'm creating a customer phone list, so the fields I need are on the **Customers** table.

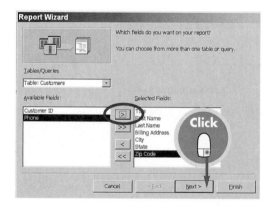

3 Choose a Grouping Category

From the left pane, choose a field to use as a grouping category and click the **>** button. Click **Next** to continue. I want to organize the list by ZIP Code, so I'll choose that field.

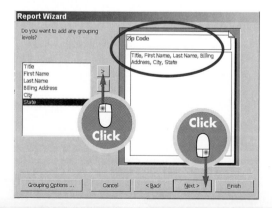

4 Choose a Sort

You can sort by as many as four fields, either in ascending or descending order. From the first drop-down list, select the field to use for the primary sort and continue until you have chosen as many sort fields as needed. Click **Next** to continue.

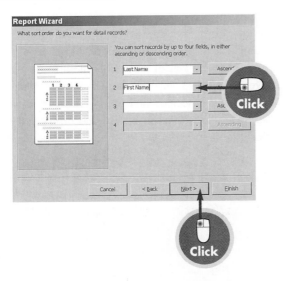

5 Select a Layout

Select a layout option to see an example of how your report will look. When you have decided on the layout options, you're ready to move on. Click **Next**.

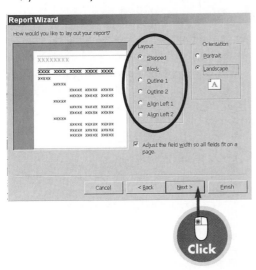

6 Select a Style

As you did with the layout options in step 5, you can click to see examples of the different report styles available. Choose a style for your report and click **Next**.

7 Assign a Title

In the final wizard dialog box, type a report title and click **Finish**. Your new report is created and displayed as its own separate window onscreen. To print the report, click the **Print** button in the toolbar.

Customers by Zip Code					
Zip Code	**Last Name**	**First Name**	**Title**	**Billing Address**	**City**
42828					
	Bounds	Adam	Mr.	4843 Windridge Drive	Indianapol
	Flynn	Katerina	Ms.	4984 Wander Wood Lan	Indianapol
46003					
	Fedor	Joshua	Mr.	1869 E. 72nd Street	Indian Bla
	Kuntz	Rhoda	Mrs.	587 W. 72nd Street	Indian Bla
46032					
	Johnson	Tyrell	Mr.	11794 Southland Ave.	Wayne's T
	Navarro	Maria	Mrs.	3847 Shipshore Drive	Indianapol
	Nuniez	Juan	Mr.	2184 Keystone Ave.	Indian Bla
	Powell	Anne	Mrs.	861 Village Drive	Westland
	Rulen	Jody	Mrs.	3717 Shelbourne Ct	Indianapol
	Trout	Eileen	Ms.	14807 Beacon Blvd	Indian Bla
46215					
	Howard	Addie	Mrs.	7960 Susan Drive, S.	Westland
	Navarro	Tony	Mr.	7898 Maple Ave.	Westland
46217					
	Starr	Brenda	Mrs.	8331 S. Harding Street	Westland

How to Modify a Report in Design View

To customize the report, open the report in **Design** view. The report comprises up to six sections in **Design** view. The **Report Header** contains information that appears only at the very beginning of the report, the **Page Header** section contains information that appears at the top of each page, the **Group Header** contains information that appears at the top of each group (if applicable), **Detail** contains the actual report data, the **Page Footer** section contains information appearing at the bottom of each page, and **Report Footer** contains information that appears at the bottom of the last page.

1 Open the Report in Design View

To begin, open the **Database** window, click **Reports** in the **Objects** bar, select the report, and click the **Design** button.

2 Add a Label

To add a text label such as a company name to the report, click the **Label** tool on the floating **Toolbox**. Move the mouse pointer to the section where you want to insert the text (such as the **Report Header**), click and hold down the left mouse button, and drag out a label box. Type your text in the label box and press **Enter**.

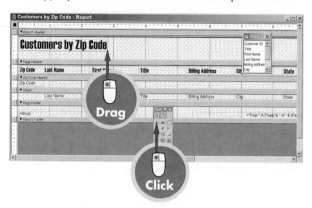

3 Change the Font

To change the font size, select the label box by clicking it, and then make your selections from the **Font** and **Font Size** boxes on the **Formatting** toolbar. You can apply other attributes as well, such as italics or bold. Resize the label box if needed by dragging one of the selection handles.

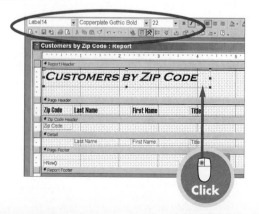

4 Add a Graphic

To add a graphic to your report, select the **Image** tool from the **Toolbox**. Move the mouse pointer to the section of the report where you want to add the graphic, hold down the left mouse button, and drag out an image box. As soon as you release the mouse button, the **Insert Picture** dialog box opens.

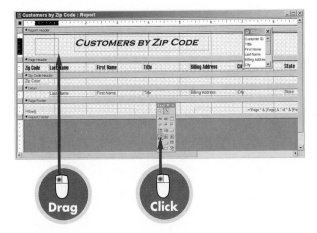

5 Select the Graphic File

Using the **Insert Picture** dialog box, locate the graphic file you want to use. Double-click the graphic name to insert the graphic in your report. (You might have to adjust the size of the image box by dragging its selection handles.)

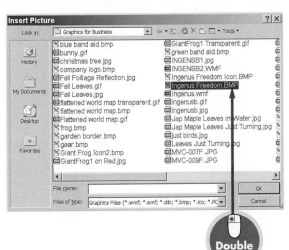

6 Remove Objects

To remove any object from a report (including a label, field, or graphic), select it and press the **Delete** key.

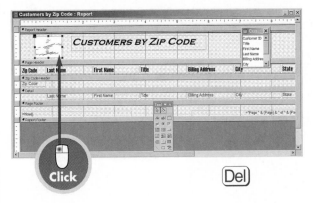

How-to Hint

No Toolbox?

You'll need the Access floating **Toolbox** to perform several of the steps in this task. If the floating **Toolbox** isn't displayed, click the **Toolbox** button on the **Form Design** toolbar to open it.

Opening the Properties

You can open an object's properties sheet by right-clicking the object and selecting **Properties** from the shortcut menu. You might want to change an object's properties to change its formatting, for example.

Previewing First

To preview your changes before saving the modified report, choose **View**, **Layout Preview** from the menu bar.

Entering Multiple Lines

To use two or more lines in a label box, press **Shift+Enter** to start a new line of text.

① How to Draw Basic Shapes 670

② How to Insert Clip Art 672

③ How to Insert an Object 674

④ How to Insert a WordArt Image 676

⑤ How to Move, Size, and Rotate an Object 678

⑥ How to Change Image Formatting 680

⑦ How to Add Shadow Effects 682

⑧ How to Group and Ungroup Objects 684

⑨ How to Insert a Diagram 686

Task

27

Working with Office's Graphics Tools

The Office programs share a lot of features, but many users aren't aware of the graphics tools available in each program. Each application enables you to add objects to your files, such as clip art, shapes, WordArt, and more. You can dress up a Word document or a PowerPoint slide with a piece of clip art from the Microsoft Clip Gallery, for example. You can insert an image file from another program into your Outlook email message. You can draw your own shapes to include in Excel charts or PowerPoint slides. All these various types of items are considered objects that can be manipulated in your Office programs.

In this part, you'll learn how to use the Office graphics tools to enhance your documents, worksheets, database tables and forms, slides, and more. You'll also learn how to draw basic shapes, insert pictures and clip art, create a WordArt image, and manipulate and format graphics objects. Don't be intimidated by the thought of creating and adding visual objects to your files. The Office graphics tools make it easy to illustrate any Office item you create.

How to Draw Basic Shapes

One of the easiest ways to add visual appeal to an Office project is to add a shape (such as a rectangle or oval) or a line. Shapes and lines can draw attention to parts of your text or other data, create a nice background effect, or function as a design element. You can also add arcs and freeform shapes using the drawing tools. The Drawing Canvas, a new addition to the Office XP programs, appears by default when you use the drawing tools. It's a framed area that keeps your shapes separate from the rest of the document area and allows you to move and resize them as a group. You can draw numerous shapes and lines inside the Drawing Canvas frame.

❶ Display the Drawing Toolbar

The Office drawing tools are accessible from Word, Excel, and PowerPoint. To view them, open the **Drawing** toolbar. Right-click over any toolbar and choose **Drawing** from the context menu. Or, click the **Drawing** button on the **Standard** toolbar. Note that the **Drawing** toolbar is displayed by default in PowerPoint.

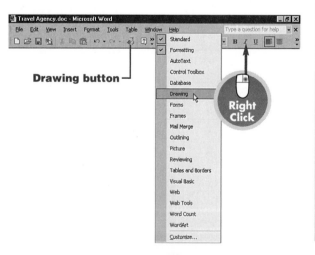

Drawing button

❷ Select a Drawing Tool

In the **Drawing** toolbar, click the tool for the shape you want to draw. To draw a rectangle, for example, click the **Rectangle** tool. Your mouse pointer takes the shape of a crosshair, and the Drawing Canvas appears onscreen.

Line ┘ └ Oval
Arrow ┘ └ Rectangle

❸ Drag the Shape

Click and drag the mouse to draw the shape inside the Drawing Canvas. When the shape reaches the desired shape and size, release the mouse button. You can now resize, rotate, move, or format the shape object as needed.

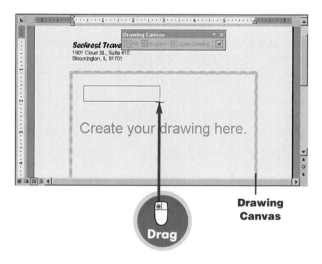

Drawing Canvas

4 Resize the Drawing Canvas

To adjust the Drawing Canvas to fit the size of the shape you've drawn, click and drag a resize handle on the Drawing Canvas or choose an option from the **Drawing Canvas** toolbar. For example, you can resize the Drawing Canvas frame to fit tightly around the shape you've drawn, or you can expand the canvas to allow more space around the shape.

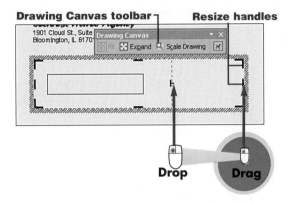

Drawing Canvas toolbar   **Resize handles**

Drop   **Drag**

5 Set a Wrap Style

You can set a text-wrap style for your shape by clicking the **Text Wrapping** button on the **Drawing Canvas** toolbar. *Wrapping* refers to how text flows around or through an object. For example, if you want the shape to appear behind the text, click the **Text Wrapping** button on the **Drawing Canvas** toolbar and choose **Behind Text** from the drop-down list.

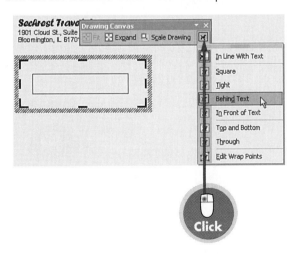

Click

6 Deactivate the Drawing Canvas

When you finish drawing a shape on the Drawing Canvas, click anywhere outside its frame. The Drawing Canvas frame closes, as does the **Drawing Canvas** toolbar.

Click

Using AutoShapes

If you're not too keen on drawing your own shapes, use the available predrawn shapes. Click the **AutoShapes** button on the **Drawing** toolbar to display a list of categories. Select the category you want to use; a palette of custom shapes appears. Select the shape you want to draw, and then you're ready to start drawing onscreen.

Drawing without the Drawing Canvas

You don't have to draw inside the Drawing Canvas frame, although it's helpful for organizing any objects you draw. You can draw shapes anywhere on your document.

Turning the Drawing Canvas Off

To turn the Drawing Canvas feature off, choose **Tools**, **Options** to open the **Options** dialog box. On the **General** tab, deselect the **Automatically Create Drawing Canvas When Inserting AutoShapes** check box.

How to Insert Clip Art

Another way to add visual impact to your Office files is to insert clip art images, which are ready-made drawings covering a wide range of topics and categories. You can insert clip art into any Office item you create, such as a letter, a worksheet, a database form, an Outlook note, or a slide. In the **Insert Clip Art** task pane, you can search for clip art and photographs, as well as sound and video clips. Clip art is organized into collections, including a collection that comes with Office XP. You can download other collections from the Web.

1 Open the Insert Clip Art Task Pane

Choose **Insert**, **Picture**, **Clip Art** to open the **Insert Clip Art** task pane. You can also click the **Insert Clip Art** button on the **Drawing** toolbar to open the task pane.

2 Conduct a Search

Click in the **Search text** box and type a keyword or phrase for the type of artwork you want to use in your file.

3 Choose a Collection

Use the **Search in** and **Results should be** drop-down lists to narrow your search by specifying a collection or media type to search for.

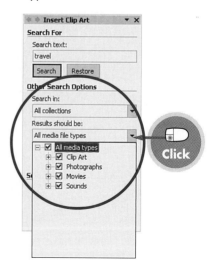

④ Start the Search

Click the **Search** button to begin the search for items that match the keyword you've entered.

⑤ Choose a Picture

The search results appear as a scrollable list with thumbnail versions of the possible matches. Scroll through the results until you find the clip art you want to use. If your keyword search doesn't reveal the results you're looking for, conduct another search. Click the **Modify** button in the task pane and start a new search using another keyword or phrase.

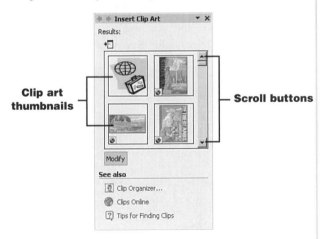

Clip art thumbnails

Scroll buttons

⑥ Insert an Item

To insert a specific piece of clip art, click its thumbnail in the task pane. That image is inserted into your document immediately. You can then resize or move the clip art as necessary (see Task 5, "How to Move, Size, and Rotate an Object").

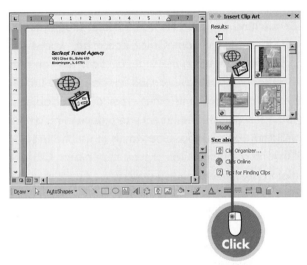

How-to Hint

Finding Clip Art on the Web

You can find more clip art images on Microsoft's Web site. Click the **Clips Online** link at the bottom of the **Insert Clip Art** task pane to open your Web browser to the clip art page at the Microsoft site. (You must connect to your Internet account first.)

Using the Clip Organizer

The **Clip Organizer** window lets you browse through clip art collections. To open the window, click the **Clip Organizer** link at the bottom of the **Insert Clip Art** task pane. Double-click the folder for the collection or category you want to view.

How to Insert an Object

If you have a picture file from another program, you can insert it into your Office document, worksheet, database form, email message, or slide. You can also insert objects such as scanned images, Word tables, Excel worksheets, and other types of visual objects. You insert objects in different ways, depending on the program you're using. One way is to use the **Insert**, **Object** command. This opens the **Insert Object** dialog box, where you can access a variety of visual objects.

1 Open the Insert Object Dialog Box

Choose **Insert**, **Object** to open the **Insert Object** dialog box.

2 Choose Create from File

To insert an existing object file in PowerPoint, click the **Create from file** option. If you're using Word or Excel, click the **Create from File** tab.

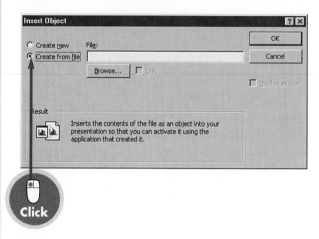

3 Open the Browse Dialog Box

To find the object file you want to insert, click the **Browse** button to open the **Browse** dialog box.

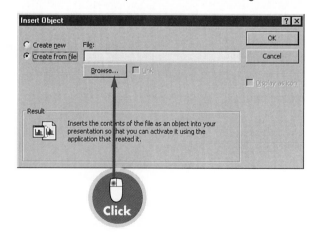

④ Locate the Object File

Locate the picture file or other visual object file you want to use. When you find the file, select it and click **OK** (in PowerPoint) or click **Insert** (in Word and Excel) to return to the **Insert Object** dialog box.

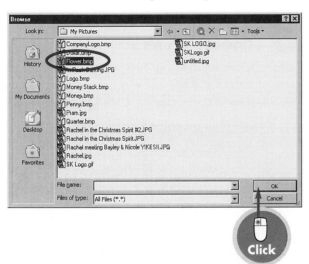

⑤ Click OK

When you're ready to insert the object file, click **OK** in the **Insert Object** dialog box.

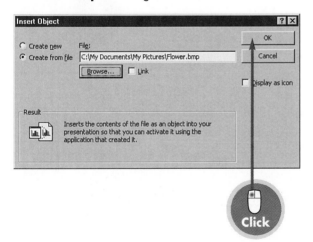

⑥ View the Results

The object appears in your file. You can now resize or move it as necessary.

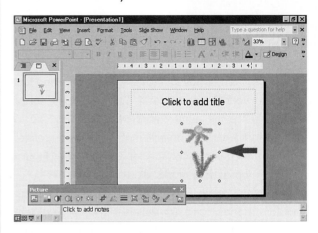

How-to Hint

Resizing and Moving

After you insert the picture, you can resize it or move it around. Learn how in Task 5, "How to Move, Size, and Rotate an Object," later in this chapter.

An Insert Trick

If you need to add the same picture file to several Word documents, you can add it to Word's AutoCorrect collection. First, insert the picture file into a document and select the graphic. Then choose **Tools**, **AutoCorrect**. In the **AutoCorrect** dialog box, type the picture's filename in the **With** box and type a text entry for the picture in the **Replace** box. If it's a company logo, for example, you might type `mylogo`. Click **Add** to add the entry to the list and then click **OK**. The next time you type `mylogo`, the picture will replace the text.

How to Insert a WordArt Image

WordArt is a handy tool for creating interesting text effects in your Office projects. You create art out of words, hence the name WordArt. It enables you to turn text into graphic objects that bend, twist, rotate, and assume a variety of special effects. You can turn ordinary words into works of art. WordArt is especially helpful when you need to create a company logo or a banner for a newsletter or flyer, or when you want draw attention to important words, such as *sale* or *urgent*. Once you've designed a WordArt object, you can move and resize it as needed.

❶ Open the WordArt Gallery

Choose **Insert**, **Picture**, **WordArt** to open the **WordArt Gallery** dialog box. Or you can click the **WordArt** button, if the **Drawing** toolbar is displayed.

❷ Choose an Effect

Select a WordArt style that best suits your needs. The samples show the shape and effect of the style, but not the actual text that will appear. Click **OK** to continue.

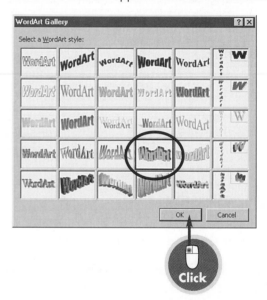

❸ Enter Your Own Text

In the **Edit WordArt Text** dialog box, type the text you want to use as your WordArt object.

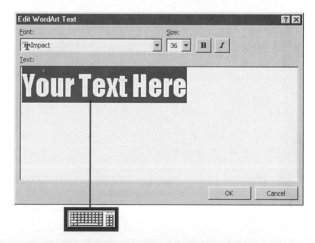

④ Format the Text

Use the **Font** drop-down list box to select another font style, if necessary. You can also change the font size and apply bold and italic. When you've finished making your formatting selections, click **OK**.

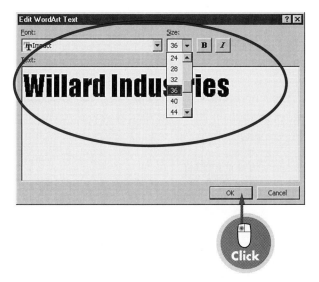

Click

⑤ WordArt Is Created

The WordArt object appears in your Office file, along with the WordArt toolbar. Use the toolbar buttons to fine-tune your WordArt object. (Refer to the How-To Hints that follow for suggestions.) You may have to move or resize the WordArt object. To learn more about moving and resizing objects, see Task 5, "How to Move, Size, and Rotate an Object."

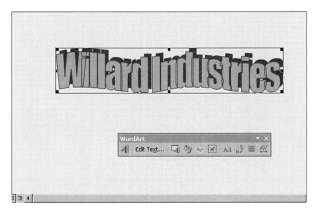

How-to Hint

Editing WordArt

Any time you need to edit your WordArt object, double-click it to reopen the **Edit WordArt Text** dialog box. You can also use the tools on the WordArt toolbar to format the object.

Try Them All!

To change your WordArt's shape or style, select the WordArt object and click the **WordArt Gallery** button on the WordArt toolbar. This opens the **WordArt Gallery** dialog box again. Choose a new style to apply. You might need to experiment with several styles before you find one you like.

I Changed My Mind!

If you open the WordArt Gallery and change your mind about using it, click **Cancel**. If you've already started creating an image and change your mind, click outside the picture. To remove a WordArt image you've already created, click to select it and then press the **Delete** key.

Endless Selections

By changing the text effects, fonts, sizes, and formatting attributes, you can create different WordArt shapes and designs. To reverse any of the changes you make, click **Undo** in the **Standard** toolbar.

How to Move, Size, and Rotate an Object

You can resize, move, and rotate any visual object that you add to your Office file. Objects include graphic images, clip art, WordArt, and any other drawing or shape you can create. When you select an object, selection handles appear around it. You can drag these handles in any direction to resize the object. You can also drag the object to a new location. To rotate the object, drag its rotation handle. The tricky part is knowing exactly where to click to perform any of these actions. In this task, you'll learn how to move, resize, and rotate any object.

❶ Select the Object

Select the object you want to move or resize. It's surrounded by tiny boxes, called selection handles or resize handles.

Selection handles

❷ Drag to Move

Hover the mouse pointer over the selected object until you see a four-headed arrow. Drag the object to a new location and drop the object in place. Notice that the dotted black lines show you exactly where you're moving the object.

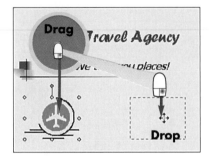

❸ Resize in One Dimension

To resize a selected object in one dimension—that is, to stretch or shrink it—use only the resizing handles that appear along the sides of the object. To stretch the object, for example, hover your mouse pointer over the handle on the right side and drag the handle. When the object is stretched the way you want it, release the mouse button.

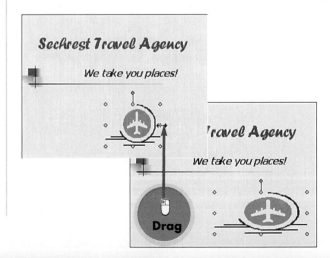

④ Resize in Two Dimensions

To resize the object in two dimensions, use any of the corner handles. Dragging a corner enables you to resize both the object's height and width at the same time. Hover the mouse pointer over a corner handle and drag. When the size is right, release the mouse button.

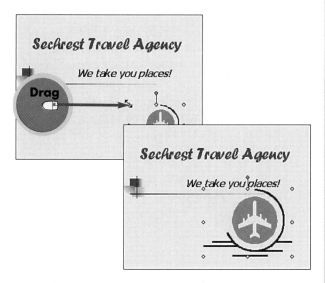

⑤ Rotate an Object

You can use the rotation handle at the top of a selected object to rotate it. Move the mouse pointer over the rotation handle until the pointer becomes a rotation icon. Click and drag the rotation handle in the direction you want to rotate the image.

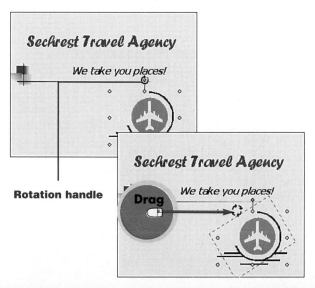

Rotation handle

⑥ Release the Mouse Button

Release the mouse button and view the object in its rotated position.

Copying and Pasting

You can easily copy and paste objects that you draw or insert with the Office graphics tools. Select the object and use the **Cut**, **Copy**, and **Paste** commands to move it to a new location. You can also copy the object and place it in a new location. Use the **Cut**, **Copy**, and **Paste** buttons on the **Standard** toolbar or find these options on the **Edit** menu.

Keeping the Size Proportional

You can maintain an object's height-to-width ratio while resizing if you hold down the **Shift** key while dragging a corner selection handle. To resize in two dimensions at once from the center of the object outward, hold down the **Ctrl** key and drag a corner selection handle.

How to Change Image Formatting

Many of the visual objects you add can be enhanced with formatting tools. You can format the shapes you draw, for example, by changing the fill color or line style. Adjusting your object's formatting can completely change its look. You can tone down an object's loud primary colors by using pastel colors instead. You can also change the importance of the line you've drawn by making its line weight thicker. The **Format** dialog box has formatting options for all kinds of object types.

1 Select the Object

First, click to select the object whose formatting you want to change.

2 Choose the Format Command

Right-click the object to display the shortcut menu, and then select the **Format** command at the bottom of the menu. The name of the command will depend on the type of visual object you selected in step 1. If you right-clicked a shape, for example, the command appears as **Format AutoShape**. If you right-clicked a text box, the command says **Format Text Box**.

3 Use the Format Dialog Box

The **Format** dialog box for the type of visual object you selected appears. Click the **Colors and Lines** tab to find options for changing the color or line style of the object.

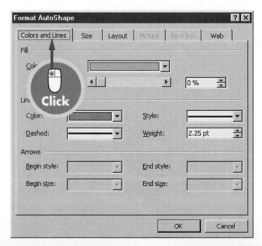

④ Change the Fill Color

The fill color is the color or pattern that appears within a shape. To change the fill color, click the **Fill Color** drop-down list button and choose another color from the palette.

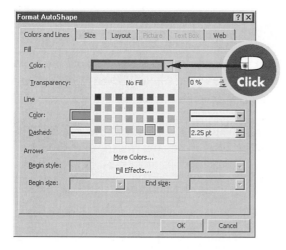

⑤ Change the Line Weight

If your object contains an outline or border, or if the object itself is a line or arc, use the **Line** options in the **Colors and Lines** tab to change the line's color, style, or weight (thickness). Click the **Style** drop-down arrow to display a list of line styles, for example.

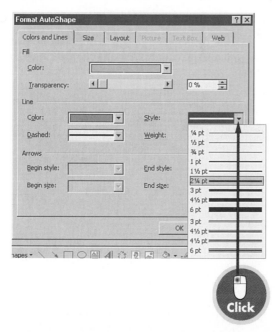

⑥ Wrap Text Around Objects

If you want the visual object to appear in the middle of a block of text, you can apply wrapping commands to designate how the text flows around (or through) the object. Click the **Layout** tab and choose a wrapping style to apply. Click **OK** to exit the dialog box and apply the new formatting settings you've selected.

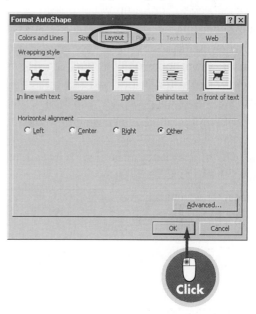

How-to Hint

Other Formatting Options

Be sure to check out the other tabs in the **Format** dialog box. You can apply numerous other options, depending on the visual object you've selected.

Using the Drawing Toolbar

The **Drawing** toolbar contains formatting tools you can apply directly to the objects you select. To fill an object with a color, for example, click the **Fill Color** button. To choose another line style to use, click the **Line Style** button.

How to Add Shadow Effects

Another way to spruce up visual objects is to add shadow effects. A shadow can give a 3-D effect to any text box, shape, clip art picture, line, WordArt design, or other visual object. With the drawing tool's **Shadow Settings** toolbar, you can control exactly where the shadow appears, you can set its color, and you can turn it off if you don't like it anymore.

1 Select the Object

To add a shadow effect to any object, first click to select the object.

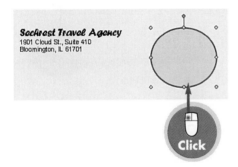

2 Click the Shadow Button

Click the **Shadow** button on the **Drawing** toolbar to display a palette of shadow effects. To apply an effect to the selected object, click the one you want.

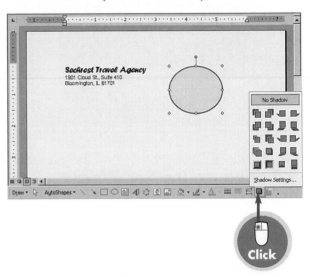

3 The Shadow Is Applied

The shadow effect is applied to the object.

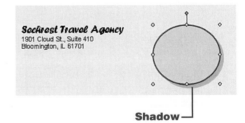

Shadow

4 Open the Shadow Settings Toolbar

For more control over the shadow, display the **Shadow Settings** toolbar. Click the **Shadow** button in the **Drawing** toolbar and select **Shadow Settings** from the palette.

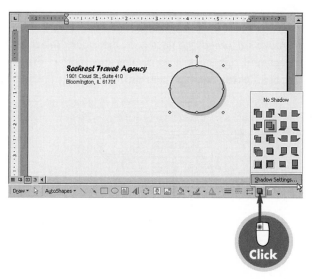

5 Nudge the Shadow

Use the **Shadow Settings** toolbar buttons to place your shadow exactly where you want it to fall. Use the **Nudge** buttons to nudge the shadow effect in the direction you want it to go. Click a button several times to nudge the shadow in that direction.

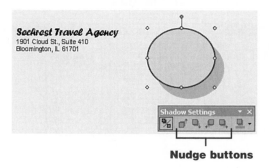

Nudge buttons

6 Choose a Shadow Color

To change the shadow's color, click the **Shadow Color** button and select a new color. This applies the color to the shadow. To close the **Shadow Settings** toolbar, click its **Close** button.

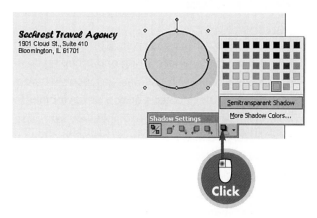

How-to Hint

Instant 3-D Effects

You can apply instant 3-D effects to your visual objects. Click the **3-D** button on the **Drawing** toolbar to display a palette of 3-D effects you can apply. To open the **3-D Settings** floating toolbar, choose **3-D Settings** from the palette. Now you can fine-tune the effects until you find just the right effect for your object.

Turning Off the Shadow

Click the **Shadow On/Off** button on the **Shadow Settings** toolbar to turn the shadow effect on or off.

How to Group and Ungroup Objects

A unique aspect of working with graphics objects in Office is that you can use layering and grouping commands to change the way the objects appear in a document. You can stack objects on top of each other to create interesting effects. For example, you can position a WordArt effect over a shape object to create a logo. You can also group objects together to treat them as a single object. Suppose that you have several objects stacked in place and want to move them over a bit. Rather than moving each object separately and layering them again, use the **Grouping** command to move the entire group as one object. After you've moved the group, you can break the objects apart and edit them separately.

① Layer the Objects

To layer objects, start by moving them on top of each other to create an effect. You might place a WordArt object on top of a shape you've drawn, for example, or stack a clip art object onto a larger shape to act as a background.

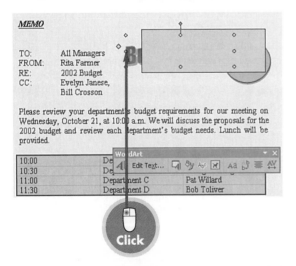

② Bring an Object to the Front

To move an object to the top of the stack, select the object and right-click it to display the shortcut menu. Choose **Order**, **Bring to Front**.

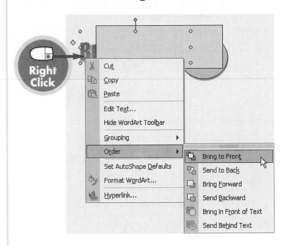

③ Move an Object to the Back

To move an object to the bottom of the stack, select the object, right-click it to display the shortcut menu, and choose **Order**, **Send to Back**.

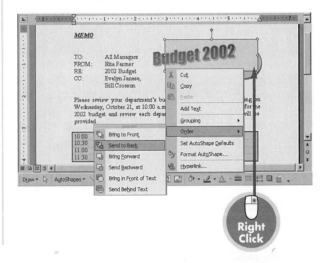

4 Select the Objects to Group

To group several objects together, click to select the first object, hold down the **Shift** key, and click to select each additional object to be grouped. (Notice that each object's selection handles are active.)

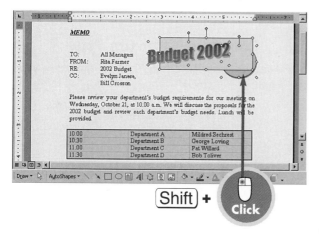

Shift + Click

5 Use the Group Command

Right-click any of the selected objects and choose **Grouping**, **Group** from the shortcut menu.

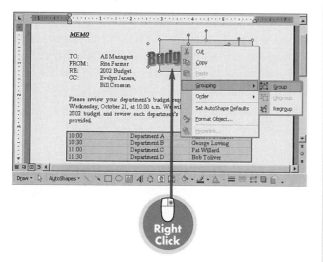

Right Click

6 Ungroup the Objects

The objects are now grouped and surrounded by a single set of selection handles. To break the objects apart again, right-click the grouped object and select **Grouping**, **Ungroup**.

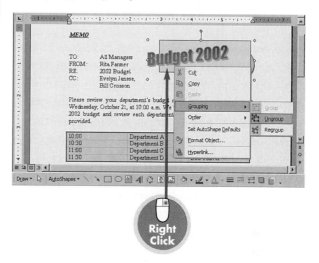

Right Click

How-to Hint

Layer by Layer

To move layers forward or backward one layer at a time, use the **Order**, **Bring Forward** or **Order**, **Send Backward** command, available from the object's shortcut menu.

A Group Shortcut

After you've layered a group of objects correctly, you might need to move them to another position. Click the **Select Objects** tool (the arrow icon on the **Drawing** toolbar), and then click and drag the mouse to create a rectangle that encloses all the objects. When you release the mouse, you've created a group. Drag this group to another part of the document—the layers stay in place. Click anywhere outside the group to break the objects apart.

How to Insert a Diagram

Use the new Office XP Diagram feature to add all kinds of diagrams to your Office projects. This feature can help you illustrate concepts, such as workflow or corporate hierarchy. When you add a diagram to your document, it opens within a drawing border or frame, along with a **Diagram** toolbar that has options for editing the diagram. You can add text elements to the diagram and rearrange the diagram shapes to suit your needs. The Diagram feature offers five different types of common diagrams: Organization, Venn, Cycle, Pyramid, Target, and Radial.

❶ Display the Diagram Gallery

Choose **Insert**, **Diagram** to open the **Diagram Gallery** dialog box.

Click

❷ Choose a Diagram Type

Select the diagram type you want to insert into your document and click **OK**.

Click

❸ View the Diagram

A diagram appears in your document along with the Diagram toolbar. You can edit the various elements that correspond to the type of diagram you selected in step 2. For example, to edit a text box element, click the box and type some text.

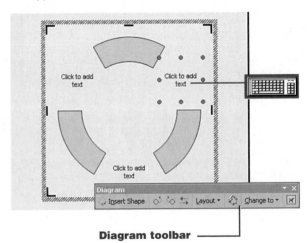

Diagram toolbar

④ Add a Shape

To add a shape to the diagram, click the **Insert Shape** button on the **Diagram** toolbar.

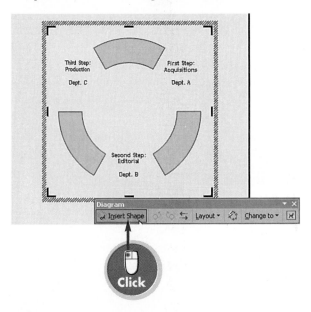

⑤ A New Shape Appears

Another shape element is added to the diagram. Depending on the diagram type, another text element may be added to correspond with the new shape.

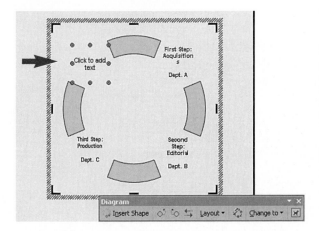

⑥ Deactivate the Diagram

When you finish building the diagram, click anywhere outside the frame. The diagram frame and the **Diagram** toolbar close, leaving just the diagram in your document.

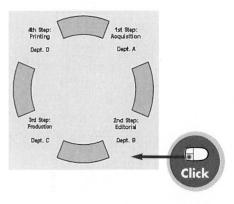

Changing the Diagram

To change the diagram to another type, click the **Change to** button on the **Diagram** toolbar and choose another type.

Repositioning Diagram Shapes

You can edit the arrangement of shapes in your diagram by clicking the **Move Shape Forward** or **Move Shape Backward** buttons on the **Diagram** toolbar. To completely reverse the flow of the diagram, click the **Reverse Diagram** button.

Editing Diagram Colors

Double-click the diagram to open the **Format Diagram** dialog box, which you can use to change the fill colors and lines used in the diagram. Double-click a shape within the diagram to open the **Format AutoShape** dialog box, where you can change colors and lines as well.

Glossary

SYMBOLS

3D card   A graphics card, used primarily for games, which enables realistic 3D motion.

802.11   The standard that governs how information is sent across a wireless network. Actually, several different 802.11 standards exist, not all of which are compatible with one another. Also known as **Wi-Fi**.

A

access number   The phone number your computer will dial to connect to the Internet. If this number is a long-distance call, you'll be running up long-distance charges every time you use the Internet, so you should choose the number carefully when setting up an account with an Internet service provider or America Online.

activate   Windows XP requires that you activate your product within a set number of days or you won't be able to continue using it. Activation is a separate process from registration. During activation, a small snapshot of key pieces of hardware on your system is sent to Microsoft. No personal information is required, and none of the hardware information can be used to identify you. In theory, activation prevents people from installing the same copy of Windows on more than one computer—an action that violates the software licensing agreement. *See also* **register**.

adapter card   *See* **expansion card**.

add-in card   *See* **expansion card**.

address bar   The text field along the top edge of a Web browser where you can type a Web page's URL and press **Enter** to load the page.

address book   A personal database of your email correspondents that is created in Outlook Express. Most other email programs offer a similar feature, including Qualcomm Eudora and PocoMail.

administrator   A user account created during Windows installation that gives full permission to use the computer and modify settings. Administrator is also a title given to a person who manages a computer network or system.

AGP (Accelerated Graphics Port)   A bus specification that enables 3D graphics to display quickly on a computer. The AGP bus is dedicated solely to graphics and offers more bandwidth than the PCI bus. It is required for graphically demanding applications.

antivirus software   Software that checks a computer for viruses and eradicates them if it finds them.

applet   A small program. In Windows, the programs you can access from the Control Panel window (Display, System, and Mouse, for example) are often called applets.

application   A program, such as Microsoft Word, that is separate from Windows.

archive   A collection of files copied to a specific location as a backup. When you install a Windows XP service pack, you have the option of archiving Windows files that the service pack will replace so that you can uninstall the service pack later.

associate   A document file is "associated with" the program that created it. Files of a certain type (for example, text files with the file extension .txt) are associated with the Windows applet Notepad. If you double-click a file to open it, the program associated with that file type launches and opens the selected file.

ATA A series of standards for IDE drives and devices. It covers a wide variety of features, including how the controller is integrated onto the drive itself.

ATAPI An IDE disk interface standard for devices such as CD-ROM or tape drives.

attachment A file that is inserted into an email message and sent to a recipient.

ATX A commonly accepted standard for the layout and form factor of the motherboard and power supply for PCs.

audio cable A cable that runs between a CD-ROM drive and a sound card and enables the sound card to play audio CDs.

Automated System Recovery A feature of the Windows XP Backup utility, Automated System Recovery backs up certain system files and then creates an emergency rescue floppy disk that you can use to restore your system following a failure.

automatic updating You can configure Windows XP to automatically monitor the Windows Update Site for updates and even to download them automatically when it finds them.

autosearch An Internet Explorer feature that enables search text to be typed in the browser's Address bar. Internet Explorer looks for the site (or sites) that best match the text.

B

back up To copy files from your primary computer to separate media (such as a floppy disk or Zip disk) in case the hard disk on the primary computer fails.

backplate A metal plate that helps secure add-in cards to the motherboard.

backward compatibility The ability of hardware or software to work with older versions of the same hardware or software.

baud The prevalent measure for data transmission speed until replaced by a more accurate term: bps (bits per second).

bidirectional parallel port A parallel port enabling data to flow in two directions between the PC and printer.

BIOS (Basic Input/Output System) The system that performs all the basic functions of your computer, such as sending information from your keyboard to your PC. The system BIOS is contained on the BIOS chip.

BIOS chip A chip that contains a system's BIOS. On many systems, it can be updated with a flash utility.

bookmarks Shortcuts to your favorite Web sites, also called *favorites*. This feature is available in Netscape Navigator, Internet Explorer, Opera, and other Web browsers. You can save bookmarks to sites you visit often, making it easier to load them in your browser.

boot To start a computer. During the boot process, the many files that make up the Windows operating system are loaded into memory.

boot disk A floppy disk that can be used to boot your computer. Boot disks are often used to recover from a system failure or to install Windows.

bootup screen The first screen you see when you start your computer.

briefcase A special folder designed primarily for users who want to transfer files to another computer. The briefcase contains functions for moving and synchronizing files.

broadband connection A connection to the Internet that's at least 10–20 times faster than you can get using a dial-up modem. Most broadband connections are made using television cable or DSL telephone line technology and cost about $40 to $70 per month. Contact your local cable or telephone company to see if it offers high-speed Internet connections. Broadband connections do not use your computer's modem. They require special hardware that might need to be set up by a professional such as a cable TV or phone installer.

browser A program, such as Internet Explorer, that can display a Web page. Some browsers can display text, graphics, and frames; other browsers can display only text. Popular browsers other than Internet Explorer include Netscape Navigator and Opera.

Buddy List A feature of America Online that enables you to keep track of friends, relatives, and other acquaintances who also use the service. The Buddy List lets you know when someone is connected to AOL or AOL Instant Messenger so that you can send the person an instant message.

bus A pathway in the PC over which data travels.

C

cable connection   *See* **broadband connection**.

cable modem   A device that enables your computer to access the Internet at high speed via the cable TV system. Although called a modem, it uses technology different from modems that use traditional telephone lines.

cache memory   Random access memory (RAM) that a computer microprocessor can access more quickly than regular RAM.

cascade   A way to arrange multiple windows on the screen. The multiple windows are layered, one on top of the other, so that the title bars of all the windows can be seen.

CD-R drive   A CD-ROM drive that lets you write data one time per a special CD.

CD-ROM   A type of optical disc that stores up to one gigabyte of data. The setup files for most applications today come on CD-ROM discs.

CD-ROM drive   A device that can run CD-ROMs.

CD-RW drive   A CD-ROM drive that lets you write data many times per a special CD.

chat   The most immediate way to communicate with someone over the Internet. A chat is a live (real time), back-and-forth discussion that takes place between two or more people over the Internet instead of over voice telephone lines or in person. *See also* **chat room**.

chat room   Also called simply a *chat*. The "place" in cyberspace where people gather to discuss a particular topic. In reality, people sit at their computers, separated by huge distances, and type questions, comments, and criticisms. Other users respond to those comments in real time. Although the discussion may be hampered by slow typing speeds, the effect is as if you are sitting in a coffee bar someplace talking over the events of the day with other people who share your interests. *See also* **chat**.

chip puller   A tool for removing chips from your PC.

clean installation   An installation of Windows onto a blank, formatted hard disk. *See also* **upgrade**.

click   To position the mouse pointer over a file or folder and click the left button on the mouse once. Clicking is used to select files in Windows and to follow a link on the Internet.

Close button   The button with the X on it, found in the upper-right corner of most windows and dialog boxes. Click the Close button to close a window.

CMOS battery   A small battery that provides power to the CMOS chip.

CMOS chip   A chip containing a record of the hardware installed on your PC. The CMOS battery supplies it with power, so the data remains stored even when the computer is off. The CMOS stores the information contained in the BIOS settings as well as maintains the clock. On older systems, there will be a separate chip; on newer systems, the function is integrated onto the motherboard chipset.

CMOS setup screen   A screen that enables you to change your CMOS settings.

cold boot   Starting a computer from a state in which the power is off.

collection   A group of associated pictures or video clips in Windows Media Player. Collections are used for organizational purposes.

color depth   The number of colors displayed on your screen. Common color depths include 16 colors, 256 colors, 16,000 colors (24-bit), and millions of colors (32-bit). Change the color depth used by Windows using the Display Properties dialog box.

community   *See* **MSN Community**.

COM port   *See* **Serial port**.

compression   A way to store data so that it takes up less disk space than normal. Windows XP offers built-in compression that does not require a separate application.

computer name   A name of up to 15 characters given to a computer. On a network, this name helps distinguish the computer from other computers.

Control Panel   A special folder that contains applets used to configure various Windows settings, such as display, mouse use, and sound.

Controller   A device found on an add-in card or on the motherboard that connects the motherboard to a hard drive.

Controller card   An add-in card that has a controller on it. *See also* **Controller**.

cookie   A special browser file stored on your system that a Web site can use to personalize your visit to the site. Web sites can read the cookie files they have created, which enables a site to recognize who you are when you visit. By design, browsers send cookies only to the site that created them.

CPU (Central Processing Unit)   The main processor on a PC, such as a Pentium or Athlon chip.

cradle   A device into which a PDA is inserted that allows it to synchronize its data with a PC's.

D

daisy-chain   A configuration in which devices are connected one to another in a chain-like fashion, one attached to the next. USB devices can be connected in a daisy chain.

decryption   To remove the encryption from a file or folder. *See also* **encryption**.

default   A setting automatically selected by Windows or another program if you do not specify another setting.

defragment   *See* **fragmentation**.

Defragmenter   Software that allows a hard disk to run more quickly by *defragmenting* it—placing all related pieces of files next to one another so they can be called into memory more quickly.

desktop   The metaphor used by Windows to display your file system. The desktop is the main screen in Windows, on which various icons are displayed.

desktop theme   A coordinated collection of background colors, wallpaper, mouse pointers, and sounds used to provide a unique feel to your desktop.

device driver   A file that controls and is required for running a particular type of device attached to your computer. Device drivers exist for printers, displays, CD-ROM readers, disk drives, and so on.

Device Manager   An application used to control the settings for hardware on your computer. The Device Manager is used to enable and disable hardware devices, as well as to control driver versions and other settings.

DHCP (Dynamic Host Configuration Protocol) A computer protocol that assigns a different IP address to a computer each time it connects to the Internet.

When you set up a home network to share a high-speed Internet connection, such as a cable modem, you often must also set up DHCP.

dialog box   A small window that opens on your computer as a program is running, often to ask a single question that can be answered by clicking a button containing a label such as Yes, No, or Cancel.

dial-up connection   A way of connecting to the Internet using a phone modem and an ordinary phone line. Your computer dials the number of an Internet service provider's modem and attempts to make a connection. No one else can use the phone line while you're connected to the Internet; as a result, many people add a second line that's strictly for use by a computer.

digital camera   A camera that records and stores photographic images in digital format, which can be read by a computer.

DIMM (dual inline memory module)   A type of RAM used in newer PCs, it attaches to the motherboard via a series of pins.

DIN connector   A connector between the keyboard and the computer.

DIP (dual inline package)   A type of RAM used in older computers.

DIP switch   A switch on an add-in card or on the motherboard used to configure a computer or peripherals.

disable   In a list of check-box options (as in a dialog box), to remove a check mark from the check box for a particular option. In contrast, you enable an option by clicking an empty check box to place a check mark in the check box.

display adapter   *See* **graphics card**.

DMA (Direct Memory Access)   A way in which data moves between a device and system memory without the use of the CPU.

docking station   A piece of hardware attached to a laptop that enables the laptop to use expansion cards and devices such as external monitors and keyboards. It is sometimes called a port replicator.

domain   A way of grouping computers and users in a fairly complicated network. Domains are often used at large companies, where powerful computers called "servers" provide security, Internet access, file storage, and much more to less powerful computers called *workstations*. If your computer is on a Windows network, it will either be part of a domain or part of a workgroup. *See also* **workgroup**.

double-click   To position the mouse pointer over a file or folder and click the left mouse button twice in rapid succession. Double-clicking opens, or launches, a file or folder.

download   To copy a file from another computer to your system, using a network such as the Internet or another means of connecting computers. You can download data files, programs, and many other types of files from sites all over the Internet to your local server or hard drive. A word of caution: Downloaded files are a major source of computer viruses, so you should have up-to-date antivirus software on any computer to which you are actively downloading files. You also should download files only from sources you know and trust.

DPI (dots per inch)   A measurement of the quality of the output of a scanner or printer, or of a computer monitor. The more dots per inch, the higher the quality.

draft mode   To print a document in a special mode offered by many programs that reduces the amount of ink used during printing and also reduces the quality of the printed document.

drive bay   A bay inside a PC into which you install devices such as hard disks, floppy disks, and CD-ROM drives.

driver   A piece of software used to enable a peripheral, such as a printer or video card, to work with your PC.

DSL connection   *See* **broadband connection**.

DSL modem   A device that enables your computer to access the Internet at high speed via special DSL lines. Although called a modem, it uses technology different from modems that use traditional telephone lines.

dual-boot   A computer on which two operating systems have been installed. When a computer is configured to dual-boot, you are presented with a menu when the computer first starts that prompts you to choose the operating system you want to use.

DVD decoder card   An add-in card that helps play DVDs.

DVD drive   A drive that can run DVD discs or play DVD movies.

DVD-RW drive   A DVD-ROM drive that lets you write data to special DVDs.

E

eBay   A popular Web site where members buy and sell items using auctions that usually last from 7 to 10 days. A unique bidding method keeps a prospective buyer's maximum bid secret until it is needed to outbid someone else. To visit the site, type the URL http://www.ebay.com into a Web browser's Address bar and press Enter.

EDO RAM (extended data output RAM)   A type of random access memory.

email   Electronic mail messages sent between different users on a network, such as the Internet. Some email systems are configured only on a local network, and email messages can only be sent between other users on the network.

enable   In a list of check-box options (as in a dialog box), to place a check mark in the check box for a particular option. In contrast, you disable an option by clicking a check mark to make the check box empty.

encryption   To translate data into a secret code that only certain users can access. Windows XP provides built-in encryption. After a user encrypts a file, only that user can decrypt the file. A way to encode data so that it remains confidential. Some Web servers can encrypt Web pages and other data so that you can enter confidential information on a site, such as when you are buying a product online and want to transmit your credit card information.

enhanced parallel port   A parallel port that offers transfer rates of up to 2MB per second. It can be used for printers and other devices.

enhanced parallel port cable   A cable you must use to take advantage of the enhanced parallel port. The numbers and IEEE 1284 are printed on the side of an enhanced parallel port cable.

EPP/ECP (Enhanced Parallel Port/Enhanced Capability Port)   A type of parallel port offering transfer rates of up to 2MB per second, for use with peripherals other than the printer. It enables higher data transfer rates than the original parallel port. EPP is for nonprinter peripherals; ECP is for printers and scanners. *See also* **enhanced parallel port** and **enhanced parallel port cable**.

Ethernet   A standard for tying together computers in a local area network.

Ethernet card   A network card that adheres to the Ethernet standard. Virtually all network cards sold for the PC are Ethernet cards.

Everyone group   A special security group that includes all users of the network. By default, the Everyone group is given read access to all files and folder on your computer that you share with the network. It is best to remove this group and narrow the focus of users to whom you allow access to a resource.

event   An occurrence in Windows, such as when you delete a file or empty the Recycle Bin. An event can also be an occurrence you don't cause, such as when Windows displays an error message. Most such occurrences can be associated with sounds.

expansion card   Also called adapters or add-in cards, these plug into the motherboard on expansion slots and expand how your PC can be used. Video cards, disk controllers, and graphics cards are just a few of the expansion cards you can add to a PC.

expansion slot   A slot on the motherboard into which expansion cards can be plugged.

Explorer   *See* **Windows Explorer**.

extension   The three-letter suffix following the dot in a filename. The extension usually identifies the type of file (for example, a .doc extension identifies the file as a Microsoft Word document, a .jpg extension identifies the file a s a JPEG image file).

Extranet   A company network built using Internet technologies that is available to business partners of a company as well as to the company itself.

F

FAT (file allocation table)   Maintained on a hard disk by an operating system, it's a table that provides a map of the clusters (the basic unit of logical storage on a hard disk), detailing where files have been stored.

FAT32   A version of the File Allocation Table (FAT) disk format used mainly in Windows 98 and Windows Me. Windows XP can also use the FAT32 file system. When using FAT32, Windows XP cannot use several advanced features, such as encryption and compression. For that reason, it is best to use the NTFS file system with Windows XP whenever possible.

favorites   A special folder that contains links to favorite Web pages in Internet Explorer. *See also* **bookmarks**.

feedback rating   A numeric ranking that is listed with every eBay buyer or seller, so that you can evaluate whether or not you want to do business with that person. *See also* **eBay**.

file   A collection of data that is stored as a single unit on a disk drive and given a name. Almost all information stored on a computer, including Windows itself, is stored as files.

file sharing   The practice of downloading files from other people and making your own files available to others, which is most popular among people who are exchanging MP3 files. Millions of people use file-sharing programs such as WinMX or services such as AudioGalaxy and Gnutella, a source of ongoing controversy because these services do nothing to stop people from exchanging copyrighted music by popular musicians.

firewall   A system designed to prevent unauthorized access to a computer or an entire network. Firewalls can be hardware-based or software-based. Windows XP comes with a software firewall. Using a personal firewall is a good idea when setting up a home network connected to the Internet because it can prevent attacks. *See also* **proxy server**.

FireWire   A standard that enables devices to be easily connected to a PC without having to open the case, and that allows devices to communicate at high speeds. It is also called IEEE 1394.

Flash memory   A type of memory easily updated by running a patch or piece of software. BIOS chips often contain flash memory, and so easily can be updated by running software. Flash memory is also called flash ROM.

floppy disk   A removable disk that can hold up to 1.44MB of data. Floppy disks are commonly used to transfer information between computers and to back up small amounts of data.

floppy drive   A drive that stores information on removable disks that hold 1.44MB of data.

folder   A Windows object that can contain files and other folders. Folders are used to organize storage. (On older, nongraphical systems, folders are called directories.)

format   To prepare a storage medium, such as a hard disk or floppy disk, for writing data. Windows includes utilities for formatting disks.

fragmentation   When data is deleted from a hard drive, the data is not actually removed. Instead, it is marked so that it can be overwritten. When new data is stored, it is written to any empty spaces on the drive. These spaces are not necessarily contiguous, which leads to a condition known as fragmentation. Fragmented drives are usable, but can slow down a system. Windows XP includes a defragmenting program that rewrites the data on a drive so that it is contiguous.

frames   A way of dividing a single Web page into separate sections, each of which can have its own scrollbar and border. Clicking a hyperlink in one frame often causes a page to be opened in a different frame.

G-H

game port   A port into which you plug a joystick or other gaming device.

graphics accelerator   A graphics card, chip, or chipset that speeds up the display of graphics on a PC.

graphics card   An add-in card that gives your computer the capability to display graphics and video on your monitor.

handle   A screen name that identifies you to the Internet-using public. Comparable to a CB radio handle, an Internet handle can say something about your personality (Grumpy1), your career (BeanCount), or your hobbies (QuiltingB). Of course, it can also be an easy-to-remember moniker such as *FirstName.LastName*.

hard drive   Where data and programs are stored, even when you turn off your computer.

hardware driver   *See* **driver**.

heatsink   A device attached to a CPU that cools down the CPU so that it doesn't overheat.

home page   The first page your browser loads when you start up the browser. Your browser's home page is often a page on MSN or one hosted by your computer's manufacturer. There are many portals you might want to consider as candidates for your home page. You can specify the home page that loads when you start up the browser. Web sites also have home pages; these pages are the first page you see when you visit a Web site. *See also* **portal**.

host   In the context of the World Wide Web, to make pages and other documents (a Web site) available to users of the Internet. Many Internet service providers offer a limited amount of free space on their servers for you to publish your Web pages; companies are also available that will host sites for free. The provider's server then becomes the host for your site.

hover   To position the mouse pointer over an area without clicking the mouse button. Hovering the mouse pointer over a hyperlink on a Web page displays the filename or the URL of the page that will load if you click that hyperlink. Hovering over an area in a program window will frequently display a ScreenTip or a ToolTip.

HTML (Hypertext Markup Language)   The text formatting and presentation language used to create most Web pages.

hyperlink   Text, graphics or other elements of a Web page that you can click to load a new document into your Web browser. When you click a hyperlink, your browser loads the document to which the link refers; that document can be a Web page, a graphics file, or some other type of information. When you create your own Web page, you can include hyperlinks to any other file—whether that file is a graphics file on your local hard drive or a sound file on somebody else's Web site, for example.

hypertext   Text on a Web page you can click to load a new document and jump to a particular location within that document.

I

icon A small picture on the desktop or in a folder that represents a file or folder. The icon usually helps indicate what kind of file or folder an object is.

ICQ The software that pioneered the instant messaging style of communication. The program is named for the phrase *I Seek You*. An estimated 100 million people have downloaded ICQ's free software, making it one of the most popular instant messaging services on the Internet.

IDE (Integrated Drive Electronics) A standard that details the way in which a computer's motherboard communicates with storage devices, such as hard disks.

IDE/EIDE hard drive A hard drive that connects to the motherboard via an IDE/EIDE controller card.

IEEE-1394 *See* **FireWire**.

inbox The folder in an email program to which new messages are delivered.

indicator light The light or lights on the front of the PC that show when the computer is turned on, or when the hard disk or CD-ROM drive is being used.

ink cartridge A cartridge for inkjet printers.

install To load software (such as Windows or Microsoft Office) onto your computer. Most programs are installed using a setup program that guides you through the installation step by step. The word *install* is also used to refer to the process of setting up other devices and software configurations on a computer. For example, configuring a printer to work on your computer is often referred to as "installing the printer." Hooking up a new hard drive inside your computer is referred to as "installing the hard drive."

instant messaging A style of chat in which you keep track of people you know who are using the same software. A server tells you when selected people are online and provides the same information about you to others. You can send private messages that are received instantly on another user's computer.

Internet Explorer The Web browser built into Windows XP.

Internet service provider (ISP) A company that offers access to the Internet through your computer's modem. You can find local ISPs in your local Yellow Pages; national ISPs such as America Online, AT&T WorldNet, and EarthLink are also options. All ISPs offer assistance in setting up your computer to work with the Internet.

intranet A private network of computers that are connected together at a business, school, or another organization. If you are connecting to the Internet using a computer on an intranet, you may have to consult your network administrator for details on how to access the World Wide Web, email, and other services.

IP address A set of numbers, such as 150.2.123.134, that identifies each computer connected to the Internet. To use many Internet services, each computer must have a unique IP address.

IRQ (interrupt request) A connection between a device and a controller. Only one device at a time can use a particular IRQ.

ISP (Internet service provider) A company that provides access to the Internet for a monthly fee.

J-K

JPEG A graphics file format that makes use of lossy compression techniques, which means that image quality is degraded when you compress the file.

joystick A device for playing games that plugs into the game port.

jumper A small set of pins set in a particular way on the motherboard or add-in card to configure devices to work with a PC.

keyboard port A port into which the keyboard is plugged. Most often, it is a PS/2 port.

L

LAN (local area network) A network of computers connected together so they can share files and printers and also share a high-speed Internet connection, such as a cable modem. This enables them all to access the Internet from one connection. LANs can be connected to one another to form a wide area network (WAN).

lasso The dotted rectangle that follows the mouse pointer when you drag around a group of objects. The lasso encircles the objects and selects all the objects at once.

LCD (liquid crystal display) The kind of display used in laptop computers.

link On a Web page, a selection of text or a graphic that, when clicked, causes the Web browser to load another Web page.

local printer A printer that is connected directly to a computer. This differs from a network printer that may be connected to a different computer on a network or directly to the network itself.

logon Because it is a secure system, Windows XP requires that you enter a username and password so that it can register you with the network and determine the permissions you have been given on a computer.

lossless compression The condition in which no elements of a picture are lost during compression, resulting in higher picture quality and often larger size of picture files.

lossy compression The condition in which certain elements of a picture are lost during compression, resulting in lower size of picture files but also reduced quality of pictures.

LPT1 The name given to the primary parallel port on a computer. The first printer attached to a computer usually uses the LPT1 port.

M

Mac address A number that identifies a network card. Each network card has a unique Mac address so that it's the only one in the world with that address. When you install a cable modem, you must tell your cable provider your network card's Mac address; otherwise, you cannot connect to the Internet.

mailing list A group discussion that takes place entirely with email. People who are interested in a list's topic send an email message to a specific address to subscribe. If the list allows public participation (as many do), you can use a special email address to send a message to all list subscribers. Any message sent by another member to the list of subscribers appears in your inbox.

Makebt32 The program used to make the set of floppy disks used for Windows XP installation. Makebt32 can be found in the BOOTDISK folder on the Windows XP installation CD.

map To create a shortcut to a shared resource on the network by telling your computer to treat the resource as a separate drive on your computer. Because not all programs know how to work with Network Place shortcuts, you can "fool" these programs into working with these shared resources by making them think that the resource is on a different drive on your computer.

maximize To enlarge a window on your desktop to maximum size, filling your screen.

memory bank A series of slots or sockets on the motherboard that holds RAM.

memory socket A socket on the motherboard into which RAM is installed.

menu A collection of related commands in a program that is accessed by clicking once on the menu's title.

microprocessor *See* **CPU**.

Microsoft Passport A free account you can use on all Microsoft Web sites and more than 125 other sites. On Windows XP, you can associate a different Passport account with each person who uses your computer. To set up a Passport, you must have an email account.

minimize To remove a window on your desktop from view. After it's minimized, you can access the window using its taskbar button.

modem Short for modulator/demodulator. A device for connecting a computer to other computers or the Internet. Modems can be located outside the computer (called an external modem), or inside the computer (called an internal modem).

motherboard The main part of the PC—a very large board into which the CPU, add-in cards, chips, RAM, and many other devices are plugged.

mounting rails Rails inside a drive bay to which hard drives and other storage devices are attached.

mounting screws Screws that secure a drive into a drive bay.

mouse port A port into which the mouse is plugged.

MP3 (MPEG-1 Audio Layer 3) A popular format for presenting recorded sound on a computer. The format was developed with the goal of preserving sound quality while making files as small as possible.

MP3 file   A computer file ending in the extension .mp3 that when run plays music. The MP3 standard compresses music so that the files are relatively small but still retain the high quality of the music.

MP3 player   A small portable device that can play MP3 files.

MSN   MSN is a free Web portal that includes news, email, travel and consumer information, instant messaging, and Web hosting. To visit the site, type the URL http://www.msn.com into your browser's Address bar and press Enter.

MSN Community   Web sites created by MSN members that can include message boards, photo albums, a place for files, and other features. There's no cost to set up these sites, which require a Microsoft Passport.

MSN Explorer   A simplified Web browser that provides quick access to many MSN-related services, such as Web-based email, calendar, and personalized Web services.

MSN Messenger   An instant messaging program, much like ICQ or AOL Instant Messenger, that can be used to communicate directly with another person on a network or the Internet.

My Computer   A special folder located on the Windows desktop that contains all the drives (hard disks, floppy disks, CD-ROM, and network drives) available on a computer.

My Documents   A special folder located on the Windows desktop meant to hold all documents and personal files you create.

My Network Places   A special folder located on the Windows desktop used to browse other computers available on the network.

My Pictures   A special folder in the My Documents folder that has special features for viewing and working with pictures.

N

nanosecond   The speed at which RAM is rated. The lower the nanosecond rating, the faster the memory. For example, a 7-nanosecond chip is faster than a 12-nanosecond chip.

netiquette   Commonly accepted standards for behavior on the Internet.

NetCam   *See* **WebCam**.

network   Several computers (and sometimes other devices) that are connected together so that they can share software, data files, and resources. See also **local area network** and **wide area network**.

network card (NIC)   An add-in card that enables a computer to be connected to a network or to the cable system or DSL line to get a high-speed Internet connection.

network drive   A shared resource, such as a folder, treated as a drive on your computer. A network drive gets its own drive letter and shows up in the My Computer window.

network hub   A device to which PCs are connected that enables them to communicate with one another as part of a local area network. Also, each PC can access the Internet through the hub.

Network Place   A shortcut to a resource (a file, folder, or a device) on the network. The shortcut you set up to that location works only on your computer; other computers on the network may or may not have the same Network Places you do.

network printer   A printer that is connected to another computer on the network or to the network itself and for which an icon is created in the Printers and Faxes folder on your computer.

news server   An Internet site that can send and receive Usenet newsgroup messages.

news   In the context of Usenet, public messages contributed to the newsgroup.

newsgroup   An Internet-based forum in which you can participate in threaded discussions. *See also* **Usenet**.

NIC (network interface card)   *See* **network card**.

NNTP   A protocol used by servers that offer Usenet, a form of discussion on the Internet. When you subscribe to an Internet service provider, you might be given the name of an NNTP server. Use this name to set up newsgroups on Outlook Express or another program that offers access to Usenet.

nonparity RAM chips RAM chips that do not perform error checking to see whether any other memory chips are not functioning properly. Most RAM sold today is nonparity.

NTFS The native file system format used by Windows XP. See also **FAT32**.

O

object An item on your screen (usually an icon) that represents a program, file, or folder.

OEM (original equipment manufacturer) A company that buys computers in bulk, customizes them, and then sells them under its own name.

offline folders Folders that have been marked to be accessible when your computer is not connected to the network. Files in offline folders are periodically synchronized with the actual files on the network.

offline viewing Looking at a Web document while not actually connected to the Internet. If your telephone and your computer share the same line, you can look at pages offline as you're talking on the phone—which you can't do if you're viewing online.

operating system A program or group of programs that controls the file system, drive access, and input for a computer. Windows XP is an example of an operating system.

Outlook Express The email and newsreader program included with Windows XP.

P

Palm A small, handheld computer commonly used for keeping track of contacts, appointments, to-do lists and similar items. It uses the Palm operating system.

palmtop A generic name for a PDA. See **PDA**.

parallel port A port into which the printer is plugged. It also can be used for scanners and other external devices. See also **LPT1**.

parity RAM chips RAM chips that perform error checking to see whether any other memory chips are not functioning properly. This is generally an older type of memory. Usually, 486 PCs and Pentiums use memory that is nonparity. Parity RAM chips have nine chips on them, instead of the eight found on nonparity memory.

partition A separate portion of a hard drive. It can also be used as a verb: You divide a hard drive into sections by partitioning it.

parent folder In a hierarchical list of folders on your computer, the parent folder is the folder above (and thus the folder that contains) the folder you are currently in.

Passport See **Microsoft Passport**.

password A word, phrase, or combination of letters, numbers, and punctuation that you must use to gain access to a Web site, online store, Internet service provider, or another service on the Internet. It's a good idea to make your passwords impossible for others to guess; one way to do this is to make a password two unrelated words separated by a punctuation mark (such as **eve*school** or **ace!radar**). See also **username**.

path The description of the location of a file or folder on your computer or on a network. A typical path might include the drive letter, folders, and name of the file (for example, C:\My Documents\invoice.doc).

pause printing To stop a document in the print queue from printing. The document remains in the print queue but does not print until you choose to resume printing. Other documents waiting in the queue continue to print. See also **restart printing**.

PC card A credit card-size add-in card that plugs into a laptop computer and gives it extra functionality. Modems and network cards are common PC cards.

PCI (Peripheral Component Interconnect) A bus standard developed by Intel that allows for fast bus speeds.

PC slot A slot into which a PC card is plugged.

PCMCIA card An older term for PC card.

PCMCIA slot An older term for PC slot.

PDA A generic name for a small, handheld computer, designed to keep track of contacts, appointments, to-do lists and similar items.

peer On networks where there is no main server, all computers are part of a workgroup and are considered peers that can share their own resources and access other resources on the network.

peripheral A general term that refers to any device, such as a printer, modem, scanner, or others, that isn't required for the basic functioning of a computer but that can be used to enhance the way it works or to give it extra functionality.

permission On a secure system such as Windows XP, users are given specific rights (such as the ability to read or change a file) on objects.

phishing An attempt to steal a user's password or credit card information. On America Online and other places where instant messages and chat are popular, a person might masquerade as a system administrator who needs your password or credit card number because of a problem of some kind. This is always a hoax: No legitimate employee of an Internet provider asks for this information in email, instant messages, or a chat room.

phone jack A connector into which you plug a telephone wire to connect your modem to the telephone system.

pickup tool A tool for picking up small objects that have fallen into your computer.

pointer A small graphic (an arrow, by default) indicating the placement of the mouse on your screen.

POP3 (Post Office Protocol version 3) A protocol used by servers that deliver email. When you set up an account with an Internet service provider, your provider will often give you the name of a POP3 server to use when receiving mail. Save this information; you need it to set up an email program such as Outlook Express.

pop-under window An extra browser window that opens as you are visiting a Web page but is immediately minimized and out-of-view. The window shows up on your taskbar with other browser windows that have been opened but are not currently visible. Like pop-up windows, these are used most often for advertising purposes.

pop-up window An extra browser window that opens as you are visiting a Web page, usually to display advertising. The name comes from the way they pop up on the screen in front of the page you're trying to view.

port A connection on your computer into which you plug a cable, connector, or device.

port replicator See **docking station**.

portal A commercial Web site that functions as a gateway to the Internet. If you designate a portal as your browser's home page, you can start every online session on that page, giving some structure to your Internet experience.

power cable A cable that connects the power supply and provides power to devices in the PC, such as hard drives and floppy drives.

power supply A device inside your PC that provides power by converting the current from your wall outlet to the type of power that can be used by your PC and all its components.

presets Shortcuts to your favorite Web radio stations in Windows Media Player 7. Click a preset to begin listening to a particular station.

print device In Microsoft lingo, the actual printer hardware connected to a computer is referred to as the print device and the icon in the Printers and Faxes folder that represents the device is referred to as a printer.

print queue A list of documents waiting for their turn to be printed by a specific printer.

printer See **print device**.

priority The status a document has in a print queue. A document's priority governs when it prints related to other documents in the print queue. By default, all documents being printed are given a priority of 1, the lowest priority available. The highest priority is 99. Increasing a document's priority causes it to print before other waiting documents.

product activation New versions of Windows require that you register and activate the operating system over the Internet or by phone so that you may continue use beyond a short trial period.

product identification key The serial number found on the back of the Windows CD-ROM case and entered during the installation process that helps identify you as the proper owner of the software.

Program Access and Defaults A feature included with Windows XP Service Pack 1 that lets you control the default applications associated with certain files (such as Web pages) and activities (such as email). This feature also lets you specify whether icons for Microsoft versions of certain built-in programs are shown on your desktop and Start menu.

Properties A dialog box available for most files and folders that contains various settings relating to the object. You can access this dialog box for most objects by right-clicking the object and choosing the Properties command from the shortcut menu.

proxy server   A server set up between your computer and the Internet (generally in an office or academic environment). To get to the Internet, you have to go through the proxy server, which performs security checks to make sure that outsiders cannot access your company's network illegally. Also called a **firewall**.

publish   To upload files to a Web server to make those files available to users of the Internet. One way to design Web pages is to create them on your computer and then publish the pages to a Web server that has direct access to the Internet.

Q-R

queue   A list of the documents waiting their turn to be printed.

RAM (random access memory)   Memory where programs are run and data is stored while the data is being manipulated. When you turn off your computer, any information in RAM is lost.

RAM cache   Memory that sits between your CPU and your main RAM. Information is shuttled here from the main RAM to be available more quickly to the CPU. Cache is faster than normal RAM and includes intelligence. It is not part of the main memory in a PC and on most cases is not found directly on the motherboard.

RAMBUS   A type of high-speed RAM.

Recent Documents   A special folder available on the Start menu that contains shortcuts to the documents you have most recently opened.

Recycle Bin   A special folder on your desktop that temporarily holds files you delete from your computer. When the Recycle Bin becomes full, the oldest files are permanently deleted to make room for new files to be added. You can also empty the Recycle Bin manually, permanently deleting all files inside.

register   During registration of Windows, you provide certain personal information (name, address, phone number, and so on) to Microsoft so that the company can record you as the owner of a Windows license. Registering is optional. When you register, you are eligible for technical support, warranty, and software bulletins; you also might receive special promotions from Microsoft on other products. *See also* **activate**.

removable drive   A device that stores data permanently like a hard drive or a floppy drive does, but on removable disks. These disks commonly hold several hundred megabytes or more of data.

Reset button   A button that turns off your computer and then automatically turns it back on.

resolution   The dimensions of your screen. Common resolutions include 640×480 pixels, 800×600 pixels, and 1024×768 pixels. You can change the resolution of your screen using the Display applet on the Control Panel.

restart printing   To begin printing a paused document again from the beginning. Restarting a print job can be useful if, for example, you start to print a document and then realize the wrong paper is loaded in the printer. You can pause the document, change the paper, and then restart the document. *See also* **pause printing**.

restore point   A special backup of system files and settings used by the System Restore application to return your computer to a particular state.

ribbon cable   A wide ribbon-like cable that connects a drive to a disk controller.

right-click   To hold the mouse pointer over a certain object and click the right mouse button once. Right-clicking an object usually opens a shortcut menu that contains commands relating to the object.

RIMM (RDRAM inline memory module)   A form of high-speed memory used by the newest, most powerful computers.

ROM (read-only memory)   Memory that is not *volatile*: It can be read but not changed, or can only be changed under specific conditions.

ROM BIOS chip   A chip that holds the code necessary for starting up your computer and for basic functions of receiving and sending data to and from hardware devices, such as the keyboard and disk drives.

router   A device that can connect networks and that routes information to and from the Internet. Routers are commonly combined with hubs in home networking devices to allow PCs to be networked and share an Internet connection.

S

scheduled task   A job (such as launching a program or backing up files) defined in the Task Scheduler application to run at a certain time.

screen name   *See* **username**.

screen resolution   *See* **resolution**.

screen saver   A small program that displays graphics on your screen when the computer has been idle for a certain amount of time. Although designed to prevent images displayed too long from permanently burning themselves into your monitor (a phenomenon that does not often occur on newer monitors), screen savers are mainly used for entertainment and for security in conjunction with a screen saver password.

ScreenTip   A small pop-up box containing text that defines or describes a particular area of the screen. You can display a ScreenTip by hovering the mouse cursor over the area of the screen in question. Some applications call the ScreenTips that appear for toolbar buttons ToolTips.

scroll   To move the display in a window horizontally or vertically to view information that cannot fit on a single screen.

SCSI (small computer systems interface)   A hardware interface for connecting hard disks, scanners, CD-ROM drives, and other devices to a PC.

SDRAM (synchronous dynamic random access memory)   A generic name for various kinds of DRAM synchronized with the clock speed for which the microprocessor is optimized.

search engines   World Wide Web sites that use computers to catalog millions of Web pages, which you can use to search for specific text. Some of the most popular search engines are AltaVista (`http://www.altavista.com`), Google (`http://www.google.com`), and HotBot (`http://hotbot.lycos.com`).

secure system   A computer that can be assigned a password so that unauthorized users are denied access.

secure Web server   Most often used for online shopping. A secure server encrypts information (such as a credit card number) that is sent to the server and received from it so that confidential information is hidden from anyone who might try to view it. These servers make use of Secure Sockets Layer (SSL), a protocol for protecting private information over the Internet.

security certificate   A special browser window that vouches for the authenticity of a program's author. After you see the security certificate, you can decide whether you want to let the program run on your machine. A security certificate is required only when you're working with ActiveX technology; Java doesn't require this kind of direct action by the user.

select   To click once and bring the focus to an object. For example, in a list of files displayed in an open folder window, you can click a file to select that file. Information about the selected object is frequently displayed.

Send to   A submenu available on the shortcut menu for most files and folders that contains commands for quickly sending files to certain locations, such as the floppy drive, desktop, and My Documents folder.

serial port   A port into which modems and other devices are plugged.

service pack   A collection of updates and features issued by Microsoft since the original release of a Windows operating system. Service packs are numbered (Service Pack 1, Service Pack 2, and so on) and are cumulative. For example, Service Pack 3 would contain all the updates found in Service Packs 1 and 2. At the time of this writing, Service Pack 1 is the only service pack issued for Windows XP, though more recent individual updates may be found on the Windows Update site.

server   A computer that sends information to other computers, either in response to a request or through an automated schedule. A popular type of server on the Internet is a Web server.

share   To allow network access to a file or folder on your computer. After you share an object, you can define which users can access the object and exactly what they can do with it.

shortcut   A small file that targets another file on your computer. Double-clicking the shortcut launches the target file.

shortcut menu   The menu available by right-clicking most files and folders. The shortcut menu contains different commands that are associated with the particular object.

signature file   Text that is automatically appended to email, Usenet postings, and similar documents. These files often contain your name, email address, favorite quote, and other personal information.

SIMMs (single inline memory modules)   A kind of RAM. They attach to the motherboard via a series of pins.

SMTP (Simple Mail Transfer Protocol)   Like POP3, a protocol used by email servers. When you sign up with an Internet service provider, your provider will often give you the name of an SMTP server to use when sending mail. You need this information to set up an email program such as Outlook Express.

socket   The way certain Intel Pentium microprocessors plug into a computer motherboard so they make contact with the motherboard's built-in wires or data bus. A number of different socket standards include Sockets 7, 8, 370, 423 and A.

sound card   An add-in card enabling your computer to play music and sounds.

spam   A kind of unsolicited Internet marketing in which thousands of email messages are sent out to anyone with an email account. An electronic version of junk mail, spam often promotes unsavory businesses and is forged so that the sender's identity is hidden. Spam is a widely loathed practice that is illegal to send in a few jurisdictions. The name was inspired by a Monty Python comedy sketch and is unrelated to the Hormel spiced meat product of the same name.

SSL   *See* **secure Web server**.

Start menu   The menu that opens when you click the Start button at the lower-left corner of your screen. The Start menu provides access to all your programs, special folders, and Windows settings.

standby   When your computer enters a mode in which the power to the monitor, hard drive, CD-ROM drive, and most other elements is turned off or reduced. Just enough power is fed to the computer's memory so that Windows remembers what programs were running and what windows were open. When your computer leaves standby, it should return to the same state it was in before it went to standby.

status area   *See* **system tray**.

streaming audio   Sound on the Internet that begins playing as soon as the file is selected rather than at the end of a complete download of the sound file. This format is especially well suited for concerts and live radio.

synchronization   In Outlook Express, the process of receiving new messages in Usenet newsgroups you have subscribed to.

synchronize   To cause offline files or folders to be in unison with the actual files and folders they represent. Files in either location with newer modification dates replace files with older modification dates.

System Restore   A Windows application that creates restore points (backups of certain system settings) and that can restore Windows to any particular restore point. *See also* **restore point**.

system tray   The part of your Windows taskbar that's next to the current time (usually in the lower-right corner of the display screen). This is also called the *status area*, and it may contain icons representing your Internet connection, speaker volume, antivirus software, and other programs that are running on your computer.

T

tape drive   A drive enabling data to be copied to a tape. The tape can hold hundreds of megabytes of data and is commonly used to back up data and hard disks.

taskbar   The strip along the bottom or side of your Windows display screen in which appear the Start button, the buttons for all active programs, the current system time, and the system tray.

TCP/IP (Transmission Control Protocol/ Internet Protocol)   The basic communication language or protocol of the Internet. It also can be used as a communications protocol in the private networks called intranets, and in extranets.

terminator   Attaches to a device on the end of a SCSI daisy-chain that lets the chain know the device is the first or last device in the chain.

thread   A group of replies to a single message in a newsreader program such as Outlook Express. When you reply to a message, your reply becomes part of the thread.

ticker symbol   A short, unique code assigned to a company by the stock exchange on which that company trades.

tile   A way to arrange multiple windows on the screen. The multiple windows are reduced in size so that some portion of each of them appears on the screen at once. You can tile windows either horizontally or vertically on the screen.

toner cartridge   An ink cartridge for laser printers.

ToolTip   *See* **ScreenTip**.

troubleshooter   A special file in the Windows Help program that walks you through steps to take in determining the cause of a problem with Windows. The troubleshooter frequently suggests resolutions to these problems or points you toward more information about the problem.

U-V

UART (Universal Asynchronous Receiver/Transmitter)   The chip that controls a computer's serial port and the interface to serial devices such as modems.

uniform resource locator (URL)   The address of a Web page. The URL for a Web page generally includes the type of file (such as http), the computer on which the file is located (such as www.microsoft.com), the folder on that computer where the file is located (such as /Windows/) and the name of the actual file (such as default.htm).

Universal Serial Bus (USB)   A standard that enables devices to be easily connected to a PC without having to open the case.

upgrade   To install Windows XP over an existing installation of a previous version of Windows (such as Windows 98/Me/2000/NT).

Uplink port   A port on a network hub that connects the hub to a cable modem or other external device for accessing the Internet.

URL (uniform resource locator)   *See* **uniform resource locator**.

USB hub   A device that enables many USB devices to connect to a computer at the same time.

USB port   A port that uses the USB standard and enables USB devices to easily connect to a PC.

Usenet   A collection of public discussion groups covering a diverse range of topics. Usenet groups, which also are called **newsgroups**, are distributed by thousands of Internet sites around the world.

username   A short version of your name, nickname, or handle that identifies you on a Web site or another service offered on the Internet. On America Online, a username is called a *screen name*. A username is usually paired with a password, and many Web sites such as Yahoo! require both of these when you are logging in to access the personalized features of the site.

V.90   A standard that allows 56 Kbps modems to communicate.

V.92   A standard that builds on the V.90 standard and adds features such as those that make connections more quickly.

video port   A port on the back of a graphics card to which the monitor is connected.

virus   A program that creates copies of itself, usually without permission, and could cause damage to files on your computer or reveal personal data to others. Viruses can be spread on floppy disks and by email, so you should protect yourself by installing an antivirus program on your computer. You also should not open any attached file you receive in email unless you know the sender (especially if the file is a program).

visualization   In a sound player such as the Windows Media Player or WinAMP, an animated program that reacts to sound as it is being played.

volume label   The name of a disk. When formatting a floppy disk, you can provide a volume label for the disk if you want; alternatively, you can leave the disk unnamed, as most people do.

W

wallpaper   A picture displayed on the Windows desktop behind any icons.

warm boot   Restarting a computer by using software rather than either turning the power off and back on or pressing a reset button.

Web browser   The tool that lets you view pages on the World Wide Web. After you connect to the Internet, you load a browser; then you can see and interact with pages on the Web. Some of the most popular browsers are Microsoft Internet Explorer, Netscape Navigator, and Opera. Internet Explorer 6 is used in many of the tasks in this book. *See also* **browser**.

Web directory World Wide Web sites that use human editors to categorize thousands of Web sites according to their content and make recommendations about the best sites. The main way to use these directories is to navigate to the categories you are interested in. Web directories include Yahoo! (http://www.yahoo.com), Lycos (http://www.lycos.com), and the Open Directory Project (http://www.dmoz.org).

Web page A document that is usually one of many related documents that make up a Web site and that is available for anyone to view with a Web browser such as Internet Explorer.

Web server A server on the Internet that sends Web pages and other documents in response to requests by Web browsers. Everything you view on the World Wide Web is delivered by a Web server to your browser. *See also* **server**.

Web site A group of related Web pages. When you are creating related Web pages in a program such as FrontPage Express, you should make an effort to link all the pages together as a site.

WebCam A small, inexpensive video camera that attaches to your computer and lets other people see videos of you live over the Internet.

weblog A Web site that's published as a series of diary-style entries, usually with the most recent entry listed first. Weblogs are often used to link to interesting Web sites and share personal details of the publisher's life. Two good examples: CamWorld at the URL http://www.camworld.com, and MetaFilter at the URL http://www.metafilter.com.

wide area network (WAN) Two or more LANs connected together over a distance. *See also* **local area network (LAN)**.

Wi-Fi *See* **802.11**.

Windows Explorer A tree-based application used to browse the file system on your computer.

Windows Media Player A program installed with Windows XP that is used to display picture files, music files, and movie files of various formats.

Windows Messenger Instant-messaging software from Microsoft that has an estimated 25 million users. You can send and receive instant messages, keep a list of contacts you communicate with regularly, and send email when one of the contacts is not connected to Messenger.

Windows Movie Maker A program installed with Windows XP that is used to create movie files out of still pictures and recorded video and audio.

wireless base station A hub/router the connects PCs wirelessly with one another and lets them communicate and share resources and an Internet connection, using the 802.11 wireless communications protocol, also called **Wi-Fi**. A small radio transceiver in the base station sends and receives data via RF frequencies in the 2.4 gigahertz range.

wireless network A network that allows PCs to communicate with one another without wires. Most wireless networks are based on the 802.11 wireless communications protocol, also called **Wi-Fi**.

wizard A Windows program that walks you through the steps involved in the installation or configuration of a Windows component or program. Most software developed by Microsoft includes an installation wizard that simplifies the process of setting up the program on your computer.

workgroup A group of computers operating as peers on a network. *See also* **peer** and **domain**.

X-Y-Z

Y2K bug The incapability of certain computers or computer functions to work when the year 2000 occurred.

ZIF (zero insertion force) socket A socket that lets you insert or remove a chip without using a special device.

Zip drive A model of disk drive made by Iomega with a removable disk roughly the size of a floppy disk that holds either 100MB or 250MB of data, depending on the exact model. Zip drives have become a popular way of backing up data on home computers.

Index

SYMBOLS

_ (underscore), 556
3D graphics effects, 683
3-D Settings toolbar, 683

A

absolute cell addresses, 572-573
Accept or Reject Changes command (Track Changes menu), 589
accepting document changes, 501
acceleration, 191
Access databases, 643
  creating, 646-647
  Database Wizard, 646-647
  Datasheet view, 649
  entering data in, 648-649
  fields
    adding to forms, 657
    creating, 651-652
    defined, 644
    deleting, 653, 656
    moving, 657
    properties, 653
    renaming, 651-653
    reordering, 653
  forms
    AutoForm options, 655
    closing, 649
    creating, 649, 654-655
    defined, 645
    Design view, 656
    fields, 656-657

Form Wizard, 654-655
headers/footers, 657
modifying, 656-657
naming, 655
navigating, 649
opening, 648, 656
saving, 657
naming, 646
planning, 645
queries
  creating, 662-663
  defined, 645
  filtering, 663
  naming, 662
  running, 663
  wildcards, 663
records
  creating, 648
  defined, 644
  filtering, 660-661
  sorting, 658-659
reports
  creating, 664-665
  customizing, 666-667
  defined, 645
  fonts, 666
  graphics, 667
  grouping categories, 664
  labels, 666
  layouts, 665
  previewing, 667
  removing objects from, 667
  report styles, 665
  Report Wizard, 664-665
  sorting, 665
  titles, 665

tables
  adding data to, 651
  closing, 653
  creating, 650-651
  defined, 644
  designing from scratch, 651
  modifying, 652-653
  naming, 651
  opening, 652
  Table Wizard, 650
Toolbox, 657
access numbers (ISPs), 280, 285-286
accessibility options, 208-209
Accessibility Options dialog box, 208-209
accounting programs, 17-19
accounts
  logging off, 73
  MSN Chat, 388-389
  selecting, 50
  switching, 70
  user accounts
    changing, 129
    creating, 128
    naming, 128
    opening, 128
    selecting, 50
Actions menu commands
  New All Day Event, 514
  New Mail Message Using, 527
  New Recurring Appointment, 512
  Plan a Meeting, 516

activating Windows XP, 270-271

Activation Wizard, 270-271

Add Data command (Chart menu), 599

Add Data dialog box, 599

Add Favorite dialog box, 299

Add Network Place Wizard, 134-135

Add Printer Wizard, 116-121

Add Schedule Task icon, 216-217

Add to My Stations (Windows Media Player), 167

Add/Remove Programs applet, 228-231

Add/Remove Windows Components button, 232

adding. *See* **installing**

Address bar (Internet Explorer), 296-297, 290

addresses
email, 362-363, 413
Web sites
.com, 310
.edu, 311
.gov, 311
.org, 310
searching, 310-311
viewing, 291
worksheet cells, 572-573

administrative tools. *See* **system tools**

Advanced Attributes dialog box, 224-225

Advanced Find dialog box, 535

Align Left button (Formatting toolbar), 470, 615

Align Right button (Formatting toolbar), 470, 615

alignment
text
PowerPoint slides, 614-615
Word documents, 470-471
worksheet cells, 578-579

All Programs button, 56

ancestry, researching online, 326-327

Ancestry.com Web site, 327

Animation Schemes command (Slide Show menu), 634

animations, adding to PowerPoint slides, 634-635

antivirus software, 342-345

AOL Instant Messenger, 379

Appearance tab (Display Properties dialog box), 186

Apple Macintosh computers, 11

applications. *See* **programs**

Apply Filter button, 661

Appointment Recurrence dialog box, 512

Appointment window, 510-513

appointments
editing, 513
recurring appointments, 512-513
reminders, 511-513
scheduling, 510-511

archives
email messages, 535
newsgroups, 410-411

Arrange Icons By command (View menu), 83

arrow keys, 30

art. *See* **images**

Ask A Question feature, 438

ASR (Automated System Recovery), 262-263

associated Web pages, printing, 307

AT&T WorldNet ISP, 279

attachments (email), 532-533
creating, 532-533
receiving, 360-361
sending, 358-359
virus dangers, 361

audio. *See* **sound**

authentication (Outlook), 351

auto-expanding, 77

auto-scrolling, 77

AutoArchive, 535

AutoComplete, 541

AutoContent Wizard, 602-603

AutoCorrect, 498-499, 675

AutoCorrect Options command (Tools menu), 458, 498

AutoFill, 546-547

AutoFilter, 562-563

AutoForm, 655

AutoFormat command (Format menu), 463, 584

AutoFormat, 463, 584-585

Automated System Recovery, 262-263

AutoPreview command (View menu), 528

Autosearch (Internet Explorer), 296, 311, 320

AutoShapes, 671
AutoSum, 568-569
AutoText command (Insert menu), 458-459
AutoText, 458-459

B

Back button (Internet Explorer), 295
Background command (Format menu), 607
Background dialog box, 626-627
backgrounds
    Excel worksheet cells, 580-581
    sending objects to, 684
    PowerPoint slides, 626-627
    watermarks, 492-493
backing up files, 257-258
    Automated System Recovery, 262-263
    Backup Wizard, 258-259
    floppy disks, 100-101
Backspace key, 33, 451
Backup Wizard, 258-259
BellSouth ISP, 279
Berners-Lee, Tim, 293
blank fields, searching for, 663
blank PowerPoint presentations, creating, 606-607
blocking
    instant messages, 384-385
    Web site content, 334-335
Bold button (Formatting toolbar), 460, 614
bold text
    PowerPoint slides, 614
    Word documents, 460
boot process
    boot program, 26-27
    Selective Startup, 248-249

BOOTDISK folder, 272
borders
    Excel worksheet cells, 580-581
    Word documents, 480-481
Borders and Shading command (Format menu), 480
Borders and Shading dialog box, 480-481
Break command (Insert menu), 486
Break dialog box, 486
Break key, 38
briefcases, 146-151
    copying, 148-149
    creating, 146-147
    moving, 148-149
    opening, 146-147
    placing documents in, 146-147
    renaming, 147
    updating files in, 150-151
Bring Forward command (Order menu), 685
Bring to Front command (Order menu), 684
broadband connections, 280-281
browsers. See Internet Explorer
browsing
    computers on networks, 134-135
    disk drives, 64-65
    files, 77
    folders, 76, 197
    networks, 132, 136-137
    system information, 220-221
    for themes, 183
    Web sites
        addresses, 296-297
        browser settings, 304
        Favorites list, 298-299
        finding sites, 310-311

home pages, 302-303
hyperlinks, 294-295
offline browsing, 300-301
printing pages, 306-307
recently visited sites, 312-313
saving Web pages to hard drive, 308-309
searching sites, 314-315, 317
bulleted lists
    PowerPoint, 610
    Word, 472-473
bulletin boards. See MSN Chat
Bullets and Numbering command (Format menu), 473
Bullets and Numbering dialog box, 473
Bullets button (Formatting toolbar), 472
Business.com Web site, 321
buttons
    Add/Remove Windows Components, 232
    Align Left, 470, 615
    Align Right, 470, 615
    Apply Filter, 661
    AutoShapes, 671
    AutoSum, 568-569
    Bold, 460, 614
    Bullets, 472
    Center, 578
    Chart Type, 594
    Columns, 477
    Comma Style, 577
    Copy from CD, 164
    Copy, 454
    Copy Music, 165
    Create New Folder, 81
    Currency Style, 576
    Cut, 454
    Decrease Decimal, 577
    Decrease Indent, 470
    displaying, 425

Error Checking, 574
Evaluate Formula, 575
Field List, 657
Fill Color, 595, 681
Filter By Form, 661
Filter By Selection, 660
Font Color, 461
Font Size, 595
Format Painter, 462-463, 582
Get Names, 164
Increase Indent, 470
Insert Chart, 620
Insert Clip Art, 618, 672
Insert Table, 478, 622
Increase Decimal, 577
Increase Indent, 579
Index, 67
Italic, 460, 614
Justify, 470
Line Spacing, 468
Line Style, 681
Maximize, 57
Merge, 578
mouse buttons, 41
My Shortcuts, 508
New Record, 648
New Slide, 628
Numbering, 472
Outlook Shortcuts, 508
Outside Border, 481
Pause, 162
Percent Style, 576
Play, 162
Print Preview, 467
Remove Filter, 660
Restore, 57
Run Query, 663
Paste, 455
Search, 137, 436
Shadow, 683
Show Desktop, 59
Show/Hide, 451
Sort Ascending, 560, 658
Sort Descending, 560, 658
Spelling and Grammar, 497
Start, 206

Stop, 162
Style, 488
Tables and Borders, 479
Text Box, 616
Text Wrapping, 671
Trace Dependents, 575
Trace Precedents, 575
Troubleshoot, 189
Underline, 460, 614
Undo, 561
Update All, 151
Volume, 163
WordArt, 676
Zoom, 448

bypassing proxy servers, 289

C

cable modems, 280

cables, 124-125

Calendar (Outlook)
appointments
editing, 513
recurring appointments, 512-513
reminders, 513
scheduling, 510-511
events, 514-515
meetings, 516-517
opening, 510
tasks, 518-519

canceling print jobs, 110-111

canvas, 671

Caps Lock key, 29, 451

carbon copies (email messages), 526

CareerBuilder Web site, 324-325

cascading windows, 58

case of text, changing, 490-491

CD-ROMs, 21

CDs
installing Windows components from, 232-233
saving PowerPoint presentations to, 640-641
tracks, selecting/deselecting, 163-165

cells (Excel worksheets)
absolute cell addresses, 572-573
alignment, 578-579
AutoFormat, 584-585
background patterns, 580-581
borders, 580-581
clearing, 552-553
copying
cell formatting, 582-583
entire cells, 541, 548-549
deleting, 552-553
editing data in, 541
entering data into, 540-541
inserting, 551
moving, 548-549
range names, 556-557
relative cell addresses, 572-573
selecting, 540, 544-545

Cells command (Format menu), 577-580

Center button (Formatting toolbar), 578

certificates
authenticity, 336-337
inspecting, 336
Thawte, 336-337
VeriSign, 336-337

chairs, choosing, 47

Change Case command (Format menu), 491

Change Case dialog box, 491

changing. *See editing*

Chart command (Insert menu), 620

Chart menu commands
Add Data, 599
Chart Options, 597
Chart Type, 595, 621
Source Data, 599

Chart Options command (Chart menu), 597

Chart Options dialog box, 597

Chart Type button, 594

Chart Type command (Chart menu), 595, 621

Chart Type dialog box, 595, 621

Chart Wizard, 590-591

charts
adding to PowerPoint presentations, 611, 620-621
chart types, 594-595, 621
Chart Wizard, 590-591
creating, 590-591
deleting, 593
editing, 598-599
moving, 592-593
options, 597
printing, 599
resizing, 592-593
titles, 596-597

chat
instant messaging, 377
blocking messages, 384-385
contact lists, 378-379
discouraging messages, 385
inviting others to use, 380-381
photographs, 383
remote assistance, 383
sending invitations, 380-381
sending messages, 382-383

MSN Chat, 387
accounts, 388-389
joining, 390-391
participating, 392-393
private conversations, 393
profiles, 389
Whisper mode, 393
Usenet newsgroups, 399
downloading messages, 404
finding, 408-409
Outlook Express configuration, 400-401
posting messages to, 406-407
reading, 402-405
searching archives, 410-411
synchronizing, 405
Usenet news services, 401
weblogs, 397
Yahoo chat, 393

checking
hardware installation, 236-237
service pack installation, 238-239

choosing computers, 13

Clean Installation option (Windows XP), 264

clean systems, 257

cleaning up Outlook Mailbox, 534-535

Clear command (Edit menu), 552

clearing
Internet Explorer History folder, 297
worksheet cells, 552-553
worksheet number formatting, 577

clicking mouse buttons, 42-43, 191

Clip Art command (Picture menu), 672

clip art. *See* images

Clip Gallery, 618

Clip Organizer, 673

Clipboard, 440-441, 455

clips (movie), 170

clock settings, 62-63

Close command (File menu), 433

Close Program dialog box, 39

closing
Drawing Canvas, 671
files, 432-433
forms, 649
Office Assistant, 439
Office programs, 419
pop-up windows, 295
tables, 653
task panes, 423
windows, 57
Windows XP, 44-45

colleges, .edu Web addresses, 311

color
depth, 188
desktop, 187
diagrams, 687
fill color, 681
font colors, 461
quality, 188
PowerPoint color schemes, 607, 626-627
shadow effects, 683
worksheet titles, 597

Colors and Lines tab (Format dialog box), 680-681

Colors dialog box, 626

Column Width dialog box, 554

columns
Excel worksheet columns
inserting, 550-551
selecting, 545
width of, 554-555
Word documents, 476-477

Columns button (Standard toolbar), 477

Columns command
Format menu, 476, 554
Insert menu, 623

Columns dialog box, 476-477

.com addresses, 310

Command Style button (Formatting toolbar), 577

commands
Actions menu
New All Day Event, 514
New Mail Message Using, 527
New Recurring Appointment, 512
Plan a Meeting, 516
Chart menu
Add Data, 599
Chart Options, 597
Chart Type, 595, 621
Source Data, 599
Data menu
Filter, 562
Sort, 560
Edit menu
Clear, 552
Copy, 440
Cut, 440
Delete Slide, 629
Find, 494, 558
Go To, 543
Paste, 441
Paste Special, 442
Repeat Font Formatting, 463
Replace, 495
File menu
Close, 433
Delete, 95

Exit, 419
Import and Export, 522
Map Network Drive, 143
New, 84, 456
Open, 87, 106, 432
Pack and Go, 640
Page Setup, 466, 502, 581, 587
Print, 106, 306, 434, 599, 639
Print Preview, 107
Rename, 92
Save, 89, 430
Save As, 88, 308, 430
Format menu
AutoFormat, 463, 584
Background, 607
Borders and Shading, 480
Bullets and Numbering, 473
Cells, 577-580
Change Case, 491
Column, 554
Columns, 476
Drop Cap, 490
Font, 461
Paragraph, 468
Row, 555
Slide Design, 607
Slide Layout, 610
Style, 489
Tabs, 475
Grouping menu, 685
Help menu, 439
Insert menu
AutoText, 458-459
Break, 486
Chart, 620
Columns, 623
Comment, 484, 586
Diagram, 686
Object, 674
Page Numbers, 487
Picture, 619, 672
Reference, 485
Rows, 623

Slides, 629
Symbol, 464
Table, 622
keyboard shortcuts, 35
msconfig, 248
Name menu, 557
New menu
Folder, 80
Shortcut, 419
Order menu
Bring Forward, 685
Bring to Front, 684
Send Backward, 685
Send to Back, 684
Picture menu
Clip Art, 672
WordArt, 676
selecting, 53
Send menu
Link by Email, 356
Page by Email, 357
Shortcut to Desktop, 357
Slide Show menu
Animation Schemes, 634
Custom Animation, 635
Rehearse Timings, 637
Set Up Show, 636
Start menu
New Office Document, 428
Search, 138
Toolbars menu, Customize, 426
Tools menu
AutoCorrect Options, 458, 498
Customize, 424
Email Accounts, 527
Formula Auditing, 574
Internet Options, 332
Mailbox Cleanup, 534
Options, 421-423
Spelling and Grammar, 497
Synchronize, 156
Track Changes, 500, 588

Track Changes menu
  Accept or Reject
    Changes, 589
  Highlight Changes, 588
View menu
  Arrange Icons By, 83
  AutoPreview, 528
  Comments, 587
  Details, 82
  Folder List, 508
  Form Header/Footer,
    657
  Grid and Guidelines,
    617
  Header and Footer, 482
  Layout Preview, 667
  List, 82
  Preview Pane, 528
  Ruler, 615
  Task Pane, 423
  Thumbnail, 83
  Toolbars, 425
  Zoom, 448

**Comment command
(Insert menu), 484, 586**

comments
  Excel worksheets, 586-587
  Word documents, 484-485

**Comments command
(View menu), 587**

communities (MSN Chat)
  joining, 394-395
  reading/sending messages
    in, 396-397
  viewing, 394

company Web sites
  Business.com Web site,
    321
  finding, 320-321

components (Windows)
  installing from CD,
    232-233
  installing from Internet,
    234-235
  updating automatically,
    234-235

**composing email, 352,
526-527**

**compressing files/folders,
224-225**

computer basics
  Apple Macintosh comput-
    ers, 11
  choosing computers, 13
  computer names, 268
  computer networks, 11
  how computers work,
    10-11
  IBM-compatible computers,
    12
  learning about computers,
    8-9
  personal computers, 11
  programs
    accounting programs,
      17, 19
    browsers, 18
    database management
      programs, 18
    DTP (desktop-publishing
      programs), 16
    games, 19
    graphics programs, 18
    how programs work, 14
    installed programs, 15
    maximum number of
      stored programs, 15
    presentation programs,
      19
    running multiple, 15
    spreadsheet programs,
      17-19
    word-processing pro-
      grams, 16
  scanning for viruses, 346
  sturdiness of computers, 6-7
  turning off computers,
    44-45
  user interfaces, 12

configuring
  Hotmail, 366-373
  Internet connections,
    278-281
    shared Internet connec-
      tions, 130-131
    via proxy servers,
      288-289
  Internet Explorer, 330-331
  networks
  Internet connections,
    130-131, 278-281,
    288-289
    small networks, 124-127
    user accounts, 128-129
  Outlook Express
    authentication, 351
    email address set up,
      350
    mail server identification,
      351
    passwords, 351
    Usenet newsgroup partic-
      ipation, 400-401
    usernames, 350
  printers
    default printers, 112-113
    network printers,
      120-121
    shared printers, 114-115
  programs, 228-229,
    242-243
  Windows XP
    accessibility options,
      208-209
    desktop appearance,
      186-187
    desktop themes,
      182-183
    display settings,
      188-189
    folder options, 196-197
    keyboard settings,
      192-193
    mouse settings, 190-191
    power options, 198-199
    Quick Launch bar,
      204-205

screen savers, *180-181*
Start menu items, *202-203*
Startup folder, *206-207*
system sounds, *200-201*
taskbar, *194-195*
volume, *178-179*
wallpaper, *184-185*

Connect dialog box, 286

connections (Internet)
choosing, 131
configuring, 278-281
disconnecting, 287
firewalls, 281
modem speeds, 287
proxy servers, 288-289
sharing, 127, 130
starting, 286-287, 291

contact lists (Windows Messenger), 378-379

Contact window (Outlook), 520-521

contacts (Outlook)
creating, 520-521
finding, 509
importing, 522-523
saving, 521

Content Advisor (Internet Explorer), 334-335

content copy protection, 165

Control key, 35

Control Panel
Add or Remove Programs, 252-253
Event Viewer, 254-255
Internet Connections, 278-281
Network and Internet Connections, 282-285

cookies, 338-339

Copy button (Standard toolbar), 454

Copy command (Edit menu), 440

Copy from CD button (Windows Media Player), 164

Copy Music button (Windows Media Player), 165

copying, 440-441
briefcases, 148-149
Excel worksheets, 565
files, 96-97, 101
folders, 96-97
objects, 679
PowerPoint slides, 631
text, 454-455
text formatting, 462-463
worksheet cell formatting, 582-583
worksheet cells, 541, 548-549
worksheet number formatting, 577

crashes, troubleshooting, 38-39

Create an Offline File shortcut, 159

Create AutoText dialog box, 458-459

Create command (Name menu), 557

Create Name dialog box, 557

Create New Folder button, 81

Create Shortcut Wizard, 419

credit card numbers, phishing practices, 390

Currency Style button (Formatting toolbar), 576

cursors
accessibility options, 209
blink rate, 193
compared to insertion points, 31
cursor movement keys, 30-31

Custom Animation command (Slide Show menu), 635

Custom AutoFilter dialog box, 563

Customize command
Toolbars menu, 426
Tools menu, 424

Customize dialog box
customizing menus, 424-425
customizing toolbars, 426-427

customizing
borders, 481
bullets, 473
Internet Explorer security settings, 332-333
locales, 268
menus, 424
Outlook Today, 509
PowerPoint animations, 635
PowerPoint design templates, 605
reports, 666-667
symbols, 465
toolbars, 426-427
Word templates, 457

Cut button (Standard toolbar), 454

Cut command (Edit menu), 440

cutting data, 440-441

D

data encryption, 333

Data menu commands
Filter, 562
Sort, 560

database management programs, 18

Database tab (Templates dialog box), 646

Database Wizard, 646-647

databases (Access), 643
 creating, 646-647
 Database Wizard, 646-647
 Datasheet view, 649
 entering data in, 648-649
 fields
  adding to forms, 657
  creating, 651-652
  defined, 644
  deleting, 653, 656
  moving, 657
  properties, 653
  renaming, 651-653
  reordering, 653
 forms
  AutoForm options, 655
  closing, 649
  creating, 649, 654-655
  defined, 645
  Design view, 656
  fields, 656-657
  Form Wizard, 654-655
  headers/footers, 657
  modifying, 656-657
  naming, 655
  navigating, 649
  opening, 648, 656
  saving, 657
 naming, 646
 planning, 645
 queries
  creating, 662-663
  defined, 645
  filtering, 663
  naming, 662
  running, 663
  wildcards, 663
 records
  creating, 648
  defined, 644
  filtering, 660-661
  sorting, 658-659
 reports
  creating, 664-665
  customizing, 666-667

 defined, 645
 fonts, 666
 graphics, 667
 grouping categories, 664
 labels, 666
 layouts, 665
 previewing, 667
 removing objects from, 667
 report styles, 665
 Report Wizard, 664-665
 sorting, 665
 titles, 665
 tables
  adding data to, 651
  closing, 653
  creating, 650-651
  defined, 644
  designing from scratch, 651
  modifying, 652-653
  naming, 651
  opening, 652
  Table Wizard, 650
 Toolbox, 657

Datasheet view (databases), 649

date/time settings, 269

decompressing files/folders, 225

Decrease Decimal button (Formatting toolbar), 577

Decrease Indent button (Formatting toolbar), 470

default fonts, 305

default printers, 112-113

default tabs, 475

Define command (Name menu), 557

Define Name dialog box, 557

defragmenting hard disks, 214-215

Del key, 37

 defined, 645

Delete command (File menu), 95

Delete dialog box, 553

Delete key, 95, 451

Delete Slide command (Edit menu), 629

deleting
 address requests, 297
 AutoText entries, 459
 comments, 485
 email messages, 535
 Excel charts, 593
 Excel worksheets, 564
 fields, 653, 656
 files, 94-95, 212-213, 304
 folders, 94-95, 525
 objects, 68-69
 page breaks, 451
 PowerPoint slides, 628-629
 programs, 231
 range names, 557
 report objects, 667
 tabs, 475
 templates, 457
 text, 33
 text boxes, 617
 worksheet cells, 552-553
 worksheet comments, 587
 worksheet rows, 550-551
 worksheet titles, 596

Dell Computers Web site, 310

deselecting text, 453

design templates (PowerPoint), 604-605

Design view (forms), 656

desk ergonomics, 47

desktop (Windows XP), 25, 49
 arranging windows, 58-59
 color, 187
 customizing, 183
 desktop appearance, 186-187
 desktop themes, 182-183
 display settings, 188-189

effects, 187
fonts, 187
icons, 54-55
moving items around, 53
notification area, 62-63
printing documents from, 108-109
programs
    starting, 56-57
    switching between, 60-61
Recycle Bin, 68-69, 94-95
styles, 186
wallpaper, 184-185

Desktop tab (Display Properties dialog box), 184

desktop-publishing programs (DTP), 16

Details command (View menu), 82

Details view, 82

Device Manager, 236-237

Diagram command (Insert menu), 686

Diagram Gallery dialog box, 686-687

Diagram toolbar, 686

diagrams
adding to files, 686-687
formatting, 687

dial-up connections, 280

dialing ISP access numbers, 286

dialog boxes
Accessibility Options, 208-209
Add Data, 599
Add Favorite, 299
Advanced Attributes, 224-225
Advanced Find, 535
Appointment Recurrence, 512
AutoCorrect, 498

AutoFormat, 463, 584-585
Background, 626-627
Borders and Shading, 480-481
Break, 486
Bullets and Numbering, 473
Change Case, 491
Chart Options, 597
Chart Type, 595, 621
Close Program, 39
Colors, 626
Column Width, 554
Columns, 476-477
Connect, 286
Create AutoText, 458-459
Create Name, 557
Custom AutoFilter, 563
Customize, 425-427
Define Name, 557
Delete, 553
Diagram Gallery, 686-687
Display Properties, 180-181
    Appearance tab, 186-187
    Desktop tab, 184-185
    Settings tab, 188-189
    Themes tab, 182-183
Drop Cap, 490
Edit Junk Senders, 537
Edit WordArt Text, 676-677
Envelope Options, 504
Envelopes and Labels, 504-505
Error Checking, 575
File Download, 319
File New Database, 646
Fill Effects, 607, 627
Find and Replace, 494-495, 558-559
Find People, 362-363
Folder Options, 83, 158-159, 196-197
Font, 461
Footnote and Endnote, 485
Format, 99, 680-681

Format Cells, 577-580
Format Diagram, 687
Function Arguments, 570-571
Go To, 543
Grid and Guidelines, 617
Highlight Changes, 588
Insert, 551
Insert Attachment, 358
Insert File, 532
Insert Function, 570
Insert Item, 533
Insert Object, 674-675
Insert Picture, 492, 619, 667
Insert Table, 622
Internet Accounts, 370
Internet Options, 302-305, 330-332
Internet Properties, 278, 282
Items to Synchronize, 156-157
Keyboard Properties, 192-193
Mailbox Cleanup, 534
Modify Style, 489
Mouse Properties, 190-192
New Folder, 524
New Form, 654
New Office Document, 428-429
Newsgroup Subscriptions, 408
Office Assistant, 439
Open, 106
Open Attachment, 361
Open File, 432-433
Open Office Document, 433
Open With, 102-103
Options, 421
Page Numbers, 487
Page Setup, 466, 502-503, 581, 587
Paragraph, 450, 468-469
Paste Special, 442-443
Power Options Properties, 198-199

Print, 106, 306, 434-435, 599, 639
Printed Watermark, 492-493
Save As, 88-89, 430-431
Save Attachments, 361
Save Web Page, 308
Select Picture, 618
Select Users or Groups, 115
Set Up Show, 636-637
Share, 140-141
Slide Finder, 629
Sort, 560-561
Sounds and Audio Device Properties, 200-201
Source Data, 599
Spelling, 496
Spelling and Grammar, 497
Symbol, 464-465
Tabs, 475
Taskbar and Start Menu, 194-195
Templates, 456-457, 646
Volume, 178-179
WordArt Gallery, 676-677
Zoom, 448

disabling
Drawing Canvas, 671
macros, 429
programs, 246-247
screensavers, 181
services, 249

disconnecting from Internet, 287

discs
CD-ROMs, 21
CDs
installing Windows components from, 232-233
saving PowerPoint presentations to, 640-641
tracks, selecting/deselecting, 163-165

Disk Cleanup, 212-213

Disk Defragmenter, 214-215

disk drives. *See* **drives**

disk space, freeing up, 212-213

disks, floppy, 21
ASR (Automated System Recovery) disks, 262-263
formatting, 98-99
invalid system disk errors, 27
saving files to, 100-101
saving PowerPoint presentations to, 640-641
setup floppy disks, 272-273

Display Properties dialog box, 180-181
Appearance tab, 186-187
Desktop tab, 184-185
Settings tab, 188-189
Themes tab, 182-183

display settings, 188-189

display troubleshooter, 189

displaying
events, 515
file associations, 103
gridlines, 479
MSN communities, 394
page breaks, 486
tasks, 519
toolbar buttons, 425
toolbars, 425
Usenet newsgroup messages, 402-405
Web sites
Internet Explorer, 294
offline browsing, 300-301
recently visited, 312-313
Windows Messenger contact lists, 378
worksheet comments, 587

documents (Word), 447
AutoCorrect feature, 498-499
closing, 432-433
creating, 428-429
envelopes, 504-505
finding, 436-437
grammar-checking, 496-497
Insert mode, 451
line spacing, 468-469
locating, 84
margins, 466-467
opening, 432-433
Overtype mode, 451
page breaks, 451, 486-487
page numbers, 486-487
paper size, 502-503
previewing, 433, 435
printing, 107, 434-435
canceling print jobs, 110-111
pausing print jobs, 111
print job management, 110-111
printer settings, 112-113
from programs, 106-107
restarting print jobs, 111
shared printers, 114-115
from Windows desktop, 108
saving, 81, 430-431
searching/replacing, 494-495
spell-checking, 496-497
styles, 488-489
templates, 429, 456-457
text
aligning, 470-471
AutoText, 458-459
borders, 480-481
color, 461
columns, 476-477
comments, 484-485
copying, 454-455
copying text formatting, 462-463

deselecting, *453*
drop caps, *490-491*
editing, *450-451*
endnotes, *484-485*
entering, *450-451*
fonts, *460-461*
footers, *482-483*
footnotes, *484-485*
formatting, *460-461*
headers, *482-483*
indenting, *470-471*
lists, *472-473*
moving, *454-455*
selecting, *452-453*
shading, *480-481*
symbols, *464-465*
tables, *478-479*
tabs, *474-475*
text case, *490-491*
tracking changes to, 500-501
views, 448-449
watermarks, 492-493
zooming in/out, 448-449

domains, 126, 269

DOS, 23

double-clicking mouse, 43

Download.com Web site, 318-319

downloading
email attachments, 360-361
MSN Chat software, 391
software, 319
Usenet newsgroup messages, 404
Web pages, 301
Windows Messenger, 377

dragging and dropping data, 43, 53, 441

drawing shapes, 670-671

Drawing Canvas, 671

Drawing toolbar, 616
displaying, 670
Fill Color button, 681
Insert Clip Art button, 618, 672
Line Style button, 681
Rectangle tool, 670
Shadow button, 683
Text Box button, 616
WordArt button, 676

drives
browsing, 64-65
defragmenting, 214-215
disk space, freeing up, 212-213
formatting, 267
mapping, 142-143
protecting, 6
selecting, 64

Drop Cap command (Format menu), 490

Drop Cap dialog box, 490

drop caps, 490-491

DSL modems, 280

DTP (desktop-publishing programs), 16

dual-boot configuration, 257

due dates (Outlook tasks), 518

DVDs, selecting tracks in, 163

E

EarthLink ISP, 279

Edit Junk Senders dialog box, 537

Edit menu commands
Clear, 552
Copy, 440
Cut, 440
Delete Slide, 629
Find, 494, 558
Go To, 543
Paste, 441
Paste Special, 442
Repeat Font Formatting, 463
Replace, 495

Edit WordArt Text dialog box, 676-677

editing
appointments, 513
chart types, 594-595
default fonts, 305
embedded objects, 443
events, 515
Excel worksheets, 541
charts, 598-599
comments, 587
titles, 596
files, 85
forms, 656-657
Internet Explorer settings, 304-305
reports, 666-667
PowerPoint slide text, 612-613
programs, 230-231
tables, 652-653
Word documents, 450-451

.edu addresses, 311

edutainment programs, 19

email, 349
addresses
falsifying, 413
finding, 362-363
searching, 323
selecting for ISP accounts, 285
attachments, 532-533
creating, 532-533
receiving, 360-361
sending, 358-359
virus dangers, 361
Hotmail, 370-371
ISP accounts, 349
mailing lists
Netly-L Web site, 365
subscribing to, 364
Topica Web site, 365
unsubscribing from, 365

messages
  archiving, 535
  attaching files to, 532-533
  carbon copies, 526
  creating, 526-527
  deleting, 535
  forwarding, 530-531
  headers, 529
  Mailbox Cleanup, 534-535
  moving, 529
  printing, 374-375
  reading, 528-529
  replying to, 530-531
  screening junk mail, 536-537
  sending, 526-527
  stationery patterns, 527
Outlook Express, 527
  composing, 352
  configuring, 350-351
  file attachments, 358-361
  forwarding, 355
  HTML formatting, 353
  priority status, 353
  receiving, 354-355
  replying to, 355
  sending, 352-353
  sending Web pages with, 356-357
  shortcuts to, 56
  signatures, 412
  spam, 373, 412-413
  Web-based email accounts, 366-369, 372-373
Email Accounts command (Tools menu), 527
embedding data, 443
emboss effects, 615
emergency repair process, 263
employment-related Web sites, 324-325

Empty Recycle Bin shortcut, 213
emptying Recycle Bin, 69, 213
enabling macros, 429
encryption, 333
End key, 31
endnotes, 484-485
Enter key, 29, 37, 450
entertainment programs, 19
Envelope Options dialog box, 504
envelopes, printing, 504-505
Envelopes and Labels dialog box, 504-505
ergonomics, 46-47
Error Checking button (Formula Auditing toolbar), 574
Error Checking dialog box, 575
errors
  formula errors, 574-575
  troubleshooting, 38-39
Evaluate Formula button (Formula Auditing toolbar), 575
evaluating formulas, 575
Event Viewer, 254-255
Event window (Outlook), 514-515
events, 200-201
  editing, 515
  Event Viewer, 254-255
  scheduling, 514-515
  turning appointments into, 515
Excel worksheets, 539
  AutoComplete, 541
  AutoFill, 546-547
  AutoFormat, 584-585
  AutoSum, 568-569

cells
  absolute cell addresses, 572-573
  alignment, 578-579
  background patterns, 580-581
  borders, 580-581
  clearing, 552-553
  copying, 541, 548-549
  copying cell formatting, 582-583
  deleting, 552-553
  editing data in, 541
  entering data into, 540-541
  inserting, 551
  moving, 548-549
  range names, 556-557
  relative cell addresses, 572-573
  selecting, 540, 544-545
  workbooks, 539
charts
  chart types, 594-595
  creating, 590-591
  deleting, 593
  editing, 598-599
  moving, 592-593
  printing, 599
  resizing, 592-593
  titles, 596-597
columns
  inserting, 550-551
  selecting, 545
  width of, 554-555
comments, 586-587
copying, 565
custom lists, 547
data
  editing, 541
  entering, 540-541
  filtering, 562-563
  finding, 558-559
  replacing, 558-559
  sorting, 560-561
deleting, 564
Format Painter, 582-583

formulas
  creating, *566-567*
  evaluating, *575*
  fixing errors in, *574-575*
  testing, *567*
functions
  arguments, *570-571*
  entering, *570-571*
  SUM, *568-569*
inserting, *565*
moving, *565*
navigating, *542-543*
number formats, *576-577*
renaming, *564*
rows
  deleting, *550-551*
  height of, *554-555*
  selecting, *545*
switching between, *564*
tracking changes to, *588-589*
undoing mistakes, *553*

Excite Web site, 315

Exit command (File menu), 419

Explorer. *See* **Internet Explorer; Windows Explorer**

eye strain, 47

F

F1 key, 67

F2 key, 93

falsifying email addresses, 413

Favorites list (Internet Explorer), 298-299

Field List button, 657

fields. *See also* **columns**
adding to forms, 657
creating, 651-652
defined, 644
deleting, 653, 656
moving, 657
properties, 653

renaming, *651-653*
reordering, *653*

file associations, 103

file attachments (email), 532-533
creating, 532-533
receiving, 360-361
sending, 358-359
virus dangers, 361

File Download dialog box, 319

File menu commands
Close, 433
Delete, 95
Exit, 419
Import and Export, 522
Map Network Drive, 143
New, 84, 456
Open, 87, 106, 432
Pack and Go, 640
Page Setup, 466, 502, 581, 587
Print, 106, 306, 434, 599, 639
Rename, 92
Print Preview, 107
Save, 89, 430
Save As, 88, 308, 430

File New Database dialog box, 646

files, 75
adding graphics to
  clip art, *672-673*
  diagrams, *686-687*
  objects, *674-675*
  WordArt, *676-677*
adding to briefcases, 146-147
.asf format, 162
associations, 103
attaching to email messages, 532-533
.avi format, 162
backing up, 257-258
  Automated System Recovery, *262-263*
  Backup Wizard, *258-259*

browsing, 77
closing, 432-433
compressing, 224-225
copying, 96-97
  to another drive, *77*
  to floppy disks, *101*
creating, 84-85, 90, 428-429
decompressing, 225
deleting, 94-95, 213
downloading, 319
editing, 85
extensions, 85
finding, 78-79, 138-139, 436-437
most recently opened, 86
moving, 77, 96-97
.mp3 format, 162
.mpg format, 162
naming, 88-89, 93
offline files, 159
opening, 65, 86-87, 432-433
  Open command, *106*
  from different programs, *102-103*
previewing, 433-435
printing, 434-435
recovering, 94
renaming, 85, 92-93
restoring from backups, 260-261
saving, 73, 88-89, 100-101, 430-431
searching, 87
selecting groups of, 94
shared files
  making available offline, *152-153*
  modifying, *141*
  opening, *133*
sharing, 127, 140-141
synchronizing, 156-157, 159
templates, 429
temporary files, 212-213
updating in briefcase, 150-151
.wav format, 162

fill color, **681**

Fill Color button
Drawing toolbar, 681
Formatting toolbar, 595

fill effects, 595, 607, 627

Fill Effects dialog box, 607, 627

Filmstrip command, 173

Filter By Form button, 661

Filter By Selection button, 660

Filter command (Data menu), 562

filtering
queries, 663
records, 660-661
advanced filtering, 661
by exclusion, 661
by form, 661
by selection, 660
worksheet data, 562-563

FilterKeys options, 208

Find and Replace dialog box, 494-495, 558-559

Find command (Edit menu), 494, 558

Find More Stations (Windows Media Player), 167

Find People dialog box, 362-363

finding. *See also* **searching**
email addresses, 362-363
files, 436-437
ISPs (Internet Service Providers), 283-284
Outlook contacts, 509
people, 322-323
PowerPoint design templates, 605
software, 318-319
text, 494-495
Usenet newsgroups, 408-409

Web sites, 310-311
worksheet data, 558-559

firewalls
configuring, 131, 288-289
enabling, 281
Internet Connection Firewall, 340-341
Norton Internet Security, 340-341
ZoneAlarm, 340-341

fixing mistakes. *See* **troubleshooting**

floppy disks, 21
ASR (Automated System Recovery) disks, 262-263
formatting, 98-99
invalid system disk errors, 27
naming, 99
saving files to, 100-101
saving PowerPoint presentations to, 640-641
setup floppy disks, 272-273

Folder command (New menu), 80

Folder List (Outlook), 508

Folder List command (View menu), 508

Folder Options dialog box, 83, 158-159, 196-197

folders, 75
arranging contents of, 83
auto-expanding, 77
BOOTDISK, 272
browsing, 76, 197
compressing, 224-225
copying, 96-97
creating, 80-81, 90
decompressing, 225
deleting, 94-95
moving, 96-97
My Pictures folder, 172-173
naming, 81
navigating, 65

opening, 65, 76-77
options, 196-197
Outlook folders, 524-525
parent folders, 84, 96
Printers folder, 109
Program Files folder, 94, 229
renaming, 80, 92-93
saving files to, 89
searching for, 78-79
shared folders
list of, 132
making available offline, 152-155
opening, 133
sharing, 127, 140-141
Startup, 206-207
synchronizing, 156-157
viewing items in, 82-83
Windows Classic, 83

Font Color button (Formatting toolbar), 461

Font command (Format menu), 461

Font dialog box, 461

Font Size button (Formatting toolbar), 595

fonts
default fonts, 305
Excel worksheets, 577-579
PowerPoint presentations, 614-615
reports, 666
Word documents, 460-461

footers
forms, 657
Word documents, 482-483

Footnote and Endnote dialog box, 485

footnotes, 484-485

foreground, bringing objects to, 684

Form Header/Footer command (View menu), 657

Form Wizard, 654-655

Format Cells dialog box, 577-580

Format Diagram dialog box, 687

Format dialog box, 99, 680-681

Format menu commands
AutoFormat, 463, 584
Background, 607
Borders and Shading, 480
Bullets and Numbering, 473
Cells, 577-580
Change Case, 491
Columns, 476, 554
Drop Cap, 490
Font, 461
Paragraph, 468
Row, 555
Slide Design, 607
Slide Layout, 610
Style, 489
Tabs, 475

Format Painter (Excel), 582-583

Format Painter button (Standard toolbar), 462-463, 582

formatting
diagrams, 687
floppy disks, 98-99
graphics, 680-681
hard drives, 267
slide text, 614-615
text, 460-461

Formatting toolbar, 614
Align Left button, 470, 615
Align Right button, 470, 615
Bold button, 460, 614
Bullets button, 472
Center button, 578
Comma Style button, 577
Currency Style button, 576
Decrease Decimal button, 577
Decrease Indent button, 470

Fill Color button, 595
Font Color button, 461
Font Size button, 595
Increase Decimal button, 577
Increase Indent button, 470, 579
Italic button, 460, 614
Justify button, 470
Line Spacing button, 468
Merge button, 578
Numbering button, 472
Outside Border button, 481
Percent Style button, 576
Style button, 488
Underline button, 460, 614

forms
AutoForm options, 655
closing, 649
creating, 649, 654-655
defined, 645
Design view, 656
fields, 656-657
Form Wizard, 654-655
headers/footers, 657
modifying, 656-657
naming, 655
navigating, 649
opening, 648, 656
saving, 657

Formula Auditing command (Tools menu), 574

Formula Auditing toolbar, 574-575

formulas
creating, 566-567
evaluating, 575
fixing errors in, 574-575
Formula Auditing toolbar, 574-575
testing, 567

Forward button (Internet Explorer), 295

Forward window (Outlook), 531

forwarding email, 355, 530-531

framed Web pages, printing, 307

free email accounts (Hotmail), 366-369, 372-373

frozen screens, troubleshooting, 38-39

ftp prefix (URLs), 311

Function Arguments dialog box, 570-571

function keys, 35

functions
arguments, 570-571
entering, 570-571
SUM, 568-569

G

galleries
Clip Gallery, 618
Diagram Gallery, 686-687
WordArt Gallery, 676

games, 19, 174-175

genealogy Web sites, 326-327

Get Names button (Windows Media Player), 164

glossary, 689-705

Go To command (Edit menu), 543

Go To dialog box, 543

Google Web site, 410-411
I'm Feeling Lucky button, 321
searches
company searches, 321
email addresses, 323
executing, 316-317
Usenet archives, 410
Web directory topics, 315

.gov addresses, 311

grammar, checking, 496-497

graphics, 669
 3D effects, 683
 adding to files, 672-675
 adding to PowerPoint
  slides, 610, 618-619,
  627
 adding to reports, 667
 AutoCorrect collection, 675
 bringing to front, 684
 Clip Organizer, 673
 color
  depth, 188
  desktop, 187
  diagrams, 687
  fill color, 681
  font colors, 461
  quality, 188
  *PowerPoint color
   schemes, 607,
   626-627*
  shadow effects, 683
  worksheet titles, 597
 copying and pasting, 679
 finding online, 673
 diagrams, 686-687
 Drawing Canvas, 671
 fill color, 681
 formatting, 680-681
 grouping, 684-685
 layering, 684
 line weight, 681
 moving, 678
 My Pictures folder,
  172-173
 resizing, 619, 678-679
 rotating, 679
 selecting, 678
 sending to back, 684
 sending via instant messaging, 383
 shadow effects, 682-683
 shapes, 670-671
 ungrouping, 685
 watermarks, 492-493
 WordArt, 676-677
 wrapping text around, 681
**Grid and Guidelines com-
 mand (View menu), 617**

**Grid and Guidelines dia-
 log box, 617**
grids, 479, 617
**Group command
 (Grouping menu), 685**
**grouping graphics objects,
 684-685**
**Grouping menu com-
 mands, 685**
guidelines, 617

handling spam, 412-413
**handouts (PowerPoint),
 638-639**
hard drives
 browsing, 64-65
 defragmenting, 214-215
 disk space, freeing up,
  212-213
 formatting, 267
 mapping, 142-143
 protecting, 6
 selecting, 64
**Header and Footer com-
 mand (View menu), 482**
**Header and Footer tool-
 bar, 482-483**
headers
 email messages, 529
 forms, 657
 Word documents, 482-483
**height of worksheet rows,
 554-555**
help
 Ask A Question feature,
  438
 Help and Support Center
  window, 66-67
 Instant Messenger, 383
 Office Assistant, 439
 Office on the Web feature,
  439
 Windows troubleshooters,
  218-219

**Help and Support Center
 window, 66-67**
**Help menu commands,
 439**
Hibernate, 73
**Hide the Office Assistant
 command (Help menu),
 439**
hiding
 gridlines, 479
 Microsoft Services, 249
 shadow effects, 683
 toolbars, 425
High Contrast option, 209
**Highlight Changes com-
 mand (Track Changes
 menu), 588**
**Highlight Changes dialog
 box, 588**
**History folder (Internet
 Explorer), 297, 312-313**
Home key, 31
**Home Networking
 Wizard, 131**
**home pages, 291, 294,
 302-303**
HotBot Web site, 317
Hotmail
 configuring, 370-371
 expanded account features,
  368-369
 freemail accounts,
  366-369, 372-373
 spam handling, 373
**HotSheet.com Web site,
 303**
**HTML formatting (email),
 353**
http prefix (URLs), 311
hubs, 124
hyperlinks, 291, 294-295
hypertext, 293

I

I'm Feeling Lucky button (Google), 321

I/O (input/output). *See* input devices

IBM-compatible computers, 13
rebooting, 39
turning off, 44-45
turning on, 26-27

icons, 97
displaying, 54-55
My Computer, 64
notification area, 63
shortcut menus, 55
turning off, 63

ICQ.com, 379

images
3D effects, 683
adding to files, 672-675
adding to PowerPoint slides, 610, 618-619, 627
adding to reports, 667
AutoCorrect collection, 675
bringing to front, 684
Clip Organizer, 673
color
depth, 188
desktop, 187
diagrams, 687
fill color, 681
font colors, 461
quality, 188
PowerPoint color schemes, 607, 626-627
shadow effects, 683
worksheet titles, 597
copying and pasting, 679
finding online, 673
diagrams, 686-687
Drawing Canvas, 671
fill color, 681
formatting, 680-681
grouping, 684-685

layering, 684
line weight, 681
moving, 678
My Pictures folder, 172-173
resizing, 619, 678-679
rotating, 679
selecting, 678
sending to back, 684
sending via instant messaging, 383
shadow effects, 682-683
shapes, 670-671
ungrouping, 685
watermarks, 492-493
WordArt, 676-677
wrapping text around, 681

Import and Export command (File menu), 522

Import and Export Wizard, 522-523

importing contact data, 522-523

Inbox (Outlook Express), 354-355

Increase Decimal button (Formatting toolbar), 577

Increase Indent button (Formatting toolbar), 470, 579

indenting text
Excel worksheet cells, 579
Word documents, 470-471

Indents and Spacing tab (Paragraph dialog box), 450

input devices
keyboards
Alt key, 35
Application key, 33
arrow keys, 30
Backspace key, 33, 451
Break key, 38
Caps Lock key, 29, 451
Control key, 35
Delete key, 33, 451

End key, 31
Enter key, 29, 450
ergonomics, 47
Escape key, 38
FilterKeys, 208
function keys, 35
Home key, 31
Insert key, 33
modifier keys, 35
MouseKeys, 209
Num Lock, 37
numeric keypad, 36-37
Page Down key, 31
Page Up key, 31
selecting text with, 452
selecting worksheet cells with, 542, 545
settings, 192-193
Shift key, 35
standard keyboards, 28
StickyKeys, 208
Tab key, 29, 450
ToggleKeys, 208
Windows Logo key, 33
mouse, 40-41, 52-53
cleaning, 41
clicking, 42-43, 191
double-clicking, 43
dragging-and-dropping, 43, 97
ergonomics, 47
insertion point, 31
IntelliMouse, 41
mouse pads, 40
MouseKeys, 209
moving, 40
pointer speed, 191
pointing, 42
pressing, 42
selecting text with, 452
selecting worksheet cells with, 542-544
settings, 190-191
pointing sticks, 41
touch pads, 41
trackballs, 41

Ins key, 37

Insert Attachment dialog box, 358

Insert Chart button (Standard toolbar), 620

Insert Clip Art button (Drawing toolbar), 618, 672

Insert Clip Art panel, 672-673

Insert dialog box, 551

Insert File dialog box, 532

Insert Function dialog box, 570

Insert Item dialog box, 533

Insert menu commands
    AutoText, 458-459
    Break, 486
    Chart, 620
    Columns, 623
    Comment, 484, 586
    Diagram, 686
    Object, 674
    Page Numbers, 487
    Picture, 619, 672
    Reference, 485
    Rows, 623
    Slides, 629
    Symbol, 464
    Table, 622

Insert mode (Word), 451

Insert Object dialog box, 674-675

Insert Picture dialog box, 492, 619, 667

Insert Table button (Standard toolbar), 478, 622

Insert Table dialog box, 622

insertion points, 30-31

installing
    antivirus software, 342-345
    broadband connections, 281

components
    from CD, 232-233
    from Internet, 234-235
firewalls, 340-341
MSN Chat software, 391
printers
    local printers, 116-119
    network printers, 120-121
programs, 228-229
service packs, 240-241
Windows XP
    Activation Wizard, 270-271
    on blank hard drives, 266-269
    setup floppy disks creating, 272-273
    upgrades, 264-265

instant messaging, 377
    blocking messages, 384-385
    contact lists, 378-379
    discouraging messages, 385
    inviting others to use, 380-381
    remote assistance, 383
    sending invitations, 380-381
    sending messages, 382-383
    sending photographs, 383

IntelliMouse, 41

International Herald Tribune Web site, 307

Internet, 277. See also email; Internet Explorer; Web sites
    connections
        choosing, 131
        configuring, 278-281
        disconnecting, 287
        firewalls, 281
        modem speeds, 287
        proxy servers, 288-289
        sharing, 127, 130
        starting, 286-287, 291

games, 175
history, 293
installing Windows components from, 234-235
instant messaging, 377
    blocking messages, 384
    contact lists, 378-379
    discouraging messages, 385
    inviting others to use, 380-381
    photographs, 383
    remote assistance, 383
    sending invitations, 380-381
    sending messages, 382-383
ISPs (Internet Service Providers)
    access numbers, 280, 285
    AT&T WorldNet, 279
    BellSouth, 279
    connections, 281, 287
    EarthLink, 279
    email accounts, 349
    finding, 283
    locating, 284
    manual set-up, 280
    method of payment, 285
    monthly subscription plans, 281
    naming, 280
    passwords, 281
    selecting, 279, 282-285
    usernames, 281
MSN Chat, 387
    accounts, 388-389
    communities, 394-397
    joining, 390-391
    message board creation, 397
    participating in chats, 392-393
    phishing, 390
    private conversations, 393
    profiles, 389
    Whisper mode, 393

playing music from,
166-167

Usenet newsgroups, 399
  downloading messages,
    404
  finding, 408-409
  Outlook Express configu-
    ration, 400-401
  posting messages to,
    406-407
  reading, 402-405
  searching archive,
    410-411
  synchronizing, 405
  Usenet news services,
    401

Yahoo chat, 393

**Internet Accounts dialog
box, 370**

**Internet Connection
Firewall, 340-341**

**Internet Connection
Wizard, 284**

Internet Explorer, 277
  Address bar, 290,
    296-297
  Autosearch, 320
  Back button, 295
  buttons
  default fonts, 305
  Favorites list, 298-299
  Forward button, 295
  History folder, 312-313
  home pages, 294,
    302-303
  Menu bar, 290
  MSN Search Engine,
    290-291
  Offline Favorite Wizard,
    300
  opening, 290
  Refresh button, 295
  security, 330-331
    blocking content,
      334-335
    certificates, 336-337
    cookies, 338-339

customizing, 332-333
levels, 330-331
settings, 304-305
Stop button, 295
temporary files, 304
temporary folders, 305
Toolbar, 290
Web sites
  finding, 310-311
  loading, 290-291
  offline browsing,
    300-301
  opening in new win-
    dows, 295
  printing, 306-307
  recently visited sites,
    312-313
  saving, 308-309
  searching, 314-315,
    317
  viewing, 294

**Internet Options com-
mand (Tools menu), 332**

**Internet Options dialog
box, 302-305, 330-332**

**Internet Properties dialog
box, 278, 282**

**invalid system disk errors,
27**

**inviting others to use
Instant Messenger,
380-381**

**ISPs (Internet Service
Providers)**
  access numbers, 280, 285
  AT&T WorldNet, 279
  BellSouth, 279
  connections
    configuring, 281
    disconnecting, 287
  EarthLink, 279
  email accounts, 349
  finding, 283
  locating, 284
  manual set-up, 280
  method of payment, 285

monthly subscription plans,
  281
naming, 280
passwords, 281
selecting, 279, 282-285
usernames, 281

**Italic button (Formatting
toolbar), 460, 614**

italicizing text
  PowerPoint slides, 614
  Word documents, 460

**Items to Synchronize dia-
log box, 156-157**

J

Jabber.com, 379

**Jezebel.com Web site,
291**

**job-hunting Web sites,
324-325**

joining
  domains, 269
  MSN Chat, 390-391
  MSN communities,
    394-395
  workgroups, 269

junk email
  decreasing, 412-413
  screening, 536-537

**Junk Senders list
(Outlook), 537**

**Justify button (Formatting
toolbar), 470**

K

Keyboard icon, 192

**Keyboard Properties dia-
log box, 192-193**

keyboard shortcuts, 35
  Ctrl+', 541
  Ctrl+B, 461
  Ctrl+C, 455
  Ctrl+E, 470
  Ctrl+End, 543

Ctrl+Home, 543
Ctrl+I, 461
Ctrl+J, 470
Ctrl+L, 470
Ctrl+R, 470
Ctrl+Shift+D, 461
Ctrl+Shift+Down Arrow, 453
Ctrl+Shift+End, 453
Ctrl+Shift+Home, 453
Ctrl+Shift+Left Arrow, 453
Ctrl+Shift+Right Arrow, 453
Ctrl+Shift+Up Arrow, 453
Ctrl+Tab, 479
Ctrl+U, 461
Ctrl+V, 455
Ctrl+X, 455
Shift+Tab, 479

keyboards, 28. See also keyboard shortcuts
Alt key, 35
Application key, 33
arrow keys, 30
Backspace key, 33, 451
Break key, 38
Caps Lock key, 29, 451
Control key, 35
Delete key, 33, 451
End key, 31
Enter key, 29, 450
ergonomics, 47
Escape key, 38
FilterKeys, 208
function keys, 35
Home key, 31
Insert key, 33
modifier keys, 35
MouseKeys, 209
Num Lock, 37
numeric keypad, 36-37
Page Down key, 31
Page Up key, 31
selecting text with, 452
selecting worksheet cells with, 542, 545
settings, 192-193
Shift key, 35

standard keyboards, 28
StickyKeys, 208
Tab key, 29, 450
ToggleKeys, 208
Windows Logo key, 33
keypad (numeric), 36-37

L

labels, 666
lasso, 94
launching. See opening
layering graphics objects, 684
Layout Preview command (View menu), 667
Layout tab (Format dialog box), 681
layouts
PowerPoint slides, 624-625
reports, 665
leader tabs, 475
learning about computers, 8-9
licensing agreement (Windows XP), 264
lighting workstations, 47
line spacing, 468-469
Line Spacing button (Formatting toolbar), 468
Line Style button (Drawing toolbar), 681
line weight, 681
Link by Email command (Send menu), 356
linking data, 443
List command (View menu), 82
List view, 82
lists
PowerPoint, 610
Word documents, 472-473

LiveUpdate (Norton AntiVirus 2002), 344-345
loading Web pages, 290-291
local printers, 116-119
locales, customizing, 268
locating. See finding
locking taskbar, 194
logging off, 71-73
logging on, 27, 50-51
Lycos Web site, 317

M

Macintosh computers, 11
macros, 429
mail. See email
Mailbox Cleanup command (Tools menu), 534
Mailbox Cleanup dialog box, 534-535
mailing lists
Netly-L Web site, 365
subscribing to, 364
Topica Web site, 365
unsubscribing from, 365
Make Available Offline command, 155
MAKEBT32 program, 272
Map Network Drive command (File menu), 143
Map Network Drive dialog box, 143
mapping network drives, 142-143
margins, 466-467
math operators, entering, 37
Maximize button, 57
Maximize button (windows), 420

maximizing windows, 420

McAfee VirusScan 6.0, 343

media clips, adding to PowerPoint slides, 611

Media Guide (Windows Media Player), 166

meetings (Outlook), 516-517

menu bars, 290, 420

menus, 424. See also commands

Merge button (Formatting toolbar), 578

message boards
  creating, 397
  MSN communities, 394-395
    joining, 394
    reading/sending messages, 396-397
    viewing, 394

Message window (Outlook), 526-527

messages
  email messages
    archiving, 535
    attaching files to, 532-533
    carbon copies, 526
    creating, 526-527
    deleting, 535
    forwarding, 530-531
    headers, 529
    Mailbox Cleanup, 534-535
    moving, 529
    printing, 374-375
    reading, 528-529
    replying to, 530-531
    screening junk mail, 536-537
    sending, 526-527
    stationery patterns, 527

instant messages, 377
  blocking, 384-385
  contact lists, 378-379
  discouraging, 385
  inviting others to use, 380-381
  remote assistance, 383
  sending, 382-383
  sending invitations, 380-381
  sending photographs, 383

MSN Chat, 387
  accounts, 388-389
  communities, 394-397
  joining chat rooms, 390-391
  message board creation, 397
  participating in chats, 392-393
  phishing, 390
  private conversations, 393
  profiles, 389
  sending, 392-393
  Whisper mode, 393

Usenet newsgroups, 399
  downloading, 404
  finding, 408-409
  newsgroup synchronization, 405
  Outlook Express configuration, 400-401
  posting, 406-407
  reading, 402-405
  searching archive, 410-411
  Usenet news services, 401
  weblogs, 397
  Yahoo chat, 393

MetaCrawler Web site, 317

MetaFilter Weblog Web site, 397

.mht file extension, 308-309

Microsoft Office programs. See Office programs

Microsoft Services, hiding, 249

Minimize All Windows command, 59

minimizing windows, 59

mistakes, undoing, 7. See also troubleshooting

modems
  connection speeds, 287
  dial-up connections, 280

modifier keys, 35

Modify Style dialog box, 489

modifying. See changing

monitoring services, 251

monitors
  burn-in, 180
  color depth setting, 188
  frozen screens, 38-39
  magnifying items on, 208
  positioning, 47
  size of items displayed on, 189

mouse, 40-41, 52-53
  cleaning, 41
  clicking, 42-43, 191
  double-clicking, 43
  dragging-and-dropping, 43, 97
  ergonomics, 47
  insertion point, 31
  IntelliMouse, 41
  mouse pads, 40
  MouseKeys option, 209
  moving, 40
  pointer speed, 191
  pointing, 42
  pressing, 42
  selecting text with, 452
  selecting worksheet cells with, 542-544
  settings, 190-191

Mouse icon, 190

mouse pads, 40
Mouse Properties dialog box, 190-191
MouseKeys options, 209
movies, 168-171
moving
  briefcases, 148-149
  email messages, 529
  Excel worksheets, 565
    cells, 548-549
    charts, 592-593
    titles, 596
  fields, 657
  files, 96-97
  folders, 96-97
  graphics objects, 96-97, 678, 684
  insertion point, 30-31
  mouse, 40
  PowerPoint slides, 630-631
  PowerPoint tables, 623
  text, 454-455
  windows, 58
msconfig command, 248
MSN Chat
  accounts, 388-389
  communities
    joining, 394-395
    message board creation, 397
    reading/sending messages, 396-397
    viewing, 394
  joining, 390-391
  participating, 392-393
  phishing dangers, 390
  private conversations, 393
  profiles, 389
  software, 391
  Web site, 388
  Whisper mode, 393
MSN Search Engine, 290-291, 296
multikey sorting, 560-561
multimedia movies, 168-171

multiple programs, running, 15
music
  finding online, 166-167
  playing, 162-163, 166-167
  recording, 164-165
Mute option, 178
My Computer window, 64
My Music folder, 165
My Network Places window
  adding network places to, 134-135
  adding shared folders to, 134-135
  browsing networks, 136-137
  opening, 132
  View workgroup computers link, 138-139
My Pictures folder, 172
My Recent Documents option, 86
My Shortcuts button, 508

N

Name menu commands, 557
naming
  briefcases, 147
  computers, 268
  databases, 646
  fields, 651
  files, 85, 92-93
  floppy disks, 99
  folders, 80-81, 92-93
  forms, 655
  Outlook folders, 524
  queries, 662
  shortcuts, 91
  tables, 651
  worksheet ranges, 556-557
  worksheets, 564

navigation, 30-31
  Excel worksheets, 542-543
  forms, 649
  Office programs
    menu bars, 420
    scrollbars, 421
    status bars, 420
    task panes, 421-423
    title bars, 420
    toolbars, 421
    window controls, 420
    work area, 421
  Web sites, 294-295
netiquette, 406-407
Netly-L Web site, 365
network cards, 124-126
network printers, 120-121
Network Setup Wizard, 130-131
networks, 11. See also Internet
  browsing, 136-137
  configuring, 124-127
    shared Internet connections, 130-131
    user accounts, 128-129
  domains, 126
  drive mapping, 142-143
  files
    finding, 138-139
    sharing, 133, 140-141
  firewalls, 131, 340-341
  folder sharing, 132-133, 138-141
  hubs, 124
  logging in, 27
  My Network Places, 132-138
  naming computers, 126
  printers, 120-121, 127
  routers, 125
  searching, 137
  setting up, 125
  switches, 124
  user accounts, 128-129

Windows XP installation, 125

workgroups, 126

New All Day Event command (Actions menu), 514

New Briefcase window, 146-147

New command (File menu), 84, 456

New Connection Wizard, 279-281

New Document task pane, 428-429, 456

New Folder dialog box, 524

New Form dialog box, 654

New Mail Message Using command (Actions menu), 527

New menu commands
Folder, 80
Shortcut, 419

New Office Document command (Start menu), 428

New Office Document dialog box, 428-429

New Presentation task pane, 602-604

New Record button, 648

New Recurring Appointment command (Action menu), 512

New Slide button (Standard toolbar), 628

Newsgroup Subscriptions dialog box, 408

newsgroups (Usenet), 399
downloading messages, 404
finding, 408-409
netiquette, 406-407

Outlook Express configuration, 400-401, 405
posting messages to, 406-407
reading, 402-405
searching archives, 410-411
searching Web directories, 409
synchronizing, 405

Newsguy Web site, 401

newspaper-style columns (Word), 476-477

non-system disk errors, 27

Normal view (PowerPoint), 608

Northern Light Web site, 317

Norton AntiVirus
installing, 342-345
LiveUpdate, 344-345
virus scan procedure, 346-347

Norton Internet Security, 340-341

Notes Page view (PowerPoint), 638

notification area, 62-63

Num Lock key, 37

numbered lists, 472-473

Numbering button (Formatting toolbar), 472

numbers
Excel formats, 576-577
numbered lists, 472-473
page numbers, 486-487

numeric keypad, 36-37

Object command (Insert menu), 674

object linking and embedding (OLE), 442-443

objects
deleting, 68-69
graphics objects
3D effects, 683
adding to AutoCorrect collection, 675
adding to files, 674-675
bringing to front, 684
clip art, 672-673
copying and pasting, 679
diagrams, 686-687
fill color, 681
formatting, 680-681
grouping, 684-685
layering, 684
line weight, 681
resizing, 678-679
rotating, 679
selecting, 678
sending to back, 684
shadow effects, 682-683
shapes, 670-671
ungrouping, 685
WordArt, 676-677
wrapping text around, 681
moving, 53, 96-97, 678
OLE (object linking and embedding), 442-443
opening, 52
rotating, 679
selecting, 52
tables
adding data to, 651
closing, 653
creating, 650-651
defined, 644
designing from scratch, 651
modifying, 652-653
naming, 651
opening, 652
Table Wizard, 650

Office Assistant, 439

Office Assistant dialog box, 439

Office Clipboard, 440-441

Office on the Web command (Help menu), 439

Office programs, 417. *See also* **Access databases; Excel spreadsheets; Outlook; PowerPoint presentations; Word documents**
  adding/removing features, 444-445
  closing, 419
  copying data, 440-441
  cutting data, 440-441
  dragging and dropping data, 441
  files
    closing, 432-433
    creating, 428-429
    finding, 436-437
    opening, 432-433
    previewing, 433-435
    printing, 434-435
    saving, 430-431
  graphics, 669
    3D effects, 683
    bringing to front, 684
    clip art, 672-673
    copying and pasting, 679
    diagrams, 686-687
    fill color, 681
    formatting, 680-681
    grouping, 684-685
    layering, 684
    line weight, 681
    moving, 678
    resizing, 678-679
    rotating, 679
    selecting, 678
    sending to back, 684
    shadow effects, 682-683
    shapes, 670-671
    ungrouping, 685
    WordArt, 676-677
    wrapping text around, 681
  help, 438-439
  menus, 424

OLE (object linking and embedding), 442-443
  pasting data, 440-441
  scrollbars, 421
  shortcut icons, 419
  starting, 418-419
  switching between, 419
  task panes, 421-422
    activating features in, 422
    closing, 423
    New Document, 428-429
    opening, 423
    scrolling, 422
    startup mode, 423
    switching between, 422-423
  templates, 429
  toolbars, 421
    buttons, 425
    customizing, 426-427
    displaying/hiding, 425
  uninstalling, 445
  windows, 420
  work area, 421

offline tasks
  offline files/folders, 159
  Web site browsing, 300-301
  working offline, 152-155
    offline settings, 158-159
    permissions, 155
    synchronizing files, 156-157

Offline Favorite Wizard (Internet Explorer), 300

offline files/folders, 159

Offline Files tab (Folder Options dialog box), 158-159

OLE (object linking and embedding), 442-443

online communities (MSN Chat)
  joining, 394-395
  message board creation, 397

reading/sending messages, 396-397
  viewing, 394

Open Attachment dialog box, 361

Open command (File menu), 87, 106, 432

Open dialog box, 87, 106

Open Directory Project Web site, 314-315

Open File dialog box, 432-433

Open Office Document dialog box, 433

Open With dialog box, 102-103

opening
  briefcases, 149
  Explorer, 76
  files, 102-103, 432-433
  folders, 76
  forms, 648, 656
  Form Wizard, 654
  Internet connections, 286-287
  Internet Explorer, 290
  menus, 53, 424
  Office Assistant, 439
  Office programs, 418-419
  Outlook Calendar, 510
  Outlook Express, 350, 364
  print queues, 110
  programs, 23, 56-57
  Restore Wizard, 260
  Simple Query Wizard, 662
  tables, 652
  task panes, 423
  Web sites, 295

operating systems, 22-23
  booting, 26-27
  DOS, 23
  Windows XP. *See* Windows XP

Options command (Tools menu), 421, 423

Options dialog box, 165, 421

Order menu commands
  Bring Forward, 685
  Bring to Front, 684
  Send Backward, 685
  Send to Back, 684

.org addresses, 310

Outline view
  PowerPoint, 609
  Word, 449

Outlining toolbar, 612-613

Outlook 2002, 507. *See also* **Outlook Express**
  appointments
    editing, 513
    recurring appointments, 512-513
    reminders, 511-513
    scheduling, 510-511
  Calendar
    appointments, 510-513
    events, 514-515
    meetings, 516-517
    opening, 510
    tasks, 518-519
  compared to Outlook Express, 351
  contacts
    creating, 520-521
    finding, 509
    importing, 522-523
    saving, 521
  email accounts, 527
  events, 514-515
  Folder List, 508
  folders, 524-525
  Mailbox Cleanup, 534-535
  meetings, 516-517
  messages
    archiving, 535
    attaching files to, 532-533
    carbon copies, 526
    creating, 526-527
    deleting, 535

    forwarding, 530-531
    headers, 529
    moving, 529
    reading, 528-529
    replying to, 530-531
    screening junk mail, 536-537
    sending, 526-527
    stationery patterns, 527
  My Shortcuts button, 508
  Outlook Bar, 508
  Outlook Shortcuts, 508-509
  tasks, 518-519
  views, 509

Outlook Bar, 508

Outlook Express. *See also* **Outlook 2002**
  compared to Outlook 2002, 351
  configuring, 350-351, 370-371
  email
    address/people locator, 362-363
    composing, 352
    file attachments, 358-361
    forwarding, 355
    HTML formatting, 353
    printing messages, 374-375
    priority status, 353
    receiving, 354-355
    replying to, 355
    sending, 352-353
    sending Web pages with, 356-357
  mailing lists, 364-365
  opening, 350, 364
  spam, 412-413
  Usenet newsgroup service
    configuring, 400-401
    downloading messages, 404
    finding newsgroups, 408-409

    posting newsgroups, 406-407
    reading newsgroups, 402-405
    searching newsgroup archives, 410-411
    synchronizing newsgroups, 405

Outlook Shortcuts button, 508

Outlook Today view, 509

Outside Border button (Formatting toolbar), 481

Overtype mode (Word), 451

P

Pack and Go command (File menu), 640

Pack and Go Wizard, 640-641

page breaks (Word), 451, 486-487

Page by email command (Send menu), 357

Page Down key, 31

page layout (printers), 113

page numbers, 486-487

Page Numbers command (Insert menu), 487

Page Numbers dialog box, 487

Page Setup command (File menu), 466, 502, 581, 587

Page Setup dialog box, 466, 502-503, 581, 587

paper size (Word), 502-503

paper source (printers), 113

Paragraph command (Format menu), 468

Paragraph dialog box, 450, 468-469

parent folders, 84, 96

passwords, 51
entering, 50
ISPs (Internet Service Providers), 281
phishing practices, 390
screensavers, 71

Paste button (Standard toolbar), 455

Paste command (Edit menu), 441

Paste Special command (Edit menu), 442

Paste Special dialog box, 442-443

pasting data, 440-441
objects, 679
text, 455

Pause button (Windows Media Player), 162

pausing print jobs, 111

PCs (IBM-compatible computers), 13
rebooting, 39
turning off, 44-45
turning on, 26-27

people locators, 322-323

Percent Style button (Formatting toolbar), 576

permissions
offline, 155
printer sharing, 115

personal computers, 11

phishing, 390

photographs. See images

Picture command (Insert menu), 619, 672

Picture menu commands
Clip Art, 672
WordArt, 676

Picture Tasks list, 173

pictures. See images

placeholders (PowerPoint), 605

Plan a Meeting command (Actions menu), 516

Plan a Meeting window (Outlook), 516-517

planning
databases, 645
meetings, 516-517

Play button (Windows Media Player), 162

playing
games, 174-175
music/videos, 162-163

pointers, 191

pointing sticks, 41-42

pop-up windows, 295

ports
choosing, 117
port numbers, 289

positioning monitors, 47

POST (power on self test), 27

posting Usenet newsgroup messages, 406-407

power on self test (POST), 27

power options, 198-199

Power Options Properties dialog box (Control Panel), 198-199

PowerPoint presentations, 601
bulleted lists, 610
charts, 611, 620-621
creating
with AutoContent Wizard, 602-603
from design templates, 604-605
from scratch, 606-607
grid and guidelines, 617
handouts, 638-639

images
adding, 618-619
clip art, 610
media clips, 611
Pack and Go Wizard, 640-641
rulers, 615
running, 636-637
saving to CDs or disks, 640-641
slides
adding, 628-629
animation effects, 634-635
backgrounds, 626-627
copying, 631
deleting, 628-629
layout, 611
moving, 630-631
reordering, 630-631
slide layout, 624-625
slide timings, 637
thumbnails, 609
transitions, 632-633
speaker notes, 638-639
stopping, 637
tables, 611, 622-623
text
adding, 612-613
aligning, 614-615
editing, 612-613
formatting, 614-615
text boxes, 610, 616-617
WordArt text, 617
views, 608-609

presentations. See PowerPoint presentations

pressing mouse buttons, 42

preventing instant messages, 384-385

Preview Pane command (View menu), 528

previewing
files, 433-435
reports, 667

Print command (File menu), 106, 306, 434, 599, 639

Print dialog box, 106, 306, 434-435, 599, 639

Print Preview button (Standard toolbar), 467

Print Preview command (File menu), 107

print queues, 110-111

printed pages, previewing, 107

Printed Watermark dialog box, 492-493

printers. *See also* **printing**
  choosing, 106, 121
  configuring, 112-113, 125
  default printers, 112-113
  installing, 119
  local printers, 116-119
  network printers, 120-121
  Printers folder, 109
  properties, 107
  selecting, 306
  share names, 119
  sharing, 114-115, 127

Printers and Faxes window, 114-115

Printers folder, 109

printing, 105. *See also* **printers**
  documents
    canceling print jobs, 110-111
    pausing print jobs, 111
    print job management, 110-111
    printer settings, 112-115
    from programs, 106-107
    restarting print jobs, 111
    shared printers, 115
    from Windows desktop, 108
  email messages, 374-375
  envelopes, 504-505
  Excel charts, 599

files, 109, 434-435
PowerPoint handouts, 639
PowerPoint speaker notes, 639
print queues, 110-111
system information, 221
test pages, 119
Web sites, 306-307
worksheet comments, 587

priority of Outlook tasks, 519

private chats (MSN Chat), 393

Processes panel, 250

processes. *See* **services**

product identification key (Windows XP), 265

profiles (MSN Chat), 389

program

programs, 14. *See also* **specific programs**
  accounting programs, 17-19
  boot program, 26-27
  browsers, 18
  closing, 72
  compared to hardware, 20-21
  configuring, 228-229
  database management programs, 18
  defaults, 242-243
  deleting, 231
  disabling, 246-247
  downloading, 319
  DTP (desktop-publishing programs), 16
  finding online, 318-319
  games, 19
  graphics programs, 18
  how programs work, 14
  installing, 228-229
  MAKEBT32, 272
  maximum number of stored programs, 15
  modifying, 230-231

Office programs. *See also* Access databases; Excel spreadsheets; Outlook; PowerPoint presentations; Word documents
  adding/removing features, 444-445
  closing, 419
  copying data, 440-441
  cutting data, 440-441
  dragging and dropping data, 441
  files, 428-437
  help, 438-439
  menus, 424
  OLE (object linking and embedding), 442-443
  pasting data, 440-441
  scrollbars, 421
  shortcut icons, 419
  starting, 418-419
  switching between, 419
  task panes, 421-423, 428-429
  templates, 429
  toolbars, 421, 425-427
  uninstalling, 445
  windows, 420
  work area, 421
  presentation programs, 19
  reloading into System Tray, 247
  removing, 230
  running, 15, 56
  shareware, 318
  spreadsheet programs, 17-19
  starting, 23, 206-207
  switching between, 60-61
  uninstalling, 252-253
  windows, 57
  word-processing programs, 16

protecting disks, 6

proxy servers, 288-289

publishing, DTP (desktop-publishing programs), 16

Q

queries
creating, 662-663
defined, 645
filtering, 663
naming, 662
running, 663
wildcards, 663

queues (print), 110-111

Quick Format option, 99

Quick Launch toolbar, 56, 59, 204-205

R

Radio Tuner (Windows Media Player), 166-167

ranges (worksheet cells)
AutoFormat feature, 584-585
names, 556-557

reading
email messages, 528-529
MSN community message boards, 396-397
Usenet newsgroup messages, 402-405

rebooting, 39

receiving email, 354-355, 360-361

Recent Documents folder, 87

Record command (Windows Movie Maker), 168

Record Narration Track dialog box (Windows Movie Maker), 171

recording music, 164-165

records
creating, 648
defined, 644
fields, 644, 651

filtering, 660-661
advanced filtering, 661
by exclusion, 661
by form, 661
by selection, 660
sorting, 658-659

recovering files
Automated System Recovery, 262-263
Restore Wizard, 260-261
System Restore tool, 222-223

Rectangle tool, 670

recurring appointments, scheduling, 512-513

Recycle Bin, 94, 213
allocating space, 69
disabling, 95
emptying, 69
opening, 68
settings, 95

Reference command (Insert menu), 485

Refresh button (Internet Explorer), 295

registering Windows XP, 271

Rehearse Timings command (Slide Show menu), 637

reinstalling devices, 237

rejecting changes (Word), 501

relative cell addresses (Excel), 572-573

reloading programs into System Tray, 247

reminders
enabling, 159
for appointments, 511-513

remote access, 145
briefcases
copying, 148-149
moving, 148-149
opening, 149

placing documents in, 146-147
updating files in, 150-151
working offline, 152-155
offline settings, 158-159
synchronizing files, 156-157

remote assistance (Instant Messenger), 383

Remove Filter button, 660

removing
filters, 660
Office components, 444-445
programs, 230
text, 33

Rename command (File menu), 92

Rename Field button, 651

renaming
briefcases, 147
fields, 651, 653
files, 85, 92-93
folders, 80-81, 92-93
shortcuts, 91
worksheets, 564

reordering
fields, 653
PowerPoint slides, 630-631

Repeat Font Formatting command (Edit menu), 463

Replace command (Edit menu), 495

replacing
text, 494-495
worksheet data, 558-559

Reply Message window (Outlook), 530

replying to email, 355, 530-531

Report Wizard, 664-665

reports
creating, 664-665
customizing, 666-667
defined, 645
fonts, 666
graphics, 667
grouping categories, 664
labels, 666
layouts, 665
previewing, 667
removing objects from, 667
report styles, 665
Report Wizard, 664-665
sorting, 665
titles, 665

Reset button, 39

resetting commands, 425

resizing
clip art, 619
Drawing Canvas, 671
Excel charts, 592-593
objects, 678-679
panes, 609
PowerPoint tables, 623
temporary folders, 305
windows, 58

Restart button, 72

restarting
computers, 72
print jobs, 111

Restore button (windows), 420

Restore buttons, 57

restore points, 222-223

Restore Wizard, 260-261

restoring files
Automated System
Recovery, 262-263
Restore Wizard, 260-261
System Restore tool, 222-223

Reviewing toolbar, 485, 500-501

right-clicking mouse, 42-43

RootsWeb Web site, 326-327

rotating objects, 679

routers, 125

Row command (Format menu), 555

rows
Word tables, 479
worksheet rows
deleting, 550-551
height of, 554-555
selecting, 545

Rows command (Insert menu), 623

RSACi ratings, 334-335

Ruler command (View menu), 615

rulers (PowerPoint), 615

Run Query button, 663

running
PowerPoint slide shows, 636-637
programs, 56
queries, 663

S

Safe Mode, 45

Save As command (File menu), 88, 308, 430

Save As dialog box, 88-89, 430-431

Save Attachments dialog box, 361

Save command (File menu), 89, 430

Save Movie dialog box (Windows Movie Maker), 171

Save Web Page dialog box, 308

saving
contacts, 521
documents, 81

files, 88-89, 100-101, 430-431
forms, 657
PowerPoint presentations, 640-641
Web sites, 308-309

scanning
for updates, 234
for viruses, 346-347

Scheduled Task Wizard, 216-217

scheduling
appointments, 510-513
events, 514-515
tasks, 216-217
Web page downloads, 301

screen resolution, 189

screening email messages, 536-537

screens. *See* monitors

screensavers, 71, 180-181

scrollbars, 421

scrolling
automatic scrolling, 77
scrollbars, 421
task panes, 422

Search button, 137, 436

Search command (Start menu), 138

search engines
Google, 316-317
HotBot, 317
Lycos, 317
MetaCrawler, 317
MSN, 290-291
Northern Light, 317
WebCrawler, 317

searching, 78-79
computers, 137
email addresses, 323, 362-363
files, 87, 436-437
Help, 66

Outlook contacts, 509
software, 318
text, 494-495
Usenet newsgroups, 405,
    410-411
Web sites
    Autosearch feature, 311
    companies, 320-321
    employment resources,
        324-325
    genealogical resources,
        326-327
    people locators,
        322-323
    search engines,
        290-291, 316-317
    URL entry, 310-311
    Web directories,
        314-315
worksheet data, 558-559
security
    backups
        creating, 257-259,
            262-263
        restoring files from,
            260-261
    encryption, 333
    firewalls, 281, 340-341
    Internet Explorer
        certificates, 336-337
        configuring, 330-333,
            338-339
        content, blocking,
            334-335
    phishing dangers, 390
    printer sharing, 114-115
    viruses, 343, 347
Select Picture dialog box,
    618
Select Users or Groups
    dialog box, 115
selecting
    copying and pasting, 679
    groups of files, 94
    home pages, 303
    ISPs (Internet Service
        Providers), 279, 282-285

moving, 678
objects, 678
printers, 306
resizing, 678-679
rotating, 679
text, 452-453
worksheet cells, 540,
    544-545
worksheet columns, 545
worksheet rows, 545
Selective Startup, 248-249
Send Backward command
    (Order menu), 685
Send menu commands
    Link by Email, 356
    Page by Email, 357
    Shortcut to Desktop, 357
Send to Back command
    (Order menu), 684
sending
    compressed files, 225
    email, 526-527
        file attachments,
            358-359
        Outlook Express,
            352-353
        Web pages, 356-357
    instant messages, 382-383
    MSN messages, 396-397
    photographs, 383
servers, proxy servers,
    288-289
service packs
    checking installation of,
        238-239
    installing, 240-241
services
    disabling, 249
    hiding, 249
    monitoring, 251
    stopping, 250-251
Services Panel, 248
Set Up Show command
    (Slide Show menu), 636
Set Up Show dialog box,
    636-637

setting up. *See* configur-
    ing
setup floppy disks,
    272-273
shading Word documents,
    480-481
Shadow button (Drawing
    toolbar), 683
shadow effects, 682-683
Shadow Settings toolbar,
    682-683
shapes, drawing,
    670-671
Share dialog box,
    140-141
Share Name option,
    114-115
share names, 119
Share this folder option,
    140
shareware, 318
sharing
    files/folders, 140-141
    Internet connections,
        130-131
    printers, 114-115
Shift key, 35
Shortcut command (New
    menu), 419
shortcut menus, 53
Shortcut to Desktop com-
    mand (Send menu), 357
shortcuts. *See* keyboard
    shortcuts
Show Desktop button, 59
Show on the Desktop
    command, 55
Show the Office Assistant
    command (Help menu),
    439
Show/Hide button
    (Standard toolbar), 451
ShowSounds option, 209

shutting down
computers, 44-45, 72-73
Windows XP, 51

Simple Query Wizard, 662

sites. *See* **Web sites**

sizing
clip art, 619
Drawing Canvas, 671
Excel charts, 592-593
objects, 678-679
panes, 609
PowerPoint tables, 623
windows, 58

Slate Web site, 307

Slide Design command (Format menu), 607

Slide Finder dialog box, 629

Slide Layout command (Format menu), 610

Slide Layout task pane, 624-625

Slide Show menu commands
Animation Schemes, 634
Custom Animation, 635
Rehearse Timings, 637
Set Up Show, 636

Slide Show view (PowerPoint), 608

slide shows (PowerPoint), 601
bulleted lists, 610
charts, 611, 620-621
creating
with AutoContent Wizard, 602-603
from design templates, 604-605
from scratch, 606-607
grid and guidelines, 617
handouts, 638-639
images
adding, 618-619
clip art, 610

media clips, 611
Pack and Go Wizard, 640-641
rulers, 615
running, 636-637
saving to CDs or disks, 640-641
slides
adding, 628-629
animation effects, 634-635
backgrounds, 626-627
copying, 631
deleting, 628-629
layout, 611
moving, 630-631
reordering, 630-631
slide layout, 624-625
slide timings, 637
thumbnails, 609
transitions, 632-633
speaker notes, 638-639
stopping, 637
tables, 611, 622-623
text
adding, 612-613
aligning, 614-615
editing, 612-613
formatting, 614-615
text boxes, 610, 616-617
WordArt text, 617
views, 608-609

Slide Sorter toolbar, 631-632

Slide Sorter view (PowerPoint), 608-609

Slide Transition task pane, 632

Slides command (Insert menu), 629

Smart Tags, 441

software. *See* **programs**

Solitaire, 174

Sort Ascending button, 560, 658

Sort command (Data menu), 560

Sort Descending button, 560, 658

Sort dialog box, 560-561

sorting
records, 658-659
reports, 665
worksheet data, 560-561

sound
accessibility options, 209
modifying, 200-201
music
finding online, 166-167
playing, 162-163, 166-167
recording, 164-165
Mute option, 178
schemes, 201
volume, 178-179

Sounds and Audio Device icon, 200

Sounds and Audio Device Properties dialog box, 200-201

SoundSentry option, 209

Source Data command (Chart menu), 599

Source Data dialog box, 599

spacing Word documents
line spacing, 468-469
margins, 466-467

spam, 373, 412-413, 536-537

speaker notes (PowerPoint), 638-639

speakers, 200-201

special characters, 85, 92

special keys, 32-33

spell-checking text, 496-497

Spelling and Grammar command (Tools menu), 497

Spelling and Grammar dialog box, 497

Spelling dialog box, 496

spreadsheet programs, 17-19. *See also* **Excel worksheets**

standard keyboards, 28

Standard toolbar
AutoSum button, 568-569
Chart Wizard button, 590
Columns button, 477
Copy button, 454
Cut button, 454
Format Painter button, 462-463, 582
Insert Chart button, 620
Insert Table button, 478, 622
New Slide button, 628
Paste button, 455
Print Preview button, 467
Search button, 436
Show/Hide button, 451
Sort Ascending button, 560
Sort Descending button, 560
Spelling and Grammar button, 497
Tables and Borders button, 479
Undo button, 561
Zoom control, 448

Standby, 73

Start button, 206

Start menu
adding items to, 202-203
creating folders in, 81
New Office Document command, 428
opening, 54
Search command, 138

starting. *See also* **opening**
Automated System Recovery, 262
Backup Wizard, 258
computers, 26-27
Form Wizard, 654

MAKEBT32 program, 272
Office Assistant, 439
Office programs, 418-419
programs, 23, 56-57
Restore Wizard, 260
Simple Query Wizard, 662
Windows XP, 27

startup
Selective Startup, 248-249
Startup folder, 206-207
startup mode, 423
Startup programs, 206-207

stationery (Outlook), 527

status bars, 420

StickyKeys options, 208

Stop button
Internet Explorer, 295
Windows Media Player, 162

stopping
PowerPoint slide shows, 637
services, 250-251

storyboards (movies), 170

Style and Formatting task pane, 489

Style button (Formatting toolbar), 488

Style command (Format menu), 489

styles (Word documents), 488-489

subfolders, 525

subscribing
to mailing lists, 364
to Usenet newsgroups, 402-405

SUM function, 568-569

Supernews.com Web site, 401

switches, 124

switching between
programs, 60-61, 419
task panes, 422-423
worksheets, 564

Symbol command (Insert menu), 464

Symbol dialog box, 464-465

symbols
adding to Word documents, 464-465
entering, 37

Synchronization Settings dialog box, 157

Synchronize command (Tools menu), 156

synchronizing
files, 156-159
folders, 156-157
Usenet newsgroups, 405

System Information tool, 220-221

System Restore tool, 222-223

system tools, 211
Automated System Recovery, 262-263
Backup Wizard, 258-259
compression tool, 224-225
Device Manager, 236-237
Disk Cleanup, 212-213
Disk Defragmenter, 214-215
Event Viewer, 254-255
Restore Wizard, 260-261
Scheduled Task Wizard, 216-217
System Information, 220-221
System Restore, 222-223
Windows troubleshooters, 218-219

System Tray, 246-247

T

Tab key, 29, 450

Table and Borders toolbar, 623

Table command (Insert menu), 622

Table Wizard, 650

tables

adding data to, 651

adding to PowerPoint presentations, 622-623

closing, 653

creating, 478-479, 650-651

defined, 644

designing from scratch, 651

fields, 652-653

modifying, 652-653

naming, 651

opening, 652

PowerPoint presentations, 611

Table Wizard, 650

Tables and Borders button (Standard toolbar), 479

Tables and Borders toolbar, 479

tabs, 474-475

Tabs command (Format menu), 475

Tabs dialog box, 475

Task Pane command (View menu), 423

task panes, 421-422

activating features in, 422

closing, 423

New Document, 428-429, 456

New Presentation, 602, 604

opening, 423

resizing, 609

scrolling, 422

Slide Layout, 624-625

Slide Transition, 632

startup mode, 423

Style and Formatting, 489

switching between, 422-423

Task window (Outlook), 518-519

taskbar

automatic scrolling, 194

buttons, 61

clock, 195

customizing, 194-195

grouping buttons, 195

hiding, 194

icons, 195

locking, 194

notification area, 62

placement, 195

properties, 194-195

resizing, 60

switching between programs, 60

System Tray, 246-247

unlocking, 61

Taskbar and Start Menu Properties dialog box, 194-195

TaskPad, 519

tasks

creating, 518-519

managing, 519

running automatically, 216-217

TaskPad, 519

viewing, 519

templates

defined, 429

PowerPoint templates, 604-605

Word templates, 456-457

Templates dialog box, 456-457, 646

temporary files, 212-213, 304

temporary folders, 305

testing formulas, 567

text. *See also* **Word documents**

aligning, 470-471

AutoCorrect, 498-499

AutoText, 458-459

borders, 480-481

color, 461

columns, 476-477

comments, 484-485

copying, 454-455

copying text formatting, 462-463

deleting, 33

deselecting, 453

drop caps, 490-491

editing, 450-451

endnotes, 484-485

entering into Word documents, 450-451

fonts, 460-461

footers, 482-483

footnotes, 484-485

formatting, 460-461

grammar-checking, 496-497

headers, 482-483

indenting, 470-471

inserting, 33

lists, 472-473

moving, 454-455

selecting, 452-453

shading, 480-481

slide text

adding, 612-613

aligning, 614-615

editing, 612-613

formatting, 614-615

text boxes, 610, 616-617

WordArt text, 617

spell-checking, 496-497

styles, 488-489

symbols, 464-465

tables, 478-479

tabs, 474-475

text case, 490-491

WordArt, 676-677

worksheet titles, 596-597

wrapping, 671, 681

Text Box button (Drawing toolbar), 616

Text Wrapping button, 671

textures (PowerPoint backgrounds), 627

**Thawte certificate author-
ity, 336-337**

**Themes tab (Display
Properties dialog box),
182**

**Thumbnail command
(View menu), 83**

thumbnails, 83, 609

tiling windows, 59

time/date settings, 269

timelines (movies), 170

**timing PowerPoint slide
shows, 637**

title bars, 420

titles
   Excel charts, 596-597
   Outlook tasks, 518
   reports, 665

ToggleKeys option, 208

**Toolbar (Internet
Explorer), 290**

toolbars, 421
   3-D Settings, 683
   AutoText, 459
   Chart toolbar, 594
   customizing, 426-427
   Diagram, 686
   displaying/hiding, 425
   Drawing toolbar, 616
     displaying, 670
     Fill Color button, 681
     *Insert Clip Art button,
     618, 672*
     Line Style button, 681
     Rectangle tool, 670
     Shadow button, 683
     Text Box button, 616
     WordArt button, 676
   Formatting toolbar
     *Align Left button, 470,
     615*
     *Align Right button, 470,
     615*
     Bold button, 460, 614
     Bullets button, 472
     Center button, 578

*Comma Style button,
577*
*Currency Style button,
576*
*Decrease Decimal but-
ton, 577*
*Decrease Indent button,
470*
Fill Color button, 595
Font Color button, 461
Font Size button, 595
*Increase Decimal button,
577*
*Increase Indent button,
470, 579*
Italic button, 460, 614
Justify button, 470
*Line Spacing button,
468*
Merge button, 578
Numbering button, 472
*Outside Border button,
481*
Percent Style button, 576
Style button, 488
*Underline button, 460,
614*
Formula Auditing toolbar,
574-575
Header and Footer,
482-483
Outlining toolbar, 612-613
Quick Launch toolbar, 56,
59
Reviewing toolbar, 485,
500-501
Shadow Settings toolbar,
682-683
Slide Sorter toolbar,
631-632
Standard toolbar
   *AutoSum button,
   568-569*
   *Chart Wizard button,
   590*
   Columns button, 477
   Copy button, 454
   Cut button, 454

*Format Painter button,
462-463, 582*
Insert Chart button, 620
*Insert Table button, 478,
622*
New Slide button, 628
Paste button, 455
*Print Preview button,
467*
Show/Hide button, 451
*Sort Ascending button,
560*
*Sort Descending button,
560*
*Spelling and Grammar
button, 497*
*Tables and Borders but-
ton, 479*
Undo button, 561
Zoom control, 448
Tables and Borders toolbar,
479, 623

**Toolbars command (View
menu), 425**

**Toolbars menu com-
mands, Customize, 426**

**tools. *See* system tools;
toolbars; wizards**

Tools menu commands
   AutoCorrect Options, 458,
   498
   Customize, 424
   Email Accounts, 527
   Formula Auditing, 574
   Internet Options, 332
   Mailbox Cleanup, 534
   Options, 421, 423
   Spelling and Grammar,
   497
   Synchronize, 156
   Track Changes, 500, 588

Topica Web site, 365

touch pads, 41

**Trace Dependents button
(Formula Auditing tool-
bar), 575**

Trace Precedents button (Formula Auditing toolbar), 575

Track Changes command (Tools menu), 500, 588

Track Changes menu commands
Accept or Reject Changes, 589
Highlight Changes, 588

trackballs, 41

tracking changes
Excel worksheets, 588-589
Word documents, 500-501

transitions between PowerPoint slides, 632-633

trash can. *See* **Recycle Bin**

Troubleshoot button, 189

troubleshooting, 218-219, 245
Event Viewer, 254-255
formulas, 574-575
frozen screens, 38-39
programs
disabling, 246-247
reloading into System Tray, 247
uninstalling, 252-253
Selective Startup, 248-249
services
disabling, 249
monitoring, 251
stopping, 250-251
System Tray, 246-247
undoing mistakes, 7, 553

Turn Off Computer window, 72

turning on/off
computers, 26-27, 44-45, 72-73
Drawing Canvas, 671
gridlines, 479
Num Lock, 37
shadow effects, 683

U

Underline button (Formatting toolbar), 460, 614

underlined text
PowerPoint slides, 614
Word documents, 460

underscore (_), 556

Undo button (Standard toolbar), 561

undoing mistakes, 7, 553

Ungroup command (Grouping menu), 685

ungrouping graphics objects, 685

UNICEF Web site, 310

uninstalling
Office programs, 445
programs, 252-253

universities, .edu Web addresses, 311

unlocking taskbars, 61

unsubscribing from mailing lists, 365

Update All button, 151

Update window, 151

updating Windows components, 234-235

upgrading to Windows XP, 264-265

URLs, 291, 296-297, 310-311

Usenet newsgroups, 399
downloading messages, 404
finding, 408-409
netiquette, 406-407
Outlook Express configuration, 400-401, 405
posting messages to, 406-407
reading, 402-405

searching archives, 410-411
synchronizing, 405
Usenet news services, 401
Web directories, 409

user accounts
changing, 129
creating, 128
naming, 128
opening, 128
selecting, 50

User Accounts window, 128

user interfaces, 12

user names, 51, 281

V

VeriSign certificate authority, 336-337

videos, 162-163

View menu commands
Arrange Icons By, 83
AutoPreview, 528
Comments, 587
Details, 82
Folder List, 508
Form Header/Footer, 657
Grid and Guidelines, 617
Header and Footer, 482
Layout Preview, 667
List, 82
Preview Pane, 528
Ruler, 615
Task Pane, 423
Thumbnail, 83
Toolbars, 425
Zoom, 448

View workgroup computers link, 132

viewing
events, 515
file associations, 103
gridlines, 479
MSN communities, 394
page breaks, 486

tasks, 519
toolbar buttons, 425
toolbars, 425
Usenet newsgroup messages, 402-405
Web sites
  Internet Explorer, 294
  offline browsing, 300-301
  recently visited, 312-313
Windows Messenger contact lists, 378
worksheet comments, 587

views
Datasheet View, 649
Details, 82
List, 82
Outlook, 509
PowerPoint, 608-609
Thumbnails, 83
Word, 448-449

viruses, 342-347

visual presentations. *See* PowerPoint presentations

visualizations, 163

volume, 63, 163, 178-179

Volume button (Windows Media Player), 163

Volume dialog box, 178-179

W

wallpaper, 184-185

watermarks, 492-493

Web browsers. *See* Internet Explorer

Web directories
Excite, 315
Google, 315
Open Directory Project, 314-315
people locators, 322-323
site searches, 314-315

topic categories, 315
Usenet newsgroups, 409
Yahoo!, 315

Web sites, 277. *See also* Internet
addresses, 291, 296-297
Ancestry.com, 327
AOL Instant Messenger, 379
AT&T WorldNet, 279
BellSouth, 279
blocking content of, 334-335
Business.com, 321
CareerBuilder, 324-325
Dell Computers, 310
Download.com, 318-319
EarthLink, 279
emailing, 356-357
employment resources, 324-325
Excite, 315
Favorites list, 298-299
genealogical resources, 326-327
Google
  company searches, 321
  search engine features, 316-317
  Usenet archives, 410
  Web directory topics, 315
history of, 293
HotBot, 317
Hotmail, 366-369, 372-373
HotSheet.com, 303
hyperlinks, 291, 294-295
ICQ.com, 379
International Herald Tribune, 307
Jabber.com, 379
Jezebel.com, 291
loading, 290-291
Lycos, 317
MetaCrawler, 317
MetaFilter Weblog, 397
MSN Chat, 388

Netly-L, 365
Newsguy, 401
Northern Light, 317
offline browsing, 300-301
Open Directory Project, 314-315
people locators, 322-323
pop-up windows, 295
printing, 306-307
recently visited pages, viewing, 312-313
RootsWeb, 326-327
saving, 308-309
searching
  search engines, 290-291, 316-317
  Web directories, 314-315
security certificates, 336-337
Slate, 307
software, 318-319
Supernews.com, 401
temporary files, 304
Topica, 365
UNICEF, 310
viewing, 294
WebCrawler, 317
White House, 311
Windows Update, 234
WindowsMedia.com, 166
Yahoo!, 315, 320, 379
Zone.com, 175
ZoneAlarm, 341

Web-based email accounts, 366-369, 372-373

WebCrawler Web site, 317

weblogs, 397

Whisper mode (MSN Chat), 393

White House Web site, 311

width of worksheet columns, 554-555

wildcards, 663

windows, 420
arranging on desktop, 58-59
cascading, 58
cleaning up, 83
closing, 57
Help and Support Center, 66-67
maximizing, 57, 420
menu bars, 420
minimizing, 57-59
moving, 58
My Computer, 64
Outlook
   Appointment window, 510-513
   Contact window, 520-521
   Event window, 514-515
   Forward window, 531
   Message window, 526-527
   Plan a Meeting window, 516-517
   Reply Message window, 530
   Task window, 518-519
resizing, 58
status bars, 420
tiling, 59
title bars, 420

Windows Classic style, 83, 186-187

Windows Explorer, 76-77

Windows Media Player, 162-167
Add to My Stations, 167
Copy from CD button, 164
Copy Music button, 165
Find More Stations, 167
Get Names button, 164
Media Guide, 166
My Music folder, 165
opening, 164
Radio Tuner, 166-167

Windows Messenger
blocking messages, 384-385
contact lists, 378-379
discouraging messages, 385
downloading, 377
inviting others to use, 380-381
remote assistance, 383
sending invitations, 380-381
sending messages, 382-383

Windows Movie Maker, 168-171

Windows Update Web site, 234

Windows XP
activating, 270-271
closing, 44-45
components
   installing from CD, 232-233
   installing from Internet, 234-235
desktop, 25, 49
   arranging windows, 58-59
   color, 187
   customizing, 183
   desktop appearance, 186-187
   desktop themes, 182-183
   display settings, 188-189
   effects, 187
   fonts, 187
   icons, 54-55
   moving items around, 53
   notification area, 62-63
   printing documents from, 108-109
   programs, 56-57, 60-61
   Recycle Bin, 68-69, 94-95
   styles, 186
   wallpaper, 184-185

dual-boot configuration, 257
games, 174-175
Help, 66-67
installation, 264-265
   Activation Wizard, 270-271
   on blank hard drives, 266-269
   setup floppy disks, 272-273
Internet connections
   configuring, 278, 281
   disconnecting, 287
   ISPs (Internet Service Providers), 282-285
   proxy servers, 288-289
logging on/off, 50-51, 70-71
registering, 271
service packs
   checking installation of, 238-239
   installing, 240-241
services
   disabling, 249
   monitoring, 251
   stopping, 250-251
settings, 177
   Accessibility options, 208-209
   desktop appearance, 186-187
   desktop theme, 182-183
   display settings, 188-189
   folder options, 196-197
   mouse properties, 190-193
   power options, 198-199
   Quick Launch bar, 204-205
   screensavers, 180-181
   Start menu items, 202-203
   Startup folder, 206-207
   system sounds, 200-201
   taskbar, 194-195

volume, 178-179
wallpaper, 184-185
shutting down, 51
starting, 27
system tools, 211
   *Automated System
     Recovery, 262-263*
   *Backup Wizard,
     258-259*
   *compression tool,
     224-225*
   *Device Manager,
     236-237*
   Disk Cleanup, 212-213
   *Disk Defragmenter,
     214-215*
   Event Viewer, 254-255
   *Restore Wizard,
     260-261*
   *Scheduled Task Wizard,
     216-217*
   *System Information,
     220-221*
   System Restore, 222-223
   *Windows troubleshoot-
     ers, 218-219*
System Tray, 246-247
troubleshooting, 245
   Event Viewer, 254-255
   programs, 252-253
   *Selective Startup,
     248-249*
   services, 249-251
   System Tray, 246-247
upgrading to, 264-265

**Windows XP style,
186-187**

**WindowsMedia.com Web
site, 166**

wizards
Activation Wizard,
   270-271
Add Network Place
   Wizard, 134-135
Add Printer Wizard,
   116-121
AutoContent Wizard,
   602-603

Automated System
   Recovery, 262-263
Backup Wizard, 258-259
Chart Wizard, 590-591
Create Shortcut Wizard,
   419
Database Wizard,
   646-647
Form Wizard, 654-655
Home Networking Wizard,
   131
Import and Export Wizard,
   522-523
Network Setup Wizard,
   130-131
Pack and Go Wizard,
   640-641
Report Wizard, 664-665
Restore Wizard, 260-261
Scheduled Task Wizard,
   216-217
Simple Query Wizard, 662
Table Wizard, 650

Word documents, 447
AutoCorrect feature,
   498-499
closing, 432-433
creating, 428-429
envelopes, 504-505
finding, 436-437
grammar-checking,
   496-497
Insert mode, 451
line spacing, 468-469
locating, 84
margins, 466-467
opening, 432-433
Overtype mode, 451
page breaks, 451,
   486-487
page numbers, 486-487
paper size, 502-503
previewing, 433, 435
printing, 107, 434-435
   *canceling print jobs,
     110-111*
   pausing print jobs, 111
   *print job management,
     110-111*

   printer settings, 112-113
   from programs, 106-107
   restarting print jobs, 111
   shared printers, 114-115
   *from Windows desktop,
     108*
saving, 81, 430-431
searching/replacing,
   494-495
spell-checking, 496-497
styles, 488-489
templates, 429, 456-457
text
   aligning, 470-471
   AutoText, 458-459
   borders, 480-481
   color, 461
   columns, 476-477
   comments, 484-485
   copying, 454-455
   *copying text formatting,
     462-463*
   deselecting, 453
   drop caps, 490-491
   editing, 450-451
   endnotes, 484-485
   entering, 450-451
   fonts, 460-461
   footers, 482-483
   footnotes, 484-485
   formatting, 460-461
   headers, 482-483
   indenting, 470-471
   lists, 472-473
   moving, 454-455
   selecting, 452-453
   shading, 480-481
   symbols, 464-465
   tables, 478-479
   tabs, 474-475
   text case, 490-491
tracking changes to,
   500-501
views, 448-449
watermarks, 492-493
zooming in/out, 448-449

**WordArt, adding to files,
617, 676-677**

WordArt button (Drawing toolbar), 676

WordArt command (Picture menu), 676

WordArt Gallery dialog box, 676-677

work area, 421

work breaks, 47

workbooks (Excel), 539

workgroups, 126, 269

worksheets (Excel), 539
  AutoComplete, 541
  AutoFill, 546-547
  AutoFormat, 584-585
  AutoSum, 568-569
  cells
    absolute cell addresses, 572-573
    alignment, 578-579
    background patterns, 580-581
    borders, 580-581
    clearing, 552-553
    copying, 541, 548-549
    copying cell formatting, 582-583
    deleting, 552-553
    editing data in, 541
    entering data into, 540-541
    inserting, 551
    moving, 548-549
    range names, 556-557
    relative cell addresses, 572-573
    selecting, 540, 544-545
    workbooks, 539
  charts
    chart types, 594-595
    creating, 590-591
    deleting, 593
    editing, 598-599
    moving, 592-593
    printing, 599
    resizing, 592-593
    titles, 596-597

  columns
    inserting, 550-551
    selecting, 545
    width of, 554-555
  comments, 586-587
  copying, 565
  custom lists, 547
  data
    editing, 541
    entering, 540-541
    filtering, 562-563
    finding, 558-559
    replacing, 558-559
    sorting, 560-561
  deleting, 564
  Format Painter, 582-583
  formulas
    creating, 566-567
    evaluating, 575
    fixing errors in, 574-575
    testing, 567
  functions
    arguments, 570-571
    entering, 570-571
    SUM, 568-569
  inserting, 565
  moving, 565
  navigating, 542-543
  number formats, 576-577
  renaming, 564
  rows
    deleting, 550-551
    height of, 554-555
    selecting, 545
  switching between, 564
  tracking changes to, 588-589
  undoing mistakes, 553

workstation ergonomics, 46-47

World Wide Web. *See* Web sites

wrapping text, 579, 681

wrist position, 47

writing email messages, 526-527

X-Z

Yahoo!
  chat, 393
  company searches, 320
  People Search, 322-323
  Web directory topics, 315
  Yahoo! Messenger, 379

Zone.com Web site, 175

ZoneAlarm (firewalls), 340-341

Zoom command (View menu), 448

Zoom dialog box, 448

zooming in/out
  PowerPoint views, 609
  Word, 448-449